D0948832

BEING AND EVENT

Also available from Continuum:

Infinite Thought, Alain Badiou (translated by Oliver Feltham and Justin Clemens)

Theoretical Writings, Alain Badiou (edited and translated by Alberto Toscano and Ray Brassier)

BEING AND EVENT

Alain Badiou

Translated by Oliver Feltham

continuum

Continuum

The Tower Building	80 Maiden Lane
11 York Road	Suite 704
London SE1 7NX	New York
www.continuumbooks.com	NY 10038

Originally published in French as *L'être et l'événement* © Editions du Seuil, 1988

This English language translation © Continuum 2005
First published by Continuum 2006
Paperback edition 2007

Ouvrage publié avec l'aide du Ministère français chargé de la Culture – Centre national du livre.

This book is supported by the French Ministry for Foreign Affairs, as part of the Burgess programme headed for the French Embassy in London by the Institut Français du Royaume-Uni.

British Library Cataloguing in Publication Data
A catalogue record for this book is available from the British Library.

ISBN-10: HB: 0-8264-5831-9
          PB: 0-8264-9529-X
ISBN-13: HB: 978-0-8264-5831-5
          PB: 978-0-8264-9529-7

Library of Congress Cataloging-in-Publication Data

A catolog record for this book is available from the Library of Congress.

Typeset by Interactive Sciences Ltd, Gloucester
Printed and bound in the USA

Contents

Part III *Being: Nature and Infinity. Heidegger/ Galileo*

Part IV *The Event: History and Ultra-one*

Part V *The Event: Intervention and Fidelity.*
Pascal/Choice; Hölderlin/Deduction

Part VI *Quantity and Knowledge. The Discernible*
(or Constructible): Leibniz/Gödel

Part VII *The Generic: Indiscernible and Truth. The Event—P. J. Cohen*

Part VIII *Forcing: Truth and the Subject. Beyond Lacan*

Author's Preface

Soon it will have been twenty years since I published this book in France. At that moment I was quite aware of having written a 'great' book of philosophy. I felt that I had actually achieved what I had set out to do. Not without pride, I thought that I had inscribed my name in the history of philosophy, and in particular, in the history of those philosophical systems which are the subject of interpretations and commentaries throughout the centuries.

That almost twenty years later the book is to be published in English, after having been published in Portuguese, Italian and Spanish, and just before it is published in German, is certainly not a proof of immortality! But even so, it is a proof of consistency and resistance; far more so than if I had been subject to immediate translation—which can always be a mere effect of fashion.

In fact, at the time of its publication, this book did not lend itself to immediate comprehension. We were at the end of the eighties, in full intellectual regression. What was fashionable was moral philosophy disguised as political philosophy. Anywhere you turned someone was defending human rights, the respect for the other, and the return to Kant. Indignant protests were made about 'totalitarianism' and a united front was assembled against radical Evil. A kind of flabby reactionary philosophy insinuated itself everywhere; a companion to the dissolution of bureaucratic socialism in the USSR, the breakneck expansion of the world finance market, and the almost global paralysis of a political thinking of emancipation.

The situation was actually quite paradoxical. On one hand, dominating public opinion, one had 'democracy'—in its entirely corrupt representative and electoral form—and 'freedom' reduced to the freedom to trade and consume. These constituted the abstract universality of our epoch. That is, this alliance between the market and parliamentarism—what I call 'capitalo-parliamentarism'—functioned as if the only possible doctrine, and on a worldwide scale. On the other hand, one had the widespread presence of relativism. Declarations were made to the effect that all cultures were of the same value, that all communities generated values, that every production of the imaginary was art, that all sexual practices were forms of love, etc. In short, the context combined the violent dogmatism of mercantile 'democracy' with a thoroughgoing scepticism which reduced the effects of truth to particular anthropological operations. Consequently, philosophy was reduced to being either a laborious justification of the universal character of democratic values, or a linguistic sophistry legitimating the right to cultural difference against any universalist pretension on the part of truths.

My book, however, by means of a weighty demonstrative apparatus, made four affirmations that went entirely against the flow of this ordinary philosophy.

1. Situations are nothing more, in their being, than pure indifferent multiplicities. Consequently it is pointless to search amongst differences for anything that might play a normative role. If truths exist, they are certainly indifferent to differences. Cultural relativism cannot go beyond the trivial statement that different situations exist. It does not tell us anything about what, among the differences, legitimately matters to subjects.

2. The structure of situations does not, in itself, deliver any truths. By consequence, nothing normative can be drawn from the simple realist examination of the becoming of things. In particular, the victory of the market economy over planned economies, and the progression of parliamentarism (which in fact is quite minor, and often achieved by violent and artificial means), do not constitute arguments in favour of one or the other. A truth is solely constituted by rupturing with the order which supports it, never as an effect of that order. I have named this type of rupture which opens up truths 'the event'. Authentic philosophy begins, not in structural facts (cultural, linguistic, constitutional, etc), but uniquely in what takes

place and what remains in the form of a strictly incalculable emergence.

3. A subject is nothing other than an active fidelity to the event of truth. This means that a subject is a militant of truth. I philosophically founded the notion of 'militant' at a time when the consensus was that any engagement of this type was archaic. Not only did I found this notion, but I considerably enlarged it. The militant of a truth is not only the political militant working for the emancipation of humanity in its entirety. He or she is also the artist-creator, the scientist who opens up a new theoretical field, or the lover whose world is enchanted.

4. The being of a truth, proving itself an exception to any pre-constituted predicate of the situation in which that truth is deployed, is to be called 'generic'. In other words, although it is situated in a world, a truth does not retain anything expressible from that situation. A truth concerns everyone inasmuch as it is a multiplicity that no particular predicate can circumscribe. The infinite work of a truth is thus that of a 'generic procedure'. And to be a Subject (and not a simple individual animal) is to be a local active dimension of such a procedure.

I attempted to argue for these theses and link them together in a coherent manner: this much I have said. What is more, I placed a rather sophisticated mathematical apparatus at their service. To think the infinity of pure multiples I took tools from Cantor's set theory. To think the generic character of truths I turned to Gödel and Cohen's profound thinking of what a 'part' of a multiple is. And I supported this intervention of mathematical formalism with a radical thesis: insofar as being, qua being, is nothing other than pure multiplicity, it is legitimate to say that ontology, the science of being qua being, is nothing other than mathematics itself.

This intrusion of formalism placed me in a paradoxical position. It is well known that for decades we have lived in an artificial opposition between Anglo-American philosophy, which is supposedly rationalist, based on the formal analysis of language and mathematized logic, and continental philosophy, supposedly on the border of irrationalism, and based on a literary and poetic sense of expression. Quite recently Sokal thought it possible to show that 'continental' references to science, such as those of Lacan, Deleuze, or even mine, were nothing more than unintelligible impostures.

However, if I use mathematics and accord it a fundamental role, as a number of American rationalists do, I also use, to the same extent, the resources of the poem, as a number of my continental colleagues do.

In the end it turned out that due to my having kept company with literature, the representatives of analytic philosophy, including those in France, attempted to denigrate my use of mathematical formalism. However, due to that very use, the pure continentals found me opaque and expected a literary translation of the mathemes.

Yet there is no difference between what I have done and what such philosophers as Plato, Descartes, Leibniz, or Hegel have done, a hundred times over since the very origins of our discipline: reorganizing a thorough, if not creative, knowledge of mathematics, by means of all the imaging powers of language. To know how to make thought pass through demonstrations as through plainsong, and thus to steep an unprecedented thinking in disparate springs.

For what I want to emphasize here is that I present nothing in mathematics which has not been established; I took some care to reproduce the demonstrations, in order that it not be thought that I glossed from a distance. In the same manner, my recourse to the poets is based on an interminable frequentation of their writings.

Thus one cannot corner me in some supposed ignorance, neither in the matter of the formal complexities I require, from Cantor to Groethendick, nor in the matter of innovative writing, from Mallarmé to Beckett.

But it is true that these usages, which break with the horrific academic destiny of specialization, renewing the tie to the absolute opening without which philosophy is nothing, could quite easily have been surprising in those times of reaction and intellectual weakness.

Perhaps today we are entering into new times. In any case, this is one of the possible senses of the publication of my book in English.

This publication owes everything, it must be said, to my principal translator, Oliver Feltham, and to his amicable advisor, Justin Clemens. It is no easy matter to transport the amplitude that I give to French syntax into the ironic concision of their language. Furthermore, I thank those who have taken the risk of distributing such a singular commodity: Continuum Books.

I would like this publication to mark an obvious fact: the nullity of the opposition between analytic thought and continental thought. And I would like this book to be read, appreciated, staked out, and contested as much by the inheritors of the formal and experimental grandeur of the sciences or of the law, as it is by the aesthetes of contemporary nihilism, the refined amateurs of literary deconstruction, the wild militants of a de-alienated world, and by those who are deliciously isolated by amorous constructions. Finally, that they say to themselves, making the difficult effort to read me: that man, in a sense that he invents, is all of us at once.

Alain Badiou, January 2005

Translator's Preface

This translation of *L'être et l'événement* is one way of prolonging the dynamic it sets in motion. At the source of that dynamic we find two fundamental propositions: the first is that mathematics is ontology, and the second is that the new happens in being under the name of the event. The global consequences of these propositions are an explorative dethroning of philosophy, the infinite unfolding of a materialist ontology, and the development of a new thought of praxis, and it is these consequences which give Badiou's philosophy its singular shape.

I. 'Mathematics is ontology'

In Badiou's terms, the proposition 'mathematics is ontology' is a philosophical idea conditioned by an event and its consequent truth procedure in the domain of science. The event was Cantor's invention of set theory and the truth procedure its subsequent axiomatization by Zermelo and Fraenkel.[1] The first element one should examine here is 'conditioning':

---

1 Badiou uses ZFC axiomatization of set theory (Zermelo–Fraenkel with the Axiom of Choice). Of course, there are other axiomatizations of set theory, such as W. V. O. Quine's, but this multiplicity simply reveals the contingency of philosophy's conditioning: a conditioning that can only be contrasted by developing another metaontology on the basis of another axiomatization of set theory.

what does it mean for a philosophical idea to be 'conditioned' by an event in a heterogeneous domain?

Conditioning is a philosophical operation that names and thinks truth procedures which occur outside philosophy. According to Badiou, both the existence and the timeliness of *a* philosophy depend upon its circulation between current truth procedures *and* philosophy's own concepts such as those of truth, the subject and appearing. Badiou does not identify which truth procedures should concern contemporary philosophy—outside his own examples—but he does stipulate that they occur in four domains alone: art, politics, science and love. He then assigns a central task to philosophy: it must think the *compossibility* of contemporary truth procedures in the four domains; that is, it must construct a conceptual space which is such that it can accommodate the diversity of the various truth procedures without being rendered inconsistent: it must act as a kind of clearing house for truths. In order to do so philosophy must name and conceptually 'seize' contemporary truth procedures in the four domains. It is this conceptual capture which transforms these independent truth procedures into 'conditions' of philosophy. In *Being and Event*, Badiou names the Zermelo–Fraenkel axiomatization of set theory as a truth procedure that follows upon the 'Cantor-event'. He thus transforms it into a 'condition' for his philosophy. The philosophical result of this set-theoretical conditioning is what Badiou terms his 'metaontology'.

Badiou's separation of philosophy from its conditions is designed to prevent what he terms a 'disaster'. A disaster occurs, in his eyes, when philosophy attempts to fuse itself with one of its conditions; that is, when philosophy tries to become political in itself, or scientific, or tries to rival literature, or winds itself around the phenomenon of transference love between the master and the disciple. These attempts at fusion constitute a recurring problem that afflicts philosophy. The best known examples concern philosophy and politics, and they include Heidegger's nomination of the truth of National Socialist politics in his Rectorship Address, and Marxism's declaration of the primacy of the proletarian viewpoint in philosophy. One should also mention logical positivism's attempted fusion between philosophy and science. In each of these 'disasters' Badiou would diagnose the desire of philosophy to produce the truth of a domain which is external to it. If there are certain strictures present in Badiou's work, then they have their source in a *renunciation* of this desire to detain truth within philosophy. As Heiner Muller says, for something to come, something has to go. For Badiou, one must maintain that truth occurs *outside* and *independently* of philosophy. This is why, in his terms, philosophy itself is not a generic truth procedure, though it may—through its conditioning—imitate many features of truth procedures.[2] The corollary of this stricture is that a strict division is required between philosophy and its 'outsides'.

Well before Badiou actually elaborated the idea, he practised philosophy as an intersection for its conditions. In *Théorie du sujet*, he developed lines of argument from the thinking of Mao, Mallarmé, and Lacan. Individual mathematicians are conspicuously absent from this list, and looking back at Badiou's early work, one can say that the political condition of Maoist –Leninist politics dominated his philosophy. On the basis of his own presentation of the development of his thought in the Introduction to *Being and Event*, it is clearly possible to speak of a 'mathematical turn' in his thought. One should note, however, that this turn is clearly inscribed, for Badiou, within the enduring problematic of thinking the relation between change and being.[3] Indeed it may be argued that it is the subsequent predominance of the scientific condition of set theory that saves Badiou's own philosophy from near fusion with politics. There is a fine line between thinking what is at stake in a particular condition and merging with that condition, and this is why Badiou states philosophy must remain mobile by circulating between a plurality of its conditions and its own history.

The general consequence of this definition of philosophy in terms of both its conditions *and* its history is that philosophy is dethroned from its classical position of sovereignty over other discourses *without* being enslaved to truth procedures. That is, by maintaining a reference to philosophy's own history and concepts, Badiou renders philosophy not fully but *partially* dependent on the occurrence of events in heterogeneous domains. In other words, philosophy no longer completely determines its objects; the concept of generic multiple, for example, is initially deter-mined in mathematics as an indiscernible set, and then, through Badiou's

---

2 As he notes in 'The Definition of Philosophy' in A. Badiou, *Infinite Thought: Truth and the Return of Philosophy* (J. Clemens & O. Feltham, (eds & trans.); London: Continuum, 2003), 165–8.

3 See P. Hallward, *Badiou: A Subject to Truth* (Minneapolis: University of Minnesota Press, 2003), 49. Bruno Bosteels also comments on this idea of a 'mathematical turn' in 'On the Subject of the Dialectic' in P. Hallward (ed.), *Think Again: Alain Badiou and the Future of Philosophy* (London: Continuum, 2004), 150–164.

work, it becomes a philosophical concept. Of course philosophy is not thereby reduced to the role of a passive receptacle: it does retain a choice over which truth procedures it names as the conditions for its conceptual construction, and this construction must remain consistent. Philosophy thus remains an active partner in the affair.

It is the multiplication of philosophy's conditions which allows Badiou to pull off the difficult trick of affirming the tasks and scope of philosophy—to think occurrences of thought in art, politics, science and love—without circumscribing its realm and assigning it a set of proper objects. In other words, Badiou manages to renew and affirm the specificity of philosophy without unifying its field: truth procedures cannot be assigned to any unified totality, and cannot, in their particularity, be predicted and thus limited.

For example, although the proposition 'mathematics is ontology' may have the *scope* of speculative metaphysics, it is non-speculative precisely because it subjects philosophy to unforeseeable non-philosophical constraints: those inherent to axiomatized set theory in its determination of a possible thought of inconsistent multiplicity. In Lacanian terms, it subjects philosophy to the *real* of mathematics, and in two forms: first, in that of the impasses—such as Russell's paradox—which forced the axiomatization of set theory and determined its shape; and second, in the form of unpredictable future events in the field of mathematics that may have implications for the metaontological apparatus set out in *Being and Event*.[4]

Badiou's proposed relation between philosophy and its conditions has certainly given rise to controversy. Deleuze, no less, objected that Badiou's philosophy was dominated by analogical thinking; that is, that it determines its own structures and then 'discovers' them outside itself, in the real of other discourses.[5] Insofar as Badiou's metaontology attempts to construct philosophical concepts which are parallel to the structures of set theory, then Badiou does engage in analogical thinking. But, if analogical

---

4 See Quentin Meillassoux, who argues that these implications include obsolescence, in his 'Nouveauté et événement' in C. Ramond (ed.), *Alain Badiou: Penser le multiple* (Paris: Harmattan, 2002), 21.

5 Badiou himself reports this objection in *Deleuze: 'La clameur de l'être'* (Paris: Hachette, 1997), 116. For the clearest exposition of Deleuze's critique of analogical thought see the third chapter 'Images of thought' of his *Difference and Repetition* (P. Patton (trans.); New York: Columbia University Press, 1995).

thinking means matching relationships between *already existing* elements in the philosophical domain to relationships between elements in the mathematical domain—Ph1:Ph2 = Ma1:Ma2—then Badiou is innocent as charged since he introduces *new elements* into philosophy on the basis of the mathematics, such as the concepts of evental site, generic multiple and natural situation. Not only that, but the *subjection* of philosophy to its conditions *results in new relationships* being constructed between already existing philosophical concepts on the basis of existing mathematical elements and relationships, such as Badiou's articulation of subject and truth on the basis of Cohen's operation of forcing.

In general, objections to a supposed philosophical imperialism present in 'conditioning' may be met with the reply that in Badiou's conception, philosophy certainly engages in the construction of its *own* concepts, but does so on the basis of its encounters with the singular *real* of *heterogeneous* procedures such as Cantorian set theory and Mallarmé's poetry. More importantly, the accusation of imperialism is itself analogical, and supposes a transitivity between the philosophical and the political realm; that is, it presupposes that not only are the same structures present in both realms, but there is an inmixing of these structures such that actions in one realm may have effects in the other. Hence it flirts with disaster, almost fusing philosophy to politics. Badiou, on the other hand, as mentioned above, is careful to maintain the difference between the philosophical and political realms. The supposition of transitivity can only lead—in the academy—to piety (respect for inert differences), inactive activism, and the posture of the radical professor.

If we use Badiou's own categories to deal with problems around the philosophy-conditions relationship, we can say that the latter is an example of the fraught relationship between representation and presentation. In other words, when philosophy names, for example, Zermelo–Fraenkel set theory as one of its conditions, it places itself in the position of philosophically representing set theory. Therefore, according to the schema of the excess of the powerset over its set and Easton's theorem, the number of ways one can philosophically represent a set theoretical presentation immeasurably exceeds the number of elements in the original presentation. Badiou terms this immeasurable excess 'the impasse of being', and argues that thought, faced with this impasse, has historically distributed itself into four grand orientations which each attempt to bridge or avoid this impasse: the transcendental, the constructivist, the generic and the praxiological. Badiou champions the fourth orientation, which he claims is operative in Marx and Freud's thought: the orientation which states that there is no unique response but a plurality of responses to the gap between representation and presentation, and the only place they are to be found is in practice. Evidently we can adopt this orientation of thought in regard to the question of the gap between Badiou's sense-laden metaontology and set theory's senseless inscriptions of multiplicity. The result of our adoption is that the only responses to this question to be found are those in the philosophical practice of conditioning; that is, in *other* philosophical responses to events in mathematics, *other* philosophical acts of nomination.[6]

Now that we have examined the nature of conditioning we may return to the status of the proposition 'mathematics is ontology': it is a nomination, a *philosophical idea*; that is, it is a decision, a principle and a hypothesis. First, although the proposition is philosophically comprehensible, given the arguments on being as inconsistent multiplicity, it is a *decision* in that it does require a certain leap from their conclusions—otherwise it would merely be a calculated or derived result.[7] Second, it is a *principle* in that it opens up new realms for thought. It leads to the construction of new concepts, such as a 'generic truth procedure', and to the elaboration of new relationships between classical ontological categories such as the One and the Many, foundation and alterity, representation and presentation. Third, it is a *hypothesis*, but not in the sense that it can be tested by physical experiment or any appeal to experience: it is itself an experience of thought to be traversed until it breaks or is interrupted by other such decisions.

If conditioning works as an encounter, then philosophy is opened up to contingent transformation and reworking. For millennia, philosophy has attempted to ground itself on One Eternal Necessity such as the prime

---

6 Monique David-Menard affirms, in relation to this question of conditioning, that 'The junction of the discourse to the matheme is neither thematized nor transcendentally determined . . . it is this excess of the practice of thought over the rules that it defines which gives it its scope.' See her 'Être et existence dans la pensée d'Alain Badiou' in Ramond, *Alain Badiou: Penser le multiple*.

7 One can trace lineages, albeit twisted, from the thesis 'being is inconsistent multiplicity' back to the work of philosophers such as Heidegger (the task is to name being without objectifying it), Derrida (there is no outside-of-the-text), and Deleuze (the plane of immanence)—and all this without the mathematics.

mover, or the dialectic of history. Here it consciously chooses to ground itself on the shifting sands of emergent truths.

With an end to ontological speculation via one last speculative proposition, the abandonment of any single ground of necessity, philosophy thus abdicates via its own magisterial gesture of naming its conditions and subjecting itself both to their necessities and their impossibilities—such as the insistence of love within the impossibility of the sexual relation. Badiou is the King Lear of philosophy, but a Lear who retains a part, a part to which one may return after voyaging through the diverse realms opened up by new artistic, political, scientific and amorous procedures.

Philosophy is thus dethroned, and it wanders over the heath, open to the storms of evental reworking, but at the same time, the ensuing multiplication and dynamism of its domains amounts to a serene affirmation of the freedom and power of thought.

If mathematics is ontology, what kind of ontology is it?

Badiou names Cantor's invention of set theory as an event, and its Zermelo–Fraenkel axiomatization as a conditioning truth procedure for his philosophy. The result is materialist, non-representational but schematic ontology: an ontology that does not claim to re-present or express being as an external substantiality or chaos, but rather to unfold being *as* it inscribes it: being as inconsistent multiplicity, a-substantial, equivalent to 'nothing'. By 'unfolding' I mean that in Badiou's reading the extension of the set theoretical universe is strictly equivalent to the actual writing of each of its formulas; it does not pre-exist set theory itself.

The materialism of set theory ontology is anchored in the axiom of separation, which states that all sets corresponding to formulas—all multiples which correspond to the limits of language—presume the prior existence of an undefined set—a multiple in excess of language. Being, as inconsistent multiplicity, is thus both in excess of the powers of language to define and differentiate it, and it must be presupposed as such in order for language to differentiate any multiple whatsoever.[8] Badiou thus identifies this axiom as inscribing a critical delimitation of the powers of language, which allows him to counter what he sees as the contemporary form of idealism in philosophy: the primacy accorded to language.

8 Badiou, *Infinite Thought*, 177.

Set theory ontology is non-representational in that it does not posit being outside itself but detains it within its inscriptions; in other words, it unfolds being performatively, in the elaboration of its formulas and their pre-suppositions. It avoids *positing* being inasmuch as there is no explicit definition of sets in Zermelo–Fraenkel set theory. As Robert Blanché argues, axiomatic systems comport 'implicit definitions', whereby the definition arises as the global result of a series of regulated operations.[9] This non-thetic relation to being may also be understood in a pragmatic sense: Peirce wrote, 'Consider what effects, that might conceivably have practical bearings, we conceive the object of our conception to have. Then, our conception of these effects is the whole of our conception of the object.'[10] In these terms, it is the effects that sets have *through* their manipulation by the axioms, and the real limits that sets impose on such manipulation, that determine our conception of inconsistent multiplicity, and thus of presented-being. These effects and their limits have no other place than the axioms, theorems and formulas of set theory, and so this is how set theory ontology may be said to be an ontology of immanence, retaining being *within* its inscriptions. In other words, Badiou assumes the original Parmenidean dispensation such that set theory, in its materiality—its letters—presents being as pure multiplicity. Badiou states: 'In mathematics, being, thought, and consistency are one and the same thing.'[11]

Another way of understanding this immanent unfolding of being as inconsistent multiplicity is to characterize set theory ontology as performative in that it *enacts* what it speaks of. Certainly, one may object that this is an ancient philosophical fantasy: to do what one is talking of, to ensure a perfect equivalence between action and discourse, practice and theory, to become the philosopher-king. However, unlike Derrida's texts which deconstruct other texts as they speak of deconstruction, unlike Hegel, who historically achieves absolute knowledge as he represents its historical progress, and finally unlike Deleuze who sets into motion his own nomadic war machine as he extols the virtues thereof, the performativity of set theory is *not* self-reflexive: set theory does not reflect its own performance, its own efficacy. This is so for two reasons: first, thanks to

9 R. Blanché, *L'axiomatique* (Paris: Quadrige/PUF, 1955), 38.

10 C. S. Peirce, 'How to Make Our Ideas Clear' in *Philosophical Writings of Peirce* (J. Buchler (ed.); New York: Dover Publications, 1955).

11 See A. Badiou, 'Platonism and Mathematical Ontology' in R. Brassier & A. Toscano (eds & trans.) *Theoretical Writings* (London: Continuum, 2004).

Godel's incompleteness theorem, we know a theory cannot prove its own consistency—its efficacy. Second, set theory cannot re-present itself in its totality because that would require a set of all sets, the total-set, and such a set is strictly non-existent: there is no Whole in set theory. Set theory ontology is thus a performative yet non-specular unfolding of being.

Although set theory ontology is non-representational in its relation to being, Badiou does claim that it is schematic: that is, not only does it present inconsistent multiplicity but it also presents the *structure* of non-ontological situations. Badiou discerns three basic structures of situations—natural, historical and neutral—and each is determined by a particular relationship between a set's elements and its subsets. These structures are said to ontologically differentiate non-ontological situations, such as forests and nations. This is precisely where the abstraction of set theory ontology risks being fleshed out: note that such fleshing out is in fact native to set theory in that any number of 'models' of it can be created by assigning fixed values to its variables. However, when it comes to Badiou's metaontological fleshing out, one operates in the opposite direction, selecting a non-ontological situation and then trying to determine its set-theoretical schema. A certain method is thus required to make the passage from a concrete analysis of a situation to an ontological description. The existence of such a method hinges on whether one can securely identify evental-sites regardless of the occurrence of an event, since it is such sites which differentiate historical from natural situations. However, Badiou stipulates that an evental-site, strictly speaking, is only evental inasmuch as an event occurs at its location. This suggests that it is undecidable whether a site is evental in the absence of an event. The method for the ontological analysis of situations thus cannot follow a verificationist model; we must accept that it will be heuristic and pragmatic. In another context, I have argued that indigenous politics in Australia constitutes a generic truth procedure, and the indigenous peoples themselves constitute an evental site in the situation of Australian politics.[12] In Australian governmental discourse the indigenous peoples are always said to be either excessive or lacking: excessive in their political demands, their drain on the public purse, their poverty; lacking in their recognition of the government's 'good intentions', in their community

12 See O. Feltham, 'Singularity in Politics: the Aboriginal Tent Embassy, Canberra 1972', in D. Hoens (ed.), *Miracles do Happen* (*Communication and Cognition*, Vol. 37, no. 1, 2004).

health standards, in their spirit of enterprise and individual responsibility, etc. It is possible to generalize these structural characteristics of excess and lack by arguing that inasmuch as the state has no measure of the contents of an evental site, the site itself will continually appear to be radically insufficient or in excess of any reasonable measure. One can thus adopt the criteria for the existence of an evental-site that it marks the place of unacceptable excess or lack in the eyes of the state.

The ultimate result of Badiou's structural differentiation of situations is that he is able to anchor his conception of praxis—of generic truth procedures—in particular types of situation. That is, only those political, scientific, artistic and interpersonal situations which comport evental-sites may give rise to a situation-transforming truth procedure. This is one of the significant strategic advantages set theory ontology possesses: rather than locating a permanent source of potential change in a general and omnipresent category (such as Negri and Hardt's 'multitudes'), it singles out a particular type of situation as a potential site of transformation. Any theory of praxis requires some form of structural differentiation to anchor the practical analyses made by the subjects involved: whether they be political (the concrete analysis of a conjuncture), artistic (the nomination of the avant-garde), or psychoanalytic (diagnostic categories). For Badiou, it is the structure of historical situations alone that provides a possible location for an event and thus for the unfolding of a praxis. But the existence of an evental-site is not enough to ensure the development of a praxis; for that, an event must occur.

II. 'The new happens in being, under the name of the event'

Events happen in certain times and places which, unlike the minor contingencies of everyday life, rupture with the established order of things. If they are recognized as harbouring implications for that order, then a transformation of the situation in which they occur may be initiated. For Badiou, there is no ground to these events: they have no assignable cause, nor do they emerge from any other situation, hence their belonging to the category of 'what-is-not-being-qua-being'. This is how Badiou places the *absolute contingency* of events: the most important feature of his new theory of praxis with regard to the withered Marxist model and its determinism.

This second fundamental proposition of Badiou's philosophy, like the first, is not the result of a philosophical deduction. However, there is certainly a philosophical context for it and its place in Badiou's thought: the encounter between epistemology, psychoanalysis and Marxism that occurred in Louis Althusser's work and in that of the *Cercle d'épistémologie* group at the École Normale Supérieure in the mid 1960's.[13] Moreover, the concept of a rupture and an ensuing structural change of a situation could be compared to the notion of an epistemological break, drawn from the lineage of Bachelard, Koyré, Canguilheim and Foucault. The problem of differentiating praxis from the repetition of social structure can be identified as emerging from the encounter between structuralism and Marxism. Finally, the problematic of the emergence of a subject separate from the ego and its interests within a praxis is a properly Lacanian problematic: the subject of desire emerges in response to the 'cut' of analytic interpretation which also provides the measure of unconscious structure. Yet in *Being and Event* none of these discourses or authors are privileged in the emergence of the thought of the event; instead Badiou turns to Mallarmé. His analysis of the structure of the event is conditioned by the poem *A Cast of Dice . . .* , and it is in this poem that he finds the Mallarméan name of the event: 'the Unique number which cannot be another'.

The proposition 'the new happens in being' therefore does not result from a philosophical deduction, but rather from a conditioning of philosophy, and, as with all conditioning, its resulting status is finally that of a philosophical idea: a hypothesis, a principle and a decision. The consequences of denying this hypothesis are as clear as they are undesirable. One could deny it, for example, by arguing that Badiou's philosophy merely presents a sophisticated take on the romantic conception of modernism with its avant-garde heroes and its ruptures of the status quo.[14] The fundamental position underlying such an argument is that named in Ecclesiastes: there is nothing new under the sun. But rather than repeating

13 The group responsible for the journal *Cahiers pour l'analyse*.

14 Badiou himself is well aware of the risk of romanticism; to the point of arguing that it still presents the major site for philosophical thought today. See his 'Philosophy and Mathematics: Infinity and the End of Romanticism' in Badiou, cf. n. 11 *Theoretical Writings*, 21–38. The most rigorous delimitation of the fragments of romanticism which remain inherent to Badiou's thought can be found in Justin Clemens' work: *The Romanticism of Contemporary Theory: Institutions, Aesthetics, Nihilism* (London: Ashgate, 2003).

the romantic conception of immediate invention, Badiou condemns it under the name of speculative leftism and its dream of an absolute beginning. What he presents, on the contrary, is a detailed study of the *long slow process of supplementation* that may follow the occurrence of an event.

Apart from this theoretical difference, the global consequences for philosophy of the Ecclesiastes position must be named. I myself hold these consequences to be three, an unholy trinity of destinies for philosophy: scholastic specialization, philosophy as consolation or therapy, and finally philosophy as fashion. Philosophy, of course, does require rigorous analysis and knowledge, it does produce affect and modify the subject, and it does require an attention to what is new in its field, but none of these requirements univocally determines its destiny. If philosophy cedes to such univocal determination—as specialization, therapy or fashion—it does remove a large part of uncertainty from its practice, but it also dies a certain death. There is far more animation to be found in Badiou's conception of philosophy in that it embraces a certain anxiety, obsession and desire: the mix which fuels its circulation between the history of philosophy, a theory of the subject, truth and appearing, and contemporary truth procedures.

A theory of praxis

Badiou's theory of praxis is timely. Much of contemporary critical philosophy arrives sooner or later at the problematic of praxis, precisely because such philosophy attempts to critically delimit capitalism and identify those practices that escape the cold rule of egoistic calculation. One can think of Derrida's work on a new type of faith, Jean-Luc Nancy's idea of a writing of the unworking of community, and Foucault's late conception of the self-styling of subjects. The significance of Badiou's conception is that it manages to develop a *practical* model of praxis insofar as we can already identify examples of such praxis at work in the world. The fundamental source of the 'practicality' of Badiou's theory of praxis is his placing it under the signs of possibility and contingency: there *may* be an evental site in a situation, an event *may* happen at that site, someone *may* intervene and name that event, others *may* identify an operator of fidelity, series of enquiries *may* develop, and finally, at a global level, these enquiries *may* be generic. We can also understand the practicality of Badiou's conception as the result of his subtraction of praxis from any form of the One—thus repeating the fundamental gesture of his ontology: the One of historical determinism (the dialectic of the class struggle); the One of eschatology (the ideal or goal of a classless society); and the One of a privileged and necessary agent (the proletariat as *the* subject of history). The results of these three subtractions from the One are: first, that generic truth procedures may take any number of historical forms; second, that they are infinite and do not possess a single goal or limit; and finally, that any subject whatsoever may carry out the work of the enquiries.

What survives this process of subtraction is language. This is another significant strength of Badiou's conception of praxis; because it includes a certain use of language—forcing—it is *transmissible between subjects*. This is what allows Badiou, when removing the determinism of the Marxist model, to avoid embracing some form of mysticism or a spontaneous participation in truth on the part of an initiated elite. Not only is a generic truth procedure an eminently practical affair which takes time, but it unfolds according to principles—an operator of fidelity, the names gen-erated by the enquiries—which can be transmitted from subject to subject and thus remain the property of no one in particular. This transmissibility of principles removes any seat for the institution of hierarchy within the praxis; indeed Badiou argues that equality, just as universality, is an immanent axiom of truth procedures.

Badiou thus removes everything from his model of praxis that could either give rise to dogmatism or retain assumptions about the shape that history—or rather histories—might take. However, there is a problem which is often mentioned in the commentary on Badiou's work, a problem about belief, action, and ideas: inasmuch as a subject retroactively assigns sense to the event, and there are no objective criteria determining whether the procedure the subject is involved in is generic or not, there is no distinction between subjectivization in a truth procedure and ideological interpellation.[15] In fact, Badiou has built in one safeguard to prevent the confusion of truth procedures and ideologies, and that is that the former is initiated by the occurrence of an event *at an evental site*. He recognizes that many practical procedures occur which invoke a certain fidelity—his example is Nazism—but he argues that they neither originate from an evental site, nor are they generic, being fully determined by existing

15 The most developed form of this objection may be found in S. Zizek, 'Psychoanalysis in Post-Marxism: The Case of Alain Badiou' in *South Atlantic Quarterly* 97:2 (Spring 1998): 235–61, which is reworked in S. Zizek, *The Ticklish Subject* (London: Verso, 1999).

knowledge. However, Badiou also says that there is no guarantee that a procedure is generic, and so we do not possess a sure-fire method for identifying evental sites. Consequently, the only answer to whether an evental site is at the origin of a procedure or not is local: that is, it depends on a concrete analysis of the locality of the procedure. The distinction between generic truth procedures and ideologies is thus a *practical* matter, to be dealt with by those locally engaged in the procedure. There is no global guarantee of the absence of ideology.

Perhaps the most questionable position here is that of the philosophers in their *abstract* fear of ideology. Let's take it for granted that we bathe daily in ideology, if only at the level of obeying the imperative Slavoj Zizek, following Lacan, identified as 'Enjoy!' According to Badiou, the only guarantee of working against such ideology is not to be found in an abstract fear or wariness, but rather in the principled engagement in particular praxes which *may* be generic.

A generic truth procedure is thus a praxis which slowly transforms and supplements a historical situation by means of separating out those of its elements which are connected to the name of the event from those which are not. This is an infinite process, and it has no assignable overall function or goal save the transformation of the situation according to *immanent* imperatives derived from the operator of fidelity and the actual enquiries.

Such is the result of Badiou's second fundamental proposition—'the new happens in being, under the name of the event'—a renovated theory of praxis. But Badiou does not rest there, for then he would risk reintroducing a dualism between the static ontological regime of the multiple, and the dynamic practical regime of truth procedures. Badiou joins the two regimes by sketching the *ontological schema* of a situation-transforming praxis, and this, in the end, is the most astonishing consequence of Badiou's identification of mathematics as ontology. Thanks to the event—within mathematics—of Paul Cohen's work on the continuum hypothesis, it is possible to mathematically write a generic or indiscernible set. In other words, Cohen develops a rigorous formalization of what is vague, indeterminate and anything-whatsoever; it is possible to speak of what is *strictly* indiscernible *without* discerning it. Some readers may have been struck by Badiou's taste for hard and fast categories—philosophy is not a truth procedure, truths take place in four domains, all appeals to a One are theological—but it is here that Badiou finally places a real difficulty with categorizing: the generic set inscribes the emergence of the new insofar as it is strictly uncategorizable.

Badiou is thus able to join his thought of being to his thought of concrete change via the mathematical concept of the generic multiple. This is the grand synthesis and challenge of Badiou's philosophy, crystallized in the title of this work, being *and* event; the task is to think being *and* event, not the being of the event, nor the event of being. The concepts Badiou employs to think this synthesis of being and event are those of a 'generic multiple' and 'forcing', and he draws them from the work of a mathematician, Paul Cohen. However, these mathematical concepts then lead Badiou to a classical philosophical concept: the subject. The reason for this turn in the argument is that for Badiou the only way to develop a modern de-substantialized non-reflective concept of the subject is to restrict it to that of a subject of praxis. Consequently, the 'and' of being and event finally names the space of the subject, the subject of the work of change, fragment of a truth procedure—the one who unfolds new structures of being and thus *writes the event into being*.[16]

Badiou's subject of praxis is not identical to an individual person; in his view, subjects are constituted by works of art, scientific theorems, political decisions, and proofs of love. Despite this, a 'subject' is not an abstract operator; any individual may form part of such a subject by their principled actions subsequent to an event.

The 'and' of 'being and event' is thus up to the subject: it's open. Alain Badiou's philosophy certainly makes a call upon one—not least to understand some set theory—and the call is made through a forceful affirmation of eveyone's capacity for truth. One can always, as Celan says, cast oneself out of one's outside, and recognize an event.

Notes on the translation

In this translation I have tried to retain some echoes of the particularities of Badiou's syntax without losing fluidity. The reason behind this choice is that, as Louise Burchill remarks (translator of Badiou's *Deleuze*), Badiou's syntax is not innocent; it does some philosophical work. Usually this work

16 This idea is developed in O. Feltham 'And being and event and . . . : philosophy and its nominations' in *The Philosophy of Alain Badiou* in *Polygraph 16* (2005).

simply amounts to establishing a hierarchy of importance between the terms in a sentence, hence the necessity of finding some equivalent to his syntax in English. One syntactic structure in particular is worth mentioning: Badiou often separates the subject of the sentence from the main verb, or the object of the verb, by inserting long subordinate phrases. One could say these phrases interrupt the 'situation' of the sentence, much like an event. Now for specific terms:

Beings/existents, being qua being. I have translated *étant* as 'being' or 'beings' and occasionally, to avoid confusion with the ontological sense of being, as 'existents'. *L'étant-en-totalité* is rendered by 'being-in-totality'. I have translated *l'être-en-tant-qu'être* as 'being-qua-being' rather than as 'being as being', since the latter is a little flat. Complications arise occasionally, such as in Meditation 20, with formulations such as *l'être-non-étant*, translated as 'non-existent-being' rather than as 'non-being-being'. The term *l'étant-en-tant-qu'étant* is translated as 'beings-qua-beings' to avoid confusion with 'being-qua-being'. The main problems reside in passages in Meditations 2 and 13 where Badiou exploits the distinction between *étant* and *être*. For example, in Meditation 13 he finally forms the term *l'être-étant-de-l'un*. Though the term 'beings' is retained for *étant* throughout the entire passage, I found myself obliged to translate the latter as 'the being-existent-of-the-one'.

Evental site translates the technical term *site événementiel*. The adjective 'eventful' is inappropriate due to its connotations of activity and busyness and so I have adopted Peter Hallward's neologism (translator of Badiou's *Ethics*).

Fidelity translates the technical term *fidelité* which is drawn from the domain of love to designate all generic procedures in which a subject commits him or herself to working out the consequences of the occurrence of an event in a situation for the transformation of that situation.

Thought. The French substantive *pensée* refers to the activity and process of thinking whereas 'thought' generally refers to a single idea or notion. I have translated *pensée* with 'thought' or 'thinking' because neither 'theory' nor 'account' nor 'philosophy' are adequate. Moreover, the Heideggerean echoes of the term should be retained.

The errancy of the void translates *l'errance du vide*. I chose errancy over wandering, deeming the latter too romantic and German for a French subtractive ontology.

Unpresentation. Badiou uses the neologism *impresentation* for which unpresentability, connoting a lack of manners or dress, is entirely unsuitable, hence the neologism 'unpresentation'.

Veracity/veridical. Badiou employs a distinction between *le veridique/ veridicité* and *le vrai*. Veracity, veridicity and veridical are employed, as distinct from truth, despite not being in current usage.

What is presented/what presents itself. These syntagms are used to translate *ce qui se présente*. Since it can be translated in both the active and the passive voice, it suggests the middle voice—unavailable in English —which possesses the advantage of avoiding any suggestion of an external agent of the verb.

Translator's Acknowledgements

I would like to first thank Alain Badiou for providing me with the inestimable opportunity to translate this work and for his patience. I am also very grateful to friends, family and colleagues for their continual encouragement, enthusiasm and assistance: Jason Barker, Bruno Besana, Ray Brassier, Chris, Val, Lex and Bryony Feltham, Peter Hallward, Dominiek Hoens, Sigi Jottkandt, Alberto Toscano, and Ben Tunstall. Two people deserve special mention for their attention to detail and innumerable suggestions when reading the drafts, Justin Clemens and Isabelle Vodoz. Lastly, thank you Barbara Formis—a true partner in the daily practice of translation.

Introduction

1

Let's premise the analysis of the current global state of philosophy on the following three assumptions:

1. Heidegger is the last universally recognizable philosopher.
2. Those programmes of thought—especially the American—which have followed the developments in mathematics, in logic and in the work of the Vienna circle have succeeded in conserving the figure of scientific rationality as a paradigm for thought.
3. A post-Cartesian doctrine of the subject is unfolding: its origin can be traced to non-philosophical practices (whether those practices be political, or relating to 'mental illness'); and its regime of interpretation, marked by the names of Marx and Lenin, Freud and Lacan, is complicated by clinical or militant operations which go beyond transmissible discourse.

What do these three statements have in common? They all indicate, in their own manner, the closure of an entire epoch of thought and its concerns. Heidegger thinks the epoch is ruled by an inaugural forgetting and proposes a Greek return in his deconstruction of metaphysics. The 'analytic' current of English-language philosophy discounts most of classical philosophy's propositions as senseless, or as limited to the exercise of a language game. Marx announces the end of philosophy and its realization in practice. Lacan speaks of 'antiphilosophy', and relegates speculative totalization to the imaginary.

On the other hand, the disparity between these statements is obvious. The paradigmatic position of science, such as it organizes Anglo-Saxon thought (up to and including its anarchistic denial), is identified by Heidegger as the ultimate and nihilistic effect of the metaphysical disposition, whilst Freud and Marx conserve its ideals and Lacan himself rebuilds a basis for mathemes by using logic and topology. The idea of an emancipation or of a salvation is proposed by Marx and Lenin in the guise of social revolution, but considered by Freud or Lacan with pessimistic scepticism, and envisaged by Heidegger in the retroactive anticipation of a 'return of the gods', whilst the Americans *grosso modo* make do with the consensus surrounding the procedures of representative democracy.

Thus, there is a general agreement that speculative systems are inconceivable and that the epoch has passed in which a doctrine of the knot *being/non-being/thought* (if one allows that this knot, since Parmenides, has been the origin of what is called 'philosophy') can be proposed in the form of a complete discourse. The time of thought is open to a different regime of understanding.

There is disagreement over knowing whether this opening—whose essence is to close the metaphysical age—manifests itself as a *revolution*, a *return* or a *critique*.

My own intervention in this conjuncture consists in drawing a diagonal through it: the trajectory of thought that I attempt here passes through three sutured points, one in each of the three places designated by the above statements.

- Along with Heidegger, it will be maintained that philosophy as such can only be re-assigned on the basis of the ontological question.
- Along with analytic philosophy, it will be held that the mathematico-logical revolution of Frege-Cantor sets new orientations for thought.
- Finally, it will be agreed that no conceptual apparatus is adequate unless it is homogeneous with the theoretico-practical orientations of the modern doctrine of the subject, itself internal to practical processes (clinical or political).

This trajectory leads to some entangled periodizations, whose unification, in my eyes, would be arbitrary, necessitating the unilateral choice of one of the three orientations over the others. We live in a complex, indeed confused, epoch: the ruptures and continuities from which it is woven cannot be captured under one term. There is not 'a' revolution today (nor 'a' return, nor 'a' critique). I would summarize the disjointed temporal multiple which organizes our site in the following manner.

1. We are the contemporaries of a *third epoch* of science, after the Greek and the Galilean. The caesura which opens this third epoch is not (as with the Greek) an invention—that of demonstrative mathematics—nor is it (like the Galilean) a break—that which mathematized the discourse of physics. It is a split, through which the very nature of the base of mathematical rationality reveals itself, as does the character of the decision of thought which establishes it.

2. We are equally the contemporaries of a *second epoch* of the doctrine of the Subject. It is no longer the founding subject, centered and reflexive, whose theme runs from Descartes to Hegel and which remains legible in Marx and Freud (in fact, in Husserl and Sartre). The contemporary Subject is void, cleaved, a-substantial, and ir-reflexive. Moreover, one can only suppose its existence in the context of particular processes whose conditions are rigorous.

3. Finally, we are contemporaries of a *new departure* in the doctrine of truth, following the dissolution of its relation of organic connection to knowledge. It is noticeable, after the fact, that to this day *veracity,* as I call it, has reigned without quarter: however strange it may seem, it is quite appropriate to say that truth is a new word in Europe (and elsewhere). Moreover, this theme of truth crosses the paths of Heidegger (who was the first to subtract it from knowledge), the mathematicians (who broke with the object at the end of the last century, just as they broke with adequation), and the modern theories of the subject (which displace truth from its subjective pronunciation).

The initial thesis of my enterprise—on the basis of which this entanglement of periodizations is organized by extracting the sense of each—is the following: the science of being qua being *has existed* since the Greeks—such is the sense and status of mathematics. However, it is only today that we have the means to *know* this. It follows from this thesis that philosophy is not centred on ontology—which exists as a separate and exact discipline—rather, it *circulates* between this ontology (thus, mathematics), the modern theories of the subject and its own history. The contemporary complex of the conditions of philosophy includes everything referred to in my first three statements: the history of 'Western' thought, post-Cantorian mathematics, psychoanalysis, contemporary art and politics. Philosophy does not coincide with any of these conditions; nor does it map out the totality to which they belong. What philosophy must do is propose a conceptual framework in which the contemporary compossibility of these conditions can be grasped. Philosophy can only do this—and this is what frees it from any foundational ambition, in which it would lose itself—by designating amongst its own conditions, as a singular discursive situation, ontology itself in the form of pure mathematics. This is precisely what delivers philosophy and ordains it to the care of truths.

The categories that this book deploys, from the pure multiple to the subject, constitute the general order of a thought which is such that it can be *practised* across the entirety of the contemporary system of reference. These categories are available for the service of scientific procedures just as they are for those of politics or art. They attempt to organize an abstract vision of the requirements of the epoch.

2

The (philosophical) statement that mathematics *is* ontology—the science of being qua being—is the trace of light which illuminates the speculative scene, the scene which I had restricted, in my *Théorie du sujet*, by presupposing purely and simply that there 'was some' subjectivization. The compatibility of this thesis with ontology preoccupied me, because the force—and absolute weakness—of the 'old Marxism', of dialectical materialism, had lain in its postulation of just such a compatibility in the shape of the generality of the laws of the dialectic, which is to say the isomorphy between the dialectic of nature and the dialectic of history. This (Hegelian) isomorphy was, of course, still-born. When one still battles today, alongside Prigogine and within atomic physics, searching for dialectical corpuscles, one is no more than a survivor of a battle which never seriously took place save under the brutal injunctions of the Stalinist state. Nature and its dialectic have nothing to do with all that. But that the process-subject be compatible with what is pronounceable—or pronounced—of being, there is a serious difficulty for you, one, moreover, that I pointed out in the question posed directly to Lacan by Jacques-Alain Miller in 1964: 'What is your ontology?' Our wily master responded with an allusion to non-being, which was well judged, but brief. Lacan, whose obsession with mathematics did nothing but grow with time, also indicated that pure logic was the 'science of the real'. Yet the real remains a category of the subject.

I groped around for several years amongst the impasses of logic—developing close exegeses of the theorems of Gödel, Tarski, and Löwenheim-Skolem—without surpassing the frame of *Theorie du sujet* save in technical subtlety. Without noticing it, I had been caught in the grip of a logicist thesis which holds that the necessity of logico-mathematical statements is formal due to their complete eradication of any effect of sense, and that in any case there is no cause to investigate what these statements account for, outside their own consistency. I was entangled in the consideration that if one supposes that there is a referent of logico-mathematical discourse, then one cannot escape the alternative of thinking of it either as an 'object' obtained by abstraction (empiricism), or as a super-sensible Idea (Platonism). This is the same dilemma in which one is trapped by the universally recognized Anglo-Saxon distinction between 'formal' and 'empirical' sciences. None of this was consistent with the clear Lacanian doctrine according to which the real is the impasse of formalization. I had mistaken the route.

It was finally down to the chance of bibliographic and technical research on the discrete/continuous couple that I came to think that it was necessary to shift ground and formulate a radical thesis concerning mathematics. What seemed to me to constitute the essence of the famous 'problem of the continuum' was that in it one touched upon an *obstacle* intrinsic to mathematical thought, in which the very impossibility which founds the latter's domain is said. After studying the apparent paradoxes of recent investigations of this relation between a multiple and the set of its parts, I came to the conclusion that the sole manner in which intelligible figures could be found within was if one first accepted that the Multiple, for mathematics, was not a (formal) concept, transparent and constructed, but a real whose internal gap, and impasse, were deployed by the theory.

I then arrived at the certainty that it was necessary to posit that mathematics writes that which, of being itself, is pronounceable in the field of a pure theory of the Multiple. The entire history of rational thought appeared to me to be illuminated once one assumed the hypothesis that mathematics, far from being a game without object, draws the exceptional severity of its law from being bound to support the discourse of ontology. In a reversal of the Kantian question, it was no longer a matter of asking:

'How is pure mathematics possible?' and responding: thanks to a transcendental subject. Rather: pure mathematics being the science of being, how is a subject possible?

3

The productive consistency of the thought termed 'formal' cannot be entirely due to its logical framework. It is not—exactly—a form, nor an episteme, nor a method. It is a *singular* science. This is what sutures it to being (void), the point at which mathematics detaches itself from pure logic, the point which establishes its historicity, its successive impasses, its spectacular splits, and its forever-recognized unity. In this respect, for the philosopher, the decisive break—in which mathematics blindly pronounces on its own essence—is Cantor's creation. It is there alone that it is finally declared that, despite the prodigious variety of mathematical 'objects' and 'structures', they can *all* be designated as pure multiplicities built, in a regulated manner, on the basis of the void-set alone. The question of the exact nature of the relation of mathematics to being is therefore entirely concentrated—for the epoch in which we find ourselves—in the axiomatic decision which authorizes set theory.

That this axiomatic system has been itself in crisis, ever since Cohen established that the Zermelo–Fraenkel system could not determine the type of multiplicity of the continuum, only served to sharpen my conviction that something crucial yet completely unnoticed was at stake there, concerning the power of language with regard to what could be mathematically expressed of being qua being. I found it ironic that in *Théorie du sujet* I had used the 'set-theoretical' homogeneity of mathematical language as a mere paradigm of the categories of materialism. I saw, moreover, some quite welcome consequences of the assertion 'mathematics = ontology'.

First, this assertion frees us from the venerable search for the foundation of mathematics, since the apodeictic nature of this discipline is wagered directly by being itself, which it pronounces.

Second, it disposes of the similarly ancient problem of the nature of mathematical objects. Ideal objects (Platonism)? Objects drawn by abstraction from sensible substance (Aristotle)? Innate ideas (Descartes)? Objects constructed in pure intuition (Kant)? In a finite operational intuition (Brouwer)? Conventions of writing (formalism)? Constructions transitive to pure logic, tautologies (logicism)? If the argument I present here holds up, the truth is that *there are no* mathematical objects. Strictly speaking, mathematics *presents nothing*, without constituting for all that an empty game, because not having anything to present, besides presentation itself—which is to say the Multiple—and thereby never adopting the form of the ob-ject, such is certainly a condition of all discourse on being *qua being*.

Third, in terms of the 'application' of mathematics to the so-called natural sciences (those sciences which periodically inspire an enquiry into the foundation of their success: for Descartes and Newton, God was required; for Kant, the transcendental subject, after which the question was no longer seriously practised, save by Bachelard in a vision which remained constitutive, and by the American partisans of the stratification of languages), the clarification is immediately evident if mathematics is the science, in any case, of everything that is, *insofar as it is*. Physics, itself, enters into presentation. It requires more, or rather, something else, but its compatibility with mathematics is a matter of principle.

Naturally, this is nothing new to philosophers—that there must be a link between the existence of mathematics and the question of being. The paradigmatic function of mathematics runs from Plato (doubtless from Parmenides) to Kant, with whom its usage reached both its highest point and, via 'the Copernican revolution', had its consequences exhausted: Kant salutes in the birth of mathematics, indexed to Thales, a salvatory event for all humanity (this was also Spinoza's opinion); however, it is the *closure* of all access to being-in-itself which founds the (human, all too human) universality of mathematics. From that point onwards, with the exception of Husserl—who is a great classic, if a little late—modern (let's say post-Kantian) philosophy was no longer haunted by a paradigm, except that of history, and, apart from some heralded but repressed exceptions, Cavaillès and Lautman, it abandoned mathematics to Anglo-Saxon linguistic sophistry. This was the case in France, it must be said, until Lacan.

The reason for this is that philosophers—who think that they alone set out the field in which the question of being makes sense—have placed mathematics, ever since Plato, as a model of certainty, or as an example of identity: they subsequently worry about the special *position* of the objects articulated by this certitude or by these idealities. Hence a relation, both permanent and biased, between philosophy and mathematics: the former oscillating, in its evaluation of the latter, between the eminent dignity of the rational paradigm and a distrust in which the insignificance of its 'objects' were held. What value could numbers and figures have—categories of mathematical 'objectivity' for twenty-three centuries—in comparison to Nature, the Good, God, or Man? What value, save that the 'manner of thinking' in which these meagre objects shone with demonstrative assurance appeared to open the way to less precarious certitudes concerning the otherwise glorious entities of speculation.

At best, if one manages to clarify what Aristotle says of the matter, Plato imagined a mathematical architecture of being, a transcendental function of ideal numbers. He also recomposed a cosmos on the basis of regular polygons: this much may be read in the *Timaeus*. But this enterprise, which binds being as Totality (the fantasy of the World) to a given state of mathematics, can only generate perishable images. Cartesian physics met the same end.

The thesis that I support does not in any way declare that being is mathematical, which is to say composed of mathematical objectivities. It is not a thesis about the world but about discourse. It affirms that mathematics, throughout the entirety of its historical becoming, pronounces what is expressible of being qua being. Far from reducing itself to tautologies (being is that which is) or to mysteries (a perpetually postponed approximation of a Presence), ontology is a rich, complex, unfinishable science, submitted to the difficult constraint of a *fidelity* (deductive fidelity in this case). As such, in merely trying to organize the discourse of what subtracts itself from any presentation, one faces an infinite and rigorous task.

The philosophical rancour originates uniquely in the following: if it is correct that the philosophers have formulated the question of being, then it is not themselves but the mathematicians who have come up with the answer to that question. All that we know, and can ever know of being qua being, is set out, through the mediation of a theory of the pure multiple, by the historical discursivity of mathematics.

Russell said—without believing it, of course, no one in truth has ever believed it, save the ignorant, and Russell certainly wasn't such—that mathematics is a discourse in which one does not know what one is talking about, nor whether what one is saying is true. Mathematics is rather the *sole* discourse which 'knows' absolutely what it is talking about: being, as such, despite the fact that there is no need for this knowledge to be reflected in an intra-mathematical sense, because being is not an object, and nor does it generate objects. Mathematics is also the sole discourse, and this is well known, in which one has a complete guarantee and a criterion of the truth of what one says, to the point that this truth is unique inasmuch as it is the only one ever to have been encountered which is fully transmissible.

4

The thesis of the identity of mathematics and ontology is disagreeable, I know, to both mathematicians and philosophers.

Contemporary philosophical 'ontology' is entirely dominated by the name of Heidegger. For Heidegger, science, from which mathematics is not distinguished, constitutes the hard kernel of metaphysics, inasmuch as it annuls the latter in the very loss of that forgetting in which metaphysics, since Plato, has founded the guarantee of its objects: the forgetting of being. The principal sign of modern nihilism and the neutrality of thought is the technical omnipresence of science—the science which installs the forgetting of the forgetting.

It is therefore not saying much to say that mathematics—which to my knowledge he only mentions laterally—is not, for Heidegger, a path which opens onto the original question, nor the possible vector of a return towards dissipated presence. No, mathematics is rather blindness itself, the great power of the Nothing, the foreclosure of thought by knowledge. It is, moreover, symptomatic that the Platonic institution of metaphysics is accompanied by the institution of mathematics as a paradigm. As such, for Heidegger, it may be manifest from the outset that mathematics is internal to the great 'turn' of thought accomplished between Parmenides and Plato. Due to this turn, that which was in a position of opening and veiling became fixed and—at the price of forgetting its own origins—manipulable in the form of the Idea.

The debate with Heidegger will therefore bear simultaneously on ontology and on the essence of mathematics, then consequently on what is signified by the site of philosophy being 'originally Greek'. The debate can be opened in the following way:

1. Heidegger still remains enslaved, even in the doctrine of the withdrawal and the un-veiling, to what I consider, for my part, to be the essence of metaphysics; that is, the figure of being as endowment and gift, as presence and opening, and the figure of ontology as the offering of a trajectory of proximity. I will call this type of ontology *poetic*; ontology

haunted by the dissipation of Presence and the loss of the origin. We know what role the poets play, from Parmenides to René Char, passing by Hölderlin and Trakl, in the Heideggerean exegesis. I attempted to follow in his footsteps—with entirely different stakes—in *Théorie du sujet*, when I convoked Aeschylus and Sophocles, Mallarmé, Hölderlin and Rimbaud to the intricacy of the analysis.

2. Now, to the seduction of poetic proximity—I admit, I barely escaped it—I will oppose the radically subtractive dimension of being, foreclosed not only from representation but from all presentation. I will say that being qua being does not in any manner let itself be approached, but solely allows itself to be *sutured* in its void to the brutality of a deductive consistency without aura. Being does not diffuse itself in rhythm and image, it does not reign over metaphor, it is the null sovereign of inference. For poetic ontology, which—like History—finds itself in an impasse of an excess of presence, one in which being conceals itself, it is necessary to substitute mathematical ontology, in which dis-qualification and unpresentation are realized through writing. Whatever the subjective price may be, philosophy must designate, insofar as it is a matter of being qua being, the genealogy of the discourse on being—and the reflection on its possible essence—in Cantor, Gödel, and Cohen rather than in Hölderlin, Trakl and Celan.

3. There is well and truly a Greek historicity to the birth of philosophy, and, without doubt, that historicity can be assigned to the question of being. However, it is not in the enigma and the poetic fragment that the origin may be interpreted. Similar sentences pronounced on being and non-being within the tension of the poem can be identified just as easily in India, Persia or China. If philosophy—which is the disposition for designating exactly where the joint questions of being and of what-happens are at stake—was born in Greece, it is because it is there that ontology established, with the first *deductive* mathematics, the necessary form of its discourse. It is the philosophico-mathematical nexus—legible even in Parmenides' poem in its usage of apagogic reasoning—which makes Greece the original site of philosophy, and which defines, until Kant, the 'classic' domain of its objects.

At base, affirming that mathematics accomplishes ontology unsettles philosophers because this thesis absolutely discharges them of what remained the centre of gravity of their discourse, the ultimate refuge of their identity. Indeed, mathematics today has no need of philosophy, and thus one can say that the discourse on being continues 'all by itself'.

Moreover, it is characteristic that this 'today' is determined by the creation of set theory, of mathematized logic, and then by the theory of categories and of *topoi*. These efforts, both reflexive and intra-mathematical, sufficiently assure mathematics of its being—although still quite blindly—to henceforth provide for its advance.

5

The danger is that, if philosophers are a little chagrined to learn that ontology has had the form of a separate discipline since the Greeks, the mathematicians are in no way overjoyed. I have met with scepticism and indeed with amused distrust on the part of mathematicians faced with this type of revelation concerning their discipline. This is not affronting, not least because I plan on establishing in this very book the following: that it is of the essence of ontology to be carried out in the reflexive foreclosure of its identity. For someone who actually *knows* that it is from being qua being that the truth of mathematics proceeds, doing mathematics—and especially inventive mathematics—demands that this knowledge be at no point represented. Its representation, placing being in the general position of an object, would immediately corrupt the necessity, for any ontological operation, of de-objectification. Hence, of course, the attitude of those the Americans call *working mathematicians*: they always find general considerations about their discipline vain and obsolete. They only trust whomever works hand in hand with them grinding away at the latest mathematical problem. But this trust—which is the practico-ontological subjectivity itself—is in principle unproductive when it comes to any rigorous description of the generic essence of their operations. It is entirely devoted to particular innovations.

Empirically, the mathematician always suspects the philosopher of not knowing enough about mathematics to have earned the right to speak. No-one is more representative of this state of mind in France than Jean Dieudonné. Here is a mathematician unanimously known for his encyclopaedic mastery of mathematics, and for his concern to continually foreground the most radical reworkings of current research. Moreover, Jean Dieudonné is a particularly well-informed historian of mathematics. Every debate concerning the philosophy of his discipline requires him. However, the thesis he continually advances (and it is entirely correct in the facts) is that of the terrible backwardness of philosophers in relation to living mathematics, a point from which he infers that what they do have to say about it is devoid of contemporary relevance. He especially has it in for those (like me) whose interest lies principally in logic and set theory. For him these are finished theories, which can be refined to the *nth* degree without gaining any more interest or consequence than that to be had in juggling with the problems of elementary geometry, or devoting oneself to calculations with matrices ('those absurd calculations with matrices' he remarks).

Jean Dieudonné therefore concludes in one sole prescription: that one must master the active, modern mathematical corpus. He assures that this task is possible, because Albert Lautman, before being assassinated by the Nazis, not only attained this mastery, but penetrated further into the nature of leading mathematical research than a good number of his mathematician-contemporaries.

Yet the striking paradox in Dieudonné's praise of Lautman is that it is absolutely unclear whether he approves of Lautman's *philosophical* statements any more than of those of the ignorant philosophers that he denounces. The reason for this is that Lautman's statements are of a great radicalism. Lautman draws examples from the most recent mathematics and places them in the service of a transplatonist vision of their schemas. Mathematics, for him, realizes in thought the descent, the procession of dialectical Ideas which form the horizon of being for all possible rationality. Lautman did not hesitate, from 1939 onwards, to relate this process to the Heideggerean dialectic of being and beings. Is Dieudonné prepared to validate Lautman's high speculations, rather than those of the 'current' epistemologists who are a century behind? He does not speak of this.

I ask then: what good is exhaustivity in mathematical knowledge —certainly worthwhile in itself, however difficult to conquer—for the philosopher, if, in the eyes of the mathematicians, it does not even serve as a particular guarantee of the validity of his philosophical conclusions?

At bottom, Dieudonné's praise for Lautman is an aristocratic procedure, a knighting. Lautman is recognized as belonging to the brotherhood of genuine scholars. But that it be philosophy which is at stake remains, and will always remain, in excess of that recognition.

Mathematicians tell us: be mathematicians. And if we are, we are honoured for that alone without having advanced one step in convincing them of the essence of the site of mathematical thought. In the final analysis, Kant, whose mathematical referent in the *Critique of Pure Reason* did not go much further than the famous '7 + 5 = 12', benefitted, on the part of Poincaré (a mathematical giant), from more *philosophical* recognition than Lautman, who referred to the *nec plus ultra* of his time, received from Dieudonné and his colleagues.

We thus find ourselves, for our part, compelled to suspect mathematicians of being as demanding concerning mathematical knowledge as they are lax when it comes to the philosophical designation of the essence of that knowledge.

Yet in a sense, they are completely right. If mathematics *is* ontology, there is no other solution for those who want to participate in the actual development of ontology: they must study the mathematicians of their time. If the kernel of 'philosophy' is ontology, the directive 'be a mathematician' is correct. The new theses on being qua being are indeed nothing other than the new theories, and the new theorems to which *working mathematicians*—'ontologists without knowing so'—devote themselves; but this lack of knowledge is the key to their truth.

It is therefore essential, in order to hold a reasoned debate over the usage made here of mathematics, to assume a crucial consequence of the identity of mathematics and ontology, which is that *philosophy is originally separated from ontology*. Not, as a vain 'critical' knowledge would have us believe, because ontology does not exist, but rather because it exists fully, to the degree that what is sayable—and said—of being qua being does not in any manner arise from the discourse of philosophy.

Consequently, our goal is not an ontological presentation, a treatise on being, which is never anything other than a mathematical treatise: for example, the formidable *Introduction to Analysis*, in nine volumes, by Jean Dieudonné. Only such a will to presentation would require one to advance into the (narrow) breach of the most recent mathematical problems. Failing that, one is a chronicler of ontology, and not an ontologist.

Our goal is to establish the meta-ontological thesis that mathematics is the historicity of the discourse on being qua being. And the goal of this goal is to assign philosophy to the thinkable articulation of two discourses (and practices) which *are not it*: mathematics, science of being, and the intervening doctrines of the event, which, precisely, designate 'that-which-is-not-being-qua-being'.

The thesis 'ontology = mathematics' is meta-ontological: this excludes it being mathematical, or ontological. The stratification of discourses must be admitted here. The demonstration of the thesis prescribes the usage of certain mathematical fragments, yet they are commanded by philosophical rules, and not by those of contemporary mathematics. In short, the part of mathematics at stake is that in which it is historically pronounced that every 'object' is reducible to a pure multiplicity, itself built on the unpresentation of the void: the part called set theory. Naturally, these fragments can be read as a particular type of ontological marking of meta-ontology, an index of a discursive de-stratification, indeed as *an evental occurrence of being*. These points will be discussed in what follows. All we need to know for the moment is that it is non-contradictory to hold these morsels of mathematics as almost inactive—as theoretical devices—*in* the development of ontology, in which it is rather algebraic topology, func-tional analysis, differential geometry, etc., which reign—and, at the same time, to consider that they remain singular and necessary supports for the theses of meta-ontology.

Let's therefore attempt to dissipate the misunderstanding. I am not pretending in any way that the mathematical domains I mention are the most 'interesting' or significant in the current state of mathematics. That ontology has followed its course well beyond them is obvious. Nor am I saying that these domains are in a foundational position for mathematical discursivity, even if they generally occur at the beginning of every systematic treatise. To begin is not to found. My problem is not, as I have said, that of foundations, for that would be to advance within the internal architecture of ontology whereas my task is solely to indicate its site. However, what I do affirm is that historically these domains are *symptoms*, whose interpretation validates the thesis that mathematics is only assured of its truth insofar as it organizes what, of being qua being, allows itself to be inscribed.

If other more active symptoms are interpreted then so much the better, for it will then be possible to organize the meta-ontological debate within a recognizable framework. With perhaps, perhaps . . . a knighting by the mathematicians.

Thus, to the philosophers, it must be said that it is on the basis of a definitive ruling on the ontological question that the freedom of their genuinely specific procedures may be derived today. And to the mathema-ticians, that the ontological dignity of their research, despite being constrained to blindness with respect to itself, does not exclude, once unbound from the being of the *working mathematician*, their becoming interested in what is happening in meta-ontology, according to other rules, and towards other ends. In any case, it does not exclude them from being persuaded that the truth is at stake therein, and furthermore that it is the act of trusting them for ever with the 'care of being' which separates truth from knowledge and opens it to the event. Without any other hope, but it is enough, than that of mathematically inferring justice.

6

If the establishment of the thesis 'mathematics is ontology' is the basis of this book, it is in no way its goal. However radical this thesis might be, all it does is *delimit* the proper space of philosophy. Certainly, it is itself a meta-ontological or philosophical thesis necessitated by the current cumulative state of mathematics (after Cantor, Gödel and Cohen) and philosophy (after Heidegger). But its function is to introduce specific themes of modern philosophy, particularly—because mathematics is the guardian of being qua being—the problem of 'what-is-not-being-qua-being'. More-over, it is both too soon and quite unproductive to say that the latter is a question of non-being. As suggested by the typology with which I began this Introduction, the domain (which *is not* a domain but rather an incision, or, as we shall see, a supplement) of what-is-not-being-qua-being is organized around two affiliated and essentially new concepts, those of truth and subject.

Of course, the link between truth and the subject appears ancient, or in any case to have sealed the destiny of the first philosophical modernity whose inaugural name is Descartes. However, I am claiming to reactivate these terms within an entirely different perspective: this book founds a doctrine which is effectively post-Cartesian, or even post-Lacanian, a doctrine of what, for thought, both un-binds the Heideggerean connection between being and truth and institutes the subject, not as support or origin, but as *fragment* of the process of a truth.

If one category had to be designated as an emblem of my thought, it would be neither Cantor's pure multiple, nor Gödel's constructible, nor the void, by which being is named, nor even the event, in which the supplement of what-is-not-being-qua-being originates. It would be the *generic*.

This very word 'generic': by way of a kind of frontier effect in which mathematics mourned its foundational arrogance I borrowed it from a mathematician, Paul Cohen. With Cohen's discoveries (1963), the great monument of thought begun by Cantor and Frege at the end of the nineteenth century became complete. Taken bit by bit, set theory proves inadequate for the task of systematically deploying the entire body of mathematics, and even for resolving its central problem, which tormented Cantor under the name of the continuum hypothesis. In France, the proud enterprise of the Bourbaki group foundered.

Yet the philosophical reading of this completion authorizes *a contrario* all philosophical hopes. I mean to say that Cohen's concepts (genericity and forcing) constitute, in my opinion, an intellectual *topos* at least as fundamental as Godel's famous theorems were in their time. They resonate well beyond their technical validity, which has confined them up till now to the academic arena of the high specialists of set theory. In fact, they resolve, within their own order, the old problem of the indiscernibles: they refute Leibniz, and open thought to the subtractive seizure of truth and the subject.

This book is also designed to broadcast that an intellectual revolution took place at the beginning of the sixties, whose vector was mathematics, yet whose repercussions extend throughout the entirety of possible thought: this revolution proposes completely new tasks to philosophy. If, in the final meditations (from 31 to 36), I have recounted Cohen's operations in detail, if I have borrowed or exported the words 'generic' and 'forcing' to the point of preceding their mathematical appearance by their philosophical deployment, it is in order to finally discern and orchestrate this Cohen-event; which has been left devoid of any intervention or sense—to the point that there is practically no version, even purely technical, in the French language.

7

Both the ideal recollection of a truth and the *finite* instance of such a recollection that is a subject in my terms, are therefore attached to what I will term *generic procedures* (there are four of them: love, art, science, and politics). The thought of the generic supposes the complete traversal of the categories of being (multiple, void, nature, infinity, . . .) and of the event (ultra-one, undecidable, intervention, fidelity, . . .). It crystallizes concepts to such a point that it is almost impossible to give an image of it. Instead, it can be said that it is bound to the profound problem of the indiscernible, the unnameable, and the absolutely indeterminate. A generic multiple (and the *being* of a truth is always such) is subtracted from knowledge, disqualified, and unpresentable. However, and this is one of the crucial concerns of this book, it can be demonstrated that it may be thought.

What happens in art, in science, in true (rare) politics, and in love (if it exists), is the coming to light of an indiscernible of the times, which, as such, is neither a known or recognized multiple, nor an ineffable singularity, but that which detains in its multiple-being all the common traits of the collective in question: in this sense, it is the truth of the collective's being. The mystery of these procedures has generally been referred either to their representable conditions (the knowledge of the technical, of the social, of the sexual) or to the transcendent beyond of their One (revolutionary hope, the lovers' fusion, poetic ec-stasis . . .). In the category of the generic I propose a contemporary thinking of these procedures which shows that they are simultaneously indeterminate and complete; because, in occupying the gaps of available encyclopaedias, they manifest the common-being, the multiple-essence, of the place in which they proceed.

A subject is then a finite moment of such a manifestation. A subject *is manifested locally*. It is solely supported by a generic procedure. Therefore, *stricto sensu*, there is no subject save the artistic, amorous, scientific, or political.

To think authentically what has been presented here merely in the form of a rough sketch, the first thing to understand is how being can be supplemented. The existence of a truth is suspended from the occurrence of an event. But since the event is only *decided* as such in the retroaction of an intervention, what finally results is a complex trajectory, which is reconstructed by the organization of the book, as follows:

1. Being: multiple and void, or Plato/Cantor. Meditations 1 to 6.
2. Being: excess, state of a situation. One/multiple, whole/parts, or $\in$/$\subset$? Meditations 7 to 10.
3. Being: nature and infinity, or Heidegger/Galileo. Meditations 11 to 15.
4. The event: history and ultra-one. What-is-not-being-qua-being. Meditations 16 to 19.
5. The event: intervention and fidelity. Pascal/axiom of choice. Hölderlin/deduction. Meditations 20 to 25.
6. Quantity and knowledge. The discernible (or constructible): Leibniz/Gödel. Meditations 26 to 30.
7. The generic: indiscernible and truth. The event – P. J. Cohen. Meditations 31 to 34.
8. Forcing: truth and subject. Beyond Lacan. Meditations 34 to 37.

It is clear: the necessary passage through fragments of mathematics is required in order to *set off*, within a point of excess, that symptomatic torsion of being which is a truth within the perpetually total web of knowledges. Thus, let it be understood: my discourse is never epistemological, nor is it a philosophy *of* mathematics. If that were the case I would have discussed the great modern schools of epistemology (formalism, intuitionism, finitism, etc.). Mathematics is *cited* here to let its ontological essence become manifest. Just as the ontologies of Presence cite and comment upon the great poems of Hölderlin, Trakl and Celan, and no-one finds matter for contestation in the poetic text being thus spread out and dissected, here one must allow me, without tipping the enterprise over into epistemology (no more than that of Heidegger's enterprise into a simple aesthetics), the right to cite and dissect the mathematical text. For what one expects from such an operation is less a knowledge of mathematics than a determination of the point at which the saying of being occurs, in a temporal excess over itself, as *a* truth—always artistic, scientific, political or amorous.

It is a prescription of the times: the possibility of citing mathematics is due such that truth and the subject be thinkable in their being. Allow me to say that these citations, all things considered, are more universally accessible and univocal than those of the poets.

8

This book, in conformity to the sacred mystery of the Trinity, is 'three-in-one'. It is made up of thirty-seven meditations: this term recalls the characteristics of Descartes' text—the order of reasons (the conceptual linkage is irreversible), the thematic autonomy of each development, and a method of exposition which avoids passing by the refutation of established or adverse doctrines in order to unfold itself in its own right. The reader will soon remark, however, that there are three different types of meditation. Certain meditations expose, link and unfold the organic concepts of the proposed trajectory of thought. Let's call them the purely conceptual meditations. Other meditations interpret, on a singular point, texts from the great history of philosophy (in order, eleven names: Plato, Aristotle, Spinoza, Hegel, Mallarmé, Pascal, Hölderlin, Leibniz, Rousseau, Descartes and Lacan). Let's call these the textual meditations. Finally, there are meditations based on fragments of mathematical—or ontological—discourse. These are the meta-ontological meditations. How dependent are these three strands upon one another, the strands whose tress is the book?

- It is quite possible, but dry, to read only the conceptual meditations. However, the proof that mathematics is ontology is not entirely delivered therein, and even if the interconnection of many concepts is established, their actual origin remains obscure. Moreover, the pertinence of this apparatus to a transversal reading of the history of philosophy—which could be opposed to that of Heidegger—is left in suspense.
- It is almost possible to read the textual meditations alone, but at the price of a sentiment of interpretative discontinuity, and without the place of the interpretations being genuinely understandable. Such a reading would transform this book into a collection of essays, and all that would be understood is that it is sensible to read them in a certain order.
- It is possible to read uniquely the meta-ontological meditations. But the risk is that the weight proper to mathematics would confer the value of mere scansions or punctuations upon the philosophical interpretations once they are no longer tied to the conceptual body. This book would be transformed into a close study and commentary of a few crucial fragments of set theory.

For philosophy *here* to become a circulation through the referential—as I have advanced—one must make one's way through all the meditations. Certain pairs, however (conceptual + textual, or, conceptual + meta-ontological), are no doubt quite practical.

Mathematics has a particular power to both fascinate and horrify which I hold to be a social construction: there is no intrinsic reason for it. Nothing is presupposed here apart from attention; a free attention disengaged *a priori* from such horror. Nothing else is required other than an elementary familiarity with formal language—the pertinent principles and conventions are laid out in detail in the 'technical note' which follows Meditation 3.

Convinced, along with the epistemologists, that a mathematical concept only becomes intelligible once one come to grips with its use in demonstrations, I have made a point of reconstituting many demonstrations. I have also left some more delicate but instructive deductive passages for the appendixes. In general, as soon as the technicality of the proof ceases to transport thought that is useful beyond the actual proof, I proceed no further with the demonstration. The five mathematical 'bulwarks' used here are the following:

- The axioms of set theory, introduced, explained and accompanied by a philosophical commentary (parts I and II, then IV and V). There is really no difficulty here for anyone, save that which envelops any concentrated thought.
- The theory of ordinal numbers (part III). The same applies.
- A few indications concerning cardinal numbers (Meditation 26): I go a bit quicker here, supposing practice in everything which precedes this section. Appendix 4 completes these indications; moreover, in my eyes, it is of great intrinsic interest.
- The constructible (Meditation 29)
- The generic and forcing (Meditations 33, 34, and 36).

These last two expositions are both decisive and more intricate. But they are worth the effort and I have tried to use a mode of presentation open to all efforts. Many of the technical details are placed in an appendix or passed over.

I have abandoned the system of constraining, numbered footnotes: if you interrupt the reading by a number, why not put into the actual text whatever you are inviting the reader to peruse? If the reader asks him or herself a question, he or she can go to the end of the book to see if I have given a response. It won't be their fault, for having missed a footnote, but rather mine for having disappointed their demand.

At the end of the book a dictionary of concepts may be found.

PART I

Being: Multiple and Void.
Plato/Cantor

MEDITATION ONE
The One and the Multiple: *a priori* conditions of any possible ontology

Since its Parmenidean organization, ontology has built the portico of its ruined temple out of the following experience: what *presents* itself is essentially multiple; *what* presents itself is essentially one. The reciprocity of the one and being is certainly the inaugural axiom of philosophy —Leibniz's formulation is excellent; 'What is not *a* being is not a *being*'—yet it is also its impasse; an impasse in which the revolving doors of Plato's *Parmenides* introduce us to the singular joy of never seeing the moment of conclusion arrive. For if being is one, then one must posit that what is not one, the multiple, *is not*. But this is unacceptable for thought, because what is presented is multiple and one cannot see how there could be an access to being outside all presentation. If presentation is not, does it still make sense to designate what presents (itself) as being? On the other hand, if presentation is, then the multiple necessarily is. It follows that being is no longer reciprocal with the one and thus it is no longer necessary to consider as one *what* presents itself, inasmuch as it is. This conclusion is equally unacceptable to thought because presentation is only *this* multiple inasmuch as what it presents can be counted as one; and so on.

We find ourselves on the brink of a decision, a decision to break with the arcana of the one and the multiple in which philosophy is born and buried, phoenix of its own sophistic consumption. This decision can take no other form than the following: the one *is not*. It is not a question, however, of abandoning the principle Lacan assigned to the symbolic; that *there is* Oneness. Everything turns on mastering the gap between the presupposition (that must be rejected) of a being of the one and the thesis of its 'there is'. What could there be, which is not? Strictly speaking, it is already too much to say 'there is Oneness' because the 'there', taken as an errant localization, concedes a point of being to the one.

What has to be declared is that the one, which is not, solely exists as *operation*. In other words: there is no one, only the count-as-one. The one, being an operation, is never a presentation. It should be taken quite seriously that the 'one' is a number. And yet, except if we pythagorize, there is no cause to posit that being qua being is number. Does this mean that being is not multiple either? Strictly speaking, yes, because being is only multiple inasmuch as it occurs in presentation.

In sum: the multiple is the regime of presentation; the one, in respect to presentation, is an operational result; being is what presents (itself). On this basis, being is neither one (because only presentation itself is pertinent to the count-as-one), nor multiple (because the multiple is *solely* the regime of presentation).

Let's fix the terminology: I term *situation* any presented multiplicity. Granted the effectiveness of the presentation, a situation is the place of taking-place, whatever the terms of the multiplicity in question. Every situation admits its own particular operator of the count-as-one. This is the most general definition of a *structure*; it is what prescribes, for a presented multiple, the regime of its count-as-one.

When anything is counted as one in a situation, all this means is that it belongs to the situation in the mode particular to the effects of the situation's structure.

A structure allows number to occur within the presented multiple. Does this mean that the multiple, as a figure of presentation, is not 'yet' a number? One must not forget that every situation is structured. The multiple is retroactively legible therein as *anterior* to the one, insofar as the count-as-one is always a *result*. The fact that the one is an operation allows us to say that the domain of the operation is not one (for the one *is not*), and that therefore this domain is multiple; since, *within presentation*, what is not one is necessarily multiple. In other words, the count-as-one (the structure) installs the universal pertinence of the one/multiple couple for any situation.

What will have been counted as one, on the basis of not having been one, turns out to be multiple.

It is therefore always in the after-effect of the count that presentation is uniquely thinkable as multiple, and the numerical inertia of the situation is set out. Yet there is no situation without the effect of the count, and therefore it is correct to state that presentation as such, in regard to number, is multiple.

There is another way of putting this: the multiple is the inertia which can be retroactively discerned starting from the fact that the operation of the count-as-one must effectively operate in order for there to be Oneness. The multiple is the inevitable predicate of what is structured because the structuration—in other words, the count-as-one—is an effect. The one, which is not, cannot present itself; it can only operate. As such it founds, 'behind' its operation, the status of presentation—it is of the order of the multiple.

The multiple evidently splits apart here: 'multiple' is indeed said of presentation, in that it is retroactively apprehended as non-one as soon as being-one is a result. Yet 'multiple' is also said of the composition of the count, that is, the multiple as 'several-ones' counted by the action of structure. There is the multiplicity of inertia, that of presentation, and there is also the multiplicity of composition which is that of number and the effect of structure.

Let's agree to term the first *inconsistent multiplicity* and the second *consistent multiplicity*.

A situation (which means a structured presentation) is, relative to the same terms, their double multiplicity; inconsistent and consistent. This duality is established in the distribution of the count-as-one; inconsistency before and consistency afterwards. Structure is both what obliges us to consider, via retroaction, that presentation is a multiple (inconsistent) and what authorizes us, via anticipation, to compose the terms of the presentation as units of a multiple (consistent). It is clearly recognizable that this distribution of obligation and authorization makes the one—which is not—into a *law*. It is the same thing to say of the one that it is not, and to say that the one is a law of the multiple, in the double sense of being what constrains the multiple to manifest itself as such, and what rules its structured composition.

What form would a discourse on being—qua being—take, in keeping with what has been said?

There is nothing apart from situations. Ontology, if it exists, is *a* situation. We immediately find ourselves caught in a double difficulty.

On the one hand, a situation is a presentation. Does this mean that *a* presentation of being as such is necessary? It seems rather that 'being' is included in what any presentation presents. One cannot see how it could be presented *qua being*.

On the other hand, if ontology—the discourse on being qua being—is a situation, it must admit a mode of the count-as-one, that is, a structure. But wouldn't the count-as-one *of being* lead us straight back into those aporias in which sophistry solders the reciprocity of the one and being? If the one is not, being solely the operation of the count, mustn't one admit that being *is not one*? And in this case, is it not subtracted from every count? Besides, this is exactly what we are saying when we declare it heterogeneous to the opposition of the one and the multiple.

This may also be put as follows: there is no structure of being.

It is at this point that the Great Temptation arises, a temptation which philosophical 'ontologies', historically, have not resisted: it consists in removing the obstacle by posing that ontology is not actually a situation.

To say that ontology is not a situation is to signify that being cannot be signified within a structured multiple, and that only an experience situated beyond all structure will afford us an access to the veiling of being's presence. The most majestic form of this conviction is the Platonic statement according to which the Idea of the Good, despite placing being, as being-supremely-being, in the intelligible region, is for all that ἐπέχεινα τῆς οὐσίας, 'beyond substance'; that is, unpresentable within the configuration of that-which-is-maintained-there. It is an Idea which is not an Idea, whilst being that on the basis of which the very ideality of the Idea maintains its being (τὸ εἶναι), and which therefore, not allowing itself to be known within the articulations of the place, can only be seen or contemplated by a gaze which is the result of an initiatory journey.

I often come across this path of thought. It is well known that, at a *conceptual* level, it may be found in negative theologies, for which the exteriority-to-situation of being is revealed in its heterogeneity to any presentation and to any predication; that is, in its radical alterity to both the multiple form of situations and to the regime of the count-as-one, an alterity which institutes the One of being, torn from the multiple, and nameable exclusively as absolute Other. From the point of view of *experience*, this path consecrates itself to mystical annihilation; an annihilation in which, on the basis of an interruption of all presentative situations, and at the end of a negative spiritual exercise, a Presence is gained, a presence which is exactly that of the being of the One as non-being, thus the annulment of all functions of the count of One. Finally, in terms of *language*, this path of thought poses that it is the poetic resource of language alone, through its sabotage of the law of nominations, which is capable of forming an exception—within the limits of the possible—to the current regime of situations.

The captivating grandeur of the effects of this choice is precisely what calls me to *refuse* to cede on what contradicts it through and through. I will maintain, and it is the wager of this book, that *ontology is a situation*. I will thus have to resolve the two major difficulties ensuing from this option —that of the presentation within which being qua being can be rationally spoken of and that of the count-as-one—rather than making them vanish in the promise of an exception. If I succeed in this task, I will refute, point by point, the consequences of what I will name, from here on, the ontologies of presence—for presence is the exact contrary of presentation. *Conceptually*, it is within the positive regime of predication, and even of formalization, that I will testify to the existence of an ontology. The *experience* will be one of deductive invention, where the result, far from being the absolute singularity of saintliness, will be fully transmissible within knowledge. Finally, the *language*, repealing any poem, will possess the potential of what Frege named ideography. Together the ensemble will oppose—to the temptation of presence—the rigour of the subtractive, in which being is said solely as that which cannot be supposed on the basis of any presence or experience.

The 'subtractive' is opposed here, as we shall see, to the Heideggerean thesis of a withdrawal of being. It is not in the withdrawal-of-its-presence that being foments the forgetting of its original disposition to the point of assigning us—us at the extreme point of nihilism—to a poetic 'over-turning'. No, the ontological truth is both more restrictive and less prophetic: it is in being foreclosed from presentation that being as such is constrained to be sayable, for humanity, within the imperative effect of a law, the most rigid of all conceivable laws, the law of demonstrative and formalizable inference.

Thus, the direction we will follow is that of taking on the apparent paradoxes of ontology as a situation. Of course, it could be said that even a book of this size is not excessive for resolving such paradoxes, far from it. In any case, let us begin.

If there cannot be *a* presentation *of* being because being occurs in every presentation—and this is why it does not present *itself*—then there is one solution left for us: that the ontological situation be *the presentation of presentation*. If, in fact, this is the case, then it is quite possible that what is at stake in such a situation is being qua being, insofar as no access to being is offered to us except presentations. At the very least, a situation whose presentative multiple is that of presentation itself could constitute the place from which all possible access to being is grasped.

But what does it mean to say that a presentation is the presentation of presentation? Is this even conceivable?

The only predicate we have applied to presentation so far is that of the multiple. If the one is not reciprocal with being, the multiple, however, is reciprocal with presentation, in its constitutive split into inconsistent and consistent multiplicity. Of course, in a structured situation—and they are all such—the multiple of presentation is *this* multiple whose terms let themselves be numbered on the basis of the law that is structure (the count-as-one). Presentation 'in general' is more latent on the side of inconsistent multiplicity. The latter allows, within the retroaction of the count, a kind of inert irreducibility of the presented-multiple to appear, an irreducibility of the domain of the presented-multiple for which the operation of the count occurs.

On this basis the following thesis may be inferred: if an ontology is possible, that is, a presentation of presentation, then it is the situation of the pure multiple, of the multiple 'in-itself'. To be more exact; ontology can be solely *the theory of inconsistent multiplicities as such*. 'As such' means that what is presented in the ontological situation is the multiple without any other predicate than its multiplicity. Ontology, insofar as it exists, must necessarily be the science of the multiple qua multiple.

Even if we suppose that such a science exists, what could its structure be, that is, the law of the count-as-one which rules it as a conceptual situation? It seems unacceptable that the multiple qua multiple be composed of ones, since presentation, which is what must be presented, is in itself multiplicity—the one is only there as a result. To compose the multiple according to the one of a law—of a structure—is certainly to lose being, if being is solely 'in situation' as presentation of presentation in general, that is, of the multiple qua multiple, subtracted from the one in its being.

For the multiple to be presented, is it not necessary that it be inscribed in the very law itself that the one *is not*? And that therefore, in a certain manner, the multiple—despite its destiny being that of constituting the place in which the one operates (the 'there is' of 'there is Oneness')—be itself without-one? It is such which is glimpsed in the inconsistent dimension of the multiple of any situation.

But if in the ontological situation the composition that the structure authorizes does not weave the multiple out of ones, what will provide the basis of its composition? What is it, in the end, which is counted as one?

The *a priori* requirement imposed by this difficulty may be summarized in two theses, prerequisites for any possible ontology.

1. The multiple from which ontology makes up its situation is composed solely of multiplicities. There is no one. In other words, every multiple is a multiple of multiples.
2. The count-as-one is no more than the system of conditions through which the multiple can be recognized as multiple.

Mind: this second requirement is extreme. What it actually means is that what ontology counts as one is not 'a' multiple in the sense in which ontology would possess an explicit operator for the gathering-into-one of the multiple, a definition of the multiple-qua-one. This approach would cause us to lose being, because it would become reciprocal to the one again. Ontology would dictate the conditions under which a *multiple* made up *a* multiple. No. What is required is that the operational structure of ontology discern the multiple without having to make a one out of it, and therefore without possessing a definition of the multiple. The count-as-one must stipulate that everything it legislates on is multiplicity of multiplicities, and it must prohibit anything 'other' than the pure multiple —whether it be the multiple of this or that, or the multiple of ones, or the form of the one itself—from occurring within the presentation that it structures.

However, this prescription-prohibition cannot, in any manner, be explicit. It cannot state 'I only accept pure multiplicity', because one would then have to have the criteria, the definition, of what pure multiplicity is. One would thus count it as one and being would be lost again, since the presentation would cease to be presentation of presentation. The prescription is therefore totally implicit. It operates such that it is only ever a matter of pure multiples, yet there is no defined concept of the multiple to be encountered anywhere.

What is a law whose objects are implicit? A prescription which does not name—in its very operation—that alone to which it tolerates application? It is evidently a system of axioms. An axiomatic presentation consists, on the basis of non-defined terms, in prescribing the rule for their manipulation. This rule counts as one in the sense that the non-defined terms are nevertheless defined by their composition; it so happens that there is a *de facto* prohibition of every composition in which the rule is broken and a *de facto* prescription of everything which conforms to the rule. An explicit definition of *what* an axiom system counts as one, or counts as its object-ones, is never encountered.

It is clear that only an axiom system can structure a situation in which what is presented is presentation. It alone avoids having to make a one out of the multiple, leaving the latter as what is implicit in the regulated consequences through which it manifests itself as multiple.

It is now understandable why an ontology proceeds to invert the consistency-inconsistency dyad with regard to the two faces of the law, obligation and authorization.

The axial theme of the doctrine of being, as I have pointed out, is inconsistent multiplicity. But the effect of the axiom system is that of making the latter consist, as an inscribed deployment, however implicit, of pure multiplicity, presentation of presentation. This axiomatic transformation into consistency avoids composition according to the one. It is therefore absolutely specific. Nonetheless, its obligation remains. Before its operation, what it prohibits—without naming or encountering it—in-consists. But what thereby in-consists is nothing other than *impure* multiplicity; that is, the multiplicity which, composable according to the one, or the particular (pigs, stars, gods . . .), in any non-ontological presentation—any presentation in which the presented is not presentation itself—consists according to a defined structure. To accede axiomatically to the presentation of their presentation, these consistent multiples of particular presentations, once purified of all particularity—thus seized before the count-as-one of the situation in which they are presented—must no longer possess any other consistency than that of their pure multiplicity, that is, their mode of inconsistency within situations. It is therefore certain that their primitive consistency is *prohibited* by the axiom system, which is to say it is ontologically inconsistent, whilst their inconsistency (their pure presentative multiplicity) is *authorized* as ontologically consistent.

Ontology, axiom system of the particular inconsistency of multiplicities, seizes the in-itself of the multiple by forming into consistency all inconsistency and forming into inconsistency all consistency. It thereby deconstructs any one-effect; it is faithful to the non-being of the one, so as to unfold, without explicit nomination, the regulated game of the multiple such that it is none other than the absolute form of presentation, thus the mode in which being proposes itself to any access.

MEDITATION TWO
Plato

'If the one is not, nothing is.'
Parmenides

My entire discourse originates in an axiomatic decision; that of the non-being of the one. The dialectical consequences of this decision are painstakingly unfolded by Plato at the very end of the *Parmenides*. We know that this text is consecrated to an 'exercise' of pure thought proposed by the elderly Parmenides to the young Socrates, and that the stakes of this exercise are the consequences that ensue for both the one and for that which is not one (named by Plato 'the others'), from each of the possible hypotheses concerning the being of the one.

What are usually designated as hypotheses six, seven, eight and nine, under the condition of the thesis 'the one is not', proceed to the examination:

- of the one's qualifications or positive participations (hypothesis six);
- of its negative qualifications (hypothesis seven);
- of the others' positive qualifications (hypothesis eight);
- of the others' negative qualifications (hypothesis nine, the last of the entire dialogue).

The impasse of the *Parmenides* is that of establishing that both the one and the others do and do not possess all thinkable determinations, that they are totally everything (πάντα πάντως ἐστί) and that they are not so (τε καὶ οὐκ ἔστι). We are thus led to a general ruin of thought as such by the entire dialectic of the one.

I shall interrupt, however, the process of this impasse at the following symptomatic point: the absolute indetermination of the non-being-one is not established according to the same procedures as the absolute indetermination of the others. In other words, under the hypothesis of the non-being of the one, there is a fundamental asymmetry between the analytic of the multiple and the analytic of the one itself. The basis of this asymmetry is that the non-being of the one is solely analysed as non-being, and nothing is said of the concept of the one, whilst for the other-than-one's, it is a matter of being, such that the hypothesis 'the one is not' turns out to be the one which *teaches us about the multiple*.

Let's see, via an example, how Plato operates with the one. Basing his discourse on a sophistic matrix drawn from the work of Gorgias, he claims that one cannot pronounce 'the one is not' without giving the one that minimal participation in being which is 'to-be-non-being' (τὸ εἶναι μὴ ὄν). This being-non-being is actually the link (δεσμὸν) by means of which the one, if it is not, can be attached to the non-being that it is. In other words, it is a law of rational nomination of non-being to concede—to what is not—the being in eclipse of this non-being of which it is said that it is not. *What* is not possesses, at the very least, the being whose non-being may be indicated; or, as Plato says, it is necessary for the one to *be* the non-being-one (ἔστιν τὸ ἕν οὐκ ὄν).

Yet there is nothing here which concerns the one in respect of its proper concept. These considerations derive from a general ontological theorem: if one can declare that something is not presented, then the latter must at the very least propose its proper name to presentation. Plato explicitly formulates this theorem in his terminology: 'non-being certainly participates in the non-being-ness of not-being-non-being, but, if it is to completely not be, it also participates in the being-ness of to-be-non-being.' It is easy to recognize, in the one(which-is-not)'s paradoxical participation in the being-ness of to-be-non-being, the absolute necessity of marking in some space of being *that* of which the non-being is indicated. It is thus clearly the pure name of the one which is subsumed here as the minimal being of the non-being-one.

Concerning the one itself, however, nothing is thought here, save that the declaration that it is not must be subjected to a law of being. There is no reflection of the one as a concept beyond the hypothetical generality of its non-being. If it were a matter of anything else, and we supposed that it was not, the same consequence of the same theorem would ensue: the paradox of non-being's access to being by means of a name. This paradox is therefore in no way a paradox of the one, because it does nothing more than repeat, with respect to the one, Gorgias' paradox on non-being. Granted, a *determinate* non-being must possess at the very least the being of its determination. But to say such does not determine in any manner the determination whose being is affirmed. That it is the one which is at stake here is beside the point.

The procedure is quite different when it comes to what is not the non-being-one, that is, those 'others', with respect to which the hypothesis of the non-being of the one delivers, on the contrary, a very precious conceptual analysis; in truth, a complete theory of the multiple.

First of all, Plato remarks that what is not the one—that is, the others (ἄλλα)—must be grasped in its difference, its heterogeneity. He writes τά ἄλλα ἕτερα ἔστιν which I would translate as 'the others are Other', simple alterity (the other) here referring back to foundational alterity (the Other), which is to say, to the thought of pure difference, of the multiple as heterogeneous dissemination, and not as a simple repetitive diversity. However, the Other, the ἕτερος, cannot designate the gap between the one and the other-than-one's, because the one is not. The result is that it is in regard to themselves that the others are Others. From the one not being follows the inevitable inference that the other is Other than the other *as* absolutely pure multiple and total dissemination of self.

What Plato is endeavouring to think here, in a magnificent, dense text, is evidently inconsistent multiplicity, which is to say, pure presentation, anterior to any one-effect, or to any structure (Meditation 1). Since being-one is prohibited for the others, *what* presents itself is immediately, and entirely, infinite multiplicity; or, to be more precise, if we maintain the sense of the Greek phrase ἄπειρός πλήθει, multiplicity deprived of any limit to its multiple-deployment. Plato thus formulates an essential ontological truth; that in absence of any being of the one, the multiple in-consists in the presentation of a multiple of multiples without any foundational stopping point. Dissemination without limits is the presentative law itself: 'For whoever thinks in proximity and with accuracy, each one appears as multiplicity without limits, once the one, not being, is lacking.'

The essence of the multiple is to multiply itself in an immanent manner, and such is the mode of the coming-forth of being for whoever thinks *closely* (ἐγγύθεν) on the basis of the non-being of the one. That it be impossible to compose the multiple-without-one, the multiple-in-itself; that, on the contrary, its very being be de-composition, this is precisely what Plato courageously envisaged in the astonishing metaphor of a speculative dream: 'If one took the point of being which seemed to be the smallest, much like a dream within sleep, it would immediately appear multiple instead of its semblance of one, and instead of its extreme smallness, it would appear enormous, compared to the dissemination that it is starting from itself.'

Why is the infinite multiplicity of the multiple like the image of a dream? Why this nocturne, this sleep of thought, to glimpse the dissemination of all supposed atoms? Simply because the inconsistent multiple is actually unthinkable as such. All thought supposes a situation of the thinkable, which is to say a structure, a count-as-one, in which the presented multiple is consistent and numerable. Consequently, the inconsistent multiple is solely—before the one-effect in which it is structured—an ungraspable horizon of being. What Plato wants to get across here—and this is where he is pre-Cantorian—is that there is no form of object for thought which is capable of gathering together the pure multiple, the multiple-without-one, and making it consist: the pure multiple scarcely occurs in presentation before it has already dissipated; its non-occurrence is like the flight of scenes from a dream. Plato writes: 'It is necessary that the entirety of disseminated being shatter apart, as soon as it is grasped by discursive thought.' Wakeful thought ($\delta\iota\acute{\alpha}\nu o\iota\alpha$)—apart from pure set theory—obtains no grasp whatsoever on this below-the-presentable that is multiple-presentation. What thought needs is the—non-being—mediation of the one.

However—and this is the apparent enigma of the end of the *Parmenides*—is it really the multiple which is at stake in the flight and debris metaphorized by the dream? The ninth hypothesis—the ultimate coup de théâtre in a dialogue which is so tense, so close to a drama of the concept—seems to ruin everything which I have just said, by refuting the idea that the alterity of the other-than-one's can be thought—if the one is not—as multiple: 'neither will (the others) be many [$\pi o\lambda\lambda\acute{\alpha}$]. For in many-beings, there would also be the one . . . Given that the one is not among the others, these others will neither be many nor one.' Or, more formally: 'Without the one, it is impossible to have an opinion of the 'many'.'

Thus, after having summoned the dream of the multiple as unlimited inconsistency of the multiple of multiples, Plato abrogates plurality and apparently assigns the others—once the one is not—to not being able to be Others according to either the one or the multiple. Hence the totally nihilist conclusion, the very same evoked in Claudel's *The Town*, by the engineer Isidore de Besme, on the edge of insurrectional destruction: 'If the one is not, nothing [οὐδέν] is.'

But what is the nothing? The Greek language speaks more directly than ours, which is encumbered by the incision of the Subject, legible, since Lacan, in the expletive 'ne'. For 'rien n'est' ('nothing is') is actually said 'οὐδέν ἔστιν', that is, as: 'rien est' ('(the) nothing is'). Therefore, what should be thought here is rather that 'nothing' is the name of the void: Plato's statement should be transcribed in the following manner; if the one is not, what occurs in the place of the 'many' is the pure name of the void, insofar as it alone subsists *as being*. The 'nihilist' conclusion restores, in diagonal to the one/multiple opposition (ἕν/πολλὰ), the point of being of the nothing, the presentable correlate—as name—of this unlimited or inconsistent multiple (πλῆθος) whose dream is induced by the non-being of the one.

And this draws our attention to a variation in Plato's terminology which sheds some light on the enigma: it is not the same Greek word which is used to designate the unlimitedness of the multiple of multiples—whose debris is glimpsed as an eclipse of discursive thought—and to designate the many—a determination that the others cannot tolerate given the one's non-being. The former is said πλῆθος, which alone merits to be translated as 'multiplicity', whilst the latter is said πολλὰ, the many, plurality. The contradiction between the analytic of the pure multiple and the rejection of any plurality—in both cases on the hypothesis of the non-being of the one—is then a mere semblance. The term πλῆθος should be thought as designating the inconsistent multiple, the multiple-without-one, pure presentation, whilst πολλὰ designates the consistent multiple, the composition of ones. The first is subtractive with regard to the one; not only is it compatible with the non-being of the one, but it is only accessible, be it within a dream, on the basis of the ontological abrogation of the one. The second term, πολλὰ, supposes that a count is possible, and thus that a count-as-one structures the presentation. Yet structure, far from supposing the being-of-the-one, the τὸ ἕν ὄν, dismisses it in a pure operational 'there is', and solely allows, as being-qua-being come to presentation, the inconsistent multiple, which it then renders unthinkable. Only the operating 'there is' of the one enables the many (πολλὰ) to be; whereas before its effect, according to the pure non-being of the one, unpresentable multiplicity, πλῆθος, appears so as to disappear. For the Greeks, the unlimitedness—ἄπειρός—of unpresentable multiplicity indicates that it is not supported by any thinkable situation.

If one allows that being is being-in-situation—which means unfolding its limit for the Greeks—it is quite true that in suppressing the 'there is' of the one, one suppresses everything, since 'everything' is necessarily 'many'. The sole result of this suppression is nothingness. But if one is concerned with being-qua-being, the multiple-without-one, it is true that the non-being of the one is that particular truth whose entire effect resides in establishing the dream of a multiple disseminated without limits. It is this 'dream' which was given the fixity of thought in Cantor's creation.

Plato's aporetic conclusion can be interpreted as an impasse of being, situated at the deciding point of the couple of the inconsistent multiple and the consistent multiple. 'If the one is not, (the) nothing is' also means that it is only in completely thinking through the non-being of the one that the name of the void emerges as the unique conceivable presentation of what supports, as unpresentable and as pure multiplicity, any plural presentation, that is, any one-effect.

Plato's text sets four concepts to work on the basis of the apparent couple of the one and the others: the one-being, the there-is of the one, the pure multiple (πλῆθος) and the structured multiple (πολλὰ). If the knot of these concepts remains undone in the final aporia, and if the void triumphs therein, it is solely because the gap between the supposition of the one's being and the operation of its 'there is' remains unthought.

This gap, however, is named by Plato many times in his work. It is precisely what provides the key to the Platonic concept par excellence, participation, and it is not for nothing that at the very beginning of the *Parmenides*, before the entrance of the old master, Socrates has recourse to this concept in order to destroy Zeno's arguments on the one and the multiple.

In Plato's work, as we know, the Idea is the occurrence in beings of the thinkable. There lies its point of being. But on the other hand, it has to support participation, which is to say, the fact that I think, on the basis of its being, existing multiples as one. Thus, these men, these hairs, and these muddy puddles are only presentable to thought insofar as a one-effect occurs among them, from the standpoint of ideal being in which Man, Hair and Mud ek-sist in the intelligible region. The in-itself of the Idea is its ek-sisting being, and its participative capacity is its 'there-is', the crux of its operation. It is in the Idea itself that we find the gap between the supposition of its being (the intelligible region) and the recognition of the one-effect that it supports (participation)—pure 'there is' in excess of its being—with regard to sensible presentation and worldly situations. The

Idea is, and, furthermore, there is Oneness both on its basis and outside it. It is its being, and also the non-being of its operation. On the one hand, it precedes all existence, and therefore all one-effects, and on the other hand, it alone *results* in there being actually thinkable compositions of ones.

One can then understand why *there is not, strictly speaking, an Idea of the one*. In the *Sophist*, Plato enumerates what he calls the supreme genres, the absolutely foundational dialectical Ideas. These five Ideas are: being, movement, rest, the same and the other. The Idea of the one is not included, for no other reason than the one is not. No separable being of the one is conceivable, and in the end this is what the *Parmenides* establishes. The one may solely be found *at* the principle of any Idea, grasped in its operation—of participation—rather than in its being. The 'there is Oneness' concerns any Idea whatsoever, inasmuch as it carries out the count of a multiple and brings about the one, being that on the basis of which it is ensured that such or such an existing thing is this or that.

The 'there-is' of the one has no being, and thus it guarantees, for any ideal being, the efficacy of its presentational function, its structuring function, which splits, before and after its effect, the ungraspable πλῆθος—the plethora of being—from the thinkable cohesion of πολλὰ—the reign of number over effective situations.

MEDITATION THREE
Theory of the Pure Multiple: paradoxes and critical decision

It is quite remarkable that, in the very moment of creating the mathematical theory of the pure multiple—termed 'set theory'—Cantor thought it possible to 'define' the abstract notion of set in the following famous philosopheme: 'By set what is understood is the grouping into a totality of quite distinct objects of our intuition or our thought.' Without exaggeration, Cantor assembles in this definition every single concept whose decomposition is brought about by set theory: the concept of totality, of the object, of distinction, and that of intuition. What makes up a set is not a totalization, nor are its elements objects, nor may distinctions be made in some infinite collections of sets (without a special axiom), nor can one possess the slightest intuition of each supposed element of a modestly 'large' set. 'Thought' alone is adequate to the task, such that what remains of the Cantorian 'definition' basically takes us back—inasmuch as under the name of set it is a matter of being—to Parmenides' aphorism: 'The same, itself, is both thinking and being.'

A great theory, which had to show itself capable of providing a universal language for all branches of mathematics, was born, as is customary, in an extreme disparity between the solidity of its reasoning and the precariousness of its central concept. As had already happened in the eighteenth century with the 'infinitesimally small', this precariousness soon manifested itself in the form of the famous paradoxes of set theory.

In order to practise a philosophical exegesis of these paradoxes—which went on to weaken mathematical certainty and provoke a crisis which it would be wrong to imagine over (it concerns the very essence of mathematics, and it was pragmatically abandoned rather than victoriously resolved) one must first understand that the development of set theory, intricated as it was with that of logic, soon overtook the conception formulated in Cantor's definition, a conception retrospectively qualified as 'naive'. What was presented as an 'intuition of objects' was recast such that it could only be thought as the extension of a concept, or of a property, itself expressed in a partially (or indeed completely, as in the work of Frege and Russell) formalized language. Consequently, one could say the following: given a property, expressed by a formula $\lambda(\alpha)$ with a free variable, I term 'set' all those terms (or constants, or proper names) which possess the property in question, which is to say those terms for which, if l is a term, $\lambda(l)$ is true (demonstrable). If, for example, $\lambda(\alpha)$ is the formula 'α is a natural whole number', I will speak of 'the set of whole numbers' to designate the multiple of what validates this formula; that is, to designate the whole numbers. In other words, 'set' is what counts-as-one a formula's multiple of validation.

For complete understanding of what follows, I recommend that the reader refer without delay to the technical note found at the end of this meditation. It explains the formal writing. The mastery of this writing, acquired after Frege and Russell, enabled advances in two directions.

1. It became possible to rigorously specify the notion of property, to formalize it by reducing it—for example—to the notion of a predicate in a first-order logical calculus, or to a formula with a free variable in a language with fixed constants. I can thus avoid, by means of restrictive constraints, the ambiguities in validation which ensue from the blurred borders of natural language. It is known that if my formula can be 'α is a horse which has wings', then the corresponding set, perhaps reduced to Pegasus alone, would engage me in complex existential discussions whose ground would be that I would have recognized the existence of the One—the very thesis in which every theory of the multiple soon entangles itself.

2. Once the object-language (the formal language) was presented which will be that of the theory in which I operate, it became legitimate to allow that for any formula with a free variable there corresponds the set of terms which validate it. In other words, the naive optimism shown by Cantor concerning the power of intuition to totalize its objects is transferred here to the security that can be guaranteed by a well-constructed language. Such security amounts to the following: control of language (of writing) equals control of the multiple. This is Frege's optimism: every concept

which can be inscribed in a totally formalized language (an ideography) prescribes an 'existent' multiple, which is that of the terms, themselves inscribable, which fall under this concept. The speculative presupposition is that nothing of the multiple can occur in excess of a well-constructed language, and therefore that being, inasmuch as it is constrained to present itself to language as the referent-multiple of a property, cannot cause a breakdown in the architecture of this language if the latter has been rigorously constructed. The master of words is also the master of the multiple.

Such was the thesis. The profound signification of the paradoxes from which set theory was obliged to emerge recast and refounded, or rendered axiomatic, is that this thesis is false. It so happens that a multiplicity (a set) can only correspond to certain properties and certain formulas at the price of the destruction (the incoherency) of the very language in which these formulas are inscribed.

In other words: the multiple does not allow its being to be prescribed from the standpoint of language alone. Or, to be more precise: I do not have the power to count as one, to count as 'set', everything which is subsumable by a property. It is not correct that for *any* formula $\lambda(\alpha)$ there is a corresponding one-set of terms for which $\lambda(\alpha)$ is true or demonstrable.

This ruined the second attempt to define the concept of set, this time on the basis of properties and their extension (Frege) rather than on the basis of intuition and its objects (Cantor). The pure multiple slipped away again from its count-as-one, supposedly accomplished in a clear definition of what a multiple (a set) is.

If one examines the structure of the most well-known paradox, Russell's paradox, one notices that the actual formula in which the failure occurs, that of the constitutive power of language over being-multiple, is quite banal; it is not extraordinary at all. Russell considers the property: 'α is a set which is not an element of itself', that is, $\sim(\alpha \in \alpha)$. It is a quite acceptable property in that all known mathematical sets possess it. For example, it is obvious that the set of whole numbers is not itself a whole number, etc. The counter-examples, however, are a little strange. If I say: 'the set of everything I manage to define in less than twenty words', the very definition that I have just written satisfies itself, having less than twenty words, and thus it is an element of itself. But it feels a bit like a joke.

Thus, forming a set out of all the sets α for which $\sim(\alpha \in \alpha)$ is true seems perfectly reasonable. However, to envisage *this* multiple is to ruin the language of set theory due to the incoherency that may be inferred from it.

That is; say that p (for 'paradoxical') is this set. It can be written $p = \{a \ / \ \sim(a \in a)\}$, which reads, 'all a's such that a is not an element of itself'. What can be said about this p?

If it contains itself as an element, $p \in p$, then it must have the property which defines its elements; that is, $\sim(p \in p)$.

If it does not contain itself as an element, $\sim(p \in p)$, then it has the property which defines its elements; therefore, it is an element of itself: $p \in p$.

Finally, we have: $(p \in p) \rightarrow \sim(p \in p)$.

This equivalence of a statement and its negation annihilates the logical consistency of the language.

In other words: the induction, on the basis of the formula $\sim(a \in a)$, of the set-theoretical count-as-one of the terms which validate it is impossible if one refuses to pay the price—in which all mathematics is abolished—of the incoherency of the language. Inasmuch as we suppose that it counts a multiple as one, the 'set' p is in excess, here, of the formal and deductive resources of the language.

This is what is registered by most logicians when they say that p, precisely due to the banality of the property $\sim(a \in a)$ from which it is supposed to proceed, is 'too large' to be counted as a set in the same way as the others. 'Too large' is the metaphor of an excess of being-multiple over the very language from which it was to be inferred.

It is striking that Cantor, at this point of the impasse, forces a way through with his doctrine of the absolute. If some multiplicities cannot be totalized, or 'conceived as a unity' without contradiction, he declares, it is because they are absolutely infinite rather than transfinite (mathematical). Cantor does not step back from associating the absolute and inconsistency. There where the count-as-one fails, stands God:

> On the one hand, a multiplicity may be such that the affirmation according to which *all* its elements 'are together' leads to a contradiction, such that it is impossible to conceive the multiplicity as a unity, as a 'finite thing'. These multiplicities, I name them *absolutely infinite multiplicities*, or *inconsistent* . . .
>
> When, on the other hand, the totality of the elements of a multiplicity can be thought without contradiction as 'being together', such that their

collection in '*a* thing' is possible, I name it a *consistent multiplicity* or a *set*.

Cantor's ontological thesis is evidently that inconsistency, mathematical impasse of the one-of-the-multiple, orientates thought towards the Infinite as supreme-being, or absolute. That is to say—as can be seen in the text—the idea of the 'too large' is much rather an excess-over-the-one-multiple than an excess over language. Cantor, essentially a theologian, therein ties the absoluteness of being *not* to the (consistent) presentation of the multiple, but to the transcendence through which a divine infinity in-consists, as one, gathering together and numbering any multiple whatsoever.

However, one could also argue that Cantor, in a brilliant anticipation, saw that the absolute point of being of the multiple is not its consistency —thus its dependence upon a procedure of the count-as-one—but its inconsistency, a multiple-deployment that no unity gathers together.

Cantor's thought thus wavers between onto-theology—for which the absolute is thought as a supreme infinite being, thus as trans-mathematical, in-numerable, as a form of the one so radical that no multiple can consist therein—and mathematical ontology, in which consistency provides a theory *of* inconsistency, in that what proves an obstacle to it (paradoxical multiplicity) is its point of impossibility, and thus, quite simply, *is not*. Consequently, it fixes the point of non-being from whence it can be established that there is *a* presentation of being.

It is indeed certain that set theory legislates (explicitly) on what is not, if, that is, it is true that set theory provides a theory of the multiple as the general form of the presentation of being. Inconsistent or 'excessive' multiplicities are nothing more than what set theory ontology designates, prior to its deductive structure, as pure non-being.

That it be in the place of this non-being that Cantor pinpoints the absolute, or God, allows us to isolate the decision in which 'ontologies' of Presence, non-mathematical 'ontologies', ground themselves: the decision to declare that beyond the multiple, even in the metaphor of its inconsistent grandeur, the one is.

What set theory enacts, on the contrary, under the effect of the paradoxes—in which it registers its particular non-being as obstacle (which, by that token, is *the* non-being)—is that the one is not.

It is quite admirable that the same man, Cantor, solely reflected this enactment or operation—in which the one is the non-being of multiple-being, an operation which he invented—in the folly of trying to save God—the one, that is—from any absolute presumption of the multiple.

The real effects of the paradoxes are immediately of two orders:

a. It is necessary to abandon all hope of explicitly defining the notion of set. Neither intuition nor language are capable of supporting the pure multiple—such as founded by the sole relation 'belonging to', written ∈—being counted-as-one in a univocal concept. By consequence, it is of the very essence of set theory to only possess an implicit mastery of its 'objects' (multiplicities, sets): these multiplicities are deployed in an axiom-system in which the property 'to be a set' does not figure.

b. It is necessary to prohibit paradoxical multiples, which is to say, the non-being whose ontological inconsistency has as its sign the ruin of the language. The axiom-system has therefore to be such that what it authorizes to be considered as a set, that is, everything that it speaks of—since, to distinguish sets from anything else within this 'everything', to distinguish the multiple (which is) from the one (which is not), and finally to distinguish being from non-being, a concept of the multiple would be required, a criterion of the set, which is excluded—is *not* correlate to formulas such as ~$(a \in a)$, formulas which induce incoherency.

Between 1908 and 1940 this double task was taken in hand by Zermelo and completed by Fraenkel, von Neumann and Gödel. It was accomplished in the shape of the formal axiom-system, the system in which, in a first-order logic, the pure doctrine of the multiple is presented, such that it can still be used today to set out every branch of mathematics.

I would insist on the fact that, it being set theory at stake, axiomatization is not an artifice of exposition, but an intrinsic necessity. Being-multiple, if trusted to natural language and to intuition, produces an undivided pseudo-presentation of consistency and inconsistency, thus of being and non-being, because it does not clearly separate itself from the presumption of the being of the one. Yet the one and the multiple do not form a 'unity of contraries', since the first is not whilst the second is the very form of any presentation of being. Axiomatization is required such that the multiple, left to the implicitness of its counting rule, be delivered *without concept*, that is, *without implying the being-of-the-one*.

The axiomatization consists in fixing the usage of the relation of belonging, ∈, to which the entire lexicon of mathematics can finally be reduced, if one considers that equality is rather a logical symbol.

The first major characteristic of the Zermelo–Fraenkel formal system (the ZF system) is that its lexicon contains solely one relation, ∈, and therefore no unary predicate, no property in the strict sense. In particular, this system excludes any construction of a symbol whose sense would be 'to be a set'. The multiple is implicitly designated here in the form of a logic of belonging, that is, in a mode in which the 'something = α' in general is presented according to a multiplicity β. This will be inscribed as α ∈ β, α is an element of β. What is counted as *one* is not the concept of the multiple; there is no inscribable thought of what *one*-multiple is. The one is assigned to the sign ∈ alone; that is, to the operator of denotation for the relation between the 'something' in general and the multiple. The sign ∈, *unbeing* of any one, determines, in a uniform manner, the presentation of 'something' as indexed to the multiple.

The second major characteristic of the ZF system immediately revokes it being, strictly speaking, *a* 'something' which is thereby disposed according to its multiple presentation. Zermelo's axiom system contains one type of variable alone, one list of variables. When I write 'α belongs to β', α ∈ β, the signs α and β are variables from the same list, and can thus be substituted for by specifically indistinguishable terms. If one admits, with a grain of salt, Quine's famous formula, 'to be is to be the value of a variable', one can conclude that the ZF system postulates that there is only one type of presentation of being: the multiple. The theory does not distinguish between 'objects' and 'groups of objects' (as Cantor did), nor even between 'elements' and 'sets'. That there is only one type of variable means: all is multiple, everything is a set. If, indeed, the inscription without concept of that-which-is amounts to fixing it as what can be bound, by belonging, to the multiple, and if what can be thus bound cannot be distinguished, in terms of the status of its inscription, from what it is bound to—if, in α ∈ β, α only has the possibility of being an element of the set β inasmuch as it is of the same scriptural type as β, that is, a set itself—then that-which-is is uniformly pure multiplicity.

The theory thus posits that what it presents—its terms—within the axiomatic articulation, and whose concept it does not deliver, is always of the type 'set'; that what belongs to a multiple is always a multiple; and that being an 'element' is not a status of being, an intrinsic quality, but the simple relation, to-be-element-of, through which a multiplicity can be presented by another multiplicity. By the uniformity of its variables, *the theory indicates, without definition, that it does not speak of the one*, and that all *that* it presents, in the implicitness of its rules, is multiple.

Any multiple is intrinsically multiple of multiples: this is what set theory deploys. The third major characteristic of Zermelo's work concerns the procedure it adopts to deal with the paradoxes, and which amounts to the following: a property only determines a multiple under the supposition that there is already a presented multiple. Zermelo's axiom system subordinates the induction of a multiple by language to the existence, prior to that induction, of an initial multiple. The axiom of separation (or of comprehension, or of sub-sets) provides for this.

It is often posited in the critique (and the modern critique) of this axiom that it proposes an arbitrary restriction of the 'dimension' of the multiplicities admitted. Yet this is based on an excessively literal reading of the metaphor 'too large' by which mathematicians designate paradoxical, or inconsistent multiplicities—those whose existential position is in excess of the coherency of the language. One could point out, of course, that Zermelo himself ratifies this restrictive vision of his own enterprise when he writes: 'the solution of these difficulties [must be seen] solely in a suitable restriction of the notion of set.' Yet such a symptom—of an inspired mathematician making do with a metaphorical conceptual relation to what he has created—does not constitute, in my eyes, a philosophically decisive argument. The essence of the axiom of separation is not that of prohibiting multiplicities which are 'too large'. Certainly, this axiom results in there being a bar on excess; but what governs it concerns the knot of language, existence and the multiple.

What are we actually told by the thesis (Fregean) which encounters the paradoxes? That one can infer, on the basis of a property $\lambda(\alpha)$ correctly constructed in a formal language, the existence of a multiple whose terms possess it. That is, there exists a set such that *every* term α for which $\lambda(\alpha)$ is demonstrable is an element of this set:

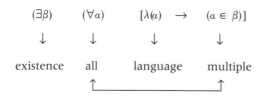

45

The essence of this thesis—which aims to secure the multiple, without ruinous excess, within the grasp of language—is that it is directly existential: for every formula λ(α) the existence of a multiple is automatically and uniformly guaranteed; the multiple which gathers together *all* the terms which validate the formula.

Russell's paradox cuts the coherency of the language with a contradiction: in doing so, it undoes the existence-multiple-language triplet such as it is inscribed—under the primacy of existence (of the existential quantifier)—in the statement above.

Zermelo proposes the same triplet, but tied into a different knot.

The axiom of separation says that, given a multiple, or rather, for any multiple supposed given (supposed presented or existent), there exists the sub-multiple of terms which possess the property expressed by the formula λ(α). In other words, what is induced by a formula of the language is not directly an existence, a presentation of multiplicity, but rather—on the condition that there is already a presentation—the 'separation', within that presentation, and supported by it, of a subset constituted from the terms (thus the multiplicities, since every multiple is a multiple of multiples) which validate the formula.

At a formal level it follows that the axiom of separation, in contrast to the preceding statement, is not existential, since it only infers an existence from its already-being-there in the form of some multiplicity whose presentation has been supposed. The axiom of separation says that for any supposed given multiplicity there exists the part (the sub-multiplicity) whose elements validate λ(α). It thereby reverses the order of the quantifiers: it is a universal statement, in which all supposed existence induces, on the basis of language, an implied existence:

$$\underset{\substack{\uparrow \\ \text{implied existence}}}{} $$

$$(\forall \alpha)\ (\exists \beta)\ (\forall \gamma)\ [[(\gamma \in \alpha)\ \&\ \lambda(\gamma)]\ \rightarrow\ (\gamma \in \beta)]$$

implied existence
↓
$(\forall \alpha)\ (\exists \beta)\ (\forall \gamma)\ [[(\gamma \in \alpha)\ \&\ \lambda(\gamma)]\ \rightarrow\ (\gamma \in \beta)]$

supposed existence   language   multiple

In contrast to Frege's statement which draws the existence of β directly from λ(α), the axiom of separation, on its own, does not allow any conclusion concerning existence. The declaration made by its implicative structure amounts to the following: if there is an α then there is a

β—which is a part of α—whose elements validate the formula $\lambda(\gamma)$. But is there an α? The axiom says nothing of this: it is only a mediation by language from (supposed) existence to (implied) existence.

What Zermelo proposes as the language-multiple-existence knot no longer stipulates that on the basis of language the existence of a multiple is inferred; but rather that language separates out, within a supposed given existence (within some already presented multiple), the existence of a sub-multiple.

Language cannot induce existence, solely a split within existence.

Zermelo's axiom is therefore materialist in that it breaks with the figure of idealinguistery—whose price is the paradox of excess—in which the existential presentation of the multiple is directly inferred from a well-constructed language. The axiom re-establishes that it is solely within the presupposition of existence that language operates—separates—and that what it thereby induces in terms of consistent multiplicity is supported in its being, in an anticipatory manner, by a presentation which is already there. The existence-multiple anticipates what language retroactively separates out from it as implied existence-multiple.

The power of language does not go so far as to institute the 'there is' of the 'there is'. It confines itself to posing that there are some distinctions within the 'there is'. The principles differentiated by Lacan may be remarked therein: that of the real (there is) and that of the symbolic (there are some distinctions).

The formal stigmata of the *already* of a count, in the axiom of separation, is found in the universality of the initial quantifier (the first count-as-one), which subordinates the existential quantifier (the separating count-as-one of language).

Therefore, it is not essentially the dimension of sets which is restricted by Zermelo, but rather the presentative pretensions of language. I said that Russell's paradox could be interpreted as an excess of the multiple over the capacity of language to present it without falling apart. One could just as well say that it is language which is excessive in that it is able to pronounce properties such as $\sim(\alpha \in \alpha)$—it would be a little forced to pretend that these properties can institute a multiple presentation. Being, inasmuch as it is the pure multiple, is subtracted from such forcing; in other words, the rupture of language shows that nothing can accede to consistent presentation in such a manner.

The axiom of separation takes a stand within ontology—its position can be summarized quite simply: the theory of the multiple, as general form of presentation, cannot presume that it is on the basis of its pure formal rule alone—well-constructed properties—that the existence of a multiple (a presentation) is inferred. Being must be already-there; some pure multiple, as multiple of multiples, must be presented in order for the rule to then separate some consistent multiplicity, itself presented subsequently by the gesture of the initial presentation.

However, a crucial question remains unanswered: if, within the framework of axiomatic presentation, it is not on the basis of language that the existence of the multiple is ensured—that is, on the basis of the presentation that the theory presents—then where is the absolutely initial point of being? Which initial multiple has its existence ensured such that the separating function of language can operate therein?

This is the whole problem of the subtractive suture of set theory to being qua being. It is a problem that language cannot avoid, and to which it leads us by foundering upon its paradoxical dissolution, the result of its own excess. Language—which provides for separations and compositions—cannot, alone, institute the existence of the pure multiple; it cannot ensure that what the theory presents is indeed presentation.

Technical Note:
the conventions of writing

The abbreviated or formal writing used in this book is based on what is called first-order logic. It is a question of being able to inscribe statements of the genre: 'for all terms, we have the following property', or 'there does not exist any term which has the following property', or 'if this statement is true, then this other statement is also true.' The fundamental principle is that the formulations 'for all' and 'there exists' only affect terms (individuals) and never properties. In short, the stricture is that properties are not capable, in turn, of possessing properties (this would carry us into a second-order logic).

The graphic realization of these requisites is accomplished by the fixation of five types of sign: variables (which inscribe individuals), logical connectors (negation, conjunction, disjunction, implication and equivalence), quantifiers (universal: 'for all', and existential: 'there exists'), properties or relations (there will only be two of these for us: equality and belonging), and punctuations (parentheses, braces, and square brackets).

- The variables for individuals (for us, multiples or sets) are the Greek letters α, β, γ, δ, π and, sometimes, λ. We will also use indices if need be, to introduce more variables, such as α_1, γ_3, etc. These signs designate *that which* is spoken of, that of which one affirms this or that.
- The quantifiers are the signs $\forall$ (universal quantifier) and $\exists$ (existential quantifier). They are always followed by a variable: $(\forall \alpha)$ reads: 'for all α'; $(\exists \alpha)$ reads: 'there exists α'.

- The logical connectors are the following: ~ (negation), → (implication), *or* (disjunction), & (conjunction), ↔ (equivalence).
- The relations are = (equality) and ∈ (belonging). They always link two variables: $\alpha = \beta$, which reads 'α is equal to β', and $\alpha \in \beta$ which reads 'α belongs to β.'
- The punctuation is comprised of parentheses ( ), braces { }, and square brackets [ ].

A formula is an assemblage of signs which obeys rules of correction. These rules can be strictly defined, but they are intuitive: it is a matter of the formula being readable. For example: $(\forall\alpha)(\exists\beta)[(\alpha \in \beta) \rightarrow \sim(\beta \in \alpha)]$ reads without a problem; 'For all α, there exists at least one β such that if α belongs to β, then β does not belong to α.'

An indeterminate formula will often be noted by the letter λ.

One very important point is the following: in a formula, a variable is either quantified or not. In the formula above, the two variables α and β are quantified (α universally, β existentially). A variable which is not quantified is a free variable. Let's consider, for example, the following formula:

$$(\forall\alpha)[(\beta = \alpha) \leftrightarrow (\exists\gamma)[(\gamma \in \beta) \,\&\, (\gamma \in \alpha)]]$$

It reads intuitively: 'For all α, the equality of β and α is equivalent to the fact that there exists a γ such that γ belongs to β and γ also belongs to α.' In this formula α and γ are quantified but β is free. The formula in question expresses a *property* of β; namely the fact that being equivalent to β is equivalent to such and such (to what is expressed by the piece of the formula: $(\exists\gamma)[(\gamma \in \beta) \,\&\, (\gamma \in \alpha)]$). We will often write $\lambda(\alpha)$ for a formula in which α is a free variable. Intuitively, this means that the formula λ expresses a property of the variable α. If there are two free variables, one writes $\lambda(\alpha,\beta)$, which expresses a relation between the free variables α and β. For example, the formula $(\forall\gamma)[(\gamma \in \alpha) \,or\, (\gamma \in \beta)]$, which reads 'all γ belong either to α or to β, or to both of them' (the logical *or* is not exclusive), fixes a particular relation between α and β.

We will allow ourselves, as we go along, to *define* supplementary signs on the basis of primitive signs. For that it will be necessary to fix via an equivalence, the possibility of retranslating these signs into formulas which contain primitive signs alone. For example, the formula: $\alpha \subset \beta \leftrightarrow (\forall\gamma)[(\gamma \in \alpha) \rightarrow (\gamma \in \beta)]$ defines the relation of inclusion between α and β. It is equivalent to the complete formula: 'for all γ, if γ belongs to

α, then γ belongs to β.' It is evident that the new writing $\alpha \subset \beta$ is merely an abbreviation for a formula $\lambda(\alpha, \beta)$ written uniquely with primitive signs, and in which α and β are free variables.

In the body of the text the reading of the formulas should not pose any problems, moreover, they will always be introduced. Definitions will be explained. The reader can trust the intuitive sense of the written forms.

MEDITATION FOUR
The Void: Proper name of being

Take any situation in particular. It has been said that its structure—the regime of the count-as-one—splits the multiple which is presented there: splits it into consistency (the composition of ones) and inconsistency (the inertia of the domain). However, inconsistency is not actually presented as such since all presentation is under the law of the count. Inconsistency as pure multiple is solely the presupposition that prior to the count the one is not. Yet what is explicit in any situation is rather that the one is. In general, a situation is not such that the thesis 'the one is not' can be presented therein. On the contrary, because the law is the count-as-one, nothing is presented in a situation which is not counted: the situation envelops existence with the one. Nothing is presentable in a situation otherwise than under the effect of structure, that is, under the form of the one and its composition in consistent multiplicities. The one is thereby not only the regime of structured presentation but also the regime of the possible of presentation itself. In a non-ontological (thus non-mathematical) situation, the multiple is possible only insofar as it is explicitly ordered by the law according to the one of the count. Inside the situation there is no graspable inconsistency which would be subtracted from the count and thus a-structured. Any situation, seized in its immanence, thus reverses the inaugural axiom of our entire procedure. It states that the one is and that the pure multiple—inconsistency—is not. This is entirely natural because an indeterminate situation, not being the presentation of presentation, necessarily identifies being with what is presentable, thus with the possibility of the one.

It is therefore *veridical* (I will found the essential distinction between the true and the veridical much further on in Meditation 31) that, inside what a situation establishes as a form of knowledge, being is being in the possibility of the one. It is Leibniz's thesis ('What is not *a* being is not a *being*') which literally governs the immanence of a situation and its horizon of verity. It is a thesis of the law.

This thesis exposes us to the following difficulty: if, in the immanence of a situation, its inconsistency does not come to light, nevertheless, its count-as-one being an operation itself indicates that the one is a result. Insofar as the one is a result, by necessity 'something' of the multiple does not absolutely coincide with the result. To be sure, there is no antecedence of the multiple which would give rise to presentation because the latter is always already-structured such that there is only oneness or consistent multiples. But this 'there is' leaves a remainder: the law in which it is deployed is discernible as operation. And although there is never anything other—in a situation—*than* the result (everything, in the situation, is counted), what thereby results marks out, before the operation, a must-be-counted. It is the latter which causes the structured presentation to waver towards the phantom of inconsistency.

Of course, it remains certain that this phantom—which, on the basis of the fact that being-one results, subtly unhinges the one from being in the very midst of the situational thesis that only the one is—cannot in any manner be presented itself, because the regime of presentation is consistent multiplicity, the result of the count.

By consequence, since everything is counted, yet given that the one of the count, obliged to be a result, leaves a phantom remainder—of the multiple not originally being in the form of the one—one has to allow that inside the situation the pure or inconsistent multiple is both excluded from everything, and thus from the presentation itself, and included, in the name of what 'would be' the presentation itself, the presentation 'in-itself', if what the law does not authorize to think was thinkable: that the one is not, that the being of consistency is inconsistency.

To put it more clearly, once the entirety of a situation is subject to the law of the one and consistency, it is necessary, from the standpoint of immanence to the situation, that the pure multiple, absolutely unpresentable according to the count, be *nothing*. But being-nothing is as distinct from non-being as the 'there is' is distinct from being.

Just as the status of the one is decided between the (true) thesis 'there is oneness' and the (false) thesis of the ontologies of presence, 'the one is', so is the status of the pure multiple decided, in the immanence of a non-ontological situation: between the (true) thesis 'inconsistency is nothing', and the (false) structuralist or legalist thesis 'inconsistency is not.'

It is quite true that prior to the count there is nothing because everything is counted. Yet this being-nothing—wherein resides the illegal inconsistency of being—is the base of there being the 'whole' of the compositions of ones in which presentation takes place.

It must certainly be assumed that the effect of structure is complete, that what subtracts itself from the latter is nothing, and that the law does not encounter singular islands in presentation which obstruct its passage. In an indeterminate situation there is no rebel or subtractive presentation of the pure multiple upon which the empire of the one is exercised. Moreover this is why, within a situation, the search for something that would feed an intuition of being qua being is a search in vain. The logic of the lacuna, of what the count-as-one would have 'forgotten', of the excluded which may be positively located as a sign or real of pure multiplicity, is an impasse—an illusion—of thought, as it is of practice. A situation never proposes anything other than multiples woven from ones, and the law of laws is that nothing limits the effect of the count.

And yet, the correlate thesis also imposes itself; that there is a being of nothing, as form of the unpresentable. The 'nothing' is what names the unperceivable gap, cancelled then renewed, between presentation as structure and presentation as structured-presentation, between the one as result and the one as operation, between presented consistency and inconsistency as what-will-have-been-presented.

Naturally it would be pointless to set off in search of the nothing. Yet it must be said that this is exactly what poetry exhausts itself doing; this is what renders poetry, even at the most sovereign point of its clarity, even in its peremptory affirmation, complicit with death. If one must—alas!—concede that there is some sense in Plato's project of crowning the poets in order to then send them into exile, it is because poetry propagates the idea of an intuition of the nothing in which being would reside when there is not even the site for such intuition—they call it Nature—because everything is consistent. The only thing we can affirm is this: every situation implies the nothing of its all. But the nothing is neither a place nor a term of the situation. For if the nothing were a term that could only mean one thing; that it had been counted as one. Yet everything which has been counted is within the consistency of presentation. It is thus ruled out that the nothing—which here names the pure will-have-been-counted as distinguishable from the effect of the count, and thus distinguishable from presentation—be taken as a term. There is not a-nothing, there is 'nothing', phantom of inconsistency.

By itself, the nothing is no more than the name of unpresentation in presentation. Its status of being results from the following: one has to admit that if the one results, then 'something'—which is not an in-situation-term, and which is thus nothing—has not been counted, this 'something' being that it was necessary that the operation of the count-as-one operate. Thus it comes down to exactly the same thing to say that the nothing is the operation of the count—which, as source of the one, is not itself counted—and to say that the nothing is the pure multiple upon which the count operates—which 'in-itself', as non-counted, is quite distinct from how it turns out according to the count.

The nothing names that undecidable of presentation which is its unpresentable, distributed between the pure inertia of the domain of the multiple, and the pure transparency of the operation thanks to which there is oneness. The nothing is as much that of structure, thus of consistency, as that of the pure multiple, thus of inconsistency. It is said with good reason that nothing is subtracted from presentation, because it is on the basis of the latter's double jurisdiction, the law and the multiple, that the nothing is the nothing.

For an indeterminate situation, there is thus an equivalent to what Plato named, with respect to the great cosmological construction of the *Timaeus*—an almost carnivalesque metaphor of universal presenta-tion—the 'errant cause', recognizing its extreme difficulty for thought. What is at stake is an unpresentable yet necessary figure which designates the gap between the result-one of presentation and that 'on the basis of which' there is presentation; that is, the non-term of any totality, the non-one of any count-as-one, the nothing particular to the situation, the unlocalizable void point in which it is manifest both that the situation is sutured to being and that the *that-which*-presents-itself wanders in the presentation in the form of a subtraction from the count. It would already be inexact to speak of this nothing as a point because it is neither local nor global, but scattered all over, nowhere and everywhere: it is such that no encounter would authorize it to be held as presentable.

I term *void* of a situation this suture to its being. Moreover, I state that every structured presentation unpresents 'its' void, in the mode of this non-one which is merely the subtractive face of the count.

I say 'void' rather than 'nothing', because the 'nothing' is the name of the void correlative to the *global* effect of structure (*everything* is counted); it is more accurate to indicate that not-having-been-counted is also quite *local* in its occurrence, since it is not counted *as one*. 'Void' indicates the failure of the one, the not-one, in a more primordial sense than the not-of-the-whole.

It is a question of names here—'nothing' or 'void'—because being, designated by these names, is neither local nor global. The name I have chosen, the void, indicates precisely that nothing is presented, no term, and also that the designation of that nothing occurs 'emptily', it does not locate it structurally.

The void is the name of being—of inconsistency—according to a situation, inasmuch as presentation gives us therein an unpresentable access, thus non-access, to this access, in the mode of what is not-one, nor composable of ones; thus what is qualifiable within the situation solely as the errancy of the nothing.

It is essential to remember that no term within a situation designates the void, and that in this sense Aristotle quite rightly declares in the *Physics* that the void is not; if one understands by 'being' what can be located within a situation, that is, a term, or what Aristotle called a substance. Under the normal regime of presentation it is veridical that one cannot say of the void, non-one and unsubstantial, that it is.

I will establish later on (Meditation 17) that for the void to become localizable at the level of presentation, and thus for a certain type of intra-situational assumption of being qua being to occur, a dysfunction of the count is required, which results from an excess-of-one. The event will be this ultra-one of a hazard, on the basis of which the void of a situation is retroactively discernible.

But for the moment we must hold that in a situation there is no conceivable encounter with the void. The normal regime of structured situations is that of the imposition of an absolute 'unconscious' of the void.

Hence one can deduce a supplementary prerequisite for ontological discourse, if it exists, and if it is—as I maintain—a situation (the mathematical situation). I have already established:

> *a*. that ontology is necessarily presentation of presentation, thus theory of the pure multiple without-one, theory of the multiple of multiples;

b. that its structure can only be that of an implicit count, therefore that of an axiomatic presentation, without a concept-one of its terms (without a concept of the multiple).

We can now add that *the sole term from which ontology's compositions without concept weave themselves is necessarily the void.*

Let's establish this point. If ontology is the particular situation which presents presentation, it must also present the law of all presentation—the errancy of the void, the unpresentable as non-encounter. Ontology will only present presentation inasmuch as it provides a theory of the presentative suture to being, which, speaking veridically, from the standpoint of any presentation, is the void in which the originary inconsistency is subtracted from the count. Ontology is therefore required to propose a theory of the void.

But if it is theory of the void, ontology, in a certain sense, can *only* be theory of the void. That is, if one supposed that ontology axiomatically presented other terms than the void—irrespective of whatever obstacle there may be to 'presenting' the void—this would mean that it distinguished between the void and other terms, and that its structure thus authorized the count-as-one of the void as such, according to its specific difference to 'full' terms. It is obvious that this would be impossible, since, as soon as it was counted as one in its difference to the one-full, the void would be filled with this alterity. If the void is thematized, it must be according to the presentation of its errancy, and not in regard to some singularity, necessarily full, which would distinguish it as one within a differentiating count. The only solution is for *all* of the terms to be 'void' such that they are composed from the void alone. The void is thus distributed everywhere, and everything that is distinguished by the implicit count of pure multiplicities is a modality-according-to-the-one of the void itself. This alone would account for the fact that the void, in a situation, is the unpresentable of presentation.

Let's rephrase this. Given that ontology is the theory of the pure multiple, what exactly could be composed by means of its presentative axiom system? What *existent* is seized upon by the Ideas of the multiple whose axioms institute the legislating action upon the multiple qua multiple? Certainly not the one, which is not. Every multiple is composed of multiples. This is the first ontological law. But where to start? What is the absolutely original existential position, the first count, if it cannot be a first *one*? There is no question about it: the 'first' presented multiplicity without concept has to be a multiple of nothing, because if it was a multiple of something, that something would then be in the position of the one. And it is necessary, thereafter, that the axiomatic rule solely authorize compositions on the basis of this multiple-of-nothing, which is to say on the basis of the void.

Third approach. What ontology theorizes is the inconsistent multiple of any situation; that is, the multiple subtracted from any particular law, from any count-as-one—the a-structured multiple. The proper mode in which inconsistency wanders within the whole of a situation is the nothing, and the mode in which it un-presents itself is that of subtraction from the count, the non-one, the void. The absolutely primary theme of ontology is therefore the void—the Greek atomists, Democritus and his successors, clearly understood this—but it is also its final theme—this was not their view—because in the last resort, *all* inconsistency is unpresentable, thus void. If there are 'atoms', they are not, as the materialists of antiquity believed, a second principle of being, the one after the void, but compositions of the void itself, ruled by the ideal laws of the multiple whose axiom system is laid out by ontology.

Ontology, therefore, can only count the void as existent. This statement announces that ontology deploys the ruled order—the consistency—of what is nothing other than the suture-to-being of any situation, the *that which* presents itself, insofar as inconsistency assigns it to solely being the unpresentable of any presentative consistency.

It appears that in this way a major problem is resolved. I said that if being is presented as pure multiple (sometimes I shorten this perilously by saying being is multiple), being *qua being*, strictly speaking, is neither one nor multiple. Ontology, the supposed science of being qua being, being submitted to the law of situations, *must* present; at best, it must present presentation, which is to say the pure multiple. How can it avoid deciding, in respect to being qua being, in favour of the multiple? It avoids doing so inasmuch as its own point of being is the void; that is, this 'multiple' which is neither one nor multiple, being the multiple of nothing, and therefore, as far as it is concerned, presenting *nothing* in the form of the multiple, no more than in the form of the one. This way ontology states that presentation is certainly multiple, but that the being of presentation, the that which is presented, being void, is subtracted from the one/multiple dialectic.

The following question then arises: if that is so, what purpose does it serve to speak of the void as 'multiple' in terms such as the 'multiple of nothing'? The reason for such usage is that ontology is a situation, and thus everything that it presents falls under its law, which is to know nothing apart from the multiple-without-one. The result is that the void is *named* as multiple even if, composing nothing, it does not actually fit into the intra-situational opposition of the one and the multiple. Naming the void as multiple is the only solution left by not being able to name it as one, given that ontology sets out as its major principle the following: the one is not, but any structure, even the axiomatic structure of ontology, establishes that there are uniquely ones and multiples—even when, as in this case, it is in order to annul the being of the one.

One of the acts of this annulment is precisely to posit that the void is multiple, that it is the first multiple, the very being from which any multiple presentation, when presented, is woven and numbered.

Naturally, because the void is indiscernible as a term (because it is not-one), its inaugural appearance is a pure act of nomination. This name cannot be specific; it cannot place the void under anything that would subsume it—this would be to reestablish the one. The name cannot indicate that the void is this or that. The act of nomination, being a-specific, consumes itself, indicating nothing other than the unpresentable as such. In ontology, however, the unpresentable occurs within a presentative forcing which disposes it as the nothing from which everything proceeds. The consequence is that the name of the void is a pure *proper name*, which indicates itself, which does not bestow any index of difference within what it refers to, and which auto-declares itself in the form of the multiple, despite there being *nothing* which is numbered by it.

Ontology commences, ineluctably, once the legislative Ideas of the multiple are unfolded, by the pure utterance of the arbitrariness of a proper name. This name, this sign, indexed to the void, is, in a sense that will always remain enigmatic, the proper name of being.

MEDITATION FIVE
The Mark ∅

The execution of ontology—which is to say of the *mathematical* theory of the multiple, or set theory—can only be presented, in conformity with the requisition of the concept (Meditation 1), as a system of axioms. The grand Ideas of the multiple are thus inaugural statements concerning variables α, β, γ, etc., in respect of which it is implicitly agreed that they denote pure multiples. This presentation excludes any explicit definition of the multiple—the sole means of avoiding the existence of the One. It is remarkable that these statements are so few in number: nine axioms or axiom-schemas. One can recognize in this economy of presentation the sign that the 'first principles of being', as Aristotle said, are as few as they are crucial.

Amongst these statements, one alone, strictly speaking, is existential; that is, its task is to directly inscribe an existence, and not to regulate a construction which presupposes there already being a presented multiple. As one might have guessed, this statement concerns the void.

In order to think the singularity of this existential statement on the void, let's first rapidly situate the principal Ideas of the multiple, those with a strictly operational value.

1. THE SAME AND THE OTHER: THE AXIOM OF EXTENSIONALITY

The axiom of extensionality posits that two sets are equal (identical) if the multiples of which they are the multiple, the multiples whose set-theoretical count as one they ensure, are 'the same'. What does 'the same' mean? Isn't there a circle here which would found the same upon the same? In natural and inadequate vocabulary, which distinguishes between 'elements' and 'sets', a vocabulary which conceals that there are only multiples, the axiom says: 'two sets are identical if they have the same elements.' But we know that 'element' does not designate anything intrinsic; all it indicates is that a multiple γ is presented by the presentation of another multiple, α, which is written $\gamma \in \alpha$. The axiom of extensionality thus amounts to saying: if every multiple presented in the presentation of α is presented in that of β, and the inverse, then these two multiples, α and β, are the same.

The logical architecture of the axiom concerns the universality of the assertion and not the recurrence of the same. It indicates that if, for every multiple γ, it is equivalent and thus indifferent to affirm that it belongs to α or to affirm that it belongs to β, then α and β are indistinguishable and can be completely substituted for each other. The *identity* of multiples is founded on the *indifference* of belonging. This is written:

$$(\forall \gamma)[(\gamma \in \alpha) \leftrightarrow (\gamma \in \beta)] \rightarrow (\alpha = \beta)$$

The differential marking of the two sets depends on what belongs to their presentations. But the 'what' is always a multiple. That such a multiple, say γ, maintains a relation of belonging with α—being one of the multiples from which α is composed—and does not maintain such a relation with β, entails that α and β are counted as different.

This purely extensional character of the regime of the same and the other is inherent to the nature of set theory, being theory of the multiple-without-one, the multiple as multiple of multiples. What possible source could there be for the existence of difference, if not that of a multiple lacking from a multiple? No particular quality can be of use to us to mark difference here, not even that the one can be distinguished from the multiple, because the one is not. What the axiom of extension does is reduce the same and the other to the strict rigour of the count such that it structures the presentation of presentation. The same is the same of the count of multiples from which all multiples are composed, once counted as one.

However, let us note: the law of the same and the other, the axiom of extensionality, does not tell us in any manner whether anything exists. All it does is fix, for any possibly existent multiple, the canonical rule of its differentiation.

2. THE OPERATIONS UNDER CONDITION: AXIOMS OF THE POWERSET, OF UNION, OF SEPARATION AND OF REPLACEMENT

If we leave aside the axioms of choice, of infinity, and of foundation—whose essential metaontological importance will be set out later on—four other 'classic' axioms constitute a second category, all being of the form: 'Take any set α which is supposed existent. There then exists a second set β, constructed on the basis of α, in such a manner.' These axioms are equally compatible with the non-existence of anything whatsoever, with absolute non-presentation, because they solely indicate an existence under the condition of another existence. The purely conditional character of existence is again marked by the logical structure of these axioms, which are all of the type 'for all α, there exists β such that it has a defined relation to α.' The 'for all α' evidently signifies: if there exists an α, then in all cases there exists a β, associated to α according to this or that rule. But the statement does not decide upon the existence or non-existence of even one of these α's. Technically speaking, this means that the *prefix*—the initial quantifier—of these axioms is of the type 'for all . . . there exists . . . such that . . . ', that is, $(\forall\alpha)(\exists\beta)[\ \ldots\ ]$. It is clear, on the other hand, that an axiom which affirmed an unconditioned existence would be of the type 'there exists . . . such that', and would thus commence with the existential quantifier.

These four axioms—whose detailed technical examination would be of no use here—concern guarantees of existence for constructions of multiples on the basis of certain internal characteristics of supposed existent multiples. Schematically:

a. The axiom of the powerset (the set of subsets)

This axiom affirms that given a set, the subsets of that set can be counted-as-one: they are a set. What is a subset of a multiple? It is a multiple such that all the multiples which are presented in its presentation (which 'belong' to it) are also presented by the initial multiple α, *without the inverse being necessarily true* (otherwise we would end up with extensional identity again). The logical structure of this axiom is not one of equivalence but one of implication. The set β is a subset of α—this is written $\beta \subset \alpha$—if, when γ is an element of β, that is, $\gamma \in \beta$, it is then also element of α, thus $\gamma \in \alpha$. In other words, $\beta \subset \alpha$—which reads 'β is included in α'—is an abbreviation of the formula: $(\forall\gamma)[(\gamma \in \beta) \rightarrow (\gamma \in \alpha)]$.

In Meditations 7 and 8, I will return to the concept of subset or sub-multiple, which is quite fundamental, and to the distinction between *belonging* (∈) and *inclusion* (⊂).

For the moment it is enough to know that the axiom of the powerset guarantees that *if* a set exists, *then* another set also exists that counts as one all the subsets of the first. In more conceptual language: if a multiple is presented, then another multiple is also presented whose terms (elements) are the sub-multiples of the first.

b. The axiom of union

Since a multiple is a multiple of multiples, it is legitimate to ask if the power of the count via which *a* multiple is presented also extends to the unfolded presentation of the multiples which compose it, grasped in turn as multiples of multiples. Can one internally disseminate the multiples out of which a multiple makes the one of the result? This operation is the inverse of that guaranteed by the axiom of the powerset.

The latter ensures that the multiple of all the regroupings is counted as one; that is, the multiple of all the subsets composed from multiples which belong to a given multiple. There is the result-one (the set) of all the possible *compositions*—all the inclusions—of what maintains with a given set the relation of belonging. Can I systematically count the *decompositions* of the multiples that belong to a given multiple? Because if a multiple is a multiple of multiples, then it is also a multiple of multiples of multiples of multiples, etc . . .

This is a double question:

- *a.* Does the count-as-one extend to decompositions? Is there an axiom of dissemination just as there is one of composition?
- *b.* Is there a halting point—given that the process of dissemination, as we have just seen, appears to continue to infinity?

The second question is very profound and the reason for this depth is obvious. Its object is to find out where presentation is sutured to some fixed point, to some atom of being that could no longer be decomposed. This would seem to be impossible if being-multiple is the absolute form of presentation. The response to this question will be set out in two stages; by the axiom of the void, a little further on, and then by the examination of the axiom of foundation, in Meditation 18.

The first question is decided here by the axiom of union which states that each step of the dissemination is counted as one. That is, it states that the multiples from which the multiples which make up a one-multiple are composed, form a set themselves (remember that the word 'set', which is neither defined nor definable, designates what the axiomatic presentation authorizes to be counted as one).

Using the metaphor of elements—itself a perpetually risky substantialization of the relation of belonging—the axiom is phrased as such: for every set, there exists the set of the elements of the elements of that set. That is, if α is presented, a certain β is also presented to which all the δ's belong which also belong to some γ which belongs to α. In other words: if $\gamma \in \alpha$ and $\delta \in \gamma$, there then exists a β such that $\delta \in \beta$. The multiple β gathers together the first dissemination of α, that obtained by decomposing into multiples the multiples which belong to it, thus by *un-counting* α:

$$(\forall \alpha)(\exists \beta)[(\delta \in \beta) \leftrightarrow (\exists \gamma)[(\gamma \in \alpha) \ \& \ (\delta \in \gamma)]]$$

Given α, the set β whose existence is affirmed here will be written $\cup \, \alpha$ (*union* of α). The choice of the word 'union' refers to the idea that this axiomatic proposition exhibits the very essence of what a multiple 'unifies'—multiples—and that this is exhibited by 'unifying' the second multiples (in regard to the initial one) from which, in turn, the first multiples—those from which the initial one results—are composed.

The fundamental homogeneity of being is supposed henceforth on the basis that $\cup \, \alpha$, which disseminates the initial one-multiple and then counts as one what is thereby disseminated, is no more or less a multiple itself than the initial set. Just like the powerset, the union set does not in any way remove us from the concept-less reign of the multiple. Neither lower down, nor higher up, whether one disperses or gathers together, the theory does not encounter any 'thing' which is heterogeneous to the pure multiple. Ontology announces herein neither One, nor All, nor Atom; solely the uniform axiomatic count-as-one of multiples.

c. The axiom of separation, or of Zermelo

Studied in detail in Meditation 3.

d. The axiom-schema of replacement (or of substitution)

In its natural formulation, the axiom of replacement says the following: if you have a set and you replace its elements by other elements, you obtain a set.

In its metaontological formulation, the axiom of replacement says rather: if a multiple of multiples is presented, another multiple is also presented which is composed from the substitution, one by one, of new multiples for the multiples presented by the first multiple. The new multiples are supposed as having been presented themselves elsewhere.

The idea—singular, profound—is the following: if the count-as-one operates by giving the consistency of being one-multiple to some multiples, it will also operate if these multiples are replaced, term by term, by others. This is equivalent to saying that *the consistency of a multiple does not depend upon the particular multiples whose multiple it is*. Change the multiples and the one-consistency—which is a result—remains, as long as you operate, however, your substitution multiple by multiple.

What set theory affirms here, purifying again what it performs as presentation of the presentation-multiple, is that the count-as-one of multiples is indifferent to *what* these multiples are multiples of; provided, of course, that it be guaranteed that nothing other than multiples are at stake. In short, the attribute 'to-be-*a*-multiple' transcends the particular multiples which are elements of a given multiple. The making-up-a-multiple (the 'holding-together' as Cantor used to say), ultimate structured figure of presentation, maintains itself as such, even if everything from which it is composed is replaced.

One can see just how far set theory takes its vocation of presenting the pure multiple alone: to the point at which the count-as-one organized by its axiom system institutes its operational permanence on the theme of the bond-multiple in itself, devoid of any specification of what it binds together.

The multiple is genuinely presented as form-multiple, invariant in any substitution which affects its terms; I mean, invariant in that it is always disposed in the one-bond of the multiple.

More than any other axiom, the axiom of replacement is suited—even to the point of over-indicating it—to the mathematical situation being presentation of the pure presentative form in which being occurs as that-which-is.

However, no more than the axioms of extensionality, separation, subsets or union does the axiom of replacement induce the existence of any multiple whatsoever.

The axiom of extensionality fixes the regime of the same and the other.

The powerset and the union-set regulate internal compositions (subsets) and disseminations (union) such that they remain under the law of the count; thus, nothing is encountered therein, neither lower down nor higher up, which would prove an obstacle to the uniformity of presentation as multiple.

The axiom of separation subordinates the capacity of language to present multiples to the fact of there already being presentation.

The axiom of replacement posits that the multiple is under the law of the count qua form-multiple, incorruptible idea of the bond.

In sum, these five axioms or axiom-schemas fix the system of Ideas under whose law any presentation, as form of being, lets itself be presented: belonging (unique primitive idea, ultimate signifier of presented-being), difference, inclusion, dissemination, the language/existence couple, and substitution.

We definitely have the entire material for an ontology here. Save that none of these inaugural statements in which the law of Ideas is given has yet decided the question: 'Is there something rather than nothing?'

3. THE VOID, SUBTRACTIVE SUTURE TO BEING

At this point the axiomatic decision is particularly risky. What privilege could *a* multiple possess such that it be designated as the multiple whose existence is inaugurally affirmed? Moreover, if it is *the* multiple from which all the others result, by compositions in conformity with the Ideas of the multiple, is it not in truth that *one* whose non-being has been the focus of our entire effort? If, on the other hand, it is a multiple-counted-as-one, thus a multiple of multiples, how could it be the absolutely first multiple, already being the result of a composition?

This question is none other than that of the suture-to-being of a theory—axiomatically presented—of presentation. The existential index to be found is that by which the legislative system of Ideas—which ensures that nothing affects the purity of the multiple—proposes itself as the inscribed deployment of being-qua-being.

But to avoid lapsing into a non-ontological situation, there is a prerequisite for this index: it cannot propose *anything* in particular; consequently, it can neither be a matter of the one, which is not, nor of the composed multiple, which is never anything but a result of the count, an effect of structure.

The solution to the problem is quite striking: maintain the position that nothing is delivered by the law of the Ideas, but *make* this nothing *be* through the assumption of a proper name. In other words: *verify, via the excedentary choice of a proper name, the unpresentable alone as existent*; on its basis the Ideas will subsequently cause all admissible forms of presentation to proceed.

In the framework of set theory what is presented is multiple of multiples, the form of presentation itself. For this reason, the unpresentable can only figure within language as what is 'multiple' of *nothing*.

Let's also note this point: the difference between two multiples, as regulated by the axiom of extensionality, can only be marked by those multiples that actually belong to the two multiples to be differentiated. A multiple-of-nothing thus has no conceivable differentiating mark. The unpresentable is inextensible and therefore in-different. The result is that the inscription of this in-different will be necessarily negative because no possibility—no multiple—can indicate that it is on *its* basis that existence is affirmed. This requirement that the absolutely initial existence be that of a negation shows that being is definitely sutured to the Ideas of the multiple in the subtractive mode. Here begins the expulsion of any presentifying assumption of being.

But what is it that this negation—in which the existence of the unpresentable as in-difference is inscribed—is able to negate? Since the primitive idea of the multiple is belonging, and since it is a matter of negating the multiple as multiple of multiples—without, however, resurrecting the one—it is certain that it is belonging as such which is negated. The unpresentable is that to which nothing, no multiple, belongs; consequently, it cannot present itself in its difference.

To negate belonging is to negate presentation and therefore existence because existence is being-in-presentation. The structure of the statement that inscribes the 'first' existence is thus, in truth, the negation of any existence according to belonging. This statement will say something like: 'there exists that to which no existence can be said to belong'; or, 'a 'multiple' exists which is subtracted from the primitive Idea of the multiple.'

This singular axiom, the sixth on our list, is *the axiom of the void-set*.

In its natural formulation—this time actually contradicting its own clarity—it says: 'There exists a set which has no element'; a point at which the subtractive of being causes the intuitive distinction between elements and sets to break down.

In its metaontological formulation the axiom says: the unpresentable is presented, as a subtractive term of the presentation of presentation. Or: a multiple is, which is not under the Idea of the multiple. Or: being lets itself be named, within the ontological situation, as that from which existence does not exist.

In its technical formulation—the most suitable for conceptual exposition—the axiom of the void-set will begin with an existential quantifier (thereby declaring that being invests the Ideas), and continue with a negation of existence (thereby un-presenting being), which will bear on belonging (thereby unpresenting being as multiple since the idea of the multiple is $\in$). Hence the following (negation is written $\sim$):

$$(\exists \beta)[\sim(\exists \alpha)(\alpha \in \beta)]$$

This reads: there exists β such that there does not exist any α which belongs to it.

Now, in what sense was I able to say that this β whose existence is affirmed here, and which is thus no longer a simple Idea or a law but an ontological suture—the existence of an inexistent—was in truth a proper name? A proper name requires its referent to be unique. One must carefully distinguish between the *one* and *unicity*. If the one is solely the implicit effect, without being, of the count, thus of the axiomatic Ideas, then there is no reason why unicity cannot be an attribute of the multiple. It indicates solely that a multiple is different from any other. It can be controlled by use of the axiom of extensionality. However, the null-set is inextensible, in-different. How can I even think its unicity when nothing belongs to it that would serve as a mark of its difference? The mathematicians say in general, quite light-handedly, that the void-set is unique 'after the axiom of extensionality'. Yet this is to proceed as if 'two' voids can be identified like two 'something's', which is to say two multiples of multiples, whilst the law of difference is conceptually, if not formally, inadequate to them. The truth is rather this: the unicity of the void-set is immediate because nothing differentiates it, not because its difference can be attested. An irremediable unicity based on in-difference is herein substituted for unicity based on difference.

What ensures the uniqueness of the void-set is that in wishing to think of it as a species or a common name, in supposing that there can be 'several' voids, I expose myself, within the framework of the ontological theory of the multiple, to the risk of overthrowing the regime of the same and the other, and so to *having to found difference on something other than belonging*. Yet any such procedure is equivalent to restoring the being of the one. That is, 'these' voids, being inextensible, are indistinguishable as multiples. They would therefore have to be differentiated as ones, by means of an entirely new principle. But, the one is not, and thus I cannot assume that being-void is a property, a species, or a common name. There are not 'several' voids, there is only one void; rather than signifying the presentation of the one, this signifies the unicity of the unpresentable such as marked within presentation.

We thus arrive at the following remarkable conclusion: *it is because the one is not that the void is unique.*

Saying that the null-set is unique is equivalent to saying that its mark is a proper name. Being thus invests the Ideas of the presentation of the pure multiple in the form of unicity signalled by a proper name. To write it, this name of being, this subtractive point of the multiple—of the general form in which presentation presents itself and thus *is*—the mathematicians searched for a sign far from all their customary alphabets; neither a Greek, nor a Latin, nor a Gothic letter, but an old Scandinavian letter, ∅, emblem of the void, zero affected by the barring of sense. As if they were dully aware that in proclaiming that the void alone is—because it alone in-exists from the multiple, and because the Ideas of the multiple only live on the basis of what is subtracted from them—they were touching upon some sacred region, itself liminal to language; as if thus, rivalling the theologians for whom supreme being has been the proper name since long ago, yet opposing to the latter's promise of the One, and of Presence, the irrevocability of un-presentation and the un-being of the one, the mathematicians had to shelter their own audacity behind the character of a forgotten language.

MEDITATION SIX
Aristotle

'Absurd (out of place) (to suppose) that the point is void.'
Physics, Book IV

For almost three centuries it was possible to believe that the experimentation of rational physics had rendered Aristotle's refutation of the existence of the void obsolete. Pascal's famous leaflet *New Experiments concerning the Void*, the title alone being inadmissible in Aristotle's system, had to endow—in 1647—Torricelli's prior work with a propagandistic force capable of mobilizing the non-scientific public.

In his critical examination of the concept of the void (*Physics*, Book IV, Section 8), Aristotle, in three different places, exposes his argument to the possibility of the experimental production of a counterexample on the part of positive science. First, he explicitly declares that it is the province of the physicist to theorize on the void. Second, his own approach cites experiments such as that of plunging a wooden cube into water and comparing its effects to those of the same cube supposed empty. Finally, his conclusion is entirely negative; the void has no conceivable type of being, neither separable nor inseparable (οὔτε ἀχώρῐστον οὔτε κεχωρισμένον).

However, thanks to the light shed on this matter by Heidegger and some others, we can no longer be satisfied today with this manner of dealing with the question. Upon a close examination, one has to accord that Aristotle leaves at least *one* possibility open: that the void be another name for matter conceived as matter (ἡ ὕλη ᾗ τοι αὕτη), especially matter as the concept of the potential being of the light and the heavy. The void would thus name the material cause of transport, not—as with the atomists—as a universal milieu of local movement, but rather as an undetermined ontological virtuality immanent to natural movement which carries the light upwards and the heavy downwards. The void would be the latent in-difference of the natural differentiation of movements, such as they are prescribed by the qualified being—light or heavy—of bodies. In this sense there would definitely be a being of the void, but a pre-substantial being; therefore unthinkable as such.

Besides, an experiment in Aristotle's sense bears no relation to the conceptual artifacts materialized in Torricelli's or Pascal's water and mercury tubes in which the mathematizable mediation of measure prevails. For Aristotle, an experiment is a current example, a sensible image, which serves to decorate and support a demonstration whose key resides entirely in the production of a correct definition. It is quite doubtful that a common referent exists, even in the shape of an in-existent, thinkable as unique, for what Pascal and Aristotle call the void. If one wants to learn from Aristotle, or even to refute him, then one must pay attention to the space of thought within which his concepts and definitions function. For the Greek, the void is not an experimental difference but rather an ontological category, a supposition relative to what *naturally* proliferates as figures of being. In this logic, the *artificial* production of a void is not an adequate response to the question of whether nature allows, according to its own opening forth, 'a place where nothing is' to occur, because such is the Aristotelian definition of the void (τὸ κενὸν τόπος ἔν ᾧ μηδέν ἔστιν).

This is because the 'physicist' in Aristotle's sense is in no way the archaeological form of the modern physicist. He only appears to be such due to the retroactive illusion engendered by the Galilean revolution. For Aristotle, a physicist studies nature; which is to say that region of being (we will say: that type of situation) in which the concepts of movement and rest are pertinent. Better still: that with which the theoretical thought of the physicist is in accord is that which causes movement and rest to be *intrinsic* attributes of that-which-is in a 'physical' situation. Provoked movements (Aristotle terms them 'violent') and thus, in a certain sense, everything which can be produced via the artifice of an experiment, via a technical apparatus, are excluded from the physical domain in Aristotle's sense. Nature is the being-qua-being of that whose presentation implies movement; it is not the law of movement, it *is* movement. Physics attempts to think the there-is of movement as a figure of the natural coming-to-be of being; physics sets itself the following question: why is there movement rather than absolute immobility? Nature is the principle (ἀρχή), the cause (αἰτία), of self-moving and of being-at-rest, which reside primordially in being-moved or being-at-rest, and this in and for itself (καθ αὐτὸ) and not by accident. Nothing herein is capable of excluding Pascal or Torricelli's void—not being determined as essentially belonging to what-is-presented in its natural originality—from being an in-existent with regard to nature, a physical non-being (in Aristotle's sense); that is, a forced or accidental production.

It is thus appropriate—in our ontological project—to reconsider Aristotle's question: our maxim cannot be that of Pascal, who, precisely with respect to the existence of the void, declared that if on the basis of a hypothesis 'something follows which is contrary to one phenomenon alone, that is sufficient proof of its falsity.' To this ruin of a conceptual system by the unicity of the fact—in which Pascal anticipates Popper—we must oppose the internal examination of Aristotle's argumentation; we for whom the void is in truth the name of being, and so can neither be cast into doubt nor established via the effects of an experiment. The facility of physical refutation—in the modern sense—is barred to us, and consequently we have to discover the ontological weak point of the apparatus inside which Aristotle causes the void to absolutely in-exist.

Aristotle himself dismisses an ontological facility which is symmetrical, in a certain sense, to the facility of experimentation. If the latter prides itself on producing an empty space, the former—imputed to Melissos and Parmenides—contents itself with rejecting the void as pure non-being: τὸ δὲ κενὸν οὐ τῶν ὄντων, the void does not make up one of the number of beings, it is foreclosed from presentation. This argument does not suit Aristotle: for him—quite rightly—first one must think the correlation of the void and 'physical' presentation, or the relation between the void and movement. The void 'in-itself' is literally unthinkable and thus irrefutable. Inasmuch as the question of the void belongs to the theory of nature, it is on the basis of its supposed disposition within self-moving that the critique must commence. In my language: the void must be examined *in situation*.

The Aristotelian concept of a natural situation is place. Place itself does not exist; it is what envelops any existent insofar as the latter is assigned to a natural site. The void 'in situation' would thus be a place in which there was nothing. The immediate correlation is not that of the void and non-being, it is rather that of the void and the nothing via the mediation—non-being, however natural—of place. But the naturalness of place is that of being the site towards which the body (the being) whose place it is, moves.

Every place is that of a body, and what testifies to this is that if one removes a body from its place, it tends to return to that place. The question of the existence of the void thus comes down to that of its function in respect to self-moving, the polarity of which is place.

The aim of Aristotle's first major demonstration is to establish that the void excludes movement, and that it thus excludes itself from being-qua-being grasped in its natural presentation. The demonstration, which is very effective, employs, one after the other, the concepts of difference, unlimitedness (or infinity), and incommensurability. There is great profundity in positing the void in this manner; as in-difference, as in-finite, and as un-measured. This triple determination specifies the errancy of the void, its subtractive ontological function and its inconsistency with regard to any presented multiple.

a. In-difference. Any movement grasped in its natural being requires the differentiation of place; the place that situates the body which moves. Yet the void as such possesses no difference (ἡ γάρ κενόν, οὐκ ἔχει διαφοράν). Difference, in fact, supposes that the differentiated multiples—termed 'bodies' by Aristotle—are counted as one according to the naturalness of their local destination. Yet the void, which names inconsistency, is 'prior' to the count-as-one. It cannot support difference (cf. Meditation 5 on the mathematics of this point), and consequently forbids movement. The dilemma is the following: 'Either there is no natural transport (φορά) anywhere, for any being, or, if there is such transport, then the void is not.' But the exclusion of movement is absurd, for movement is presentation itself as the natural coming forth of being. And it would be—and this is Aristotle's expression itself—ridiculous (γελοῖον) to demand proof of the existence of presentation, since all existence is assured on the basis of presentation. Furthermore: 'It is evident that, amongst beings, there is a plurality of beings arising from nature.' If the void thus excludes difference, it is 'ridiculous' to ensure its being as natural being.

b. In-finite. For Aristotle there is an *intrinsic* connection between the void and infinity, and we shall see (in Meditations 13 and 14 for example) that he is entirely correct on this point: the void is the point of being of infinity. Aristotle makes this point according to the subtractive of being, by posing that in-difference is common to the void and infinity as species of both the nothing and non-being: 'How could there be natural movement if, due to the void and infinity, no difference existed? . . . For there is no difference on the basis of the nothing (τοῦ μηδενὸς), no more than on the basis of non-being (τοῦ μὴ ὄντος). Yet the void seems to be a non-being and a privation (στέρησις).'

However, what is infinity, or more exactly, the unlimited? For a Greek, it is the negation of presentation itself, because what-presents-itself affirms its being within the strict disposition of its limit (πέρας). To say that the void is intrinsically infinite is equivalent to saying that it is outside situations, unpresentable. As such, the void is in excess of being as a thinkable disposition, and especially as natural disposition. It is such in three manners.

– First, supposing that there is movement, and thus natural presentation, in the void, or according to the void: one would then have to conceive that bodies are necessarily transported to infinity (εἰς ἄπειρον ἀνάγκη φέρεσθαι), since no difference would dictate their coming to a halt. The physical exactitude of this remark (in the modern sense) is an ontological—thus physical—impossibility in its Aristotelian sense. It indicates solely that the hypothesis of a natural being of the void immediately exceeds the inherent limit of any effective presentation.

– Second, given that the in-difference of the void cannot determine any natural direction for movement, the latter would be 'explosive', which is to say multi-directional; transport would take place 'everywhere' (πάντη). Here again the void exceeds the always *orientated* character of natural disposition. It ruins the topology of situations.

— Finally, if we suppose that it is a body's *internal* void which lightens it and lifts it up; if, therefore, the void is the cause of movement, it would also have to be the latter's goal: the void transporting itself towards its own natural place, which one would suppose to be, for example, upwards. There would thus be a reduplication of the void, an excess of the void over itself thereby entailing its own mobility towards itself, or what Aristotle calls a 'void of the void' (κενοῦ κενόν). Yet the indifference of the void prohibits it from differentiating itself from itself—which is in fact an ontological theorem (cf. Meditation 5)—and consequently from presupposing itself as the destination of its natural being.

To my mind, the ensemble of these remarks is entirely coherent. It is the case—and politics in particular shows this—that the void, once named 'in situation', exceeds the situation according to its own infinity; it is also the case that its evental occurrence proceeds 'explosively', or 'everywhere', within a situation; finally, it is exact that the void pursues its own particular trajectory—once unbound from the errancy in which it is confined by the state. Evidently, we must therefore conclude with Aristotle that the void *is not*; if by 'being' we understand the limited order of presentation, and in particular what is natural of such order.

c. Un-measure. Every movement is measurable in relation to another according to its speed. Or, as Aristotle says, there is always a proportion, a ratio (λόγος) between one movement and another, inasmuch as they are within time, and all time is finite. The natural character of a situation is also its proportionate or numerable character in the broader sense of the term. This is actually what I will establish by linking natural situations to the concept of ordinal multiplicity (Meditations 11 and 12). There is a reciprocity between nature (φύσις) and proportion, or reason (λόγος). One element which contributes to this reciprocity as a power of obstruction —and thus of a limit—is the resistance of the milieu in which there is movement. If one allows that this resistance can be zero, which is the case if the milieu is void, movement will lose all measure; it will become incomparable to any other movement, it will tend towards infinite speed. Aristotle says: 'The void bears no ratio to the full, such that neither does movement [in the void].' Here again the conceptual mediation is accomplished subtractively, which is to say by means of the nothing: 'There is no ratio in which the void is exceeded by bodies, just as there is no ratio between the nothing (τὸ μηδὲν) and number.' The void is in-numerable, hence the movement which is supposed therein does not have a thinkable nature, possessing no reason on the basis of which its comparison to other movements could be ensured.

Physics (in the modern sense) must not lead us astray here. What Aristotle is inviting us to think is the following: every reference to the void produces an excess over the count-as-one, an irruption of inconsistency, which propagates—metaphysically—within the situation at infinite speed. The void is thus incompatible with the slow order in which every situation re-ensures, in their place, the multiples that it presents.

It is this triple negative determination (in-difference, in-finite, un-measured) which thus leads Aristotle to refuse any *natural* being for the void. Could it, however, have a *non-natural* being? Three formulas must be interrogated here; wherein resides the possible enigma of an unpresentable, pre-substantial void whose being, unborn and non-arriving, would however be the latent illumination of what is, insofar as it is.

The first of these formulas—attributed in truth by Aristotle to those 'partisans of the void' that he sets out to refute—declares that 'the same being (*étant*) pertains to a void, to fullness, and to place, but the same being (*étant*) does not belong to them when they are considered from the standpoint of being (*être*).' If one allows that place can be thought as situation in general, which is to say not as *an* existence (a multiple), but as the site of existing such that it circumscribes every existing term, then Aristotle's statement designates identity to the situation of both fullness (that of an effective multiple), and of the void (the non-presented). But it also designates their non-identity once these three names—the void, fullness, and place—are assigned to their difference *according to being*. It is thus imaginable that a situation, conceived as a structured multiplicity, simultaneously brings about consistent multiplicity (fullness), inconsistent multiplicity (the void), and itself (place), according to an immediate identity which is that of being-in-totality, the complete domain of experience. But, on the other hand, what can be said via these three terms of being-qua-being is not identical, since on the side of place we have the one, the law of the count; on the side of fullness the multiple as counted-as-one; and on the side of the void, the without-one, the unpresented. Let's not forget that one of Aristotle's major axioms is 'being is said in several manners.' Under these conditions, the void would be being as non-being—or un-presentation—fullness, being as being—consistency—and place, being as the non-existing-limit of its being—border of the multiple by the one.

The second formula is Aristotle's concession to those who are absolutely (πάντως) convinced of the role of the void as cause of transport. He allows that one could admit the void is 'the matter of the heavy and the light as such'. To concede that the void could be a *name* for matter-in-itself is to attribute an enigmatic existence to it; that of the 'third principle', the subject-support (τὸ ὑποκείμενον), whose necessity is established by Aristotle in the first book of the *Physics*. The being of the void would share with the being of matter a sort of precariousness, which would suspend it between pure non-being and being-effectively-being, which for Aristotle can only be a specifiable term, a something (τὸ τόδε τι). Let's say that failing presentation in the consistency of a multiple, the void is the latent errancy of the being of presentation. Aristotle explicitly attributes this errancy of being—on the underside and at the limit of its presented consistency—to matter when he says that matter is certainly a non-being, but solely by accident (κατὰ συμβεσηκός), and especially—in a striking formula—that it is 'in some manner a quasi-substance' (ἐγγὺς καὶ οὐσίαν πως). To admit that the void can be another name for matter is to confer upon it the status of an almost-being.

The last formula evokes a possibility that Aristotle rejects, and this is where we part from him: that the void, once it is unlocalizable (or 'outside-situation'), must be thought as a pure *point*. We know that this is the genuine ontological solution because (cf. Meditation 5) the empty set, such that it exists solely by its name, $\varnothing$, can however be qualified as unique, and thus cannot be represented as space or extension, but rather as punctuality. The void is the unpresentable *point of being* of any presentation. Aristotle firmly dismisses such a hypothesis: '῎Ατοπον δὲ εἰ ἡ στιγμὴ κενόν', 'absurd (out of place) that the point be void'. The reason for this dismissal is that it is unthinkable for him to completely separate the question of the void from that of place. If the void is not, it is because one cannot think an empty place. As he explains, if one supposed the punctuality of the void, this point would have to 'be a place in which there was the extension of a tangible body'. The in-extension of a point does not make any place for a void. It is precisely here that Aristotle's acute thought encounters its own point of impossibility: that it is necessary to think, under the name of the void, the outside-place on the basis of which any place—any situation—maintains itself with respect to its being. That the without-place (ἄτοπον) signifies the absurd causes one to forget that the point, precisely in not being a place, can mitigate the aporias of the void.

It is because the void is the point of being that it is also the almost-being which haunts the situation in which being consists. The insistence of the void in-consists as de-localization.

Part II

Being: Excess,
State of the situation,
One/Multiple, Whole/Parts,
or $\in$/$\subset$?

MEDITATION SEVEN
The Point of Excess

---

1. BELONGING AND INCLUSION

In many respects set theory forms a type of foundational interruption of the labyrinthine disputes over the multiple. For centuries, philosophy has employed two dialectical couples in its thought of presented-being, and their conjunction produced all sorts of abysses, the couples being the one and the multiple and the part and the whole. It would not be an exaggeration to say that the entirety of speculative ontology is taken up with examinations of the connections and disconnections between Unity and Totality. It has been so from the very beginnings of metaphysics, since it is possible to show that Plato essentially has the One prevail over the All whilst Aristotle made the opposite choice.

Set theory sheds light on the fecund frontier between the whole/parts relation and the one/multiple relation; because, at base, it suppresses both of them. The multiple—whose concept it thinks without defining its signification—for a post-Cantorian is neither supported by the existence of the one nor unfolded as an organic totality. The multiple consists from being without-one, or multiple of multiples, and the categories of Aristotle (or Kant), Unity and Totality, cannot help us grasp it.

Nevertheless, set theory distinguishes two possible relations between multiples. There is the originary relation, *belonging*, written ∈, which indicates that a multiple is counted as element in the presentation of another multiple. But there is also the relation of *inclusion*, written ⊂, which indicates that a multiple is a sub-multiple of another multiple: we made reference to this relation (Meditation 5) in regard to the power-set axiom. To recap, the writing $\beta \subset \alpha$, which reads β is included in α, or β is a subset of α, signifies that every multiple which belongs to β also belongs to α: $(\forall\gamma)[(\gamma \in \beta) \rightarrow (\gamma \in \alpha)]$

One cannot underestimate the conceptual importance of the distinction between belonging and inclusion. This distinction directs, step by step, the entire thought of quantity and finally what I will term later the great orientations of thought, prescribed by being itself. The meaning of this distinction must thus be immediately clarified.

First of all, note that a multiple is not thought differently according to whether it supports one or the other of these relations. If I say 'β belongs to α', the multiple α is exactly the same, a multiple of multiples, as when I say 'γ is included in α.' It is entirely irrelevant to believe that α is first thought as One (or set of elements), and then thought as Whole (or set of parts). Symmetrically, nor can the set which belongs, or the set which is included, be qualitatively distinguished on the basis of their relational position. Of course, I will say if β belongs to α it is an element of α, and if γ is included in α it is a subset of α. But these determinations—element and subset—do not allow one to think anything intrinsic. In every case, the element β and the subset γ are pure multiples. What varies is their position alone with regard to the multiple α. In one case (the case $\in$), the multiple falls under the count-as-one which is the other multiple. In the other case (the case $\subset$), every element presented by the first multiple is also presented by the second. But being-multiple remains completely unaffected by these distinctions of relative position.

The power-set axiom also helps to clarify the ontological neutrality of the distinction between belonging and inclusion. What does this axiom state (cf. Meditation 5)? That if a set α exists (is presented) then there also exists the set of all its subsets. What this axiom—the most radical, and in its effects, the most enigmatic of axioms (and I will come back to this at length)—affirms, is that between $\in$ and $\subset$ there is at least the correlation that all the multiples *included* in a supposedly existing α *belong* to a β; that is, they form a set, a multiple counted-as-one:

$$(\forall\alpha)(\exists\beta)[(\forall\gamma)[(\gamma \in \beta) \leftrightarrow (\gamma \subset \alpha)]]$$

Given α, the set β whose existence is affirmed here, the set of subsets of α, will be written $p(\alpha)$. One can thus also write:

$[\gamma \in p(\alpha)] \leftrightarrow (\gamma \subset \alpha)$

The dialectic which is knotted together here, that of belonging and inclusion, extends the power of the count-as-one to what, in a multiple, can be distinguished in terms of internal multiple-presentations, that is, compositions of counts 'already' possible *in* the initial presentation, on the basis of the same multiplicities as those presented in the initial multiple.

As we shall see later, it is of capital importance that in doing so the axiom does not introduce a special operation, nor any *primitive* relation other than that of belonging. Indeed, as we have seen, inclusion can be defined on the basis of belonging alone. Wherever I write $\beta \subset \alpha$, I could decide not to abbreviate and write: $(\forall \gamma)[(\gamma \in \beta) \rightarrow (\gamma \in \alpha)]$. This amounts to saying that even if for commodity's sake we sometimes use the word 'part' to designate a subset, there is no more a concept of a whole, and thus of a part, than there is a concept of the one. There is solely the relation of belonging.

The set $p(\alpha)$ of all the subsets of the set α is *a multiple essentially distinct from α itself*. This crucial point indicates how false it is to sometimes think of α as forming a one out of its elements (belonging) and sometimes as the whole of its parts (inclusion). The set of multiples that belong to α is nothing other than α itself, multiple-presentation of multiples. The set of multiples included in α, or subsets of α, is a *new* multiple, $p(\alpha)$, whose existence—once that of α is supposed—is solely guaranteed by a special ontological Idea: the power-set axiom. The gap between α (which counts-as-one the belongings, or elements) and $p(\alpha)$ (which counts-as-one the inclusions, or subsets) is, as we shall see, the point in which the impasse of being resides.

Finally, belonging and inclusion, with regard to the multiple α, concern two distinct operators of counting, and not two different ways to think the being of the multiple. The structure of α is α itself, which forms a one out of all the multiples which belong to it. The set of all the subsets of α, $p(\alpha)$, forms a one out of all the multiples included in α, but this second count, despite being related to α, is absolutely distinct from α itself. It is therefore a metastructure, another count, which 'completes' the first in that it gathers together all the sub-compositions of internal multiples, all the inclusions. The power-set axiom posits that this second count, this metastructure, always exists if the first count, or presentative structure, exists. Meditation 8 will address the necessity of this reduplication or requirement—countering the danger of the void—that every count-as-one be doubled by a count of the count, that every structure call upon a metastructure. As always, the mathematical axiom system does not think this necessity: rather, it *decides* it.

However, there is an immediate consequence of this decision: the *gap* between structure and metastructure, between element and subset, between belonging and inclusion, is a permanent question for thought, an intellectual provocation of being. I said that a and $p(a)$ were distinct. In what measure? With what effects? This point, apparently technical, will lead us all the way to the Subject and to truth. What is sure, in any case, is that no multiple a can coincide with the set of its subsets. Belonging and inclusion, in the order of being-existent, are irreducibly disjunct. This, as we shall see, is *demonstrated* by mathematical ontology.

2. THE THEOREM OF THE POINT OF EXCESS

The question here is that of establishing that given a presented multiple the one-multiple composed from its subsets, whose existence is guaranteed by the power-set axiom, is essentially 'larger' than the initial multiple. This is a crucial ontological theorem, which leads to a real impasse: it is literally impossible to assign a 'measure' to this superiority in size. In other words, the 'passage' to the set of subsets is an operation in *absolute* excess of the situation itself.

We must begin at the beginning, and show that the multiple of the subsets of a set necessarily contains at least one multiple which does not belong to the initial set. We will term this *the theorem of the point of excess*.

Take a supposed existing multiple a. Let's consider, amongst the multiples that a forms into a one—all the β's such that $\beta \in a$—those which have the property of not being 'elements of themselves'; that is, which do not present themselves as multiples in the one-presentation that they are.

In short, we find here, again, the basis of Russell's paradox (cf. Meditation 3). These multiples β therefore first possess the property of belonging to a, $(\beta \in a)$, and second the property of not belonging to themselves, $\sim(\beta \in \beta)$.

Let's term the multiplicities which possess the property of not belonging to themselves $(\sim(\beta \in \beta))$ *ordinary* multiplicities, and for reasons made clear in Meditation 17, those which belong to themselves $(\beta \in \beta)$ *evental* multiplicities.

Take all the elements of α which are ordinary. The result is obviously a subset of α, the 'ordinary' subset. This subset is a multiple which we can call γ. A simple convention—one which I will use often—is that of writing: $\{\beta \mid \ldots \}$ to designate the multiple made up of all the β's which have this or that property. Thus, for example, γ, the set of all ordinary elements of α, can be written: $\gamma = \{\beta \mid \beta \in \alpha \;\&\; {\sim}(\beta \in \beta)\}$. Once we suppose that α exists, γ also exists, by the axiom of separation (*cf.* Meditation 3): I 'separate' in α all the β's which have the property of being ordinary. I thereby obtain an *existing* part of α. Let's term this part the *ordinary subset* of α.

Since γ is *included* in α, $(\gamma \subset \alpha)$, γ *belongs* to the set of subsets of α, $(\gamma \in p(\alpha))$.

But, on the other hand, γ *does not* belong to α itself. If γ did belong to α, that is, if we had $\gamma \in \alpha$, then one of two things would come to pass. Either γ is ordinary, ${\sim}(\gamma \in \gamma)$, and it thus belongs to the ordinary subset of α, the subset which is nothing other than γ itself. In that case, we have $\gamma \in \gamma$, which means γ is evental. But if it is evental, such that $\gamma \in \gamma$, being an element of the ordinary subset γ, it has to be ordinary. This equivalence for γ of $(\gamma \in \gamma)$, the evental, and ${\sim}(\gamma \in \gamma)$, the ordinary, is a formal contradiction. It obliges us to reject the initial hypothesis: thus, γ does not belong to α.

Consequently, there is always—whatever α is—at least one element (here γ) of $p(\alpha)$ which is not an element of α. This is to say, *no multiple is capable of forming-a-one out of everything it includes*. The statement 'if β is *included* in α, then β *belongs* to α' is false for all α. Inclusion is in irremediable excess of belonging. In particular, the included subset made up of all the ordinary elements of a set constitutes a definitive point of excess over the set in question. It never belongs to the latter.

The immanent resources of a presented multiple—if this concept is extended to its subsets—thus surpass the capacity of the count whose result-one is itself. To number this resource another power of counting, one different from itself, will be necessary. The existence of this other count, this other one-multiple—to which this time the multiples included in the first multiple will tolerate belonging—is precisely what is stated in the power-set axiom.

Once this axiom is admitted, one is *required* to think the gap between simple presentation and this species of re-presentation which is the count-as-one of subsets.

3. THE VOID AND THE EXCESS

What is the retroactive effect of the radical distinction between belonging and inclusion upon the proper name of being that is the mark $\emptyset$ of the empty set? This is a typical ontological question: establish the effect upon a point of being (and the only one we have available is $\emptyset$) of a conceptual distinction introduced by an Idea (an axiom).

One might expect there to be no effect since the void does not present anything. It seems logical to suppose that the void does not include anything either: not having any elements, how could it have a subset? This supposition is wrong. The void maintains with the concept of inclusion two relations that are essentially new with respect to the nullity of its relation with belonging:

– the void is a subset of any set: it is universally included;
– the void possesses a subset, which is the void itself.

Let's examine these two properties. This examination is also an onto-logical exercise, which links a thesis (the void as proper name of being) to a crucial conceptual distinction (belonging and inclusion).

The first property testifies to the omnipresence of the void. It reveals the errancy of the void in all presentation: the void, to which nothing belongs, is by this very fact included in everything.

One can intuitively grasp the ontological pertinence of this theorem, which states: 'The void-set is a subset of any set supposed existent.' For if the void is the unpresentable point of being, whose unicity of inexistence is marked by the existent proper name $\emptyset$, then no multiple, by means of its existence, can prevent this inexistent from placing itself within it. On the basis of everything which is not presentable it is inferred that the void is presented everywhere in its lack: not, however, as the one-of-its-unicity, as immediate multiple counted by the one-multiple, but as *inclusion*, because subsets are the very place in which a multiple of nothing can err, just as the nothing itself errs within the all.

In the deductive presentation of this fundamental ontological theorem—in what we will term the regime of fidelity of the ontological situation—it is remarkable that it appear as a consequence, or rather as a particular case, of the logical principle '*ex falso sequitur quodlibet*'. This is not surprising if we remember that the axiom of the empty set states, in substance, that there exists a negation (there exists a set for which 'to not belong to it' is a universal attribute, an attribute of every multiple). On the basis of this true negative statement, if it is denied in turn—if it is falsely supposed that a multiple belongs to the void—one necessarily infers anything, and in particular, that this multiple, supposedly capable of belonging to the void, is certainly capable of belonging to any other set. In other words, the absurd chimera—or idea without being—of an 'element of the void' implies that this element—radically non-presented of course —would, if it were presented, be an element of any set whatsoever. Hence the statement: 'If the void presents a multiple α, then any multiple β whatsoever also presents that α.' One can also say that a multiple which would belong to the void would be that ultra-nothing, that ultra-void with regard to which no existence-multiple could oppose it being presented by itself. Since every belonging which is supposed for the void is extended to every multiple, we do not need anything more to conclude: the void is indeed included in everything.

This argument may be formally presented in the following manner:

Take the logical tautology $\sim A \rightarrow (A \rightarrow B)$ which is the principle I mentioned above in Latin: if a statement A is false (if I have non-A) and if I affirm the latter (if I posit A), then it follows that anything (any statement B whatsoever) is true.

Let's consider the following variation (or particular case) of this tautology: $\sim(\alpha \in \varnothing) \rightarrow [(\alpha \in \varnothing) \rightarrow (\alpha \in \beta)]$ in which α and β are any multiples whatsoever supposed given. This variation is itself a logical tautology. Its antecedent, $\sim(\alpha \in \varnothing)$, is axiomatically true, because no α can belong to the empty set. Therefore its consequent, $[(\alpha \in \varnothing) \rightarrow (\alpha \in \beta)]$, is equally true. Since α and β are indeterminate free variables, I can make my formula universal: $(\forall \alpha)(\forall \beta)[(\alpha \in \varnothing) \rightarrow (\alpha \in \beta)]$. But what is $(\forall \alpha)(\forall \beta)$ $[(\alpha \in \varnothing) \rightarrow (\alpha \in \beta)]$ if it is not the very definition of the relation of inclusion between $\varnothing$ and β, the relation $\varnothing \subset \beta$?

Consequently, my formula amounts to the following: $(\forall \beta)[\varnothing \subset \beta]$, which reads, as predicted: of any supposed given multiple β, $\varnothing$ is a subset.

The void is thus clearly in a position of universal inclusion.

It is on this very basis that it is inferred that the void, which has no element, does however have a subset.

In the formula $(\forall \beta)[\varnothing \subset \beta]$, which marks the universal inclusion of the void, the universal quantifier indicates that, without restriction, every existent multiple admits the void as subset. The set $\varnothing$ itself *is* an existent-multiple, the multiple-of-nothing. Consequently, $\varnothing$ is a subset of itself: $\varnothing \subset \varnothing$.

At first glance this formula is completely enigmatic. This is because intuitively, and guided by the deficient vocabulary which shoddily distinguishes, via the vague image of 'being-inside', between belonging and inclusion, it seems as though we have, by this inclusion, 'filled' the void with something. But this is not the case. Only belonging, $\in$, the unique and supreme Idea of the presented-multiple, 'fills' presentation. Moreover, it would indeed be absurd to imagine that the void can belong to itself —which would be written $\varnothing \in \varnothing$—because nothing belongs to it. But in reality the statement $\varnothing \subset \varnothing$ solely announces that everything which is presented, including the proper name of the unpresentable, forms a subset of itself, the 'maximal' subset. This reduplication of identity by inclusion is no more scandalous when one writes $\varnothing \subset \varnothing$ than it is when one writes $a \subset a$ (which is true in all cases). That this maximal subset of the void is itself void is the least of things.

Now, given that the void admits at least one subset—itself—there is reason to believe that the power-set axiom can be applied here: there must exist, since $\varnothing$ exists, the set of its subsets, $p(\varnothing)$. Structure of the nothing, the name of the void calls upon a metastructure which counts its subsets.

The set of subsets of the void is the set to which everything *included* in the void *belongs*. But only the void is included in the void: $\varnothing \subset \varnothing$. Therefore, $p(\varnothing)$, set of subsets of the void, is that multiple to which the void, and the void alone, belongs. Mind! The set to which the void alone belongs cannot be the void itself, because *nothing* belongs to the void, not even the void itself. It would already be excessive for the void to have an element. One could object: but given that this element is void there is no problem. No! This element would not be the void as the nothing that it is, as the unpresentable. It would be the *name* of the void, the existent mark of the unpresentable. The void would no longer be void if its name belonged to it. Certainly, the name of the void can be *included* in the void, which amounts to saying that, in the situation, it is equal to the void, since the unpresentable is solely presented by its name. Yet, equal to its name, the void cannot make a one out of its name without differentiating itself from itself and thus becoming a non-void.

Consequently, the set of subsets of the void is the non-empty set whose unique element is the name of the void. From now on we will write $\{\beta_1, \beta_2, \ldots \beta_n \ldots \}$ for the set which is composed of (which makes a one out of) the marked sets between the braces. In total, the elements of this set are precisely β_1, β_2, etc. Since $p(\varnothing)$ has as its unique element $\varnothing$, this gives us: $p(\varnothing) = \{\varnothing\}$, which evidently implies $\varnothing \in p(\varnothing)$.

However, let's examine this new set closely, $p(\varnothing)$, our second existent-multiple in the 'genealogical' framework of the set-theory axiomatic. It is written $\{\varnothing\}$, and $\varnothing$ is its sole element, fine. But first of all, what is signified by 'the void' being an element of a multiple? We understood that $\varnothing$ was a subset of any supposed existent multiple, but 'element'? Moreover, this must mean, it being a matter of $\{\varnothing\}$, that $\varnothing$ is both subset and element, included and belonging—that we have $\varnothing \subset \{\varnothing\}$ and also $\varnothing \in \{\varnothing\}$. Doesn't this infringe the rule according to which belonging and inclusion cannot coincide? Secondly, and more seriously: this multiple $\{\varnothing\}$ has as its unique element the name-of-the-void, $\varnothing$. Therefore, wouldn't this be, quite simply, *the one* whose very being we claimed to call into question?

There is a simple response to the first question. The void does not have any element; it is thus unpresentable, and we are concerned with its proper name alone, which presents being in its lack. It is not the 'void' which belongs to the set $\{\varnothing\}$, because the void belongs to no presented multiple, being the being itself of multiple-presentation. What belongs to this set is the proper name which constitutes the suture-to-being of the axiomatic presentation of the pure multiple; that is, the presentation of presentation.

The second question is not dangerous either. The non-coincidence of inclusion and belonging signifies that there is an excess of inclusion over belonging; that it is impossible that every part of a multiple belongs to it. On the other hand, it is in no way ruled out that everything which belongs to a multiple is also included in it. The implicative dissymmetry travels in one direction alone. The statement $(\forall a)[(a \subset \beta) \rightarrow (a \in \beta)]$ is certainly false for any multiple β (theorem of the point of excess). However the 'inverse' statement; $(\forall a)[(a \in \beta) \rightarrow (a \subset \beta)]$, *can* be true, for certain multiples. It is particularly true for the set $\{\varnothing\}$, because its unique element, $\varnothing$, is also one of its subsets, $\varnothing$ being universally included. There is no paradox here, rather a singular property of $\{\varnothing\}$.

I now come to the third question, which clarifies the problem of the One.

4. ONE, COUNT-AS-ONE, UNICITY AND FORMING-INTO-ONE

There are four meanings concealed beneath the single signifier 'one'. Their differentiation—a task in which mathematical ontology proves to be a powerful tool—serves to clarify a number of speculative, and in particular, Hegelian, aporias.

The one as such, as I said, is not. It is always the result of a count, the effect of a structure, because the presentative form in which all access to being is to be had is the multiple, as multiple of multiples. As such, in set theory, what I count as one under the name of a set α, is multiple-of-multiples. It is thus necessary to distinguish the *count-as-one, or structure*, which produces the one as a nominal seal of the multiple, and *the one as effect*, whose fictive being is maintained solely by the structural retroaction in which it is considered. In the case of the null-set, the count-as-one consists in fixing a proper name for the negation of any presented multiple; thus a proper name for the unpresentable. The fictive one-effect occurs when, via a shortcut whose danger has already been mentioned, I allow myself to say that ∅ is 'the void', thereby assigning the predicate of the one to the suture-to-being that is the name, and presenting the unpresentable *as such*. The mathematical theory itself is more rigorous in its paradox: speaking of the 'void-set', it maintains that this name, which does not present anything, is nevertheless that of a multiple, once, as name, it is submitted to the axiomatic Ideas of the multiple.

As for *unicity*, it is not a being, but a predicate of the multiple. It belongs to the regime of the same and the other, such as its law is instituted by any structure. A multiple is unique inasmuch as it is other than any other. The theologians, besides, already knew that the thesis 'God is One' is quite different from the thesis 'God is unique.' In Christian theology, for example, the triplicity of the person of God is internal to the dialectic of the One, but it never affects his unicity (mono-theism). Thus, the name of the void being unique, once it is retroactively generated as a-name for the multiple-of-nothing, does not signify in any manner that 'the void is one.' It solely signifies that, given that the void, 'unpresentable', is solely presented as a name, the existence of 'several' names would be incompatible with the extensional regime of the same and the other, and would in fact constrain us to presuppose the being of the one, even if it be in the mode of one-voids, or pure atoms.

Finally, it is always possible to count as one an already counted one-multiple; that is, to apply the count to the one-result of the count. This amounts, in fact, to submitting to the law, in turn, the names that it produces as seal-of-the-one for the presented multiple. In other words: any name, which marks that the one results from an operation, can be taken in the situation as a multiple to be counted as one. The reason for this is that the one, such as it occurs via the effect of structure upon the multiple, and causes it to consist, is not transcendent to presentation. As soon as it results, the one is presented in turn and taken as a term, thus as a multiple. The operation by which the law indefinitely submits to itself the one which it produces, counting it as one-multiple, I term *forming-into-one*. Forming-into-one is not *really* distinct from the count-as-one; it is rather a modality of the latter which one can use to describe the count-as-one applying itself to a result-one. It is clear that forming-into-one confers no more being upon the one than does the count. Here again, the being-of-the-one is a retroactive fiction, and what is presented always remains a multiple, even be it a multiple of names.

I can thus consider that the set {∅}, which counts-as-one the result of the originary count—the one-multiple which is the name of the void—is the forming-into-one of this name. Therein the one acquires no further being than that conferred upon it operationally by being the structural seal of the multiple. Furthermore, {∅} is a multiple, a set. It so happens that what belongs to it, ∅, is unique, that's all. But unicity is not the one.

Note that once the existence of {∅}—the forming-into-one of ∅—is guaranteed via the power-set axiom applied to the name of the void, then the operation of forming-into-one is uniformly applicable to any multiple already supposed existent. It is here that the value of the axiom of replacement becomes evident (cf. Meditation 5). In substance this axiom states that if a multiple exists, then there also exists the multiple obtained by replacing each of the elements of the first by other existing multiples. Consequently, if in {∅}, which exists, I 'replace' ∅ by the supposed existent set δ, I get {δ}; that is, the set whose unique element is δ. This set exists because the axiom of replacement guarantees the permanence of the existent one-multiple for any term-by-term substitution of what belongs to it.

We thus find ourselves in possession of our first derived law within the framework of axiomatic set theory: if the multiple δ exists (is presented), then the multiple {δ} is also presented, to which δ alone belongs, in other words, the name-one 'δ' that the multiple which it is received, having been counted-as-one. This law, δ → {δ}, is the forming-into-one of the multiple δ; the latter already being the one-multiple which results from a count. We will term the multiple {δ}, result-one of the forming-into-one, the *singleton* of δ.

The set {∅} is thus simply the first singleton.

To conclude, let's note that because forming-into-one is a law applicable to any existing multiple, and the singleton $\{\varnothing\}$ exists, the latter's forming-into-one, which is to say the forming-into-one of the forming-into-one of $\varnothing$, also exists: $\{\varnothing\} \rightarrow \{\{\varnothing\}\}$. This singleton of the singleton of the void has, like every singleton, one sole element. However, this element is not $\varnothing$, but $\{\varnothing\}$, and these two sets, according to the axiom of extension, are different. Indeed, $\varnothing$ is an element of $\{\varnothing\}$ rather than being an element of $\varnothing$. Finally, it appears that $\{\varnothing\}$ and $\{\{\varnothing\}\}$ are also different themselves.

This is where the unlimited production of new multiples commences, each drawn from the void by the combined effect of the power-set axiom—because the name of the void is a part of itself—and forming-into-one.

The Ideas thereby authorize that starting from one simple proper name alone—that, subtractive, of being—the complex proper names differentiate themselves, thanks to which one is marked out: that on the basis of which the presentation of an infinity of multiples structures itself.

MEDITATION EIGHT
The State, or Metastructure,
and the Typology of Being
(normality, singularity, excrescence)

All multiple-presentation is exposed to the danger of the void: the void is its being. The consistency of the multiple amounts to the following: the void, which is the name of inconsistency in the situation (under the law of the count-as-one), cannot, in itself, be presented or fixed. What Heidegger names the care of being, which is the ecstasy of beings, could also be termed the situational anxiety of the void, or the necessity of warding off the void. The apparent solidity of the world of presentation is merely a result of the action of structure, even if *nothing* is outside such a result. It is necessary to prohibit that catastrophe of presentation which would be its encounter with its own void, the presentational occurrence of inconsistency as such, or the ruin of the One.

Evidently the guarantee of consistency (the 'there is Oneness') cannot rely on structure or the count-as-one alone to circumscribe and prohibit the errancy of the void from *fixing* itself, and being, on the basis of this very fact, as presentation of the unpresentable, the ruin of every donation of being and the figure subjacent to Chaos. The fundamental reason behind this insufficiency is that *something*, within presentation, escapes the count: this something is nothing other than the count itself. The 'there is Oneness' is a pure operational result, which transparently reveals the very operation from which the result results. It is thus possible that, subtracted from the count, and by consequence a-structured, the structure itself be the point where the void is given. In order for the void to be prohibited from presentation, *it is necessary that structure be structured*, that the 'there is Oneness' be valid for the count-as-one. The consistency of presentation thus requires that all structure be *doubled* by a metastructure which secures the former against any fixation of the void.

The thesis that all presentation is structured twice may appear to be completely *a priori*. But what it amounts to, in the end, is something that each and everybody observes, and which is philosophically astonishing: the being of presentation is inconsistent multiplicity, but despite this, it is never chaotic. All I am saying is this: it is on the basis of Chaos not being the form of the donation of being that one is obliged to think that there is a reduplication of the count-as-one. The prohibition of any presentation of the void can only be immediate and constant if this vanishing point of consistent multiplicity—which is precisely its consistency as operational result—is, in turn, stopped up, or closed, by a count-as-one of the operation itself, a count of the count, a metastructure.

I would add that the investigation of any effective situation (any region of structured presentation), whether it be natural or historical, reveals the real operation of the second count. On this point, concrete analysis converges with the philosophical theme: all situations are structured twice. This also means: there is always both presentation and representation. To think this point is to think the requisites of the errancy of the void, of the non-presentation of inconsistency, and of the danger that being-qua-being represents; *haunting* presentation.

The anxiety of the void, otherwise known as the care of being, can thus be recognized, in all presentation, in the following: the structure of the count is reduplicated in order to verify itself, to vouch that its effects, for the entire duration of its exercise, are complete, and to unceasingly bring the one into being within the un-encounterable danger of the void. Any operation of the count-as-one (of terms) is in some manner doubled by a count of the count, which guarantees, at every moment, that the gap between the consistent multiple (such that it results, composed of ones) and the inconsistent multiple (which is solely the presupposition of the void, and does not present anything) is veritably null. It thus ensures that there is no possibility of that disaster of presentation ever occurring which would be the presentational occurrence, in torsion, of the structure's own void.

The structure of structure is responsible for establishing, in danger of the void, that it is universally attested that, in the situation, the one is. Its necessity resides entirely in the point that, given that the one is not, it is only on the basis of its operational character, exhibited by its double, that the one-effect can deploy the guarantee of its own veracity. This veracity is literally the fictionalizing of the count via the imaginary being conferred upon it by it undergoing, in turn, the operation of a count.

What is induced by the errancy of the void is that structure—the place of risk due to its pure operational transparency and due to the doubt occasioned, as for the one, by it having to operate upon the multiple —must, in turn, be strictly fixed within the one.

Any ordinary situation thus contains a structure, both secondary and supreme, by means of which the count-as-one that structures the situation is in turn counted-as-one. The guarantee that the one *is* is thus completed by the following: that from which its being proceeds—the count—*is*. 'Is' means 'is-one', given that the law of a structured presentation dictates the reciprocity of 'being' and 'one' therein, by means of the consistency of the multiple.

Due to a metaphorical affinity with politics that will be explained in Meditation 9, I will hereinafter term *state of the situation* that by means of which the structure of a situation—of any structured presentation what-soever—is counted as one, which is to say the one of the one-effect itself, or what Hegel calls the One-One.

What exactly is the operational domain of the state of a situation? If this metastructure did nothing other than count the *terms* of the situation it would be indistinguishable from structure itself, whose entire role is such. On the other hand, *defining* it as the count of the count alone is not sufficient either, or rather, it must be accorded that the latter can solely be a final result of the operations of the state. A structure is precisely not a term of the situation, and as such it cannot be counted. A structure exhausts itself in its effect, which is that there is oneness.

Metastructure therefore cannot simply re-count the terms of the situa-tion and re-compose consistent multiplicities, nor can it have pure operation as its operational domain; that is, it cannot have forming a one out of the one-effect as its direct role.

If the question is approached from the other side—that of the concern of the void, and the risk it represents for structure—we can say the following: the void—whose spectre must be exorcised by declaring that structural integrity *is* integral, by bestowing upon structure, and thus the one, a being-of-itself—as I mentioned, can be neither local nor global. There is no risk of the void being *a* term (since it is the Idea of what is subtracted from the count), nor is it possible for it to be the whole (since it is precisely the nothing of this whole). If there is a risk of the void, it is neither a local risk (in the sense of *a* term) nor is it a global risk (in the sense of the structural integrality of the situation). What is there, being neither local nor global, which could delimit the domain of operation for the second and supreme count-as-one, the count that defines the state of the situation? Intuitively, one would respond that there are *parts* of a situation, being neither points nor the whole.

Yet, conceptually speaking, what is a 'part'? The first count, the structure, allows the designation within the situation of terms that are one-multiples; that is, consistent multiplicities. A 'part' is intuitively a multiple which would be composed, in turn, of such multiplicities. A 'part' would generate compositions out of the very multiplicities that the structure composes under the sign of the one. A part is a sub-multiple.

But we must be very careful here: either this 'new' multiple, which is a sub-multiple, could form a one in the sense of structure, and so in truth it would merely be a term; a composed term, granted, but then so are they all. That this term be composed of already composed multiples, and that all of this be sealed by the one, is the ordinary effect of structure. Or, on the other hand, this 'new' multiple may not form a one; consequently, in the situation, it would purely and simply not exist.

In the interest of simplifying thought let's directly import set theory categories (Meditation 7). Let's say that a consistent multiplicity, counted as one, *belongs* to a situation, and that a sub-multiple, a composition of consistent multiplicities, is *included* in a situation. Only what belongs to the situation is presented. If what is included is presented, it is because it belongs. Inversely, if a sub-multiple does not belong to the situation, it can definitely be said to be abstractly 'included' in the latter; it is not, in fact, presented.

Apparently, either a sub-multiple, because it is counted-as-one in the situation, is only a term, and there is no reason to introduce a new concept, or it is not counted, and it does not exist. Again, there would be no reason to introduce a new concept, save if it were possible that what in-exists in this manner is the very place of the risk of the void. If inclusion can be distinguished from belonging, is there not some part, some non-unified composition of consistent multiplicities, whose inexistence lends a latent figure to the void? The pure errancy of the void is one thing; it is quite another to realize that the void, conceived as the limit of the one, could in fact 'take place' within the inexistence of a composition of consistent multiplicities upon which structure has failed to confer the seal of the one.

In short, if it is neither a one-term, nor the whole, the void would seem to have its place amongst the sub-multiples or 'parts'.

However, the problem with this idea is that structure could well be capable of conferring the one upon everything found within it that is composed from compositions. Our entire artifice is based on the distinction between belonging and inclusion. But why not pose that any composition of consistent multiplicities is, in turn, consistent, which is to say granted one-existence in the situation? And that by consequence inclusion implies belonging?

For the first time we have to employ here an *ontological theorem*, as demonstrated in Meditation 7; the theorem of the point of excess. This theorem establishes that within the framework of the pure theory of the multiple, or set theory, it is formally impossible, whatever the situation be, for *everything* which is included (every subset) to belong to the situation. There is an irremediable excess of sub-multiples over terms. Applied to a situation—in which 'to belong' means: to be a consistent multiple, thus to be presented, or to exist—the theorem of the point of excess simply states: there are always sub-multiples which, despite being included in a situation as compositions of multiplicities, cannot be counted in that situation as terms, and which therefore do not exist.

We are thus led back to the point that 'parts'—if we choose this simple word whose precise sense, disengaged from the dialectic of parts and the whole, is: 'sub-multiple'—must be recognized as the place in which the void may receive the latent form of being; because there are always parts which in-exist in a situation, and which are thus subtracted from the one. An inexistent part is the possible support of the following—which would ruin structure—the one, somewhere, is not, inconsistency is the law of being, the essence of structure is the void.

The definition of the state of a situation is then clarified immediately. *The domain of metastructure is parts*: metastructure guarantees that the one holds for inclusion, just as the initial structure holds for belonging. Put more precisely, given a situation whose structure delivers consistent one-multiples, there is always a metastructure—the state of the situation —which counts as one *any* composition of these consistent multiplicities.

What is *included* in a situation *belongs* to its state. The breach is thereby repaired via which the errancy of the void could have fixed itself to the multiple, in the inconsistent mode of a non-counted part. Every part receives the seal of the one from the state.

By the same token, it is true, *as final result*, that the first count, the structure, is counted by the state. It is evident that amongst all the 'parts' there is the 'total part', which is to say the complete set of everything generated by the initial structure in terms of consistent multiplicities, of everything it counts as one. If the state structures the entire multiple of parts, then this totality also belongs to it. The completeness of the initial one-effect is thus definitely, in turn, counted as one by the state in the form of its effective whole.

The state of a situation is the riposte to the void obtained by the count-as-one of its parts. This riposte is apparently complete, since it both numbers what the first structure allows to in-exist (supernumerary parts, the excess of inclusion over belonging) and, finally, it generates the One-One by numbering structural completeness itself. Thus, for both poles of the danger of the void, the in-existent or inconsistent multiple and the transparent operationality of the one, the state of the situation proposes a clause of closure and security, through which the situation consists according to the one. This is certain: the resource of the state alone permits the outright affirmation that, in situations, the one is.

We should note that the state is a structure which is intrinsically *separate* from the original structure of the situation. According to the theorem of the point of excess, parts exist which in-exist for the original structure, yet which belong to the state's one-effect; the reason being that the latter is fundamentally distinct from any of the initial structure's effects. In an ordinary situation, special operators would thus certainly be required, characteristic of the state; operators capable of yielding the one of those parts which are subtracted from the situation's count-as-one.

On the other hand, the state is always that *of* a situation: what it presents, under the sign of the one, as consistent multiplicities, is in turn solely composed of what the situation presents; since what is *included* is composed of one-multiples which *belong*.

As such, the state of a situation can either be said to be separate (or transcendent) or to be attached (or immanent) with regard to the situation and its native structure. This connection between the separated and the attached characterizes the state as metastructure, count of the count, or one of the one. It is by means of the state that structured presentation is furnished with a fictional *being*; the latter banishes, or so it appears, the peril of the void, and establishes the reign, since completeness is numbered, of the universal security of the one.

The degree of connection between the native structure of a situation and its statist metastructure is variable. This question of a *gap* is the key to the analysis of being, of the typology of multiples-in-situation.

Once counted as one in a situation, a multiple finds itself *presented* therein. If it is also counted as one by the metastructure, or state of the situation, then it is appropriate to say that it is *represented*. This means that it belongs to the situation (presentation), and that it is equally included in the situation (representation). It is a term-part. Inversely, the theorem of the point of excess indicates that there are included (represented) multiples which are not presented (which do not belong). These multiples are parts and not terms. Finally, there are presented terms which are not represented, because they do not constitute a part of the situation, but solely one of its immediate terms.

I will call *normal* a term which is both presented and represented. I will call *excrescence* a term which is represented but not presented. Finally, I will term *singular* a term which is presented but not represented.

It has always been known that the investigation of beings (thus, of what is presented) passes by the filter of the presentation/representation dialectic. In our logic—based directly on a hypothesis concerning being —normality, singularity and excrescence, linked to the gap between structure and metastructure, or between belonging and inclusion, form the decisive concepts of a typology of the donations of being.

Normality consists in the re-securing of the originary one by the state of the situation in which that one is presented. Note that a normal term is found both in presentation (it belongs) and in representation (it is included).

Singular terms are subject to the one-effect, but they cannot be grasped as parts because they are composed, as multiples, of elements which are not accepted by the count. In other words, a singular term is definitely a one-multiple of the situation, but it is 'indecomposable' inasmuch as what it is composed of, or at least part of the latter, is not presented anywhere in the situation in a *separate manner*. This term, unifying ingredients which are not necessarily themselves terms, cannot be considered a part. Although it belongs to it, this term cannot be included in the situation. As such, an indecomposable term will not be re-secured by the state. For the state, not being a part, this term is actually not one, despite it being evidently one in the situation. To put it differently; this term exists—it is presented—but its existence is not directly verified by the state. Its existence is only verified inasmuch as it is 'carried' by parts that exceed it. The state will not have to register this term as one-of-the-state.

Finally, an excrescence is a one of the state that is not a one of the native structure, an existent of the state which in-exists in the situation of which the state is the state.

We thus have, within the complete—state-determined—space of a situation, three fundamental types of one-terms: the normal, which are presented and represented; the singular, which are presented and not represented; and the excrescent, which are represented and not presented. This triad is inferred on the basis of the separation of the state, and by extension, of the necessity of its power for the protection of the one from any fixation-within-the-multiple of the void. These three types structure what is essentially at stake in a situation. They are the most primitive concepts of any experience whatsoever. Their pertinence will be demonstrated in the following Meditation using the example of historico-political situations.

Of all these inferences, what particular requirements result for the situation of ontology? It is evident that as a theory of presentation it must also provide a theory of the state, which is to say, mark the distinction between belonging and inclusion and make sense out of the count-as-one of parts. Its particular restriction, however, is that of having to be 'stateless' with regard to itself.

If indeed there existed a state of the ontological situation, not only would pure multiples be presented therein, but also represented; consequently there would be a rupture, or an order, between a first 'species' of multiples, those presented by the theory, and a second 'species', the sub-multiples of the first species, whose axiomatic count would be ensured by the state of the ontological situation alone, its theoretical metastructure. More importantly, there would be meta-multiples that the state of the situation *alone* would count as one, and which would be compositions of simple-multiples, the latter presented directly by the theory. Or rather; there would be *two* axiom systems, one for elements and one for parts, one of belonging ($\in$), and the other of inclusion ($\subset$). This would certainly be inadequate since the very stake of the theory is the axiomatic presentation of the multiple of multiples as the *unique* general form of presentation.

In other words, it is inconceivable that the implicit presentation of the multiple by the ontological axiom system imply, in fact, two disjoint axiom systems, that of structured presentation, and that of the state.

To put it differently, ontology cannot have its own *excrescences*— 'multiples' that are represented *without ever having been presented as multiples*—because what ontology presents is presentation.

By way of consequence, ontology is obliged to construct the concept of subset, draw all the consequences of the gap between belonging and inclusion, and not fall under the regime of that gap. *Inclusion must not arise on the basis of any other principle of counting than that of belonging.* This is the same as saying that ontology must proceed on the basis that the count-as-one of a multiple's subsets, whatever that multiple may be, is only ever another term within the space of the axiomatic presentation of the pure multiple, and this requirement must be accepted without limitation.

The state of the ontological situation is thus inseparable, which is to say, inexistent. This is what is signified (Meditation 7) by the existence of the set of subsets being an axiom or an Idea, *just like the others*: all it gives us is a multiple.

The price to be paid is clear: in ontology, the state's 'anti-void' functions are not guaranteed. In particular, not only is it possible that the fixation of the void occur somewhere within the parts, but it is inevitable. The void is necessarily, in the ontological apparatus, the subset par excellence, because nothing therein can ensure its expulsion by special operators of the count, distinct from those of the situation in which the void roams. Indeed, in Meditation 7 we saw that in set theory the void is universally included.

The integral realization, on the part of ontology, of the non-being of the one leads to the inexistence of a state of the situation that it is; thereby infecting inclusion with the void, after already having subjected belonging to having to weave with the void alone.

The unpresentable void herein sutures the situation to the non-separation of its state.

Table 1: Concepts relative to the presentation/representation couple

SITUATION		STATE OF THE SITUATION	
Philosophy	Mathematics	Philosophy	Mathematics
– A term of a situation is what that situation presents and counts as one.	– The set β is an element of the set α if it enters into the multiple-composition of α. It is then said that β belongs to α. This is written: $\beta \in \alpha$.	– The state secures the count-as-one of all the sub-multiples, or subsets, or parts of the situation. It re-counts the terms of the situation inasmuch as they are presented by such sub-multiples.	– There exists a set of all the subsets of a given set α. It is written: $p(\alpha)$. Every element of $p(\alpha)$ is a subset (English terminology) or a part (French terminology) of the set α.
– 'To belong to a situation' means: to be presented by that situation, to be one of the elements it structures.	– $\in$ is the sign of belonging. It is the fundamental sign of set theory. It allows one to think the pure multiple without recourse to the One.	– 'To be included in a situation' means: to be counted by the state of the situation.	– To be a subset (or a part) is said: γ is included in α. This is written: $\gamma \subset \alpha$.
– Belonging is thus equivalent to presentation, and a term which belongs will also be said to be an element.	$\beta \in \alpha$	– Inclusion is thus equivalent to representation by the state. We will say of an included—thus, represented—term that it is a part.	– $\subset$ is the sign of inclusion. It is a derived sign. It can be defined on the basis of $\in$. $\gamma \subset \alpha$ or $\gamma \in p(\alpha)$

Thus it must be understood that:

– presentation, count-as-one, structure, belonging and element are *on the side of the situation*;

– representation, count of the count, metastructure, inclusion, subset and part are *on the side of the state of the situation*.

MEDITATION NINE
The State of the Historical-social Situation

In Meditation 8 I said that every structured presentation supposes a metastructure, termed the state of the situation. I put forward an empirical argument in support of this thesis; that every effectively presented multiplicity reveals itself to be submitted to this reduplication of structure or of the count. I would like to give an example of such reduplication here, that of historico-social situations (the question of Nature will be treated in Meditations 11 & 12). Besides the verification of the concept of the state of the situation, this illustrative meditation will also provide us with an opportunity to employ the three categories of presented-being: normality, singularity, and excrescence.

One of the great advances of Marxism was no doubt it having understood that the State, in essence, does not entertain any relationship with individuals; the dialectic of its existence does not relate the one of authority to a multiple of subjects.

In itself, this was not a new idea. Aristotle had already pointed out that the *de facto* prohibition which prevents thinkable constitutions—those which conform to the equilibrium of the concept—from becoming a reality, and which makes politics into such a strange domain—in which the pathological (tyrannies, oligarchies and democracies) regularly prevails over the normal (monarchies, aristocracies and republics)—is in the end the existence of the rich and the poor. Moreover, it is before this particular existence, this ultimate and real impasse of *the political* as pure thought, that Aristotle hesitates; not knowing how it might be suppressed, he hesitates before declaring it entirely 'natural', since what he most desires to see realized is the extension—and, rationally, the universality—of the middle class. He thus clearly recognizes that real states relate less to the social bond than to its un-binding, to its internal oppositions, and that in the end *politics* does not suit the philosophical clarity of *the political* because the state, in its concrete destiny, defines itself less by the balanced place of citizens than by the great masses—the parts which are often parties—both empirical and in flux, that are constituted by the rich and the poor.

Marxist thought relates the State directly to sub-multiples rather than to terms of the situation. It posits that the count-as-one ensured by the State is not originally that of the multiple of individuals, but that of the multiple of classes of individuals. Even if one abandons the terminology of classes, the formal idea that the State—which is the state of the historico-social situation—deals with collective subsets and not with individuals remains essential. This idea must be understood: the essence of the State is that of not being obliged to recognize individuals—when it is obliged to recognize them, in concrete cases, it is always according to a principle of counting which does not concern the individuals as such. Even the coercion that the State exercises over such or such an individual—besides being for the most part anarchic, unregulated and stupid—does not signify in any way that the State is *defined* by the coercive 'interest' that it directs at this individual, or at individuals in general. This is the underlying meaning that must be conferred upon the vulgar Marxist idea that 'the State is always the State of the ruling class.' The interpretation I propose of this idea is that the State solely exercises its domination according to a law destined to form-one out of the *parts* of a situation; moreover, the role of the State is to qualify, one by one, each of the compositions of compositions of multiples whose general consistency, in respect of *terms*, is secured by the situation, that is, by a historical presentation which is 'already' structured.

The State is simply the necessary metastructure of every historico-social situation, which is to say the law that guarantees that there is Oneness, not in the immediacy of society—that is always provided for by a non-state structure—but amongst the set of its subsets. It is this one-effect that Marxism designates when it says that the State is 'the State of the ruling class'. If this formula is supposed to signify that the State is an instrument 'possessed' by the ruling class, then it is meaningless. If it does mean something, it is inasmuch as the effect of the State—to yield the one amongst the complex parts of historico-social presentation—is always a structure, and inasmuch as it is clearly necessary that there be a law of the count, and thus a *uniformity of effect*. At the very least, the term 'ruling class' designates this uniformity, whatever the semantic pertinence of the expression might be.

There is another advantage to the Marxist statement: if it is grasped purely in its form, in posing that the State is that *of* the ruling class, it *indicates that the State always re-presents what has already been presented*. It indicates the latter all the more given that the definition of the ruling classes is not statist, it is rather economic and social. In Marx's work, the presentation of the bourgeoisie is not elaborated in terms of the State; the criteria for the bourgeoisie are possession of the means of production, the regime of property, the concentration of capital, etc. To say of the State that it is that *of* the bourgeoisie has the advantage of underlining that the State re-presents something that has already been historically and socially presented. This re-presentation evidently has nothing to do with the character of government as constitutionally representational. It signifies that in attributing the one to the subsets or parts of the historico-social presentation, in qualifying them according to the law which it is, the State is always defined by the representation—according to the multiples of multiples to which they belong, thus, according to their belonging to what is *included* in the situation—of the terms presented by the situation. Of course, the Marxist statement is far too restrictive; it does not entirely grasp the State as state (of the situation). Yet it moves in the right direction insofar as it indicates that whatever the form of count-as-one of parts operated by the State, the latter is always consecrated to re-presenting presentation: the State is thus the structure of the historico-social structure, the guarantee that the one results *in everything*.

It then becomes evident why the State is both absolutely tied to historico-social presentation and yet also separated from it.

The State is tied to presentation in that the parts, whose one it constructs, are solely multiples of multiples already counted-as-one by the structures of the situation. From this point of view, the State is historically linked to society in the very movement of presentation. The State, solely capable of re-presentation, cannot bring forth a null-multiple—null-term—whose components or elements would be absent from the situation. This is what clarifies the administrative or management function of the State; a function which, in its diligent uniformity, and in the specific constraints imposed upon it by being the state *of the situation*, is far more structural and permanent than the coercive function. On the other hand, because the parts of society exceed its terms on every side, because what is included in a historical situation cannot be reduced to what belongs to it, the State—conceived as operator of the count and guarantee of the universal reinforcement of the one—is necessarily a separate apparatus. Like the state of any situation whatsoever, the State of a historico-social situation is subject to the theorem of the point of excess (Meditation 7). What it deals with—the gigantic, infinite network of the situation's subsets—forces the State to not identify itself with the original structure which lays out the consistency of presentation, which is to say the immediate social bond.

The bourgeois State, according to the Marxist, is separated from both Capital and from its general structuring effect. Certainly, by numbering, managing and ordering subsets, the State re-presents terms which are already structured by the 'capitalistic' nature of society. However, as an operator, it is distinct. This separation defines the coercive function, since the latter relates to the immediate structuring of terms according to a law which 'comes from elsewhere'. This coercion is a matter of principle: it forms the very mode in which the one can be reinforced in the count of parts. If, for example, an individual is 'dealt with' by the State, whatever the case may be, this individual is not counted as one as 'him' or 'herself', which solely means, as that multiple which has received the one in the structuring immediacy of the situation. This individual is considered *as a subset*; that is—to import a mathematical (ontological) concept (cf. Meditation 5)—as the singleton of him or herself. Not as Antoine Dombasle—the proper name of an infinite multiple—but as {Antoine Dombasle}, an indifferent figure of unicity, constituted by the forming-into-one of the name.

The 'voter', for example, is not the subject John Doe, it is rather the part that the separated structure of the State re-presents, according to its own one; that is, it is the set whose sole element is John Doe and not the multiple whose immediate-one is 'John Doe'. The individual is always —patiently or impatiently—subject to this elementary coercion, to this atom of constraint which constitutes the possibility of every other type of constraint, including inflicted death. This coercion consists in not being held to be someone who belongs to society, but as someone who is *included* within society. The State is fundamentally indifferent to belonging yet it is constantly concerned with inclusion. Any consistent subset is immediately counted and considered by the State, for better or worse, because it is matter for representation. On the other hand, despite the protestations and declarations to the contrary, it is always evident that in the end, when it is a matter of people's *lives*—which is to say, of the multiple whose one they have received—the State is not concerned. Such is the ultimate and ineluctable depth of its separation.

It is at this point, however, that the Marxist line of analysis progressively exposes itself to a fatal ambiguity. Granted, Engels and Lenin definitively underlined the separate character of the State; moreover they showed —and they were correct—that coercion is reciprocal with separation. Consequently, for them the essence of the State is finally its bureaucratic and military machinery; that is, the structural visibility of its *excess* over social immediacy, its character of being monstrously *excrescent*—once examined from the sole standpoint of the immediate situation and its terms.

Let's concentrate on this word 'excrescence'. In the previous meditation I made a general distinction between three types of relation to the situational integrity of the one-effect (taking both belonging and inclusion into consideration): normality (to be presented and represented); singularity (to be presented but not represented); excrescence (to be represented but not presented). Obviously what remains is the void, which is neither presented nor represented.

Engels quite clearly remarks signs of excrescence in the State's bureaucratic and military machinery. There is no doubt that such parts of the situation are re-presented rather than presented. This is because they themselves have to do with the operator of re-presentation. Precisely! The ambivalence in the classic Marxist analysis is concentrated in one point: thinking—since it is solely from the standpoint of the State that there are excrescences—that the State *itself* is an excrescence. By consequence, as political programme, the Marxist proposes the revolutionary suppression of the State; thus the end of representation and the universality of simple presentation.

What is the source of this ambivalence? What must be recalled here is that for Engels the separation of the State does not result directly from the simple existence of classes (parts); it results rather from the antagonistic nature of their interests. There is an irreconcilable conflict between the most significant classes—in fact, between the two classes which, according to classical Marxism, produce the very consistency of historical presentation. By consequence, if the monopoly on arms and structured violence were not separate in the form of a State apparatus, there would be a permanent state of civil war.

These classical statements must be quite carefully sorted because they contain a profound idea: *the State is not founded upon the social bond, which it would express, but rather upon un-binding, which it prohibits.* Or, to be more precise, the separation of the State is less a result of the consistency of presentation than of the danger of inconsistency. This idea goes back to Hobbes of course (the war of all against all necessitates an absolute transcendental authority) and it is fundamentally correct in the following form: if, in a situation (historical or not), it is necessary that the parts be counted by a metastructure, it is because their excess over the terms, escaping the initial count, designates a potential place for the fixation of the void. It is thus true that the separation of the State pursues the integrality of the one-effect beyond the terms which belong to the situation, to the point of the mastery, which it ensures, of *included* multiples: so that the void and the gap between the count and the counted do not become identifiable, so that the inconsistency that consistency *is* does not come to pass.

It is not for nothing that governments, when an emblem of their void wanders about—generally, an inconsistent or rioting crowd—prohibit 'gatherings of more than three people', which is to say they explicitly declare their non-tolerance of the one of such 'parts', thus proclaiming that the function of the State is to number inclusions such that consistent belongings be preserved.

However, this is not exactly what Engels said: roughly speaking, for Engels, using Meditation 8's terminology, the bourgeoisie is a normal term (it is presented economically and socially, and re-presented by the State), the proletariat is a singular term (it is presented but not represented), and the State apparatus is an excrescence. The ultimate foundation of the State is that singular and normal terms maintain a sort of antagonistic non-liaison between themselves, or a state of un-binding. The State's excrescence is therefore a result which refers not to the unpresentable, but rather to differences in presentation. Hence, on the basis of the modification of these differences, it is possible to hope for the disappearance of the State. It would suffice for the singular to become universal; this is also called the end of classes, which is to say the end of parts, and thus of any necessity to control their excess.

Note that from this point of view, communism would in reality be the unlimited regime of the individual.

At base, the classical Marxist description of the State is formally correct, but not its general dialectic. The two major parameters of the state of a situation—the unpresentable errancy of the void, and the irremediable excess of inclusion over belonging, which necessitate the re-securing of the one and the structuring of structure—are held by Engels to be particularities of presentation, and of what is numbered therein. The void is reduced to the non-representation of the proletariat, thus, unpresentability is reduced to a modality of non-representation; the separate count of parts is reduced to the non-universality of bourgeois interests, to the presentative split between normality and singularity; and, finally, he reduces the machinery of the count-as-one to an excrescence because he does not understand that the excess which it treats is ineluctable, for it is a theorem of being.

The consequence of these theses is that politics can be defined therein as an assault against the State, whatever the mode of that assault might be, peaceful or violent. It 'suffices' for such an assault to mobilize the singular multiples against the normal multiples by arguing that excrescence is intolerable. However, if the government and even the material substance of the State apparatus can be overturned or destroyed; even if, in certain circumstances it is politically useful to do so, one must not lose sight of the fact that the State as such—which is to say the re-securing of the one over the multiple of parts (or parties)—cannot be so easily attacked or destroyed. Scarcely five years after the October Revolution, Lenin, ready to die, despaired over the obscene permanence of the State. Mao himself, more phlegmatic and more adventurous, declared—after twenty-five years in power and ten years of the Cultural Revolution's ferocious tumult—that not much had changed after all.

This is because even if the route of political change—and I mean the route of the radical dispensation of justice—is always bordered by the State, it cannot in any way let itself be guided by the latter, for the State is precisely non-political, insofar as it cannot change, save hands, and it is well known that there is little strategic signification in such a change.

It is not antagonism which lies at the origin of the State, because one cannot think the dialectic of the void and excess as antagonism. No doubt politics itself must originate in the very same place as the state: in that dialectic. But this is certainly not in order to seize the State nor to double the State's effect. On the contrary, politics stakes its existence on its capacity to establish a relation to both the void and excess which is essentially different from that of the State; it is this difference alone that subtracts politics from the one of statist re-insurance.

Rather than a warrior beneath the walls of the State, a political activist is a patient watchman of the void instructed by the event, for it is only when grappling with the event (see Meditation 17) that the State blinds itself to its own mastery. There the activist constructs the means to sound, if only for an instant, the site of the unpresentable, and the means to be thenceforth faithful to the proper name that, afterwards, he or she will have been able to give to—or hear, one cannot decide—this non-place of place, the void.

MEDITATION TEN
Spinoza

> *'Quicquid est in Deo est'* or : all situations have the same state.
>
> *Ethics*, Book I

Spinoza is acutely aware that presented multiples, which he calls 'singular things' (*res singulares*), are generally multiples of multiples. A composition of multiple individuals (*plura individua*) is actually one and the same singular thing provided that these individuals contribute to one unique action, that is, insofar as they simultaneously cause a unique effect (*unius effectus causa*). In other words, for Spinoza, the count-as-one of a multiple, structure, *is causality*. A combination of multiples is a one-multiple insofar as it is the one of a causal action. Structure is retroactively legible: the one of the effect validates the one-multiple of the cause. The time of incertitude with respect to this legibility distinguishes individuals, whose multiple, supposed inconsistent, receives the seal of consistency once the unity of their effect is registered. The inconsistency, or disjunction, of individuals is then received as the consistency of the singular thing, one and the same. In Latin, inconsistency is *plura individua*, consistency is *res singulares*: between the two, the count-as-one, which is the *unius effectus causa*, or *una actio*.

The problem with this doctrine is that it is circular. If in fact I can only determine the one of a singular thing insofar as the multiple that it is produces a unique effect, then I must already dispose of a criterion of such unicity. What is this 'unique effect'? No doubt it is a complex of individuals in turn—in order to attest its one, in order to say that it is *a* singular thing, I must consider its effects, and so on. The retroaction of the one-effect according to causal structure is suspended from the anticipation of the effects of the effect. There appears to be an infinite oscillation between the inconsistency of individuals and the consistency of the singular thing; insofar as the operator of the count which articulates them, causality, can only be vouched for, in turn, by the count of the effect.

What is surprising is that Spinoza does not in any way appear to be perturbed by this impasse. What I would like to interpret here is not so much the apparent difficulty as the fact that it is not one for Spinoza himself. In my eyes, the key to the problem is that according to his own fundamental logic, *the count-as-one in the last resort is assured by the metastructure*, by the state of the situation, which he calls God or Substance. Spinoza represents the most radical attempt ever in ontology to identify structure and metastructure, to assign the one-effect directly to the state, and to in-distinguish belonging and inclusion. By the same token, it is clear that this is the philosophy *par excellence* which *forecloses the void*. My intention is to establish that this foreclosure fails, and that the void, whose metastructural or divine closure should ensure that it remains in-existent and unthinkable, is well and truly named and placed by Spinoza under the concept of *infinite mode*. One could also say that the infinite mode is where Spinoza designates, despite himself—and thus with the highest uncon-scious awareness of his task—the point (excluded everywhere by him) at which one can no longer avoid the supposition of a Subject.

To start with, the essential identity of belonging and inclusion can be directly deduced from the presuppositions of the definition of the singular thing. The thing, Spinoza tells us, is what results as one in the entire field of our experience, thus in presentation in general. It is what has a 'determinate existence'. But what exists is either being-qua-being, which is to say the one-infinity of the unique substance—whose other name is God—or an immanent modification of God himself, which is to say an effect of substance, an effect whose entire being is substance itself. Spinoza says: 'God is the immanent, not the transitive, cause of all things.' A thing is thus a mode of God, a thing necessarily belongs to these 'infinities in infinite modes' (*infinita infinitis modis*) which 'follow' divine nature. In other words, *Quicquid est in Deo est*; whatever the thing be that is, it is in God. The *in* of belonging is universal. It is not possible to separate another relation from it, such as inclusion. If you combine several things—several individuals—according to the causal count-as-one for example (on the basis of the one of their effect), you will only ever obtain another thing, that is, a mode which belongs to God. It is not possible to distinguish an element or a term of the situation from what would be a part of it. The 'singular thing', which is a one-multiple, belongs to substance in the same manner as the individuals from which it is composed; it is a mode of substance just as they are, which is to say an internal 'affection', an immanent and partial effect. Everything that belongs is included and everything that is included belongs. The absoluteness of the supreme count, of the divine state, entails that everything presented is represented and reciprocally, *because presentation and representation are the same thing*. Since 'to belong to God' and 'to exist' are synonymous, the count of parts is secured by the very movement which secures the count of terms, and which is the inexhaustible immanent productivity of substance.

Does this mean that Spinoza does not distinguish situations, that there is only one situation? Not exactly. If God is unique, and if being is uniquely God, the *identification* of God unfolds an infinity of intellectually separable situations that Spinoza terms the attributes of substance. The attributes are substance itself, inasmuch as it allows itself to be identified in an infinity of different manners. We must distinguish here between being-qua-being (the substantiality of substance), and what thought is able to conceive of as constituting the differentiable identity—Spinoza says: the essence—of being, which is plural. An attribute consists of 'what the intellect (*intellectus*) perceives of a substance, as constituting its essence'. I would say the following: the one-of-being is thinkable through the multiplicity of situations, each of which 'expresses' that one, because if that one was thinkable in one manner alone, then it would have difference external to it; that is, it would be counted itself, which is impossible, because it *is* the supreme count.

In themselves, the situations in which the one of being is thought as immanent differentiation are of infinite 'number', for it is of the being of being to be infinitely identifiable: God is indeed 'a substance consisting of infinite attributes', otherwise it would again be necessary that differences be externally countable. For us, however, according to human finitude, two situations are separable: those which are subsumed under the attribute thought (*cogitatio*) and those under the attribute of extension (*extensio*). The being of this particular mode that is a human animal is to co-belong to these two situations.

It is evident, however, that the presentational structure of situations, being reducible to the divine metastructure, is unique: the two situations in which humans exist are structurally (that is, in terms of the state) unique; *Ordo et connexio idearum idem est, ac ordo et connexio rerum*, it being understood that 'thing' (*res*) designates here an existent—a mode—of the situation 'extension', and that 'idea' (*idea*) an existent of the situation 'thought'. This is a striking example, because it establishes that a human, even when he or she belongs to two separable situations, can count as one insofar as the state of the two situations is the same. One could not find a better indication of the degree to which statist excess subordinates the presentative immediacy of situations (attributes) to itself. This *part* that is a human, body and soul, intersects two separable types of multiple, *extensio* and *cogitatio*, and thus is apparently included in their union. In reality it belongs solely to the modal regime, because the supreme metastructure directly guarantees the count-as-one of everything which exists, whatever its situation may be.

From these presuppositions there immediately follows the foreclosure of the void. On one hand, the void cannot *belong* to a situation because it would have to be counted as one therein, yet the operator of the count is causality. The void, which does not contain any individual, cannot contribute to any action whose result would be a unique effect. The void is therefore inexistent, or unpresented: 'The void is not given in Nature, and all parts must work together such that the void is not given.' On the other hand, the void cannot be *included* in a situation either, it cannot be a part of it, because it would have to be counted as one by its state, its metastructure. In reality, the metastructure is *also* causality; this time understood as the immanent production of the divine substance. It is impossible for the void to be subsumed under this count (of the count), which is identical to the count itself. The void can thus neither be presented nor can exceed presentation in the mode of the statist count. It is neither presentable (belonging) nor unpresentable (point of excess).

Yet this deductive foreclosure of the void does not succeed—far from it—in the eradication of any possibility of its errancy in some weak point or abandoned joint of the Spinozist system. Put it this way: the danger is notorious when it comes to the consideration, with respect to the count-as-one, of the disproportion between the infinite and the finite.

'Singular things', presented, according to the situations of Thought and Extension, to human experience, are finite; this is an essential predicate, it is given in their definition. If it is true that the ultimate power of the count-as-one is God, being both the state of situations and immanent presentative law, then there is apparently no measure between the count and its result because God is 'absolutely infinite'. To be more precise, does not causality—by means of which the one of the thing is recognized in the one of its effect—risk introducing the void of a measurable non-relation between its infinite origin and the finitude of the one-effect? Spinoza posits that 'the knowledge of the effect depends on, and envelops, the knowledge of the cause.' Is it conceivable that the knowledge of a finite thing envelop the knowledge of an infinite cause? Would it not be necessary to traverse the void of an absolute loss of reality between cause and effect if one is infinite and the other finite? A void, moreover, that would necessarily be immanent, since a finite thing is a modality of God himself? It seems that the excess of the causal source re-emerges at the point at which its intrinsic qualification, absolute infinity, cannot be represented on the same axis as its finite effect. Infinity would therefore designate the statist excess over the presentative belonging of singular finite things. And the correlate, ineluctable because the void is the ultimate foundation of that excess, is that the void would be the errancy of the incommensurability between the infinite and the finite.

Spinoza categorically affirms that, 'beyond substance and modes, nothing is given (*nil datur*).' Attributes are actually not 'given', they name the situations of donation. If substance is infinite, and modes are finite, the void is ineluctable, like the stigmata of a split in presentation between substantial being-qua-being and its finite immanent production.

To deal with this re-emergence of the unqualifiable void, and to maintain the entirely affirmative frame of his ontology, Spinoza is led to posit that *the couple substance/modes, which determines all donation of being, does not coincide with the couple infinite/finite*. This structural split between presentative nomination and its 'extensive' qualification naturally cannot occur on the basis of there being a finitude of substance, since the latter is 'absolutely infinite' by definition. There is only one solution; that *infinite modes* exist. Or, to be more precise—since, as we shall see, it is rather the case that these modes in-exist—the immediate cause of a singular finite thing can only be another singular finite thing, and, *a contrario*, a (supposed) infinite thing can only produce the infinite. The effective causal liaison being thus exempted from the abyss between the infinite and the finite, we come back to the point—within presentation—where excess is cancelled out, thus, the void.

Spinoza's deductive procedure (propositions 21, 22, and 28 of Book I of *The Ethics*) then runs as follows:

– Establish that 'everything which follows from the absolute nature of any of God's attributes . . . is infinite.' This amounts to saying that if an effect (thus a mode) results directly from the infinity of God, such as identified in a presentative situation (an attribute), then that effect is necessarily infinite. It is an immediate infinite mode.

– Establish that everything which follows from an infinite mode—in the sense of the preceding proposition—is, in turn, infinite. Such is a mediate infinite mode.

Having reached this point, we know that the infinity of a cause, whether it be directly substantial or already modal, solely engenders infinity. We therefore avoid the loss of equality, or the non-measurable relation between an infinite cause and a finite effect, which would have immediately provided the place for a fixation of the void.

The converse immediately follows:

– The count-as-one of a singular thing on the basis of its supposed finite effect immediately designates it as being finite itself; for if it were infinite, its effect, as we have seen, would also have to be such. In the structured presentation of singular things there is a causal recurrence of the finite:

> Any singular thing, for example something which is finite and has a determinate existence, can neither exist, nor be determined to produce an effect unless it is determined to exist and produce an effect by another cause, which is also finite and has a determinate existence; and again, this cause also can neither exist nor be determined to produce an effect unless it is determined to exist and produce an effect by another, which is also finite and has a determinate existence, and so on, to infinity.

Spinoza's feat here is to arrange matters such that the excess of the state—the infinite substantial origin of causality—is not discernible as such in the presentation of the causal chain. The finite, in respect to the count of causality and its one-effect, refers back to the finite alone. The rift between the finite and the infinite, in which the danger of the void resides, does not traverse the presentation of the finite. This essential homogeneity of presentation expels the un-measure in which the dialectic of the void and excess might be revealed, or encountered, within presentation.

But this can only be established if we suppose that another causal chain 'doubles', so to speak, the recurrence of the finite; the chain of infinite modes, immediate then mediate, itself intrinsically homogeneous, but entirely disconnected from the presented world of 'singular things'.

The question is that of knowing in which sense these infinite modes *exist*. In fact, very early on, there were a number of curious people who asked Spinoza exactly what these infinite modes were, notably a certain Schuller, a German correspondent, who, in his letter of 25 July 1675, begged the 'very wise and penetrating philosopher Baruch de Spinoza' to give him 'examples of things produced immediately by God, and things produced mediately by an infinite modification'. Four days later, Spinoza replied to him that 'in the order of thought' (in our terms; in the situation, or attribute, thought) the example of an immediate infinite mode was 'absolutely infinite understanding', and in the order of extension, movement and rest. As for mediate infinite modes, Spinoza only cites one, without specifying its attribute (which one can imagine to be extension). It is 'the figure of the entire universe' (*facies totius universi*).

Throughout the entirety of his work, Spinoza will not say anything more about infinite modes. In the *Ethics*, Book II, lemma 7, he introduces the idea of presentation as a multiple of multiples—adapted to the situation of extension, where things are bodies—and develops it into an infinite hierarchy of bodies, ordered according to the complexity of each body as a multiple. If this hierarchy is extended to infinity (*in infinitum*), then it is possible to conceive that 'the whole of Nature is one sole Individual (*totam Naturam unum esse Individuum*) whose parts, that is, all bodies, vary in an infinity of modes, without any change of the whole Individual.' In the *scholium* for proposition 40 in Book V, Spinoza declares that 'our mind, insofar as it understands, is an eternal mode of thought (*aeternus cogitandi modus*), which is determined by another eternal mode of thought, and this again by another, and so on, to infinity, so that all together, they constitute the eternal and infinite understanding of God.'

It should be noted that these assertions do not make up part of the demonstrative chain. They are isolated. They tend to present Nature as the infinite immobile totality of singular moving things, and the divine Understanding as the infinite totality of particular minds.

The question which then emerges, and it is an insistent one, is that of the existence of these totalities. The problem is that the principle of the Totality which is obtained by addition *in infinitum* has nothing to do with the principle of the One by which substance guarantees, in radical statist excess, however immanent, the count of every singular thing.

Spinoza is very clear on the options available for establishing an existence. In his letter 'to the very wise young man Simon de Vries' of March 1663, he distinguishes two of them, corresponding to the two instances of the donation of being; substance (and its attributive identifications) and the modes. With regard to substance, existence is not distinguished from essence, and so it is *a priori* demonstrable on the basis of the definition alone of the existing thing. As proposition 7 of Book I of the

Ethics clearly states; 'it pertains to the nature of a substance to exist.' With regard to modes, there is no other recourse save experience, for 'the existence of modes [cannot] be concluded from the definition of things.' The existence of the universal—or statist—power of the count-as-one is originary, or *a priori*; the existence in situation of particular things is *a posteriori* or to be experienced.

That being the case, it is evident that the existence of infinite modes cannot be established. Since they are modes, the correct approach is to experience or test their existence. However, it is certain that we have no experience of movement or rest *as infinite modes* (we solely have experience of particular finite things in movement or at rest); nor do we have experience of Nature in totality or *facies totius universi*, which radically exceeds our singular ideas; nor, of course, do we have experience of the absolutely infinite understanding, or the totality of minds, which is strictly unrepresentable. *A contrario*, if, there where experience fails *a priori* deduction might prevail, if it therefore belonged to the defined essence of movement, of rest, of Nature in totality, or of the gathering of minds, to exist, then these entities would no longer be modal but substantial. They would be, at best, identifications of substance, situations. They would not be given, but would constitute the places of donation, which is to say the attributes. In reality, it would not be possible to distinguish Nature in totality from the attribute 'extension', nor the divine understanding from the attribute 'thought'.

We have thus reached the following impasse: in order to avoid any direct causal relation between the infinite and the finite—a point in which a measureless errancy of the void would be generated—one has to suppose that the direct action of infinite substantiality does not produce, in itself, anything apart from infinite modes. But it is impossible to justify the existence of even one of these modes. It is thus necessary to pose either that these infinite modes exist, but are inaccessible to both thought and experience, or that they do not exist. The first possibility creates an underworld of infinite things, an intelligible place which is totally unpresentable, thus, a void *for us* (for our situation), in the sense that the only 'existence' to which we can testify in relation to this place is that of a name: 'infinite mode'. The second possibility directly creates a void, in the sense in which the proof of the causal recurrence of the finite—the proof of the homogeneity and consistency of presentation—is founded upon an inexistence. Here again, 'infinite mode' is a pure name whose referent is eclipsed; it is cited only inasmuch as it is required by the proof, and then it is cancelled from all finite experience, the experience whose unity it served to found.

Spinoza undertook the ontological eradication of the void by the appropriate means of an absolute unity of the situation (of presentation) and its state (representation). I will designate as *natural* (or ordinal) multiplicities those that incarnate, in a given situation, the maximum in this equilibrium of belonging and inclusion (Meditation 11). These natural multiples are those whose terms are all *normal* (cf. Meditation 8), which is to say represented in the very place of their presentation. According to this definition, *every* term, for Spinoza, is natural: the famous '*Deus, sive Natura*' is entirely founded. But the rule for this foundation hits a snag; the necessity of having to convoke a void term, whose name without a testifiable referent ('infinite mode') inscribes errancy in the deductive chain.

The great lesson of Spinoza is in the end the following: even if, via the position of a supreme count-as-one which fuses the state of a situation and the situation (that is, metastructure and structure, or inclusion and belonging), you attempt to annul excess and reduce it to a unity of the presentative axis, you will not be able to avoid the errancy of the void; you will have to place its name.

Necessary, but inexistent: the infinite mode. It fills in—the moment of its conceptual appearance being also the moment of its ontological disappearance—the causal abyss between the infinite and the finite. However, it only does so in being the technical name of the abyss: the signifier 'infinite mode' organizes a subtle misrecognition of this void which was to be foreclosed, but which insists on erring beneath the nominal artifice itself from which one deduced, in theory, its radical absence.

PART III

Being: Nature and Infinity.
Heidegger/Galileo

MEDITATION ELEVEN
Nature: Poem or matheme?

The theme of 'nature'—and let's allow the Greek term φύσις to resonate beneath this word—is decisive for ontologies of Presence, or poetic ontologies. Heidegger explicitly declares that φύσις is a 'fundamental Greek word for being'. If this word is fundamental, it is because it designates being's vocation for presence, in the mode of its appearing, or more explicitly of its non-latency (ἀλήθεια). Nature is not a region of being, a register of being-in-totality. It is the appearing, the bursting forth of being itself, the coming-to of its presence, or rather, the 'stance of being'. What the Greeks received in this word φύσις, in the intimate connection that it designates between being and appearing, was that being does not *force* its coming to Presence, but coincides with this matinal advent in the guise of appearance, of the pro-position. If being is φύσις, it is because it is 'the appearing which resides in itself'. Nature is thus not objectivity nor the given, but rather the gift, the gesture of opening up which unfolds its own limit as that in which it resides without limitation. Being is 'the opening up which holds sway, φύσις'. It would not be excessive to say that φύσις designates being-present according to the offered essence of its auto-presentation, and that nature is therefore being itself such as its proximity and its un-veiling are maintained by an ontology of presence. 'Nature' means: presentification of presence, offering of what is veiled.

Of course, the word 'nature', especially in the aftermath of the Galilean rupture, is commensurate with a complete forgetting with regard to what is detained in the Greek word φύσις. How can one recognize in this nature 'written in mathematical language' what Heidegger wants us to hear again when he says 'φύσις is the remaining-there-in-itself'? But the forgetting, under the word 'nature', of everything detained in the word φύσις in the sense of coming forth and the open, is far more ancient than what is declared in 'physics' in its Galilean sense. Or rather: the 'natural' objectivity which physics takes as its domain was only possible on the basis of the metaphysical subversion that began with Plato, the subversion of what is retained in the word φύσις in the shape of Presence, of being-appearing. The Galilean reference to Plato, whose vector, let's note, is none other than mathematicism, is not accidental. The Platonic 'turn' consisted, at the ambivalent frontiers of the Greek destiny of being, of proposing 'an interpretation of φύσις as ἰδέα'. But in turn, the Idea, in Plato's sense, can also only be understood *on the basis of* the Greek conception of nature, or φύσις. It is neither a denial nor a decline. It *completes* the Greek thought of being as appearing, it is the 'completion of the beginning'. For what is the Idea? It is the *evident* aspect of what is offered—it is the 'surface', the 'façade', the offering to the regard of what opens up as nature. It is still, of course, appearing as the aura-like being of being, but within the delimitation, the cut-out, of a visibility *for us*.

From the moment that this 'appearing in the second sense' detaches itself, becomes a measure of appearing itself, and is isolated as ἰδέα, from the moment that this slice of appearing is taken for the being of appearing, the 'decline' indeed begins, which is to say the loss of everything there is of presence and non-latency (ἀλήθεια) in presentation. What is decisive in the Platonic turn, following which nature forgets φύσις, 'is not that φύσις should have been characterised as ἰδέα, but that ἰδέα should have become the sole and decisive interpretation of being'.

If I return to Heidegger's well-known analyses, it is to underline the following, which in my eyes is fundamental: the trajectory of the forgetting which founds 'objective' nature, submitted to mathematical Ideas, as loss of opening forth, of φύσις, consists finally in substituting lack for presence, subtraction for pro-position. From the moment when being as Idea was promoted to the rank of veritable entity—when the evident 'façade' of what appears was promoted to the rank of appearing—'[what was] previously dominant, [was] degraded to what Plato calls the μή ὄν, what in truth should not be.' Appearing, repressed or compressed by the evidence of the ἰδέα, ceases to be understood as opening-forth-into-presence, and becomes, on the contrary, that which, forever unworthy —because unformed—of the ideal paradigm, must be figured as *lack of being*: 'What appears, the phenomenon, is no longer φύσις, the holding sway of that which opens forth . . . what appears is *mere* appearance, it is actually an illusion, which is to say a lack.'

If 'with the interpretation of being as ἰδέα there is a rupture with regard to the authentic beginning', it is because what gave an indication, under the name of φύσις, of an originary link between being and appearing—presentation's guise of presence—is reduced to the rank of a subtracted, impure, inconsistent given, whose sole consistent opening forth is the cut-out of the Idea, and particularly, from Plato to Galileo—and Cantor—the mathematical Idea.

The Platonic *matheme* must be thought here precisely as a *disposition* which is separated from and forgetful of the preplatonic *poem*, of Parmenides' poem. From the very beginning of his analysis, Heidegger marks that the authentic thought of being as φύσις and the 'naming force of the word' are linked to 'the great poetry of the Greeks'. He underlines that 'for Pindar φυά constitutes the fundamental determination of being-there.' More generally, the work of art, τέχνη in the Greek sense, is founded on nature as φύσις: 'In the work of art considered as appearing, what comes to appear is the holding sway of the opening forth, φύσις.'

It is thus clear that at this point two directions, two orientations command the entire destiny of thought in the West. One, based on nature in its original Greek sense, welcomes—in poetry—appearing as the coming-to-presence of being. The other, based on the Idea in its Platonic sense, submits the lack, the subtraction of all presence, to the matheme, and thus disjoins being from appearing, essence from existence.

For Heidegger, the poetico-natural orientation, which lets-be presentation as non-veiling, is the authentic origin. The mathematico-ideal orientation, which subtracts presence and promotes evidence, is the metaphysical closure, the first step of the forgetting.

What I propose is not an overturning but *another* disposition of these two orientations. I willingly admit that absolutely originary thought occurs in poetics and in the letting-be of appearing. This is proven by the immemorial character of the poem and poetry, and by its established and constant suture to the theme of nature. However, this immemoriality testifies against the evental emergence of philosophy in Greece. Ontology strictly speaking, as native figure of Western philosophy, is not, and cannot be, the arrival of the poem in its attempt to name, in brazen power and coruscation, appearing as the coming-forth of being, or non-latency. The latter is both far more ancient, and with regard to its original sites, far more multiple (China, India, Egypt . . .). What constituted the Greek event is rather the *second* orientation, which thinks being subtractively in the mode of an ideal or axiomatic thought. The particular invention of the Greeks is that being is expressible once a decision of thought subtracts it from any instance of presence.

The Greeks did not invent the poem. Rather, they *interrupted* the poem with the matheme. In doing so, in the exercise of deduction, which is fidelity to being such as named by the void (cf. Meditation 24), the Greeks opened up the infinite possibility of an ontological text.

Nor did the Greeks, and especially Parmenides and Plato, think being as φύσις or nature, whatever decisive importance this word may have possessed for them. Rather, they originally *untied* the thought of being from its poetic enchainment to natural appearing. The advent of the Idea designates this unchaining of ontology and the opening of its infinite text as the historicity of mathematical deductions. For the punctual, ecstatic and repetitive figure of the poem they substituted the innovatory accumulation of the matheme. For presence, which demands an initiatory return, they substituted the subtractive, the void-multiple, which commands a transmissible thinking.

Granted, the poem, interrupted by the Greek event, has nevertheless never ceased. The 'Western' configuration of thought combines the accumulative infinity of subtractive ontology and the poetic theme of natural presence. Its scansion is not that of a forgetting, but rather that of a *supplement*, itself in the form of a caesura and an interruption. The radical change introduced by the mathematical supplementation is that the immemorial nature of the poem—which was full and innate donation—became, after the Greek event, the *temptation* of a return, a temptation that Heidegger believed—like so many Germans—to be a nostalgia and a loss, whereas it is merely the permanent play induced in thought by the unrelenting novelty of the matheme. Mathematical ontology—labour of the text and of inventive reason—retroactively constituted poetic utterance *as* an auroral temptation, *as* nostalgia for presence and rest. This nostalgia, latent thereafter in every great poetic enterprise, is not woven from the forgetting of being: on the contrary, it is woven from the pronunciation of being in its subtraction by mathematics in its effort of thought. The victorious mathematical enunciation entails the belief that the poem says a lost presence, a threshold of sense. But this is merely a divisive illusion, a correlate of the following: being is expressible from the unique point of its empty suture to the demonstrative text. The poem entrusts itself nostalgically to nature solely because it was once interrupted by the matheme, and the 'being' whose presence it pursues is solely the impossible *filling in* of the void, such as amidst the arcana of the pure multiple, mathematics indefinitely discerns therein what can, in truth, be subtractively pronounced of being itself.

What happens—for that part of it which has not been entrusted to the poem—to the concept of 'nature' in this configuration? What is the fate and the scope of this concept within the framework of mathematical ontology? It should be understood that this is an ontological question and has nothing to do with physics, which establishes the laws for particular domains of presentation ('matter'). The question can also be formulated as follows: is there a pertinent concept of nature in the doctrine of the multiple? Is there any cause to speak of 'natural' multiplicities?

Paradoxically, it is again Heidegger who is able to guide us here. Amongst the general characteristics of φύσις, he names 'constancy, the stability of what has opened forth of itself'. Nature is the 'remaining there of the stable'. The constancy of being which resonates in the word φύσις can also be found in linguistic roots. The Greek φύω, the Latin *fui*, the French *fus*, and the German *bin* (am) and *bist* (are) are all derived from the Sanscrit *bhu* or *bheu*. The Heideggerean sense of this ancestry is 'to come to stand and remain standing of itself'.

Thus, being, thought as φύσις, is the stability of maintaining-itself-there; the constancy, the equilibrium of that which maintains itself within the opening forth of its limit. If we retain this concept of nature, we will say that a pure multiple is 'natural' if it attests, in its form-multiple itself, a particular con-sistency, a specific manner of holding-together. A natural multiple is a superior form of the internal cohesion of the multiple.

How can this be reflected in our own terms, within the typology of the multiple? I distinguished, in structured presentation, normal terms (presented and represented) from singular terms (presented but not represented) and excrescences (represented but not presented) (Meditation 8). Already, it is possible to think that *normality*—which balances presentation (belonging) and representation (inclusion), and which symmetrizes structure (what is presented in presentation) and metastructure (what is counted as one by the state of the situation)—provides a pertinent concept of equilibrium, of stability, and of remaining-there-in-itself. For us stability necessarily derives from the count-as-one, because all consistency proceeds from the count. What could be more stable than what is, as multiple, counted twice in its place, by the situation and by its state? Normality, the maximum bond between belonging and inclusion, is well suited to thinking the natural stasis of a multiple. Nature is what is normal, the multiple re-secured by the state.

But a multiple is in turn multiple of multiples. If it is normal in the situation in which it is presented and counted, the multiples from which it is composed could, in turn, be singular, normal or excrescent with respect to it. The stable remaining-there of a multiple could be *internally* contradicted by singularities, which are presented by the multiple in question but not re-presented. To thoroughly think through the stable consistency of natural multiples, no doubt one must prohibit these internal singularities, and posit that a normal multiple is composed, in turn, of normal multiples alone. In other words, such a multiple is both presented and represented within a situation, and furthermore, inside it, all the multiples which belong to it (that it presents) are also included (represented); moreover, all the multiples which make up these multiples are also normal, and so on. A natural presented-multiple (a natural situation) is the recurrent form-multiple of a special equilibrium between belonging and inclusion, structure and metastructure. Only this equilibrium secures and re-secures the consistency of the multiple. Naturalness is the intrinsic normality of a situation.

We shall thus say the following: a situation is *natural* if all the term-multiples that it presents are normal and if, moreover, all the multiples presented by its term-multiples are also normal. Schematically, if N is the situation in question, every element of N is also a sub-multiple of N. In ontology this will be written as such: when one has $n \in N$ (belonging), one also has $n \subset N$ (inclusion). In turn, the multiple n is also a natural situation, in that if $n' \in n$, then equally $n' \subset n$. We can see that a natural multiple counts as one normal multiples, which themselves count as one normal multiples. This normal stability ensures the *homogeneity* of natural multiples. That is, if we posit reciprocity between nature and normality, the consequence—given that the terms of a natural multiple are themselves composed of normal multiples—is that nature remains homogeneous *in dissemination*; what a natural multiple presents is natural, and so on. Nature never internally contradicts itself. It is self-homogeneous self-presentation. Such is the formulation within the concept of being as pure multiple of what Heidegger determines as φύσις, 'remaining-there-in-itself'.

But for the poetic categories of the auroral and the opening-forth we substitute the structural and conceptually transmissible categories of the maximal correlation between presentation and representation, belonging and inclusion.

Heidegger holds that being 'is as φύσις'. We shall say rather: being consists maximally as natural multiplicity, which is to say as homogeneous normality. For the non-veiling whose proximity is lost, we substitute this aura-less proposition: nature is what is rigorously normal in being.

MEDITATION TWELVE
The Ontological Schema of Natural Multiples and the Non-existence of Nature

Set theory, considered as an adequate thinking of the pure multiple, or of the presentation of presentation, *formalizes* any situation whatsoever insofar as it reflects the latter's being as such; that is, the multiple of multiples which makes up any presentation. If, within this framework, one wants to formalize *a* particular situation, then it is best to consider *a* set such that its characteristics—which, in the last resort, are expressible in the logic of the sign of belonging alone, $\in$—are comparable to that of the structured presentation—the situation—in question.

If we wish to find the ontological schema of natural multiplicities such as it is thought in Meditation 11; that is, as a set of normal multiplicities, themselves composed of normal multiplicities—thus the schema of the maximum equilibrium of presented-being—then we must first of all formalize the concept of normality.

The heart of the question lies in the re-securing performed by the state. It is on the basis of this re-securing, and thus on the basis of the disjunction between presentation and representation, that I categorized terms as singular, normal, or excrescent, and defined natural situations (every term is normal, and the terms of the terms are also normal).

Do these Ideas of the multiple, the axioms of set-theory, allow us to formalize, and thus to think, this concept?

1. THE CONCEPT OF NORMALITY: TRANSITIVE SETS

To determine the central concept of normality one must start from the following: a multiple α is normal if every *element* β of this set is also a *subset*;

that is, $\beta \in \alpha \rightarrow \beta \subset \alpha$.

One can see that α is considered here as the situation in which β is presented, and that the implication of the formula inscribes the idea that β is counted-as-one *twice* (in α); once as element and once as subset, by presentation and by the state, that is, according to α, and according to $p(\alpha)$.

The technical concept which designates a set such as α is that of a *transitive* set. A transitive set is a set such that everything which belongs to it ($\beta \in \alpha$) is also included in it ($\beta \subset \alpha$).

In order not to overburden our terminology, and once it is understood that the couple belonging/inclusion does *not* coincide with the couple One/All (cf. on this point the table following Meditation 8), from this point on, along with French mathematicians, we will term all subsets of α *parts* of α. In other words we will read the mark $\beta \subset \alpha$ as 'β is a part of α.' For the same reasons we will name $p(\alpha)$, which is the set of subsets of α (and thus the state of the situation α), 'the set of parts of α.' According to this convention a transitive set will be a set such that all of its *elements* are also *parts*.

Transitive sets play a fundamental role in set theory. This is because transitivity is in a certain manner *the maximum correlation between belonging and inclusion*: it tells us that 'everything which belongs is included.' Thanks to the theorem of the point of excess we know that the inverse proposition would designate an impossibility: it is not possible for everything which is included to belong. Transitivity, which is the ontological concept of the ontic concept of equilibrium, amounts to the primitive sign of the one-multiple, $\in$, being here—in the immanence of the set α—translatable into inclusion. In other words, in a transitive set in which every element is a part, what is presented to the set's count-as-one is also re-presented to the set of parts' count-as-one.

Does at least one transitive set exist? At this point of our argument, the question of existence is strictly dependent upon the existence of the name of the void, the sole existential assertion which has so far figured in the axioms of set theory, or the Ideas of the multiple. I established (Meditation 7) the existence of the singleton of the void, written $\{\varnothing\}$, which is the formation-into-one of the name of the void; that is, the multiple whose sole element is $\varnothing$. Let's consider the set of subsets of this $\{\varnothing\}$, that is, $p\{\varnothing\}$, which we will now call the set of parts of the singleton of the void. This set exists because $\{\varnothing\}$ exists and the axiom of parts is a conditional guarantee of existence (if α exists, $p(\alpha)$ exists: cf. Meditation 5). What would the parts of $p(\varnothing)$ be? Doubtless there is $\{\varnothing\}$ itself, which is, after all, the 'total part'.

There is also ∅, because the void is universally included in every multiple (∅ is a part of every set, cf. Meditation 7). It is evident that there are no other parts. The multiple $p(∅)$, set of parts of the singleton {∅}, is thus a multiple which has *two* elements, ∅ and {∅}. Here, woven from nothing apart from the void, we have the ontological schema of the Two, which can be written: {∅, {∅}}.

This Two is a transitive set. Witness:

– the element ∅, being a universal part, is part of the Two;

– the element {∅} is also a part since ∅ is an *element* of the Two (it belongs to it). Therefore the *singleton* of ∅, that is, the part of the Two which has ∅ as its sole element, is clearly included in the Two.

Consequently, the two elements of the Two are also two parts of the Two and the Two is transitive insofar as it makes a one solely out of multiples that are also parts. The mathematical concept of transitivity, which formalizes normality or stable-multiplicity, is therefore thinkable. Moreover, it subsumes existing multiples (whose existence is deduced from the axioms).

2. NATURAL MULTIPLES: ORDINALS

There is better to come. Not only is the Two a transitive set, but its elements, ∅ and {∅}, are also transitive. As such, we recognize that, as a normal multiple composed of normal multiples, the Two formalizes *natural* existent-duality.

To formalize the natural character of a situation not only is it necessary that a pure multiple be transitive, but also that all of its elements turn out to be transitive. This is transitivity's recurrence 'lower down' which rules the natural equilibrium of a situation, since such a situation is normal and everything which it presents is equally normal, relative to the presentation. So, how does this happen?

– The element {∅} has ∅ as its unique element. The void is a universal part. This element ∅ is thus also a part.

– The element ∅, proper name of the void, does not present any element and consequently—and it is here that the difference according to indifference, characteristic of the void, really comes into play—nothing inside it *is not* a part. There is no obstacle to declaring ∅ to be transitive.

As such, the Two is transitive, and all of its elements are transitive.

A set that has this property will be called an *ordinal*. The Two is an ordinal. An ordinal ontologically reflects the multiple-being of natural situations. And, of course, ordinals play a decisive role in set theory. One of their main properties is that *every multiple which belongs to them is also an ordinal*, which is the law of being of our definition of Nature; everything which belongs to a natural situation can also be considered as a natural situation. Here we have found the homogeneity of nature again.

Let's demonstrate this point just for fun.

Take α, an ordinal. If $\beta \in \alpha$, it first follows that β is transitive, because every element of an ordinal is transitive. It then follows that $\beta \subset \alpha$, because α is transitive, and thus everything which *belongs to* it is also *included in* it. But if β is included in α, by the definition of inclusion, every element of β belongs to α. Therefore, $(\gamma \in \beta) \to (\gamma \in \alpha)$. But if γ belongs to α, it is transitive because α is an ordinal. Finally, every element of β is transitive, and given that β itself is transitive, β must be an ordinal.

An ordinal is thus a multiple of multiples which are themselves ordinals. This concept literally provides the backbone of all ontology, because it is the very concept of Nature.

The doctrine of Nature, from the standpoint of the thought of being-qua-being, is thus accomplished in the theory of ordinals. It is remarkable that despite Cantor's creative enthusiasm for ordinals, since his time they have not been considered by mathematicians as much more than a curiosity without major consequence. This is because modern ontology, unlike that of the Ancients, does not attempt to lay out the architecture of being-in-totality in all its detail. The few who devote themselves to this labyrinth are specialists whose presuppositions concerning onto-logy, the link between language and the sayable of being, are particularly restrictive; notably—and I will return to this—one finds therein the tenants of *constructibility*, which is conceived as a programme for the complete mastery of the connection between formal language and the multiples whose existence is tolerated.

One of the important characteristics of ordinals is that their definition is intrinsic, or structural. If you say that a multiple is an ordinal—a transitive set of transitive sets—this is an *absolute* determination, indifferent to the situation in which the multiple is presented.

The ontological criterion for natural multiples is their stability, their homogeneity; that is, as we shall see, their immanent order. Or, to be more precise, the fundamental relation of the thought of the multiple, belonging ($\in$), connects all natural multiples together in a specific manner. Natural multiples are universally intricated via the sign in which ontology concentrates presentation. Or rather: natural consistency—to speak like Heidegger—is the 'holding sway', throughout the entirety of natural multiples, of the original Idea of multiple-presentation that is belonging. Nature belongs to itself. This point—from which far-reaching conclusions will be drawn on number, quantity, and thought in general—demands our entrance into the web of inference.

3. THE PLAY OF PRESENTATION IN NATURAL MULTIPLES OR ORDINALS

Consider a natural multiple, α. Take an element β of that multiple, $\beta \in \alpha$. Since α is normal (transitive), by the definition of natural multiples, the element β is also a part, and thus we have $\beta \subset \alpha$. The result is that every element of β is also an element of α. Let's note, moreover, that due to the homogeneity of nature, every element of an ordinal is an ordinal (see above). We attain the following result: if an ordinal β is an element of an ordinal α, and if an ordinal γ is an element of the ordinal β, then γ is also an element of α: $[(\beta \in \alpha) \ \& \ (\gamma \in \beta)] \rightarrow (\gamma \in \alpha)$.

One can therefore say that belonging 'transmits itself' from an ordinal to any ordinal which presents it in the one-multiple that it is: the element of the element is also an element. If one 'descends' within natural presentation, one remains within such presentation. Metaphorically, a cell of a complex organism and the constituents of that cell are constituents of that organism just as naturally as its visible functional parts are.

So that natural language might guide us—and despite the danger that intuition presents for subtractive ontology—we shall adopt the convention of saying that an ordinal β is *smaller than* an ordinal α if one has $\beta \in \alpha$. Note that in the case of α being different to β, 'smaller than' causes belonging and inclusion to coincide here: by virtue of the transitivity of α, if $\beta \in \alpha$, one also has $\beta \subset \alpha$, and so the element β is equally a part. That an ordinal be smaller than another ordinal means indifferently that it either belongs to the larger, or is included in the larger.

Must 'smaller than' be taken in a *strict sense*, excluding the statement 'α is smaller than α'? We will allow here that, in a general manner, it is unthinkable that a set belong to itself. The writing $\alpha \in \alpha$ is marked as forbidden. The reasons of thought which lie behind this prohibition are profound because they touch upon the question of the event: we shall study this matter in Meditations 17 and 18. For the moment all I ask is that the prohibition be accepted as such. Its consequence, of course, is that no ordinal can be smaller than itself, since 'smaller than' coincides, for natural multiples, with 'to belong to'.

What we have stated above can also be formulated, according to the conventions, as such: if an ordinal is smaller than another, and that other is smaller than a third, then the first is also smaller than the third. This is the banal law of an *order*, yet this order, and such is the foundation of natural homogeneity, is nothing other than the order of presentation, marked by the sign $\in$.

Once there is an order, a 'smaller than', it makes sense to pose the question of the 'smallest' multiple which would have such or such a property, according to this order.

This question comes down to knowing whether, given a property Ψ expressed in the language of set theory, such or such multiple:

- first, possesses the said property;
- second, given a relation of order, is such that no multiple which is 'smaller' according to that relation, has the said property.

Since 'smaller', for ordinals or natural multiples, is said according to belonging, this signifies that an α exists which is such that it possesses the property Ψ itself, but no multiple which belongs to it possesses the latter property. It can be said that such a multiple is $\in$-minimal for the property.

Ontology establishes the following theorem: given a property Ψ, *if* an ordinal possesses it, *then* there exists an ordinal which is $\in$-minimal for that property. This connection between the ontological schema for nature and minimality according to belonging is crucial. What it does is orientate thought towards a natural 'atomism' in the wider sense: if a property is attested for at least one natural multiple, then there will always exist an *ultimate* natural element with this property. For every property which is discernible amongst multiples, nature proposes to us a halting point, beneath which nothing natural may be subsumed under the property.

The demonstration of this theorem requires the use of a principle whose conceptual examination, linked to the theme of the event, is completed solely in Meditation 18. The essential point to retain is the principle of minimality: whatever is accurately thought about an ordinal, there will always be another ordinal such that this thought can be 'minimally' applied to it, and such that no smaller ordinal (thus no ordinal belonging to the latter ordinal) is pertinent to that thought. There is a halting point, *lower down*, for every natural determination. This can be written:

$$\Psi(\alpha) \rightarrow (\exists\beta)[(\Psi\beta) \ \& \ (\gamma \in \beta) \rightarrow \sim(\Psi\gamma)]$$

In this formula, the ordinal β is the natural minimal validation of the property Ψ. Natural stability is embodied by the 'atomic' stopping point that it links to any explicit characterization. In this sense, all natural consistency is atomic.

The principle of minimality leads us to the theme of the *general connection* of all natural multiples. For the first time we thus meet a *global* ontological determination; one which says that every natural multiple is connected to every other natural multiple by presentation. There are no holes in nature.

I said that *if* there is the relation of belonging between ordinals, it functions like a relation of order. The key point is that in fact there is *always*, between two different ordinals, the relation of belonging. If α and β are two ordinals such that $\alpha \neq \beta$, then either $\alpha \in \beta$ or $\beta \in \alpha$. Every ordinal is a 'portion' of another ordinal (because $\alpha \in \beta \rightarrow \alpha \subset \beta$ by the transitivity of ordinals) save if the second is a portion of the first.

We saw that the ontological schema of natural multiples was essentially homogeneous, insofar as every multiple whose count-as-one is guaranteed by an ordinal is itself an ordinal. The idea that we have now come to is much stronger. It designates the universal intrication, or co-presentation, of ordinals. Because every ordinal is 'bound' to every other ordinal by belonging, it is necessary to think that multiple-being presents nothing *separable* within natural situations. Everything that is presented, by way of the multiple, in such a situation, is either contained within the presentation of other multiples, or contains them within its own presentation. This major ontological principle can be stated as follows: Nature does not know any independence. In terms of the pure multiple, and thus according to its being, the natural world requires each term to inscribe the others, or to be inscribed by them. Nature is thus universally *connected*; it is an assemblage of multiples intricated within each other, without a separating void ('void' is not an empirical or astrophysical term here, it is an ontological metaphor).

The demonstration of this point is a little delicate, but it is quite instructive at a conceptual level due to its extensive usage of the principle of minimality. Normality (or transitivity), order, minimality and total connection thus show themselves to be organic concepts of natural-being. Any reader who is discouraged by demonstrations such as the following can take the result as given and proceed to section four.

Suppose that two ordinals, α and β, however different they are, share the property of *not* being 'bound' by the relation of belonging. Neither one belongs to the other: $\sim(\alpha \in \beta)$ & $\sim(\beta \in \alpha)$ & $\sim(\alpha = \beta)$. Two ordinals then exist, say γ and δ, which are $\in$-minimal for this property. To be precise, this means:

– that the ordinal γ is $\in$-minimal for the property 'there exists an ordinal α such that $\sim(\alpha \in \gamma)$ & $\sim(\gamma \in \alpha)$ & $\sim(\alpha = \gamma)$', or, 'there exists an ordinal disconnected from the ordinal in question';
– that, such an $\in$-minimal γ being fixed, δ is $\in$-minimal for the property; $\sim(\delta \in \gamma)$ & $\sim(\gamma \in \delta)$ & $\sim(\delta = \gamma)$.

How are this γ and this δ 'situated' in relation to each other, given that they are $\in$-minimal for the supposed property of *disconnection* with regard to the relation of belonging? I will show that, at all events, one is *included* in the other, that $\delta \subset \gamma$. This comes down to establishing that every element of δ is an element of γ. This is where minimality comes into play. Because δ is $\in$-minimal for the disconnection with γ, it follows that one *element* of δ is itself actually connected. Thus, if $\lambda \in \delta$, λ is connected to γ, which means either:

– that $\gamma \in \lambda$, but this is impossible because $\in$ is a relation of order between ordinals, and from $\gamma \in \lambda$ and $\lambda \in \delta$, we would get $\gamma \in \delta$, which is forbidden by the disconnection of γ and δ;
– or that $\gamma = \lambda$, which is met by the same objection since if $\lambda \in \delta$, $\gamma \in \delta$ which cannot be allowed;
– or that $\lambda \in \gamma$. This is the only solution. Therefore, $(\lambda \in \delta) \to (\lambda \in \gamma)$, which clearly means that δ is a part of γ (every element of δ is an element of γ).

Note, moreover, that $\delta \subset \gamma$ is a *strict* inclusion, because δ and γ are excluded from being equal by their disconnection. I therefore have the right to consider an element of the *difference* between δ and γ, since that difference is not empty. Say π is that element. I have $\pi \in \gamma$ & $\sim(\pi \in \delta)$.

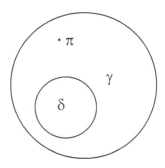

Since γ is $\in$-minimal for the property 'there exists an ordinal which is disconnected from the ordinal under consideration', *every* ordinal is connected to an element of γ (otherwise, γ would not be $\in$-minimal for that property). In particular, the ordinal δ is connected to π, which is an element of γ. We thus have:

– either $\delta \in \pi$, which is impossible, for given that $\pi \in \gamma$, we would have to have $\delta \in \gamma$ which is forbidden by the disconnection of δ & γ;

– or $\delta = \pi$, same objection;

– or $\pi \in \delta$, which is forbidden by the choice of π outside δ.

This time we have reached an impasse. All the hypotheses are unworkable. The initial supposition of the demonstration—that there exist two disconnected ordinals—must therefore be abandoned, and we must posit that, given two different ordinals, either the first belongs to the second, or the second to the first.

4. ULTIMATE NATURAL ELEMENT (UNIQUE ATOM)

The fact that belonging, between ordinals, is a total order completes the principle of minimality—the atomism of ultimate natural elements which possess a given property. It happens that an ultimate element, $\in$-minimal for the property Ψ, is finally *unique*.

Take an ordinal α which possesses a property φ and which is $\in$-minimal for that property. If we consider any other ordinal β, different from α, we know that it is connected to α by belonging. Thus: either $\alpha \in \beta$, and β—if it has the property—is not $\in$-minimal for it, because β contains α, which possesses the property in question; or, $\beta \in \alpha$, and then β does not possess the property, because α is $\in$-minimal. It follows that α is the *unique* $\in$-minimal ordinal for that property.

This remark has wide-ranging consequences, because it authorizes us—for a natural property, which suits natural multiples—to speak of *the* unique ordinal which is the 'smallest' element for which the property is appropriate. We are thus now able to identify an 'atom' for every natural property.

The ontological schema of natural multiples clarifies our constant tendency—present in physics as it is elsewhere—to determine the concept of the ultimate constituent capable of 'bearing' an explicit property. The unicity of being of the minimum is the foundation of the conceptual unicity of this constituent. The examination of nature can anchor itself, as a law of its pure being, in the certitude of a unique halting point in the 'descent' towards ultimate elements.

5. AN ORDINAL IS THE NUMBER OF THAT OF WHICH IT IS THE NAME

When one names 'a' an ordinal, which is to say the pure schema of a natural multiple, one seals the one of the multiples which belong to it. But these multiples, being ordinals, are entirely ordered by belonging. An ordinal can therefore be 'visualized' as a chain of belonging, which, starting from the name of the void, continues up till a without including it, because $a \in a$ is forbidden. In sum, the situation is the following:

$$\varnothing \in \ ..... \ \in \ ..... \ \in \beta \in \ ..... \in a$$

All the elements aligned according to belonging are also those which make up the multiple a. The signifier 'a' designates the interruption, at the rank a, of a chain of belonging; an interruption which is also the reassemblage in a multiple of all the multiples ordered in the chain. One can thus say that there are a elements in the ordinal a, because a is the ath term of the ordered chain of belongings.

An ordinal is thus the number of its name. This is a possible definition of a natural multiple, thought according to its being: the one-multiple that it is, signified in the re-collection of an order such that this 'one' is an interruption of the latter at the very point of its multiple-extension. 'Structure' (of order) and 'multiple', both referring back to the primitive sign of the multiple, ∈, are in a position of equivocity in the name. There is a balance of being and of order which justifies the Cantorian name 'ordinal'.

A natural multiple structures into number the multiple whose one it forms, and its name-one coincides with this number-multiple.

It is thus true that 'nature' and 'number' are substitutable.

6. NATURE DOES NOT EXIST

If it is clear that a natural being is that which possesses, as its ontological schema of presentation, an ordinal, what then is *Nature*, that Nature which Galileo declared to be written in 'mathematical language'? Grasped in its pure multiple-being, nature should be natural-being-in-totality; that is, the multiple which is composed of *all* the ordinals, thus of all the pure multiples which are proposed as foundations of possible being for every presented or presentable natural multiplicity. The set of all the ordinals—of all the name-numbers—defines, in the framework of the Ideas of the multiple, the ontological substructure of Nature.

However, a new theorem of ontology declares that such a set is not compatible with the axioms of the multiple, and could not be admitted as existent within the frame of onto-logy. Nature has no sayable being. There are only *some* natural beings.

Let's suppose the existence of a multiple which makes a one out of all the ordinals, and say that this multiple is O. It is certain that O is transitive. If $\alpha \in O$, α is an ordinal, and so all of its elements are ordinals, and consequently belong to O. Therefore α is also a part of O: $\alpha \in O \rightarrow \alpha \subset O$. Moreover, all the elements of O, being ordinals, are themselves transitive. The multiple O thereby satisfies the definition of ordinals. Being an ordinal, O, the supposed set of all ordinals, must belong to itself, $O \in O$. Yet auto-belonging is forbidden.

The ontological doctrine of natural multiplicities thus results, on the one hand, in the recognition of their universal intrication, and on the other hand, in the inexistence of their Whole. One could say: everything (which is natural) is (belongs) in everything, save that there is no everything. The homogeneity of the ontological schema of natural presentations is realized in the unlimited opening of a chain of name-numbers, such that each is composed of all those which precede it.

MEDITATION THIRTEEN
Infinity: the other, the rule, and the Other

The compatibility of divine infinity with the essentially finite ontology of the Greeks, in particular that of Aristotle, is the point at which light may be shed upon the question of whether it makes any sense, and what sense in particular, to say that being qua being is infinite. That the great medieval philosophers were able to graft the idea of a supreme infinite being without too much damage on to a substantialist doctrine wherein being unfolded according to the disposition of its proper limit, is a sufficient indication that it is at the very least possible to think being as the finite opening of a singular difference whilst placing, at the summit of a representable hierarchy, an excess of difference such that, under the name of God, a being is supposed for whom none of the finite limiting distinctions proposed to us by created Nature are pertinent.

It must be admitted that, in a certain sense, Christian monotheism, despite its designation of God as infinite, does not immediately and radically rupture with Greek finitism. The thought of being as such is not fundamentally affected by a transcendence which is hierarchically representable as beyond—yet deducible from—the natural world. The possibility of such continuity in the orientation of ontological discourse is evidently founded on the following: in the metaphysical age of thought, which fuses the question of being to that of the supreme being, the infinity of the God-being can be based on a thinking in which being, qua being, remains essentially finite. Divine infinity solely designates the transcendent 'region' of being-in-totality wherein *we no longer know* in what sense the essential finitude of being is manifested. The in-finite is the punctual limit to the exercise of *our* thought of finite-being. Within the framework of what Heidegger names ontotheology (the metaphysical dependency of the thought of being on the supremely-being), the difference between the infinite and the finite—a difference amongst beings or *ontical* difference—strictly speaking, does not declare anything about being as such, and can conserve the design of Greek finitude perfectly. That the infinite/finite couple is non-pertinent within the space of *ontological* difference is finally the key to the compatibility of a theology of the infinite with an ontology of the finite. The couple infinite/finite *distributes* being-in-totality within the unshaken framework of substantialism, which figures being, whether it is divine or natural, as τόδε τι, singular essence, thinkable solely according to the affirmative disposition of its limit.

The infinite God of medieval Christianity *is*, qua being, essentially finite. This is evidently the reason why there is no unbridgeable abyss between Him and created Nature, since the reasoned observation of the latter furnishes us with proof of His existence. The real operator of this proof is moreover the distinction, specifically linked to natural existence, between the reign of movement—proper to natural substances said to be finite—and that of immobility—God is the immobile supreme mover—which characterizes infinite substance. At this point we should note that when he was on the point of recognizing the infinity of created Nature itself, under the effect of the Galileo event, Descartes also had to *change proofs* as to the existence of God.

The effective infinity of being cannot be recognized according to the unique metaphysical punctuality of the substantial infinity of a supreme being. The thesis of the infinity of being is necessarily post-Christian, or, if you like, post-Galilean. It is historically linked to the ontological advent of a mathematics of the infinite, whose intimate connection with the subject of Science—the void of the Cogito—ruins the Greek limit and in-disposes the supremacy of the being in which the finite ontological essence of the infinite itself was named God.

The consequence is that the radicality of any thesis on the infinite does not—paradoxically—concern God but rather Nature. The audacity of the moderns certainly did not reside in their introduction of the concept of infinity, for the latter had long since been adapted to Greek thought by the Judeo-Christian foundation. Their audacity lay in ex-centring the use of this concept, in redirecting it from its function of distributing the regions of being in totality towards a characterization of beings-qua-beings: nature, the moderns said, is infinite.

This thesis of the infinity of nature is moreover only superficially a thesis concerning the world—or the Universe. For 'world' can still be conceived as a being-of-the-one, and as such, as shown by Kant in the cosmological antinomy, it merely constitutes an illusory impasse. The speculative possibility of Christianity was an attempt to think infinity as an attribute of the One-being whilst universally guarding ontological finitude, and reserving the ontical sense of finitude for the multiple. It is through the mediation of a supposition concerning the being of the One that these great thinkers were able to simultaneously turn the infinite (God) into a being, turn the finite (Nature) into a being, and maintain a finite ontological substructure in both cases. This ambiguity of the finite, which ontically designates creatures and ontologically designates being, God included, has its source in a gesture of Presence which guarantees that the One is. If the infinity of Nature solely designates the infinity of the world or the 'infinite universe' in which Koyré saw the modern rupture, then it is still possible to conceive this universe as an accomplishment of the being-existent-of-the-one; that is, as nothing other than a depunctualized God. Moreover, the finitist substructure of ontology would persist within this avatar, and ontical infinity would fall from its transcendental and personal status in favour of a cosmological spacing—without, for all that, opening up to a radical statement on the essential infinity of being.

What must therefore be understood is that the infinity of nature only designates the infinity of the One-world imaginarily. Its real sense—since the one is not—concerns the pure multiple, which is to say presentation. If, historically, even in a manner originally misrecognized, the concept of infinity was only revolutionary in thought once it was declared to apply to Nature, this is because everyone felt that what was touched upon there was the ontotheological edifice itself, specifically in its encounter with the infinite/finite couple: what was at stake was the ruin of the simple criterion of the regional distinction, within being-in-totality, between God and created Nature. The meaning of this tremor was the reopening of the ontological question itself, as can be seen in philosophy from Descartes to Kant: an absolutely new anxiety infected the finitist conviction. If, after all, infinity is natural, if it is not the negative name of the supreme-being, the sign of an exception in which a hierarchical punctuality is distinguished that is thinkable as the being-of-the-one, then is it not possible that this predicate is appropriate to being insofar as it is presented, thus to the multiple in itself? It is from the standpoint of a hypothesis, not of *an* infinite being, but of numerous infinite multiples, that the intellectual revolution of the sixteenth and seventeenth centuries provoked, in thought, the risky reopening of the interrogation of being, and the irreversible abandon of the Greek disposition.

In its most abstract form, the recognition of the infinity of being is first of all the recognition of the infinity of situations, the supposition that the count-as-one concerns infinite multiplicities. What, however, is an infinite multiplicity? In a certain sense—and I will reveal why—the question has not yet been entirely dealt with today. Moreover, it is the perfect example of an intrinsically ontological—mathematical—question. There is *no* infra-mathematical concept of infinity, only vague images of the 'very large'. Consequently, not only is it necessary to affirm that being is infinite but that *it alone* is; or rather, that infinite is a predicate which is solely appropriate to being qua being. If, indeed, it is only in mathematics that one finds univocal conceptualizations of the infinite, this is because this concept is only suitable to what mathematics is concerned with, which is being qua being. It is evident to what degree Cantor's oeuvre completes and accomplishes the historical Galilean gesture: there at the very point where, in Greek and then Greco-Christian thought, an essential appropriation of being as finite was based—infinity being the ontic attribute of the divine difference—it is on the contrary of being as such and of it alone that infinity is from this point on predicated, in the form of the notion of an 'infinite set', and it is the finite which serves to think the empirical or intrasituational differences which concern beings.

We should add that, necessarily, the mathematical ontologization of the infinite separates it absolutely from the one, which is not. If pure multiples are what must be recognized as infinite, it is ruled out that there be some one-infinity. There will necessarily be *some* infinite multiples. But what is more profound still is that there is no longer any guarantee that we will be able to recognize a simple concept of the infinite-multiple, for if such a concept were legitimate, the multiples appropriate to it would, in some manner, be supreme, being no 'less multiple' than others. In this case infinity would lead us back to the supremely-being, in the mode of a halting point which would be assigned to the thought of the pure multiple, given that there would be nothing beyond the infinite multiples. There-fore, what must be expected instead is that there be infinite multiples which can be differentiated from each other *to infinity*. The ontologization of infinity, besides abolishing the one-infinite, also abolishes the unicity of infinity; what it proposes is the vertigo of an infinity of infinities distinguishable within their common opposition to the finite.

What are the means of thought available for rendering effective the thesis 'there exists an infinity of presentation'? By 'means' we understand methods via which infinity would occur within the thinkable *without the mediation of the one*. Aristotle already recognized that the idea of infinity (for him, the ἄπειρον, the un-limited) requires an intellectual operator of passage. For him, 'infinity' was being such that it could not be exhausted by the procession of thought, given a possible method of exhaustion. This necessarily means that between one stage of the procedure, whatever it is, and the goal—that is, the supposed limit of the being under consideration—there always exists 'still more' (*encore*). The physical embodiment (*en-corps*) of the being is here the 'still more' of the procedure, at whatever stage it may be of the attempted exhaustion. Aristotle denied that such a situation was realizable for the obvious reason that the already-there of the being under consideration included the disposition of its limit. For Aristotle, the singular 'already' of an indeterminate being excludes any invariant or eternal reduplication of the 'still-more'.

This dialectic of the 'already' and the 'still-more' is central. It amounts to the following: for a procedure of exhaustion which concerns a multiple to have any meaning, it is necessary that that multiple be presented. But if the latter is already effectively presented, how can the traversal of its presentation require it being always still to come?

The ontology of infinity—which is to say of the infinite multiple, and not of the transcendent One—finally requires three elements:

   a. an 'already', a point-of-being—thus a presented or existent multiple;

   b. a procedure—a rule—which is such that it indicates how I 'pass' from one presented term to another, a rule which is necessary since its failure to traverse the entirety of a multiple will reveal the latter's infinity;

   c. the report of the invariant existence—on the basis of the already, and according to the rule, to the rule's 'still-more'—of a term still-not-yet traversed.

But this is not sufficient. Such a situation will only reveal the impotence of the rule, it will not reveal *the existence of a cause of this impotence*. What is therefore necessary, in addition, is:

  d. a second existent (besides the 'already') which acts as cause of the failure of the procedure of exhaustion; that is, a multiple which is supposed such that the 'still-more' is reiterated inside it.

Without this supposition of existence, the only possibility is that the rule—whose every procedural stage would generate the finite, however numerous they were—be itself empirically incapable of reaching the limit. If the exhaustion, rather than being empirical, is one of principle, then it is necessary that the reduplication of the 'still-more' be attestable within the place of an existent; that is, within a presented multiple.

The rule will not present this multiple, since it is by failing to completely traverse it that the rule qualifies it as infinite. It is thus necessary that it be presented 'elsewhere', as the place of the rule's impotence.

Let's put this differently. The rule tells me how I pass from one term to another. This other is also the same, because, after it, the 'still-more' is reiterated due to which this term will solely have been the mediation between its other (the first term) and the other term to come. Only the absolutely initial 'already' was in-different, according to the rule, to what preceded it. However, this initial 'already' is retroactively aligned with what follows it; since, starting out from it, the rule had already found its 'still-one-more'. All of these terms are on the edge of 'still-yet-an-other' and this is what makes each of these others into the same as its other. The rule restricts the other to its identity of impotence. When I posit that a multiple exists such that *inside it* this becoming-the-same of the others proceeds according to the 'still-yet-an-other', a multiple such that all of the others are contained within it, I cause the advent, not of 'still-yet-an-other', but rather of that Other on the basis of which it so happens that there is some other, that is, some same.

The Other is, on the one hand, in the position of place for the other-sames; it is the domain of both the rule's exercise and its impotence. On the other hand, it is what none of these others are, what the rule does not allow to traverse; it is therefore *the* multiple subtracted from the rule, and it is also what, if reached by the rule, would interrupt its exercise. It is clearly in the position of *limit* for the rule.

An infinite multiple is thus a presented multiple which is such that a rule of passage may be correlated to it, for which it is simultaneously the place of exercise and limit. Infinity is the Other on the basis of which there is—between the fixity of the already and the repetition of the still-more—a rule according to which the others are the same.

The existential status of infinity is double. What is required is both the being-already-there of an initial multiple and the being of the Other which can never be inferred from the rule. This double existential seal is what distinguishes real infinity from the imaginary of the one-infinity, which was posited in a single gesture.

Finally, infinity establishes a connection between a point of being, an automatism of repetition and a second existential seal. In infinity, the origin, the other and the Other are joined. The referral of the other to the Other occurs in two modes: that of place (every other is presented by the Other, as the same which belongs to it); and that of limit (the Other is none of those others whose traversal is authorized by the rule).

The second existential seal forbids one from imagining that the infinite can be deduced from the finite. If one terms 'finite' whatever can be entirely traversed by a rule—thus whatever, in a point, subsumes its Other as an other—then it is clear that infinity cannot be inferred from it, because infinity requires that the Other originate from elsewhere than any rule concerning the others.

Hence the following crucial statement: the thesis of the infinity of being is necessarily an ontological decision, which is to say an axiom. Without such a decision it will remain for ever possible for being to be essentially finite.

And this is precisely what was decided by the men of the sixteenth and seventeenth centuries when they posited that nature is infinite. It was not possible, in any manner, to deduce this point on the basis of observations, of new astronomical telescopes, etc. What it took was a pure courage of thought, a voluntary incision into the—eternally defendable—mechanism of ontological finitism.

By consequence, ontology, limited historially, must bear a trace of the following: the only genuinely atheological form of the statement on the infinity of being concerned nature.

I stated (Meditation 11) that *natural* multiplicities (or ordinals) were those which realized the maximum equilibrium between belonging (the regime of the count-as-one) and inclusion (the regime of the state). The ontological decision concerning infinity can then be simply phrased as: an infinite natural multiplicity exists.

This statement carefully avoids any reference to *Nature*, in which it is still too easy to read the substitutive reign of the cosmological one, after the centuries-long reign of the divine one-infinity. It solely postulates that at least one natural multiple—a transitive set of transitive sets—is infinite.

This statement may disappoint, inasmuch as the adjective 'infinite' is mentioned therein without definition. Thus, it will rather be said: there exists a natural multiple such that a rule is linked to it on the basis of which, at any moment of its exercise, there is always 'still-yet-an-other', yet the rule is such that it is not any of these others, in spite of them all belonging to it.

This statement may appear prudent, inasmuch as it solely anticipates the existence, in any attestable situation, of *one* infinite multiple. It will be the task of ontology to establish that if there is one, then there are others, and the Other of those others, and so on.

This statement may appear restrictive and perilous, inasmuch as it only delivers a concept of infinity. Again, it will be the task of ontology to prove that if there exists an infinite multiple, then others exist, which, according to a precise norm, are incommensurable to it.

It is by these means that the historical decision to maintain the possible infinity of being is structured. This infinity—once subtracted from the empire of the one, and therefore in default of any ontology of Presence—proliferates beyond everything tolerated by representation, and designates—by a memorable inversion of the anterior age of thought—the finite itself as being the exception. Solely an impoverishment—no doubt vital—of contemplation would maintain, concerning us, the fraternal precariousness of this exception.

A human is that being which prefers to represent itself within finitude, whose sign is death, rather than knowing itself to be entirely traversed and encircled by the omnipresence of infinity.

At the very least, one consolation remains; that of discovering that nothing actually obliges humanity to acquire this knowledge, because at this point the sole remit for thought is to the school of decision.

MEDITATION FOURTEEN
The Ontological Decision:
'There is some infinity in natural multiples'

The ontological schema of natural multiples is the concept of ordinals. The historicity of the decision on the being of infinity is inscribed in the thesis 'nature is infinite' (and not in the thesis 'God is infinite'). For these reasons, an axiom on infinity would logically be written as: 'there exists an infinite ordinal'. However, this axiom is meaningless: it remains circular—it implies infinity in the position of its being—as long as the notion of infinity has not been transformed into a predicative formula written in set theory language and compatible with the already received Ideas of the multiple.

One option is forbidden to us, the option of defining natural infinity as the *totality* of ordinals. In Meditation 12, we showed that under such a conception Nature has no being, because the multiple which is supposed to present all the ordinals—all possible beings whose form is natural—falls foul of the prohibition on self-belonging; by consequence, it does not exist. One must acknowledge, along with Kant, that a cosmological conception of the Whole or the Totality is inadmissible. If infinity exists, it must be under the category of one or of several natural beings, not under that of the 'Grand Totality'. In the matter of infinity, just as elsewhere, the one-multiple, result of presentation, prevails over the phantom of the Whole and its Parts.

The obstacle that we then come up against is the homogeneity of the ontological schema of natural multiples. If the qualitative opposition infinite/finite traverses the concept of ordinal, it is because there are two fundamentally different *species* of natural multiple-being. If, in fact, a decision is required here, it will be that of assuming this specific difference, and thus that of rupturing the presentative homogeneity of natural being. To stipulate the place of such a decision is to think about where, in the definition of ordinals, the split or conceptual discontinuity lies; the discontinuity which, founding two distinct species, requires legislation upon their existence. We shall be guided herein by the historico-conceptual investigation of the notion of infinity (Meditation 13).

1. POINT OF BEING AND OPERATOR OF PASSAGE

In order to think the existence of infinity I said that three elements were necessary: an initial point of being, a rule which produces some same-others, and a second existential seal which fixes the place of the Other for the other.

The absolutely initial point of being for ontology is the name of the void, $\varnothing$. The latter can also be termed the name of a natural multiple, since nothing prohibits it from being such (cf. Meditation 12). It is, besides, the only existential Idea which we have retained up to this point; those multiples which are admitted into existence on the basis of the name of the void—like, for example, $\{\varnothing\}$—are done so in conformity with the constructive Ideas—the other axioms of the theory.

A rule of passage for natural multiples must allow us, on the basis of $\varnothing$, to ceaselessly construct other existing ordinals—to always say 'still one more'—that is, to construct other transitive sets whose elements are equally transitive, and which are acceptable according to the axiomatic Ideas of the presentation of the pure multiple.

Our reference point will be the existent figure of the Two (Meditation 12); that is, the multiple $\{\varnothing,\{\varnothing\}\}$, whose elements are the void and its singleton. The axiom of replacement says that once this Two exists then it is the case that every set obtained by replacing its elements by other (supposed existent) elements exists (Meditation 5). This is how we secure the abstract concept of the Two: if α and β exist, then the set $\{\alpha,\beta\}$ also exists, of which α and β are the sole elements (in the existing Two, I replace $\varnothing$ with α, and $\{\varnothing\}$ with β). This set, $\{\alpha,\beta\}$, will be called the *pair* of α and β. It is the 'forming-into-two' of α and β.

It is on the basis of this pair that we shall define the classic operation of the union of two sets, $\alpha \cup \beta$—the elements of the union are those of α and those of β 'joined together'. Take the pair $\{\alpha,\beta\}$. The axiom of union (cf. Meditation 5) stipulates that the set of the elements of the elements of a given set exists—its dissemination. If the pair $\{\alpha,\beta\}$ exists, then its union $\cup \ \{\alpha,\beta\}$ also exists; as its elements it has the elements of the elements of the pair, that is, the elements of α and β. This is precisely what we wanted. We will thus posit that $\alpha \cup \beta$ is a canonical formulation for $\cup \ \{\alpha,\beta\}$. Moreover we have just seen that if α and β exist, then $\alpha \cup \beta$ also exists.

Our rule of passage will then be the following: $\alpha \rightarrow \alpha \cup \{\alpha\}$.

This rule 'produces', on the basis of a given ordinal, the multiple union of itself and its own singleton. The elements of this union are thus, on the one hand, those of α itself, and on the other hand, α in person, the unique element of its singleton. In short, we are adding α's own proper name to itself, or in other words, we are adding the one-multiple that α is to the multiples that it presents.

Note that we definitely produce an *other* in this manner. That is, α, as I have just said, is an element of $\alpha \cup \{\alpha\}$; however, it is not itself an element of α, because $\alpha \in \alpha$ is prohibited. Therefore, α is different from $\alpha \cup \{\alpha\}$ by virtue of the axiom of extensionality. They differ by one multiple, which is precisely α itself.

In what follows, we shall write $\alpha \cup \{\alpha\}$ in the form $S(\alpha)$, which we will read: the *successor* of α. Our rule enables us to 'pass' from an ordinal to its successor.

This 'other' that is the successor, is also a 'same' insofar as *the successor of an ordinal is an ordinal*. Our rule is thus a rule of passage which is immanent to natural multiples. Let's demonstrate this.

On the one hand, the elements of $S(\alpha)$ are certainly all transitive. That is, since α is an ordinal, both itself and its elements are transitive. It so happens that, $S(\alpha)$ is composed precisely of the elements of α to which one adds α.

On the other hand, $S(\alpha)$ is itself also transitive. Take $\beta \in S(\alpha)$:

– either $\beta \in \alpha$, and consequently $\beta \subset \alpha$ (because α is transitive). But since $S(\alpha) = \alpha \cup \{\alpha\}$, it is clear that $\alpha \subset S\{\alpha\}$. Since a part of a part is also a part, we have $\beta \subset S(\alpha)$;

– or $\beta = \alpha$, and thus $\beta \subset S(\alpha)$ because $\alpha \subset S(\alpha)$.

So, every multiple which *belongs* to $S(\alpha)$ is also *included* in it. Therefore, $S(\alpha)$ is transitive.

As a transitive multiple whose elements are transitive, $S(\alpha)$ is an ordinal (as long as α is).

Moreover, there is a precise sense in saying that $S(\alpha)$ is *the* successor of α, or the ordinal—the 'still one more'—which comes immediately 'after' α. No other ordinal β can actually be placed 'between' α and $S(\alpha)$. According to which law of placement? To that of belonging, which is a total relation of order between ordinals (cf. Meditation 12). In other words, no ordinal exists such that $\alpha \in \beta \in S(\alpha)$.

Since $S(\alpha) = \alpha \cup \{\alpha\}$, the statement '$\beta \in S(\alpha)$' signifies:

– either $\beta \in \alpha$, which excludes $\alpha \in \beta$, because belonging, as a relation of order between ordinals, is transitive, and from $\beta \in \alpha$ and $\alpha \in \beta$ one can draw $\beta \in \beta$ which is impossible;

– or $\beta \in \{\alpha\}$, which amounts to $\beta = \alpha$, α being the unique element of the singleton $\{\alpha\}$. But $\beta = \alpha$ obviously excludes $\alpha \in \beta$, again due to the prohibition on self-belonging.

In each case it is impossible to insert β between α and $S(\alpha)$. The rule of succession is therefore univocal. It allows us to pass from one ordinal to *the* unique ordinal which follows it according to the total relation of order, belonging.

On the basis of the initial point of being, $\varnothing$, we construct, in the following manner, the sequence of *existing* ordinals (since $\varnothing$ exists):

$$\varnothing,\ S(\varnothing),\ S(S(\varnothing)),\ ...,\ \overbrace{S(S(...\ (S(\varnothing)))\ ...\ )}^{n\ \text{times}},\ ...$$

Our intuition would readily tell us that we have definitely 'produced' an infinity of ordinals here, and thus decided in favour of a natural infinity. Yet this would be to succumb to the imaginary prestige of Totality. All the classical philosophers recognized that via this repetition of the effect of a rule, I only ever obtain the indefinite of same-others, and not an existing infinity. On the one hand, *each* of the ordinals thus obtained is, in an intuitive sense, manifestly finite. Being the nth successor of the name of the void, it has n elements, all woven from the void alone via the reiteration of forming-into-one (as required by ontology, cf. Meditation 4). On the other hand, no axiomatic Idea of the pure multiple authorizes us to form-one out of *all* the ordinals that the rule of succession allows us to attain. Each exists according to the still-one-more to come, according to which its being-other is retroactively qualifiable as the same; that is, as a one-between-others which resides on the border of the repetition, which it supports, of the rule. However, the Totality is inaccessible. There is an abyss here that solely a decision will allow us to bridge.

2. SUCCESSION AND LIMIT

Amongst those ordinals whose existence is founded by the sequence constructed via the rule of succession, $\varnothing$ is the first to distinguish itself; it is exceptional in all regards, just as it is for ontology in its entirety. Within the sequence the ordinals which differ from $\varnothing$ are all *successors* of another ordinal. In a general manner, one can say that an ordinal α is a successor ordinal—which we will note $Sc(\alpha)$—if there exists an ordinal β which α succeeds: $Sc(\alpha) \leftrightarrow (\exists\beta)[\alpha = S(\beta)]$.

There can be no doubt about the existence of successor ordinals because I have just exhibited a whole series of them. The problem in which the ontological decision concerning infinity will be played out is that of the existence of *non-successor ordinals*. We will say that an ordinal α is a *limit ordinal*, written $lim(\alpha)$, if it does not succeed any ordinal β:

$$lim(\alpha) \leftrightarrow \sim Sc(\alpha) \leftrightarrow \sim(\exists\beta)[\alpha = S(\beta)]$$

The internal structure of a limit ordinal—supposing that one exists—is essentially different from that of a successor ordinal. This is where we encounter a qualitative discontinuity in the homogeneous universe of the ontological substructure of natural multiples. The *wager* of infinity turns on this discontinuity: a limit ordinal is the place of the Other for the succession of same-others which belong to it.

The crucial point is the following: if an ordinal belongs to a limit ordinal, its successor also belongs to that limit ordinal. That is, if $\beta \in \alpha$ (α supposed as limit ordinal), one cannot have $\alpha \in S(\beta)$, since α would then be inserted between β and $S(\beta)$, and we established this to be impossible above. Furthermore, we cannot have $S(\beta) = \alpha$, because α, being a limit ordinal, is not the successor of any ordinal. Since belonging is a total relation of order between ordinals, the impossibility of $\alpha \in S(\beta)$ and of $\alpha = S(\beta)$ imposes that $S(\beta) \in \alpha$.

The result of these considerations is that between a limit ordinal and the ordinal β which belongs to it, an infinity (in the intuitive sense) of ordinals insert themselves. That is, if $\beta \in \alpha$, and α is limit, $S(\beta) \in \alpha$ and $S(S(\beta)) \in \alpha$, and so on. The limit ordinal is clearly the Other-place in which the other of succession insists on being inscribed. Take the sequence of successor ordinals which can be constructed, via the rule S, on the basis of an ordinal which belongs to a limit ordinal. This entire sequence unfolds itself 'inside' that limit ordinal, in the sense that all the terms of the sequence belong to the latter. At the same time, the limit ordinal itself is Other, in that it can never be the still-one-more which succeeds an other.

We could also mention the following structural difference between successor and limit ordinals: the first possess a maximum multiple within themselves, whilst the second do not. For if an ordinal α is of the form $S(\beta)$, that is, $\beta \cup \{\beta\}$, then β, which belongs to α, is the largest of all the ordinals which make up α (according to the relation of belonging). We have seen that no ordinal can be inserted between β and $S(\beta)$. The ordinal β is thus, absolutely, the maximum multiple contained in $S(\beta)$. However, no maximum term of this type ever belongs to a limit ordinal: once $\beta \in \alpha$, if α is limit, then there exists a γ such that $\beta \in \gamma \in \alpha$. As such, the ontological schema 'ordinal'—if a successor is at stake—is appropriate for a strictly hierarchical natural multiple in which one can designate, in an unambiguous and immanent manner, the dominant term. If a limit ordinal is at stake, the natural multiple whose substructure of being is formalized by such an ordinal is 'open' in that its internal order does not contain any maximum term, any closure. It is the limit ordinal itself which dominates such an order, but it only does so from the exterior: not belonging to itself, it ex-sists from the sequence whose limit it is.

The identifiable discontinuity between successor ordinals and limit ordinals finally comes down to the following; the first are determined on the basis of the *unique* ordinal which they succeed, whilst the second, being the very place of succession, can only be indicated beyond a 'finished' sequence—though unfinishable according to the rule—of ordinals previously passed through. The successor ordinal has a *local* status with regard to ordinals smaller than it ('smaller than', let's recall, means: which belong to it; since it is belonging which totally orders the ordinals). Indeed, it is the successor of one of these ordinals. The limit ordinal, on the contrary, has a *global* status, since none of the ordinals smaller than it is any 'closer' to it than another: it is the Other of all of them.

The limit ordinal is subtracted from the part of the same that is detained within the other under the sign of 'still-one-more'. The limit ordinal is the non-same of the entire sequence of successors which precedes it. It is not still-one-more, but rather the One-multiple within which the insistence of the rule (of succession) ex-sists. With regard to a sequence of ordinals such as those we are moving through, in passing via succession from an ordinal to the following ordinal, a limit ordinal is what stamps into ek-sistence, beyond the existence of each term of the sequence, the passage itself, the support-multiple in which all the ordinals passed through mark themselves, step by step. In the limit ordinal, the *place* of alterity (all the terms of the sequence belong to it) and the *point* of the Other (its name, α, designates *an* ordinal situated beyond all those which figure in the sequence) are fused together. This is why it is quite correct to name it a *limit*: that which gives a series both its principle of being, the one-cohesion of the multiple that it is, and its 'ultimate' term, the one-multiple towards which the series tends without ever reaching nor even approaching it.

This fusion, at the limit, between the place of the Other and its one, referred to an initial point of being (here, ∅, the void) and a rule of passage (here, succession) is, literally, the general concept of infinity.

3. THE SECOND EXISTENTIAL SEAL

Nothing, at this stage, obliges us to admit the existence of a limit ordinal. The Ideas of the multiple put in play up till now (extensionality, parts, separation, replacement and void), even if we add the idea of foundation (Meditation 18) and that of choice (Meditation 22), are perfectly compatible with the inexistence of such an ordinal. Certainly, we have recognized the existence of a sequence of ordinals whose initial point of existence is ∅ and whose traversal cannot be completed via the rule of succession. However, strictly speaking, it is not the sequence which exists, but each of its (finite) terms. Only an absolutely new axiomatic decision would authorize us to compose a *one* out of the sequence itself. This decision, which amounts to deciding in favour of infinity at the level of the ontological schema of natural multiples, and which thus formalizes the historical gesture of the seventeenth-century physicists, is stated quite simply: there exists a limit ordinal. This 'there exists', the first pronounced by us since the assertion of the existence of the name of the void, is the second existential seal, in which the infinity of being finds its foundation.

4. INFINITY FINALLY DEFINED

This 'there exists a limit ordinal' is our second existential assertion after that of the name of the void. However, it does not introduce a second suture of the framework of the Ideas of the multiple to being qua being.

Just as for the other multiples, the original point of being for the limit ordinal is the void and its elements are solely combinations of the void with itself, as regulated by the axioms. From this point of view, infinity is not in any way a 'second species' of being which would be woven together with the effects of the void. In the language of the Greeks, one would say that although there are two existential axioms, there are not two Principles (the void and infinity). The limit ordinal is only secondarily 'existent', on the supposition that, already, the void belongs to it—we have marked this in the axiom which formalizes the decision. What the latter thus causes to exist is the place of a repetition, the Other of others, the domain for the exercise of an operator (of succession), whilst $\emptyset$ summons being as such to ontological presentation. Deciding whether a limit ordinal exists concerns the *power* of being rather than its being. Infinity does not initiate a doctrine of mixture, in which being would result, in sum, from the dialectical play of two heterogeneous forms. There is only the void, and the Ideas. In short, the axiom 'there exists a limit ordinal' is an Idea hidden under an assertion of existence; the Idea that an endless repetition—the still-one-more —convokes the fusion of its site and its one to a second existential seal: the point exemplarily designated by Mallarmé; 'as far as a place fuses with a beyond'. And since, in ontology, to exist is to be a one multiple, the form of recognition of a place which is also a beyond would be the adjunction of a multiple, an ordinal.

Be that as it may, *we have not yet defined infinity*. A limit ordinal exists; that much is given. Even so, we cannot make the concept of infinity and that of a limit ordinal coincide; consequently, nor can we identify the concept of finitude with that of a successor ordinal. If a is a limit ordinal, then $S(a)$, its successor, is 'larger' than it, since $a \in S(a)$. This finite successor—if we pose the equation successor = finite—would therefore be larger than its infinite predecessor—if we pose that limit = infinite—however, this is unacceptable for thought, and it suppresses the irreversibility of the 'passage to infinity'.

If the *decision* concerning the infinity of natural being does bear upon the limit ordinal, then the *definition* supported by this decision is necessarily quite different. A further proof that the real, which is to say the obstacle, of thought is rarely that of finding a correct definition; the latter rather follows from the singular and eccentric point at which it became necessary to wager upon sense, even when its direct link to the initial problem was not apparent. The law of the hazardous detour thereby summons the subject to a strictly incalculable distance from its object. This is why there is no Method.

In Meditation 12 I indicated a major property of ordinals, minimality: if there exists an ordinal which possesses a given property, there exists a unique ordinal which is ∈-minimal for this property (that is, such that no ordinal belonging to it has the said property). It happens that 'to be a limit ordinal' is a property, which is expressed—appropriately—in a formula $\lambda(a)$ with a free variable. Moreover, the axiom 'there exists a limit ordinal' tells us precisely that at least one existent ordinal possesses this property. By consequence, a unique ordinal exists which is ∈-minimal for the said property. What we have here is *the smallest limit ordinal*, 'below' which, apart from the void, there are *solely* successor ordinals. This ontological schema is fundamental. It marks the threshold of infinity: it is, since the Greeks, the exemplary multiple of mathematical thought. We shall call it ω_0 (it is also called $\aleph$ or aleph-zero). This proper name, ω_0, convokes, in the form of *a* multiple, the first existence supposed by the decision concerning the infinity of being. It carries out that decision in the form of a specified pure multiple. The structural fault which opposes, within natural homogeneity, the order of successors (hierarchical and closed) to that of limits (open, and sealed by an ex-sistent), finds its *border* in ω_0.

The definition of infinity is established upon this border. We will say that *an ordinal is infinite if it is ω_0, or if ω_0 belongs to it*. We will say that *an ordinal is finite if it belongs to ω_0*.

The name of the distribution and division of the finite and the infinite, in respect to natural multiples, is therefore ω_0. The matheme of infinity, in the natural order, supposes solely that ω_0 is specified by the minimality of the limit—which defines a *unique* ordinal and justifies the usage of a proper name:

$$lim(\omega_0) \ \& \ (\forall a)[[(a \in \omega_0) \ \& \ (a \neq \varnothing)] \rightarrow Sc(a)];$$

since the following definitions of *Inf* (infinite) and *Fin* (finite) are proposed:

$$Inf(a) \leftrightarrow [(a = \omega_0) \ or \ (\omega_0 \in a)],$$

$$Fin(a) \leftrightarrow (a \in \omega_0).$$

What ω_0 presents are natural finite multiples. Everything *which* presents ω_0 is infinite. The multiple ω_0, in part both finite and infinite, will be said to be infinite, due to it being on the side of the limit, not succeeding anything.

Amongst the infinite sets, certain are successors: for example, $\omega_0 \cup \{\omega_0\}$, the successor of ω_0. Others are limits: for example, ω_0. Amongst finite sets, however, all are successors except $\varnothing$. The crucial operator of disjunction within natural presentation (limit/successor) is therefore not restituted in the defined disjunction (infinite/finite).

The exceptional status of ω_0 should be taken into account in this matter. Due to its minimality, it is the only infinite ordinal to which no other limit ordinal belongs. As for the other infinite ordinals, ω_0 at least belongs to them; ω_0 does not belong to itself. Thus between the finite ordinals—those which belong to ω_0—and ω_0 itself, there is an abyss without mediation.

This is one of the most profound problems of the doctrine of the multiple—known under the name of the theory of 'large cardinals'—that of knowing whether such an abyss can be repeated within the infinite itself. It is a matter of asking whether an infinite ordinal superior to ω_0 can exist which is such that there is no available procedure for reaching it; such that between it and the infinite multiples which precede it, there is a total absence of mediation, like that between the finite ordinals and their Other, ω_0.

It is quite characteristic that such an existence demands a *new decision*: a new axiom on infinity.

5. THE FINITE, IN SECOND PLACE

In the order of *existence* the finite is primary, since our initial existent is $\varnothing$, from which we draw $\{\varnothing\}$, $S\{\varnothing\}$, etc., all of them 'finite'. However, in the order of the *concept*, the finite is secondary. It is solely under the retroactive effect of the existence of the limit ordinal ω_0 that we qualify the sets $\varnothing$, $\{\varnothing\}$, etc., as finite; otherwise, the latter would have no other attribute than that of being existent one-multiples. The matheme of the finite, $Fin(\alpha) \leftrightarrow (\alpha \in \omega_0)$, suspends the criteria of finitude from the decision on existence which strikes the limit ordinals. If the Greeks were able to identify finitude with being, it is because that which is, in the absence of a decision on infinity, is found to be finite. The essence of the finite is thus solely multiple-being as such. Once the historical decision to bring infinite natural multiples into being is taken, the finite is qualified as a *region* of being, a minor form of the latter's presence. It then follows that the concept of finitude can only be fully elucidated on the basis of the intimate nature of infinity. One of Cantor's great intuitions was that of positing that the mathematical reign of Thought had as its 'Paradise'—as Hilbert remarked—the proliferation of infinite presentations, and that the finite came second.

Arithmetic, queen of Greek thought before Eudoxas' geometrizing revolution, is in truth the science of the first limit ordinal alone, ω_0. It is ignorant of the latter's function as Other: it resides *within* the elementary immanence of what belongs to ω_0—finite ordinals. The strength of arithmetic lies in its calculatory domination, which is obtained by the foreclosure of the limit and the pure exercise of the interconnection of same-others. Its weakness lies in its ignorance of the presentative essence of the multiples with which it calculates: an essence revealed only in deciding that there is only the series of others within the site of the Other, and that every repetition supposes the point at which, interrupting itself in an abyss, it summons beyond itself the name of the one-multiple that it is. Infinity is that name.

MEDITATION FIFTEEN
Hegel

'Infinity is in itself the other of the being-other void.'
The Science of Logic

The ontological impasse proper to Hegel is fundamentally centred in his holding that there is a being of the One; or, more precisely, that *presentation generates structure*, that the pure multiple detains in itself the count-as-one. One could also say that Hegel does not cease to write the in-difference of the other and the Other. In doing so, he renounces the possibility of ontology being a situation. This is revealed by two consequences which act as proof:

– Since it is infinity which articulates the other, the rule and the Other, it is calculable that the impasse emerge around this concept. The disjunction between the other and the Other—which Hegel tries to eliminate—reappears in his text in the guise of two developments which are both disjoint and identical (quality and quantity).

– Since it is mathematics which constitutes the ontological *situation*, Hegel will find it necessary to devalue it. As such, the chapter on quantitative infinity is followed by a gigantic 'remark' on mathematical infinity, in which Hegel proposes to establish that mathematics, in comparison to the concept, represents a state of thought which is 'defective in and for-itself', and that its 'procedure is non scientific'.

1. THE MATHEME OF INFINITY REVISITED

The Hegelian matrix of the concept of infinity is stated as follows: 'Concerning qualitative and quantitative infinity, it is essential to remark that the finite is not surpassed by a third but that it is determinateness as dissolving itself within itself which surpasses itself'.

The notions which serve as the architecture of the concept are thus determinateness (*Bestimmtheit*), starting point of the entire dialectic, and surpassing (*hinausgehen über*). It is easy to recognize therein both the initial point of being and the operator of passage, or what I also termed the 'already' and the 'still more' (cf. Meditation 13). It would not be an exaggeration to say that all of Hegel can be found in the following: the 'still-more' is immanent to the 'already'; everything that is, is already 'still-more'.

'Something'—a pure presented term—is determinate for Hegel only insofar as it can be thought as other than an other: 'The exteriority of being-other is the proper interiority of the something.' This signifies that the law of the count-as-one is that the term counted possesses *in itself* the mark-other of its being. Or rather: the one is only said of being inasmuch as being is its own proper non-being, is what it is not. For Hegel, there is an identity in becoming of the 'there is' (pure presentation) and the 'there is oneness' (structure), whose *mediation is the interiority of the negative*. Hegel posits that 'something' must detain the mark of its own identity. The result is that every point of being is 'between' itself and its mark. Determinateness comes down to the following: in order to found the Same it is necessary that there be some Other within the other. Infinity originates therein.

The analytic here is very subtle. If the one of the point of being—the count-as-one of a presented term—that is, its limit or what discerns it, results from it detaining its mark-other in interiority—it is what it isn't—then the being of this point, as one-thing, is to cross that limit: 'The limit, which constitutes the determination of the something, but such that it is determined at the same time as its non-being, is a frontier.'

The passage from the pure limit (*Grenze*) to the frontier (*Schranke*) forms the resource of an infinity directly *required* by the point of being.

To say of a thing that it is marked in itself as one has two senses, for the thing instantly becomes both the gap between its being and the one-of-its-being. On one side of this gap, it is clearly it, the thing, which is one, and thus limited by what is not it. There we have the static result of marking, *Grenze*, the limit. But on the other side of the gap, the one of the thing is not its being, the thing is in itself other than itself. This is *Schranke*, its frontier. But the frontier is a dynamic result of the marking, because the thing, necessarily, passes beyond its frontier. In fact, the frontier is the non-being through which the limit occurs. Yet the thing *is*. Its being is accomplished by the crossing of non-being, which is to say by passing through the frontier. The profound root of this movement is that the one, if it marks being *in itself*, is surpassed by the being that it marks. Hegel possesses a profound intuition of the count-as-one being a law. But because he wants, at any price, this law to be a law *of being*, he transforms it into duty. The being-of-the-one consists in *having* the frontier *to* be passed beyond. The thing is determinateness inasmuch as it has-to-be that one that it is in not being it: 'The being-in-itself of determination, in this relation to the limit, I mean to itself as frontier, is *to-have-to-be*.'

The one, inasmuch as it is, is the surpassing of its non-being. Therefore, being-one (determinateness) is realized as crossing the frontier. But by the same token, it is pure having-to-be: its being is the imperative to surpass its one. The point of being, always discernible, possesses the one in itself; and so it directly entails the surpassing of self, and thus the dialectic of the finite and the infinite: 'The concept of the finite is inaugurated, in general, in having-to-be; and, at the same time, the act of transgressing it, the infinite, is born. Having-to-be contains what presents itself as progress towards infinity.'

At this point, the essence of the Hegelian thesis on infinity is the following. the point of being, since it is always intrinsically discernible, *generates* out of itself the operator of infinity; that is, the surpassing, which combines, as does any operator of this genre, the step-further (the still-more)—here, the frontier—and the automatism of repetition—here, the having-to-be.

In a subtractive ontology it is tolerable, and even required, that there be some exteriority, some extrinsic-ness, since the count-as-one is not inferred from inconsistent presentation. In the Hegelian doctrine, which is a generative ontology, everything is intrinsic, since being-other is the one-of-being, and everything possesses an identificatory mark in the shape of the interiority of non-being. The result is that, for subtractive ontology, infinity is a *decision* (of ontology), whilst for Hegel it is a *law*. On the basis that the being-of-the-one is internal to being in general, it follows—in the Hegelian analysis—that it is of the essence-one of being to be infinite.

Hegel, with an especial genius, set out to co-engender the finite and the infinite on the basis of the point of being alone. Infinity becomes an internal reason of the finite itself, a simple attribute of experience in general, because it is a consequence of the regime of the one, of the between in which the thing resides, in the suture of its being-one and its being. Being *has to* be infinite: 'The finite is therefore itself that passing over of itself, it is itself the fact of being *infinite*.'

2. HOW CAN AN INFINITY BE BAD?

However, which infinity are we dealing with? The limit/frontier schism founds the finite's insistence on surpassing itself, its having-to-be. This having-to-be results from the operator of passage (the passing-beyond) being a direct derivative of the point of being (determinateness). But is there solely one infinity here? Isn't there solely the *repetition* of the finite, under the law of the one? In what I called the matheme of infinity, the repetition of the term as same-other is not yet infinity. For there to be infinity, it is necessary for the Other *place* to exist in which the other insists. I called this requisite that of the second existential seal, via which the initial point of being is convoked to inscribe its repetition within the place of the Other. Solely this *second* existence merits the name of infinity. Now, it is clear how Hegel, under the hypothesis of a fixed and internal identity of the 'something', engenders the operator of passage. But how can he *leap* from this to the gathering together of the complete passage?

This difficulty is evidently one that Hegel is quite aware of. For him, the have-to-be, or progress to infinity, is merely a mediocre transition, which he calls—quite symptomatically—the bad infinity. Indeed, once surpassing is an internal law of the point of being, the infinity which results has no other being than that of this point. That is, it is no longer the finite which is infinite, it is rather the infinite which is finite. Or, to be exact—a strong description—the infinite is merely the void in which the repetition of the finite operates. Each step-further convokes the void in which it repeats itself: 'In this void, what is it that emerges? . . . this new limit is itself only something to pass over or beyond. As such, the void, the nothing, emerges again; but this determination can be posed in it, a new limit, *and so on to infinity.*'

We thus have nothing more than the pure alternation of the void and the limit, in which the statements 'the finite is infinite' and 'the infinite is finite' succeed each other in having-to-be, like 'the monotony of a boring and forever identical repetition'. This boredom is that of the bad infinity. It requires a higher duty: that the passing-beyond be passed beyond; that the law of repetition be *globally* affirmed; in short, that the Other come forth.

But this time the task is of the greatest difficulty. After all, the bad infinity is bad due to the very same thing which makes it good in Hegelian terms: it does not break the ontological immanence of the one; better still, it derives from the latter. Its limited or finite character originates in its being solely defined locally, by the still-more of this already that is determinateness. However, this local status ensures the grasp of the one, since a term is always locally counted or discerned. Doesn't the passage to the global, and thus to the 'good infinity', impose a disjunctive decision in which the being of the one will falter? The Hegelian artifice is at its apogee here.

3. THE RETURN AND THE NOMINATION

Since it is necessary to resolve this problem without undoing the dialectical continuity, we will now turn, with Hegel, to the 'something'. Beyond its being, its being-one, its limit, its frontier, and finally the having-to-be in which it insists, what resources does it dispose of which would authorize us, in passing beyond passing-beyond, to conquer the non-void plenitude of a global infinity? Hegel's stroke of genius, if it is not rather a matter of supreme dexterity, is to abruptly return to pure presentation, towards inconsistency as such, and to declare that what constitutes the good infinity is the *presence* of the bad. That the bad infinity is *effective* is precisely what its badness cannot account for. Beyond repeating itself, the something detains, in excess of that repetition, the essential and presentable capacity to repeat itself.

The objective, or bad infinity is the repetitive oscillation, the tiresome encounter of the finite in having-to-be and the infinite as void. The veritable infinity is subjective in that it is the virtuality contained in the pure presence of the finite. The objectivity of objective repetition is thus an affirmative infinity, a presence: 'The unity of the finite and the infinite . . . is itself *present*.' Considered as presence of the repetitive process, the 'something' has broken its external relation to the other, from which it drew its determinateness. It is now relation-to-self, pure immanence, because the other has become effective *in the mode of the infinite void in which the something repeats itself*. The good infinity is finally the following: the repetitional of repetition, as other of the void; 'Infinity is . . . as other of the void being-other . . . return to self and relation to self.'

This subjective, or for-itself, infinity, which is the good presence of the bad operation, is no longer representable, for what represents it is the repetition of the finite. What a repetition cannot repeat is its own presence, it repeats itself *therein* without repetition. We can thus see a dividing line drawn between:

– the bad infinity: objective process, transcendence (having-to-be), representation;

– the good infinity: subjective virtuality, immanence, unrepresentable.

The second term is like the double of the first. Moreover, it is striking that in order to think it, Hegel has recourse to the foundational categories of ontology: pure presence and the void.

What has not yet been explained is why presence or virtuality persists in being called 'infinity' here, even in the world of the *good* infinity. With the bad infinity, the tie to the matheme is clear: the initial point of being (determinateness) and the operator of repetition (passing-beyond) are both recognizable. But what about the good?

In reality, this nomination is the result of the entire procedure, which can be summarised in six steps:

a. The something is posited as one on the basis of an external difference (it is other than the other).

b. But since it must be intrinsically discernible, it must be thought that it has the other-mark of its one in itself. Introjecting external difference, it *voids* the other something, which becomes, no longer *an*-other term, but a void space, an other-void.

c. Having its non-being in itself, the something, which is, sees that its limit is also a frontier, that its entire being is to pass beyond (to be as to-have-to-be).

d. The passing-beyond, due to point b, occurs in the void. There is an alternation between this void and the repetition of the something (which redeploys its limit, then passes beyond it again as frontier). This is the bad infinity.

e. This repetition is present. The pure presence of something detains—virtually—presence and the law of repetition. It is the global of that of which the local is each oscillation of the finite (determinateness)/ infinite (void) alternation.

f. To name this virtuality I must *draw the name from the void*, since pure presence as relation to self is, at this point, the void itself. Given that the void is the trans-finite polarity of the bad infinity, it is necessary that this name be: infinity, the good infinity.

Infinity is therefore the contraction in virtuality of repetition in the presence of that which repeats itself: a contraction named 'infinity' on the basis of the void in which the repetition exhausts itself. The good infinity is the name of what transpires within the repeatable of the bad: a name drawn from the void bordered by what is certainly a tiresome process, but, once the latter is treated as presence, we also know that it must be declared subjectively infinite.

It seems that the dialectic of infinity is thoroughly complete. On what basis then does it start all over again?

4. THE ARCANA OF QUANTITY

Infinity was split into bad and good. But here it is split again into qualitative infinity (whose principle we have just studied) and quantitative infinity.

The key to this turnstile resides in the maze of the One. If it is necessary to take up the question of infinity again, it is because the being-of-the-one does not operate in the same manner in quantity as in quality. Or rather, the point of being—determinateness—is constructed quantitatively in an inverse manner to its qualitative structure.

I have already indicated that, at the end of the first dialectic, the thing no longer had any relation save to itself. In the good infinity, being is for-itself, it has 'voided' its other. How can it detain the mark of the-one-that-it-is? The qualitative 'something' is, itself, discernible insofar as it has its other in itself. The quantitative 'something' is, on the other hand, without other, and consequently *its determinateness is indifferent*. Let's understand this as stating that the quantitative One is the being of the pure One, which does not differ from anything. It is not that it is indiscernible: *it is discernible amidst everything, by being the indiscernible of the One.*

What founds quantity, what discerns it, is literally the indifference of difference, the anonymous One. But if quantitative being-one is without difference, it is clearly because its limit is not a limit, because every limit, as we have seen, results from the introjection of an other. Hegel will speak of 'determinateness which has become indifferent to being, a limit which is just as much not one'. Only, a limit which is also not a limit is porous.

The quantitative One, the indifferent One, which is number, is also multiple-ones, because its in-difference is also that of proliferating the same-as-self outside of self: the One, whose limit is immediately a non-limit, realizes itself 'in the multiplicity external to self, which has as its principle or unity the indifferent One'.

One can now grasp the difference between the movements in which qualitative and quantitative infinity are respectively generated. If the essential time of the qualitative something is *the introjection of alterity* (the limit thereby becoming frontier), that of the quantitative something is *the externalization of identity*. In the first case, the one plays with being, the between-two in which the duty is to pass beyond the frontier. In the second case, the One makes itself into multiple-Ones, a unity whose repose lies in spreading itself beyond itself. Quality is infinite according to a dialectic of *identification*, in which the one proceeds from the other. Quantity is infinite according to a dialectic of *proliferation*, in which the same proceeds from the One.

The exterior of number is therefore not the void in which a repetition insists. The exterior of number is itself as multiple proliferation. One can also say that the operators are not the same in quality and quantity. The operator of qualitative infinity is passing-beyond. The quantitative operator is duplication. One re-posits the something (still-more), the other im-poses it (always). In quality, what is repeated is that the other be that interior which has to cross its limit. In quantity, what is repeated is that the same be that exterior which has to proliferate.

One crucial consequence of these differences is that the good quantitative infinity cannot be pure presence, interior virtuality, the subjective. The reason is that the same of the quantitative One also proliferates inside itself. If, outside itself, it is incessantly number (the infinitely large), inside itself it remains external: it is the infinitely small. The dissemination of the One in itself balances its proliferation. There is no presence in interiority of the quantitative. Everywhere the same dis-poses the limit, because it is indifferent. Number, the organization of quantitative infinity, seems to be universally bad.

Once confronted with this impasse concerning presence (and for us this is a joyful sight—number imposing the danger of the subtractive, of un-presence), Hegel proposes the following line of solution: thinking that the indifferent limit finally produces some real difference. The true—or good—quantitative infinity will be *the forming-into-difference of indifference*. One can, for example, think that the infinity of number, beyond the One which proliferates and composes this or that number, is that of *being* a number. Quantitative infinity is quantity qua quantity, the proliferator of proliferation, which is to say, quite simply, the quality of quantity, the quantitative such as discerned qualitatively from any other determination.

But in my eyes this doesn't work. What exactly doesn't work? It's the nomination. I have no quarrel with there being a qualitative essence of quantity, but why name it 'infinity'? The name suits qualitative infinity *because it was drawn from the void*, and the void was clearly the transfinite polarity of the process. In numerical proliferation there is no void because the exterior of the One *is* its interior, the pure law which causes the same-as-the-One to proliferate. The radical absence of the other, indifference, renders illegitimate here any declaration that the essence of finite number, its numericity, is infinite.

In other words, *Hegel fails to intervene on number.* He fails because the nominal equivalence he proposes between the pure presence of passing-beyond in the void (the good qualitative infinity) and the qualitative concept of quantity (the good quantitative infinity) is a trick, an illusory scene of the speculative theatre. There is no symmetry between the same and the other, between proliferation and identification. However heroic the effort, it is *interrupted de facto* by the exteriority itself of the pure multiple. Mathematics occurs here as discontinuity within the dialectic. It is this lesson that Hegel wishes to mask by suturing under the same term—infinity—two disjoint discursive orders.

5. DISJUNCTION

It is at this point that the Hegelian enterprise encounters, as its real, the impossibility of pure disjunction. On the basis of the very same premises as Hegel, one must recognize that the repetition of the One in number cannot arise from the interiority of the negative. What Hegel cannot think is the difference between the same and the same, that is, the pure position of two letters. In the qualitative, everything originates in the impurity which stipulates that the other marks the point of being with the one. In the quantitative, the expression of the One cannot be marked, such that any number is both disjoint from any other and composed from the same. If it is infinity that is desired, nothing can save us here from making a decision which, in one go, disjoins the place of the Other from any insistence of same-others. In wishing to maintain the continuity of the dialectic right through the very chicanes of the pure multiple, and to make the entirety proceed from the point of being alone, Hegel cannot rejoin infinity. One cannot for ever dispense with the second existential seal.

Dismissed from representation and experience, the disjoining decision makes its return in the text itself, by a split between two dialectics, quality and quantity, so similar that the only thing which frees us from having to fathom the abyss of their twinhood, and thus discover the paradox of their non-kindred nature, is that fragile verbal footbridge thrown from one side to the other: 'infinity'.

The 'good quantitative infinity' is a properly Hegelian hallucination. It was on the basis of a completely different psychosis, in which God in-consists, that Cantor had to extract the means for legitimately naming the infinite multiplicities—at the price, however, of transferring to them the very proliferation that Hegel imagined one could reduce (it being bad) through the artifice of its differentiable indifference.

PART IV
The Event: History and Ultra-one

MEDITATION SIXTEEN
Eventual Sites and Historical Situations

Guided by Cantor's invention, we have determined for the moment the following categories of being-qua-being: the multiple, general form of presentation; the void, proper name of being; the excess, or state of the situation, representative reduplication of the structure (or count-as-one) of presentation; nature, stable and homogeneous form of the standing-there of the multiple; and, infinity, which decides the expansion of the natural multiple beyond its Greek limit.

It is in this framework that I will broach the question of 'what-is-not-being-qua-being'—with respect to which it would not be prudent to immediately conclude that it is a question of non-being.

It is striking that for Heidegger that-which-is-not-being-qua-being is distinguished by its negative counter-position to art. For him, it is φύσις whose opening forth is set to work by the work of art and by it alone. Through the work of art we know that 'everything else which appears' —apart from appearing itself, which is nature—is only confirmed and accessible 'as not counting, as a nothing'. The nothing is thus singled out by its 'standing there' not being coextensive with the dawning of being, with the natural gesture of appearing. It is what is dead through being separated. Heidegger founds the position of the nothing, of the that-which-is-not-being, within the holding-sway of φύσις. The nothing is the inert by-product of appearing, the non-natural, whose culmination, dur-ing the epoch of nihilism, is found in the erasure of any natural appearing under the violent and abstract reign of modern technology.

I shall retain from Heidegger the germ of his proposition: that the *place* of thought of that-which-is-not-being is the non-natural; that which is presented *other* than natural or stable or normal multiplicities. The place of the other-than-being is the abnormal, the instable, the antinatural. I will term *historical* what is thus determined as the opposite of nature.

What is the abnormal? In the analytic developed in Meditation 8 what are initially opposed to normal multiplicities (which are presented and represented) are singular multiplicities, which are presented but not represented. These are multiples which belong to the situation without being included in the latter: they are elements but not subsets.

That a presented multiple is not at the same time a subset of the situation necessarily means that certain multiples from which this multiple is composed do not, themselves, belong to the situation. Indeed, if *all* the terms of a presented multiple are themselves presented in a situation, then the collection of these terms—the multiple itself—is a *part* of the situation, and is thus counted by the state. In other words, the necessary and sufficient condition for a multiple to be both presented and represented is that all of its terms, in turn, be presented. Here is an image (which in truth is merely approximate): a family of people is a presented multiple of the social situation (in the sense that they live together in the same apartment, or go on holiday together, etc.), and it is also a represented multiple, a part, in the sense that *each* of its members is registered by the registry office, possesses French nationality, and so on. If, however, one of the members of the family, physically tied to it, is not registered and remains clandestine, and due to this fact never goes out alone, or only in disguise, and so on, it can be said that this family, despite being presented, is not represented. It is thus *singular*. In fact, one of the members of the presented multiple that this family is, remains, himself, un-presented *within the situation*.

This is because a term can only be presented in a situation by a multiple to which it belongs, without directly being itself a multiple of the situation. This term falls under the count-as-one of presentation (because it does so according to the one-multiple to which it belongs), but it is not separately counted-as-one. The belonging of such terms to a multiple singularizes them.

It is rational to think the ab-normal or the anti-natural, that is, history, as an omnipresence of singularity—just as we have thought nature as an omnipresence of normality. The form-multiple of historicity is what lies entirely within the instability of the singular; it is that upon which the state's metastructure has no hold. It is a point of subtraction from the state's re-securing of the count.

I will term *eventual site* an entirely abnormal multiple; that is, a multiple such that none of its elements are presented in the situation. The site, itself, is presented, but 'beneath' it nothing from which it is composed is presented. As such, the site is not a part of the situation. I will also say of such a multiple that it is *on the edge of the void*, or *foundational* (these designations will be explained).

To employ the image used above, it would be a case of a concrete family, *all* of whose members were clandestine or non-declared, and which presents itself (manifests itself publicly) *uniquely* in the group form of family outings. In short, such a multiple is solely presented as the multiple-that-it-is. None of its terms are counted-as-one as such; only the multiple of these terms forms a one.

It becomes clearer why an evental site can be said to be 'on the edge of the void' when we remember that from the perspective of the situation this multiple is made up exclusively of non-presented multiples. Just 'beneath' this multiple—if we consider the multiples from which it is composed—there is *nothing*, because none of its terms are themselves counted-as-one. A site is therefore the *minimal* effect of structure which can be conceived; it is such that it belongs to the situation, whilst what belongs to it in turn does not. The border effect in which this multiple touches upon the void originates in its consistency (its one-multiple) being composed solely from what, with respect to the situation, in-consists. Within the situation, this multiple is, but *that of which* it is multiple is not.

That an evental (or on the edge of the void) site can be said to be foundational is clarified precisely by such a multiple being minimal for the effect of the count. This multiple can then naturally enter into consistent combinations; it can, in turn, *belong* to multiples counted-as-one in the situation. But being purely presented such that nothing which belongs to it is, it cannot itself result from an internal combination of the situation. One could call it a primal-one of the situation; a multiple 'admitted' into the count without having to result from 'previous' counts. It is in this sense that one can say that in regard to structure, it is an undecomposable term. It follows that evental sites block the infinite regression of combinations of multiples. Since they are on the edge of the void, one cannot think the underside of their presented-being. It is therefore correct to say that sites *found* the situation because they are the absolutely primary terms therein; they interrupt questioning according to combinatory origin.

One should note that the concept of an evental site, unlike that of natural multiplicity, is neither intrinsic nor absolute. A multiple could quite easily be singular in one situation (its elements are not presented therein, although it is) yet normal in another situation (its elements happen to be presented in this new situation). In contrast, a natural multiple, which is normal and all of whose terms are normal, conserves these qualities wherever it appears. Nature is absolute, historicity relative. One of the profound characteristics of singularities is that they can always be *normalized*: as is shown, moreover, by socio-political History; any evental site can, in the end, undergo a state normalization. However, it is impossible to singularize natural normality. If one admits that for there to be historicity evental sites are necessary, then the following observation can be made: history can be naturalized, but nature cannot be historicized. There is a striking dissymmetry here, which prohibits—outside the framework of the ontological thought of the pure multiple—any unity between nature and history.

In other words, the *negative* aspect of the definition of evental sites—to not be represented—prohibits us from speaking of a site 'in-itself'. A multiple is a site relative to the situation in which it is presented (counted as one). A multiple is a site solely *in situ*. In contrast, a natural situation, normalizing all of its terms, is definable intrinsically, and even if it becomes a sub-situation (a sub-multiple) within a larger presentation, it conserves its character.

It is therefore essential to retain that the definition of evental sites is *local*, whilst the definition of natural situations is *global*. One can maintain that there are only site-*points*, inside a situation, in which certain multiples (but not others) are on the edge of the void. In contrast, there are situations which are globally natural.

In *Théorie du sujet*, I introduced the thesis that History does not exist. It was a matter of refuting the vulgar Marxist conception of the meaning of history. Within the abstract framework which is that of this book, the same idea is found in the following form: there are in situation evental sites, but there is no evental situation. We can think the *historicity* of certain multiples, but we cannot think *a* History. The practical—political—consequences of this conception are considerable, because they set out a differential topology of action. The idea of an overturning whose origin would be a state of a totality is imaginary. Every radical transformational action originates *in a point*, which, inside a situation, is an evental site.

Does this mean that the concept of situation is indifferent to historicity? Not exactly. It is obvious that not all thinkable situations necessarily contain evental sites. This remark leads to a typology of situations, which would provide the starting point of what, for Heidegger, would be a doctrine, not of the being-of-beings, but rather of beings 'in totality'. I will leave it for later: it alone would be capable of putting some order into the classification of knowledges, and of legitimating the status of the conglomerate once termed the 'human sciences'.

For the moment, it is enough for us to distinguish between situations in which there are evental sites and those in which there are not. For example, in a natural situation there is no such site. Yet the regime of presentation has many other states, in particular ones in which the distribution of singular, normal and excrescent terms bears neither a natural multiple nor an evental site. Such is the gigantic reservoir from which our existence is woven, the reservoir of *neutral* situations, in which it is neither a question of life (nature) nor of action (history).

I will term situations in which at least one evental site occurs *historical*. I have chosen the term 'historical' in opposition to the intrinsic stability of natural situations. I would insist upon the fact that historicity is a local criterion: one (at least) of the multiples that the situation counts and presents is a site, which is to say it is such that none of its proper elements (the multiples from which it forms a one-multiple) are presented in the situation. A historical situation is therefore, in at least one of its points, on the edge of the void.

Historicity is thus presentation at the punctual limits of its being. In opposition to Heidegger, I hold that it is by way of historical localization that being comes-forth within presentative proximity, because something is subtracted from representation, or from the state. Nature, structural stability, equilibrium of presentation and representation, is rather that from which being-there weaves the greatest oblivion. Compact excess of presence and the count, nature buries inconsistency and turns away from the void. Nature is too global, too normal, to open up to the evental convocation of its being. It is solely in the point of history, the representative precariousness of evental sites, that it will be revealed, via the chance of a supplement, that being-multiple inconsists.

MEDITATION SEVENTEEN
The Matheme of the Event

The approach I shall adopt here is a constructive one. The event is not actually internal to the analytic of the multiple. Even though it can always be *localized* within presentation, it is not, as such, presented, nor is it presentable. It is—not being—supernumerary.

Ordinarily, conceptual construction is reserved for structures whilst the event is rejected into the pure empiricity of what-happens. My method is the inverse. The count-as-one is in my eyes the evidence of presentation. It is the event which belongs to conceptual construction, in the double sense that it can only be *thought* by anticipating its abstract form, and it can only be *revealed* in the retroaction of an interventional practice which is itself entirely thought through.

An event can always be localized. What does this mean? First, that no event immediately concerns a situation in its entirety. An event is always in a point of a situation, which means that it 'concerns' *a* multiple presented in the situation, whatever the word 'concern' may mean. It is possible to characterize in a general manner the type of multiple that an event *could* 'concern' within an indeterminate situation. As one might have guessed, it is a matter of what I named above an evental site (or a foundational site, or a site on the edge of the void). We shall posit once and for all that there are no natural events, nor are there neutral events. In natural or neutral situations, there are solely *facts*. The distinction between a fact and an event is based, in the last instance, on the distinction between natural or neutral situations, the criteria of which are global, and historical situations, the criterion of which (the existence of a site) is local. There are events uniquely in situations which present at least one site. The event is attached, in its very definition, to the place, to the point, in which the historicity of the situation is concentrated. Every event has a site which can be singularized in a historical situation.

The site designates the local type of the multiplicity 'concerned' by an event. It is not because the site exists in the situation that there is an event. But *for* there to be an event, there must be the local determination of a site; that is, a situation in which at least one multiple on the edge of the void is presented.

The confusion of the existence of the site (for example, the working class, or a given state of artistic tendencies, or a scientific impasse) with the necessity of the event itself is the cross of determinist or globalizing thought. The site is only ever a *condition of being* for the event. Of course, if the situation is natural, compact, or neutral, the event is impossible. But the existence of a multiple on the edge of the void merely opens up the possibility of an event. It is always possible that no event actually occur. Strictly speaking, a site is only 'evental' insofar as it is retroactively qualified as such by the occurrence of an event. However, we do know one of its ontological characteristics, related to the form of presentation: it is always an abnormal multiple, on the edge of the void. Therefore, there is no event save relative to a historical situation, even if a historical situation does not *necessarily* produce events.

And now, *hic Rhodus, hic salta.*

Take, in a historical situation, an evental site X.

I term event of the site X a multiple such that it is composed of, on the one hand, elements of the site, and on the other hand, itself.

The inscription of a *matheme of the event* is not a luxury here. Say that S is the situation, and $X \in S$ (X belongs to S, X is presented by S) the evental site. The event will be written e_x (to be read 'event of the site X'). My definition is then written as follows:

$$e_x = \{x \in X, e_x\}$$

That is, the event is a one-multiple made up of, on the one hand, all the multiples which belong to its site, and on the other hand, the event itself.

Two questions arise immediately. The first is that of knowing whether the definition corresponds in any manner to the 'intuitive' idea of an event. The second is that of determining the consequences of the definition with regard to the place of the event in the situation whose event it is, in the sense in which its site is an absolutely singular multiple of that situation.

I will respond to the first question with an image. Take the syntagm 'the French Revolution'. What should be understood by these words? One could certainly say that the event 'the French Revolution' forms a one out of everything which makes up its site; that is, France between 1789 and, let's say, 1794. There you'll find the electors of the General Estates, the peasants of the Great Fear, the sans-culottes of the towns, the members of the Convention, the Jacobin clubs, the soldiers of the draft, but also, the price of subsistence, the guillotine, the effects of the tribunal, the massacres, the English spies, the Vendeans, the *assignats* (banknotes), the theatre, the *Marseillaise*, etc. The historian ends up including in the event 'the French Revolution' everything delivered by the epoch as traces and facts. This approach, however—which is the inventory of all the elements of the site—may well lead to the one of the event being undone to the point of being no more than the forever infinite numbering of the gestures, things and words that co-existed with it. The halting point for this dissemination is *the mode in which the Revolution is a central term of the Revolution itself*; that is, the manner in which the conscience of the times—and the retroactive intervention of our own—filters the entire site through the one of its evental qualification. When, for example, Saint-Just declares in 1794 'the Revolution is frozen', he is certainly designating infinite signs of lassitude and general constraint, but he adds to them that *one-mark* that is the Revolution itself, as this signifier of the event which, being qualifiable (the Revolution is 'frozen'), proves that it is itself a *term* of the event that it is. Of the French Revolution as event it must be said that it both presents the infinite multiple of the sequence of facts situated between 1789 and 1794, and, *moreover*, that it presents itself as an immanent résumé and one-mark of its own multiple. The Revolution, even if it is interpreted as being such by historical retroaction, is no less, in itself, supernumerary to the sole numbering of the terms of its site, despite it presenting such a numbering. The event is thus clearly the multiple which both presents its entire site, and, by means of the pure signifier of itself immanent to its own multiple, manages to present the presentation itself, that is, the one of the infinite multiple that it is. This empirical evidence clearly corresponds with our matheme which posits that, apart from the terms of its site, the mark of itself, e_x, belongs to the evental multiple.

Now, what are the consequences of all this in regard to the relation between the event and the situation? And first of all, is the event or is it not a *term* of the situation in which it has its site?

I touch here upon the bedrock of my entire edifice. For it so happens that it is impossible—at this point—to respond to this simple question. If there exists an event, *its belonging to the situation of its site is undecidable from the standpoint of the situation itself.* That is, the signifier of the event (our e_x) is necessarily supernumerary to the site. Does it correspond to a multiple effectively presented in the situation? And what is this multiple?

Let's examine carefully the matheme $e_x \{x \mid x \in X, e_x\}$. Since X, the site, is on the edge of the void, its elements x, in any case, are *not* presented in the situation; only X itself is (thus, for example, 'the peasants' are certainly presented in the French situation of 1789–1790, but not *those* peasants of the Great Fear who seized castles). If one wishes to verify that the event is presented, there remains the other element of the event, which is the signifier of the event itself, e_x. The basis of this undecidability is thus evident: it is due to the circularity of the question. In order to verify whether an event is presented in a situation, it is first necessary to verify whether it is presented as an element of itself. To know whether the French Revolution is really *an* event in French history, we must first establish that it is definitely a term immanent to itself. In the following chapter we shall see that only an *interpretative intervention* can declare that an event *is* presented in a situation; as the arrival in being of non-being, the arrival amidst the visible of the invisible.

For the moment we can only examine the consequences of two possible hypotheses, hypotheses separated in fact by the entire extent of an interpretative intervention, of a *cut*: either the event belongs to the situation, or it does not belong to it.

– *First hypothesis*: the event belongs to the situation. From the standpoint of the situation, being presented, it *is*. Its characteristics, however, are quite special. First of all, note that the event is a *singular* multiple (in the situation to which we suppose it belongs). If it was actually normal, and could thus be represented, the event would be a *part* of the situation. Yet this is impossible, because elements of its site belong to it, and such elements—the site being on the edge of the void—are not, themselves, presented. The event (as, besides, intuition grasps it), therefore, cannot be thought in state terms, in terms of parts of the situation. The state does not count any event.

However, *if the event belongs to the situation*—if it is presented therein—it is not, itself, on the edge of the void. For, having the essential characteristic of belonging to itself, $e_x \in e_x$, it presents, as multiple, at least one multiple which is presented, namely itself. In our hypothesis, the event blocks its *total* singularization by the belonging of its signifier to the multiple that it is. In other words, an event is not (does not coincide with) an evental-site. It 'mobilizes' the elements of its site, but it adds its own presentation to the mix.

From the standpoint of the situation, if the event belongs to it, as I have supposed, the event is separated from the void by itself. This is what we will call being 'ultra-one'. Why 'ultra-one'? Because the sole and unique term of the event which guarantees that it is not—unlike its site—on the edge of the void, is the-one-that-it-is. And it *is* one, because we are supposing that the situation presents it; thus that it falls under the count-as-one.

To declare that an event belongs to the situation comes down to saying that it is conceptually distinguished from its site by the interposition of itself between the void and itself. This interposition, tied to self-belonging, is the ultra-one, because it counts the same thing as one *twice*: once as a presented multiple, and once as a multiple presented in its own presentation.

– *Second hypothesis*: the event does *not* belong to the situation. The result: 'nothing has taken place except the place.' For the event, apart from itself, solely presents the elements of its site, which are not presented in the situation. If it is not presented there either, *nothing* is presented by it, from the standpoint of the situation. The result is that, inasmuch as the signifier e_x 'adds itself', via some mysterious operation within the borderlands of a site, to a situation which does not present it, *only the void* can possibly be subsumed under it, because no presentable multiple responds to the call of such a name. And in fact, if you start posing that the 'French Revolution' is merely a pure word, you will have no difficulty in *demonstrating*, given the infinity of presented and non-presented facts, that *nothing* of such sort ever took place.

Therefore: either the event is in the situation, and it ruptures the site's being 'on-the-edge-of-the-void' by interposing itself between itself and the void; or, it is not in the situation, and its power of nomination is solely addressed, if it is addressed to 'something', to the void itself.

The undecidability of the event's belonging to the situation can be interpreted as a double function. On the one hand, the event would evoke the void, on the other hand, it would interpose itself between the void and itself. It would be both a name of the void, and the ultra-one of the presentative structure. And it is this ultra-one-naming-the-void which would deploy, in the interior-exterior of a historical situation, in a torsion of its order, the being of non-being, namely, *existing*.

It is at this very point that the interpretative intervention has to both detain and decide. By the declaration of the belonging of the event to the situation it bars the void's irruption. But this is only in order to force the situation itself to confess its own void, and to thereby let forth, from inconsistent being and the interrupted count, the incandescent non-being of an existence.

MEDITATION EIGHTEEN
Being's Prohibition of the Event

The ontological (or mathematical) schema of a natural situation is an ordinal (Meditation 12). What would the ontological schema be of an eventual site (a site on the edge of the void, a foundational site)? The examination of this question leads to surprising results, such as the following: on the one hand, in a certain sense, *every* pure multiple, every thinkable instance of being-qua-being is 'historical', but on the condition that one allows that the name of the void, the mark ∅, 'counts' as a historical situation (which is entirely impossible in situations other than ontology itself); on the other hand, the event is forbidden, ontology rejects it as 'that-which-is-not-being-qua-being'. We shall register once again that the void—the proper name of being—subtractively supports contradictory nominations; since in Mediation 12 we treated it as a natural multiple, and here we shall treat it as a site. But we shall also see how the symmetry between nature and history ends with this indifference of the void: ontology admits a complete doctrine of normal or natural multiples—the theory of ordinals—yet it does not admit a doctrine of the event, and so, strictly speaking, it does not admit historicity. With the event we have the first concept *external* to the field of mathematical ontology. Here, as always, ontology decides by means of a special axiom, the axiom of foundation.

1. THE ONTOLOGICAL SCHEMA OF HISTORICITY AND INSTABILITY

Meditation 12 allowed us to find the ontological correlates of normal multiples in transitive sets (every element is also a subset, belonging implies inclusion). Historicity, in contrast, is founded on singularity, on the 'on-the-edge-of-the-void,' on what belongs without being included.

How can this notion be formalized?

Let's use an example. Let α be a non-void multiple submitted to one rule alone: it is not an element of itself (we have: $\sim(\alpha \in \alpha)$). Consider the set $\{\alpha\}$ which is the forming-into-one of α, or its singleton: the set whose unique element is α. We can recognize that α is on the edge of the void for the situation formalised by $\{\alpha\}$. In fact, $\{\alpha\}$ has only α as an element. It so happens that α is not an element of itself. Therefore $\{\alpha\}$, which presents α alone, certainly does not present any other element of α, because they are all different from α. As such, within the situation $\{\alpha\}$, the multiple α is an evental site: it is presented, but nothing which belongs to it is presented (within the situation $\{\alpha\}$).

The multiple α being a site in $\{\alpha\}$, and $\{\alpha\}$ thus formalizing a historical situation (because it has an evental site as an element), can be expressed in the following manner—which causes the void to appear: the intersection of $\{\alpha\}$ (the situation) and α (the site) is void, because $\{\alpha\}$ does not present any element of α. The element α being a site for $\{\alpha\}$ means that the void alone names what is common to α and $\{\alpha\}$: $\{\alpha\} \cap \alpha = \varnothing$.

Generally speaking, the ontological schema of a historical situation is a multiple such that there belongs to it at least one multiple whose intersection with the initial multiple is void: in α there is β such that $\alpha \cap \beta = \varnothing$. It is quite clear how β can be said to be on the edge of the void relative to α: the void names what β presents *in* α, namely nothing. This multiple, β, formalizes an evental site in α. Its existence qualifies α as a historical situation. It can also be said that β *founds* α, because belonging to α finds its halting point in what β presents.

2. THE AXIOM OF FOUNDATION

However, and this is the crucial step, it so happens that this foundation, this on-the-edge-of-the-void, this site, constitutes in a certain sense a general law of ontology. An idea of the multiple (an axiom), introduced rather tardily by Zermelo, an axiom quite properly named the axiom of foundation, poses that in fact every pure multiple is historical, or contains at least one site. According to this axiom, within an existing one-multiple, there always exists a multiple presented by it such that this multiple is on the edge of the void relative to the initial multiple.

Let's start with the technical presentation of this new axiom.

Take a set α, and say that β is an element of α, $(\beta \in \alpha)$. If β is on the edge of the void according to α, this is because no element of β is itself an element of α: the multiple α presents β but it does not present in a separate manner any of the multiples that β presents.

This signifies that β and α have *no common element*: no multiple presented by the one-multiple α is presented by β, despite β itself, as one, being presented by α. That two sets have no element in common can be summarized as follows: the intersection of these two sets can only be named by the proper name of the void: $\alpha \cap \beta = \varnothing$.

This relation of total disjunction is a concept of alterity. The axiom of extension announces that a set is other than another set if at least one element of one is not an element of the other. The relation of disjunction is stronger, because it says that *no* element belonging to one belongs to the other. As multiples, they have *nothing* to do with one another, they are two absolutely heterogeneous presentations, and this is why this relation—of non-relation—can only be thought under the signifier of being (of the void), which indicates that the multiples in question have nothing in common apart from *being* multiples. In short, the axiom of extensionality is the Idea of the other and total disjunction is the idea of the Other.

It is evident that an element β which is a site in α is an element of α which is Other than α. Certainly β belongs to α, but the multiples out of which β forms-one are heterogeneous to those whose one is α.

The axiom of foundation thus states the following: given any existing multiple whatsoever (thus a multiple counted as one in accordance with the Ideas of the multiple and the existence of the name of the void), there always belongs to it—if, of course, it is not the name of the void itself in which case nothing would belong to it—a multiple on the edge of the void within the presentation that it is. In other words: every non-void multiple contains some Other:

$$(\forall \alpha)[(\alpha \neq \varnothing) \rightarrow (\exists \beta)[(\beta \in \alpha) \,\&\, (\beta \cap \alpha = \varnothing)]]$$

The remarkable conceptual connection affirmed here is that of the Other and foundation. This new Idea of the multiple stipulates that a non-void set is founded inasmuch as a multiple always belongs to it which is Other than it. Being Other than it, such a multiple guarantees the set's immanent foundation, since 'underneath' this foundational multiple, there is nothing which belongs to the initial set. Therefore, belonging cannot infinitely regress: this halting point establishes a kind of original finitude—situated 'lower down'—of any presented multiple in regard to the primitive sign of the multiple, the sign ∈.

The axiom of foundation is the ontological proposition which states that every existent multiple—besides the name of the void—occurs according to an immanent origin, positioned by the Others which belong to it. It adds up to the historicity of every multiple.

Set theory ontology thereby affirms, through the mediation of the Other, that even though presentation can be infinite (cf. Meditations 13 & 14) it is always marked by finitude *when it comes to its origin*. Here, this finitude is the existence of a site, on the edge of the void; historicity.

I now turn to the critical examination of this Idea.

3. THE AXIOM OF FOUNDATION IS A METAONTOLOGICAL THESIS OF ONTOLOGY

The multiples actually *employed* in current ontology—whole numbers, real numbers, complex numbers, functional spaces, etc.—are all founded in an evident manner, without recourse to the axiom of foundation. As such, this axiom (like the axiom of replacement in certain aspects) is surplus to the *working mathematician's* requirements, and so to historical ontology. Its range is thus more reflexive, or conceptual. The axiom indicates an essential structure of the theory of being, rather than being required for particular results. What it declares concerns in particular the relation between the science of being and the major categories of situations which classify being-in-totality. Its usage, for the most part, is metatheoretical.

4. NATURE AND HISTORY

Yet one could immediately object that the effect of the axiom of foundation is actually entirely the opposite. If, beside the void, every set admits some Otherness, and thus presents a multiple which is the schema of a site in the presentation, this is because, in terms of ontological matrices, *every situation is historical*, and there are historical multiples *everywhere*. What then happens to the classification of being-in-totality? What happens in particular to stable natural situations, to ordinals?

Here we touch on nothing less than *the ontological difference between being and beings*, between the presentation of presentation—the pure multiple—and presentation—the presented multiple. This difference comes down to the following: the ontological situation originally names the void as an existent multiple, whilst every other situation consists only insofar as it ensures the non-belonging of the void, a non-belonging controlled, moreover, by the state of the situation. The result is that the ontological matrix of a natural situation, which is to say an ordinal, is definitely founded, but it is done so uniquely *by the void*. In an ordinal, the Other *is* the name of the void, and it alone. We will thus allow that a stable natural situation is ontologically reflected as a multiple whose historical or foundational term is the name of the void, and that a historical situation is reflected by a multiple which possesses in any case *other* founding terms, non-void terms.

Let's turn to some examples.

Take the Two, the set $\{\varnothing, \{\varnothing\}\}$, which is an ordinal (Meditation 12). What is the Other in it? Certainly not $\{\varnothing\}$ because $\varnothing$ belongs to it, which also belongs to the Two. Therefore, it must be $\varnothing$, to which nothing belongs, and which thus certainly has no element in common with the Two. Consequently, the void founds the Two.

In general, *the void alone founds an ordinal*; more generally, it alone founds a transitive set (this is an easy exercise tied to the definition of transitivity).

Now take our earlier example, the singleton $\{a\}$ where a is non-void. We saw that a was the schema of a site in that set, and that $\{a\}$ was the schema of a historical situation (with one sole element!). We have $a \cap \{a\} = \varnothing$. But this time the foundational element (the site), which is a, is non-void by hypothesis. The schema $\{a\}$, not being founded by the void, is thus distinct from ordinals, or schemas of natural situations, which are *solely* founded by the void.

In *non-ontological* situations, foundation via the void is impossible. Only *mathematical ontology* admits the thought of the suture to being under the mark $\varnothing$.

For the first time, a gap is noticeable between ontology and the thought of other presentations, or beings, or non-ontological presentations, a gap which is due to the position of the void. In general, what is natural is stable or normal; what is historical contains some multiples on-the-edge-of-the-void. In ontology, however, what is natural is what is founded solely by the void; all the rest schematizes the historical. Recourse to the void is what institutes, in the thought of the nature/history couple, an *ontico-ontological difference*. It unfolds in the following manner:

a. A situation-being is natural if it does not present any singular term (if all of its terms are normal), and if none of its terms, considered in turn as situations, present singular terms either (if normality is recurrent downwards). It is a *stability of stabilities.*

– In the ontological situation, a pure multiple is natural (is an ordinal) if it is founded by the void alone, and if everything which belongs to it is equally founded by the void alone (since everything which belongs to an ordinal is an ordinal). It is a *void-foundation of void-foundations.*

b. A situation-being is historical if it contains at least one evental, foundational, on-the-edge-of-the-void site.

– In the ontological situation, according to the axiom of foundation, to every pure multiple there *always* belongs at least one Other-multiple, or site. However, we will say that a set formalizes a historical situation if at least one Other multiple belongs to it *which is not the name of the void.* This time it is thus a simple foundation by the other-than-void.

Since ontology uniquely admits founded multiples, which contain schemas of event-sites (though they may be void), one could come to the hasty conclusion that it is entirely orientated towards the thought of a being of the event. We shall see that it is quite the contrary which is the case.

5. THE EVENT BELONGS TO THAT-WHICH-IS-NOT-BEING-QUA-BEING

In the construction of the concept of the event (Meditation 17) the belonging to itself of the event, or perhaps, rather, the belonging of the signifier of the event to its signification, played a special role. Considered as a multiple, the event contains, besides the elements of its site, itself; thus being presented by the very presentation that it is.

If there existed an ontological formalization of the event it would therefore be necessary, within the framework of set theory, to allow the existence, which is to say the count-as-one, of a set such that it belonged to itself: $a \in a$.

It is in this manner, moreover, that one would formalize the idea that the event results from an excess-of-one, an ultra-one. In fact, the *difference* of this set a, after the axiom of extensionality, must be established via the examination of its elements, therefore, if a belongs to itself, via the examination of a itself. As such, a's identity can only be specified on the basis of a itself. The set a can only be recognized inasmuch as it has already been recognized. This type of self-antecedence in identification indicates the effect of the ultra-one in that the set a, such that $a \in a$, is solely identical to itself inasmuch as it *will have been* identical to itself.

Sets which belong to themselves were baptized *extraordinary* sets by the logician Mirimanoff. We could thus say the following: an event is onto-logically formalized by an extraordinary set.

We could. But the axiom of foundation forecloses *extraordinary sets from any existence, and ruins any possibility of naming a multiple-being of the event.* Here we have an essential gesture: that by means of which ontology declares that the event is not.

Let's suppose the existence of a set a which belongs to itself, a multiple which presents the presentation that it is: $a \in a$. If this a exists, its singleton $\{a\}$ also exists, because forming-into-one is a general operation (cf. Meditation 7). However, this singleton would not obey the Idea of the multiple stated by the axiom of foundation: $\{a\}$ would have no Other in itself, no *element* of $\{a\}$ such that its intersection with $\{a\}$ was void.

In other words: to $\{a\}$, a alone belongs. However, a belongs to a. Therefore, the intersection of $\{a\}$ and its unique element a *is not void*; it is equal to a: $[a \in \{a\} \,\&\, (a \in a)] \rightarrow (a \cap \{a\} = a)$. The result is that $\{a\}$ is not founded as the axiom of foundation requires it to be.

Ontology does not allow the existence, or the counting as one as sets in its axiomatic, of multiples which belong to themselves. There is no acceptable ontological matrix of the event.

What does this mean, this consequence of a law of the discourse on being-qua-being? It must be taken quite literally: ontology has nothing to say about the event. Or, to be more precise, ontology demonstrates that the event is not, in the sense in which it is a theorem of ontology that all self-belonging contradicts a fundamental Idea of the multiple, the Idea which prescribes the foundational finitude of origin for all presentation.

The axiom of foundation de-limits being by the prohibition of the event. It thus brings forth that-which-is-not-being-qua-being as a point of impossibility of the discourse on being-qua-being, and it exhibits its signifying emblem: the multiple such as it presents itself, in the brilliance, in which being is abolished, of the mark-of-one.

MEDITATION NINETEEN
Mallarmé

       ' . . . or was the event brought about in view of every null result'

A Cast of Dice . . .

A poem by Mallarmé always fixes the place of an aleatory event; an event to be interpreted on the basis of the traces it leaves behind. Poetry is no longer submitted to action, since the meaning (univocal) of the text depends on what is declared to have happened therein. There is a certain element of the detective novel in the Mallarméan enigma: an empty salon, a vase, a dark sea—what crime, what catastrophe, what enormous misadventure is indicated by these clues? Gardner Davies was quite justified in calling one of his books *Mallarmé and the Solar Drama*, for if the sunset is indeed an example of one of these defunct events whose 'there-has-been' must be reconstructed in the heart of the night, then this is generally because the poem's structure is *dramatic*. The extreme condensation of figures—a few objects—aims at isolating, upon a severely restricted stage, and such that nothing is hidden from the interpreter (the reader), a system of clues whose placement can be unified by one hypothesis alone as to what has happened, and, of which, one sole consequence authorizes the announcement of how the event, despite being abolished, will *fix* its décor in the eternity of a 'pure notion'. Mallarmé is a thinker of the event-drama, in the double sense of the staging of its appearance-disappearance (' . . . we do not have an idea of it, solely in the state of a glimmer, for it is immediately resolved . . . '), and of its interpretation which gives it the status of an 'acquisition for ever'. The non-being 'there is', the pure and cancelled occurrence of the gesture, are precisely what thought proposes to render eternal. As for the rest, reality in its massivity, it is merely imaginary, the result of false relations, and it employs language for commercial tasks alone. If poetry is an essential use of language, it is not because it is able to devote the latter to Presence; on the contrary, it is because it trains language to the paradoxical function of maintaining that which—radically singular, pure action—would otherwise fall back into the nullity of place. Poetry is the stellar assumption of that pure undecidable, against a background of nothingness, that is an action of which one can only *know* whether it has taken place inasmuch as one *bets* upon its truth.

In *A Cast of Dice . . .* , the metaphor of all evental-sites being on the edge of the void is edified on the basis of a deserted horizon and a stormy sea. Here we have, because they are reduced to the pure imminence of the nothing—of unpresentation—what Mallarmé names the 'eternal circumstances' of action. The term with which Mallarmé always designates a multiple presented in the vicinity of unpresentation is the Abyss, which, in *A Cast of Dice . . .* , is 'calm', 'blanched', and refuses in advance any departure from itself, the 'wing' of its very foam 'fallen back from an incapacity to take flight'.

The paradox of an evental-site is that it can only be recognized on the basis of what it does not present in the situation in which it is presented. Indeed, it is only due to it forming-one from multiples which are inexistent in the situation that a multiple is singular, thus subtracted from the guarantee of the state. Mallarmé brilliantly presents this paradox by composing, on the basis of the site—the deserted Ocean—a *phantom* multiple, which metaphorizes the inexistence of which the site is the presentation. Within the scenic frame, you have nothing apart from the Abyss, the sea and sky being indistinguishable. Yet from the 'flat incline' of the sky and the 'yawning deep' of the waves, the image of a ship is composed, sails and hull, annulled as soon as invoked, such that the desert of the site 'quite inwardly sketches . . . a vessel' which, itself, does not exist, being the figurative interiority of which the empty scene indicates, using its resources alone, the probable absence. The event will thus not only happen *within* the site, but on the basis of the provocation of whatever unpresentability is contained in the site: the ship 'buried in the depths', and whose abolished plenitude—since the Ocean alone is presented—authorizes the announcement that the action will take place 'from the bottom of a shipwreck'. For every event, apart from being localized by its site, initiates the latter's ruin *with regard to the situation*, because it retroactively names its inner void. The 'shipwreck' alone gives us the allusive debris from which (in the one of the site) the undecidable multiple of the event is composed.

Consequently, the *name* of the event—whose entire problem, as I have said, lies in thinking its belonging to the event itself—will be placed on the basis of one piece of this debris: the captain of the shipwrecked vessel, the 'master' whose arm is raised above the waves, whose fingers tighten around the two dice whose casting upon the surface of the sea is at stake. In this 'fist which would grip it', 'is prepared, works itself up, and mingles . . . the unique Number which cannot be an other.'

Why is the event—such that it occurs in the one of the site on the basis of 'shipwrecked' multiples that this one solely presents in their one-result—a cast of dice here? Because this gesture symbolizes the event in general; that is, that which is purely hazardous, and which cannot be inferred from the situation, yet which is nevertheless a fixed multiple, a number, that nothing can modify once it has laid out the sum—'refolded the division'—of its visible faces. A cast of dice joins the emblem of chance to that of necessity, the erratic multiple of the event to the legible retroaction of the count. The event in question in *A Cast of Dice . . .* is therefore that of the production of an absolute symbol of the event. The stakes of casting dice 'from the bottom of a shipwreck' are those of making an event out of the thought of the event.

However, given that the essence of the event is to be undecidable with regard to its belonging to the situation, an event whose content is the eventness of the event (and this is clearly the cast of dice thrown 'in eternal circumstances') cannot, in turn, have any other *form* than that of indecision. Since the master must produce the absolute event (the one, Mallarmé says, which will abolish chance, being the active, effective, concept of the 'there is'), he must suspend this production from a hesitation which is itself absolute, and which indicates that the event is that multiple in respect to which we can neither know nor observe whether it belongs to the situation of its site. We shall never see the master throw the dice because our sole access, in the scene of action, is to a hesitation as eternal as the circumstances: 'The master . . . hesitates . . . rather than playing as a hoar maniac the round in the name of the waves . . . to not open the hand clenched beyond the useless head.' 'To play the round' or 'to not open his hand'? In the first case, the essence of the event is lost because it is *decided* in an anticipatory manner that it will happen. In the second case, its essence is also lost, because 'nothing will have taken place but place.' Between the cancellation of the event by the reality of its visible belonging to the situation and the cancellation of the event by its total invisibility, the only representable figure of the concept of the event is the staging of its undecidability.

Accordingly, the entire central section of *A Cast of Dice . . .* organizes a stupefying series of metaphorical translations around the theme of the undecidable. From the upraised arm, which—perhaps—holds the 'secret' of number, a whole fan of analogies unfolds, according to the technique which has already brought forth the unpresentable of the oceanic site by superimposing upon it the image of a ghost ship; analogies in which, little by little, an equivalence is obtained between throwing the dice and retaining them; thus a metaphorical treatment of the *concept* of undecidability.

The 'supreme conjunction with probability' represented by the old man hesitating to throw the dice upon the surface of the sea is initially—in an echo of the foam traces out of which the sails of the drowned ship were woven—transformed into a wedding veil (the wedding of the situation and the event), frail material on the point of submersion, which 'will tremble/will collapse', literally sucked under by the nothingness of presentation in which the unpresentables of the site are dispersed.

Then this veil, on the brink of disappearing, becomes a 'solitary feather' which 'hovers about the gulf'. What more beautiful image of the event, impalpable yet crucial, could be found than this white feather upon the sea, with regard to which one cannot reasonably decide whether it will 'flee' the situation or 'be strewn' over it?

The feather, at the possible limit of its wandering, adjusts itself to its marine pedestal as if to a velvet hat, and under this headgear—in which a *fixed* hesitation ('this rigid whiteness') and the 'sombre guffaw' of the massivity of the place are joined—we see, in a miracle of the text, none other than Hamlet emerge, 'sour Prince of pitfalls'; which is to say, in an exemplary manner, the very subject of theatre who cannot find acceptable reasons to decide whether or not it is appropriate, and when, to kill the murderer of his father.

The 'lordly feathered crest' of the romantic hat worn by the Dane throws forth the last fires of undecidability, it 'glitters then shadows', and in this shadow in which, again, everything risks being lost, a siren and a rock emerge—poetic temptation of gesture and massivity of place—which this time will vanish together. For the 'impatient terminal scales' of the temptress serve for nothing more than causing the rock to 'evaporate into mist', this 'false manor' which pretended to impose a 'limit upon infinity'. Let this be understood: the undecidable equivalence of the gesture and the place is refined to such a point within this scene of analogies, through its successive transformations, that one supplementary image alone is enough to annihilate the correlative image: the impatient gesture of the Siren's tail, inviting a throw of the dice, can only cause the limit to the infinity of indecision (which is to say, the local visibility of the event) to disappear, and the original site to return. The original site dismisses the two terms of the dilemma, given that it was not possible to establish a stable dissymmetry between the two, on the basis of which the reason for a choice could have been announced. The mythological chance of an appeal is no longer to be found upon any discernible rock of the situation. This step backwards is admirably stylized by the reappearance of an earlier image, that of the feather, which this time will 'bury itself in the original spray', its 'delirium' (that is, the wager of being able to decide an absolute event) having advanced to the very heights of itself, to a 'peak' from which, the undecidable essence of the event figured, it falls away, 'withered by the identical neutrality of the gulf'. It will not have been able, given the gulf, to strew itself over it (cast the dice) or to escape it (avoid the gesture); it will have exemplified the impossibility of rational choice—of the abolition of chance—and, in this neutral identity, it will have quite simply abolished itself.

In the margins of this figurative development, Mallarmé gives his abstract lesson, which is announced on page eight, between Hamlet and the siren, by a mysterious 'If'. The ninth page resolves its suspense: 'If . . . it was the number, it would be chance.' If the event delivered the fixed finitude of the one-multiple that it is, this would in no way entail one having been able to rationally decide upon its relation to the situation.

The fixity of the event as result—its count-as-one—is carefully detailed by Mallarmé: it would come to *existence*, ('might it have existed other than as hallucination') it would be enclosed within its *limits* ('might it have begun and might it have ended'), having emerged amidst its own disappearance ('welling up as denied'), and having closed itself within its own appearance ('closed when shown'), it would be *multiple* ('might it have been counted'); yet it would also be *counted as one* ('evidence of the sum however little a one'). In short, the event would be within the situation, it would have been presented. But this presentation would either engulf the event within the neutral regime of indeterminate presentation ('the identical neutrality of the gulf'), allowing its evental essence to escape, *or*, having no graspable relation with this regime, it would be 'worse / no / more nor less / indifferently but as much / chance', and consequently it would not have represented either, via the event of the event, the absolute notion of the 'there is'.

Must we then conclude, in a nihilistic manner, that the 'there is' is forever un-founded, and that thought, devoting itself to structures and essences, leaves the interruptive vitality of the event outside its domain? Must we conclude that the power of place is such that at the undecidable point of the outside-place reason hesitates and cedes ground to irrationality? This is what the tenth page seems to suggest: there we find the declaration 'nothing will have taken place but place.' The 'memorable crisis'—that would have represented the absolute event symbolized in the cast of dice—would have had the privilege of escaping from the logic of the result; the event would have been realized 'in view of every result null human', which means: the ultra-one of number would have transcended the human—all too human—law of the count-as-one, which stipulates that the multiple—because the one is not—can only exist as the result of structure. By the absoluteness of a gesture, an auto-foundational interruption would have fusioned uncertainty and the count; chance would have both affirmed and abolished itself in the excess-of-one, the 'stellar birth' of an event in which the essence of the event is deciphered. But no. 'Some commonplace plashing' of the marine surface—the pure site this time lacking any interiority, even ghostly—ends up 'dispersing the empty act'. Save—Mallarmé tells us—if, by chance, the absolute event had been able to take place, the 'lie' of this act (a lie which is the fiction of a truth) would have caused the ruin of the indifference of the place, 'the perdition . . . of the indistinct'. Since the event was not able to engender itself, it seems that one must recognize that 'the indistinct' carries the day, that place is sovereign, that 'nothing' is the true name of what happens, and that poetry, language turned towards the eternal fixation of what-comes-to-pass, is not distinct from commercial usages in which names have the vile function of allowing the imaginary of relations to be exchanged, that of vain and prosperous reality.

But this is not the last word. Page eleven, opened by an 'excepted, perhaps' in which a promise may be read, suddenly inscribes, both beyond any possible calculation—thus, in a structure which is that of the event —and in a synthesis of everything antecedent, the stellar double of the suspended cast of dice: the Great Bear (the constellation 'towards . . . the Septentrion') enumerates its seven stars, and realizes 'the successive collision astrally of a count total in formation'. To the 'nothing' of the previous page responds, outside-place ('as far as a place fusions with a beyond'), the essential figure of number, and thus the concept of the event. This event has definitely *occurred* on its own ('watching over / doubting / rolling / sparkling and meditating'), and it is also a *result*, a halting point ('before halting at some last point which consecrates it').

How is this possible? To understand one must recall that at the very end of the metamorphoses which inscribe indecision (master's arm, veil, feather, Hamlet, siren), we do not arrive at non-gesture, but rather at an equivalence of gesture (casting the dice) and non-gesture (not casting the dice). The feather which returned to the original spray was thus the purified symbol of the undecidable, it did not signify the renunciation of action. That 'nothing' has taken place therefore means solely that nothing *decidable within the situation* could figure the event as such. By causing the place to prevail over the idea that an event could be calculated therein, the poem realizes the essence of the event itself, which is precisely that of being, from this point of view, incalculable. The pure 'there is' is simultaneously chance and number, excess-of-one and multiple, such that the scenic presentation of its being delivers non-being alone, since every existent, for itself, lays claim to the structured necessity of the one. As an un-founded multiple, as self-belonging, undivided signature of itself, the event can only be indicated beyond the situation, despite it being necessary to wager that it has manifested itself therein.

Consequently, the courage required for maintaining the equivalence of gesture and non-gesture—thereby risking abolishment within the site—is compensated by the supernumerary emergence of the constellation, which fixes in the sky of Ideas the event's excess-of-one.

Of course, the Great Bear—this arbitrary figure, which is the total of a four and a three, and which thus has nothing to do with the Parousia of the supreme count that would be symbolized, for example, by a double six—is 'cold from forgetting and disuse', for the eventness of the event is anything but a warm presence. However, the constellation is subtractively equivalent, 'on some vacant superior surface', to any being which *what-happens* shows itself to be capable of, and this fixes for us the task of interpreting it, since it is impossible for us to will it into being.

By way of consequence, the conclusion of this prodigious text—the densest text there is on the limpid seriousness of a conceptual drama—is a maxim, of which I gave another version in my *Théorie du sujet*. Ethics, I said, comes down to the following imperative: 'Decide from the standpoint of the undecidable.' Mallarmé writes: 'Every thought emits a cast of dice.'

On the basis that 'a cast of dice never will abolish chance', one must not conclude in nihilism, in the uselessness of action, even less in the management-cult of reality and its swarm of fictive relationships. For if the event is erratic, and if, from the standpoint of situations, one cannot decide whether it exists or not, it is given to us to bet; that is, to legislate without law in respect to this existence. Given that undecidability is a rational attribute of the event, and the salvatory guarantee of its non-being, there is no other vigilance than that of becoming, as much through the anxiety of hesitation as through the courage of the outside-place, both the feather, which 'hovers about the gulf', and the star, 'up high perhaps'.

PART V

The Event:
Intervention and Fidelity.
Pascal/Choice;
Hölderlin/Deduction

MEDITATION TWENTY

The Intervention: Illegal choice of a name of the event, logic of the two, temporal foundation

We left the question of the event at the point at which the situation gave us no base for deciding whether the event belonged to it. This undecidability is an intrinsic attribute of the event, and it can be deduced from the matheme in which the event's multiple-form is inscribed. I have traced the consequences of two possible decisions: if the event does not belong to the situation, then, given that the terms of its event-site are not presented, nothing will have taken place; if it does belong, then it will interpose itself between itself and the void, and thus be determined as ultra-one.

Since it is of the very essence of the event to be a multiple whose belonging to the situation is undecidable, deciding that it belongs to the situation is a wager: one can only hope that this wager never becomes legitimate, inasmuch as any legitimacy refers back to the structure of the situation. No doubt, the consequences of the decision will become known, but it will not be possible to return back prior to the event in order to tie those consequences to some founded origin. As Mallarmé says, wagering that something has taken place cannot abolish the chance of it having-taken-place.

Moreover, the procedure of decision requires a certain degree of preliminary separation from the situation, a coefficient of unpresentability. For the situation itself, in the plenitude of multiples that it presents as result-ones, cannot provide the means for setting out such a procedure in its entirety. If it could do so, this would mean that the event was not undecidable therein.

In other words, there cannot *exist* any regulated and necessary procedure which is adapted to the decision concerning the eventness of a multiple. In particular, I have shown that the state of a situation does not guarantee any rule of this order, because the event, happening in a site—a multiple on the edge of the void—is never resecured as part by the state. Therefore one cannot refer to a supposed *inclusion* of the event in order to conclude in its *belonging*.

I term *intervention* any procedure by which a multiple is recognized as an event.

'Recognition' apparently implies two things here, which are joined in the unicity of the interventional gesture. First, that the form of the multiple is designated as evental, which is to say in conformity with the matheme of the event: this multiple is such that it is composed from —forms a one out of—on the one hand, represented elements of its site, and on the other hand, itself. Second, that with respect to this multiple, thus remarked in its form, it is decided that it is a term of the situation, that it belongs to the latter. An intervention consists, it seems, in identifying that there has been some undecidability, and in deciding its belonging to the situation.

However, the second sense of intervention cancels out the first. For if the essence of the event is to be undecidable, the decision annuls it as event. From the standpoint of the decision, you no longer have anything other than a term of the situation. The intervention thus appears—as perceived by Mallarmé in his metaphor of the disappearing gesture—to consist of an auto-annulment of its own meaning. Scarcely has the decision been taken than what provoked the decision disappears in the uniformity of multiple-presentation. This would be one of the paradoxes of action, and its key resides in decision: what it is applied to—an aleatory exception—finds itself, by the very same gesture which designates it, reduced to the common lot and submitted to the effect of structure. Such action would necessarily fail to *retain* the exceptional mark-of-one in which it was founded. This is certainly one possible acceptation of Nietzsche's maxim of the Eternal Return of the Same. The will to power, which is the interpretative capacity of the decision, would bear within itself a certitude: that its ineluctable consequence be the prolonged repetition of the laws of the situation. Its destiny would be that of wanting the Other only in its capacity as a new support for the Same. Multiple-being, broken apart in the chance of an unpresentation that an illegal will alone can legalize, would return, along with the law of the count, to inflict the one-result upon the illusory novelty of the consequences. It is well known what kind of pessimistic political conclusions and nihilist cult of art are drawn from this evaluation of the will in 'moderate' (let's say: non-Nazi) Nietzscheism. The metaphor of the Overman can only secure, at the extreme point of the sickly revenge of the weak and amidst the omnipresence of their resentment, the definite return of the Presocratic reign of power. Man, sick with man, would find Great Health in the event of his own death, and he would decide that this event announces that 'man is what must be surpassed'. But this 'surpassing' is also the return to the origin: to be cured, even if it be of oneself, is merely to re-identify oneself according to the immanent force of life.

In reality, the paradox of the intervention is more complex because it is impossible to separate its two aspects: recognition of the evental form of a multiple, and decision with respect to its belonging to the situation.

An event of the site X belongs to itself, $e_x \in e_x$. Recognizing it as multiple supposes that it has *already* been named—for this supernumerary signifier, e_x, to be considered as an element of the one-multiple that it is. The act of nomination of the event is what constitutes it, not as real—we will always posit that this multiple has occurred—but as susceptible to a decision concerning its belonging to the situation. The essence of the intervention consists—within the field opened up by an interpretative hypothesis, whose *presented* object is the site (a multiple on the edge of the void), and which concerns the 'there is' of an event—in naming this 'there is' and in unfolding the consequences of this nomination in the space of the situation to which the site belongs.

What do we understand here by 'nomination'? Another form of the question would be: what resources connected to the situation can we count on to pin this paradoxical multiple that is the event to the signifier; thereby granting ourselves the previously inexpressible possibility of its belonging to the situation? No presented term of the situation can furnish what we require, because the effect of homonymy would immediately efface everything unpresentable contained in the event; moreover, one would be introducing an ambiguity into the situation in which all interventional capacity would be abolished. Nor can the site itself name the event, even if it serves to circumscribe and qualify it. For the site *is* a term of the situation, and its being-on-the-edge-of-the-void, although open to the possibility of an event, in no way necessitates the latter. The Revolution of 1789 is certainly 'French', yet France is not what engendered and named its eventness. It is much rather the case that it is the revolution which has since retroactively given meaning—by being inscribed, via decision, therein—to that historical situation that we call France. In the same manner, the problem of the solution by roots of equations of the fifth degree or more found itself in a relative impasse around 1840: this defined—like all theoretical impasses—an evental site for mathematics (for ontology). However, this impasse did not determine the conceptual revolution of Evariste Galois, who understood, besides, with a special acuity, that his entire role had been that of obeying the injunction contained in the works of his predecessors, since therein one found 'ideas prescribed without their authors' awareness'. Galois thereby remarked the function of the void in intervention. Furthermore, it is the theory of Galoisian extensions which retroactively assigned its true sense to the situation of 'solution by roots'.

If, therefore, it is—as Galois says—the unnoticed of the site which founds the evental nomination, one can then allow that what the situation proposes as base for the nomination is not what it presents, but what it *un*presents.

The initial operation of an intervention is to *make a name out of an unpresented element of the site to qualify the event whose site is the site*. From this point onwards, the x which indexes the event e_x will no longer be X, which names the site, existing term of the situation, but an $x \in X$ that X, which is on the edge of the void, counts as one in the situation without that x being itself presented—or existent, or one—in the situation. The name of the event is drawn from the void at the edge of which stands the intra-situational presentation of its site.

How is this possible? Before responding to this question—a response to be elaborated over the meditations to come—let's explore the consequences.

a. One must not confuse the unpresented element 'itself'—its belonging to the site of the event as element—and its function of nomination with respect to the event-multiple, a multiple to which, moreover, it belongs. If we write the matheme of the event (Meditation 17):

$$e_x = \{x \in X, e_x\}$$

we see that if e_x had to be *identified* with an element x of the site, the matheme would be redundant—e_x would simply designate the set of (represented) elements of the site, including itself. The mention of e_x would be superfluous. It must therefore be understood that the term x has a double function. On the one hand, it is $x \in X$, unpresented element of the presented one of the site, 'contained' in the void at the edge of which the site stands. On the other hand, it indexes the event to the arbitrariness of the signifier; an arbitrariness, however, that is limited by one law alone —that the name of the event must emerge from the void. The interventional capacity is bound to this double function, and it is on such a basis that the belonging of the event to the situation is decided. The intervention touches the void, and is thereby subtracted from the law of the count-as-one which rules the situation, precisely because its inaugural axiom is *not tied to the one, but to the two*. As one, the element of the site which indexes the event does not exist, being unpresented. What induces its existence is the decision by which it occurs as two, as itself absent *and* as supernumerary name.

b. It is no doubt misleading to speak of *the* term *x* which serves as name for the event. How indeed could it be distinguished within the void? The law of the void is in-difference (Meditation 5). 'The' term which serves as name for the event is, in itself, anonymous. The event has the nameless as its name: it is with regard to everything that happens that one can only say what it is by referring it to its unknown Soldier. For if the term indexing the event was chosen by the intervention from amongst existing nominations—the latter referring to terms differentiable within the situation —one would have to admit that the count-as-one entirely structures the intervention. If this were so, 'nothing would have taken place, but place'. In respect of the term which serves as index for the event, all that can be said—despite it being the one of its double function—is that it belongs to the site. Its proper name is thus the common name 'belonging to the site'. It is *an* indistinguishable of the site, projected by the intervention into the two of the evental designation.

c. This nomination is essentially illegal in that it cannot conform to any *law* of representation. I have shown that the state of a situation—its metastructure—serves to form-a-one out of any part in the space of presentation. Representation is thus secured. Given a multiple of presented multiples, its name, correlate of its one, is an *affair of the state*. But since the intervention extracts the supernumerary signifier from the void bordered on by the site, the state law is interrupted. The *choice* operated by the intervention is a non-choice for the state, and thus for the situation, because no existent rule can specify *the* unpresented term which is thereby chosen as name of the pure evental 'there is'. Of course, the term of the site which names the event is, if one likes, a *representative* of the site. It is such all the more so given that its name is 'belonging to the site'. However, from the perspective of the situation—or of its state—this representation can never be recognized, Why? Because no law of the situation thus authorizes the determination of an anonymous term for each part, a purely inde-terminate term; still less the extension of this illegal procedure, by means of which each included multiple would produce—by what miracle of a choice without rules?—a representative lacking any other quality than that of belonging to this multiple, to the void itself, such that its borders are signalled by the absolute singularity of the site. The choice of the representative cannot, within the situation, be allowed as representation. In contrast to 'universal suffrage', for example, which fixes, via the state, a uniform procedure for the designation of representatives, interventional choice projects into signifying indexation a term with respect to which nothing in the situation, no rule whatsoever, authorizes its distinction from any other.

d. Such an interruption of the law of representation inherent to every situation is evidently not possible in itself. Consequently, the inter-ventional choice is only effective as endangering the one. It is only *for the event*, thus for the nomination of a paradoxical multiple, that the term chosen by the intervenor represents the void. The name subsequently circulates within the situation according to the regulated consequences of the interventional decision which inscribes it there. It is never the name of *a* term, but of the event. One can also say that in contrast to the law of the count, an intervention only establishes the one of the event as a-non-one, given that its nomination—chosen, illegal, supernumerary, drawn from the void—only obeys the principle 'there is oneness' *in absentia*. Inasmuch as it is named e_x the event is clearly *this* event; inasmuch as its name is a representative without representation, the event remains anonymous and uncertain. The excess of one is also beneath the one. The event, pinned to multiple-being by the interventional capacity, remains sutured to the unpresentable. This is because the essence of the ultra-one is the Two. Considered, not in its multiple-being, but in its position, or its situation, an event is an *interval* rather than a term: it establishes itself, in the interventional retroaction, between the empty anonymity bordered on by the site, and the addition of a name. Moreover, the matheme inscribes this originary split, since it only determines the one-composition of the event e_x inasmuch as it distinguishes therein between itself and the represented elements of the site—from which, besides, the name originates.

The event is ultra-one—apart from it interposing itself between itself and the void—because the maxim 'there is Twoness' is founded upon it. The Two thereby invoked is not the reduplication of the one of the count, the repetition of the effects of the law. It is an originary Two, an interval of suspense, the divided effect of a decision.

e. It will be observed that the intervention, being thereby assigned to a double border effect—border of the void, border of the name—and being the basis of the named event's circulation within the situation, if it is a decision concerning belonging to the situation, remains undecidable itself. It is only recognized in the situation by its consequences. What is actually presented in the end is e_x, the name of the event. But its support, being illegal, cannot occur as such at the level of presentation. It will therefore always remain doubtful whether there has been an event or not, except to those who intervene, who decide its belonging to the situation. What there will be are consequences of a particular multiple, and they will be counted as one in the situation, and it will appear as though they were not predictable therein. In short, there will have been some chance in the situation; however, it will never be legitimate for the intervenor to pretend that the chance originated in a rupture of the law which itself arose from a decision on belonging concerning the environs of a defined site. Of course, one can always affirm that the undecidable has been decided, at the price of having to admit that it remains undecidable whether that decision on the undecidable was taken by anybody in particular. As such, the intervenor can be both entirely accountable for the regulated consequences of the event, and entirely incapable of boasting that they played a decisive role in the event itself. Intervention generates a discipline: it does not deliver any originality. There is no hero of the event.

f. If we now turn to the state of the situation, we see that it can only resecure the belonging of this supernumerary name, which circulates at random, at the price of pointing out the very void whose foreclosure is its function. What indeed are the *parts* of the event? What is included in it? Both the elements of its site and the event itself belong to the event. The elements of the site are unpresented. The only 'part' that they form for the state is thus the site itself. As for the supernumerary name, e_x, henceforth circulating due to the effect of the intervention, it possesses the property of belonging to itself. Its recognizable part is therefore its own unicity, or the singleton $\{e_x\}$ (Meditation 7). The terms registered by the state, guarantor of the count-as-one of parts, are finally the site, and the forming-into-one of the name of the event: X and $\{e_x\}$. The state thus fixes, after the intervention, the term $\{X,\{e_x\}\}$ as the canonical form of the event. What is at stake is clearly a Two (the site counted as one, and a multiple formed into one), but the problem is that between these two terms *there is no relation*. The matheme of the event, and the logic of intervention, show that between the site X and the event interpreted as e_x there is a double connection: on the one hand, the elements of the site belong to the event, considered as multiple, which is to say in its being; on the other hand, the nominal index x is chosen as illegal representative within the unpresented of the site. However, the state cannot know anything of the latter, since the illegal and the unpresentable are precisely what it expels. The state certainly captures that there has been some novelty in the situation, in the form of the representation of a Two which juxtaposes the site (already marked out) and the singleton of the event (put into circulation by the intervention). However, what is thereby juxtaposed remains essentially unrelated. From the standpoint of the state, the name has no discernible relation to the site. Between the two *there is nothing but the void*. In other words, the Two created by the site and the event formed into one is, for the state, a presented yet incoherent multiple. The event occurs for the state as the being of an enigma. Why is it necessary (and it is) to register this couple as a part of the situation when *nothing* marks out their pertinence? Why is this multiple, e_x, *erring at random, found to be essentially connected to the respectable X* which is the site? The danger of the count disfunctioning here is that the representation of the event blindly inscribes its intervallic essence by rendering it in state terms: it is a disconnected connection, an irrational couple, a one-multiple whose one is lawless.

Moreover, empirically, this is a classic enigma. Every time that a site is the theatre of a real event, the state—in the political sense, for example—recognizes that a designation must be found for the couple of the site (the factory, the street, the university) and the singleton of the event (strike, riot, disorder), but it cannot succeed in fixing the rationality of the link. This is why it is a law of the state to detect in the anomaly of this Two—and this is an avowal of the dysfunction of the count—the *hand of a stranger* (the foreign agitator, the terrorist, the perverse professor). It is not important whether the agents of the state believe in what they say or not, what counts is the necessity of the statement. For this metaphor is in reality that of the void itself: something unpresented is *at work*—this is what the state is declaring, in the end, in its designation of an external cause. The state blocks the apparition of the immanence of the void by the transcendence of the guilty.

In truth, the intervallic structure of the event is projected within a necessarily incoherent state excrescence. That it is incoherent—I have spoken of such: the void transpires therein, in the unthinkable joint between the heterogeneous terms from which it is composed. That it is an excrescence—this much can be deduced. Remember (Meditation 8), an excrescence is a term that is represented (by the state of the situation) but not presented (by the structure of the situation). In this case, what is presented is the event itself, e_x, and it alone. The representative couple, $\{X,\{e_x\}\}$, heteroclite pairing of the site and the forming-into-one of the event, is merely the mechanical effect of the state, which makes an inventory of the parts of the situation. This couple is not presented anywhere. Every event is thus given, on the statist surface of the situation, as an excrescence whose structure is a Two without concept.

g. Under what conditions is an intervention possible? What is at stake here is the commencement of a long critical trial of the reality of action, and the foundation of the thesis: there is some newness in being—an antagonistic thesis with respect to the maxim from Ecclesiastes, '*nihil novi sub sole*'.

I mentioned that intervention requires a kind of preliminary separation from the immediate law. Because the referent of the intervention is the void, such as attested by the fracture of its border—the site—and because its choice is illegal—representative without representation—it cannot be grasped as a one-effect, or structure. Yet given that what is a-non-one is precisely the event itself, there appears to be a circle. It seems that the event, as interventional placement-in-circulation of its name, can only be authorized on the basis of that other event, equally void for structure, which is the intervention itself.

There is actually no other recourse against this circle than that of splitting the point at which it rejoins itself. It is certain that the event alone, aleatory figure of non-being, founds the possibility of intervention. It is just as certain that if no intervention puts it into circulation within the situation on the basis of an extraction of elements from the site, then, lacking any being, radically subtracted from the count-as-one, the event does not exist. In order to avoid this curious mirroring of the event and the intervention—of the fact and the interpretation—*the possibility of the intervention must be assigned to the consequences of another event*. It is evental recurrence which founds intervention. In other words, there is no interventional capacity, constitutive for the belonging of an evental multiple to a situation, save within the network of consequences of a previously decided belonging. An intervention is what presents an event for the occurrence of another. It is an evental between-two.

This is to say that the theory of intervention forms the kernel of any theory of time. Time—if not coextensive with structure, if not the *sensible form of the Law*—is intervention itself, thought as the gap between two events. The essential historicity of intervention does not refer to time as a measurable milieu. It is established upon interventional capacity inasmuch as the latter only separates itself from the situation by grounding itself on the circulation—which has already been decided—of an evental multiple. This ground alone, combined with the frequentation of the site, can introduce a sufficient amount of non-being between the intervention and the situation in order for being itself, qua being, to be wagered in the shape of the unpresentable and the illegal, that is, in the final resort, as inconsistent multiplicity. Time is here, again, the requirement of the Two: for there to be an event, one must be able to situate oneself within the consequences of another. The intervention is a line drawn from one paradoxical multiple, which is already circulating, to the circulation of another, a line which scratches out. It is a *diagonal* of the situation.

One important consequence of evental recurrence is that no intervention whatsoever can legitimately operate according to the idea of a primal event, or a radical beginning. We can term *speculative leftism* any thought of being which bases itself upon the theme of an absolute commencement. Speculative leftism imagines that intervention authorizes itself on the basis of itself alone; that it breaks with the situation without any other support than its own negative will. This imaginary wager upon an absolute novelty—'to break in two the history of the world'—fails to recognize that the real of the conditions of possibility of intervention is always the circulation of an already decided event. In other words, it is the presupposition, implicit or not, that there has already been an intervention. Speculative leftism is fascinated by the evental ultra-one and it believes that in the latter's name it can reject any immanence to the structured regime of the count-as-one. Given that the structure of the ultra-one is the Two, the imaginary of a radical beginning leads ineluctably, in all orders of thought, to a Manichean hypostasis. The violence of this false thought is anchored in its representation of an imaginary Two whose temporal manifestation is signed, via the excess of one, by the ultra-one of the event, Revolution or Apocalypse. This thought is unaware that the event itself only exists insofar as it is *submitted*, by an intervention whose possibility requires recurrence—and thus non-commencement—to the ruled structure of the situation; as such, any novelty is relative, being legible solely after the fact as the hazard of an order. What the doctrine of the event teaches us is rather that the entire effort lies in following the event's consequences, not in glorifying its occurrence. There is no more an angelic herald of the event than there is a hero. Being does not commence.

The real difficulty is to be found in the following: the consequences of an event, being submitted to structure, cannot be discerned as such. I have underlined this undecidability according to which the event is only possible if special procedures conserve the evental nature of its consequences. This is why its sole foundation lies in a *discipline* of time, which controls from beginning to end the consequences of the introduction into circulation of the paradoxical multiple, and which at any moment knows how to discern its connection to chance. I will call this organised control of time *fidelity*.

To intervene is to enact, on the border of the void, being-faithful to its previous border.

MEDITATION TWENTY-ONE
Pascal

'The history of the Church should, properly speaking,
be called the history of truth'
Pensées

Lacan used to say that if no religion were true, Christianity, nevertheless, was the religion which came closest to the question of truth. This remark can be understood in many different ways. I take it to mean the following: in Christianity and in it alone it is said that the essence of truth supposes the evental ultra-one, and that relating to truth is not a matter of contemplation—or immobile knowledge—but of intervention. For at the heart of Christianity there is that event—situated, exemplary—that is the death of the son of God on the cross. By the same token, belief does not relate centrally to the being-one of God, to his infinite power; its interventional kernel is rather the constitution of the meaning of that death, and the organization of a fidelity to that meaning. As Pascal says: 'Except in Jesus Christ, we do not know the meaning of our life, or death, or God, or ourselves.'

All the parameters of the doctrine of the event are thus disposed within Christianity; amidst, however, the remains of an ontology of presence —with respect to which I have shown, in particular, that it diminishes the concept of infinity (Meditation 13).

a. The evental multiple happens in the special site which, for God, is human life: summoned to its limit, to the pressure of its void, which is to say in the symbol of death, and of cruel, tortured, painful death. The Cross is the figure of this senseless multiple.

b. Named progressively by the apostles—the collective body of intervention—as 'the death of God', this event belongs to itself, because its veritable eventness does not lie in the occurrence of death or torture, but in it being a matter of God. All the concrete episodes of the event (the flogging, the thorns, the way of the cross, etc.) solely constitute the ultra-one of an event inasmuch as God, incarnated and suffering, endures them. The interventional hypothesis that such is indeed the case interposes itself between the common banality of these details, themselves on the edge of the void (of death), and the glorious unicity of the event.

c. The ultimate essence of the evental ultra-one is the Two, in the especially striking form of a division of the divine One—the Father and the Son—which, in truth, definitively ruins any recollection of divine transcendence into the simplicity of a Presence.

d. The metastructure of the situation, in particular the Roman public power, registers this Two in the shape of the heteroclite juxtaposition of a site (the province of Palestine and its religious phenomena) and a singleton without importance (the execution of an agitator); at the very same time, it has the premonition that in this matter a void is convoked which will prove a lasting embarrassment for the State. Two factors testify to this embarrassment or to the latent conviction that madness lies therein: first, at the level of anecdote, Pilate keeps his distance (let these Jews deal with their own obscure business); and second, much later and at the level of a document, the instructions requested by Pliny the Younger from Emperor Trajan concerning the treatment reserved for Christians, clearly designated as a troublesome subjective exception.

e. The intervention is based upon the circulation, within the Jewish milieu, of another event, Adam's original sin, of which the death of Christ is the relay. The connection between original sin and redemption definitively founds the time of Christianity as a time of exile and salvation. There is an essential historicity to Christianity which is tied to the intervention of the apostles as the placement-into-circulation of the event of the death of God; itself reinforced by the promise of a Messiah which organized the fidelity to the initial exile. Christianity is structured from beginning to end by evental recurrence; moreover, it prepares itself for the divine hazard of the third event, the Last Judgement, in which the ruin of the terrestial situation will be accomplished, and a new regime of existence will be established.

f. This periodized time organizes a diagonal of the situation, in which the connection to the chance of the event of the regulated consequences it entails remains discernible due to the effect of an *institutional fidelity*. Amongst the Jews, the prophets are the special agents of the discernible. They interpret without cease, within the dense weave of presented multiples, what belongs to the consequences of the lapse, what renders the promise legible, and what belongs merely to the everyday business of the world. Amongst the Christians, the Church—the first institution in human history to pretend to universality—organizes fidelity to the Christ-event, and explicitly designates those who support it in this task as 'the faithful'.

Pascal's particular genius lies in his attempt to renovate and maintain the evental kernel of the Christian conviction under the absolutely modern and unheard of conditions created by the advent of the subject of science. Pascal saw quite clearly that these conditions would end up ruining the demonstrative or rational edifice that the medieval Fathers had elaborated as the architecture of belief. He illuminated the paradox that at the very moment in which science finally legislated upon nature via demonstration, the Christian God could only remain at the centre of subjective experience if it belonged to an entirely different logic, if the 'proofs of the existence of God' were abandoned, and if the pure evental force of faith were restituted. It would have been possible, indeed, to believe that with the advent of a mathematics of infinity and a rational mechanics, the question imposed upon the Christians was that of either renovating their proofs by nourishing them on the expansion of science (this is what will be undertaken in the eighteenth century by people like Abbot Pluché, with their apologies for the miracles of nature, a tradition which lasted until Teilhard de Chardin); or, of completely separating the genres, and establishing that the religious sphere is beyond the reach of, or indifferent to, the deployment of scientific thought (in its strict form, this is Kant's doctrine, with the radical separation of the faculties; and in its weak form, it is the 'supplement of spirituality'). Pascal is a dialectician insofar as he is satisfied with neither of these two options. The first appears to him—and rightly so—to lead solely to an abstract God, a sort of ultra-mechanic, like Descartes' God ('useless and uncertain') which will become Voltaire's clockmaker-God, and which is entirely compatible with the hatred of Christianity. The second option does not satisfy his own desire, contemporary with the flourishing of mathematics, for a unified and total doctrine, in which the strict distinction of orders (reason and charity do not actually belong to the same domain, and here Pascal anticipated Kant, all the same) must not hinder the existential unity of the Christian and the mobilization of all of his capacities in the religious will alone; for 'the God of Christians . . . is a God who fills the heart and soul of those whom he possesses . . . ; who makes them incapable of any other end but him.' The Pascalian question is thus not that of a knowledge of God contemporary with the new stage of rationality. What he asks is this: what is it that is a Christian subject today? And this is the reason why Pascal re-centres his entire apologia around a very precise point: what could cause an atheist, a libertine, to *pass* from disbelief to Christianity? One would not be exaggerating if one said that Pascal's modernity, which is still disconcerting today, lies in the fact that he prefers, by a long way, a resolute unbeliever ('atheism: proof of force of the soul') to a Jesuit, to a lukewarm believer, or to a Cartesian deist. And for what reason, if not that the nihilist libertine appears to him to be significant and modern in a different manner than the amateurs of compromise, who *adapt themselves* to both the social authority of religion, and to the ruptures in the edifice of rationalism. For Pascal, Christianity stakes its existence, under the new conditions of thought, not in its flexible capacity to maintain itself institutionally in the heart of an overturned city, but in its power of subjective capture over these typical representatives of the new world that are the sensual and desperate materialists. It is to them that Pascal addresses himself with tenderness and subtlety, having, on the contrary, only a terribly sectarian scorn for comfortable Christians, at whose service he places—in *The Provincial Letters*, for example—a violent and twisted style, an unbridled taste for sarcasm, and no little bad faith. Moreover, what makes Pascal's prose unique—to the point of removing it from its time and placing it close, in its limpid rapidity, to the Rimbaud of *A Season in Hell*—is a sort of urgency in which the work on the text (Pascal rewrote the same passage ten times) is ordained by a defined and hardened interlocutor; in the anxiety of not doing everything in his power to convince the latter. Pascal's style is thus the ultimate in interventional style. This immense writer transcended his time by means of his militant vocation: nowadays, however, people pretend that a militant vocation buries you in your time, to the point of rendering you obsolete overnight.

To grasp what I hold to be the very heart of Pascal's *provocation* one must start from the following paradox: why does this open-minded scientist, this entirely modern mind, absolutely insist upon justifying Christianity by what would appear to be its weakest point for post-Galilean rationality, that is, the doctrine of miracles? Isn't there something quite literally *mad* about choosing, as his privileged interlocutor, the nihilist libertine, trained in Gassendi's atomism and reader of Lucrece's diatribes against the supernatural, and then trying to convince him by a maniacal recourse to the historicity of miracles?

Pascal, however, holds firm to his position that 'all of belief is based on the miracles'. He refers to Saint Augustine's declaration that he would not be Christian without the miracles, and states, as an axiom, 'It would have been no sin not to have believed in Jesus Christ without the miracles.' Still better: although Pascal exalts the Christian God as the God of consolation, he excommunicates those who, in satisfying themselves with this filling of the soul by God, only pay attention to miracles for the sake of form alone. Such people, he says, 'discredit his [Christ's] miracles'. And so, 'those who refuse to believe in miracles today on account of some supposed and fanciful contradiction are not excused.' And this cry: 'How I hate those who profess to doubt in miracles!'

Let's say, without proceeding any further, that the miracle—like Mallarmé's chance—is the emblem of the pure event as resource of truth. Its function—to be in excess of proof—pinpoints and factualizes the ground from which there originates both the possibility of believing *in truth*, and God not being reducible to this pure object of knowledge with which the deist satisfies himself. The miracle is the symbol of an interruption of the law in which the interventional capacity is announced.

Pascal's doctrine on this point is very complex because it articulates, on the basis of the Christ-event, both its chance and its recurrence. The central dialectic is that of prophecy and the miracle.

Insofar as the death of Christ can only be interpreted as the incarnation of God with respect to original sin—for which it forms the relay and sublation—its meaning must be legitimated by exploring the diagonal of fidelity which unites the first event (the fall, origin of our misery) to the second (redemption, as a cruel and humiliating reminder of our greatness). The prophecies, as I said, organize this link. Pascal elaborates, in respect to them, an entire theory of interpretation. The evental between-two that they designate is *necessarily* the place of an ambiguity; what Pascal terms the obligation of figures. On the one hand, if Christ is the event that can only be named by an intervention founded upon a faithful discernment of the effects of sin, then that event must have been predicted, 'prediction' designating here the interpretative capacity itself, transmitted down the centuries by the Jewish prophets. On the other hand, for Christ to be an event, even the rule of fidelity, which organizes the intervention generative of meaning, must be *surprised* by the paradox of the multiple. The only solution is that the meaning of the prophecy be simultaneously obscure in the time of its pronunciation, and retroactively clear once the Christ-event, interpreted by the believing intervention, establishes its truth. Fidelity, which prepares for the foundational intervention of the apostles, is mostly enigmatic, or double: 'The whole question lies in knowing whether or not they [the prophecies] have two meanings.' The literal or vulgar meaning provides immediate clarity but essential obscurity. The genuinely prophetic meaning, illuminated by the interventional interpretation of Christ and the apostles, provides an essential clarity and an immediate *figure*: 'A cipher with a double meaning: one clear, and *one* in which the meaning is said to be hidden'. Pascal invented reading for symptoms. The prophecies are continually obscure in regard to their spiritual meaning, which is only revealed via Christ, but unequally so: certain passages can only be interpreted on the basis of the Christian hypothesis, and without this hypothesis their functioning, at the vulgar level of meaning, is incoherent and bizarre:

> In countless places the [true, Christian] spiritual meaning is hidden by another meaning and revealed in a very few places though nevertheless in such a way that the passages in which it is hidden are equivocal and can be interpreted in both ways; whereas the passages in which it is revealed are unequivocal and can only be interpreted in a spiritual sense.

Thus, within the prophetic textual weave of the Old Testament, the Christ-event disengages rare unequivocal symptoms, on the basis of which, by successive associations, the general coherence of one of the two meanings of prophetic obscurity is illuminated—to the detriment of what appears to be conveyed by the 'figurative' in the form of vulgar evidence.

This coherence, which founds, in the future anterior, Jewish fidelity in the between-two of original sin and redemption, does not, however, allow the recognition of that which, beyond its truth function, constitutes the very being of the Christ-event, which is to say the *eventness* of the event, the multiple which, in the site of life and death, belongs to itself. Certainly, Christ is predicted, but the 'He-has-been-predicted' is only demonstrated on the basis of the intervention which decides that this tortured man, Jesus, is indeed the Messiah-God. As soon as this interventional decision is taken, everything is clear, and the truth circulates throughout the entirety of the situation, under the emblem which names it: the Cross. However, to take this decision, the double meaning of the prophecies is not sufficient.

One must trust oneself to the event from which there is drawn, in the heart of its void—the scandalous death of God which contradicts every figure of the Messiah's glory—the provocative name. And what supports this confidence cannot be the clarity dispensed to the double meaning of the Jewish text; on the contrary, the latter depends upon the former. It is thus the miracle alone which attests, through the belief one accords to it, that one submits oneself to the realized chance of the event, and not to the necessity of prediction. Still more is required: the miracle itself cannot be so striking and so evidently addressed to everyone that submission to it becomes merely a necessary evidence. Pascal is concerned to save the vulnerability of the event, its quasi-obscurity, since it is precisely on this basis that the Christian subject is the one who decides from the standpoint of undecidability ('Incomprehensible that God be, incomprehensible that he not be'), rather than the one who is crushed by the power of either a demonstration ('The God of the Christians is not a God who is merely the author of geometrical truths') or some prodigious occurrence; the latter being reserved for the third event, the Last Judgement, when God will appear 'with such a blaze of lightning, and such an overthrow of nature, that the dead will rise and the blindest will see him for themselves'. In the miracles there is an indication that the Christ-event has taken place: these miracles are destined, by their moderation, to those whose Jewish fidelity is exerted beyond itself, for God, 'wishing to appear openly to those who seek him with all their heart, and hidden to those who flee from him with all their heart . . . tempers the knowledge of himself'.

Intervention is therefore a precisely calibrated subjective operation.

1. With respect to its *possibility*, it depends upon evental recurrence, upon the diagonal of fidelity organised by the Jewish prophets: the site of Christ is necessarily Palestine; there alone can the witnesses, the investigators, and the intervenors be found upon whom it depends that the paradoxical multiple be named 'incarnation and death of God'.

2. Intervention, however, is never *necessary*. For the event is not in the situation to verify the prophecy; it is discontinuous with the very diagonal of fidelity which reflects its recurrence. Indeed, this reflection only occurs within a figurative ambiguity, in which the symptoms themselves can only be isolated retroactively. *Consequently, it is of the essence of the faithful to divide themselves*: 'At the time of the Messiah, the people were divided . . . The Jews refused him, but not all of

them.' As a result, the intervention is always the affair of an avant-garde: 'The spiritual embraced the Messiah; the vulgar remained to bear witness to him.'

3. The belief of the intervening avant-garde bears on the eventness of the event, and it *decides* the event's belonging to the situation. 'Miracle' names this belief, and so this decision. In particular, the life and death of Christ—the event strictly speaking—cannot be legitimated by the accomplishment of prophecies, otherwise the event would not interrupt the law: 'Jesus Christ proved that he was the Messiah not by verifying his teaching against Scripture and the prophecies, but always by his miracles.' Despite being rational in a retroactive sense, the interventional decision of the apostles' avant-garde was never deducible.

4. However, within the *after-effect* of the intervention, the figurative form of the previous fidelity is entirely clarified, starting from the key-points or symptoms, or in other words, the most erratic parts of the Jewish text: 'The prophecies were equivocal: they are no longer so.' The intervention wagers upon a discontinuity with the previous fidelity solely in order to install an unequivocal continuity. In this sense, it is the minority's risk of intervention at the site of the event that, in the last resort, provides a passage for *fidelity to the fidelity*.

Pascal's entire objective is quite simply that the libertine re-intervene, and within the effects of such a wager, accede to the coherency which founds him. What the apostles did against the law, the atheist nihilist (who possesses the advantage of not being engaged in any conservative pact with the world) can redo. By way of consequence, the three grand divisions of the *Pensées* may be clearly distinguished:

a. A grand *analytic* of the modern world; the best-known and most complete division, but also that most liable to cause the confusion of Pascal with one of those sour and pessimistic 'French moralists' who form the daily bread of high school philosophy. The reason being that the task is to get as close as possible to the nihilist subject and to share with him a dark and divided vision of experience. We have Pascal's 'mass line' in these texts: that through which he co-belongs to the vision of the world of the desperate and to their mockery of the meagre chronicles of the everyday imaginary. The most novel resource for these maxims recited by everybody is that of invoking the great modern ontological decision concerning the infinity of nature (cf. Meditation 13). Nobody is more possessed by the conviction that every situation is infinite than Pascal. In a spectacular overturning of the orientation of antiquity, he clearly states that it is the finite which *results*—an imaginary cut-out in which man reassures himself —and that it is the infinite which structures presentation: 'nothing can fix the finite between the two infinities which both give it form and escape it.' This convocation of the infinity of being justifies the humiliation of the *natural* being of man, because his existential finitude only ever delivers, in regard to the multiples in which being presents itself, the 'eternal despair of ever knowing their principle or their end'. It prepares the way—via the mediation of the Christ-event—for reason to be given for this humiliation via the salvation of *spiritual* being. But this spiritual being is no longer a correlate of the infinite situation of nature; it is a subject that charity links internally to divine infinity, which is of another order. Pascal thus simultaneously thinks natural infinity, the 'unfixable' relativity of the finite, and the multiple-hierarchy of orders of infinity.

b. The second division is devoted to an *exegesis* of the Christ-event, grasped in the four dimensions of interventional capacity: the evental recurrence, which is to say the examination of the Old Testament prophecies and the doctrine of their double meaning; the Christ-event, with which Pascal, in the famous 'mystery of Jesus', succeeds in identifying; the doctrine of miracles; and, the retroaction which bestows unequivocal meaning.

This exegesis is the central point of the organization of *Pensées*, because it alone founds the truth of Christianity, and because Pascal's strategy is not that of 'proving God': his interest lies rather in unifying, by a re-intervention, the libertine with the subjective figure of the Christian. Moreover, in his eyes, this procedure alone is compatible with the modern situation, and especially with the effects of the historical decision concerning the infinity of nature.

c. The third division is an *axiology*, a formal doctrine of intervention. Once the existential misery of humanity within the infinity of situations is described, and once, from the standpoint of the Christ-event, a coherent interpretation is given in which the Christian subject is tied to the *other* infinity, that of the living God, what remains to be done is to directly address the modern libertine and urge him to reintervene, following the path of Christ and the apostles. Nothing in fact, not even the interpretative illumination of the symptoms, can render this reintervention necessary. The famous text on the wager—whose real title is 'Infinite—nothing'—

indicates solely that, since the heart of the truth is that the event in which it originates is undecidable, choice, in regard to this event, is ineluctable. Once an avant-garde of intervenors—the true Christians—has decided that Christ was the reason of the world, you cannot continue as though there were no choice to be made. The veritable essence of the wager is that one must wager, it is not that once convinced of the necessity of doing so, one chooses infinity over nothing: that much is evident.

In order to prepare the ground Pascal refers directly to the absence of proof and transforms it, by a stroke of genius, into a strength concerning the crucial point: one must choose; 'it is through their lack of proofs that they [the Christians] show that they are not lacking in sense.' For sense, attributed to the intervention, is actually subtracted from the law of 'natural lights'. Between God and us 'there is an infinite chaos which divides us'. And because sense is solely legible in the absence of the rule, choosing, according to him, 'is not voluntary': the wager has *always taken place*, as true Christians attest. The libertine thus has no grounds, according to his own principles, for saying: ' . . . I do not blame them for their choice, but for making a choice at all . . . the right thing to do is not to wager.' He would have grounds for saying such if there were some examinable proofs—always suspect—and if one had to wager on their pertinence. But there are no proofs as long as the decision on the Christ-event has not been taken. The libertine is at least constrained to recognize that he is required to decide on this point.

However, the weakness of the interventional logic lies in its finding its ultimate limit here: if choice is necessary, it must be admitted that I can declare the event itself null and opt for its non-belonging to the situation. The libertine can always say: 'I am forced to wager . . . and I am made in such a way that I cannot believe.' The interventional conception of truth permits the complete refusal of its effects. The avant-garde, by its existence alone, imposes choice, but not *its* choice.

It is thus necessary to return to the consequences. Faced with the libertine, who despairs in being made such that he cannot believe, and who, beyond the logic of the wager—the very logic which I termed 'confidence in confidence' in *Théorie du sujet*—asks Christ to give him still more 'signs of his wishes', there is no longer any other response than, 'so he has: but you neglect them'. Everything can founder on the rock of nihilism: the best one can hope for is this fugitive between-two which lies between the conviction that one must choose, and the coherence of the universe of signs; the universe which we cease to neglect—once the choice is made—and which we discover to be sufficient for establishing that this choice was definitely that of truth.

There is a secular French tradition, running from Voltaire to Valéry, which regrets that such a genius as Pascal, in the end, wasted his time and strength in wishing to salvage the Christian mumbo-jumbo. If only he had solely devoted himself to mathematics and to his brilliant considerations concerning the miseries of the imagination—he excelled at such! Though I am rarely suspected of harbouring Christian zeal, I have never appreciated this motivated nostalgia for Pascal the scholar and moralist. It is too clear to me that, beyond Christianity, what is at stake here is the militant apparatus of truth: the assurance that it is in the interpretative intervention that it finds its support, that its origin is found in the event; and the will to *draw out* its dialectic and to propose to humans that they consecrate the best of themselves to the essential. What I admire more than anything in Pascal is the effort, amidst difficult circumstances, to go *against the flow*; not in the reactive sense of the term, but in order to invent the modern forms of an ancient conviction, rather than follow the way of the world, and adopt the portable scepticism that every transitional epoch resuscitates for the usage of those souls too weak to hold that there is no historical *speed* which is incompatible with the calm willingness to change the world and to universalize its form.

MEDITATION TWENTY-TWO

The Form-multiple of Intervention:
is there a being of choice?

The rejection by set theory of any being of the event is concentrated in the axiom of foundation. The immediate implication appears to be that intervention cannot be one of set theory's concepts either. However, there is a mathematical Idea in which one can recognize, without too much difficulty, the interventional *form*—its current name, quite significantly, is 'the axiom of choice'. Moreover, it was around this Idea that one of the most severe battles ever seen between mathematicians was unleashed, reaching its full fury between 1905 and 1908. Since the conflict bore on the very essence of mathematical thought, on what can be legitimately tolerated in mathematics as a constituent operation, it seemed to allow no other solution but a split. In a certain sense, this is what happened, although the small minority termed 'intuitionist' determined their own direction according to far vaster considerations than those immediately at stake in the axiom of choice. But isn't this always the case with those splits which have a real historical impact? As for the overwhelming majority who eventually came to admit the incriminated axiom, they only did so, in the final analysis, for pragmatic reasons. Over time it became clear that the said axiom, whilst implying statements quite repugnant to 'intuition-'—such as real numbers being well ordered—was indispensable to the establishment of other statements whose disappearance would have been tolerated by very few mathematicians, statements both algebraic ('every vectorial space has a base') and topological ('the product of any family of compact spaces is a compact space'). This matter was never completely cleared up: some refined their critique at the price of a sectarian and restricted vision of mathematics; and others came to an agreement in order to save the essentials and continue under the rule of 'proof' by beneficial consequences.

What is at stake in the axiom of choice? In its final form it posits that given a multiple of multiples, there *exists* a multiple composed of *a* 'representative' of each non-void multiple whose presentation is assured by the first multiple. In other words, one can 'choose' an element from each of the multiples which make up a multiple, and one can 'gather together' these chosen elements: the multiple obtained in such a manner is consistent, which is to say it exists.

In fact, the existence affirmed here is that of a *function*, one which matches up each of a set's multiples with one of its elements. Once one supposes the existence of this function, the multiple which is its result also exists: here it is sufficient to invoke the axiom of replacement. It is this function which is called the 'function of choice'. The axiom posits that for every existent multiple α, there corresponds an existent function f, which 'chooses' a representative in each of the multiples which make up α:

$$(\forall \alpha)(\exists f)[(\beta \in \alpha) \rightarrow f(\beta) \in \beta]$$

By the axiom of replacement, the function of choice guarantees the existence of a set γ composed of *a* representative of each non-void element of α. (In the void it is obvious that f cannot 'choose' anything: it would produce the void again, $f(\varnothing) = \varnothing$.) To belong to γ—which I will term a *delegation* of α—means: to be an element of an element of α that has been selected by f:

$$\delta \in \gamma \rightarrow (\exists \beta)[(\beta \in \alpha) \,\&\, f(\beta) = \delta]$$

A delegation of α makes a one-multiple out of the one-representatives of each of multiples out of which α makes a one. The 'function of choice' f selects a delegate from each multiple belonging to α, and all of these delegates constitute an existent delegation—just as every constituency in an election by majority sends a deputy to the house of representatives.

Where is the problem?

If the set α is *finite*, there is no problem: besides, this is why there is no problem with elections in which the number of constituencies is assuredly finite. However, it is foreseeable that if this set were infinite there would be problems, especially concerning what a majority might be . . .

That there is no problem in the case of α being finite can be shown by recurrence: one establishes that the function of choice *exists* within the framework of the Ideas of the multiple that have already been presented.

There is thus no need of a supplementary Idea (of an axiom) to guarantee its being.

If I now consider an infinite set, the Ideas of the multiple do not allow me to establish the general existence of a function of choice, and thus guarantee the being of a delegation. Intuitively, there is something *un-delegatable* in infinite multiplicity. The reason is that a function of choice operating upon an infinite set must simultaneously 'choose' a representative for an infinity of 'the represented'. But we know that the conceptual mastery of infinity supposes a rule of passage (Meditation 13). If such a rule allowed the *construction* of the function, we would eventually be able to guarantee, if need be, its existence: for example, as the limit of a series of partial functions. At a general level, nothing of the sort is available. It is not at all clear *how* to proceed in order to explicitly define a function which selects *one* representative from *each* multiple of an infinite multiplicity of non-void multiples. The excess of the infinite over the finite is manifested at a point at which the representation of the first—its delegation—appears to be impracticable in general, whilst that of the second, as we have seen, is deducible. From the years 1890–1892 onwards, when people began to notice that usage had *already* been made—without it being explicit—of the idea of the existence of a function of choice for infinite multiples, mathematicians such as Peano or Bettazzi objected that there was something arbitrary or unrepresentable about such usage. Betazzi had already written: 'one must choose an object arbitrarily in each of the *infinite* sets, which does not seem rigorous; unless one wishes to accept as a postulate that such a choice can be carried out—something, however, which seems ill-advised to us.' All the terms which were to organize the conflict a little later on are present in this remark: since the choice is 'arbitrary', that is, unexplainable in the form of a defined rule of passage, it requires an axiom, which, not having any intuitive value, is itself arbitrary. Sixteen years later, the great French mathematician Borel wrote that admitting 'the legitimacy of a non-denumerable infinity of choice (successive or simultaneous)' appeared to him to be 'a completely meaningless notion'.

The obstacle was in fact the following: on the one hand, admitting the *existence* of a function of choice on infinite sets is necessary for a number of useful if not fundamental theorems in algebra and analysis, to say nothing of set theory itself; in respect of which, as we shall see (Meditation 26), the axiom of choice clarifies both the question of the hierarchy of pure multiples, and the question of the connection between being-qua-being and the natural form of its presentation. On the other hand, it is completely impossible, at the general level, to *define* such a function or to indicate its realization—even when assuming that one exists. Here we find ourselves in the difficult position of having to postulate the existence of a particular type of multiple (a function) without this postulation allowing us to exhibit a single case or construct a single example. In their book on the foundations of set theory, Fraenkel, Bar-Hillel and A. Levy indicate quite clearly that the axiom of choice—the Idea which postulates the existence, for every multiple, of a function of choice—has to do solely with existence in general, and does not promise any individual realization of such an assertion of existence:

> In fact, the axiom does not assert the possibility (with scientific resources available at present or in any future) of *constructing* a selection-set [what I term a delegation]; that is to say, of providing a rule by which in each member β of a a certain member of β can be named . . . The [axiom] just maintains the *existence* of a selection-set.

The authors term this particularity of the axiom its 'purely existential character'.

However, Fraenkel, Bar-Hillel and Levy are mistaken in holding that once the 'purely existential character' of the axiom of choice is recognized, the attacks whose target it formed will cease to be convincing. They fail to appreciate that existence is a crucial question for ontology: in this respect, the axiom of choice remains an Idea which is fundamentally *different* from all those in which we have recognized the laws of the presentation of the multiple qua pure multiple.

I said that the axiom of choice could be formalized in the following manner:

$$(\forall a)(\exists f)[(\forall \beta)[(\beta \in a \ \& \ \beta \neq \varnothing) \to f(\beta) \in \beta]]$$

The writing set out in this formula would only require in addition that one stipulate that f is the particular type of multiple termed a function; this does not pose any problem.

To all appearances we recognize therein the 'legal' form of the axioms studied in Meditation 5: following the supposition of the already given existence of a multiple a, the existence of another multiple is affirmed: here, the function of choice, f. But the similarity stops there. For in the other axioms, *the type of connection between the first multiple and the second is explicit*. For example, the axiom of the powerset tells us that every element of $p(a)$ is a part of a. The result, moreover, is that the set thus obtained is *unique*. For a given a, $p(a)$ is *a* set. In a similar manner, given a defined property $\Psi(\beta)$, the set of elements of α which possess this property—whose existence is guaranteed by the axiom of separation—is *a* fixed part of α. In the case of the axiom of choice, the assertion of existence is much more evasive: the function whose existence is affirmed is submitted solely to an intrinsic condition ($f(\beta) \in \beta$), which does not allow us to think that its connection to the internal structure of the multiple α could be made explicit, nor that the function is unique. The multiple f is thus only attached to the singularity of α by very loose ties, and it is quite normal that given the existence of a particular α, one cannot, in general, 'derive' the construction of *a* determined function f. The axiom of choice juxtaposes to the existence of a multiple the possibility of its delegation, without inscribing a rule for this possibility that could be applied to the particular form of the initial multiple. The existence whose universality is affirmed by this axiom is *indistinguishable* insofar as the condition it obeys (choosing representatives) says nothing to us about the 'how' of its realization. As such, it is an existence *without-one*; because without such a realization, the function f remains suspended from an existence that we do not know how to present.

The function of choice is subtracted from the count, and although it is declared presentable (since it exists), there is no general opening for its presentation. What is at stake here is a presentability without presentation.

There is thus clearly a conceptual enigma in the axiom of choice: that of its difference from the other Ideas of the multiple, which resides in the very place in which Fraenkel, Bar-Hillel and Levy saw innocence; its 'purely existential character'. For this 'purity' is rather the impurity of a mix between the assertion of the presentable (existence) and the ineffectual character of the presentation, the subtraction from the count-as-one.

The hypothesis I advance is the following: *within ontology, the axiom of choice formalizes the predicates of intervention*. It is a question of thinking intervention *in its being*; that is, without the event—we know ontology has nothing to do with the latter. The undecidability of the event's belonging is a vanishing point that leaves a trace in the ontological Idea in which the intervention-being is inscribed: a trace which is precisely the unassignable or quasi-non-one character of the function of choice. In other words, the axiom of choice thinks the form of being of intervention devoid of any event. What it finds therein is marked by this void in the shape of the unconstructibility of the function. Ontology declares that intervention *is*, and names this being 'choice' (and the selection, which is significant, of the word 'choice' was entirely rational). However, ontology can only do this at the price of endangering the one; that is, in suspending this being from its pure generality, thereby naming, by default, the non-one of the intervention.

The axiom of choice subsequently commands strategically important results of ontology, or mathematics: such is the exercise of deductive fidelity to the interventional form fixed to the generality of its being. The acute awareness on the part of mathematicians of the singularity of the axiom of choice is indicated by their practice of marking the theorems which depend upon the latter, thus distinguishing them from those which do not. There could be no better indication of the *discernment* in which all the zeal of fidelity is realized, as we shall see: the discernment of the *effects* of the supernumerary multiple whose belonging to the situation has been decided by an intervention. Save that, in the case of ontology, what is at stake are the effects of the belonging of a supernumerary axiom to the situation of the Ideas of the multiple, an axiom which *is* intervention-in-its-being. The conflict between mathematicians at the beginning of the century was clearly—in the wider sense—a political conflict, because its stakes were those of admitting a being of intervention; something that no known procedure or intuition justified. Mathematicians—it was Zermelo on the occasion—had to intervene for intervention to be added to the Ideas of being. And, given that it is the law of intervention, they soon became divided. The very ones who—implicitly—used this axiom *de facto* (like Borel, Lebesgue, etc.) had, in their eyes, no acceptable reason to validate its belonging *de jure* to the situation of ontology. It was neither possible for them to avoid the interventional wager, nor to subsequently support its validity within the retroactive discernment of its effects. One who made great usage of the axiom, Steinitz, having established the dependency on the axiom of the theorem 'Every field allows an algebraic closure' (a genuinely decisive theorem), summarized the doctrine of the faithful in 1910 in the following manner:

> Many mathematicians are still opposed to the axiom of choice. With the growing recognition that there are mathematical questions which cannot be decided without this axiom, resistance to it should gradually disappear. On the other hand, in the interest of methodological purity, it may appear useful to avoid the above mentioned axiom as long as the

nature of the question does not require its usage. I have resolved to clearly mark its limits.

Sustaining an interventional wager, organizing oneself so as to discern its effects, not abusing the power of a supernumerary Idea and waiting on subsequent decisions for people to rally to the initial decision: such is a reasonable ethics for partisans of the axiom of choice, according to Steinitz.

However, this ethics cannot dissimulate the abruptness of the intervention on intervention that is formalized by the existence of a function of choice.

In the first place, given that the assertion of the existence of the function of choice is not accompanied by any procedure which allows, in general, the actual exhibition of one such function, what is at stake is a declaration of the existence of representatives—a delegation—without any law of representation. In this sense, the function of choice is essentially illegal in regard to what prescribes whether a multiple can be declared existent. For its existence is affirmed despite the fact that no being can come to manifest, as _a_ being, the effective and singular character of what this function subsumes. The function of choice is pronounced as a _being_ which is not really _a_ being: it is thus subtracted from the Leibnizian legislation of the count-as-one. It exists _out of the situation_.

Second; _what_ is chosen by a function of choice remains unnameable. We know that for every non-void multiple β presented by a multiple α the function selects a representative: a multiple which belongs to β, $f(\beta) \in \beta$. But the ineffectual character of the choice—the fact that one cannot in general construct and name the multiple which the function of choice is—prohibits the donation of any singularity whatsoever to the representative $f(\beta)$. _There is_ a representative, but it is impossible to know which one it is; to the point that this representative has no other identity than that of having to represent the multiple to which it belongs. Insofar as it is illegal, the function of choice is also anonymous. No proper name isolates the representative selected by the function from amongst the other presented multiples. The name of the representative is in fact a common name: 'to belong to the multiple β and to be indiscriminately selected by f'. The representative is certainly put into circulation within the situation, since I can always say that a function f exists such that, for any given β, it selects an $f(\beta)$ which belongs to β. In other words, for an existent multiple α, I can declare the existence of the set of representatives of the multiples which make up α; the delegation of α. I subsequently reason on the basis of this existence. But I cannot, in general, *designate* a single one of these representatives; the result being that the delegation itself is a multiple with indistinct contours. In particular, determining how it *differs* from another multiple (by the axiom of extensionality) is essentially impracticable, because I would have to isolate at least one element which did not figure in the other multiple and I have no guarantee of success in such an enterprise. This type of oblique in-extensionality of the delegation indicates the anonymity of principle of representatives.

It happens that in these two characteristics—illegality and anonymity—we can immediately recognize the attributes of intervention: outside the law of the count, it has to draw the anonymous name of the event from the void. In the last resort, the key to the special sense of the axiom of choice—and the controversy it provoked—lies in the following: it does *not* guarantee the existence of multiples in the situation, but rather the existence of the intervention, grasped, however, in its pure being (the type of multiple that it is) with no reference to any event. The axiom of choice is the ontological statement relative to the particular form of presentation which is interventional activity. Since it suppresses the evental historicity of the intervention, it is quite understandable that it cannot specify, in general, the one-multiple that it is (with respect of a given situation, or, ontologically, with respect to a supposed existent set). All that it can specify is a form-multiple: that of a function, whose *existence*, despite being proclaimed, is generally not realized in any *existent*. The axiom of choice tells us: 'there are some interventions.' The existential marking—that contained in the 'there are'—cannot surpass itself towards a being, because an intervention draws its singularity from *that* excess-of-one—the event—whose non-being is declared by ontology.

The consequence of this 'empty' stylization of the being of intervention is that, via an admirable overturning which manifests the power of ontology, the ultimate effect of this axiom in which anonymity and illegality give rise to the appearance of the greatest disorder—as intuited by the mathematicians—is *the very height of order*. There we have a striking ontological metaphor of the theme, now banal, according to which immense revolutionary disorders engender the most rigid state order. The axiom of choice is actually required to establish that every multiplicity allows itself to be well-ordered. In other words, every multiple allows itself to be 'enumerated' such that, at every stage of this enumeration, one can distinguish the element which comes 'after'. Since the name-numbers which are natural multiples (the ordinals) provide the measure of any enumeration—of any well-ordering—it is finally on the basis of the axiom of choice that every multiple allows itself to be thought according to a defined connection to the order of nature.

This connection to the order of nature will be demonstrated in Meditation 26. What is important here is to grasp the effects, within the ontological text, of the a-historical character which is given to the form-multiple of the intervention. If the Idea of intervention—which is to say the intervention on the being of intervention—still retains some of the 'savagery' of illegality and anonymity, and if these traits were marked enough for mathematicians—who have no concern for being and the event—to blindly quarrel over them, the order of being reclaims them all the more easily given that events, being the basis of real interventions, and undecidable in their belonging, remain outside the field of ontology; and so the pure interventional form—the function of choice—finds itself delivered, in the suspense of its existence, to the rule in which the one-multiple is pronounced in its being. This is why the apparent interruption of the law designated by this axiom immediately transforms itself, in its principal equivalents or in its consequences, into the natural rigidity of an order.

The most profound lesson delivered by the axiom of choice is therefore that it is on the basis of the *couple* of the undecidable event and the interventional decision that time and historical novelty result. Grasped in the isolated form of its pure being, intervention, despite the illegal appearance it assumes, in being ineffective, ultimately functions in the service of order, and even, as we shall see, of hierarchy.

In other words: intervention does not draw the force of a disorder, or a deregulation of structure, from its being. It draws such from its efficacy, which requires rather the initial deregulation, the initial disfunctioning of the count which is the paradoxical eventual multiple—in respect to which everything that is pronounceable of being excludes its being.

MEDITATION TWENTY-THREE
Fidelity, Connection

I call *fidelity* the set of procedures which discern, within a situation, those multiples whose existence depends upon the introduction into circulation (under the supernumerary name conferred by an intervention) of an evental multiple. In sum, a fidelity is the apparatus which separates out, within the set of presented multiples, those which depend upon an event. To be faithful is to gather together and distinguish the becoming legal of a chance.

The word 'fidelity' refers directly to the amorous relationship, but I would rather say that it is the amorous relationship which refers, at the most sensitive point of individual experience, to the dialectic of being and event, the dialectic whose temporal ordination is proposed by fidelity. Indeed, it is evident that love—what is called love—founds itself upon an intervention, and thus on a nomination, near a void summoned by an *encounter*. Marivaux's entire theatre is consecrated to the delicate question of knowing *who* intervenes, once the evident establishment—via the chance of the encounter alone—of the uneasiness of an excessive multiple has occurred. Amorous fidelity is precisely the measure to be taken, in a return to the situation whose emblem, for a long time, was marriage, of what subsists, day after day, of the connection between the regulated multiples of life and the intervention in which the one of the encounter was delivered. How, from the standpoint of the event-love, can one separate out, under the law of time, what organizes—beyond its simple occurrence—the *world* of love? Such is the employment of fidelity, and it is here that the almost impossible agreement of a man and a woman will be necessary, an agreement on the criteria which distinguish, amidst everything presented, the effects of love from the ordinary run of affairs.

Our usage of this old word thus justified, three preliminary remarks must be made.

First, a fidelity is always particular, insofar as it depends on an event. There is no general faithful disposition. Fidelity must not be understood in any way as a capacity, a subjective quality, or a virtue. Fidelity is a situated operation which depends on the examination of situations. Fidelity is a functional relation to the event.

Second, a fidelity is not a term-multiple of the situation, but, like the count-as-one, an operation, a structure. What allows us to evaluate a fidelity is its result: the count-as-one of the regulated effects of an event. Strictly speaking, fidelity *is not*. What exists are the groupings that it constitutes of one-multiples which are *marked*, in one way or another, by the evental happening.

Third, since a fidelity discerns and groups together presented multiples, it counts the parts of a situation. The result of faithful procedures is *included* in the situation. Consequently, fidelity operates in a certain sense on the terrain of the *state* of the situation. A fidelity can appear, according to the nature of its operations, like a counter-state, or a sub-state. There is always something institutional in a fidelity, if institution is understood here, in a very general manner, as what is found in the space of representation, of the state, of the count-of-the-count; as what has to do with inclusions rather than belongings.

These three remarks, however, should be immediately qualified.

First, if it is true that every fidelity is particular, it is still necessary to philosophically think the universal *form* of the procedures which constitute it. Suppose the introduction into circulation (after the interpretative retroaction of the intervention) of the signifier of an event, e_x: a procedure of fidelity consists in employing a certain criterion concerning the connection or non-connection of any particular presented multiple to this supernumerary element e_x. The particularity of a fidelity, apart from being evidently attached to the ultra-one that is the event (which is no longer anything more for it than one existing multiple amongst the others), also depends on the criterion of connection retained. In the same situation, and for the same event, different criteria can exist which define different fidelities, inasmuch as their results—multiples grouped together due to their connection with the event—do not necessarily make up identical parts ('identical' meaning here: parts held to be identical by the state of the situation). At the empirical level, we know that there are many manners of being faithful to an event: Stalinists and Trotskyists both proclaimed their fidelity to the event of October 1917, but they massacred each other. Intuitionists and set theory axiomaticians both declared themselves faithful to the event-crisis of the logical paradoxes discovered at the beginning of the twentieth century, but the mathematics they developed were completely different. The consequences drawn from the chromatic fraying of the tonal system by the serialists and then by the neo-classicists were diametrically opposed, and so it goes.

What must be retained and conceptually fixed is that a fidelity is conjointly defined by a *situation*—that in which the intervention's effects are linked together according to the law of the count—by a particular *multiple*—the event as named and introduced into circulation—and by a *rule of connection* which allows one to evaluate the dependency of any particular existing multiple with respect to the event, given that the latter's belonging to the situation has been decided by the intervention.

From this point onwards, I will write □ (to be read; 'connected for a fidelity') for the criterion by which a presented multiple is declared to depend on the event. The formal sign □, in a given situation and for a particular event, refers to diverse procedures. Our concern here is to isolate an atom, or minimal sequence, of the operation of fidelity. The writing α □ e_x designates such an atom. It indicates that the multiple α is connected to the event e_x for a fidelity. The writing $\sim(\alpha$ □ $e_x)$ is a negative atom: it indicates that, for a fidelity, the multiple α is considered as non-connected to the event e_x—this means that α is indifferent to its chance occurrence, as retroactively fixed by the intervention. A fidelity, in its real being, its non-existent-being, is a chain of positive or negative atoms, which is to say the reports that such and such existing multiples are or are not connected to the event. For reasons which will gradually become evident, and which will find their full exercise in the meditation on truth (Meditation 31), I will term *enquiry* any *finite* series of atoms of connection for a fidelity. At base, an enquiry is a given—finite—state of the faithful procedure.

These conventions lead us immediately to the second preliminary remark and the qualification it calls for. Of course, fidelity, as procedure, is not. However, at every moment, an evental fidelity can be grasped in a provisional result which is composed of effective enquiries in which it is inscribed whether or not multiples are connected to the event. It is always acceptable to posit that the *being* of a fidelity is constituted from the multiple of multiples that it has discerned, according to its own operator of connection, as being dependent on the event from which it proceeds. These multiples always make up, from the standpoint of the state, a part of the situation—a multiple whose one is a one of inclusion—the part 'connected' to the event. One could call this part of the situation the *instantaneous being* of a fidelity. We shall note, again, that this is a state concept.

However, it is quite imprecise to consider this state projection of the procedure as an ontological foundation of the fidelity itself. At any moment, the enquiries in which the provisional result of a fidelity is inscribed form a finite set. Yet this point must enter into a dialectic with the fundamental ontological decision that we studied in Meditations 13 and 14: the declaration that, in the last resort, every situation is infinite. The completion of this dialectic in all its finesse would require us to establish the sense in which every situation involves, with regard to its being, a connection with *natural* multiples. The reason is that, strictly speaking, we have wagered the infinity of being solely in regard to multiplicities whose ontological schema is an ordinal, thus natural multiplicities. Meditation 26 will establish that every pure multiple, thus every presentation, allows itself, in a precise sense, to be 'numbered' by an ordinal. For the moment it is enough for us to anticipate one consequence of this correlation, which is that almost all situations are infinite. It follows that the state projection of a fidelity—the grouping of a finite number of multiples connected to the event—is incommensurable with the situation, and thus with the fidelity itself. Thought as a non-existent procedure, a fidelity is what opens up to the *general* distinction of one-multiples presented in the situation, according to whether they are connected to the event or not. A fidelity is therefore itself, as procedure, commensurate with the situation, and so it is infinite if the situation is such. No particular multiple limits, in principle, the exercise of a fidelity. By consequence, the instantaneous state projection—which groups together multiples *already* discerned as connected to the event into a part of the situation—is only a gross approximation of what the fidelity is capable of; in truth, it is quite useless.

On the other hand, one must recognize that this infinite capacity is not effective, since at any moment its result allows itself to be projected by the state as a finite part. One must therefore say: thought in its being—or according to being—a fidelity is a finite element of the state, a representation; thought in its non-being—as operation—a fidelity is an infinite procedure adjacent to presentation. A fidelity is thus always in non-existent excess over its being. Beneath itself, it exists; beyond itself, it inexists. It can always be said that it is an almost-nothing of the state, or that it is a quasi-everything of the situation. If one determines its concept, the famous 'so we are nothing, let's be everything' [*nous ne sommes rien, soyons tout*] touches upon this point. In the last resort it means: let's be faithful to the event that we are.

To the ultra-one of the event corresponds the Two in which the intervention is resolved. To the situation, in which the consequences of the event are at stake, corresponds, for a fidelity, both the one-finite of an effective representation, and the infinity of a virtual presentation.

Hence my third preliminary remark must be restricted in its field of application. If the result of a fidelity is statist in that it gathers together multiples connected to the event, fidelity *surpasses* all the results in which its finite-being is set out (as Hegel says, cf. Meditation 15). The thought of fidelity as counter-state (or sub-state) is itself entirely approximative. Of course, fidelity touches the state, inasmuch as it is thought according to the category of result. However, grasped at the bare level of presentation, it remains this inexistent procedure for which *all* presented multiples are available: each capable of occupying the place of the a on the basis of which either $a \, \square \, e_x$ or $\sim(a \, \square \, e_x)$ will be inscribed in an effective enquiry of the faithful procedure—according to whether the criterion $\square$ determines that a maintains a marked dependence on the event or not.

In reality, there is a still more profound reason behind the subtraction from the state, or the deinstitutionalization, of the concept of fidelity. The state is an operator of the count which refers back to the fundamental ontological relations, belonging and inclusion. It guarantees the count-as-one of parts, thus of multiples which are composed of multiples presented in the situation. That a multiple, a, is counted by the state essentially signifies that every multiple β which belongs to it, is, itself, presented in the situation, and that as such a is a part of the situation: it is included in the latter. A fidelity, on the other hand, discerns the connection of presented multiples to a particular multiple, the event, which is circulated within the situation via its illegal name. The operator of connection, $\square$, has no *a priori* tie to belonging or inclusion. It is, itself, *sui generis*: particular to the fidelity, and by consequence attached to the evental singularity. Evidently, the operator of connection, which characterizes a singular fidelity, can enter into a greater or lesser proximity to the principal ontological connections of belonging and inclusion. A *typology* of fidelities would be attached to precisely such proximity. Its rule would be the following: the closer a fidelity comes, via its operator $\square$, to the ontological connections—belonging and inclusion, presentation and representation, $\in$ and $\subset$—the more statist it is. It is quite certain that positing that a multiple is only connected to an event *if it belongs to it* is the height of statist redundancy. For in all strictness the event is the sole *presented* multiple which belongs to the event within the situation: $e_x \in e_x$. If the connection of fidelity, $\square$, is identical to belonging, $\in$, what follows is that the unique *result* of the fidelity is that part of the situation which is the singleton of the event, $\{e_x\}$. In Meditation 20, I showed that it is just such a singleton which forms the constitutive element of the relation without concept of the state to the event. In passing, let's note that the *spontaneist* thesis (roughly speaking: the only ones who can take part in an event are those who made it such) is in reality the *statist* thesis. The more the operator of fidelity is distinguished from belonging to the evental multiple itself, the more we move away from this coincidence with the state of the situation. A non-institutional fidelity is a fidelity which is capable of discerning the marks of the event at the furthest point from the event itself. This time, the ultimate and trivial limit is constituted by a universal connection, which would pretend that *every* presented multiple is in fact dependent on the event. This type of fidelity, the inversion of spontaneism, is for all that still absolutely statist: its result is the situation in its entirety, that is, the maximum part numbered by the state. Such a connection, which separates nothing, which admits no negative atoms—no $\sim(a \ \square \ e_x)$ which would inscribe the indifference of a multiple to the evental irruption—founds a *dogmatic* fidelity. In the matter of fidelity to an event, the unity of being of spontaneism (only the event is connected to itself) and dogmatism (every multiple depends on the event) resides in the coincidence of their results with special functions of the state. A fidelity is definitively distinct from the state if, in some manner, it is *unassignable* to a defined function of the state; if, from the standpoint of the state, its result is a particularly nonsensical part. In Meditation 31 I will construct the ontological schema of such a result, and I will show that it is a question of a *generic* fidelity.

The degree to which fidelity is removed as far as possible from the state is thus played out, on the one hand, in the gap between its operator of connection and belonging (or inclusion), and, on the other hand, in its genuinely separational capacity. A real fidelity establishes dependencies which for the state are without concept, and it splits—via successive finite states—the situation in two, because it also discerns a mass of multiples which are indifferent to the event.

It is at this point, moreover, that one can again think fidelity as a counter-state: what it does is organize, *within* the situation, another legitimacy of inclusions. It builds, according to the infinite becoming of the finite and provisional results, a kind of *other* situation, obtained by the division in two of the primitive situation. This other situation is that of the multiples marked by the event, and it has always been tempting for a fidelity to consider the set of these multiples, in its provisional figure, as its own body, as the acting effectiveness of the event, as the *true* situation, or flock of the Faithful. This ecclesiastical version of fidelity (the connected multiples are the Church of the event) is an ontologization whose error has been pointed out. It is, nevertheless, a necessary tendency; that is, it presents another form of the tendency to be satisfied solely with the projection of a non-existent—an erring procedure—onto the statist surface upon which its results are legible.

One of the most profound questions of philosophy, and it can be recognized in very different forms throughout its history, is that of knowing in what measure the evental constitution itself—the Two of the anonymous void bordered by the site and the name circulated by the intervention—*prescribes* the type of connection by which a fidelity is regulated. Are there, for example, events, and thus interventions, which are such that the fidelity binding itself together therein is *necessarily* spontaneist or dogmatic or generic? And if such prescriptions exist, what role does the evental-site play? Is it possible that the very nature of the site influences fidelity to events pinned to its central void? The nature of Christianity has been at stake in interminable debates over whether the Christ-event determined, and in what details, the organization of the Church. Moreover, it is open knowledge to what point the entirety of these debates were affected by the question of the Jewish site of this event. In the same manner, both the democratic and the republican figure of the state have always sought to legitimate themselves on the basis of the maxims declared in the revolution of 1789. Even in pure mathematics—in the ontological situation—a point as obscure and decisive as that of knowing which branches, which parts of the discipline are active or fashionable at a particular moment is generally referred to the consequences, which have to be faithfully explored, of a theoretical mutation, itself concentrated in an event-theorem or in the irruption of a new conceptual apparatus. Philosophically speaking, the 'topos' of this question is that of Wisdom, or Ethics, in their relation to a central illumination obtained without concept at the end of an initiatory groundwork, whatever the means may be (the Platonic ascension, Cartesian doubt, the Husserlian ἐποχή . . .). It is always a matter of knowing whether one can deduce, from the evental *conversion*, the rules of the infinite fidelity.

For my part, I will call *subject* the process itself of liaison between the event (thus the intervention) and the procedure of fidelity (thus its operator of connection). In *Théorie du sujet*—in which the approach is logical and historical rather than ontological—I foreshadowed some of these current developments. One can actually recognize, in what I then termed *subjectivization*, the group of concepts attached to intervention, and, in what I named *subjective process*, the concepts attached to fidelity. However, the order of reasons is this time that of a foundation: this is why the category of subject, which in my previous book immediately followed the elucidation of dialectical logic, arrives, in the strictest sense, *last*.

Much light would be shed upon the history of philosophy if one took as one's guiding thread such a conception of the subject, at the furthest remove from any psychology—the subject as what designates the *junction* of an intervention and a rule of faithful connection. The hypothesis I propose is that even in the absence of an explicit concept of the subject, a philosophical system (except perhaps those of Aristotle and Hegel) will always possess, as its keystone, a theoretical proposition concerning this junction. In truth, this is the problem which remains for philosophy, once the famous interrogation of being-qua-being has been removed (to be treated within mathematics).

For the moment it is not possible to go any further in the investigation of the mode in which an event prescribes—or not—the manners of being faithful to it. If, however, we suppose that there is *no relation* between intervention and fidelity, we will have to admit that the operator of connection in fact emerges *as a second event*. If there is indeed a complete hiatus between e_x, circulated in the situation by the intervention, and the faithful discernment, by means of atoms of the type $(a \; \square \; e_x)$ or $\sim (a \; \square \; e_x)$, of what is connected to it, then we will have to acknowledge that, apart from the event itself, there is *another* supplement to the situation which is the operator of fidelity. And this will be all the more true the more real the fidelity is, thus the less close it is to the state, the less institutional. Indeed, the more distant the operator of connection $\square$ is from the grand onto-logical liaisons, the more it acts as an innovation, and the less the resources of the situation and its state seem capable of dissipating its sense.

MEDITATION TWENTY-FOUR
Deduction as Operator of Ontological Fidelity

In Meditation 18, I showed how ontology, the doctrine of the pure multiple, prohibits the belonging of a multiple to itself, and consequently posits that the event is not. This is the function of the axiom of foundation. As such, there cannot be any intra-ontological—intra-mathematical—problem of fidelity, since the type of 'paradoxical' multiple which schematizes the event is foreclosed from any circulation within the ontological situation. It was decided *once and for all* that such multiples would not belong to this situation. In this matter ontology remains faithful to the imperative initially formulated by Parmenides: one must turn back from any route that would authorize the pronunciation of a being of non-being.

But from the inexistence of a mathematical concept of the event one cannot infer that mathematical events do not exist either. In fact, it is the contrary which seems to be the case. The historicity of mathematics indicates that the function of temporal foundation on the part of the event and the intervention has played a major role therein. A great mathematician is, if nothing else, an intervenor on the borders of a site within the mathematical situation inasmuch as the latter is devastated, at great danger for the one, by the precarious convocation of its void. Moreover, in Meditation 20, I mentioned the clear conscience of his particular function in this regard possessed by Evariste Galois, a mathematical genius.

If no ontological statement, no theorem, bears upon an event or evaluates the proximity of its effects, if therefore onto-logy, strictly speaking, does not legislate on fidelity, it is equally true that throughout the entire historical deployment of ontology there have been event-theorems, and by consequence, the ensuing necessity of being faithful to them. This serves as a sharp reminder: ontology, the presentation of presentation, is itself presented exclusively in time as a situation, and new propositions are what periodize this presentation. Of course, the mathematical text is intrinsically egalitarian: it does not categorize propositions according to their degree of proximity or connection to a proposition-event, to a *discovery* in which a particular site in the theoretical apparatus found itself forced to make the unpresentable appear. Propositions are true or false, demonstrated or refuted, and all of them, in the last resort, speak of the pure multiple, thus of the form in which the 'there is' of being-qua-being is realized. All the same, it is a symptom—no doubt superfluous with respect to the essence of the text, yet flagrant—that the editors of mathematical works are always preoccupied with—precisely—the categorization of propositions, according to a hierarchy of importance (fundamental theorems, simple theorems, propositions, lemmas, etc.), and, often, with the indication of the occurrence of a proposition by means of its date and the mathematician who is its author. What also forms a symptom is the ferocious quarrelling over priority, in which mathematicians fight over the honour of having been the principal intervenor —although the egalitarian universalism of the text should lead to this being a matter of indifference—with respect to a particular theoretical transformation. The empirical disposition of mathematical writings thus bears a trace of the following: despite being abolished as explicit results, it is the events of ontology that determine whatever the theoretical edifice is, at any particular moment.

Like a playwright who, in the knowledge that the lines alone constitute the stable reference of a performance for the director, desperately tries to anticipate its every detail by stage instructions which describe décor, costumes, ages and gestures, the writer-mathematician, in anticipation, stages the pure text—in which being is pronounced qua being—by means of indications of precedence and origin. In these indications, in some manner, a certain *outside* of the ontological situation is evoked. These proper names, these dates, these appellations are the eventual stage instructions of a text which forecloses the event.

The central interpretation of these symptoms concerns—inside the mathematical text this time—the identification of the operators of fidelity by means of which one can evaluate whether propositions are compatible with, dependent on, or influenced by the emergence of a new theorem, a new axiomatic, or new apparatuses of investigation. The thesis that I will formulate is simple: *deduction*—which is to say the obligation of demonstration, the principle of coherency, the rule of interconnection—is the means via which, at each and every moment, ontological fidelity to the extrinsic eventness of ontology is realized. The double imperative is that a new theorem attest its coherency with the situation (thus with existing propositions)—this is the imperative of demonstration; and that the consequences drawn from it be themselves regulated by an explicit law—this is the imperative of deductive fidelity as such.

1. THE FORMAL CONCEPT OF DEDUCTION

How can this operator of fidelity whose usage has been constituted by mathematics, and by it alone, be described? From a formal perspective —which came relatively late in the day in its complete form—a deduction is a chain of explicit propositions which, starting from axioms (for us, the Ideas of the multiple, and the axioms of first-order logic with equality), results in the deduced proposition via intermediaries such that the passage from those which precede to those which follow conforms to defined rules.

The *presentation* of these rules depends on the logical vocabulary employed, but they are always identical in substance. If, for example, one admits as primitive logical signs: negation $\sim$, implication $\rightarrow$, and the universal quantifier $\forall$—these being sufficient for our needs—there are two rules:

– *Separation*, or '*modus ponens*': if I have already deduced $A \rightarrow B$, and I have also deduced A, then I consider that I have deduced B. That is, noting $\vdash$ the fact that I have already demonstrated a proposition:

$\vdash A \rightarrow B$
$\vdash A$
_____
$\vdash B$

– *Generalization*. If α is a variable, and I have deduced a proposition of the type $B[\alpha]$ in which α is not quantified in B, I then consider that I have deduced $(\forall \alpha)B$.

Modus ponens corresponds to the 'intuitive' idea of implication: if A entails B and A is 'true', B must also be true.

Generalization also corresponds to the 'intuitive' idea of the universality of a proposition: if A is true for *any α in particular* (because α is a variable), this is because it is true for every α.

The extreme poverty of these rules contrasts sharply with the richness and complexity of the universe of mathematical demonstrations. But it is, after all, in conformity with the ontological essence of this universe that *the difficulty of fidelity lies in its exercise and not in its criterion.* The multiples presented by ontology are all woven from the void, *qualitatively* they are quite indistinct. Thus, the discernment of the deductive connection between a proposition which concerns them to another proposition could not bring extremely numerous and heterogeneous *laws* into play. On the other hand, effectively distinguishing amongst these qualitative proximities demands extreme finesse and much experience.

This still very formal perspective can be radicalized. Since the 'object' of mathematics is being-qua-being, one can expect a quite exceptional uniformity amongst the propositions which constitute its presentation. The apparent proliferation of conceptual apparatuses and theorems must in the end refer back to some indifference, the background of which would be the foundational function of the void. Deductive fidelity, which incorporates new propositions into the warp and weft of the general edifice, is definitely marked by *monotony,* once the presentative diversity of multiples is purified to the point of retaining solely from the multiple its multiplicity. Empirically speaking, moreover, it is obvious in mathematical practice that the complexity and subtlety of demonstrations can be broken up into brief sequences, and once these sequences are laid out, they reveal their repetitiveness; it becomes noticeable that they use a few 'tricks' alone drawn from a very restricted stock. The entire art lies in the general organization, in demonstrative *strategy.* Tactics, on the other hand, are rigid and almost skeletal. Besides, great mathematicians often 'step right over' the detail, and—visionaries of the event—head straight for the general conceptual apparatus, leaving the calculations to the disciples. This is particularly obvious amongst intervenors when what they introduce into circulation is exploited or even proves problematic for a long time after them, such as Fermat, Desargues, Galois or Riemann.

The disappointing formal truth is that all mathematical propositions, once demonstrated within the axiomatic framework, are, in respect of deductive syntax, *equivalent.* Amongst the purely logical axioms which support the edifice, there is indeed the tautology: $A \rightarrow (B \rightarrow A)$, an old scholastic adage which posits that a true proposition is entailed by any proposition, *ex quodlibet sequitur verum*, such that if you have the proposition *A* it follows that you also have the proposition $(B \rightarrow A)$, where *B* is any proposition whatsoever.

Now suppose that you have deduced both proposition *A* and proposition *B*. From *B* and the tautology $B \rightarrow (A \rightarrow B)$, you can also draw $(A \rightarrow B)$. But if $(B \rightarrow A)$ and $(A \rightarrow B)$ are both true, then this is because *A* is equivalent to *B*: $A \leftrightarrow B$.

This equivalence is a formal marker of the monotony of ontological fidelity. In the last resort, this monotony is founded upon the latent uniformity of those multiples that the fidelity evaluates—*via* propositions—in terms of their connection to the inventive irruption.

By no means, however, does this barren formal identity of all propositions of ontology stand in the way of subtle hierarchies, or even, in the end (through wily detours), of their fundamental non-equivalence.

It must be understood that the strategic resonance of demonstrative fidelity maintains its tactical rigidity solely as a formal guarantee, and that the real text only rarely rejoins it. Just as the strict writing of ontology, founded on the sign of belonging alone, is merely the law in which a forgetful fecundity takes flight, so logical formalism and its two operators of faithful connection—*modus ponens* and generalization—rapidly make way for procedures of identification and inference whose range and consequences are vast. I shall examine two of these procedures in order to test the gap, particular to ontology, between the uniformity of equivalences and the audacity of inferences: the usage of hypotheses, and reasoning by the absurd.

2. REASONING VIA HYPOTHESIS

Any student of mathematics knows that in order to demonstrate a proposition of the type '*A* implies *B*', one can proceed as follows: one supposes that *A* is true and one deduces *B* from it. Note, by the way, that a proposition '$A \rightarrow B$' does not take a position on the truth of *A* nor on the truth of *B*. It solely prescribes the connection between *A* and *B* whereby one implies the other. As such, one can demonstrate, in set theory, the proposition; 'If there exists a Ramsey cardinal (a type of 'very large' multiple), then the set of real constructible numbers (on 'constructible' see Meditation 29) is denumerable (that is, it belongs to the smallest type of infinity, ω_0, see Meditation 14).' However, the proposition 'there exists a

Ramsey cardinal' cannot, itself, be demonstrated; or at the very least it cannot be inferred from the Ideas of the multiple such as I have presented them. This theorem, demonstrated by Rowbottom in 1970—here I give the evental indexes—thus inscribes an implication, and simultaneously leaves in suspense the two ontological questions whose connection it secures: 'Does a Ramsey cardinal exist?', and, 'Is the set of real constructible numbers denumerable?'

In what measure do the initial operators of fidelity—*modus ponens* and generalization—authorize us to 'make the hypothesis' of a proposition A in order to draw from it the consequence B, and to conclude in the truth of the implication $A \rightarrow B$, which, as I have just said, in no way confirms the hypothesis of the truth of A? Have we not thus illegitimately *passed via non-being*, in the form of an assertion, A, which could quite easily be false, and yet whose truth we have maintained? We shall come across this problem again—that of the mediation of the false in the faithful establishment of a true connection—but in a more acute form, in the examination of reasoning by the absurd. To my eyes, it signals the gap between the strict *law* of presentation of ontological propositions—the monotonous equivalence of true propositions—and the strategies of fidelity which build effective and temporally assignable connections between these propositions from the standpoint of the event and the intervention; that is, from the standpoint of what is put into circulation, at the weak points of the previous apparatus, by great mathematicians.

Of course, however visibly and strategically distinct the *long-range* connections might be from the tactical monotony of the atoms of inference (*modus ponens* and generalization), they must, in a certain sense, become reconciled to them, because the law is the law. It is quite clear here that ontological fidelity, however inventive it may be, cannot, in evaluating connections, *break* with the count-as-one and turn itself into an exception to structure. In respect of the latter, it is rather a diagonal, an extreme loosening, an unrecognizable abbreviation.

For example, what does it mean that one can 'make the hypothesis' that a proposition A is true? This amounts to saying that given the situation (the axioms of the theory)—call the latter T—and its rules of deduction, we temporarily place ourselves in the fictive situation whose axioms are those of T plus the proposition A. Let's call this fictive situation $T + A$. The rules of deduction remaining unchanged, we deduce, within the situation $T + A$, the proposition B. Nothing is at stake so far but the normal mechanical run of things, because the rules are fixed. We are solely allowing ourselves the *supplement* which is the usage, within the demonstrative sequence, of the 'axiom' *A*.

It is here that a theorem of logic intervenes, called the 'theorem of deduction', whose strategic value I pointed out eighteen years ago in *Le concept de modèle*. Basically, this theorem states that once the normal purely logical axioms are admitted, and the rules of deduction which I mentioned, we have the following situation: if a proposition *B* is deducible in the theory *T* + *A*, then the proposition (*A* → *B*) is deducible in the theory *T*. This is so regardless of what the fictive theory *T* + *A* *is worth*; it could quite well be incoherent. This is why I can 'make the hypothesis' of the truth of *A*, which is to say *supplement* the situation by the fiction of a theory in which *A* is an axiom: in return I am guaranteed that in the 'true' situation, that commanded by the axioms of *T*—the Ideas of the multiple—the proposition *A* implies any proposition *B* deducible in the fictive situation.

One of the most powerful resources of ontological fidelity is thus found in the capacity to move to adjacent fictive situations, obtained by axiomatic supplementation. However, it is clear that once the proposition (*A* → *B*) is inscribed as a faithful consequence of the situation's axioms, nothing will remain of the mediating fiction. In order to evaluate propositions, the mathematician never ceases to haunt fallacious or incoherent universes. No doubt the mathematician spends more time in such places than on the equal plain of propositions whose truth, with respect to being-qua-being, renders them equivalent: yet the mathematician only does so in order to enlarge still further the surface of this plain.

The theorem of deduction also permits one possible identification of what an evental site is in mathematics. Let's agree that a proposition is singular, or on the edge of the void, if, within a historically structured mathematical situation, it implies many other significant propositions, yet it cannot itself be deduced from the axioms which organize the situation. In short, this proposition is presented in its consequences, but no faithful discernment manages to connect it. Say that *A* is this proposition: one can deduce all kinds of propositions of the type *A* → *B*, but not *A* itself. Note that in the fictive situation *T* + *A* all of these propositions *B* would be deduced. That is, since *A* is an axiom of *T* + *A*, and we have *A* → *B*, *modus ponens* authorizes the deduction of *B* in *T* + *A*. In the same manner, everything which is implied by *B* in *T* + *A* would also be deduced therein. For if we have *B* → *C*, since *B* is deduced, we also have *C*, again due to *modus ponens*. But the theorem of deduction guarantees for us that if such a C is deduced in $T + A$, the proposition $A \rightarrow C$ is deducible in T. Consequently, the fictive theory $T + A$ disposes of a considerable supplementary resource of propositions of the type $A \rightarrow C$, in which C is a consequence, in $T + A$, of a proposition B such that $A \rightarrow B$ has itself been demonstrated in T. We can see how the proposition A appears like a kind of source, saturated with possible consequences, in the shape of propositions of the type $A \rightarrow x$ which are deducible in T.

An event, named by an intervention, is then, at the theoretical site indexed by the proposition A, a new apparatus, demonstrative or axiomatic, such that A is henceforth clearly admissible as a proposition of the *situation*. Thus, it is in fact a protocol from which it is *decided* that the proposition A—suspended until then between its non-deducibility and the extent of its effects—belongs to the ontological situation. The immediate result, due to *modus ponens*, is that all the B's and all the C's implied by that proposition A also become part of the situation. An intervention is signalled, and this can be seen in every real mathematical invention, by a brutal *outpouring* of new results, which were all suspended, or frozen, in an implicative form whose components could not be *separated*. These moments of fidelity are paroxysmic: deductions are made without cease, separations are made, and connections are found which were completely incalculable within the previous state of affairs. This is because a substitution has been made: in place of the fictive—and sometimes quite simply unnoticed—situation in which A was only a hypothesis, we now have an evental reworking of the effective situation, such that A has been decided within it.

3. REASONING VIA THE ABSURD

Here again, and without thinking, the apprentice postulates that in order to prove the truth of A, one supposes that of non-A, and that, drawing from this supposition some absurdity, some contradiction with truths that have already been established, one concludes that it is definitely A which is required.

In its apparent form, the schema of reasoning via the absurd—or apagogic reasoning—is identical to that of hypothetical reasoning: I install myself in the fictive situation obtained by the addition of the 'axiom' non-A, and within this situation I deduce propositions. However, the ultimate resource behind this artifice and its faithful function of connection is different, and we know that apagogic reasoning was discussed at length by the intuitionist school before being categorically rejected. What lies at the heart of such resistance? It is that when reasoning via the absurd, one supposes that it is the same thing to demonstrate the proposition A and to demonstrate the negation of the negation of A. However, the strict equivalence of A and $\sim\sim A$—which I hold to be directly linked to what is at stake in mathematics, being-qua-being (and not sensible time)—is so far removed from our dialectical experience, from everything proclaimed by history and life, that ontology is simultaneously vulnerable in this point to the empiricist and to the speculative critique. This equivalence is unacceptable for both Hume and Hegel. Let's examine the details.

Take the proposition A: say that I want to establish the deductive connection—and thus, finally, the equivalence—between it and propositions already established within the situation. I install myself in the fictive situation $T + \sim A$. The strategy is to deduce a proposition B in the latter which formally contradicts a proposition already deduced in T. That is to say, I obtain in $T + \sim A$ a B such that its negation, $\sim B$, is already proven in T. I will hence conclude that A is deducible in T (it is said: I will *reject* the hypothesis $\sim A$, in favour of A). But why?

If, in $T + \sim A$, I deduce the proposition B, the theorem of deduction assures me that the proposition $\sim A \rightarrow B$ is deducible in T. On this point there is no difference from the case of hypothetical reasoning.

However, a logical axiom—again an old scholastic adage—termed *contraposition* affirms that if a proposition C entails a proposition D, I cannot deny D without denying the C which entails it. Hence the following tautology:

$$(C \rightarrow D) \rightarrow (\sim D \rightarrow \sim C)$$

Applied to the proposition $(\sim A \rightarrow B)$, which I obtained in T on the basis of the fictive situation $T + \sim A$ and the theorem of deduction, this scholastic tautology gives:

$$(\sim A \rightarrow B) \rightarrow (\sim B \rightarrow \sim\sim A)$$

If $(\sim A \rightarrow B)$ is deduced, the result, by *modus ponens*, is that $(\sim B \rightarrow \sim\sim A)$ is deduced. Now remember that B, deduced in $(T + \sim A)$, is explicitly contradictory with the proposition $\sim B$ which is deduced in T. But if $\sim B$ is deduced in T, and so is $(\sim B \rightarrow \sim\sim A)$, then, by *modus ponens*, $\sim\sim A$ is a theorem of T. This is recapitulated in Table 2:

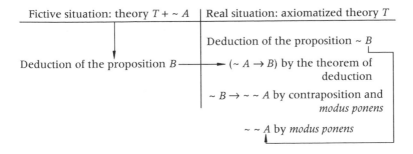

Fictive situation: theory $T + \sim A$	Real situation: axiomatized theory T
Deduction of the proposition B	Deduction of the proposition $\sim B$
	$(\sim A \to B)$ by the theorem of deduction
	$\sim B \to \sim \sim A$ by contraposition and *modus ponens*
	$\sim \sim A$ by *modus ponens*

Strictly speaking, the procedure delivers the following result: if, from the supplementary hypothesis $\sim A$, I deduce a proposition which is incoherent with regard to some other proposition that has already been established, then the negation of the negation of A is deducible. To conclude in the deducibility of A, a little extra is necessary—for example, the implication $\sim\sim A \to A$—which the intuitionists refuse without fail. For them, reasoning via the absurd does not permit one to conclude beyond the truth of $\sim\sim A$, which is a proposition of the situation quite distinct from the proposition A. Here two regimes of fidelity bifurcate: in itself, this is compatible with the abstract theory of fidelity; it is not guaranteed that the event prescribes the criterion of connection. In classical logic, the substitution of the proposition A for the proposition $\sim\sim A$ is absolutely legitimate: for an intuitionist it is not.

My conviction on this point is that intuitionism has mistaken the route in trying to apply back onto ontology criteria of connection which *come from elsewhere*, and especially from a doctrine of mentally effective operations. In particular, intuitionism is a prisoner of the empiricist and illusory representation of mathematical *objects*. However complex a mathematical proposition might be, if it is an affirmative proposition it comes down to declaring the existence of a pure form of the multiple. All the 'objects' of mathematical thought—structures, relations, functions, etc.—are nothing in the last instance but species of the multiple. The famous mathematical 'intuition' can do no more than control, *via* propositions, the connection-multiples between multiples. Consequently, if we consider a proposition A (supposed affirmative) in its onto-logical essence, even if it envelops the appearance of very singular relations and objects, it turns out to have no other meaning than that of positing that a particular multiple can be effectively postulated as existent, within the frame constituted by the Ideas of the multiple, including the existential assertions relative to the name of the void and to the limit-ordinals (to infinite multiples). Even the implicative propositions belong, in the last resort, to such a species. As such, Rowbottom's theorem, mentioned above, amounts to stating that in the situation—possibly fictive—constituted by the Ideas of the multiple supplemented by the proposition 'there exists a Ramsey cardinal', there exists a multiple which is a one-to-one correspondence between the real constructible numbers and the ordinal ω_0 (see Meditations 26 and 29 on these concepts). Such a correspondence, being a function, and thus a particular type of relation, *is* a multiple.

Now, the negation of a proposition which affirms the existence of a multiple is a declaration of non-existence. The entire question concerning the double negation $\sim\sim A$ thus comes down to knowing what it could mean to deny that a multiple—in the ontological sense—does not exist. We will agree that it is reasonable to think that this means that it exists, if it is admitted that *ontology attributes no other property to multiples than existence*, because any 'property' is itself a multiple. We will therefore not be able to determine, 'between' non-existence and existence, any specific intermediary property, which would provide a foundation for the gap between the negation of non-existence and existence. For this supposed property would have to be presented, in turn, as an existent multiple, save if it were non-existent. It is thus on the basis of the ontological vocation of mathematics that one can infer, in my view, the legitimacy of the equivalence between affirmation and double negation, between A and $\sim\sim A$, and by consequence, the conclusiveness of reasoning via the absurd.

Even better: I consider, in agreement with Szabo, the historian of mathematics, that the use of apagogic reasoning signals the originary belonging of mathematical deductive fidelity to ontological concerns. Szabo remarks that a typical form of reasoning by the absurd can be found in Parmenides with regard to being and non-being, and he uses this as an argument for placing deducible mathematics within an Eleatic filiation. Whatever the historical connection may be, the conceptual connection is convincing. For it is definitely due to it treating being-qua-being that authorization is drawn in mathematics for the use of this audacious form of fidelity that is apagogic deduction. If the *determination* of the referent was carried the slightest bit further, it would immediately force us to admit that it is not legitimate to identify affirmation and the negation of negation. Its pure multiple-indeterminateness alone allows this criterion of connection between propositions to be maintained.

What strikes me, in reasoning via the absurd, is rather the *adventurous* character of this procedure of fidelity, its freedom, the extreme uncertainty of this criterion of connection. In simple hypothetical reasoning, the strategic goal is clearly fixed. If you want to demonstrate a proposition of the type $A \rightarrow B$, you install yourself in the adjacent situation $T + A$, and *you attempt to demonstrate B*. You know where you are going, even if knowing *how* to get there is not necessarily trivial. Moreover, it is quite possible that $T + A$, although momentarily fictive, is a coherent apparatus. There is not the same obligation to infidelity, constituted by pseudo-deductive connections in an incoherent universe, a universe in which *any* proposition is deducible. On the contrary, it is just such an obligation that one voluntarily assumes in the case of reasoning via the absurd. For if you suppose that the proposition A is true—that it is discernible by deductive fidelity as a consequence of T's previous theorems—then the situation $T + \sim A$ is certainly incoherent, because A is inferred on the basis of T, and so this situation contains both A and $\sim A$. Yet it is in this situation that you install yourself. Once there, what is it that you hope to deduce? A proposition contradicting one of those that you have established. But which one? No matter, any proposition will do. The goal of the exercise is thus indistinct, and it is quite possible that you will have to search blindly, for a long time, before a contradiction turns up from which the truth of the proposition A can be inferred.

There is, no doubt, an important difference between constructive reasoning and non-constructive or apagogic reasoning. The first proceeds from deduced propositions via deduced propositions towards the proposition that it has set out to establish. It thus tests faithful connections without subtracting itself from the laws of presentation. The second immediately installs the fiction of a situation that it supposes incoherent until that incoherency manifests itself in the random occurrence of a proposition which contradicts an already established result. This difference is due less to its employment of double negation than to its strategic quality, which consists, on the one hand, of an assurance and a prudence internal to order, and, on the other hand, of an adventurous peregrination through disorder. Let's not underestimate the paradox that lies in rigorously *deducing*, thus using faithful tactics of connection between propositions, in the very place in which you suppose, via the hypothesis $\sim A$, the reign of incoherency, which is to say the vanity of such tactics. The pedantic exercise of a rule has no other use here than that of establishing—through the *encounter* with a singular contradiction—its own total inanity. This combination of the zeal of fidelity with the chance of the encounter, of the precision of the rule with the awareness of the nullity of its place of exercise, is the most striking characteristic of the procedure. Reasoning via the absurd is the most *militant* of all the conceptual procedures of the science of being-qua-being.

4. TRIPLE DETERMINATION OF DEDUCTIVE FIDELITY

That deduction—which consists in locating a *restricted* connection between propositions, and in the end their syntactic equivalence—be the criterion of ontological fidelity; this much, in a certain sense, could be proved *a priori*. Once these propositions all bear upon presentation in general, and envisage the multiple solely in its pure multiplicity—thus in its void armature—then no other rule appears to be available for the 'proximity' of new propositions and already established propositions, save that of checking their equivalence. When a proposition affirms that a pure multiple exists, it is guaranteed that this existence, being that of a *resource of being*, cannot be secured at the price of the non-existence of another of these resources, whose existence has been affirmed or deduced. Being, qua being, does not proliferate in onto-logical discourse to the detriment of itself, for it is as indifferent to life as it is to death. It has to *be* equally throughout the entire presentational resource of pure multiples: there can be no declaration of the existence of a multiple if it is not equivalent to the existence of every other multiple.

The upshot of all this is that ontological fidelity—which remains external to ontology itself, because it concerns events *of the discourse* on being and not events *of being*, and which is thus, in a certain sense, only a quasi-fidelity—receives each of the three possible determinations of any fidelity. I laid out the doctrine of these determinations in Meditation 23.

– In one sense, ontological fidelity or deductive fidelity is *dogmatic*. If, indeed, its criterion of connection is demonstrative coherency, then it is to *every* already established proposition that a new proposition is connected. If it contradicts any single one of them, its supposition must be rejected. In this manner, the name of the event ('Rowbottom's theorem') is declared to have subjected to its dependency every term of the situation: every proposition of the discourse.

– In a second sense, however, ontological fidelity is *spontaneist*. What in fact characterizes a new theorem cannot be its syntactic equivalence to any demonstrated proposition. If the latter were so, anyone—any *machine* —producing a deducible proposition, both interminable and vain, would be credited with the status of an intervenor, and we would no longer know what a mathematician was. It is rather the absolute singularity of a proposition, its irreducible power, the manner in which it, and it alone, subordinates previously disparate parts of the discourse to itself that constitutes it as the circulating name of an event of ontology. Thus conceived, ontological fidelity attempts rather to show that a great number of propositions, insofar as they are merely the new theorem's secondary consequences, will not in truth be able to claim *conceptual* equivalence to it, even if they do possess *formal* equivalence. Consequently, the 'great theorem', keystone of an entire theoretical apparatus, is only truly connected to itself. This is what will be signalled from the exterior by its attachment to the proper name of the mathematician-intervenor who introduced it into circulation, in the required form of its proof.

– Finally, in a third sense, ontological fidelity is *generic*. For what it attempts to weave, on the basis of inventions, reworkings, calculations, and in the adventurous use of the absurd, are general and polymorphous propositions situated at the junction of several branches, and whose status is that of concentrating within themselves, in a diagonal to established specialities (algebra, topology, etc.), *mathematicity* itself. To a brilliant, subtle but very singular result, the mathematician will prefer an innovative open conception, a conceptual androgyne, on the basis of which its subsumption of all sorts of externally disparate propositions may be tested—not via the game of formal equivalence, but because it, in itself, is a guardian of the variance of being, of its prodigality in forms of the pure multiple. Nor should it be a question of one of those propositions whose extension is certainly immense, but uniquely because they possess the poverty of first principles, of the Ideas of the multiple, like the axioms of set theory. Thus, it will *also* be necessary that these propositions, however polymorphic, be not connected to many others, and that they accumulate a separative force with their power of generality. This is precisely what places the 'great theorems'—name-proofs of there having been, in some site of the discourse, a convocation of its possible silence—in a general or generic position with regard to what deductive fidelity explores and distinguishes amongst their effects in the mathematical situation.

This triple determination makes deductive fidelity into the equivocal *paradigm* of all fidelity: proofs of love, ethical rigour, the coherency of a work of art, the accordance of a politics with the principles which it claims as its own—the exigency of such a fidelity is propagated everywhere: to be commensurable to the strictly implacable fidelity that rules the discourse on being itself. But one can only fail to satisfy such an exigency; because the fact that it is this type of connection which is maintained in the mathematical text—despite it being indifferent to the matter—is something which proceeds directly from being itself. What one must be able to require of oneself, at the right time, is rather that capacity for adventure to which ontology testifies, in the heart of its transparent rationality, by its recourse to the procedure of the absurd; a detour in which the extension of their solidity may be restituted to the equivalences: 'He shatters his own happiness, his excess of happiness, and to the Element which magnified it, he rends, but purer, what he possessed.'

MEDITATION TWENTY-FIVE
Hölderlin

> 'And fidelity has not been given to our soul as a vain present /
> And not for nothing was in / Our souls loyalty fixed'
> 'At the Source of the Danube'

The torment proper to Hölderlin, but also what founds the ultimate serenity, the *innocence* of his poems, is that the appropriation of Presence is mediated by an event, by a paradoxical flight from the site to itself. For Hölderlin, the generic name of the site in which the event occurs is the homeland: 'And no wonder! Your homeland and soil you are walking, / What you seek, it is near, now comes to meet you halfway.' The homeland is the site haunted by the poet, and we know the Heideggerean fortune of the maxim 'poetically man dwells, always, on earth.'

I take this occasion to declare that, evidently, any exegesis of Hölderlin is henceforth dependent on that of Heidegger. The exegesis I propose here, in respect to a particular point, forms, with the orientations fixed by the master, a sort of braid. There are few differences in emphasis to be found in it.

There is a paradox of the homeland, in Hölderlin's sense, a paradox which makes an evental-site out of it. It so happens that conformity to the presentation of the site—what Hölderlin calls 'learning to make free use of what's native and national in us'—supposes that we share in its devastation by departure and wandering. Just as great rivers have, as their being, the impetuous breaking apart of any obstacle to their flight towards the plain, and just as the site of their source is thus the void—from which we are separated solely by the excess-of-one of their élan ('Enigma, born from a pure jetting forth!')—so the homeland is first what one leaves, not because one separates oneself from it, but, on the contrary, through that superior fidelity which lies in understanding that the very *being* of the homeland is that of escaping. In the poem 'The Journey' Hölderlin indicates that his homeland, 'Most happy Swabia', proposes itself as site because there one hears 'the source sound', and 'The snowy summit drenches the earth / With purest water.' This sign of a fluvial escape is precisely what links one to the homeland. It is from residing 'close to its origin' that a 'native loyalty' explicitly proceeds. Fidelity to the site is therefore, in essence, fidelity to the event through which the site—being both source of itself and escape from itself—is migration, wandering, and the immediate proximity of the faraway. When—again in 'The Journey' —just after having evoked his 'native loyalty' to the Swabian homeland Hölderlin cries out: 'But I am bound for the Caucasus!', this Promethean irruption, far from contradicting the fidelity, is its effective procedure; just as the Rhine, in being impatient to leave—'His regal soul drove him on towards Asia'—realizes in fact its own appropriateness to Germany and to the pacific and paternal foundation of its cities.

Under these conditions, saying that the poet, by his departure and his blind voyage—blind because the freedom of the departure-event, for those demi-gods that are poets and rivers, consists in such a *fault*, 'in their soul quite naïve, not knowing *where* they are going'—is faithful to the homeland, that he takes its measure, is the same as saying that the homeland has remained faithful to the wanderer, in its maintenance of the very site from which he escaped from himself. In the poem which has this title—'The Wanderer'—it is written 'Loyal you were, and loyal remain to the fugitive even / Kindly as ever you were, heaven of the homeland, take me back.' But reciprocally, in 'The Source of the Danube', it is with respect to the poet that 'not for nothing was in / Our souls loyalty fixed'; moreover, it is the poet who guards the 'treasure itself'. Site and intervenor, homeland and poet exchange in the 'original jetting forth' of the event their rules of fidelity, and each is thereby disposed to welcome the other in this movement of return in which thing is measured to thing—when 'window-panes glitter with gold', and 'There I'm received by the house and the garden's secretive halflight / Where together with plants fondly my father reared me'—measuring the distance at which each thing maintains itself from the shadow brought over it by its essential departure.

One can, of course, marvel over this distance being in truth a primitive connection: 'Yes, the ancient is still there! It thrives and grows ripe, but no creature / Living and loving there ever abandons its fidelity.' But at a more profound level, there is a joy in thinking that one offers fidelity; that instructed by the nearby via the practice, shared with it, of the faraway, towards which it was source, one forever evaluates the veritable essence of what is there: 'Oh light of youth, oh joy! You are the one / of ancient times, but what purer spirit you pour forth, / Golden fountain welling up from this consecration!' Voyaging with the departure itself, intervenor struck by the god, the poet brings back to the site the sense of its proximity: 'Deathless Gods! . . . / Out of you originated, with you I have also voyaged, / You, the joyous ones, you, filled with more knowledge, I bring back. / Therefore pass to me now the cup that is filled, overflowing / With the wine from those grapes grown on warm hills of the Rhine.'

As a central category of Hölderlin's poetry, fidelity thus designates the poetic capacity to inhabit the site at the point of return. It is the science acquired via proximity to the fluvial, native, furious uprooting—in which the interpreter had to risk himself—from what constitutes the site, from everything which composes its tranquil light. It names, at the most placid point of Germany, drawn from the void of this very placidity, the foreign, wandering, 'Caucasian' vocation which is its paradoxical event.

What authorizes the poet to interpret Germany in such a way, in accordance not with its disposition but with its event—that is, to think the Rhine, this 'slow voyage / Across the German lands', according to its imploring, angry source—is a faithful diagonal traced from *another* event: the Greek event.

Hölderlin was certainly not the only German thinker to believe that thinking Germany on the basis of the unformed and the source requires a fidelity to the Greek formation—perhaps still further to that crucial event that was its disappearance, the flight of the Gods. What must be understood is that for him the Greek relation between the event—the savagery of the pure multiple, which he calls Asia—and the regulated closure of the site is the exact inverse of the German relation.

In texts which have seen much commentary, Hölderlin expresses the assymmetry between Greece and Germany with extreme precision. Everything is said when he writes: 'the clarity of exposition is as primordially natural to us as fire from the sky for the Greeks.' The originary and apparent disposition of the Greek world is Caucasian, unformed, violent, and the closed beauty of the Temple is conquered by an *excess of form*. On the other hand, the visible disposition of Germany is the policed form, flat and serene, and what must be conquered is the Asiatic event, towards which the Rhine would go, and whose artistic stylization is 'sacred pathos'. The poetic intervenor is not on the same *border* in Greece as in Germany: sworn to name the illegal and foundational event as luminous closure with the Greeks, the poet is also sworn, with the Germans, to deploy the measure of a furious Asiatic irruption *towards* the homeland's calm welcome. Consequently, for a Greek, interpretation is what is complex, whilst for a German the stumbling point is fidelity. The poet will be all the better armed for the exercise of a German fidelity if he has discerned and practised the fate of Greek interpretation: however brilliant it may have been, it was not able to keep the Gods; it assigned them to too strict an enclosure, to the vulnerability of an excess of form.

A fidelity to the Greeks, which is disposed *towards* intervention on the borders of the German site, does not prohibit but rather requires that one know how to discern, amongst the effects of the Greeks' formal excellence, the denial of a foundational excess and the forgetting of the Asiatic event. It thus requires that one be more faithful to the evental essence of the Greek truth than the Greek artists themselves were able to be. This is why Hölderlin exercises a superior fidelity by translating Sophocles without subjecting himself to the law of literary exactitude: 'By national conformity and due to certain faults which it has always been able to accommodate, Greek art is foreign to us; I hope to give the public an idea of it which is more lively than the usual, by accenting the oriental character that it always disowned and by rectifying, where necessary, its aesthetic faults.' Greece had the force to *place* the gods, Germany must have the force to *maintain* them, once it is ensured, by the intervention of a poetic Return, that they will descend upon the Earth again.

The diagonal of fidelity upon which the poet founds his intervention into the German site is thus the ability to distinguish, in the Greek world, between what is connected to the primordial event, to the Asiatic power of the gods, and what is merely the gold dust, elegant but vain, of legend. When 'Only as from a funeral pyre henceforth / A golden smoke, the legend of it, drifts / And glimmers on around our doubting heads / And no one knows what's happening to him', one must resort to the norm of fidelity whose keeper, guardian of the Greek event on the borders of the German site, is the poet. For 'good / indeed are the legends, for of what is the most high / they are a memory, but still is needed / The one who will decipher their sacred message.'

Here again we find the connection between interventional capacity and fidelity to *another* event that I remarked in Pascal with regard to the deciphering of the double meaning of the prophecies. The poet will be able to name the German source, and then, on its basis, establish the rule of fidelity in which the peace of the proximity of a homeland is won; insofar as he has found the key to the double meaning of the Greek world, insofar as he is already a faithful decryptor of sacred legends. On occasion, Hölderlin is quite close to a prophetic conception of this bond, and thereby exposed to the danger of imagining that Germany *fulfils* the Greek promise. He willingly evokes 'the ancient / Sign handed down', which 'far, striking, creating, rings out!' Still more dangerously, he becomes elated with the thought: 'What of the children of God was foretold in the songs of the ancients, / Look, we are it, *ourselves* . . . / Strictly it has come true, fulfilled as in men by a marvel.' But this is only the exploration of a risk, an excess of the poetic procedure, because the poet very quickly declares the contrary: ' . . . Nothing, despite what happens, nothing has the force / to act, for we are heartless.' Hölderlin always maintains the measure of his proper function: companion, instructed by the fidelity (in the Greek double sense) of the Germanic event, he attempts to unfold, in return, its foundational rule, its sustainable fidelity, the 'celebration of peace'.

I would like to show how these significations are bound together in a group of isolated lines. It is still a matter of debate amongst experts whether these lines should be attached to the hymn 'Mnemosyne' or regarded as independent, but little matter. So:

Ripe are, dipped in fire, cooked
The fruits and tried on the earth, and it is law,
Prophetic, that all must insinuate within
Like serpents, dreaming on
The mounds of heaven. And much
As on the shoulders a
Load of wood must be
Retained. But evil are
The paths, for crookedly
Like steeds go the imprisoned
Elements and ancient laws
Of the earth. And always
There is a yearning that seeks the unbound. But much
Must be retained. And fidelity is needed.

Forward, however, and back we will
Not look. Be lulled and rocked as
On a swaying skiff of the sea.

The site is described at the summit of its maturity, passed through the fire of Presence. The signs, ordinary in Hölderlin, of the bursting forth of the multiple in the calm glory of its number, are here the earth and the fruit. Such a parousia submits itself to the Law: this much may be inferred from all presentation being also the prescription of the one. But a strange uneasiness affects this Law. It is in excess of the simple organization of presentation in two different manners: first, because it enjoins each thing to insinuate itself within, as if maturity (the taste of the fruits of the earth) concealed its essence, as if some temptation of the latent void was at work within, as delivered by the disturbing image of the serpent; and second, because beyond what is exposed, the law is 'prophetic', dreamy, as if the 'mounds of Heaven' did not fulfil its expectation, nor its practice. All of this unquestionably metaphorizes the singularity of the German site, its bordering-upon-the-void, the fact that its terrestial placidity is vulnerable to a second irruption: that of the Caucasus, which is detained, within its familiar, bourgeois presentation, by the maternal Swabia. Moreover, with respect to what should be bound together in itself and calmly gathered together, it is solely on the basis of a faithful effort that its maintenance results. The maturity of the fruits, once deciphered as endangering the one by the poet, becomes a burden, a 'load of wood' under the duty of maintaining its consistency. This is precisely what is at stake: whilst Greece accomplishes its being in the excellence of form because its native site is Asiatic and furious, Germany will accomplish its being in a second fidelity, founded upon the storm, because its site is that of the golden fields, of the restrained Occident. The destiny of the German law is to *uproot itself* from its reign over conciliatory multiplicities. The German path leads astray ('But evil are / The paths'). The great call to which the peace of the evening responds is the 'yearning that seeks the un-bound'. This evental un-binding—this crookedness of 'imprisoned elements' and 'ancient laws' —prohibits any frequentation of the site in the assurance of a straight path. First serpent of its internal temptation, the site is now the 'steed' of its exile. The inconsistent multiple *demands to be* within the very law itself which regulates consistency. In a letter, after having declared that 'nature in my homeland moves me powerfully', Hölderlin cites as the first anchor of that emotion, 'the storm . . . from this very point of view, as power and as figure among the other forms of the sky'.

The duty of the poet—of the intervenor—cannot be, however, that of purely and simply giving way to this stormy disposition. What is to be saved, in definitive, is the peace of the site: 'much must be retained.' Once it is understood that the savour of the site resides uniquely in it being the serpent and steed of itself, and that its desire—ineluctably revealed in some uprooting, in some departure—is not its bound form, but the un-bound, the duty is then to anticipate the second joy, the conquered liaison, that will be given, at the most extreme moment of the uprooting, by the open return within the site; this time with the precaution of a knowledge, a norm, a capacity for maintenance and discernment. The imperative is voiced: fidelity is required. Or rather: let's examine each and every thing in the transparent light that comes after the storm.

But, and this is clear, fidelity could never be the feeble will for conservation. I have already pointed this out: the prophetic disposition which only sees in the event and its effects a verification, just like the canonical disposition which enjoins the site to remain faithful to its pacific nativity—which would force the law to not go crookedly, to no longer dream on the mounds of Heaven—is sterile. The intervenor will only found his second fidelity by trusting himself to the present of the storm, by abolishing himself in the void in which he will summon the name of what has occurred—this name, for Hölderlin, is in general the return of the gods. Consequently, it is necessary, for it not to be in vain that the maturity of the site be devastated by a dream of Asia, that one neither look forward nor back, and that one be, as close as possible to the unpresentable, 'as / On a swaying skiff of the sea'. Such is the intervenor, such is one who knows that he is required to be faithful: able to frequent the site, to share the fruits of the earth; but also, held by fidelity to the other event, able to discern fractures, singularities, the on-the-edge-of-the-void which makes the vacillation of the law possible, its dysfunction, its crookedness; but also, protected against the prophetic temptation, against the canonical arrogance; but also, confident in the event, in the name that he bestows upon it. And, finally, thus departed from the earth to the sea, embarked, able to test the fruits, to separate from their appearance the latent savour that they draw, in the future anterior, from their desire to not be bound.

PART VI

Quantity and Knowledge.
The Discernible (or Constructible):
Leibniz/Gödel

MEDITATION TWENTY-SIX
The Concept of Quantity and the Impasse of Ontology

The thought of being as *pure* multiple—or as multiple-without-one—may appear to link that thought to one of quantity. Hence the question: is being intrinsically quantifiable? Or, to be more precise: given that the form of presentation is the multiple, is there not an original link between what is presented and quantitative extension? We know that for Kant the key principle of what he termed the 'axioms of intuition' reads 'All intuitions are extensive magnitudes.' In recognizing in the pure multiple that which, of its presentation, is its being, are we not positing, symmetrically to Kant's axioms, that every presentation is intrinsically quantitative? Is every multiple numerable?

Again, as Kant says: 'the pure *schema* of *size* (*quantitatis*) . . . is *number* . . . Number is thus nothing other than the unity of the synthesis of the manifold of an intuition which is homogeneous in general.' Qua pure multiple of multiples, the ontological schema of presentation is also homogeneous for us. And inasmuch as it is subject to the effect-of-one, it is also a synthesis of the manifold. Is there thus an essential numerosity of being?

Of course, for us, the foundation of a 'quantity of being' cannot be that proposed by Kant for the quantity of the objects of intuition: Kant finds this foundation in the transcendental potentiality of time and space, whilst we are attempting to mathematically think multiple-presentation *irrespective* of time (which is founded by intervention) and space (which is a singular construction, relative to certain types of presentation). What this entails, moreover, is that the very concept of size (or of number) cannot, for us, be that employed by Kant. For him, an extensive size is 'that in which the representation of the parts makes possible the representation of the whole'. Yet I have sufficiently insisted, in particular in Meditations 3, 5 and 7, on the fact that the Cantorian Idea of the multiple, crystallized in the sign $\in$ of belonging, cannot be subsumed under the whole/parts relation. It is not possible for the number of being—if it exists—to be thought from the standpoint of this relation.

But perhaps the main obstacle is not found there. The obstacle—it separates us from Kant, with the entire depth of the Cantorian revolution—resides in the following (Meditations 13 and 14): the form-multiple of presentation is generally infinite. That being is given as infinite multiplicities would seem to weigh against its being numerable. It would rather be innumerable. As Kant says, 'such a concept of size [infinity, whether it be spatial or temporal], like that of a given infinity, is empirically impossible.' Infinity is, at best, a limit Idea of experience, but it cannot be one of the stakes of knowledge.

The difficulty is in fact the following: the extensive or quantitative character of presentation supposes that commensurable multiplicities are placed in relation to one another. In order to have the beginnings of a knowledge of quantity, one must be able to say that one multiple is 'larger' than another. But what exactly does it mean to say that one infinite multiple is larger than another? Of course, one can see how one infinite multiple *presents* another: in this manner, ω_0, the first infinite ordinal (cf. Meditation 14), belongs—for example—to its successor, the multiple $\omega_0 \cup \{\omega_0\}$, which is obtained by the addition of the name $\{\omega_0\}$ itself to the (finite) multiples which make up ω_0. Have we obtained a 'larger' multiple for all that? It has been open knowledge for centuries (Pascal used this point frequently) that adding something finite to the infinite does not change the infinite quantity if one attempts to determine this quantity *as such*. Galileo had already remarked that, strictly speaking, there were no 'more' square numbers—of the form n^2—than there were simple numbers; since for *each* whole number n, one can establish a correspondence with its square n^2. He quite wisely concluded from this, moreover, that the notions of 'more' and 'less' were not pertinent to infinity, or that infinite totalities were *not* quantities.

In the end, the apparent impasse of any ontological doctrine of quantity can be expressed as follows: the ontological schema of presentation supported by the decision on natural infinity ('there exists a limit ordinal') admits *existent* infinite multiplicities. However, there seems to be some difficulty in understanding how the latter might be comparable, or how they might belong to a unity of count which would be uniformly applicable to them. Therefore, being is not in general quantifiable.

It would not be an exaggeration to say that the dissolution of this impasse commands the destiny of thought.

1. THE QUANTITATIVE COMPARISON OF INFINITE SETS

One of Cantor's central ideas was to propose a protocol for the comparison of infinite multiples—when it comes to the finite, we have always known how to resort to those particular ordinals that are the members of ω_0, the finite ordinals, or the natural whole numbers (cf. Meditation 14); that is, we knew how to *count*. But what exactly could counting mean for infinite multiples?

What happened was that Cantor had the brilliant idea of treating positively the remarks of Galileo and Pascal—and those of the Portuguese Jesuit school before them—in which these authors had concluded in the impossibility of infinite number. As often happens, the invention consisted in turning a paradox into a concept. Since there is a correspondence, term by term, between the whole numbers and the square numbers, between the n and the n^2, why not intrepidly posit that in fact there are *just as many* square numbers as numbers? The (intuitive) obstacle to such a thesis is that square numbers form a *part* of numbers in general, and if one says that there are 'just as many' squares as there are numbers, the old Euclidean maxim 'the whole is greater than the part' is threatened. But this is exactly the point: because the set theory doctrine of the multiple does not define the multiple it does not have to run the gauntlet of the intuition of the whole and its parts; moreover, this is why its doctrine of quantity can be termed anti-Kantian. We will allow, without blinking an eye, that given that it is a matter of infinite multiples, it is possible for what is *included* (like square numbers in whole numbers) to be 'as numerous' as that in which it is included. Instead of being an insurmountable obstacle for any comparison of infinite quantities, such commensurability will become a particular property of these quantities. There is a subversion herein of the old intuition of quantity, that subsumed by the couple whole/parts: this subversion completes the innovation of thought, and the ruin of that intuition.

Galileo's remark orientated Cantor in yet another manner: if there are 'as many' square numbers as numbers, then this is because one can establish a correspondence between every whole n and its square n^2. This concept of term for term 'correspondence' between a multiple, be it infinite, and another multiple provides the key to a *procedure* of comparison: two multiples will be said to be 'as numerous' (or, a Cantorian convention, *of the same power*) as each other if there *exists* such a correspondence. Note that the concept of quantity is thus referred to that of existence, as is appropriate given the ontological vocation of set theory.

The mathematical formalization of the general idea of 'correspondence' is a function. A function f causes the elements of one multiple to 'correspond' to the elements of another. When one writes $f(a) = \beta$, this means that the element β 'corresponds' to the element a.

A suspicious reader would object that we have introduced a supplementary concept, that of function, which exceeds the pure multiple, and ruins the ontological homogeneity of set theory. Well no, in fact! A function can quite easily be represented as a pure multiple, as established in Appendix 2. When I say 'there exists a function' I am merely saying: 'there exists a multiple which has such and such characteristics', and the latter can be defined on the basis of the Ideas of the multiple alone.

The essential characteristic of a function is that it establishes a correspondence between an element and *one* other element *alone*: if I have $f(a) = \beta$ and $f(a) = \gamma$, this is because β is *the same multiple* as γ.

In order to exhaust the idea of 'term by term' correspondence, as in Galileo's remark, I must, however, improve my functional concept of correspondence. To conclude that squares are 'as numerous' as numbers, not only must a square correspond to every number, but, conversely, for every square there must also be a corresponding number (and one alone). Otherwise, I will not have practised the comparative *exhaustion* of the *two* multiples in question. This leads us to the definition of a one-to-one function (or one-to-one correspondence); the foundation for the quantitative comparison of multiples.

Say a and β are two sets. The function f of a towards β will be a *one-to-one correspondence* between a and β if:

– for every element of a, there corresponds, via f, an element of β;
– to two different elements of a correspond two different elements of β;
– and, every element of β is the correspondent, by f, of an element of a.

It is clear that in this manner the use of *f* allows us to 'replace' *all* the elements of α with *all* the elements of β by substituting for an element δ of α the *f*(δ) of β, unique, and different from any other, that corresponds to it. The third condition states that *all* the elements of β are to be used in this manner. It is quite a sufficient concept for the task of thinking that the one-multiple β does not make up one 'more' multiple than α, and that α and β are thus equal in number, or in extension, with respect to what they present.

If two multiples are such that there exists a one-to-one correspondence between them, it will be said that they have *the same power*, or that they are extensively the same.

This concept is literally that of the quantitative identity of two multiples, and it also concerns those which are infinite.

2. NATURAL QUANTITATIVE CORRELATE OF A MULTIPLE: CARDINALITY AND CARDINALS

We now have at our disposal an existential procedure of comparison between two multiples; at the least we know what it means when we say that they are the same quantitatively. The 'stable' or natural multiples that are ordinals thus become comparable to any multiple whatsoever. This comparative reduction of the multiple in general to the series of ordinals will allow us to construct what is essential for any thought of quantity: a scale of measure.

We have seen (Meditation 12) that an ordinal, an ontological schema of the natural multiple, constitutes a name-number inasmuch as the one-multiple that it is, totally ordered by the fundamental Idea of presentation—belonging—also designates the long numerable chain of all the previous ordinals. An ordinal is thus a tool-multiple, a potential measuring instrument for the 'length' of any set, once it is guaranteed, by the axiom of choice—or axiom of abstract intervention (cf. Meditation 22)—that every multiple can be well-ordered. We are going to employ this instrumental value of ordinals: its subjacent ontological signification, moreover, is that every multiple can be connected to a natural multiple, or, in other words, *being is universally deployed as nature*. Not that every presentation is natural, we know this is not the case—historical multiples exist (see Meditations 16 and 17 on the foundation of this distinction)—but every multiple can be referred to natural presentation, in particular with respect to its number or quantity.

One of ontology's crucial statements is indeed the following: every multiple has the same power as at least one ordinal. In other words, the 'class' formed out of those multiples which have the same quantity will always contain at least one ordinal. There is no 'size' which is such that one cannot find an *example* of it amongst the natural multiples. In other words, nature contains all thinkable orders of size.

However, by virtue of the ordinals' property of minimality, if there exists an ordinal which is attached to a certain class of multiples according to their size, then there exists a smallest ordinal of this type (in the sense of the series of ordinals). What I mean is that amongst all the ordinals such that a one-to-one correspondence exists between them, there is one of them, unique, which belongs to all the others, or which is $\in$-minimal for the property 'to have such an intrinsic size'. This ordinal will evidently be such that it will be impossible for there to exist a one-to-one correspondence between it and an ordinal smaller than it. It will mark, amongst the ordinals, the *frontier* at which a new order of intrinsic size commences. These ordinals can be perfectly defined: they possess the property of tolerating no one-to-one correspondence with any of the ordinals which precede them. As frontiers of power, they will be termed *cardinals*. The property of being a cardinal can be written as follows:

Card $(\alpha) \leftrightarrow$ 'α is an ordinal, and there is no one-to-one correspondence between α and an ordinal β such that $\beta \in \alpha$.'

Remember, a function, which is a one-to-one correspondence, is a relation, and *thus a multiple* (Appendix 2). This definition in no way departs from the general framework of ontology.

The idea is then to represent the class of multiples of the same size—those between which a one-to-one correspondence exists—that is, to name an *order* of size, by means of the cardinal present in that class. There is always one of them, but this in turn depends upon a crucial point which we have left in suspense: every multiple has the same power as at least one ordinal, and consequently the same power as the smallest of ordinals of the same power as it—the latter is necessarily a cardinal. Since ordinals, and thus cardinals, are totally ordered, we thereby obtain a measuring scale for intrinsic size. The further the cardinal-name of a type of size (or power) is placed in the series of ordinals, the higher this type will be. Such is the principle of a measuring scale for quantity in pure multiples, thus, for the quantitative instance of being.

We have not yet established the fundamental connection between multiples in general and natural multiples, the connection which consists of the existence for each of the former of a representative of the same power from amongst the latter; that is, the fact that *nature measures being*.

For the rest of this book, I will increasingly use what I call *accounts of demonstration*, substitutes for the actual demonstrations themselves. My motive is evident: the further we plunge into the ontological text, the more complicated the strategy of fidelity becomes, and it often does so well beyond the metaontological or philosophical interest that might lie in following it. The account of the proof which concerns us here is the following: given an indeterminate multiple λ, we consider a *function of choice* on $p(\lambda)$, whose existence is guaranteed for us by the axiom of choice (Meditation 22). We will then *construct* an ordinal such that it is in one-to-one correspondence with λ. To do this we will first establish a correspondence between the void-set, the smallest element of any ordinal, and the element λ_0, which corresponds via the function of choice to λ itself. Then, for the following ordinal—which is in fact the number 1—we will establish a correspondence with the element that the function of choice singles out in the part $[\lambda - \lambda_0]$: say the latter element is λ_1. Then, for the following ordinal, a correspondence will be established with the element chosen in the part $[\lambda - \{\lambda_0, \lambda_1\}]$, and so on. For an ordinal a, a correspondence is established with the element singled out by the function of choice in the part obtained by subtracting from λ everything which has *already* been obtained as correspondent for the ordinals which precede a. This continues up to the point of there being no longer anything left in λ; that is, up to the point that what has to be subtracted is λ itself, such that the 'remainder' is empty, and the function of choice can no longer choose anything. Say that γ is the ordinal at which we stop (the first to which nothing corresponds, for lack of any possible choice). It is quite clear that our correspondence is one-to-one between this ordinal γ and the initial multiple λ, since *all* of λ's elements have been exhausted, and each corresponds to *an* ordinal anterior to γ. It so happens that 'all the ordinals anterior to γ' is nothing other, qua one-multiple, than γ itself. QED.

Being the same size as an ordinal, it is certain that the multiple λ is the same size as a cardinal. If the ordinal γ that we have constructed is not a cardinal, this is because it has the same power as an ordinal which precedes it. Let's select the $\in$-minimal ordinal from amongst the ordinals which have the same power as γ. It is certainly a cardinal and it has the same power as γ, because whatever has the same power as whatever has the same power, has the same power as . . . (I leave the rest to you).

It is thus guaranteed that the cardinals can serve as a measuring scale for the size of sets. Let's note at this point that it is upon the interventional axiom—the existence of the illegal function of choice, of the representative without a procedure of representation—that this second victory of nature depends: the victory which lies in its capacity to *fix*, on an ordered scale—the cardinals—the type of intrinsic size of multiples. This dialectic of the illegal and the height of order is characteristic of the style of ontology.

3. THE PROBLEM OF INFINITE CARDINALS

The theory of cardinals—and especially that of infinite cardinals, which is to say those equal or superior to ω_0—forms the very heart of set theory; the point at which, having attained an apparent mastery, via the name-numbers that are natural multiples, of the quantity of pure multiples, the mathematician can deploy the technical refinement in which what he guards is forgotten: being-qua-being. An eminent specialist in set theory wrote: 'practically speaking, the most part of set theory is the study of infinite cardinals.'

The paradox is that the immense world of these cardinals 'practically' does not appear in 'working' mathematics; that is, the mathematics which deals with real and complex numbers, functions, algebraic structures, varieties, differential geometry, topological algebra, etc. And this is so for an important reason which houses the aforementioned impasse of ontology: we shall proceed to its encounter.

Certain results of the theory of cardinals are immediate:

– Every finite ordinal (every element of ω_0) is a cardinal. It is quite clear that one cannot establish any one-to-one correspondence between two different whole numbers. The world of the finite is therefore arranged, in respect to intrinsic size, according to the scale of finite ordinals: there are ω_0 'types' of intrinsic size; as many as there are natural whole numbers.

– By the same token, without difficulty, one can finally extend the distinction finite/infinite to multiples in general: previously it was reserved for natural multiples—a multiple is thus infinite (or finite) if it quantity is named by a cardinal equal or superior (or, respectively, inferior) to ω_0.

– It is guaranteed that ω_0 is itself a cardinal—the first infinite cardinal: if it were not such, there would have to be a one-to-one correspondence between it and an ordinal smaller than it, thus between it and a finite number. This is certainly impossible (demonstrate it!).

– But can one 'surpass' ω_0? Are there infinite quantities larger than other infinite quantities? Here we touch upon one of Cantor's major innovations: the infinite proliferation of *different* infinite quantities. Not only is quantity—here numbered by a cardinal—pertinent to infinite-being, but it distinguishes, within the infinite, 'larger' and 'smaller' infinite quantities. The millenary speculative opposition between the finite, quantitatively varied and denumerable, and the infinite, unquantifiable and unique, is succeeded—thanks to the Cantorian revolution—by a uniform scale of quantities which goes from the empty multiple (which numbers nothing) to an unlimited series of infinite cardinals, which number quantitatively distinct infinite multiples. Hence the achievement—in the proliferation of infinities—of the complete ruin of any being of the One.

The heart of this revolution is the recognition (authorized by the Ideas of the multiple, the axioms of set theory) that distinct infinite quantities do exist. What leads to this result is a theorem whose scope for thought is immense: Cantor's theorem.

4. THE STATE OF A SITUATION IS QUANTITATIVELY LARGER THAN THE SITUATION ITSELF

It is quite natural, in all orders of thought, to have the idea of examining the 'quantitative' relation, or relation of power, between a situation and its state. A situation presents one-multiples; the state re-presents parts or compositions of those multiples. Does the state present 'more' or 'less' part-multiples than the situation presents one-multiples (or 'as many')? The theorem of the point of excess (Meditation 7) already indicates for us that the state cannot be *the same* multiple as the situation whose state it is. Yet this alterity does not rule out the intrinsic quantity—the cardinal—of the state being identical to that of the situation. The state might be different whilst remaining 'as numerous', but no more.

Note, however, that in any case the state is *at least* as numerous as the situation: the cardinal of the set of parts of a set cannot be inferior to that of the set. This is so because given any element of a set, its singleton is a part, and since a singleton 'corresponds' to every presented element, there are at least as many parts as elements.

The only remaining question is that of knowing whether the cardinal of the set of parts is equal or superior to that of the initial set. The said theorem—Cantor's—establishes that it is always superior. The demonstration uses a resource which establishes its kinship to Russell's paradox and to the theorem of the point of excess. That is, it involves 'diagonal' reasoning, which reveals a 'one-more' (or a remainder) of a procedure which is supposed exhaustive, thus ruining the latter's pretension. It is possible to say that this procedure is typical of everything in ontology which is related to the problem of excess, of 'not-being-according-to-such-an-instance-of-the-one'.

Suppose that a one-to-one correspondence, f, exists between a set α and the set of its parts, $p(\alpha)$; that is, that the state has the same cardinal as the set (or more exactly, that they belong to the same quantitative class whose representative is a cardinal).

To every *element* β of α thus corresponds a *part* of α, which is an element of $p(\alpha)$. Since this part corresponds by f to the element β we will write it $f(\beta)$. Two cases can then be distinguished:

– either the element β is *in* the part $f(\beta)$ which corresponds to it, that is, $\beta \in f(\beta)$;
– or this is not the case: $\sim(\beta \in f(\beta))$.

One can also say that the—supposed—one-to-one correspondence f between α and $p(\alpha)$ *categorizes* α's elements into two groups, those which are internal to the part (or element of $p(\alpha)$) which corresponds to them, and those which are external to such parts. The axiom of separation guarantees us the existence of the part of α composed of all the elements which are f-external: it corresponds to the property 'β does not belong to $f(\beta)$'. This part, because f is a one-to-one correspondence between α and *the set* of its parts, corresponds via f to an element of α that we shall call δ (for 'diagonal'). As such we have: $f(\delta)$ = 'the set of all f-external elements of α'. The goal, in which the supposed existence of f is abolished (here one can recognize the scope of reasoning via the absurd, cf. Meditation 24), is to show that this element δ is incapable of being itself either f-internal or f-external.

If δ is f-internal, this means that $\delta \in f(\delta)$. But $f(\delta)$ is the set of f-external elements, and so δ, if it belongs to $f(\delta)$, cannot be f-internal: a contradiction.

If δ is f-external, we have $\sim(\delta \in f(\delta))$, therefore δ is not one of the elements which are f-external, and so it cannot be f-external either: another contradiction.

The only possible conclusion is therefore that the initial supposition of a one-to-one correspondence between α and $p(\alpha)$ is untenable. The set of parts cannot have the same cardinal as the initial set. It exceeds the latter absolutely; it is of a higher quantitative order.

The theorem of the point of excess gives a local response to the question of the relation between a situation and its state: the state counts at least one multiple which does not belong to the situation. Consequently, the state is *different* from the situation whose state it is. Cantor's theorem, on the other hand, gives a global response to this question: the power of the state—in terms of pure quantity—is superior to that of the situation. This, by the way, is what rules out the idea that the state is merely a 'reflection' of the situation. It is separated from the situation: this much has already been shown by the theorem of the point of excess. Now we know that it dominates it.

5. FIRST EXAMINATION OF CANTOR'S THEOREM: THE MEASURING SCALE OF INFINITE MULTIPLES, OR THE SEQUENCE OF ALEPHS

Since the quantity of the set of parts of a set is superior to that of the set itself, the problem that we raised earlier is solved: there necessarily exists at least one cardinal larger than ω_0 (the first infinite cardinal)—it is the cardinal which numbers the quantity of the multiple $p(\omega_0)$. Quantitatively, infinity is multiple. This consideration immediately opens up an infinite scale of distinct infinite quantities.

It is appropriate to apply the principle of minimality here, which is characteristic of ordinals (Meditation 12). We have just seen that an ordinal exists which has the property of 'being a cardinal and being superior to ω_0' ('superior' means here: which presents, or, to which ω_0 belongs, since the order on ordinals is that of belonging). Therefore, there exists a *smallest* ordinal possessing such a property. It is thus the smallest cardinal superior to ω_0, the infinite quantity which comes just after ω_0. It will be written ω_1 and called the *successor* cardinal of ω_0. Once again, by Cantor's theorem, the multiple $p(\omega_1)$ is quantitatively superior to ω_1; thus a successor cardinal of ω_1 exists, written ω_2, and so on. All of these infinite cardinals, $\omega_0, \omega_1, \omega_2 \ldots$, designate distinct, and increasing, types of infinite quantities.

The successor operation—the passage from one cardinal ω_n to the cardinal ω_{n+1}—is not the only operation of the scale of sizes. We also find here the breach between the general idea of succession and that of the limit, which is characteristic of the natural universe. For example, it is quite clear that the series $\omega_0, \omega_1, \omega_2 \ldots \omega_n, \omega_{n+1} \ldots$ is an initial scale of different cardinals which succeed one another. But consider the *set* $\{\omega_0, \omega_1, \omega_2 \ldots \omega_n, \omega_{n+1} \ldots\}$: it exists, because it is obtained by *replacing*, in ω_0 (which exists), every finite ordinal by the infinite cardinal that it indexes (the function of replacement is quite simply: $n \rightarrow \omega_n$). Consequently, there also exists the union-set of this set; that is, $\omega_{(\omega_0)} = \cup \{\omega_0, \omega_1, \ldots \omega_n \ldots\}$. I say that this set $\omega_{(\omega_0)}$ is a cardinal, the first *limit cardinal* greater than ω_0. This results, intuitively, from the fact that the elements of $\omega_{(\omega_0)}$, the dissemination of *all* the $\omega_0, \omega_1, \ldots \omega_n \ldots$, cannot be placed in a one-to-one correspondence with any ω_n in particular; there are 'too many' of them for that. The multiple $\omega_{(\omega_0)}$ is thus quantitatively superior to all the members of the series $\omega_0, \omega_1, \ldots \omega_n \ldots$, because it is composed of all the elements of all of these cardinals. It is the cardinal which comes just 'after' this series, the limit of this series (setting out this intuition in a strict form is a good exercise for the reader).

One can obviously continue: we will have the successor cardinal of $\omega_{(\omega_0)}$, that is, $\omega_{s(\omega_0)}$, and so on. Then we can use the limit again, thus obtaining $\omega_{(\omega_0)_{(\omega_0)}}$. In this manner one can attain gigantic multiplicities, such as:

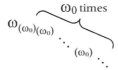

for example, which do not themselves fix any limit to the iteration of processes.

The truth is that for *each* ordinal α there thus corresponds an infinite cardinal ω_α, from ω_0 up to the most unrepresentable quantitative infinities.

This scale of infinite multiplicities—called the sequence of alephs because they are often noted by the Hebrew letter aleph ($\aleph$) followed by indexes—fulfils the double promise of the numbering of the infinities, and of the infinity of their types thus numbered. It completes the Cantorian project of a total dissemination or dis-unification of the concept of infinity.

If the series of ordinals designates, beyond the finite, an infinity of *natural* infinities, distinguished by the fact that they order what belongs to them, then the sequence of alephs names an infinity of general infinities, seized, without any order, in their raw dimension, their number of elements; that is, as the quantitative extension of what they present. And since the sequence of alephs is indexed by ordinals, one can say that there are 'as many' types of quantitative infinity as there are natural infinite multiples.

However, this 'as many' is illusory, because it links two totalities which are not only inconsistent, but inexistent. Just as the set of all ordinals cannot exist—which is said: Nature does not exist—nor can the set of all cardinals exist, the absolutely infinite Infinity, the infinity of all intrinsically thinkable infinities—which is said, this time: God does not exist.

6. SECOND EXAMINATION OF CANTOR'S THEOREM: WHAT MEASURE FOR EXCESS?

The set of parts of a set is 'more numerous' than the set itself. But by how much? What is this excess *worth*, and how can it be measured? Since we dispose of a complete scale of finite cardinals (natural whole numbers) and infinite cardinals (alephs), it makes sense to ask, if one knows the cardinal which corresponds to the quantitative class of a multiple α, what cardinal corresponds to the quantitative class of the multiple $p(\alpha)$. We know that it is superior, that it comes 'afterwards' in the scale. But where exactly?

In the finite, the problem is simple: if a set possesses n elements, the set of its parts possesses 2^n elements, which is a definite and calculable whole number. This finite combinatory exercise is open to any reader with a little dexterity.

But what happens if the set in question is infinite? The corresponding cardinal is then an aleph, say ω_β. Which is the aleph which corresponds to the set of its parts? The difficulty of the problem resides in the fact that there is certainly one, and one alone. This is the case because *every* existent multiple has the same power as a cardinal, and once the latter is determined, it is impossible that the multiple *also* have the same power as another cardinal: between two different cardinals no one-to-one correspondence—by definition—can exist.

The impasse is the following: within the framework of those Ideas of the multiple which are currently supposed—and many others whose addition to the latter has been attempted—it is *impossible* to determine where on the scale of alephs the set of parts of an infinite set is situated. To be more precise, it is quite coherent with these Ideas to suppose that this place is 'more or less' whatever one has agreed to decide upon.

Before giving a more precise expression to this errancy, to this unmeasure of the state of a situation, let's stop and try to grasp its weight. It signifies that however exact the quantitative knowledge of a situation may be, one cannot, other than by an arbitrary decision, estimate by 'how much' its state exceeds it. It is as though the doctrine of the multiple, in the case of infinite or post-Galilean situations, has to admit two regimes of presentation which cannot be sutured together within the order of quantity: the immediate regime, that of elements and belonging (the situation and its structure); and the second regime, that of parts and inclusion (the state). It is here that the formidable complexity of the question of the state—in politics, of the State—is revealed. It is articulated around this hiatus which has been uncovered by ontology in the modality of impossibility: *the natural measuring scale for multiple-presentations is not appropriate for representations*. It is not appropriate for them, despite the fact that they are certainly located upon it. The problem is, they *are unlocalizable* upon it. This paradoxical intrication of impossibility and certainty disperses the prospects of any evaluation of the power of the state. That it is necessary, in the end, to *decide* upon this power introduces randomness into the heart of what can be said of being. Action receives a warning from ontology: that it endeavours in vain when it attempts to precisely calculate the state of the situation in which its resources are disposed. Action must make a wager in this matter, rather than a calculation; and of this wager it is known—what is called knowledge—that all it can do is oscillate between overestimation and underestimation. The state is solely commensurable to the situation by chance.

7. COMPLETE ERRANCY OF THE STATE OF A SITUATION: EASTON'S THEOREM

Let's set down several conventions for our script. So that we no longer have to deal with the indexes of alephs, from now on we shall note a cardinal by the letters λ and π. We shall use the notation $|\alpha|$ to indicate the quantity of the multiple α; that is, the cardinal π which has the same power as α. To indicate that a cardinal λ is smaller than a cardinal π, we shall write $\lambda < \pi$ (which in fact signifies: λ and π are different cardinals), and $\lambda \in \pi$.

The impasse of ontology is then stated in the following manner: given a cardinal λ, what is the cardinality of its state, of the set of its parts? What is the relation between λ and $|p(\lambda)|$?

It is this relation which is shown to be rather an un-relation, insofar as 'almost' any relation that is chosen in advance is consistent with the Ideas of the multiple. Let's examine the meaning of this 'almost', and then what is signified by the consistency of this choice with the Ideas.

It is not as though we know *nothing* about the relation of size between a multiple and its state, between presentation by belonging and representation by inclusion. We know that $|p(\alpha)|$ is larger than α, whatever multiple α we consider. This absolute quantitative excess of the state over the situation is the content of Cantor's theorem.

We also know another relation, whose meaning is clarified in Appendix 3 (it states that the cofinality of the set of parts is quantitatively superior to the set itself).

To what point do we, in truth, know nothing more, in the framework of the Ideas of the multiple formulable today? What teaches us here —extreme science proving itself to be science of ignorance—is Easton's theorem.

This theorem roughly says the following: given a cardinal λ, which is either ω_0 or a successor cardinal, it is coherent with the Ideas of the multiple to choose, as the value of $|p(\lambda)|$—that is, as quantity for the state whose situation is the multiple—any cardinal π, provided that it is superior to λ and that it is a successor cardinal.

What exactly does this impressive theorem mean? (Its general demonstration is beyond the means of this book, but a particular example of it is treated in Meditation 36.) 'Coherent with the Ideas of the multiple' means: *if* these Ideas are coherent amongst themselves (thus, if mathematics is a language in which deductive fidelity is genuinely separative, and thus consistent), *then* they will remain so if you decide that, in your eyes, the multiple $p(\lambda)$ has as its intrinsic size a particular successor cardinal π—provided that it is superior to λ.

For example, with respect to the set of parts of ω_0—and Cantor wore himself out, taking his thought to the very brink, in the attempt to establish that it was equal to the successor of ω_0, to ω_1—Easton's theorem says that it is deductively acceptable to posit that it is ω_{347}, or $\omega_{(\omega_0) + 18}$, or whatever other cardinal as immense as you like, provided that it is a successor. Consequently, Easton's theorem establishes the quasi-total errancy of the excess of the state over the situation. It is as though, between the structure in which the immediacy of belonging is delivered, and the metastructure which counts as one the parts and regulates the inclusions, a chasm opens, whose filling in depends solely upon a conceptless choice.

Being, as pronounceable, is unfaithful to itself, to the point that it is no longer possible to deduce the value, in infinite extension, of the care put into every presentation in the counting as one of its parts. The un-measure of the state causes an errancy in quantity on the part of the very instance from which we expected—precisely—the guarantee and fixity of situations. The operator of the banishment of the void: we find it here letting the void reappear at the very jointure between itself (the capture of parts) and the situation. That it is necessary to tolerate the almost complete arbitrariness of a choice, that quantity, the very paradigm of objectivity, leads to pure subjectivity; such is what I would willingly call the Cantor-Gödel-Cohen-Easton symptom. Ontology unveils in its impasse a point at which thought—unconscious that it is being itself which convokes it therein—has always had to divide itself.

MEDITATION TWENTY-SEVEN
Ontological Destiny of Orientation in Thought

Since its very origins, in anticipation of its Cantorian grounding, philosophy has interrogated the abyss which separates numerical discretion from the geometrical continuum. This abyss is none other than that which separates ω_0, infinite denumerable domain of finite numbers, from the set of its parts $p(\omega_0)$, the sole set able to fix the quantity of points in space. That there is a mystery of being at stake here, in which speculative discourse weaves itself into the mathematical doctrine of number and measure, has been attested by innumerable concepts and metaphors. It was certainly not clear that in the last resort it is a matter of the relation between an infinite set and the set of its parts. But from Plato to Husserl, passing by the magnificent developments of Hegel's *Logic*, the strictly inexhaustible theme of the dialectic of the discontinuous and the continuous occurs time and time again. We can now say that it is being itself, flagrant within the impasse of ontology, which organizes the inexhaustibility of its thought; given that no measure may be taken of the quantitative bond between a situation and its state, between belonging and inclusion. Everything leads us to believe that it is *for ever* that this provocation to the concept, this un-relation between presentation and representation, will be open in being. Since the continuous—or $p(\omega_0)$—is a pure errant principle with respect to the denumerable—to ω_0—the closing down or blocking of this errancy could require the ingenuity of knowledge indefinitely. Such an activity would not be in vain, for the following reason: if the impossible-to-say of being is precisely the quantitative bond between a multiple and the multiple of its parts, and if this unpronounceable unbinding opens up the perspective of infinite choices, then it can be thought that this time what is at stake is Being itself, in default of the science of ontology. If the real is the impossible, the real of being—Being—will be precisely what is detained by the enigma of an anonymity of quantity.

Every particular orientation of thought receives as such its cause from what it usually does not concern itself with, and which ontology alone declares in the deductive dignity of the concept: this vanishing Being which supports the eclipse of being 'between' presentation and representation. Ontology establishes its errancy. Metaontology, which serves as an unconscious framework for every orientation within thought, wishes either to fix its mirage, or to abandon itself entirely to the joy of its disappearance. Thought is nothing other than the desire to finish with the exorbitant excess of the state. Nothing will ever allow one to resign oneself to the innumerable parts. Thought occurs for there to be a cessation—even if it only lasts long enough to indicate that it has not actually been obtained—of the quantitative unmooring of being. It is always a question of a measure being taken of how much the state exceeds the immediate. Thought, strictly speaking, is what un-measure, ontologically proven, cannot satisfy.

Dissatisfaction, the historical law of thought whose cause resides in a point at which being is no longer *exactly* sayable, arises in each of three great endeavours to remedy this excess, this ὕβρις, which the Greek tragedians quite rightly made into the major determinant of what happens to the human creature. Aeschylus, the greatest amongst them, proposed its subjective channelling via the immediately political recourse to a new symbolic order of justice. For it is definitely, in the desire that is thought, a question of the innumerable injustice of the state: moreover, that one must respond to the challenge of being by politics is another Greek inspiration which still reigns over us. The joint invention of mathematics and the 'deliberative form' of the State leads, amidst this astonishing people, to the observation that the saying of being would hardly make any sense if one did not immediately draw from the affairs of the City and historical events whatever is necessary to provide also for the needs of 'that-which-is-not-being'.

The first endeavour, which I will term alternatively grammarian or programmatic, holds that the fault at the origin of the un-measure lies in language. It requires the state to explicitly distinguish between what can be legitimately considered as a part of the situation and what, despite forming 'groupings' in the latter, must nevertheless be held as unformed and unnameable. In short, it is a question of severely restricting the recognizable dignity of inclusion to what a well-made language will allow to be named of it. In this perspective, the state does not count as one 'all' the parts. What, moreover, is a part? The state legislates on what it counts, the metastructure maintains 'reasonable' representations alone in its field. The state is programmed to solely recognize as a part, whose count it ensures, what the situation's resources themselves allow to be *distinguished*. Whatever is not distinguishable by a well-made language is not. The central principle of this type of thought is thus the Leibnizian principle of indiscernibles: there cannot exist two things whose difference cannot be marked. Language assumes the role of a law of being insofar as it will hold as identical whatever it cannot distinguish. Thereby reduced to counting only those parts which are commonly nameable, the state, one hopes, will become adequate to the situation again.

The second endeavour obeys the inverse principle: it holds that the excess of the state is only unthinkable because the discernment of parts is required. What is proposed this time, via the deployment of a doctrine of indiscernibles, is a demonstration that it is the latter which make up the essential of the field in which the state operates, and that any authentic thought must first forge for itself the means to apprehend the indeterminate, the undifferentiated, and the multiply-similar. Representation is interrogated on the side of what it numbers without ever discerning: parts without borders, random conglomerates. It is maintained that what is representative of a situation is not what distinctly belongs to it, but what is evasively included in it. The entire rational effort is to dispose of a matheme of the indiscernible, which brings forth in thought the innumerable parts that cannot be named as separate from the crowd of those which—in the myopic eyes of language—are absolutely identical to them. Within this orientation, the mystery of excess will not be reduced but rejoined. Its origin will be known, which is that the anonymity of parts is necessarily beyond the distinction of belongings.

The third endeavour searches to fix a stopping point to errancy by the thought of a multiple whose extension is such that it organizes everything which precedes it, and therefore sets the representative multiple in its place, the state bound to a situation. This time, what is at stake is a logic of transcendence. One goes straight to the prodigality of being in infinite presentations. One suspects that the fault of thought lies in its underestimation of this power, by bridling it either via language, or by the sole recourse to the undifferentiated. The correct approach is rather to differentiate a gigantic infinity which prescribes a hierarchical disposition in which nothing will be able to err any more. The effort, this time, is to contain the un-measure, not by reinforcing rules and prohibiting the indiscernible, but directly from above, by the conceptual practice of possibly maximal presentations. One hopes that these transcendent multiplicities will unveil the very law of multiple-excess, and will propose a vertiginous closure to thought.

These three endeavours have their correspondences in ontology itself. Why? Because each of them implies that a certain *type of being* is intelligible. Mathematical ontology does not constitute, by itself, any orientation in thought, but it must be compatible with all of them: it must discern and propose the multiple-being which they have need of.

To the first orientation corresponds the doctrine of *constructible* sets, created by Gödel and refined by Jensen. To the second orientation corresponds the doctrine of *generic* sets, created by Cohen. The correspondence for the third is the doctrine of *large cardinals*, to which all the specialists of set theory have contributed. As such, ontology proposes the schema of adequate multiples as *substructure of being* of each orientation. The constructible unfolds the being of configurations of knowledge. The generic, with the concept of the indiscernible multiple, renders possible the thought of the being of a truth. The grand cardinals approximate the virtual being required by theologies.

Obviously, the three orientations also have their philosophical correspondences. I named Leibniz for the first. The theory of the general will in Rousseau searches for the generic point, that is, the any-point-whatsoever in which political authority will be founded. All of classical metaphysics conspires for the third orientation, even in the mode of communist eschatology.

But a fourth way, discernible from Marx onwards, grasped from another perspective in Freud, is transversal to the three others. It holds that the *truth* of the ontological impasse cannot be seized or thought in immanence to ontology itself, nor to speculative metaontology. It assigns the un-measure of the state to the historial limitation of being, such that, without knowing so, philosophy only reflects it to repeat it. Its hypothesis consists in saying that one can only *render justice* to injustice from the angle of the event and intervention. There is thus no need to be horrified by an un-binding of being, because it is in the undecidable occurrence of a supernumerary non-being that every truth procedure originates, including that of a truth whose stakes would be that very un-binding.

It states, this fourth way, that on the underside of ontology, against being, solely discernible from the latter point by point (because, globally, they are incorporated, one in the other, like the surface of a Möbius strip), the unpresented procedure of the true takes place, the sole remainder left by mathematical ontology to whomever is struck by the desire to think, and for whom is reserved the name of Subject.

MEDITATION TWENTY-EIGHT
Constructivist Thought and the Knowledge of Being

Under the requisition of the hiatus in being, it is tempting to reduce the extension of the state by solely tolerating as parts of the situation those multiples whose nomination is allowed by the situation itself. What does the 'situation itself' mean?

One option would be to only accept as an included one-multiple what is already a one-multiple in the position of belonging. It is agreed that the representable is always already presented. This orientation is particularly well adapted to stable or natural situations, because in these situations every presented multiplicity is re-secured in its place by the state (cf. Meditations 11 and 12). Unfortunately it is unpracticable, because it amounts to repealing the foundational difference of the state: if representation is only a double of presentation, the state is useless. Moreover, the theorem of the point of excess shows that it is impossible to abolish all distance between a situation and its state.

However, in every orientation of thought of the constructivist type, a nostalgia for this solution subsists. There is a recurrent theme in such thought: the valorization of equilibrium; the idea that nature is an artifice which must be expressly imitated in its normalizing architecture—ordinals being, as we know, transitive intrications; the distrust of excess and errancy; and, at the heart of this framework, the systematic search for the double function, for the term which can be thought twice without having to change place or status.

But the fundamental approach in which a severe restriction of errancy can be obtained—without escaping the minimal excess imposed by the state—and a maximum legibility of the concept of 'part', is that of basing oneself on the constraints of language. In its essence, constructivist thought is a logical grammar. Or, to be exact, it ensures that language prevails as the norm for what may be acceptably recognized as one-multiple amongst representations. The spontaneous philosophy of all constructivist thought is radical nominalism.

What is understood here by 'language'? What is at stake, in fact, is a mediation of interiority, complete within the situation. Let's suppose that the presented multiples are only presented inasmuch as they have names, or that 'being-presented' and 'being-named' are one and the same thing. What's more, we have at our disposal a whole arsenal of properties, or liaison terms, which unequivocally designate that such a named thing maintains with another such a relationship, or possesses such a qualification. *Constructivist thought will only recognize as 'part' a grouping of presented multiples which have a property in common, or which all maintain a defined relationship to terms of the situation which are themselves univocally named.* If, for example, you have a scale of size at your disposal, it makes sense to consider, as parts of the situation, first, all those multiples of the situation which have *such* a fixed size; second, all those which are 'larger' than a fixed (effectively named) multiple. In the same manner, if one says 'there exists . . . ', this must be understood as saying, 'there exists a term named in the situation'; and if one says 'for all . . . ', this must be understood as, 'for all named terms of the situation'.

Why is language the medium of an interiority here? Because every *part*, without ambiguity, is assignable to an effective marking of the *terms* of the situation. It is out of the question to evoke a part 'in general'. You have to specify:

- what property or relation of language you are making use of, and you must be able to justify the application of these properties and relations to the terms of the situation;
- which fixed (and named) terms—or parameters—of the situation are implied.

In other words, the concept of part is *under condition*. The state simultaneously operates a count-as-one of parts and codifies what falls under this count: thus, besides being the master of representation in general, the state is the master of language. Language—or any comparable apparatus of recognition—is the legal filter for groupings of presented multiples. It is interposed between presentation and representation.

It is clear how only those parts which are *constructed* are *counted* here. If the multiple α is *included* in the situation, it is only on the condition that it is possible to establish, for example, that it groups together all those immediately presented multiples which maintain a relation—that is legitimate in the situation—with a multiple whose belonging to the situation is established. Here, the part results from taking into account, in successive stages, fixed multiples, admissible relations, and then the grouping-together of all those terms which can be linked to the former by means of the latter. Thus, there is always a perceptible bond between a part and terms which are recognizable within the situation. It is this bond, this *proximity* that language builds between presentation and representation, which grounds the conviction that the state does not exceed the situation by *too much*, or that it remains commensurable. I term 'language of the situation' the medium of this commensurability. Note that the language of the situation is subservient to presentation, in that it cannot cite any term, even in the general sense of 'there exists . . . ', whose belonging to the presentation cannot be verified. In this manner, through the medium of language, yet without being reduced to the latter inclusion stays *as close as possible* to belonging. The Leibnizian idea of a 'well-made language' has no other ambition than that of keeping as tight a rein as possible on the errancy of parts by means of the ordered codification of their expressible link to the situation whose parts they are.

What the constructivist vision of being and presentation hunts out is the 'indeterminate', the unnameable part, the conceptless link. The ambiguity of its relation to the state is thus quite remarkable. On the one hand, in restricting the statist metastructure's count-as-one to nameable parts, it seems to reduce its power; yet, on the other hand, it specifies its police and increases its authority by the connection that it establishes between mastery of the included one-multiple and mastery of language. What has to be understood here is that for this orientation in thought, a grouping of presented multiples which is indiscernible in terms of an immanent relation *does not exist*. From this point of view, the state legislates on existence. What it loses on the side of excess it gains on the side of the 'right over being'. This gain is all the more appreciable given that nominalism, here invested in the measure of the state, is irrefutable. From the Greek sophists to the Anglo-Saxon logical empiricists (even to Foucault), this is what has invariably made out of it the critical—or anti-philosophical—philosophy par excellence. To refute the doctrine that a part of the situation solely exists if it is constructed on the basis of properties and terms which are discernible in the language, would it not be necessary to *indicate* an absolutely undifferentiated, anonymous, inde- terminate part? But how could such a part be indicated, if not by *constructing* this very indication? The nominalist is always justified in saying that *this* counter-example, because it has been isolated and described, is in fact an example. Every example is grist to his mill if it can be indicated in the procedure which extracts its inclusion on the basis of belongings and language. The indiscernible is not. This is the thesis with which nom- inalism constructs its fortification, and by means of which it can restrict, at its leisure, any pretension to unfold excess in the world of in- differences.

Furthermore, within the constructivist vision of being, and this is a crucial point, *there is no place for an event to take place*. It would be tempting to say that on this point it coincides with ontology, which forecloses the event, thus declaring the latter's belonging to that-which-is-not-being- qua-being (Meditation 18). However this would be too narrow a conclu- sion. Constructivism has no need to *decide* upon the non-being of the event, because it does not have to know anything of the latter's undecid- ability. Nothing requires a decision with respect to a paradoxical multiple here. It is actually of the very essence of contructivism—this is its *total* immanence to the situation—to conceive neither of self-belonging, nor of the supernumerary; thus it maintains the entire dialectic of the event and intervention outside thought.

The orientation of constructivist thought cannot encounter a multiple which presents itself in the very presentation that it is—and this is the main characteristic of the eventual ultra-one—for the simple reason that if one wanted to 'construct' this multiple, one would have to have *already* examined it. This circle, which Poincaré remarked with respect to 'impredi- cative' definitions, breaks the procedure of construction and the depend- ency on language. Legitimate nomination is impossible. If you can name the multiple, it is because you discern it according to its elements. But if it is an element of itself, you would have had to have previously discerned it.

Not only that, but the case of the pure ultra-one—the multiple which has itself alone as element—leads formation-into-one into an impasse, due to the way the latter functions in this type of thought. That is, the singleton of such a multiple, which is a part of the situation, should isolate *the* multiple which possesses a property explicitly formulable in the language. But this is not possible, because the part thus obtained necessarily has the property in question *itself*. That is, the singleton, just like the multiple, has the same multiple alone as element. It cannot differentiate itself from the latter, neither extensionally, nor by any property. This case of indiscernibility between an element (a presentation) and its representative formation-into-one cannot be allowed within constructivist thought. It fails to satisfy the double differentiation of the state: by the count, and by language. In the case of a natural situation, a multiple can quite easily be both element and part: the part represented by the operation of its forming-into-one is nevertheless absolutely distinct from itself—from this 'itself' named twice, as such, by structure and metastructure. In the case of the evental ultra-one, the operation does not operate, and this is quite enough for contructivist thought to deny any being to what thereby leads the authority of language into an impasse.

With respect to the supernumerary nomination drawn from the void, in which the very secret of intervention resides, it absolutely breaks with the constructivist rules of language: the latter extract the names with which language supports the recognition of parts solely from the situation itself.

Unconstructible, the event is not. Inasmuch as it exceeds the immanence of language to the situation, intervention is unthinkable. The constructivist orientation *edifies* an immanent thought of the situation, *without deciding* its occurrence.

But if there is neither event nor intervention how can the situation change? The radical nominalism enveloped by the orientation of constructivist thought is no way disturbed by having to declare that a situation does not change. Or rather, what is called 'change' in a situation is nothing more than the constructive deployment of its parts. The *thought* of the situation evolves, because the exploration of the effects of the state brings to light previously unnoticed but linguistically controllable new connections. *The support for the idea of change is in reality the infinity of language.* A new nomination takes the role of a new multiple, but such novelty is relative, since the multiple validated in this manner is always constructible on the basis of those that have been recognized.

What then does it mean that there are different situations? *It means, purely and simply, that there are different languages.* Not only in the empirical sense of 'foreign' languages, but in Wittgenstein's sense of 'language games'. Every system of marking and binding constitutes a universe of constructible multiples, a distinct filter between presentation and representation. Since language legislates on the *existence* of parts, it is clearly within the being itself of presentation that there is difference: certain multiples can be validated—and thus exist—according to one language and not according to another. The heterogeneity of language games is at the foundation of a diversity of situations. Being is deployed multiply, because its deployment is solely presented within the multiplicity of languages.

In the final analysis, the doctrine of the multiple can be reduced to the double thesis of the infinity of each language (the reason behind apparent change) and the heterogeneity of languages (the reason behind the diversity of situations). And since the state is the master of language, one must recognize that for the constructivist change and diversity do not depend upon presentational primordiality, but upon representative functions. The key to mutations and differences resides in the State. It is thus quite possible that being qua being, is One and Immobile. However, constructivism prohibits such a declaration since it cannot be constructed on the basis of controllable parameters and relations within the situation. Such a thesis belongs to the category, as Wittgenstein puts it, of what one has to 'pass over in silence' because 'we cannot speak of [it]'. 'Being able to speak' being understood, of course, in a constructivist sense.

The orientation of constructivist thought—which responds, even if unconsciously, to the challenge represented by the impasse of ontology, the errancy of excess—forms the substructure of many particular conceptions. It is far from exercising its empire solely in the form of a nominalist philosophy. In reality, it universally regulates the dominant conceptions. The prohibition that it lays on random conglomerates, indistinct multiples and unconstructible forms suits conservation. The non-place of the event calms thought, and the fact that the intervention is unthinkable relaxes action. As such, the constructivist orientation underpins *neo-classicist* norms in art, *positivist* epistemologies and *programmatic* politics.

In the first case, one considers that the 'language' of an artistic situation—its particular system of marking and articulation—has reached a state of perfection which is such that, in wanting to modify it, or break with it, one would lose the thread of recognizable construction. The neo-classicist considers the 'modern' figures of art as promotions of chaos and the indistinct. He is right insofar as within the evental and interventional *passes* in art (let's say non-figurative painting, atonal music, etc.) there is necessarily a period of apparent barbarism, of intrinsic valorization of the complexities of disorder, of the rejection of repetition and easily discernible configurations. The deeper meaning of this period is that *it has not yet been decided exactly what the operator of faithful connection is* (cf. Meditation 23). At this point, the constructivist orientation commands us to confine ourselves —until this operator is stabilized—to the continuity of an engendering of parts regulated by the previous language. A neo-classicist is not a reactionary, he is a partisan of sense. I have shown that interventional illegality only generates sense *in* the situation when it disposes of a measure of the proximity between multiples of the situation and the supernumerary name of the event (that it has placed in circulation). This new temporal foundation is established during the previous period. The 'obscure' period is that of the overlapping of periods, and it is true that, distributed in heterogeneous periods, the first artistic productions of the new epoch only deliver a shattered or confused sense, which is solely perceptible for a transitory avant-garde. The neo-classicist fulfils the precious function of the guardianship of sense on a global scale. He testifies that there *must* be sense. When the neo-classicist declares his opposition to 'excess', it has to be understood as a warning: that no-one can remove themselves from the requisition of the ontological impasse.

In the second case, one considers that the language of positive science is the unique and definitive 'well-made' language, and that it has to name the procedures of construction, as far as possible, in every domain of experience. Positivism considers that presentation is a multiple of *factual* multiples, whose marking is experimental; and that constructible liaisons, grasped by the language of science, which is to say in a precise language, discern laws therein. The use of the word 'law' shows to what point positivism renders science a matter of the state. The hunting down of the indistinct thus has two faces. On the one hand, one must confine oneself to controllable facts: the positivist matches up clues and testimonies, experiments and statistics, in order to guarantee belongings. On the other hand, one must watch over the transparency of the language. A large part of 'false problems' result from imagining the existence of a multiple when the procedure of its construction under the control of language and under the law of facts is either incomplete or incoherent. Under the injunction of constructivist thought, positivism devotes itself to the ill-rewarded but useful tasks of the systematic marking of presented multiples, and the measurable fine-tuning of languages. The positivist is a professional in the maintenance of apparatuses of discernment.

In the third case, one posits that a political proposition necessarily takes the form of a programme whose agent of realization is the State—the latter is obviously none other than *the state of the politico-historic situation* (cf. Meditation 9). A programme is precisely a procedure for the construction of parts: political parties endeavour to show how such a procedure is compatible with the admitted rules of the language they share (the language of parliament for example). The centre of gravity of the interminable and contradictory debates over the 'possibility' (social, financial, national . . .) of measures recommended by so-and-so lies in the constructive character of the multiples whose discernment is announced. Moreover, everyone proclaims that their opposition is not 'systematic', but 'constructive'. What is at stake in this quarrel over the possible? The State. This is in perfect conformity with the orientation of constructivist thought, which renders its discourse statist in order to better grasp the commensurability between state and situation. The programme—a concentrate of the political proposition—is clearly a formula of the language which proposes a new configuration defined by strict links to the situation's parameters (budgetary, statistical, etc.), and which declares the latter *constructively* realizable—that is, recognizable—within the meta-structural field of the State.

The programmatic vision occupies the necessary role, in the field of politics, of reformatory moderation. It is a mediation of the State in that it attempts to formulate, in an accepted language, what the State is capable of. It thus protects people, in times of order, from having to recognize that what the State is capable of exceeds the very resources of that language; and that it would be more worthwhile to examine—yet it is an arid and complex demand—what they, the people, are capable of in the matter of politics and with respect to the surplus-capacity of the State. In fact the programmatic vision shelters the citizen from politics.

In short, the orientation of constructivist thought subsumes the relation to being *within the dimension of knowledge*. The principle of indiscernibles, which is its central axiom, comes down to the following: that which is not susceptible to being classified within a knowledge is not. 'Knowledge' designates here the capacity to inscribe controllable nominations in legitimate liaisons. In contrast to the radicalism of ontology, which suppresses liaisons in favour of the pure multiple (cf. Appendix 2), it is from liaisons that can be rendered explicit in a language that constructivism draws the guarantee of being for those one-multiples whose existence is ratified by the state. This is why, at the very point at which ontology revokes the bond of knowledge and faithfully connects its propositions together on the basis of the paradoxical marking of the void, constructivist thought advances step by step under the control of formulable connections, thus proposing a *knowledge of being*. This is the reason why it can hope to dominate any excess, that is, any unreasonable hole within the tissue of language.

It has to be acknowledged that this is a strong position, and that no-one can avoid it. Knowledge, with its moderated rule, its policed immanence to situations and its transmissibility, is the ordinary regime of the relation to being under circumstances in which it is not time for a new temporal foundation, and in which the diagonals of fidelity have somewhat deteriorated for lack of complete belief in the event they prophesize.

Rather than being a distinct and aggressive agenda, constructivist thought is the latent philosophy of all human sedimentation; the cumulative strata into which the forgetting of being is poured to the profit of language and the consensus of recognition it supports.

Knowledge calms the passion of being: measure taken of excess, it tames the state, and unfolds the infinity of the situation within the horizon of a constructive procedure shored up on the already-known.

No-one would wish this adventure to be permanent in which improbable names emerge from the void. Besides, it is on the basis of the exercise of knowledge that the surprise and the subjective motivation of their improbability emerges.

Even for those who wander on the borders of evental sites, staking their lives upon the occurrence and the swiftness of intervention, it is, after all, appropriate to be knowledgeable.

MEDITATION TWENTY-NINE
The Folding of Being and the Sovereignty of Language

The impasse of ontology—the quantitative un-measure of the set of parts of a set—tormented Cantor: it threatened his very desire for foundation. Accompanied by doubt, and with a relentlessness recounted in letters—letters speaking, in the morning light, of a hard night of thought and calculation—he believed that one should be able to show that the quantity of a set of parts is the cardinal which comes directly after that of the set itself, its successor. He believed especially that $p(\omega_0)$, the parts of denumerable infinity (thus, all the subsets constituted from whole numbers), had to be equal in quantity to ω_1, the first cardinal which measures an infinite quantity superior to the denumerable. This equation, written $|p(\omega_0)| = \omega_1$, is known under the name of the *continuum hypothesis*, because the multiple $p(\omega_0)$ is the ontological schema of the geometric or spatial continuum. Demonstrating the continuum hypothesis, or (when doubt had him in its grips) refuting it, was Cantor's terminal obsession: a case in which the individual is prey, at a point which he believes to be local or even technical, to a challenge of thought whose sense, still legible today, is exorbitant. For what wove and spun the dereliction of Cantor the inventor was nothing less than an errancy of being.

The equation $|p(\omega_0)| = \omega_1$ can be given a global sense. The generalized continuum hypothesis holds that, for any cardinal ω_a one has $|p(\omega_a)| = \omega_{S(a)}$. These hypotheses radically normalize the excess of the state by attributing a minimal measure to it. Since we know, by Cantor's theorem, that $|p(\omega_0)|$ in any case has to be a cardinal superior to ω_a, declaring it equal to $\omega_{S(a)}$, thus, to the cardinal which follows ω_a in the sequence of alephs, is, strictly speaking, *the least one can do*.

Easton's theorem (Meditation 26) shows that these 'hypotheses' are in reality pure decisions. Nothing, in fact, allows them to be verified or refuted, since it is coherent with the Ideas of the multiple that $\mid p(\omega_a) \mid$ take just about any value superior to ω_a.

Cantor thus had no chance in his desperate attempts to either establish or refute the 'continuum hypothesis'. The subjacent ontological challenge exceeded his inner conviction.

But Easton's theorem was published in 1970. Between Cantor's failure and Easton there are K.Gödel's results, which occurred at the end of the 1930s. These results, the ontological form of constructivist thought, already established that accepting the continuum hypothesis did not, in any manner, imply breaking with fidelity to the Ideas of the multiple: this decision is coherent with the fundamental axioms of the science of the pure multiple.

What is remarkable is that the normalization represented by the continuum hypothesis—the minimum of state excess—has its coherency guaranteed solely within the framework of a doctrine of the multiple which enslaves the latter's existence to the powers of language (on this occasion, the formalized language of logic). In this framework, moreover, it turns out that the axiom of choice is no longer a decision, because (from being an axiom in Zermelo's theory) it has become a faithfully deducible theorem. As such, the constructivist orientation, retroactively applied to ontology on the basis of the latter's own impasses, has the effect of comforting the axiom of intervention, at the price, one could say, of robbing it of its interventional value, since it becomes a necessity logically drawn from other axioms. It is no longer necessary to make an intervention with respect to intervention.

It is quite understandable that when it came to naming the voluntarily restricted version he operated of the doctrine of the multiple, Gödel chose the expression 'constructible universe', and that the multiples thereby submitted to language were called 'constructible sets'.

1. CONSTRUCTION OF THE CONCEPT OF CONSTRUCTIBLE SET

Take a set a. The general notion of the set of parts of a, $p(a)$, designates everything which is included in a. This is the origin of excess. Constructivist ontology undertakes the restriction of such excess: it envisages only admitting as *parts* of α what can be separated out (in the sense of the axiom of separation) by properties which are themselves stated in explicit formulas whose field of application, parameters, and quantifiers are solely referred to α itself.

Quantifiers: if, for example, I want to separate out (and constitute as a part of α) all the elements β of α which possess the property 'there exists a γ such that β has the relation R with γ'—$(\exists\gamma)[R(\beta,\gamma)]$—what must be understood is that the γ in question, cited by the existential quantifier, must be an element of α, and not just any existent multiple, drawn from the 'entire' universe of multiples. In other words, the proposition $(\exists\gamma)[R(\beta,\gamma)]$ must be read, in the case in question, as $(\exists\gamma)[\gamma \in \alpha \,\&\, R(\beta,\gamma)]$.

The same occurs with the universal quantifier. If I want to separate out as a part, let's say, all the elements β of α which are 'universally' linked to every multiple by a relation—$(\forall\gamma)[R(\beta,\gamma)]$—what must be understood is that $(\forall\gamma)$ means: for every γ *which belongs to* α: $(\forall\gamma)[\gamma \in \alpha \rightarrow R(\beta,\gamma)]$.

As far as parameters are concerned, a parameter is a proper name of a multiple which appears in a formula. Take, for example, the formula $\lambda(\beta,\beta_1)$, where β is a free variable and β_1 the name of a specified multiple. This formula 'means' that β entertains a definite relation with the multiple β_1 (a relation whose sense is fixed by λ). I can thus separate, as a part, all the elements β of α which effectively maintain the relation in question with the multiple named by β_1. However, in the constructivist vision (which postulates a radical immanence to the initial multiple α), this would only be legitimate if the multiple designated by β_1 belonged itself to α. For every fixed value attributed *in* α to this name β_1 I will have a part—in the constructive sense—composed of all the elements of α which maintain the relation expressed by the formula λ to this 'colleague' in belonging to α.

Finally, we will consider a *definable part* of α to be a grouping of elements of α that can be separated out by means of a formula. This formula will be said to be *restricted* to α; that is, it is a formula in which: 'there exists' is understood as 'there exists in α'; 'for all' is understood 'for all elements of α'; and all the names of sets must be interpreted as names of elements of α. We can see how the concept of part is hereby severely restricted under the concept of definable part by the double authority of language (the existence of an explicit separating formula) and the unique reference to the initial set.

We will term $D(\alpha)$—'the set of definable parts of α'—the set of parts which can be constructed in this manner. It is obvious that $D(\alpha)$ is a subset of $p(a)$, of the set of parts in the general sense. The former solely retains 'constructible' parts.

The language and the immanence of interpretations filter the concept of part here: a definable part of a is indeed *named* by the formula λ (which must be satisfied by the elements of the part), and *articulated on* a, in that the quantifiers and parameters do not import anything which is external to a. $D(a)$ is the subset of $p(a)$ whose constituents can be discerned and whose procedure of derivation, of grouping, on the basis of the set a itself, can be explicitly designated. Inclusion, by means of the logico-immanent filter, is *tightened around* belonging.

With this instrument, we can propose a hierarchy of being, the constructible hierarchy.

The idea is to constitute the void as the 'first' level of being and to pass to the following level by 'extracting' from the previous level all the constructible parts; that is, all those definable by an explicit property of the language on the previous level. Language thereby progressively enriches the number of pure multiples admitted into existence without letting anything escape from its control.

To number the levels, we will make use of the tool of nature: the series of ordinals. The concept of constructible level will be written L, and an ordinal index will indicate at what point of the procedure we find ourselves. L_a will signify the ath constructible level. Thus, the first level is void, and so we will posit $\mathsf{L}_0 = \varnothing$, the sign L_0 indicating that the hierarchy has begun. The second level will be constituted from all the *definable* parts of $\varnothing$ in L_0; that is, in $\varnothing$. In fact, there is only one such part: $\{\varnothing\}$. Therefore, we will posit that $\mathsf{L}_1 = \{\varnothing\}$. In general, when one arrives at a level L_a, one 'passes' to the level $\mathsf{L}_{S(a)}$ by taking all the explicitly definable parts of L_a (and not all the parts in the sense of ontology). Therefore, $\mathsf{L}_{S(a)} = D(\mathsf{L}_a)$. When one arrives at a limit ordinal, say ω_0, it suffices to gather together everything which is admitted to the previous levels. The *union* of these levels is then taken, that is: $\mathsf{L}_{\omega_0} = \cup\ \mathsf{L}_n$, for every $n \in \omega_0$. Or:

$\mathsf{L}_{\omega_0} = \cup\ \{\ \mathsf{L}_0, \mathsf{L}_1, \ldots\ \mathsf{L}_n, \mathsf{L}_{n+1}, \ldots\ \}$.

The constructible hierarchy is thus defined via recurrence in the following manner:

$\mathsf{L}_0 = \varnothing$

$\mathsf{L}_{S(a)} = D(\mathsf{L}_a)$ when it is a question of a successor ordinal;

$\mathsf{L}_a = \underset{\beta \in a}{\cup}\ \mathsf{L}_\beta$ when it is a question of a limit ordinal.

What each level of the constructible hierarchy does is normalize a 'distance' from the void, therefore, an increasing complexity. But the only multiples which are admitted into existence are those extracted from the inferior level by means of constructions which can be articulated in the formal language, and not 'all' the parts, including the undifferentiated, the unnameable and the indeterminate.

We will say that a multiple γ is *constructible* if it belongs to one of the levels of the constructible hierarchy. The property of being a constructible set will be written $\mathsf{L}(\gamma)$: $\mathsf{L}(\gamma) \rightarrow (\exists a)[\gamma \in \mathsf{L}_a]$, where a is an ordinal.

Note that if γ belongs to a level, it necessarily belongs to a successor level $\mathsf{L}_{s(\beta)}$ (try to demonstrate this, by showing how a limit level is only ever the union of all the inferior levels). $\mathsf{L}_{s(\beta)} = D(\mathsf{L}_\beta)$, which means that γ is a definable part of the level L_β. Consequently, for every constructible set there is an associated formula λ, which separates it out within its level of extraction (here, L_β), and possibly parameters, all of which are elements of this level. The set's *belonging* to $\mathsf{L}_{s(\beta)}$, which signifies its *inclusion* (definable) in L_β, is constructed on the basis of the tightening (within the level L_β, and under the logico-immanent control of a formula) of inclusion over belonging. We advance in counted—nameable—steps.

2. THE HYPOTHESIS OF CONSTRUCTIBILITY

At this point, 'being contructible' is merely a *possible* property for a multiple. This property can be expressed—by technical means for the manipulation of the formal language that I cannot reproduce here—in the language of set theory, the language of ontology, whose specific and unique sign is $\in$. Within the framework of ontology, one could consider that there are constructible sets and others which are not constructible. Thus, we would possess a negative criterion of the unnameable or nondescript multiple: it would be a multiple that was not constructible, and which therefore belonged to what ontology admits as multiple without belonging to any level of the hierarchy L.

There is, however, an impressive obstacle to such a conception which would reduce the constructivist restriction to being solely the examination of a particular property. It so happens that, if it is quite possible to demonstrate that some sets are constructible, *it is impossible to demonstrate that some sets are not*. The argument, in its conceptual scope, is that of nominalism, and its triumph is guaranteed: if you demonstrate that *such* a set is not constructible, it is because you were able to construct it. How indeed can one explicitly define such a multiple without, at the same time, showing it to be constructible? Certainly, we shall see that this aporia of the indeterminate, of the indiscernible, can be circumvented; that much is guaranteed—such is the entire point of the thought of the generic. But first we must give it its full measure.

Everything comes down to the following: the proposition 'every multiple is constructible' is *irrefutable* within the framework of the Ideas of the multiple that we have advanced up to this point—if, of course, these Ideas are themselves coherent. To hope to exhibit by demonstration a counter-example is therefore to hope in vain. One could, without breaking with the deductive fidelity of ontology, decide to solely accept constructible sets as existent.

This decision is known in the literature as the axiom of constructibility. It is written: 'For every multiple γ, there exists a level of the constructible hierarchy to which it belongs'; that is, $(\forall \gamma)(\exists a)[\gamma \in L_a]$, where a is an ordinal.

The demonstration of the irrefutable character of this decision—which is in no way considered by the majority of mathematicians as an axiom, as a veritable 'Idea' of the multiple—is of a subtlety which is quite instructive yet its technical details exceed the concerns of this book. It is achieved by means of an auto-limitation of the statement 'every multiple is constructible' to the constructible universe itself. The approach is roughly the following:

a. One begins by establishing that the seven main axioms of set theory (extensionality, powerset (parts), union, separation, replacement, void, and infinity) remain 'true' if the notion of set is restricted to that of constructible set. In other words, the set of constructible parts of a constructible set is constructible, the union of a constructible set is constructible, and so on. This amounts to saying that the constructible universe is a *model* of these axioms in that if one applies the constructions and the guarantees of existence supported by the Ideas of the multiple, and if their domain of application is restricted to the constructible universe, then the constructible is generated in return. It can also be said that in considering constructible multiples *alone*, one stays within the framework of the Ideas of the multiple, because the realization of these Ideas in the restricted universe will never generate anything non-constructible.

It is therefore clear that any demonstration drawn from the Ideas of the multiple can be 'relativized' because it is possible to restrict it to a demonstration which concerns constructible sets alone: it suffices to add to each of the demonstrative uses of an axiom that it must be taken in the constructible sense. When you write 'there exists α', this means 'there exists a constructible α', and so on. One then senses—though such a premonition is still vague—that it is impossible to demonstrate the existence of a non-constructible set, because the relativization of this demonstration would more or less amount to maintaining that a constructible non-constructible set exists: the supposed coherence of ontology, which is to say the value of its operator of fidelity—deduction—would not survive.

b. In fact, once the constructible universe is demonstrated to be a model of the fundamental axioms of the doctrine of the multiple, Gödel directly completes the irrefutability of the hypothesis 'every multiple is constructible' by showing that this statement is true in the constructible universe, that it is a consequence therein of the 'relativized' axioms. Common sense would say that this result is trivial: if one is inside the constructible universe, it is guaranteed that every multiple is constructible therein! But common sense goes astray in the labyrinth woven by the sovereignty of language and the folding of being within. The question here is that of establishing whether the statement $(\forall \alpha)[(\exists \beta)(\alpha \in L_\beta)]$ is a theorem of the constructible universe. In other words, *if* the quantifiers $(\forall \alpha)$ and $(\exists \beta)$ are restricted to this universe ('for every constructible α', and 'there exists a constructible β'), and *if* the writing '$\alpha \in L_\beta$'—that is, the *concept* of level—can be explicitly presented as a restricted *formula*, in the constructible sense, *then* this statement will be deducible within ontology. To peep under the veil, note that the relativization of the two quantifiers to the constructible universe generates the following:

$$(\forall \alpha)[(\exists \gamma)(\alpha \in L_\gamma)] \rightarrow (\exists \beta)[(\exists \delta)(\beta \in L_\delta) \ \& \ (\alpha \in L_\beta)]$$

For every α there exists an ordinal β such that $\alpha \in L_\beta$
which is constructible which is constructible

Two stumbling points show up when this formula is examined:

– One must be sure that the levels L_β can be indexed by constructible ordinals. In truth, *every* ordinal is constructible. The reader will find the proof of the latter, which is quite interesting, in Appendix 4. It is interesting because for thought it amounts to stating that nature is universally nameable (or constructible). This demonstration, which is not entirely trivial, was already part of Gödel's results.

– One must be sure that writings like $\alpha \in L_\gamma$ have a constructible sense; in other words, that the concept of constructible level is itself constructible. This will be verified by showing that the function which matches every ordinal α to the level L_α—thus the definition by recurrence of the levels L_α—is not modified in its results if it is relativized to the constructible universe. That is, we originally gave this definition of the constructible *within ontology,* and not within the constructible universe. It is not guaranteed that the levels L_α are 'the same' if they are defined within their own proper empire.

3. ABSOLUTENESS

It is quite characteristic that in order to designate a property or a function that remains 'the same' within ontology strictly speaking and in its relativization mathematicians employ the adjective 'absolute'. This symptom is quite important.

Take a formula $\lambda(\beta)$ where β is a free variable of the formula (if there are any). We will define the *restriction to the constructible universe* of this formula by using the procedures which served in constructing the concept of constructibility; that is, by considering that, in λ, a quantifier $(\exists \beta)$ means 'there exists a constructible β'—or $(\exists \beta)[L(\beta) \, \& \, \ldots \,]$—a quantifier $(\forall \beta)$ means 'for all constructible β'—or $(\forall \beta)[L(\beta) \rightarrow \ldots \,]$—and the variable β is solely authorised to take constructible values. The formula obtained in this manner will be written $\lambda^L(\beta)$, which reads: 'restriction of the formula λ to the constructible universe'. We previously indicated, for example, that the restriction to the constructible universe of the axioms of set theory is deducible.

We will say that a formula $\lambda(\beta)$ is *absolute for the constructible universe* if it can be demonstrated that its restriction is equivalent to itself, for fixed constructible values of variables. In other words, if we have: $L(\beta) \rightarrow [\lambda(\beta) \leftrightarrow \lambda^L(\beta)]$.

Absoluteness signifies that the formula, once tested *within* the constructible universe, has the same truth value as its restriction to that universe. If the formula is absolute, its restriction therefore does not restrict its truth, once one is in a position of immanence to the constructible universe. It can be shown, for example, that the operation 'union' is absolute for the constructible universe, in that if one has L_α, then $\cup \, \alpha = (\cup \, \alpha)^L$: the union (in the general sense) of a constructible α is *the same thing*, the same being, as union in the constructible sense.

The absolute is here the equivalence of general truth and restricted truth. Absolute is a predicate of these propositions which stipulates that their restriction does not affect their truth value.

If we return now to our problem, the point is to establish that the concept of constructible hierarchy is absolute for the constructible universe, thus in a certain sense absolute for itself. That is: $\mathsf{L}(\alpha) \rightarrow [\mathsf{L}(\alpha) \leftrightarrow \mathsf{L}^{\mathsf{L}}(\alpha)]$, where $\mathsf{L}^{\mathsf{L}}(\alpha)$ means the *constructible concept of constructibility*.

To examine this point, far more rigour in the manipulation of formal language will be required than that which has been introduced up to this point. It will be necessary to scrutinize exactly what a restricted formula is, to 'decompose' it into elementary set operations *in finite number* ('the Gödel operations'), and then to show that each of these operations is absolute for the constructible universe. It will then be established that the function which maps the correspondence, to each ordinal α, of the level L_α is itself absolute for the constructible universe. We will then be able to conclude that the statement 'every multiple is constructible', relativized to the constructible universe, is true; or, that every constructible set is constructively constructed.

The *hypothesis* that every set is constructible is thus a *theorem* of the constructible universe.

The effect of this inference is immediate: if the statement 'every multiple is constructible' is true in the constructible universe, one cannot produce any refutation of it in ontology *per se*. Such a refutation would, in fact, be relativizable (because all the axioms are), and one would be able to refute, within the constructivist universe, the relativization of that statement. Yet this is not possible because, on the contrary, that relativization is deducible therein.

The decision to solely accept the existence of constructible multiples is thus without risk. No counter-example, as long as one confines oneself to the Ideas of the multiple, could be used to ruin its rationality. The hypothesis of an ontology submitted to language—of an ontological nominalism—is irrefutable.

One empirical aspect of the question is that, of course, no mathematician could ever exhibit a non-constructible multiple. The classic sets of active mathematics (whole numbers, real and complex numbers, functional spaces, etc.) are all constructible.

Is this enough to convince someone whose desire is not only to advance ontology (that is, to be a mathematician), but to think ontological thought? Must one have the wisdom to fold being to the requisites of formal language? The mathematician, who only ever *encounters* constructible sets, no doubt also has that *other* latent desire: I detect its sign in the fact that, in general, mathematicians are reluctant to maintain the hypothesis of constructibility as an axiom in the same sense as the others—however homogeneous it may be to the reality that they manipulate.

The reason for this is that the normalizing effects of this folding of being, of this sovereignty of language, are such that they propose a flattened and correct universe in which excess is reduced to the strictest of measures, and in which situations persevere indefinitely in their regulated being. We shall see, successively, that if one assumes that every multiple is constructible, the event is not, the intervention is non-interventional (or legal), and the un-measure of the state is exactly measurable.

4. THE ABSOLUTE NON-BEING OF THE EVENT

In ontology *per se*, the non-being of the event is a decision. To foreclose the existence of sets which belong to themselves—ultra-one's—a special axiom is necessary, the axiom of foundation (Meditation 14). The delimitation of non-being is the result of an explicit and inaugural statement.

With the hypothesis of constructibility, everything changes. This time one can actually *demonstrate* that no (constructible) multiple is evental. In other words, the hypothesis of constructibility reduces the axiom of foundation to the rank of a theorem, a faithful consequence of the other Ideas of the multiple.

Take a constructible set α. Suppose that it is an element of itself, that we have $\alpha \in \alpha$. The set α, which is constructible, *appears* in the hierarchy at a certain level, let's say $\mathsf{L}_{s(\beta)}$. It appears as a definable *part* of the previous level. Thus we have $\alpha \subset \mathsf{L}_\beta$. But since $\alpha \in \alpha$, we also have $\alpha \in \mathsf{L}_\beta$, if α is a part of L_β. Therefore, α had *already* appeared at L_β when we supposed that its first level of appearance was $\mathsf{L}_{s(\beta)}$. This antecedence to self is constructively impossible. We can see here how hierarchical generation bars the possibility of self-belonging. Between cumulative construction by levels and the event, a choice has to be made. If, therefore, every multiple is constructible, no multiple is evental. We have no need here of the axiom of foundation: the hypothesis of constructibility provides for the deducible elimination of any 'abnormal' multiplicity, of any ultra-one.

Within the constructible universe, it is necessary (and not decided) that the event does not exist. This is a difference of principle. The interventional recognition of the event contravenes a special and primordial thesis of general ontology. It *refutes*, on the other hand, the very coherency of the constructible universe. In the first case, it suspends an axiom. In the second, it ruins a fidelity. Between the hypothesis of constructibility and the event, again, a choice has to be made. And the discordance is maintained in the very sense of the word 'choice': the hypothesis of constructibility takes no more account of intervention than it does of the event.

5. THE LEGALIZATION OF INTERVENTION

No more than the axiom of foundation is the axiom of choice an axiom within the constructible universe. This unheard of decision, which caused such an uproar, finds itself equally reduced to being no more than an effect of the other Ideas of the multiple. Not only can one demonstrate that a (constructible) function of choice exists, on all constructible sets, but furthermore that there exists one such function, forever identical and definable, which is capable of operating on any (constructible) multiple whatsoever: it is called a *global* choice function. The illegality of choice, the anonymity of representatives, the ungraspable nature of delegation (see Meditation 22) are reduced to the procedural uniformity of an order.

I have already revealed the duplicity of the axiom of choice. A wild procedure of representatives without any law of representation, it nevertheless leads to the conception that all multiples are susceptible to being well-ordered. The height of disorder is inverted into the height of order. This second aspect is central in the constructible universe. In the latter, one can directly demonstrate, without recourse to supplementary hypotheses, nor to any wager on intervention, that every multiple is well-ordered. Let's trace the development of this triumph of order via language. It is worthwhile glancing—without worrying about complete rigour—at the techniques of order, such as laid out under the constructivist vision on a shadowless day.

As it happens, everything, or almost everything, is extracted from the *finite* character of the explicit writings of the language (the formulas). Every constructible set is a definable part of a level L_β. The formula λ which defines the part only contains a finite number of signs. It is thus possible to rank, or order, all the formulas on the basis of their 'length' (their number of signs). One then agrees, and a bit of technical tinkering suffices to establish this convention, to order *all* constructible multiples on the basis of the order of the formulas which define them. In short, since every constructible multiple has a name (a phrase or a formula which designates it), the order of names induces a total order of these multiples. Such is the power of any dictionary: to exhibit a list of nameable multiplicities. Things are, of course, a bit more complicated, because one must also take into account that it is *at a certain level*, L_β, that a constructible multiple is definable. What will actually be combined is the order of words, or formulas, and the supposed order previously obtained upon the elements of the level L_β. Nevertheless, the heart of the procedure lies in the fact that every set of finite phrases can be well-ordered.

The result is that every level L_β is well-ordered, and thus so is the entire constructible hierarchy.

The axiom of choice is no longer anything more than a sinecure: given any constructible multiple, the 'function of choice' will only have to select, for example, its smallest element according to the well-ordering induced by its inclusion within the level L_β, of which it is a definable part. It is a uniform, determined procedure, and, I dare say, one without choice.

We have thus indicated that the existence of a function of choice on any constructible multiple can be *demonstrated*: moreover, we are actually capable of constructing or exhibiting this function. As such, it is appropriate within the constructible universe to abandon the expression 'axiom of choice' and to replace it with 'theorem of universal well-ordering'.

The metatheoretical advantage of this demonstration is that it is guaranteed from now on that the axiom of choice is (in general ontology) coherent with the other Ideas of the multiple. For if one could refute it on the basis of these Ideas, which is to say demonstrate the existence of a set without a choice function, a *relativized* version of this demonstration would exist. One could demonstrate something like: 'there exists a constructible set which does not allow a constructible choice function.' But we have just shown the contrary.

If ontology without the axiom of choice is coherent, it must also be so with the axiom of choice, because in the restricted version of ontology found in the constructible universe the axiom of choice is a faithful consequence of the other axioms.

The inconvenience, however, lies in the hypothesis of constructibility solely delivering a necessary and explicit version of 'choice'. As a deductive consequence, this 'axiom' loses everything which made it into the form-multiple of intervention: illegality, anonymity, existence without existent. It is no longer anything more than a formula in which one can decipher the total order to which language folds being, when it is allowed that language legislates upon what is admissible as a one-multiple.

6. THE NORMALIZATION OF EXCESS

The impasse of ontology is transformed into a passage by the hypothesis of constructibility. Not only is the intrinsic size of the set of parts perfectly fixed, but it is also, as I have already announced, the smallest possible such size. Nor is a decision is required to end the excessive errancy of the state. One *demonstrates* that if ω_a is a constructible cardinal, the set of its constructible parts has $\omega_{S(a)}$ as its cardinality. The generalized continuum hypothesis is true in the constructible universe. The latter, and careful here, must be read as follows: $\llcorner (\omega_a) \rightarrow [| \ p(\omega_a) \ | = \omega_{S(a)}]^\llcorner$; a writing in which everything is restricted to the constructible universe.

This time it will suffice to outline the demonstration in order to point out its obstacle.

The first remark to be made is that from now on, when we speak of a cardinal ω_a, what must be understood is: the ath *constructible* aleph. The point is delicate, but it sheds a lot of light upon the 'relativism' induced by any constructivist orientation of thought. The reason is that the concept of cardinal, in contrast to that of ordinal, *is not absolute*. What is a cardinal after all? It is an ordinal such that there is no one-to-one correspondence between it and an ordinal which precedes it (a smaller ordinal). But a one-to-one correspondence, like any relation, is only ever a multiple. In the constructible universe, an ordinal is a cardinal if there does not exist, between it and a smaller ordinal, a *constructible* one-to-one correspondence. Therefore, it is possible, given an ordinal a, that it be a cardinal in the constructible universe, and not in the universe of ontology. For that to be the case it would suffice that, between a and a smaller ordinal, there exists a non-constructible one-to-one correspondence, but no constructible one-to-one correspondence.

I said 'it is possible'. The spice of the matter is that this 'it is possible' will never be an 'it is sure'. For that it would be necessary to show the existence of a non-constructible set (the one-to-one correspondence), which is impossible. *Possible* existence, however, suffices to de-absolutize the concept of cardinal. Despite being undemonstrable, there is a risk attached to the series of constructible cardinals: that they be 'more numerous' than the cardinals in the general sense of ontology. It is possible that there are cardinals which are created by the constraint of language and the restriction it operates upon the one-to-one correspondences in question. This risk is tightly bound to the following: cardinality is defined in terms of inexistence (no one-to-one correspondence). Yet nothing is less absolute than inexistence.

Let's turn to the account of the proof.

One starts by showing that the intrinsic quantity—the cardinal—of an infinite level of the constructible hierarchy is equal to that of its ordinal index. That is, $|\mathsf{L}_\alpha| = |\alpha|$. This demonstration is quite a subtle exercise which the skilful reader can attempt on the basis of methods found in Appendix 4.

Once this result is acquired, the deductive strategy is the following:

Take a cardinal (in the constructible sense), ω_a. What we know is that $|\mathsf{L}_{\omega_a}| = \omega_a$ and that $|\mathsf{L}_{\omega_{S(a)}}| = \omega_{S(a)}$: two levels whose indexes are two successive cardinals have these cardinals respectively as their cardinality. Naturally between L_{ω_a} and $\mathsf{L}_{\omega_{S(a)}}$ there is a gigantic crowd of levels; all those indexed by the innumerable ordinals situated 'between' these two special ordinals that are cardinals, alephs. Thus, between L_{ω_0} and L_{ω_1}, we have $\mathsf{L}_{S(\omega_0)}, \mathsf{L}_{S(S(\omega_0))}, \ldots, \mathsf{L}_{\omega_0 + \omega_0}, \ldots, \mathsf{L}_{\omega_0 2}, \ldots, \mathsf{L}_{\omega_0 n}, \ldots$

What can be said about the *parts* of the cardinal ω_a? Naturally, 'part' must be understood in the constructible sense. There will be parts of ω_a that will be definable in $\mathsf{L}_{S(\omega_a)}$, and which will appear on the following level, $\mathsf{L}_{S(S(\omega_a))}$, then others on the next level, and so on. The fundamental idea of the demonstration is to establish that *all* the constructible parts of ω_a will be 'exhausted' *before* arriving at the level $\mathsf{L}_{\omega_{S(a)}}$. The result will be that all of these parts are found together in the level $\mathsf{L}_{\omega_{S(a)}}$, which, as we have seen, conserves what has been previously constructed. If all of the constructible parts of ω_a are elements of $\mathsf{L}_{\omega_{S(a)}}$, then $p(\omega_a)$ *in the constructible sense*—if you like, $p^\mathsf{L}(\omega_a)$—is itself a part of this level. But if $p^\mathsf{L}(\omega_a) \subset \mathsf{L}_{\omega_{S(a)}}$, its cardinality being at the most equal to that of the set in which it is included, we have (since $|\mathsf{L}_{\omega_{S(a)}}| = \omega_{S(a)}$): $|p(\omega_a)| < \omega_{S(a)}$. Given that Cantor's theorem tells us $\omega_a < |p(\omega_a)|$, it is evident that $|p(\omega_a)|$ is necessarily equal to $\omega_{S(a)}$, because 'between' ω_a and $\omega_{S(a)}$ there is no cardinal.

Everything, therefore, comes down to showing that a constructible part of ω_α appears in the hierarchy before the level $\mathsf{L}_{\omega_{S(\alpha)}}$. The fundamental lemma is written in the following manner: for any constructible part β of ω_α, there exists an ordinal γ such that $\gamma \in \omega_{S(\alpha)}$, with $\beta \in \mathsf{L}_\gamma$. This lemma, the rock of the demonstration, is what lies beyond the means I wish to employ in this book. It also requires a very close analysis of the formal language.

Under its condition we obtain the total domination of the state's excess which is expressed in the following formula: $\mid p(\omega_\alpha) \mid = \omega_{S(\alpha)}$; that is, the placement, in the constructible universe, of the set of parts of an aleph *just after it*, according to the power defined by the successor aleph.

At base, the sovereignty of language—if one adopts the constructivist vision—produces the following statement (in which I short-circuit quantitative explanation, and whose charm is evident): *the state succeeds the situation*.

7. SCHOLARLY ASCESIS AND ITS LIMITATION

The long, sinuous meditation passing through the scruples of the constructible, the forever incompletable technical concern, the incessant return to what is explicit in language, the weighted connection between existence and grammar: do not think that what must be read therein with boredom is an uncontrolled abandon to formal artifice. Everybody can see that the constructible universe is—in its refined procedure even more than in its result—the ontological symbol of knowledge. The ambition which animates this genre of thought is to maintain the multiple within the grasp of what can be written and verified. Being is only admitted to being within the transparency of signs which bind together its derivation on the basis of what we have already been able to inscribe. What I wished to transmit, more than the general spirit of an ontology ordained to knowledge, was the ascesis of its means, the clockwork minutiae of the filter it places between presentation and representation, or belonging and inclusion, or the immediacy of the multiple, and the construction of legitimate groupings—its passage to state jurisdiction. Nominalism reigns, I stated, in our world: it is its spontaneous philosophy. The universal valorization of 'competence', even inside the political sphere, is its basest product: all it comes down to is guaranteeing the competence of he who is capable of naming realities such as they are. But what is at stake here is a lazy nominalism, for our times do not even have the time for authentic knowledge. The exaltation of competence is rather the desire—in order to do without truth—to glorify knowledge without knowing.

Its nose to the grindstone of being, scholarly or constructible ontology is, in contrast, ascetic and relentless. The gigantic labour by means of which it refines language and passes the presentation of presentation through its subtle filters—a labour to which Jensen, after Gödel, attached his name—is properly speaking admirable. There we have the clearest view—because it is the most complex and precise—of what *of* being qua being *can be pronounced* under the condition of language and the discernible. The examination of the consequences of the hypothesis of constructibility gives us the ontological paradigm of constructivist thought and teaches us what thought is capable of. The results are there: the irrepressible excess of the state of a situation finds itself, beneath the scholarly eye which instructs being according to language, reduced to a minimal and measurable quantitative pre-eminence.

We also know the price to be paid—but is it one for knowledge itself? —the absolute and necessary annulment of any thought of the event and the reduction of the form-multiple of intervention to a definable figure of universal order.

The reason behind this trade-off, certainly, is that the constructible universe is narrow. If one can put it this way, it contains the least possible multiples. It counts as one with parsimony: real language, discontinuous, is an infinite power, but it never surpasses the denumerable.

I said that any direct evaluation of this restriction was impossible. Without the possibility of exhibiting at least one non-constructible set one cannot know to what degree constructivist thought deprives us of multiples, or of the wealth of being. The sacrifice demanded here as the price of measure and order is both intuitively enormous and rationally incalculable.

However, if the framework of the Ideas of the multiple is enlarged by the axiomatic admission of 'large' multiples, of cardinals whose existence cannot be inferred from the resources of the classic axioms alone, one realizes, from this observatory in which being is immediately magnified in its power of infinite excess, that the limitation introduced in the thought of being by the hypothesis of constructibility is quite simply draconian, and that the sacrifice is, literally, unmeasured. One can thus turn to what I termed in Meditation 27 the third orientation of thought: its exercise is to name multiples so transcendent it is expected that they order whatever precedes them, and although it often fails in its own ambition this orientation can be of some use in judging the real effects of the constructivist orientation. From my point of view, which is neither that of the power of language (whose indispensable ascesis I recognize), nor that of transcendence (whose heroism I recognize), there is some pleasure to be had in seeing how each of these orientations provides a diagnostic for the other.

In Appendix 3, I speak of the 'large cardinals' whose existence cannot be deduced within the classical set theory axioms. However, by confidence in the prodigality of presentation, one may declare their being—save if, in investigating further, one finds that in doing so the coherency of language is ruined. For example, does a cardinal exist which is both limit and 'regular' other than ω_0? It can be shown that this is a matter of decision. Such cardinals are said to be 'weakly inaccessible'. Cardinals said to be 'strongly inaccessible' have the property of being 'regular', and, moreover, of being such that they overtake in intrinsic size the set of parts of any set which is smaller than them. If π is inaccessible, and if $a < \pi$, we also have $\mid p(a) \mid < \pi$. As such, these cardinals cannot be attained by means of the reiteration of statist excess over what is inferior to them.

But there is the possibility of defining cardinals far more gigantic than the first strongly inaccessible cardinal. For example, the Mahlo cardinals are still larger than the first inaccessible cardinal π, which itself has the property of being the πth inaccessible cardinal (thus, the latter is such that the set of inaccessible cardinals smaller than it has π as its cardinality).

The theory of 'large cardinals' has been constantly enriched by new monsters. All of them must form the object of special axioms to guarantee their existence. All of them attempt to constitute within the infinite an abyss comparable to the one which distinguishes the first infinity, ω_0, from the finite multiples. None of them quite succeed.

There is a large variety of technical means for defining very large cardinals. They can possess properties of inaccessibility (this or that operation applied to smaller cardinals does not allow one to construct them), but also positive properties, which do not have an immediately visible relation with intrinsic size yet which nevertheless require it. The classic example is that of measurable cardinals whose specific property —and I will leave its mystery intact—is the following: a cardinal π is measurable if there exists on π a non-principal π-complete ultrafilter. It is clear that this statement is an assertion of existence and not a procedure of inaccessibility. One can demonstrate, however, that a measurable cardinal is a Mahlo cardinal. Furthermore, and this already throws some light upon the limiting effect of the constructibility hypothesis, one can demonstrate (Scott, 1961) that if one admits this hypothesis, there are no measurable cardinals. The constructible universe *decides*, itself, on the impossibility of being of certain transcendental multiplicities. It restricts the infinite prodigality of presentation.

Diverse properties concerning the 'partitions' of sets also lead us to the supposition of the existence of very large cardinals. One can see that the 'singularity' of a cardinal is, in short, a property of partition: it can be divided into a number, smaller than itself, of pieces smaller than itself (Appendix 3).

Consider the following property of partition: given a cardinal π, take, for each whole number n, the n-tuplets of elements of π. The set of these n-tuplets will be written $[\pi]^n$, to be read: the set whose elements are all sets of the type $\{\beta_1, \beta_2, \ldots \beta_n\}$ where $\beta_1, \beta_2, \beta_n$ are n elements of π. Now consider the union of all the $[\pi]^n$, *for* $n \to \omega_0$; in other words, the set made up of *all* the finite series of elements of π. Say that this set is divided into two: on the one side, certain n-tuplets, on the other side, others. Note that this partition cuts through each $[\pi]^n$: for example, on one side there are probably triplets of elements of π $\{\beta_1, \beta_2, \beta_3\}$, and on the other side, other triplets $\{\beta'_1, \beta'_2, \beta'_3\}$, and so it goes for every n. It is said that a subset, $\gamma \subset \pi$, of π is *n-homogeneous* for the partition if all the n-tuplets of elements of γ are in the same half. In this manner, γ is 2-homogeneous for the partition if *all* the pairs $\{\beta_1, \beta_2\}$—with $\beta_1 \in \gamma$ and $\beta_2 \in \gamma$—are in the same half.

It will be said that $\gamma \subset \pi$ is *globally homogeneous* for the partition if it is n-homogeneous for all n. This does *not* mean that all the n-tuplets, for whatever n, are in the same half. It means that, n being fixed, for that n, they are all in one of the halves. For example, all the pairs $\{\beta_1, \beta_2\}$ of elements of γ must be in the same half. All the triplets $\{\beta_1, \beta_2, \beta_3\}$ must also be in the same half (but it could be the other half, not the one in which the pairs are found), etc.

A cardinal π is a *Ramsey cardinal* if, for *any* partition defined in this manner—that is, a division in two of the set $\underset{n \in \omega_0}{\cup} [\pi]^n$—there exists a subset $\gamma \subset \pi$, whose cardinality is π which is globally homogeneous for the partition.

The link to intrinsic size is not particularly clear. However it can be shown that every Ramsey cardinal is inaccessible, that it is weakly compact (another species of monster), etc. In brief, a Ramsey cardinal is very large indeed.

It so happens that in 1971, Rowbottom published the following remarkable result: if there exists a Ramsey cardinal, for every cardinal smaller than it, the set of *constructible* parts of this cardinal has a power equal to this cardinal. In other words: if π is a Ramsey cardinal, and if $\omega_a < \pi$, we have $| p^{\llcorner}(\omega_a) | = \omega_a$. In particular, we have $| p^{\llcorner}(\omega_0) | = \omega_0$, which means that the set of constructible parts of the denumerable—that is, the real constructible numbers, the constructible continuum—does *not* exceed the denumerable itself.

The reader may find this quite surprising: after all, doesn't Cantor's theorem, whose constructible relativization certainly exists, state that $| p(\omega_a) | > \omega_a$ always and everywhere? Yes, but Rowbottom's theorem is a theorem *of general ontology* and not a theorem immanent to the constructible universe. *In* the constructible universe, we evidently have the following: 'The set of constructible parts of a (constructible) set has a power (in the constructible sense) superior (in the constructible sense) to that (in the constructible sense) of the initial set.' With such a restriction we definitely have, *in* the constructible universe, $\omega_a < | p(\omega_a) |$, which means: no *constructible* one-to-one correspondence exists between the set of constructible parts of ω_a and ω_a itself.

Rowbottom's theorem, on the other hand, deals with cardinalities in general ontology. It declares that if there exists a Ramsey cardinal, then there is definitely a one-to-one correspondence between ω_a (in the general sense) and the set of its constructible parts. One result in particular is that the *constructible* ω_1, which is constructibly equal to $| p(\omega_a) |$, is not, in general ontology with Ramsey cardinals, a cardinal in any manner (in the general sense).

If the point of view of truth, exceeding the strict law of language, is that of general ontology, and if confidence in the prodigality of being weighs in favour of admitting the existence of a Ramsey cardinal, then Rowbottom's theorem grants us a measure of the sacrifice that we are invited to make by the hypothesis of constructibility: it authorizes the existence of no more parts than there are elements in the situation, and it creates 'false cardinals'. Excess, then, is not measured but cancelled out.

The situation, and this is quite characteristic of the position of knowledge, is in the end the following. *Inside* the rules which codify the admission into existence of multiples within the constructivist vision we have a complete and totally ordered universe, in which excess is minimal, and in which the event and intervention are reduced to being no more than necessary consequences of the situation. *Outside*—that is, from a standpoint where no restriction upon parts is tolerated, where inclusion radically exceeds belonging, and where one assumes the existence of the indeterminate and the unnameable (and assuming this only means that they are not prohibited, since they cannot be *shown*)—the constructible universe appears to be one of an astonishing poverty, in that it reduces the function of excess to nothing, and only manages to stage it by means of fictive cardinals.

This poverty of knowledge—or this dignity of procedures, because the said poverty can only be seen from outside, and under risky hypotheses—results, in the final analysis, from its particular law being, besides the discernible, that of the decidable. Knowledge excludes ignorance. This tautology is profound: it designates that scholarly ascesis, and the universe which corresponds to it, is captivated by the desire for decision. We have seen how a positive decision was taken concerning the axiom of choice and the continuum hypothesis with the hypothesis of constructibility. As A. Levy says: 'The axiom of constructibility gives such an exact description of what all sets are that one of the most profound open problems in set theory is to find a natural statement of set theory which does not refer, directly or indirectly, to very large ordinals . . . and which is neither proved nor refuted by the axiom of constructibility.' Furthermore, concerning the thorny question of knowing which regular ordinals have or don't have the tree property, the same author notes: 'Notice that if we assume the axiom of constructibility then we know exactly which ordinals have the tree property; it is typical of this axiom to decide questions one way or another.'

Beyond even the indiscernible, what patient knowledge desires and seeks from the standpoint of a love of exact language, even at the price of a rarefaction of being, is that nothing be undecidable.

The ethic of knowledge has as its maxim: act and speak such that everything be clearly decidable.

MEDITATION THIRTY
Leibniz

'Every event has prior to it, its conditions, prerequisites, suitable dispositions, whose existence makes up its sufficient reason'

Fifth Writing in Response to Clarke

It has often been remarked that Leibniz's thought was prodigiously modern, despite his stubborn error concerning mechanics, his hostility to Newton, his diplomatic prudence with regard to established powers, his conciliatory volubility in the direction of scholasticism, his taste for 'final causes', his restoration of singular forms or entelechies, and his popish theology. If Voltaire's sarcasms were able, for a certain time, to spread the idea of a blissful optimism immediately annulled by any temporal engagement, who, today, would philosophically desire Candide's little vegetable garden rather than Leibniz's world where 'each portion of matter can be conceived as a garden full of plants, and as a pond full of fish', and where, once more, 'each branch of a plant, each member of an animal, each drop of its humours, is still another such garden or pond'?

What does this paradox depend on, this paradox of a thought whose conscious conservative will drives it to the most radical anticipations, and which, like God creating monads in the system, 'fulgurates' at every moment with intrepid intuitions?

The thesis I propose is that Leibniz is able to demonstrate the most implacable inventive freedom once he has *guaranteed* the surest and most controlled ontological foundation—the one which completely accomplishes, down to the last detail, the constructivist orientation.

In regard to being in general, Leibniz posits that two principles, or axioms, guarantee its submission to language.

The first principle concerns being-possible, which, besides, is, insofar as it resides as Idea in the infinite understanding of God. This principle, which rules the essences, is that of non-contradiction: everything whose contrary envelops a contradiction possesses the right to be in the mode of possibility. Being-possible is thus subordinate to pure logic; the ideal and transparent language which Leibniz worked on from the age of twenty onwards. This being, which contains—due to its accordance with the formal principle of identity—an effective possibility, is neither inert, nor abstract. It tends towards existence, as far as its intrinsic perfection—which is to say its nominal coherence—authorizes it to: 'In possible things, or in possibility itself or essence, there is a certain urge for existence, or, so to speak, a striving to being.' Leibniz's logicism is an ontological postulate: every non-contradictory multiple desires to exist.

The second principle concerns being-existent, the world, such that amongst the various possible multiple-combinations, it has actually been presented. This principle, which rules over the apparent contingency of the 'there is', is the principle of sufficient reason. It states that what is presented must be able to be thought according to a suitable reason for its presentation: 'we can find no true or existent fact, no true assertion, without there being a sufficient reason why it is thus and not otherwise.' What Leibniz absolutely rejects is chance—which he calls 'blind chance', exemplified for him, and quite rightly, in Epicurus' *clinamen*—if it means an event whose sense would have to be wagered. For any reason concerning such an event would be, in principle, insufficient. Such an interruption of logical nominations is inadmissible. Not only 'nothing happens without it being possible for someone who knows enough things to give a reason sufficient to determine why it is so and not otherwise', but analysis can and must be pursued to the point at which a reason is *also* given for the reasons themselves: 'Every time that we have sufficient reasons for a singular action, we also have reasons for its prerequisites.' A multiple, and the multiple infinity of multiples from which it is composed, can be circumscribed and thought in the absolute constructed legitimacy of their being.

Being-qua-being is thus doubly submitted to nominations and explanations:

– as essence, or possible, one can always examine, in a regulated manner, its logical coherency. Its 'necessary truth' is such that one must find its reason 'by analysis, resolving it into simpler ideas and simpler truths until we reach the primitives', the primitives being tautologies, '*identical propositions* whose opposite contains an explicit contradiction';

– as existence, it is such that 'resolution into particular reasons' is always possible. The only obstacle is that this resolution continues infinitely. But this is merely a matter for the calculation of series: presented-being, infinitely multiple, has its ultimate reason in a limit-term, God, which, at the very origin of things, practises a certain 'Divine Mathematics', and thus forms the 'reason'—in the sense of calculation—'[for] the sequence or *series* of this multiplicity of contingencies'. Presented multiples are constructible, both *locally* (their 'conditions, prerequisites, and suitable dispositions' are necessarily found), and *globally* (God is the reason for their series, according to a simple rational principle, which is that of producing the maximum of being with the minimum of means, or laws).

Being-in-totality, or the world, is thereby found to be intrinsically nameable, both in its totality and in its detail, according to a law of being that derives either from the language of logic (the universal characteristic), or from local empirical analysis, or, finally, from the global calculation of *maxima*. God designates nothing more than *the place of these laws of the nameable*: he is 'the realm of eternal truths', for he detains the principle not only of existence, but of the possible, or rather, as Leibniz said, 'of what is real in possibility', thus of the possible as regime of being, or as 'striving to existence'. God is the constructibility of the constructible, the programme of the World. Leibniz is the principal philosopher for whom God is language in its supposed completion. God is nothing more than the being of the language in which being is folded, and he can be resolved or dissolved into two *propositions*: the principle of contradiction, and the principle of sufficient reason.

But what is still more remarkable is that the entire regime of being can be inferred from the confrontation between these two axioms and one sole question: 'Why is there something rather than nothing?' For—as Leibniz remarks—'nothing is simpler and easier than something.' In other words, Leibniz proposes to extract laws, or reasons, from situations *on the sole basis of there being some presented multiples*. Here we have a schema in torsion. For on the basis of there being something rather than nothing, it has *already* been inferred that there is some being in the pure possible, or that logic desires the being of what conforms to it. It is 'since something rather than nothing exists' that one is forced to admit that 'essence in and of itself strives for existence.' Otherwise, we would have to conceive of an abyss *without reason* between possibility (the logical regime of being) and existence (the regime of presentation), which is precisely what the constructivist orientation cannot tolerate. Furthermore, it is on the basis of there being something rather than nothing that the necessity is inferred of rationally accounting for 'why things should be so and not otherwise', thus of explaining the second regime of being, the contingency of presentation. Otherwise we would have to conceive of an abyss without reason between existence (the world of presentation) and the possible inexistents, or Ideas, and this is not tenable either.

The question 'why is there something rather than nothing?' functions like a junction for all the constructible significations of the Leibnizian universe. The axioms impose the question; and, reciprocally, the complete response to the question—which supposes the axioms—validating it having been posed, confirms the axioms that it uses. The world is identity, continuous local connection and convergent, or calculable, global series: as such, it is a result of what happens when the pure 'there is' is questioned with regard to the simplicity of nothingness—the completed power of language is revealed.

Of this power, from which nothing thinkable can subtract itself, the most striking example for us is the principle of indiscernibles. When Leibniz posits that 'there are not, in nature, two real, absolute beings, *indiscernible* from each other' or, in an even stronger version, that '[God] will never choose between indiscernibles', he is acutely aware of the stakes. The indiscernible is the ontological predicate of an obstacle for language. The 'vulgar philosophers', with regard to whom Leibniz repeats that they think with 'incomplete notions'—and thus according to an open and badly made language—are mistaken when they believe that there are different things 'only because they are *two*'. If two beings are indiscernible, language cannot separate them. Separating itself from reason, whether it be logical or sufficient, this pure 'two' would introduce nothingness into being, because it would be impossible to determine one-of-the-two—remaining in-different to the other for any thinkable language—with respect to its reason for being. It would be supernumerary with regard to the axioms, effective contingency, 'superfluous' in the sense of Sartre's *Nausea*. And since God is, in reality, the complete language, he cannot tolerate this unnameable extra, which amounts to saying that he could neither have thought nor created a pure 'two': if there were two indiscernible beings, 'God and nature would act without reason in treating the one otherwise than the other'. God cannot tolerate the nothingness which is the action that has no name. He cannot lower himself to '*agendo nihil agere* because of indiscernibility'.

Why? Because it is precisely around the exclusion of the indiscernible, the indeterminate, the un-predicable, that the orientation of constructivist thought is built. If all difference is attributed on the basis of language and not on the basis of being, *presented* in-difference is impossible.

Let's note that, in a certain sense, the Leibnizian thesis is true. I showed that the logic of the Two originated in the event and the intervention, and not in multiple-being as such (Meditation 20). By consequence, it is certain that the position of the pure Two requires an operation which-is-not, and that solely the production of a supernumerary name initiates the thought of indiscernible or generic terms. But for Leibniz the impasse is double here:

– On the one hand, there is no event, since everything which happens is locally calculable and globally placed in a series whose reason is God. Locally, presentation is continuous, and it does not tolerate interruption or the ultra-one: '*The present is always pregnant with the future* and no given state is naturally explainable save by means of that which immediately preceded it. If one denies this, the world would have *hiatuses*, which would overturn the great principle of sufficient reason, and which would oblige us to have recourse to miracles or to pure chance in the explanation of phenomena.' Globally, the 'curve' of being—the complete system of its unfathomable multiplicity—arises from a nomination which is certainly transcendental (or it arises from the complete language that is God), yet it is representable: 'If one could express, by a formula of a superior characteristic, an essential property of the Universe, one would be able to read therein what the successive states would be of all of its parts at any assigned time.'

The event is thus excluded on the following basis: the complete language is the *integral calculus* of multiple-presentation, whilst a local approximation already authorizes its *differential calculus*.

– Furthermore, since one supposes a complete language—and this hypothesis is required for any constructivist orientation: the language of Gödel and Jensen is equally complete; it is the *formal* language of set theory—it cannot make any sense to speak of a supernumerary name. The intervention is therefore not possible; for if being is coextensive with a complete language, it is because it is submitted to *intrinsic* denominations, and not to an errancy in which it would be tied to a name by the effect of a wager. Leibniz's lucidity on this matter is brilliant. If he hunts out—for example—anything which resembles a doctrine of atoms (supposedly indiscernible), it is in the end because atomist nominations are arbitrary. The text is admirable here: 'It obviously follows from this perpetual substitution of indiscernible elements that in the corporeal world there can be no way of distinguishing between different momentary states. For the *denomination* by which one part of matter would be distinguished from another would be only *extrinsic*.'

Leibniz's logical nominalism is essentially superior to the atomist doctrine: being and the name are made to coincide only insofar as the name, within the place of the complete language named God, is the effective *construction* of the thing. It is not a matter of an extrinsic superimposition, but of an ontological mark, of a legal signature. In definitive: if there are no indiscernibles, if one must rationally revoke the indeterminate, it is because a being is *internally* nameable; 'For there are never two beings in nature which are perfectly alike, two beings in which it is not possible to discover an internal difference, that is, one founded on an intrinsic nomination.'

If you suppose a complete language, you suppose by the same token that the one-of-being is being itself, and that the symbol, far from being 'the murder of the thing', is that which supports and perpetuates its presentation.

One of Leibniz's great strengths is to have anchored his constructivist orientation in what is actually the origin of any orientation of thought: the problem of the continuum. He assumes the infinite divisibility of natural being without concession; he then compensates for and restricts the excess that he thus liberates within the state of the world—within the natural situation—by the hypothesis of a control of singularities, by 'intrinsic nominations'. This exact balance between the measureless proliferation of parts and the exactitude of language offers us the paradigm of constructivist thought at work. On the one hand, although imagination only perceives leaps and discontinuities—thus, the denumerable—within the natural orders and species, it must be supposed, audaciously, that there is a rigorous continuity therein; this supposes, in turn, that a precisely innumerable crowd—an infinity in radical excess of numeration—of intermediary species, or 'equivocations', populates what Leibniz terms 'regions of inflexion or heightening'. But on the other hand, this overflowing of infinity, if referred to the complete language, is commensurable, and dominated by a unique principle of progression which integrates its nominal unity, since 'all the different classes of beings whose assemblage constitutes the universe are nothing more, in the ideas of God—who knows their essential gradations distinctly—than so many coordinates of the same curve.' By the mediation of language, and the operators of 'Divine Mathematics' (series, curve, coordinates), the continuum is welded to the one, and far from being errancy and indetermination, its quantitative expansion ensures the glory of the well-made language according to which God constructed the maximal universe.

The downside of this equilibrium, in which 'intrinsic nominations' hunt out the indiscernible, is that it is unfounded, in that no void operates the suture of multiples to their being as such. Leibniz hunts down the void with the same insistence that he employs in refuting atoms, and for the same reason: the void, if we suppose it to be real, is indiscernible; its difference—as I indicated in Meditation 5—is built on in-difference. The heart of the matter—and this is typical of the superior nominalism which is constructivism—is that difference is ontologically superior to indifference, which Leibniz metaphorizes by declaring 'matter is more perfect than the void.' Echoing Aristotle (cf. Meditation 6), but under a far stronger hypothesis (that of the constructivist control of infinity), Leibniz in fact announces that *if the void exists, language is incomplete*, for a difference is missing from it inasmuch as it allows some indifference to be: 'Imagine a wholly empty space. God could have placed some matter in it without derogating, in any respect, from all other things; therefore, he did so; therefore, there is no space wholly empty; therefore, all is full.'

But if the void is not the regressive halting point of natural being, the universe is unfounded: divisibility to infinity admits chains of belonging without ultimate terms—exactly what the axiom of foundation (Meditation 18) is designed to prohibit. This is what Leibniz apparently assumes when he declares that 'each portion of matter is not only divisible to infinity . . . but is also actually subdivided without end.' Although presented-being is controlled 'higher up' by the intrinsic nominations of the integral language, are we not exposed here to its dissemination *without reason* 'lower down'? If one rejects that the name of the void is in some manner the absolute origin of language's referentiality—and that as such presented multiples can be hierarchically ordered on the basis of their 'distance from the void' (see Meditation 29)—doesn't one end up by dissolving language within the regressive indiscernibility of what in-consists, endlessly, in sub-multiplicities?

Leibniz consequently does fix halting points. He admits that 'a multitude can derive its reality only from *true unities*', and that therefore there exist 'atoms of substance . . . absolutely destitute of parts'. These are the famous monads, better named by Leibniz as 'metaphysical points'. These points do not halt the infinite regression of the material continuum: they constitute the entire real of that continuum and authorize, by their infinity, it being infinitely divisible. *Natural* dissemination is structured by a network of *spiritual* punctualities that God continuously 'fulgurates'. The main problem is obviously that of knowing how these 'metaphysical points' are discernible. Let's take it that it is not a question of parts of the real, but of absolutely indecomposable substantial unities. If, between them, there is no extensional difference (via elements being present in one and not in the other), isn't it quite simply an *infinite collection of names of the void* which is at stake? If one thinks according to ontology, it is quite possible to see no more in the Leibnizian construction than an anticipation of set theories with atoms—those which disseminate the void itself under a proliferation of names, and in whose artifice Mostowski and Fraenkel will demonstrate the independence of the axiom of choice (because, and it is intuitively reasonable, one cannot well-order the set of atoms: they are too 'identical' to each other, being merely indifferent differences). Is it not the case that these 'metaphysical points', required in order to found discernment within the infinite division of presented-being, are, amongst themselves, indiscernible? Here again we see a radical constructivist enterprise at grips with the limits of language. Leibniz will have to distinguish differences 'by figures', which monads are incapable of (since they have no parts), from differences 'by internal qualities and actions': it is the latter alone which allow one to posit that 'each monad is different from every other one.' The 'metaphysical points' are thus both quantitatively void and qualitatively full. If monads were without quality, they 'would be indiscernible from one another, since they also do not differ in quantity'. And since the principle of indiscernibles is the absolute law of any constructivist orientation, monads must be qualitatively discernible. This amounts to saying that they are unities of quality, which is to say—in my eyes—pure *names*.

The circle is closed here at the same time as this 'closure' stretches and limits the discourse: if it is possible for a language that is supposed complete to dominate infinity, it is because the primitive unities in which being occurs within presentation are themselves nominal, or constitute real universes of sense, indecomposable and disjoint. The phrase of the world, its syntax named by God, is written in these unities.

Yet it is also possible to say that since the 'metaphysical points' are solely discernible by their internal qualities, they must be thought as pure interiorities—witness the aphorism: 'Monads have no windows'—and consequently as *subjects*. Being is a phrase written in subjects. However, this subject, which is not split by any ex-centring of the Law, and whose desire is not caused by any object, is in truth a purely logical subject. What appears to happen to it is only the deployment of its qualitative predicates. It is a practical tautology, a reiteration of its difference.

What we should see in this is the instance of the subject such that constructivist thought meets its limit in being unable to exceed it: a grammatical subject; an interiority which is tautological with respect to the name-of-itself that it is; a subject required by the absence of the event, by the impossibility of intervention, and ultimately by the system of qualitative atoms. It is difficult to not recognize therein the *singleton*, such as summoned, for example—failing the veritable subject—in parliamentary elections: the singleton, of which we know that it is not the presented multiple, but its representation by the state. With regard to what is weak and conciliatory in Leibniz's political and moral conclusions, one cannot, all the same, completely absolve the audacity and anticipation of his mathematical and speculative intellectuality. Whatever genius may be manifested in unfolding the constructible figure of an order, even if this order be of being itself, the subject whose concept is proposed in the end is not the subject, evasive and split, which is capable of wagering the truth. All it can know is the form of its own Ego.

PART VII

The Generic: Indiscernible and Truth.
The Event — P. J. Cohen

MEDITATION THIRTY-ONE
The Thought of the Generic and Being in Truth

We find ourselves here at the threshold of a decisive advance, in which the concept of the 'generic'—which I hold to be crucial, as I said in the introduction—will be defined and articulated in such a manner that it will found the very being of any truth.

'Generic' and 'indiscernible' are concepts which are almost equivalent. Why play on a synonymy? Because 'indiscernible' conserves a negative connotation, which indicates uniquely, via non-discernibility, that what is at stake is subtracted from knowledge or from exact nomination. The term 'generic' positively designates that what does not allow itself to be discerned is in reality the general truth of a situation, the truth of its being, as considered as the foundation of all knowledge to come. 'Indiscernible' implies a negation, which nevertheless retains this essential point: a truth is always that which makes a hole in a knowledge.

What this means is that everything is at stake in the thought of the truth/knowledge couple. What this amounts to, in fact, is thinking the relation—which is rather a non-relation—between, on the one hand, a post-evental fidelity, and on the other hand, a fixed state of knowledge, or what I term below the encyclopaedia of the situation. The key to the problem is the mode in which the procedure of fidelity *traverses* existent knowledge, starting at the supernumerary point which is the name of the event. The main stages of this thinking—which is necessarily at its very limit here—are the following:

- the study of local or finite forms of a procedure of fidelity (enquiries);

- the distinction between the true and the veridical, and the demonstration that every truth is necessarily infinite;
- the question of the existence of the generic and thus of truths;
- the examination of the manner in which a procedure of truth subtracts itself from this or that jurisdiction of knowledge (avoidance);
- and the definition of a generic procedure of fidelity.

1. KNOWLEDGE REVISITED

The orientation of constructivist thought, and I emphasized this in Meditation 28, is the one which naturally prevails in established situations because it measures being to language such as it is. We shall suppose, from this point on, the existence, in every situation, of a language of the situation. *Knowledge* is the capacity to discern multiples within the situation which possess this or that property; properties that can be indicated by explicit phrases of the language, or sets of phrases. The rule of knowledge is always a criterion of exact nomination. In the last analysis, the constitutive operations of every domain of knowledge are *discernment* (such a presented or thinkable multiple possesses such and such a property) and *classification* (I can group together, and designate by their common property, those multiples that I discern as having a nameable characteristic in common). Discernment concerns the connection between language and presented or presentable realities. It is orientated towards presentation. Classification concerns the connection between the language and the parts of a situation, the multiples of multiples. It is orientated towards representation.

We shall posit that discernment is founded upon the capacity to judge (to speak of properties), and classification is founded upon the capacity to link judgements together (to speak of parts). Knowledge is realized as an encyclopaedia. An encyclopaedia must be understood here as a summation of judgements under a common determinant. Knowledge—in its innumerable compartmentalized and entangled domains—can therefore be thought, with regard to its being, as assigning to this or that multiple an encyclopaedic determinant by means of which the multiple finds itself belonging to a set of multiples, that is, to a part. As a general rule, a multiple (and its sub-multiples) fall under numerous determinants. These determinants are often analytically contradictory, but this is of little importance.

The encylopaedia contains a classification of parts of the situation which group together terms having this or that explicit property. One can 'designate' each of these parts by the property in question and thereby determine it within the language. It is this designation which is called a determinant of the encyclopaedia.

Remember that knowledge does not know of the event because the name of the event is supernumerary, and so it does not belong to the language of the situation. When I say that it does not belong to the latter, this is not necessarily in a material sense whereby the name would be barbarous, incomprehensible, or non-listed. What qualifies the name of the event is that it is drawn from the void. It is a matter of an evental (or historical) quality, and not of a signifying quality. But even if the name of the event is very simple, and it is definitely listed in the language of the situation, it is supernumerary *as name of the event,* signature of the ultra-one, and therefore it is foreclosed from knowledge. It will also be said that the event does not fall under any encyclopaedic determinant.

2. ENQUIRIES

Because the encyclopaedia does not contain any determinant whose referential part is assignable to something like an event, the identification of multiples connected or unconnected to the supernumerary name (circulated by the intervention) is a task which cannot be based on the encyclopaedia. A fidelity (Meditation 23) is not a matter of knowledge. It is not the work of an expert: it is the work of a militant. 'Militant' designates equally the feverish exploration of the effects of a new theorem, the cubist precipitation of the Braque–Picasso tandem (the effect of a retroactive intervention upon the Cézanne-event), the activity of Saint Paul, and that of the militants of an *Organisation Politique.* The operator of faithful connection designates *another mode of discernment*: one which, outside knowledge but within the effect of an interventional nomination, explores connections to the supernumerary name of the event.

When I recognize that *a* multiple which belongs to the situation (which is counted as one there) is connected—or not—to the name of the event I perform the *minimal* gesture of fidelity: the observation of *a* connection (or non-connection). The actual meaning of this gesture—which provides the foundation of being for the entire process constituted by a fidelity—naturally depends on the name of the event (which is itself a multiple), on the operator of faithful connection, on the multiple therein encountered, and finally on the situation and the position of its eventual-site, etc. There are infinite nuances in the phenomenology of the procedure of fidelity. But my goal is not a phenomenology, it is a Greater Logic (to remain within Hegelian terminology). I will thus place myself in the following abstract situation: *two* values alone are discerned via the operator of fidelity: connection and non-connection. This abstraction is legitimate since *ultimately*—as phenomenology shows (and such is the sense of the words 'conversion', 'rallying', 'grace', 'conviction', 'enthusiasm', 'persuasion', 'admiration' . . . according to the type of event)—a multiple either is or is not within the field of effects entailed by the introduction into circulation of a supernumerary name.

This minimal gesture of a fidelity, tied to the *encounter* between a multiple of the situation and a vector of the operator of fidelity—and one would imagine this happens initially in the environs of the event-site—has one of two meanings: there is a connection (the multiple is within the effects of the supernumerary name) or a non-connection (it is not found therein).

Using a transparent algebra, we will note $x(+)$ the fact that the multiple x is recognized as being connected to the name of the event, and $x(-)$ that it is recognized as non-connected. A report of the type $x(+)$ or $x(-)$ is precisely the minimal gesture of fidelity that we were talking about.

We will term *enquiry* any finite set of such minimal reports. An enquiry is thus a 'finite state' of the process of fidelity. The process has 'militated' around an encountered series of multiples $(x_1, x_2, \ldots x_n)$, and deployed their connections or non-connections to the supernumerary name of the event. The algebra of the enquiry notes this as: $(x_1(+), x_2(+), x_3(-), \ldots x_n(+))$, for example. Such an enquiry discerns (in my arbitrary example) that x_1 and x_2 are taken up positively in the effects of the supernumerary name, that x_3 is not taken up, and so on. In real circumstances such an enquiry would already be an entire network of multiples of the situation, combined with the supernumerary name by the operator. What I am presenting here is the ultimate sense of the matter, the ontological framework. One can also say that an enquiry discerns two finite multiples: the first, let's say $(x_1, x_2 \ldots)$, groups together the presented multiples, or terms of the situation, which are connected to the event. The second, $(x_3 \ldots)$, groups together those which are un-connected. As such, just like knowledge, an enquiry is the conjunction of a discernment—such a multiple of the situation possesses the property of being connected to the event (to its name)—and a classification—this is the class of connected multiples, and that is the class of non-connected multiples. It is thus legitimate to treat the enquiry, a finite series of minimal reports, as the veritable basic unit of the procedure of fidelity, because it combines the one of discernment with the several of classification. It is the enquiry which lies behind the *resemblance* of the procedure of fidelity *to a knowledge*.

3. TRUTH AND VERIDICITY

Here we find ourselves confronted with the subtle dialectic of knowledges and post-evental fidelity: the kernel of being of the knowledge/truth dialectic.

First let's note the following: the classes resulting from the militant discernment of a fidelity, such as those detained by *an* enquiry, are *finite* parts of the situation. Phenomenologically, this means that a given state of the procedure of fidelity—that is, a finite sequence of discernments of connection or non-connection—is realized in two classes, one positive and one negative, which respectively group the minimal gestures of the type $x(+)$ and $x(-)$. However, *every finite part of the situation is classified by at least one knowledge*: the results of an enquiry *coincide* with an encyclopaedic determinant. This is entailed by every presented multiple being nameable in the language of the situation. We know that language allows no 'hole' within its referential space, and that as such one must recognize the empirical value of the principle of indiscernibles: strictly speaking, there is no unnameable. Even if nomination is evasive, or belongs to a very general determinant, like 'it's a mountain', or 'it's a naval battle', nothing in the situation is radically subtracted from names. This, moreover, is the reason why the world is full, and, however strange it may seem at first in certain circumstances, it can always be rightfully held to be linguistically *familiar*. In principle, a finite set of presented multiples can always be enumerated. It can be thought as the class of 'the one which has this name, and the one which has that name, and . . . '. The totality of these discernments constitutes an encyclopaedic determinant. Therefore, every *finite* multiple of presented multiples is a part which falls under knowledge, even if this only be by its enumeration.

One could object that it is not according to such a principle of classification (enumeration) that the procedure of fidelity groups together—for example—a finite series of multiples connected to the name of the event. Of course, but *knowledge knows nothing of this*: to the point that one can always justify saying of such or such a finite grouping, that even if it was actually produced by a fidelity, it is merely the referent of a well-known (or in principle, knowable) encyclopaedic referent. This is why I said that the results of an enquiry necessarily coincide with an encyclopaedic determinant. Where and how will the difference between the procedures be affirmed if the result-multiple, for all intensive purposes, is *already* classified by a knowledge?

In order to clarify this situation, we will term *veridical* the following statement, which can be controlled by a knowledge: 'Such a part of the situation is answerable to such an encyclopaedic determinant.' We will term *true* the statement controlled by the procedure of fidelity, thus attached to the event and the intervention: 'Such a part of the situation groups together multiples connected (or unconnected) to the supernumerary name of the event.' What is at stake in the present argument is entirely bound up in the choice of the adjective 'true'.

For the moment, what we know is that for a given enquiry, the corresponding classes, positive and negative, being finite, fall under an encyclopaedic determinant. Consequently, they validate a veridical statement.

Although knowledge does not want to know anything of the event, of the intervention, of the supernumerary name, or of the operator which rules the fidelity—all being ingredients that are supposed in the being of an enquiry—it nevertheless remains the case that an enquiry *cannot discern the true from the veridical*: its true-result is at the same time already constituted as belonging to a veridical statement.

However, it is in no way *because* the multiples which figure in an enquiry (with their indexes + or −) fall under a determinant of the encyclopaedia that they were re-grouped as constituting the true-result of this enquiry; rather it was uniquely because the procedure of fidelity *encountered* them, within the context of its temporal insistence, and 'militated' around them, testing, by means of the operator of faithful connection, their degree of proximity to the supernumerary name of the event. Here we have the paradox of a multiple—the finite result of an enquiry—which is random, subtracted from all knowledge, and which weaves a diagonal to the situation, yet which is already part of the encyclopaedia's repertory. It is as though knowledge has the power to efface the event in its supposed effects, counted as one by a fidelity; it trumps the fidelity with a peremptory 'already-counted!'

This is the case, however, when these effects are *finite*. Hence a law, of considerable weight: *the true only has a chance of being distinguishable from the veridical when it is infinite*. A truth (if it exists) must be an infinite part of the situation, because for every finite part one can always say that it has *already* been discerned and classified by knowledge.

One can see in what sense it is the *being* of truth which concerns us here. 'Qualitatively', or as a reality-in-situation, a finite result of an enquiry is quite distinct from a part named by a determinant of the encyclopaedia, because the procedures which lead to the first remain unknown to the second. It is solely as pure multiples, that is, according to their being, that finite parts are indistinguishable, because every one of them falls under a determinant. What we are looking for is an ontological differentiation between the true and the veridical, that is, between truth and knowledge. The external qualitative characterization of procedures (event—intervention—fidelity on the one hand, exact nomination in the established language on the other) does not suffice for this task if the presented-multiples which result are *the same*. The requirement will thus be that the one-multiple of a truth—the result of true judgements—must be indiscernible and unclassifiable for the encyclopaedia. This condition founds the difference between the true and the veridical *in being*. We have just seen that one condition of this condition is that a truth be infinite.

Is this condition sufficient? Certainly not. Obviously a great number of encyclopaedic determinants exist which designate infinite parts of the situation. Knowledge, since the great ontological decision concerning infinity (cf. Meditation 13), moves easily amongst the infinite classes of multiples which fall under an encyclopaedic determinant. Statements such as 'the whole numbers form an infinite set', or 'the infinite nuances of the sentiment of love' can be held without difficulty to be veridical in this or that domain of knowledge. That a truth is infinite does not render it by the same token indiscernible from every single thing already counted by knowledge.

Let's examine the problem in its abstract form. Saying that a truth is infinite is saying that its procedure contains an infinity of enquiries. Each of these enquiries contains, in finite number, positive indications $x(+)$—that is, that the multiple x is connected to the name of the event—and negative indications $y(-)$. The 'total' procedure, that is, a certain infinite state of the fidelity, is thus, in its result, composed of two infinite classes: that of multiples with a positive connection, say $(x_1, x_2, \ldots x_n)$, and that of multiples with a negative connection, $(y_1, y_2, \ldots y_n)$. But it is quite possible that these two classes always coincide with parts which fall under encyclopaedic determinants. A domain of knowledge could exist for which $x_1, x_2, \ldots x_n$ are precisely those multiples that can be discerned as having a common property, a property which can be explicitly formulated in the language of the situation.

Vulgar Marxism and vulgar Freudianism have never been able to find a way out of this ambiguity. The first claimed that truth was historically deployed on the basis of revolutionary events by the working class. But it thought the working class as the class of workers. Naturally, 'the workers', in terms of pure multiples, formed an infinite class; it was not the sum total of empirical workers that was at stake. Yet this did not prevent knowledge (and paradoxically Marxist knowledge itself) from being for ever able to consider 'the workers' as falling under an encyclopaedic determinant (sociological, economical, etc.), the event as having nothing to do with this always-already-counted, and the supposed truth as being merely a veridicity submitted to the language of the situation. What is more, from this standpoint the truth could be annulled—the famous 'it's been done before' or 'it's old-fashioned'—because the encyclopaedia is always incoherent. It was from this coincidence, which it claimed to assume within itself—because it declared itself to be simultaneously political truth, combative and faithful, and knowledge of History, of Society—that Marxism ended up dying, because it followed the fluctuations of the encyclopaedia under the trial of the relation between language and the State. As for American Freudianism, it claimed to form a section of psychological knowledge, assigning truth to everything which was connected to a stable class, the 'adult genital complex'. Today this Freudianism looks like a state corpse, and it was not for nothing that Lacan, in order to save fidelity to Freud—who had named 'unconscious' the paradoxical events of hysteria —had to place the distinction between knowledge and truth at the centre of his thought, and severely separate the discourse of the analyst from what he called the discourse of the University.

Infinity, however necessary, will thus not be able to serve as the unique criterion for the indiscernibility of faithful truths. Are we capable of proposing a sufficient criterion?

4. THE GENERIC PROCEDURE

If we consider any determinant of the encyclopaedia, then its contradictory determinant also exists. This is entailed by the language of the situation containing negation (note that the following prerequisite is introduced here: 'there is no language without negation'). If we group all the multiples which have a certain property into a class, then there is immediately another disjoint class; that of the multiples which do not have the property in question. I said previously that all the finite parts of a situation are registered under encyclopaedic classifications. In particular, this includes those finite parts which contain multiples of which some belong to one class, and others to the contradictory class. If x possesses a property, and y does not, the finite part $\{x,y\}$ made up of x and y is the object of a knowledge just like any other finite part. However, it is indifferent to the property because one of its terms possesses it, whilst the other does not. Knowledge considers that *this* finite part, taken as a whole, is not apt for discernment via the property.

We shall say that a finite part *avoids* an encyclopaedic determinant if it contains multiples which belong to this determinant *and* others which belong to the contradictory determinant. All finite parts fall, moreover, under an encyclopaedic determinant. Thus, all finite parts which avoid a determinant are themselves determined by a domain of knowledge. Avoidance is a structure of finite knowledge.

Our goal is then to found upon this structure of knowledge (referred to the finite character of the enquiries) a characterization of truth as infinite part of the situation.

The general idea is to consider that *a truth groups together all the terms of the situation which are positively connected to the event*. Why this privilege of positive connection, of $x(+)$? Because what is negatively connected does no more than repeat the pre-eventual situation. From the standpoint of the procedure of fidelity, a term encountered and investigated negatively, an $x(-)$, has no relation whatsoever with the name of the event, and thus is it in no way 'concerned' by that event. It will not enter into the *new-multiple* that is a post-evental truth, since, with regard to the fidelity, it turns out to have no connection to the supernumerary name. As such, it is quite coherent to consider that a truth, as the total result of a procedure of fidelity, is made up of all the encountered terms which have been positively investigated; that is, all those which the operator of connection has declared to be linked, in one manner or another, to the name of the event. The $x(-)$ terms remain *indifferent,* and solely mark the repetition of the pre-evental order of the situation. But for an infinite truth thus conceived (all terms declared $x(+)$ in at least one enquiry of the faithful procedure) to genuinely be a production, a novelty, it is necessary that the part of the situation obtained by gathering the $x(+)$'s does not coincide with an encyclopaedic determinant. Otherwise, in its being, it also would repeat a configuration that had *already* been classified by knowledge. It would not be genuinely post-evental.

Our problem is finally the following: on what condition can one be sure that the set of terms of the situation which are positively connected to the event is in no manner already classified within the encyclopaedia of the situation? We cannot directly formulate this potential condition via an 'examination' of the infinite set of these terms, because this set is always to-come (being infinite) and moreover, it is randomly composed by the trajectory of the enquiries: a term is *encountered* by the procedure, and the finite enquiry in which it figures attests that it is positively connected, that it is an $x(+)$. Our condition must necessarily concern *the enquiries* which make up the very fabric of the procedure of fidelity.

The crucial remark is then the following. Take an enquiry which is such that the terms it reports as positively connected to the event (the finite number of $x(+)$'s which figure in the enquiry) form a finite part which avoids a determinant of knowledge in the sense of avoidance defined above. Then take a faithful procedure in which this enquiry figures: the infinite total of terms connected positively to the event via that procedure cannot in any manner coincide with the determinant avoided by the $x(+)$'s of the enquiry in question.

This is evident. If the enquiry is such that $x_{n_1}(+), x_{n_2}(+), \ldots x_{n_q}(+)$, that is, all the terms encountered by the enquiry which are connected to the name of the event, form, once gathered together, a finite part which avoids a determinant, this means that amongst the x_n there are terms which belong to this determinant (which have a property) and others which do not (because they do not have the property). The result is that the infinite class $(x_1, x_2, \ldots x_n \ldots)$ which totalizes the enquiries according to the positive cannot coincide with the class subsumed by the encyclopaedic determinant in question. For in the former class, one finds the $x_{n_1}(+)$, $x_{n_2}(+), \ldots x_{n_q}(+)$ of the enquiry mentioned above, since all of them were positively investigated. Thus there are elements in the class which have the property and there are others which do not. This class is therefore not the one that is defined in the language by the classification 'all the multiples discerned as having this property'.

For an infinite faithful procedure to thus generate as its positive result-multiple—as the post-evental truth—a total of (+)'s connected to the name of the event which 'diagonalize' a determinant of the encyclopaedia, it is sufficient that within that procedure there be at least *one* enquiry which avoids this determinant. The presence of this particular finite enquiry is enough to ensure that the infinite faithful procedure does not coincide with the determinant in question.

Is this a reasonable requisite? Yes, because the faithful procedure is random, and in no way predetermined by knowledge. Its origin is the event, of which knowledge knows nothing, and its texture the operator of faithful connection, which is itself also a temporal production. The multiples encountered by the procedure do not depend upon any knowledge. They result from the randomness of the 'militant' trajectory starting out from the event-site. There is no reason, in any case, for an enquiry not to exist which is such that the multiples positively evaluated therein by the operator of faithful connection form a finite part which avoids a determinant; the reason being that an enquiry, in itself, has nothing to do with any determinant whatsoever. It is thus entirely reasonable that the faithful procedure, in one of its finite states, encounter such a group of multiples. By extension to the true-procedure of its usage within knowledge, we shall say that an enquiry of this type *avoids* the encyclopaedic determinant in question. Thus: if an infinite faithful procedure contains at least one finite enquiry which avoids an encyclopaedic determinant, then the infinite positive result of that procedure (the class of $x(+)$'s will not coincide with that part of the situation whose knowledge is designated by this determinant. In other words, the property, expressed in the language of the situation which founds this determinant, cannot be used, in any case, to discern the infinite positive result of the faithful procedure.

We have thus clearly formulated a condition for the infinite and positive result of a faithful procedure (the part which totalises the $x(+)$'s) avoiding—not coinciding with—a determinant of the encyclopaedia. And this condition concerns the enquiries, the finite states of the procedure: it is enough that the $x(+)$'s of *one* enquiry of the procedure form a finite set which avoids the determinant in question.

Let's now imagine that the procedure is such that the condition above is satisfied for *every* encyclopaedic determinant. In other words, for *each* determinant at least one enquiry figures in the procedure whose $x(+)$'s avoid that determinant. For the moment I am not enquiring into the *possibility* of such a procedure. I am simply stating that *if* a faithful procedure contains, for every determinant of the encyclopaedia, an enquiry which avoids it, *then* the positive result of this procedure will not coincide with *any* part subsumable under a determinant. As such, the class of multiples which are connected to the event will not be determined by any of the properties which can be formulated in the language of the situation. It will thus be *indiscernible and unclassifiable* for knowledge. In this case, truth would be irreducible to veridicity.

We shall therefore say: *a truth is the infinite positive total—the gathering together of x(+)'s— of a procedure of fidelity which, for each and every determinant of the encyclopaedia, contains at least one enquiry which avoids it.*

Such a procedure will be said to be *generic* (for the situation).

Our task is to justify this word: generic—and on this basis, the justification of the word truth is inferred.

5. THE GENERIC IS THE BEING-MULTIPLE OF A TRUTH

If there exists an event-intervention-operator-of-fidelity complex which is such that an infinite positive state of the fidelity is generic (in the sense of the definition)—in other words, if a truth exists—the multiple-referent of this fidelity (the *one-truth*) is a *part* of the situation: the part which groups together all of the terms positively connected to the name of the event; all the x(+)'s which figure in at least one enquiry of the procedure (in one of its finite states). The fact that the procedure is generic entails the non-coincidence of this part with anything classified by an encyclopaedic determinant. Consequently, this part is unnameable by the resources of the language of the situation alone. It is subtracted from any knowledge; it has not been already-counted by any of the domains of knowledge, nor will be, if the language remains in the same state—or remains *that of* the State. This part, in which a truth inscribes its procedure as infinite result, is an *indiscernible of the situation*.

However, it is clearly a part: it is counted as one by the state of the situation. What could this 'one' be which—subtracted from language and constituted from the point of the evental ultra-one—is indiscernible? Since this part has no particular expressible property, its entire being resides in this: it is a part, which is to say it is composed of multiples effectively presented in the situation. An indiscernible *inclusion*—and such, in short, is a truth—has no other 'property' than that of referring to *belonging*. This part is anonymously that which has no other mark apart from arising from presentation, apart from being composed of terms which have nothing in common that could be remarked, save belonging to *this* situation; which, strictly speaking, is its being, qua being. But as for this 'property'—*being*; quite simply—it is clear that it is shared by *all* the terms of the situation, and that it is coexistent with every part which groups together terms. Consequently, the indiscernible part, by definition, solely possesses the 'properties' of any part whatsoever. It is rightfully declared *generic*, because, if one wishes to qualify it, all one can say is that its elements *are*. The part thus belongs to the supreme genre, the genre of the being of the situation as such—since *in* a situation 'being' and 'being-counted-as-one-in-the-situation' are one and the same thing.

It then goes without saying that one can maintain that such a part is attachable to truth. For what the faithful procedure thus rejoins is none other than the truth *of the entire situation*, insofar as the sense of the indiscernible is that of exhibiting as one-multiple the very being of what belongs insofar as it belongs. Every nameable part, discerned and classified by knowledge, refers not to being-in-situation as such, but to what language carves out therein as recognizable particularities. The faithful procedure, precisely because it originates in an event in which the void is summoned, and not in the established relation between the language and the state, disposes, in its infinite states, of the being of the situation. It is a one-truth of the situation, whilst a determinant of knowledge solely specifies veracities.

The discernible is veridical. But the indiscernible alone is true. There is no truth apart from the generic, because only a faithful generic procedure aims at the one of situational being. A faithful procedure has as its infinite horizon being-in-truth.

6. DO TRUTHS EXIST?

Evidently, everything hangs on the possibility of the existence of a generic procedure of fidelity. This question is both *de facto* and *de jure*.

De facto, I consider that in the situational sphere of the *individual*—such as psychoanalysis, for example, thinks and presents it—love (if it exists, but various empirical signs attest that it does) is a generic procedure of fidelity: its event is the encounter, its operators are variable, its infinite production is indiscernible, and its enquiries are the existential episodes that the amorous couple intentionally attaches to love. Love is thus a-truth (one-truth) of the situation. I call it 'individual' because it *interests no-one* apart from the individuals in question. Let's note, and this is crucial, that it is thus *for them* that the one-truth produced by their love is an indiscernible part of their existence; since the others do not share in the situation which I am speaking of. An-amorous-truth is un-known for those who love each other: all they do is produce it.

In 'mixed' situations, in which the means are *individual* but the transmission and effects concern the collective—it is *interested* in them—art and science constitute networks of faithful procedures: whose events are the great aesthetic and conceptual transformations; whose operators are variable (I showed in Meditation 24 that the operator of mathematics, science of being-qua-being, was deduction; it is not the same as that of biology or painting); whose infinite production is indiscernible—there is no 'knowledge' of art, nor is there, and this only seems to be a paradox, a 'knowledge of science', for science here is *its infinite being*, which is to say the procedure of invention, and not the transmissible exposition of its fragmentary results, which are *finite*; and finally whose enquiries are works of art and scientific inventions.

In collective situations—in which the collective becomes interested in itself—politics (if it exists *as generic politics*: what was called, for a long time, revolutionary politics, and for which another word must be found today) is also a procedure of fidelity. Its events are the historical caesura in which the void of the social is summoned in default of the State; its operators are variable; its infinite productions are indiscernible (in particular, they do not coincide with *any part nameable according to the State*), being nothing more than 'changes' of political subjectivity within the situation; and finally its enquiries consist of militant organized activity.

As such, love, art, science and politics generate—infinitely—truths concerning situations; truths subtracted from knowledge which are only counted by the state in the anonymity of their being. All sorts of other practices—possibly respectable, such as commerce for example, and all the different forms of the 'service of goods', which are intricated in knowledge to various degrees—do not generate truths. I have to say that philosophy does not generate any truths either, however painful this admission may be. At best, philosophy is *conditioned* by the faithful procedures of its times. Philosophy can aid the procedure which conditions it, precisely because it depends on it: it attaches itself via such intermediaries to the foundational events of the times, yet philosophy itself does not make up a generic procedure. Its particular function is to arrange multiples for a random encounter with such a procedure. However, whether such an encounter takes place, and whether the multiples thus arranged turn out to be connected to the supernumerary name of the event, does not depend upon philosophy. A philosophy worthy of the name—the name which began with Parmenides—is in any case antinomical to the service of goods, inasmuch as it endeavours to be at the service of truths; one can always endeavour to be at the service of something that one does not constitute. Philosophy is thus at the service of art, of science and of politics. That it is capable of being at the service of love is more doubtful (on the other hand, art, a mixed procedure, supports truths of love). In any case, there is no commercial philosophy.

As a *de jure* question, the existence of faithful generic procedures is a scientific question, a question of ontology, since it is not the sort of question that can be treated by a simple knowledge, and since the indiscernible occurs at the place of the being of the situation, *qua being*. It is mathematics which must judge whether it makes any sense to speak of an indiscernible part of any multiple. Of course, mathematics cannot think a procedure of truth, because mathematics eliminates the event. But it can decide whether it is compatible with ontology that there be truths. Decided at the level of fact by the entire history of humankind—because *there are* truths—the question of the being of truth has only been resolved at a *de jure* level quite recently (in 1963, Cohen's discovery); without, moreover, the mathematicians—absorbed as they are by the forgetting of the destiny of their discipline due to the technical necessity of its deployment—knowing how to name what was happening there (a point where the philosophical help I was speaking of comes into play). I have consecrated Meditation 33 to this mathematical event. I have deliberately weakened the explicit links between the present conceptual development and the mathematical doctrine of generic multiplicities in order to let ontology 'speak', eloquently, for itself. Just as the signifier always betrays something, the technical appearance of Cohen's discoveries and their investment in a problematic domain which is apparently quite narrow (the 'models of set theory') are immediately enlivened by the choice made by the founders of this doctrine of the word 'generic' to designate the non-constructible multiples and 'conditions' to designate the finite states of the procedure ('conditions' = 'enquiries').

The conclusions of mathematical ontology are both clear and measured. Very roughly:

a. If the initial situation is denumerable (infinite, but just as whole numbers are), there exists a generic procedure;

b. But this procedure, despite being *included* in the situation (it is a part of it), does not *belong* to it (it is not presented therein, solely represented: it is an excrescence—cf. Meditation 8);

c. However, one can 'force' a new situation to exist—a 'generic extension'—which contains the entirety of the old situation, and to which this time the generic procedure belongs (it is both presented and represented: it is normal). This point (forcing) is the step of the Subject (cf. Meditation 35);

d. In this new situation, if the language remains the same—thus, if the primitive givens of knowledge remain stable—the generic procedure still produces indiscernibility. Belonging to the situation this time, the generic is an intrinsic indiscernible therein.

If one attempts to join together the empirical and scientific conclusions, the following hypothesis can be made: the fact that a generic procedure of fidelity progresses to infinity entails a reworking of the situation; one that, whilst conserving all of the old situation's multiples, presents other multiples. The ultimate effect of an evental caesura, and of an intervention from which the introduction into circulation of a supernumerary name proceeds, would thus be that the truth of a situation, with this caesura as its principle, *forces the situation to accommodate it*: to extend itself to the point at which this truth—primitively no more than a part, a representation —attains belonging, thereby becoming a presentation. The trajectory of the faithful generic procedure and its passage to infinity transform the ontological status of a truth: they do so by changing the situation 'by force'; anonymous excrescence in the beginning, the truth will end up being normalized. However, it would remain subtracted from knowledge if the language of the situation was not radically transformed. Not only is a truth indiscernible, but its procedure requires that this indiscernibility *be*. A truth would force the situation to dispose itself such that this truth—at the outset anonymously counted as one by the state alone, pure indistinct excess over the presented multiples—be finally recognized as a term, and as internal. A faithful generic procedure renders the indiscernible immanent.

As such, art, science and politics do change the world, not by what they discern, but by what they indiscern therein. And the all-powerfulness of a truth is merely that of changing what is, such that this unnameable being may be, which is the very being of what-is.

MEDITATION THIRTY-TWO
Rousseau

> 'if, from these [particular] wills, one takes away the
> pluses and the minuses which cancel each other out,
> what is left as the sum of differences is the general will.'
> *Of the Social Contract*

Let's keep in mind that Rousseau does not pretend to resolve the famous problem that he poses himself: 'Man is born free, and everywhere he is in chains.' If by resolution one understands the examination of the real procedures of passage from one state (natural freedom) to another (civil obedience), Rousseau expressly indicates that he does not have such at his disposal: 'How did this change come about? I do not know.' Here as elsewhere his method is to set aside all the facts and to thereby establish a foundation for the operations of thought. It is a question of establishing under what conditions such a 'change' is *legitimate*. But 'legitimacy' here designates existence; in fact, the existence of politics. Rousseau's goal is to examine the conceptual prerequisites of politics, to think *the being of politics*. The truth of that being resides in 'the act by which a people is a people'.

That legitimacy be existence itself is demonstrated by the following: the empirical reality of States and of civil obedience does not prove in any way that there is politics. This is a particularly strong idea of Rousseau: the factual appearance of a sovereign does not suffice for it to be possible to speak of politics. The most part of the major States are a-political because they have come to the term of their dissolution. In them, 'the social pact is broken'. It can be observed that 'very few nations have laws.' Politics is rare, because the fidelity to what founds it is precarious, and because there is an 'inherent and inevitable vice which relentlessly tends to destroy the body politic from the very moment of its birth'.

It is quite conceivable that if politics, in its being-multiple (the 'body politic' or 'people'), is always on the edge of its own dissolution, this is because it has no structural base. If Rousseau for ever establishes the modern concept of politics, it is because he posits, in the most radical fashion, that politics is a procedure which originates in an event, and not in a structure supported within being. Man is not a political animal: the chance of politics is a supernatural event. Such is the meaning of the maxim: 'One always has to go back to a first convention.' The social pact is not a historically provable fact, and Rousseau's references to Greece or Rome merely form the classical ornament of that temporal absence. The social pact is the *evental form* that one must suppose if one wishes to think the truth of that aleatory being that is the body politic. In the pact, we attain the *eventness* of the event in which any political procedure finds its truth. Moreover, that nothing necessitates such a pact is precisely what directs the polemic against Hobbes. To suppose that the political convention results from the necessity of having to exit from a war of all against all, and to thus subordinate the event to the effects of force, is to submit its eventness to an extrinsic determination. On the contrary, what one must assume is the 'superfluous' character of the originary social pact, its absolute non-necessity, the rational chance (which is retroactively thinkable) of its occurrence. Politics is a *creation*, local and fragile, of collective humanity; it is never the treatment of a vital necessity. Necessity is always a-political, either beforehand (the state of nature), or afterwards (dissolved State). Politics, in its being, is solely commensurable to the event that institutes it.

If we examine the *formula* of the social pact, that is, the statement by which previously dispersed natural individuals become constituted as a people, we see that it discerns an absolutely novel term, called the general will: 'Each of us puts his person and his full power in common under the supreme direction of the general will.' It is this term which has quite rightly born the brunt of the critiques of Rousseau, since, in the *Social Contract*, it is both presupposed and constituted. Before the contract, there are only particular wills. After the contract, the pure referent of politics is the general will. But the contract itself articulates the submission of particular wills to the general will. A structure of torsion may be recognized here: *once* the general will is constituted, it so happens that it is precisely *its* being which is presupposed in such constitution.

The only standpoint from which light may be shed upon this torsion is that of considering the body politic to be a supernumerary multiple: the ultra-one of the event that is the pact. In truth, the pact is nothing other than *the self-belonging of the body politic to the multiple that it is*, as founding event. 'General will' names the durable truth of this self-belonging: 'The body politic . . . since it owes its being solely to the sanctity of the contract, can never obligate itself . . . to do anything that detracts from that primitive act . . . To violate the act by which it exists would be to annihilate itself, and what is nothing produces nothing.' It is clear that the being of politics originates from an immanent relation to self. It is 'not-detracting' from this relation—political fidelity—that alone supports the deployment of the truth of the 'primitive act'. In sum:

- the pact is the event which, by chance, supplements the state of nature;
- the body politic, or people, is the evental ultra-one which interposes itself between the void (nature is the void for politics) and itself;
- the general will is the operator of fidelity which directs a generic procedure.

It is the last point which contains all the difficulties. What I will argue here is that Rousseau clearly designates the necessity, for any true politics, to articulate itself around a generic (indiscernible) subset of the collective body; but on the other hand, he does not resolve the question of the political procedure itself, because he persists in submitting it to the law of number (to the majority).

We know that once named by the intervention the event founds time upon an originary Two (Meditation 20). Rousseau formalizes this point precisely when he posits that will is split by the event-contract. *Citizen* designates in each person his or her participation in the sovereignty of general will, whereas *subject* designates his or her submission to the laws of the state. The measure of the duration of politics is the insistence of this Two. There is politics when an internalized collective operator splits particular wills. As one might have expected, the Two is the essence of the ultra-one that is a people, the real body of politics. Obedience to the general will is the mode in which civil liberty is realized. As Rousseau says, in an extremely tense formula, 'the words *subject* and *sovereign* are identical correlatives.' This 'identical correlation' designates the citizen as support of the generic becoming of politics, as a militant, in the strict sense, of the political cause; the latter designating purely and simply the existence of politics. In the citizen (the militant), who divides the will of the individual into two, politics is realized inasmuch as it is maintained within the evental (contractual) foundation of time.

Rousseau's acuity extends to his perception that the norm of general will is *equality*. This is a fundamental point. General will is a relationship of co-belonging of the people to itself. It is therefore only effective from all the people to all the people. Its forms of manifestation—laws—are: 'a relation . . . between the entire object from one point of view and the entire object from another point of view, with no division of the whole'. Any decision whose object is particular is a decree, and not a law. It is not an operation of general will. General will never considers an individual nor a particular action. *It is therefore tied to the indiscernible.* What it speaks of in its declarations cannot be separated out by statements of knowledge. A decree is founded upon knowledge, but a law is not; a law is concerned solely with the truth. This evidently results in the general will being intrinsically egalitarian, since it cannot take persons or goods into consideration. This leads in turn to an intrinsic qualification of the division of will: 'particular will, tends, by its nature, to partiality, and general will to equality.' Rousseau thinks the essential modern link between the existence of politics and the egalitarian norm. Yet it is not quite exact to speak of a norm. As an intrinsic qualification of general will, equality *is* politics, such that, *a contrario*, any in-egalitarian statement, whatever it be, is anti-political. The most remarkable thing about the *Social Contract* is that it establishes an intimate connection between politics and equality by an articulated recourse to an evental foundation and a procedure of the indiscernible. It is because general will indiscerns its object and excludes it from the encyclopaedias of knowledge that it is ordained to equality. As for this indiscernible, it refers back to the evental character of political creation.

Finally, Rousseau rigorously proves that general will cannot be represented, not even by the State: 'The sovereign, which is solely a collective being, can be represented only by itself: power can quite easily be transferred, but not will.' This distinction between power (transmissible) and will (unrepresentable) is very profound. It frees politics from the state. As a procedure faithful to the event-contract, politics cannot tolerate delegation or representation. It resides entirely in the 'collective being' of its citizen-militants. Indeed, power is induced from the existence of politics; it is not the latter's adequate manifestation.

It is on this basis, moreover, that two attributes of general will are inferred which often give rise to suspicions of 'totalitarianism': its indivisibility, and its infallibility. Rousseau cannot admit the logic of the 'division' or 'balance' of powers, if one understands by 'power' the essence of the political phenomenon, which Rousseau would rather name will. As generic procedure, politics is indecomposable, and it is only by dissolving it into the secondary multiplicity of governmental decrees that its articulation is supposedly thought. The trace of the evental ultra-one in politics is that there is only one such politics, which no instance of power could represent or fragment. For politics, ultimately, is the existence of the people. Similarly, 'general will is always upright and always tends towards public utility'; for what *external* norm could we use to judge that this is not the case? If politics 'reflected' the social bond, one could, on the basis of the thought of this bond, ask oneself whether the reflection was adequate or not. But since it is an interventional creation, it is its own norm of itself, the egalitarian norm, and all that one can assume is that a political will which makes mistakes, or causes the unhappiness of a people, is *not* in fact a political—or general—will, but rather a particular usurpatory will. Grasped in its essence, general will is infallible, due to being subtracted from any particular knowledge, and due to it relating solely to the generic existence of the people.

Rousseau's hostility to parties and factions—and thus to any form of parliamentary representativity—is deduced from the generic character of politics. The major axiom is that 'in order to definitely have the expression of the general will, [there must] be no partial society in the State.' A 'partial society' is characterized by being discernible, or separable; as such, it is not faithful to the event-pact. As Rousseau remarks, the original pact is the result of a 'unanimous consentment'. If there are opponents, they are purely and simply external to the body politic, they are 'foreigners amongst the Citizens'. For the evental ultra-one evidently cannot take the form of a 'majority'. Fidelity to the event requires any genuinely political decision to conform to this one-effect; that is, to not be subordinated to the separable and discernible will of a subset of the people. Any subset, even that cemented by the most real of interests, is a-political, given that it can be named in an encyclopaedia. It is a matter of knowledge, and not of truth.

By the same token, it is ruled out that politics be realizable in the election of representatives since 'will does not admit of being represented.' The deputies may have particular executive functions, but they cannot have any legislative function, because 'the deputies of the people . . . are not and cannot be its representatives', and 'any law which the People has not ratified in person is null; it is not a law.' The English parliamentary system does not impress Rousseau. According to him, there is no politics to be found therein. As soon as the deputies are elected, the English people 'is enslaved; it is nothing'. If the critique of parliamentarianism is radical in Rousseau, it is because far from considering it to be a good or bad form of politics he denies it any political being.

What has to be understood is that the general will, like any operator of faithful connection, serves to evaluate the proximity, or conformity, of this or that statement to the event-pact. It is not a matter of knowing whether a statement originates from good or bad politics, from the left or the right, but of whether it *is* or is not political: 'When a law is proposed in the People's assembly, what they are being asked is not exactly whether they approve the proposal or reject it, but whether it does or does not conform to the general will, which is theirs.' It is quite remarkable that for Rousseau political decision amounts to deciding whether a statement is political, and in no way to knowing whether one is for or against it. There is a radical disjunction here between politics and opinion, via which Rousseau antici- pates the modern doctrine of politics as militant procedure rather than as changeover of power between one consensus of opinion and another. The ultimate foundation of this anticipation is the awareness that politics, being the generic procedure in which the truth of the people insists, cannot refer to the knowledgeable discernment of the social or ideological components of a nation. Evental self-belonging, under the name of the social contract, regulates general will, and in doing so it makes of it a term subtracted from any such discernment.

However, there are two remaining difficulties.

- There is only an event as named by an intervention. Who is the intervenor in Rousseau's doctrine? This is the question of the legislator, and it is not an easy one.
- If the pact is necessarily unanimous, this is not the case with the vote for subsequent laws, or with the designation of magistrates. How can the generic character of politics subsist when unanimity fails? This is Rousseau's impasse.

In the person of the legislator the generic unanimity of the event as grasped in its multiple-being inverts itself into absolute singularity. The legislator is the one who intervenes within the site of an assembled people and names, by constitutional or foundational laws, the event-pact. The supernumerary nature of this nomination is inscribed in the following manner: 'This office [that of the legislator], which gives the republic its constitution, has no place in its constitution.' The legislator does not belong to the state of nature because he intervenes in the foundational event of politics. Nor does he belong to the political state, because, it being his role to declare the laws, he is not submitted to them. His action is 'singular and superior'. What Rousseau is trying to think in the metaphor of the quasi-divine character of the legislator is in fact the convocation of the void: the legislator is the one who draws forth, out of the natural void, as retroactively created by the popular assembly, a wisdom in legal nomination that is then ratified by the suffrage. The legislator is turned towards the event, and subtracted from its effects; 'He who drafts the laws has, then, or should have no legislative power.' Not having any power, he can only lay claim to a previous fidelity, the prepolitical fidelity to the gods of Nature. The legislator 'places [decisions] in the mouth of immortals', because such is the law of any intervention: having to lay claim to a previous fidelity in order to name what is unheard of in the event, and so create names which are suitable (as it happens: laws—to name a people constituting itself and an advent of politics). One can easily recognize an interventional avant-garde in the statement in which Rousseau qualifies the paradox of the legislator: 'An undertaking beyond human force, and to execute it an authority that is nil'. The legislator is the one who ensures that the collective event of the contract, recognized in its ultra-one, is named such that politics, from that point on, exists as fidelity or general will. He is the one who changes the collective occurrence into a political duration. He is the intervenor on the borders of popular assemblies.

What is not yet known is the exact nature of the political procedure in the long term. How is general will revealed and practised? What is the practice of marking positive connections (political laws) between this or that statement and the name of the event which the legislator, supported by the contractual unanimity of the people, put into circulation? This is the problem of the political sense of the *majority*.

In a note, Rousseau indicates the following: 'For a will to be general, it is not always necessary that it be unanimous, but it is necessary that all votes be counted; any formal exclusion destroys generality.' The historical fortune of this type of consideration is well-known: the fetishism of universal suffrage. However, with respect to the generic essence of politics, it does not tell us much, apart from indicating that an indiscernible subset of the body politic—and such is the *existing* form of general will—must genuinely be a subset of this entire body, and not of a fraction. This is the trace, at a given stage of political fidelity, of the event itself being unanimous, or a relation of the people to itself as a whole.

Further along Rousseau writes: 'the vote of the majority always obligates all the rest', and 'the tally of the votes yields the declaration of the general will.' What kind of relation could possibly exist between the 'tally of the votes' and the general character of the will? Evidently, the subjacent hypothesis is that the majority of votes materially expresses an indeterminate or indiscernible subset of the collective body. The only justification Rousseau gives for such a hypothesis is the symmetrical destruction of particular wills of opposite persuasions: '[the will of all] is nothing but a sum of particular wills; but if, from these same wills, one takes away the pluses and the minuses which cancel each other out, what is left as the sum of differences is the general will.' But it is not clear why the said sum of differences, which supposedly designates the indiscernible or non-particular character of political will, should appear empirically as a majority; especially given that it is a few differing voices, as we see in parliamentary regimes, which finally decide the outcome. Why would these undecided suffrages, which are in excess of the mutual annihilation of particular wills, express the generic character of politics, or fidelity to the unanimous founding event?

Rousseau's difficulty in passing from the principle (politics finds its truth solely in a generic part of the people, every discernible part expresses a particular interest) to the realization (absolute majority is supposed to be an adequate sign of the generic) leads him to distinguish between *important* decisions and *urgent* decisions:

> Two general maxims can help to regulate these ratios: one, that the more serious and important the deliberations are, the nearer unanimity the view which prevails should be; the other, that the more rapidly the business at hand has to be resolved, the narrower should be the prescribed difference in weighting opinions: in deliberations which have to be concluded straightaway, a majority of one should suffice.

One can see that Rousseau does not make strictly absolute majority into an absolute. He envisages degrees, and introduces what will become the concept of 'qualified majority'. We know that even today majorities of two thirds are required for certain decisions, like revisions of the constitution. But these nuances depart from the principle of the generic character of the will. For *who* decides whether an affair is important or urgent? And by what majority? It is paradoxical that the (quantitative) expression of the general will is suddenly found to depend upon the empirical character of the matters in question. Indiscernibility is limited and corrupted here by the discernibility of cases and by a casuistry which supposes a classificatory encyclopaedia of political circumstances. If political fidelity is bound in its mode of practice to encyclopaedic determinants which are allocated to the particularity of situations, it loses its generic character and becomes a technique for the evaluation of circumstances. Moreover, it is difficult to see how a law—in Rousseau's sense—could *politically* organize the effects of such a technique.

This impasse is better revealed by the examination of a complexity which appears to be closely related, but which Rousseau manages to master. It is the question of the designation of the government (of the executive). Such a designation, concerning particular people, cannot be an act of the general will. The paradox is that the people must thus accomplish a governmental or executive act (naming certain people) despite there not yet being a government. Rousseau resolves this difficulty by positing that the people transforms itself from being sovereign (legislative) into a *democratic* executive organ, since democracy, for him, is government by all. (This indicates—just to open a parenthesis—that the founding contract is not democratic, since democracy is a form of the executive. The contract is a unanimous collective event, and not a democratic governmental decree.) There is thus, whatever the form of government be, an obligatory moment of democracy; that in which the people, 'by a sudden conversion of sovereignty into democracy', are authorized to take particular decisions, like the designation of government personnel. The question then arises of how these decisions are taken. But in this case, no contradiction ensues from these decisions being taken by a majority of suffrages, because it is a matter of a decree and not a law, and so the will is particular, not general. The objection that number regulates a decision whose object is discernible (people, candidates, etc.) is not valid, because this decision is not political, being governmental. Since the generic is not in question, the impasse of its majoritarian expression is removed.

On the other hand, the impasse remains in its entirety when politics is at stake; that is, when it is a question of decisions which relate the people to itself, and which engage the generic nature of the procedure, its subtraction from any encyclopaedic determinant. The general will, qualified by indiscernibility—which alone attaches it to the founding event and institutes politics as truth—cannot allow itself to be determined by number. Rousseau finally becomes so acutely aware of this that he allows that an *interruption of laws* requires the concentration of the general will in the dictatorship of one alone. When it is a question of 'the salvation of the fatherland', and the 'apparatus of laws' becomes an obstacle, it is legitimate to name (but how?) 'a supreme chief who silences all the laws'. The sovereign authority of the collective body is then suspended: not due to the absence of the general will, but on the contrary, because it is 'not in doubt', for 'it is obvious that the people's foremost intention is that the State not perish.' Here again we find the constitutive torsion that consists in the goal of political will being politics itself. Dictatorship is the adequate form of general will once it provides the sole means of maintaining politics' conditions of existence.

Moreover, it is striking that the requirement for a dictatorial interruption of laws emerges from the confrontation between the general will and events: 'The inflexibility of laws, which keeps them from bending to events, can in some cases render them pernicious.' Once again we see the evental ultra-one struggling with the fixity of the operators of fidelity. A casuistry is required, which alone will determine the material form of the general will: from unanimity (required for the initial contract) to the dictatorship of one alone (required when *existing* politics is threatened in its being). This plasticity of expression refers back to the indiscernibility of political will. If it was determined by an explicit statement of the situation, politics would have a canonical form. Generic truth suspended from an event, it is a part of the situation which is subtracted from established language, and its form is aleatoric, for it is solely an *index* of existence and not a knowledgeable nomination. Its procedure is supported uniquely by the zeal of citizen-militants, whose fidelity generates an infinite truth that no form, constitutional or organizational, can adequately express.

Rousseau's genius was to have abstractly circumscribed the nature of politics as generic procedure. Engaged, however, as he was in the classical approach, which concerns the legitimate form of sovereignty, he considered—albeit with paradoxical precautions—that the majority of suffrages was ultimately the empirical form of this legitimacy. He was not able to found this point upon the essence of politics itself, and he bequeathes us the following question: what is it that *distinguishes*, on the presentable surface of the situation, the political procedure?

The essence of the matter, however, lies in joining politics not to legitimacy but to truth—with the obstacle that those who would maintain these principles 'will have sadly told the truth, and will have flattered the people alone'. Rousseau remarks, with a touch of melancholy realism, 'truth does not lead to fortune, and the people confers no ambassador-ships, professorships or pensions.'

Unbound from power, anonymous, patient forcing of an indiscernible part of the situation, politics does not even turn you into the ambassador of a people. Therein one is the servant of a truth whose reception, in a transformed world, is not such that you can take advantage of it. Number itself cannot get its measure.

Politics is, for itself, its own proper end; in the mode of what is being produced as true statements—though forever un-known—by the capacity of a collective will.

MEDITATION THIRTY-THREE

The Matheme of the Indiscernible:
P. J. Cohen's strategy

It is impossible for mathematical ontology to dispose of a concept of truth, because any truth is post-eventum, and the paradoxical multiple that is the event is prohibited from being by that ontology. The process of a truth thus entirely escapes ontology. In this respect, the Heideggerean thesis of an originary co-belonging of being (as φύσις) and truth (as ἀλήθεια, or non-latency) must be abandoned. The sayable of being is disjunct from the sayable of truth. This is why philosophy alone thinks truth, in what it itself possesses in the way of subtraction from the subtraction of being: the event, the ultra-one, the chance-driven procedure and its generic result.

However, if the thought of being does not open to any thought of truth—because a truth is not, but comes forth from the standpoint of an undecidable supplementation—there is still a *being of the truth*, which is *not* the truth; precisely, it is the latter's being. The generic and indiscernible multiple is *in* situation; it is presented, despite being subtracted from knowledge. The *compatibility* of ontology with truth implies that the being of truth, as generic multiplicity, is ontologically thinkable, even if a truth is not. Therefore, it all comes down to this: can ontology produce the concept of a generic multiple, which is to say an unnameable, un-constructible, indiscernible multiple? The revolution introduced by Cohen in 1963 responds in the affirmative: there exists an ontological concept of the indiscernible multiple. Consequently, ontology is compatible with the philosophy of truth. It *authorizes* the existence of the result-multiple of the generic procedure suspended from the event, despite it being indiscernible within the situation in which it is inscribed. Ontology, after having being able to think, with Gödel, Leibniz's thought (constructible hierarchy and sovereignty of language), also thinks, with Cohen, its refutation. It shows that the principle of indiscernibles is a voluntarist limitation, and that the indiscernible *is*.

Of course, one cannot speak of a multiple which is indiscernible 'in-itself'. Apart from the Ideas of the multiple tolerating the supposition that every multiple is constructible (Meditation 30), indiscernibility is necessarily relative to a criterion of the discernible, that is, to a situation and to a language.

Our strategy (and Cohen's invention literally consists of this movement) will thus be the following: we shall install ourselves in a multiple which is fixed once and for all, a multiple which is very rich in properties (it 'reflects' a significant part of general ontology) yet very poor in quantity (it is denumerable). The language will be that of set theory, but restricted to the chosen multiple. We will term this multiple a *fundamental quasi-complete situation* (the Americans call it a *ground-model*). Inside this fundamental situation, we will define a procedure for the approximation of a supposed indiscernible multiple. Since such a multiple cannot be named by any phrase, we will be obliged to anticipate its nomination by a supplementary letter. This extra signifier—to which, in the beginning, nothing which is presented in the fundamental situation corresponds—is the ontological transcription of the supernumerary nomination of the event. However, ontology does not recognize any event, because it forecloses self-belonging. What stands in for an event-without-event is the supernumerary letter itself, and it is thus quite coherent that it designate nothing. Due to a predilection whose origin I will leave the reader to determine, I will choose the symbol ♀ for this inscription. This symbol will be read 'generic multiple', 'generic' being the adjective retained by mathematicians to designate the indiscernible, the absolutely indeterminate, which is to say a multiple that in a given situation solely possesses properties which are more or less 'common' to all the multiples of the situation. In the literature, what I note here as ♀ is noted G (for generic).

Given that a multiple ♀ is not nameable, the possible filling in of its absence—the construction of its concept—can only be a procedure, a procedure which must operate inside the domain of the nameable of the fundamental situation. This procedure designates discernible multiples which have a certain relation to the supposed indiscernible. Here we recognize an intra-ontological version of the procedure of enquiries, such as it—exploring by finite sequences faithful connections to the name of an event—un-limits itself within the indiscernible of a truth. But in ontology there is no procedure, only structure. There is not a-truth, but construction of the concept of the being-multiple of any truth.

We will thus start from a multiple supposed existent *in* the initial situation (the quasi-complete situation); that is, from a multiple which belongs to this situation. This multiple will function in two different manners in the construction of the indiscernible. On the one hand, its elements will furnish the substance-multiple of the indiscernible, because the latter will be a *part* of the chosen multiple. On the other hand, these elements will condition the indiscernible in that they will transmit 'information' about it. This multiple will be both the basic *material* for the construction of the indiscernible (whose elements will be extracted from it), and the place of its *intelligibility* (because the conditions which the indiscernible must obey in order to be indiscernible will be materialized by certain structures of the chosen multiple). That a multiple can both function as simple term of presentation (this term belongs to the indiscernible) and as vector of information about what it belongs to is the key to the problem. It is also an intellectual *topos* with respect to the connection between the pure multiple and sense.

Due to their second function, the elements of the base multiple chosen in the fundamental quasi-complete situation will be called *conditions* (for the indiscernible ♀).

The hope is that certain groupings of conditions, conditions which are themselves conditioned *in the language of the situation*, will make it possible to think that a multiple which counts these conditions as one is incapable, itself, of being discernible. In other words, the conditions will give us both an approximate description and a composition-one sufficient for the conclusion to be drawn that the multiple thus described and composed cannot be named or discerned in the original quasi-complete situation. It is to this conditioned multiple that we will apply the symbol ♀.

In general, the ♀ in question will not even belong to the situation. Just like the symbol attached to it, it will be supernumerary within the situation, despite *all* of the conditions which fill in its initial absence themselves belonging to the situation. The idea is then that of seeing what happens if, by force, this indiscernible is 'added' or 'joined' to the situation. One can see here that, via a retrogression typical of ontology, the supplementation of being that is the event (in non-ontological situations) comes *after* the signifying supplementation, which, in non-ontological situations, arises from the intervention at the evental site. Ontology will explore how, from a given situation, one can construct another situation by means of the 'addition' of an indiscernible multiple of the initial situation. This formalization is clearly that of politics, which, naming an unpresented of the site on the basis of the event, reworks the situation through its tenacious fidelity to that nomination. But here it is a case of a politics without future anterior, a *being* of politics.

The result, in ontology, is that the question is very delicate—'adding' the indiscernible once it has been conditioned (and not constructed or named): what does that mean? Given that you cannot discern $\female$ within the fundamental situation, what explicit procedure could possibly add it to the multiple of that situation? The solution to this problem consists in constructing, within the situation, multiples which function as *names* for every possible element of the situation obtained by the addition of the indiscernible $\female$. Naturally, in general, we will not know *which* multiple of $S(\female)$ (let's call the addition such) is named by each name. Moreover, this referent changes according to whether the indiscernible is this or that, and we do not know how to name or think this 'this or that'. But we will know that there are names for all. We will then posit that $S(\female)$ is the set of values of the names *for a fixed supposed indiscernible*. The manipulation of names will allow us to think many properties of the situation $S(\female)$. The properties will depend on $\female$ being indiscernible or generic. This is why $S(\female)$ will be termed a generic extension of S. For a fixed set of conditions, we will speak, in an entirely general manner, of 'the generic extension of S': the indiscernible leaves a trace in the form of our incapacity to discern 'an' extension obtained on the basis of a 'distinct' indiscernible (the thought of this 'distinctness', as we shall see, is severely limited by the indiscernibility of the indiscernibles).

What remains to be seen is how exactly this program is compatible with the Ideas of the multiple: thus, how exactly—and the bearing of this problem is crucial—an ontological concept of the pure indiscernible multiple exists.

1. FUNDAMENTAL QUASI-COMPLETE SITUATION

The ontological concept of a situation is an indeterminate multiple. One would suppose, however, that the intrasituational approximation of an indiscernible demands quite complex operations. Surely a simple multiple (a finite multiple, for example) does not propose the required operational resources, nor the 'quantity' of sets that these resources presuppose (since we know that an operation is no more, in its being, than a particular multiple).

In truth, the right situation must be as close as possible—with no effort spared—to the resources of ontology itself. It must *reflect* the Ideas of the multiple in the sense that the axioms, or at least the most part of them, must be veridical within it. What does it mean for an axiom to be veridical (or reflected) in a particular multiple? It means that the relativization to this multiple of the formula which expresses the axiom is veridical in this multiple; or, in the vocabulary of Meditation 29, that this formula is *absolute* for the multiple in question. Let's give a typical example: say that S is a multiple and $a \in S$ an indeterminate element of S. The axiom of foundation will be veridical in S if there exists some Other in S; in other words, if we have $\beta \in a$ and $\beta \cap a = \varnothing$, it being understood that this β must exist for an inhabitant of S—in the universe of S 'to exist' means: to belong to S. Let's now suppose that S is a transitive set (Meditation 12). This means that $(a \in S) \to (a \subset S)$. Therefore, every element of a is also an element of S. Since the axiom of foundation is true *in general ontology*, there is (for the ontologist) at least one β such that $\beta \in a$ and $\beta \cap a = \varnothing$. But, due to the transitivity of S, this β is also an element of S. Therefore, for an inhabitant of S, it is equally veridical that there exists a β with $\beta \cap a = \varnothing$. The final result is that we know that a transitive multiple S always reflects the axiom of foundation. From a standpoint inside such a multiple, there is always some Other in an existent multiple, which is to say belonging to the transitive situation in question.

This reflective capacity, by means of which the Ideas of the multiple are 'cut down' to a particular multiple and found to be veridical within it from an internal point of view, is characteristic of ontological theory.

The maximal hypothesis we can make in respect to this capacity, for a fixed multiple S, is the following:

- S verifies all the axioms of set theory which can be expressed in one formula alone; that is, extensionality, union, parts, the void, infinity, choice, and foundation;
- S verifies at least a finite number of instances of those axioms which can only be expressed by an infinite series of formulae; that is, separation and replacement (since there is actually a distinct axiom of separation for every formula $\lambda(a)$, and an axiom of replacement for

every formula $\lambda(\alpha,\beta)$ which indicates that α is replaced by β: see Meditation 5);

– S is transitive (otherwise it would be very easy to exit from it, since one could have $\alpha \in S$, but $\beta \in \alpha$ and $\sim(\beta \in S)$). Transitivity guarantees that what is presented *by* what S presents, is also presented by S. The count-as-one is homogeneous downwards.

For reasons which will turn out to be decisive later on, we will add:

– S is infinite, but denumerable (its cardinality is ω_0).

A multiple S which has these four properties will be said to be a *quasi-complete situation*. In the literature, it is designated, a little abusively, as a *model* of set theory.

Does a quasi-complete situation exist? This is a profound problem. Such a situation 'reflects' a large part of ontology in one of its terms alone: there is a multiple such that the Ideas of the multiple are veridical therein for the most part. We know that a total reflection is impossible, because it would amount to saying that we can fix *within* the theory a 'model' of all of its axioms, and consequently, after Gödel's completeness theorem, that we can demonstrate within the theory the very coherency of the theory. The theorem of incompleteness by the very same Gödel assures us that if that were the case then the theory would in fact be incoherent: any theory which is such that the statement 'the theory is coherent' may be inferred from its axioms is incoherent. The coherency of ontology—the virtue of its deductive fidelity—is in excess of what can be demonstrated by ontology. In Meditation 35 I will show that what is at stake here is a torsion which is constitutive of the subject: the law of a fidelity is not faithfully discernible.

In any case one can demonstrate—within the framework of theorems named by the mathematicians (and rightly so) the 'theorems of reflection' —that quasi-complete denumerable situations exist. Mathematicians speak of transitive denumerable models of set theory. These theorems of reflection show that ontology is capable of reflecting itself as much as is desired (that is, it reflects as many axioms as required in finite number) within *a* denumerable multiple. Given that every *current* theorem is demonstrated with a finite number of axioms, the current state of ontology allows itself to be reflected within a denumerable universe, in the sense that all the statements that mathematics has demonstrated until today are veridical for an inhabitant of that universe—and in the eyes of this inhabitant, the only multiples in existence are those which belong to her universe.

Therefore, we can maintain that what we *know* of being as such—the being of an indeterminate situation—can always be presented within the form of a denumerable quasi-complete situation. No statement is immune from such presentation with regard to its currently established veridicity.

The entire development which follows supposes that we have chosen a denumerable quasi-complete situation. It is from the inside of such a situation that we will force the addition of an indiscernible.

The main precaution is that of carefully distinguishing what is absolute for S and what is not. Two characteristic examples:

- If $\alpha \in S$, $\cup\, \alpha$, the dissemination of α, *in the sense of general ontology*, also belongs to S. This results from the elements of the elements of α (in the sense of the situation S) being the same as the elements of the elements of α in the sense of general ontology, since S is a transitive situation. Given that the axiom of union is supposed veridical in S, a quasi-complete situation, the count-as-one of the elements of its elements exists within it. It is *the same multiple* as $\cup\, \alpha$ in the sense of general ontology. Union is therefore absolute for S, insofar as if one has $\alpha \in S$, one has $\cup\, \alpha \in S$.

- In contrast, $p(\alpha)$ is not absolute for S. The reason is that for an $\alpha \in S$, if $\beta \subset \alpha$ (in the sense of general ontology), it is in no way evident that $\beta \in S$, that is, that the part β exists for an inhabitant of S. The veridicity of the axiom of the powerset in S signifies solely that when $\alpha \in S$, the set of parts of α *which belong to S* is counted as one in S. But from the outside, the ontologist can quite easily distinguish a part of α which, not existing *in S* (because it *does not belong* to S), makes up part of $p(\alpha)$ in the sense of general ontology without making up part of $p(\alpha)$ in the sense given to it by an inhabitant of S. By consequence, $p(\alpha)$ is not absolute for S.

One can find in Appendix 5 a list of terms and operations whose absoluteness can be demonstrated for a quasi-complete situation. This demonstration (which I do not reproduce) is quite interesting, considering the suspicious character, in mathematics as in philosophy, of the concept of absoluteness.

Let's solely retain three results, each revelatory. In a quasi-complete situation, the following are absolute:

- 'to be an ordinal', in the following sense: the ordinals for an inhabitant of S are exactly those ordinals which belong to S in the sense of general ontology;
- ω_0, the first limit ordinal, and thus all of its elements as well (the finite ordinals or whole numbers);
- the set of *finite* parts of α, in the sense in which if $\alpha \in S$, the set of finite parts of α is counted as one in S.

On the other hand, $p(\alpha)$ in the general sense, ω_α for $\alpha > 0$, and $\mid \alpha \mid$ (the cardinality of α), are all *not* absolute.

It is clear that absoluteness does not suit pure quantity (except if it is finite), nor does it suit the state. There is something evasive, or relative, in what is intuitively held, however, to be the most objective of givens: the quantity of a multiple. This provides a stark contrast with the absolute solidity of the ordinals, the rigidity of the ontological schema of natural multiples.

Nature, even infinite, is absolute: infinite quantity is relative.

2. THE CONDITIONS: MATERIAL AND SENSE

What would a set of conditions look like? A condition is a multiple π of the fundamental situation S which is destined to possibly belong to the indiscernible $\female$ (the function of material), and, whatever the case may be, to transmit some 'information' about this indiscernible (which will be a part of the situation S). How can a pure multiple serve as support for information? A pure multiple 'in itself' is a schema of presentation in general; it does not indicate anything apart from what belongs to it.

As it happens, we will not work—towards information, or sense—on the multiple 'in-itself'. The notion of information, like that of a code, is differential. What we will have is rather the following: a condition π_2 will be held to be more restrictive, or more precise, or stronger than a condition π_1, if, for example, π_1 is included within π_2. This is quite natural: since *all* the elements of π_1 are in π_2, and a multiple detains nothing apart from belonging, one can say that π_2 gives all the information given by π_1 plus more. The concept of *order* is central here, because it permits us to distinguish multiples which are 'richer' in sense than others; even if, in terms of belonging, they are all elements of the supposed indiscernible, $\female$.

Let's use an example that will prove extremely useful in what follows. Suppose that our conditions are finite series of 0's and 1's (where 0 is actually the multiple $\varnothing$ and 1 is the multiple $\{\varnothing\}$; by absoluteness— Appendix 5—these multiples certainly belong to S). A condition would be, for example, $<0,1,0>$. The supposed indiscernible will be a multiple whose elements are all of this type. We will have, for example, $<0,1,0> \in \female$. Let's suppose that $<0,1,0>$ gives, moreover, information about what $\female$ is—as a multiple—apart from the fact that it belongs to it. It is sure that all of this information is also contained in the condition $<0,1,0,0>$, since the 'segment' $<0,1,0>$, which constitutes the entirety of the first condition, is completely reproduced within the condition $<0,1,0,0>$ in the same places (the first three). The latter condition gives, in addition, the information (whatever it might be) transmitted by the fact that there is a zero in the fourth position.

This will be written: $<0,1,0> \subset <0,1,0,0>$. The second condition will be thought to dominate the first, and to make the nature of the indiscernible a little more precise. Such is the principle of order underlying the notion of information.

Another requisite characteristic for information is that the conditions be compatible amongst themselves. Without a criterion of the compatible and the incompatible, we would do no more than blindly accumulate information, and nothing would guarantee the preservation of the ontological consistency of the multiple in question. For the indiscernible to exist, it has to be coherent with the Ideas of the multiple. Since what we are aiming at is the description of *an* indiscernible multiple, we cannot tolerate, in reference to the same point, contradictory information. Thus, the conditions $<0,1>$ and $<0,1,0>$ are compatible, because they say the same thing as far as the first two places are concerned. On the other hand, the conditions $<0,1>$ and $<0,0>$ are incompatible, because one gives information coded by 'in the second place there is a 1', and the other gives information coded, contradictorily, by 'in the second place there is a 0'. These conditions cannot be valid *together* for the same indiscernible $\female$.

Note that if two conditions are compatible, it is always because they can be placed 'together', without contradiction, in a stronger condition which contains both of them, and which accumulates their information. In this manner, the condition $<0,1,0,1>$ 'contains' both the condition $<0,1>$ and the condition $<0,1,0>$: the latter are obligatorily, by that very fact, compatible. Inversely, no condition can contain both the condition $<0,1>$ and $<0,0>$ because they diverge on the mark occupying the second place.

Such is the principle of compatibility underlying the notion of information.

Finally, a condition is useless if it already prescribes, itself, a stronger condition; in other words, if it does not tolerate any aleatory progress in the conditioning. This idea is very important because it formalizes the freedom of conditioning which alone will lead to an indiscernible. Let's take, for example, the condition *<0,1>*. The condition *<0,1,0>* is a reinforcement of the latter (it says both the same thing and more). The same goes for the condition *<0,1,1>*. However, these two 'extensions' of *<0,1>* are incompatible between themselves because they give contradictory information concerning the mark which occupies the third place. The situation is thus the following: the condition *<0,1>* admits two incompatible extensions. The progression of the conditioning of ♀, starting from the condition *<0,1>*, is not prescribed by this condition. It could be *<0,1,0>*, it could be *<0,1,1>*, but these choices designate different indiscernibles. The growing precision of the conditioning is made up of real choices; that is, choices between incompatible conditions. Such is the principle of choice underlying the notion of information.

Without having to enter into the manner in which a multiple actually gives information, we have determined three principles which are indispensable to the multiple's generation of valuable information. Order, compatibility and choice must, in all cases, *structure* every set of conditions.

This allows us to formalize without difficulty what a *set of conditions* is: it will be written ©.

a. A set © of conditions, with © ∈ *S*, is a set of sets noted π_1, π_2, . . . π_n . . . The indiscernible ♀ will have conditions as elements. It will thus be a part of ©: ♀ ⊂ ©, and therefore a part of *S*: ♀ ⊂ *S*. Note that because the situation *S* is transitive, © ∈ *S* → © ⊂ *S*, and since π ∈ ©, we also have π ∈ *S*.

b. There is an order on these conditions, that we will note ⊂ (because in general it coincides with inclusion, or is a variant of the latter). If $\pi_1 \subset \pi_2$, we will say that the condition π_2 *dominates* the condition π_1 (it is an extension of the latter, it says more).

c. Two conditions are *compatible* if they are dominated by the same third condition. 'π_1 is compatible with π_2' thus means that: $(\exists\pi_3)[\pi_1 \subset \pi_3 \ \& \ \pi_2 \subset \pi_3]$. If this is not the case, they are incompatible.

d. Every condition is dominated by two conditions which are incompatible between themselves: $(\forall\pi_1)(\exists\pi_2)(\exists\pi_3)[\pi_1 \subset \pi_2 \, \& \, \pi_1 \subset \pi_3 \, \& \, '\pi_2$ and π_3 are incompatible'].

Statement *a* formalizes that every condition is material for the indiscernible; statement *b* that we can distinguish more precise conditions; statement *c* that the description of the indiscernible admits a principle of coherency; statement *d* that there are real choices in the pursuit of the description.

3. CORRECT SUBSET (OR PART) OF THE SET OF CONDITIONS

The conditions, as I have said, have a double function: material for an indiscernible subset, information on that subset. The intersection of these two functions can be read in a statement like $\pi_1 \in \female$. This statement 'says' both that the condition π_1 is presented by $\female$ and—same thing read differently—that $\female$ is such that π_1 belongs to it, or can belong to it; which is information about $\female$, but a 'minimal' or atomic piece of information. What interests us is knowing how certain conditions can be regulated such that they constitute a coherent subset of the set © of conditions. This 'collective' conditioning is directly tied to the principles of order, compatibility and choice which structure the set ©. It sutures the function of material to that of information, because it indicates what can or must belong *on the basis of* the conditions' structure of information.

Leave aside for the moment the indiscernible character of the part that we want to condition. We don't need the supernumerary sign $\female$ just quite yet. Let's work out, in a general manner, the following: what conditions must be imposed upon the conditions first for them to aim at the one of a multiple, or at a part δ of ©, and second for us to be able or not to decide, ultimately, whether this δ exists in the situation?

What is certain is that if a condition π_1 figures in the conditioning of a part δ of the situation, and if $\pi_2 \subset \pi_1$ (π_1 dominates π_2), the condition π_2 also figures therein, because everything that it gives us as information on this supposed multiple is *already* in π_1.

We will term *correct set* a set of conditions which aim at the one-multiple of a part δ of ©. We have just seen, and this will be the first rule for a correct set of conditions, that if a condition belongs to this set then all the conditions that the first condition dominates also belong to it. These rules of correction will be noted *Rd*. We have:

Rd_1: $[\pi_1 \in \delta \; \& \; \pi_2 \subset \pi_1] \rightarrow \pi_2 \in \delta$

What we are doing is trying to axiomatically characterize a correct part of conditions. For the moment, the fact that δ is indiscernible is not taken into account in any manner. The variable δ suffices, for an inhabitant of S, to construct the *concept* of a correct set of conditions.

A consequence of the rule is that $\varnothing$, the empty set, belongs to every correct set. Indeed, being in the position of universal inclusion (Meditation 7), $\varnothing$ is included in every condition π, or is dominated by every condition. What can be said of $\varnothing$? One can say that it is the *minimal* condition, the one which teaches us nothing about what the subset δ is. This zero-degree of conditioning is a piece of every correct part because no characteristic of δ can prevent $\varnothing$ from figuring in it, insofar as no characteristic is affirmed or contradicted by any element of $\varnothing$ (there aren't any such elements).

It is certain that a correct part must be coherent, because it aims at the one of a multiple. It cannot contain incompatible conditions. Our second rule will posit that if two conditions belong to a correct part, they are compatible; that is, they are dominated by a third condition. But given that this third condition 'accumulates' the information contained in the first two, it is reasonable to posit that it also belongs to the correct part. Our rule becomes: given two conditions of δ, there exists a condition of δ which dominates both of them. This is the second rule of correction, Rd_2:

Rd_2: $[(\pi_1 \in \delta) \; \& \; (\pi_2 \in \delta)] \rightarrow (\exists \pi_3)[(\pi_3 \in \delta) \; \& \; (\pi_1 \subset \pi_3) \; \& \; (\pi_2 \subset \pi_3)]$

Note that the concept of correct part, as founded by the two rules Rd_1 and Rd_2, is perfectly clear for an inhabitant of S. The inhabitant sees that a correct part is a certain subset of © which has to obey two rules expressed in the language of the situation. Of course, we still do not know exactly whether correct parts exist in S. For that, they would have to be parts of © which are known in S. The fact that © is an element of the situation S guarantees, by transitivity, that an *element* of © is also an element of S; however, it does not guarantee that a *part* of © is automatically such. Nevertheless, the—possibly empty—concept of a correct set of conditions is thinkable in S. It is a correct definition for an inhabitant of S.

What is not yet known is how to describe a correct part which would be an *indiscernible* part of ©, and so of S.

4. INDISCERNIBLE OR GENERIC SUBSET

Suppose that a subset δ of © is correct, which is to say it obeys the rules Rd_1 and Rd_2. What else is necessary for it to be indiscernible, thus, for this δ to be a ♀?

A set δ is discernible *for an inhabitant of S* (the fundamental quasi-complete situation) if there exists an explicit property of the language of the situation which names it completely. In other words, an explicit formula $λ(α)$ must exist, which is comprehensible for an inhabitant of S, such that 'belong to δ' and 'have the property expressed by $λ(α)$' coincide: $α \in δ \leftrightarrow λ(α)$. *All* the elements of δ have the property formulated by $λ$, and *they alone* possess it, which means that if $α$ does *not* belong to δ, $α$ does not have the property $λ$: $\sim(α \in δ) \leftrightarrow \sim λ(α)$. One can say, in this case, that $λ$ 'names' the set δ, or (Meditation 3) that it *separates* it.

Take a correct set of conditions δ. It is a part of ©, it obeys the rules Rd_1 and Rd_2. Moreover, it is discernible, and it coincides with what is separated, within ©, by a formula $λ$. We have: $π \in δ \leftrightarrow λ(π)$. Note then the following: by virtue of the principle d of conditions (the principle of choice), every condition is dominated by two incompatible conditions. In particular, for a condition $π_1 \in δ$, we have two dominating conditions, $π_2$ and $π_3$, which are incompatible between themselves. The rule Rd_2 of correct parts prohibits the two incompatible conditions from both belonging to the same correct part. It is therefore necessary that either $π_2$ or $π_3$ does not belong to δ. Let's say that it's $π_2$. Since the property $λ$ discerns δ, and $π_2$ does not belong to δ, it follows that $π_2$ *does not possess* the property expressed by $λ$. We thus have: $\sim λ(π_2)$.

We arrive at the following result, which is decisive for the characterization of an indiscernible: if a correct part δ is discerned by a property $λ$, every element of δ (every $π \in δ$) is dominated by a condition $π_2$ such that $\sim λ(π_2)$.

To illustrate this point, let's return to the example of the finite series of *1*'s and *0*'s.

The property 'solely containing the mark *1*' separates in © the set of conditions *<1>*, *<1,1>*, *<1,1,1>*, etc. It clearly discerns this subset. It so happens that this subset is correct: it obeys the rule Rd_1 (because every condition dominated by a series of *1*'s is itself a series of *1*'s); and it obeys the rule Rd_2 (because two series of *1*'s are dominated by a series of *1*'s which is 'longer' than both of them). We thus have an example of a discernible correct part.

Now, the negation of the discerning property 'solely containing the mark *1*' is expressed as: 'containing the mark *0* at least once'. Consider the set of conditions which satisfy this negation: these are conditions which have at least one *0*. It is clear that given a condition which does not have any *0*'s, it is always dominated by a condition which has a *0*: $<1,1,1>$ is dominated by $<1,1,1,0>$. It is enough to add *0* to the end. As such, the discernible correct part defined by 'all the series which only contain *1*'s' is such that in its *exterior* in ©, defined by the contrary property 'containing at least one *0*', there is always a condition which dominates any given condition in its interior.

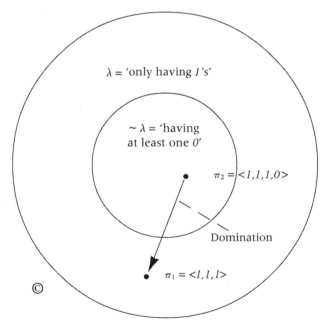

We can therefore specify the discernibility of a correct part by saying: if λ discerns the correct part δ (here λ is 'only having *1*'s'), then, for every element of δ (here, for example, $<1,1,1>$), there exists in the exterior of δ—that is, amongst the elements which verify ~λ (here, ~λ is 'having at least one *0*')—at least one element (here, for example, *<1,1,1,0>*) which dominates the chosen element of δ.

This allows us to develop a *structural* characterization of the discernibility of a correct part, without reference to language.

Let's term *domination* a set of conditions such that any condition outside the domination is dominated by at least one condition inside the domination. That is, if the domination is noted D (see diagram):

$$\sim(\pi_1 \in D) \rightarrow (\exists \pi_2)[(\pi_2 \in D) \text{ \& } (\pi_1 \subset \pi_2)]$$

This axiomatic definition of a domination no longer makes any mention of language or of properties like λ, etc.

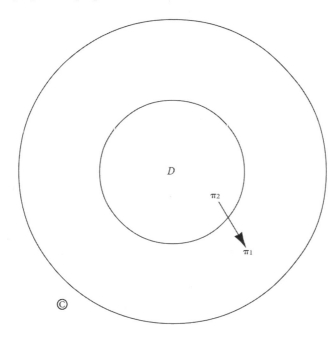

We have just seen that if a property λ discerns a correct subset δ, then the conditions which satisfy ~λ (which are not in δ) are a domination. In the example given, the series which negate the property 'only having *1*'s'; that is, all the series which have at least one *0*, form a domination, and so it goes.

One property of a correct set δ which is discernible (by λ), is that its exterior in © (itself discerned by ~λ) is a domination. *Every correct discernible set is therefore totally disjoint from at least one domination*; that is, from the domination constituted by the conditions which *do not possess* its discerning property. If δ is discerned by λ, (© − δ), the exterior of δ, discerned by ~λ, is a domination. Of course, the intersection of δ and of what remains in © when δ is removed is necessarily empty.

A contrario, if a correct set δ intersects every domination—has at least one element in common with every domination—then this is definitely because it is indiscernible: otherwise it would *not* intersect the domination which corresponds to the negation of the discerning property. The axiomatic definition of a domination is intrinsic, it does not mention language, and it is comprehensible for an inhabitant of S. Here we are on the very brink of possessing a *concept* of the indiscernible, one given strictly in the language of ontology. We will posit that ♀ *must* intersect (have at least one element in common with) *every* domination, to be understood as: all those which exist for an inhabitant of S, that is, which belong to the quasi-complete situation S. Remember that a domination is actually a *part*, D, of the set of conditions ©. Moreover, $p(©)$ is *not* absolute. Thus, there are perhaps dominations which exist in the sense of general ontology, but which do not exist for an inhabitant of S. Since indiscernibility is relative to S, domination—which supports its concept—is also relative. The idea is that, *in S*, the correct part ♀, intersecting every domination, contains, for every property supposed to discern it, one condition (at least) which does not possess this property. It is thus the exemplary place of the vague, of the indeterminate, such as the latter is thinkable within S; because it subtracts itself, in at least one of its points, from discernment by any property whatsoever.

Hence the capital definition: *a correct set ♀ will be generic for S if, for any domination D which belongs to S, we have* $D \cap ♀ \neq \emptyset$ (the intersection of D and ♀ is not empty).

This definition, despite being given in the language of general ontology (because S does *not* belong to S), is perfectly intelligible for an inhabitant of S. He knows what a domination is, because what defines it—the formula $\sim(\pi_1 \in D) \rightarrow (\exists \pi_2)[(\pi_2 \in D) \,\&\, (\pi_1 \subset \pi_2)]$—concerns conditions, which belong to S. He knows what a correct set of conditions is. He understands the phrase 'a correct set is generic if it intersects every domination'—it being understood that, for him, 'every domination' means 'every domination belonging to S', since he quantifies *in his universe*, which is S. It so happens that this phrase defines the concept of genericity for a correct part. This concept is therefore accessible to an inhabitant of *S*. It is literally the concept, inside the fundamental situation, of a multiple which is indiscernible in that situation.

To give some kind of basis for an intuition of the generic, let's consider our finite series of *1*'s and *0*'s again. The property 'having at least one *1*' discerns a domination, because any series which only has *0*'s is dominated by a series which has a *1* (a *1* is added to the initial series of *0*'s). Consequently, if a set of finite series of *0*'s and *1*'s is generic, its intersection with this domination is not void: it contains at least one series which has a *1*. But one could show, in exactly the same manner, that 'having at least two *1*'s' or 'having at least four thousand *1*'s' also discern dominations (one adds as many *1*'s as necessary to the series which do not have enough). Again, the generic set will necessarily contain series which have the sign *1* twice or four thousand times. The same remark could be made for the properties 'having at least one *0*' and 'having at least four thousand *0*'s. The generic set will therefore contain series carrying the mark *1* or the mark *0* as many times as one wishes. One could start over with more complex properties, such as 'end in a *1*' (but *not*, note, with 'begin by a *1*', which does not discern a domination—see for yourself), or 'end in ten billion *1*'s'; but also, 'have at least seventeen *0*'s and forty-seven *1*'s', etc. The generic set, obliged to intersect every domination defined by these properties, has to contain, for each property, at least one series which possesses it. One can grasp here quite easily the root of the indeterminateness, the indiscernibility of ♀: it contains 'a little bit of everything', in the sense in which an immense number of properties are each supported by at least one term (condition) which belongs to ♀. The only limit here is consistency: the indiscernible set ♀ cannot contain two conditions that two properties render incompatible, like 'begin with *1*' *and* 'begin with *0*'. Finally, the indiscernible set *only* possesses the properties necessary to its pure existence as multiple in its material (here, the series of *0*'s and *1*'s). It does not possess any particular, discerning, separative property. It is an anonymous representative of the parts of the set of conditions. At base, its sole property is that of consisting as pure multiple, or being. Subtracted from language, it makes do with its being.

MEDITATION THIRTY-FOUR

The Existence of the Indiscernible:
the power of names

---

1. IN DANGER OF INEXISTENCE

At the conclusion of Meditation 33, we dispose of a *concept* of the indiscernible multiple. But by what 'ontological argument' shall we pass from the concept to existence? To exist meaning here: *to belong to* a situation.

An inhabitant of the universe S, who has a concept of genericity, can ask herself the following question: does this multiple of conditions, which I can *think*, exist? Such existence is not automatic, for the reason evoked above: $p(©)$ not being absolute, it is quite possible that *in S*—even supposing that a correct generic part exists *for the ontologist*—there does not exist any subset of S corresponding to the criteria of such a part.

The response to the inhabitant's question, and it is extremely disappointing, is negative. If ♀ is a correct part which *belongs* to S ('belonging to S' is the ontological concept of existence for an inhabitant of the universe S), its exterior in ©, © − ♀, also belongs to S, for reasons of absoluteness (Appendix 5). Unfortunately, this exterior *is a domination*, as we have in fact already seen: every condition which belongs to ♀ is dominated by two incompatible conditions; there is thus at least one which is exterior to ♀. Therefore © − ♀ dominates ♀. But ♀, being generic, should intersect every domination which belongs to S, and so intersect its own exterior, which is absurd.

By consequence, it is impossible for ♀ to belong to S if ♀ is generic. For an inhabitant of S, no generic part exists. It looks like we have failed, and so close to the destination! Certainly, we have constructed *within* the fundamental situation a concept of a generic correct subset which is not distinguished by any formula, and which, in this sense, is indiscernible for an inhabitant of S. But since no generic subset exists in this situation, indiscernibility remains an empty concept: the indiscernible is *without being*. In reality, an inhabitant of S can only *believe* in the existence of an indiscernible—insofar as if it exists, it is outside the world. The employment of a clear concept of the indiscernible could give rise to such a faith, with which this concept's void of being might be filled. But existence changes its sense here, because it is not assignable to the situation. Must we then conclude that the thinking of an indiscernible remains vacant, or suspended from the pure concept, if one does not fill it with a transcendence? For an inhabitant of S, in any case, it seems that God alone can be indiscernible.

2. ONTOLOGICAL *COUP DE THÉÂTRE*: THE INDISCERNIBLE EXISTS

This impasse will be broken by the ontologist operating from the exterior of the situation. I ask the reader to attend, with concentration, to the moment at which ontology affirms its powers, through the domination of thought it practises upon the pure multiple, and thus upon the *concept* of situation.

For the ontologist, the situation S is a multiple, and this multiple has properties. Many of these properties are not observable from inside the situation, but are evident from the outside. A typical property of this sort is the cardinality of the situation. To say, for example, that S is denumerable—which is what we posited at the very beginning—is to signify that there is a one-to-one correspondence between S and ω_0. But this correspondence is surely not a multiple of S, if only because S, involved in this very correspondence, is *not* an element of S. Therefore, it is only from a point outside S that the cardinality of S can be revealed.

Now, from this exterior in which the master of pure multiples reigns (the thought of being-qua-being, mathematics), it can be seen—such is the eye of God—that the dominations of © which belong to S form a denumerable set. Obviously! S is denumerable. The dominations which belong to it form a part of S, a part which could not exceed the cardinality of that in which it is included. One can therefore speak of the denumerable list $D_1, D_2, \ldots$

D_n . . . of the dominations of © which belong to S.

We shall then construct a correct generic part in the following manner (via recurrence):

– π_0 is an indeterminate condition.
– If π_n is defined, one of two things must come to pass:

- either $\pi_n \in D_{n+1}$, the domination of the rank $n + 1$. If so, I posit that $\pi_{n+1} = \pi_n$.
- or $\sim(\pi_n \in D_{n+1})$. Then, by the definition of a domination, there exists a $\pi_{n+1} \in D_{n+1}$ which dominates π_n. I then take this π_{n+1}.

This construction gives me a sequence of 'enveloped' conditions:
$\pi_0 \subset \pi_1 \subset \pi_2 \subset \ldots \subset \pi_n \subset \ldots$

I define $\mathfemale$ as the set of conditions dominated by at least one π_n of the above sequence. That is: $\pi \in \mathfemale \leftrightarrow [(\exists \pi_n) \, \pi \subset \pi_n]$

I then note that:

a. $\mathfemale$ is a correct set of conditions.

- This set obeys the rule Rd_1. For if $\pi_1 \in \mathfemale$, there is π_n such that $\pi_1 \subset \pi_n$. But then, $\pi_2 \subset \pi_1 \rightarrow \pi_2 \subset \pi_n$, therefore $\pi_2 \in \mathfemale$. Every condition dominated by a condition of $\mathfemale$ belongs to $\mathfemale$.
- This set obeys the rule Rd_2. For if $\pi_1 \in \mathfemale$ and $\pi_2 \in \mathfemale$, we have $\pi_1 \subset \pi_n$ and $\pi_2 \subset \pi_{n'}$. Say, for example, that $n < n'$. By construction of the sequence, we have $\pi_n \subset \pi_{n'}$, thus $(\pi_1 \cup \pi_2) \subset \pi_{n'}$, and therefore $(\pi_1 \cup \pi_2) \in \mathfemale$. Now $\pi_1 \subset (\pi_1 \cup \pi_2)$ and $\pi_2 \subset (\pi_1 \cup \pi_2)$. Therefore, there is clearly a dominating condition in $\mathfemale$ common to π_1 and π_2.

b. $\mathfemale$ is generic.

For every domination D_n belonging to S, a π_n exists, by construction of the sequence; a π_n such that $\pi_n \in \mathfemale$ and $\pi_n \in D_n$. Thus, for every D_n, we have $\mathfemale \cap D_n \neq \emptyset$.

For general ontology there is thus no doubt that a generic part of S *exists*. The ontologist is evidently in agreement with an inhabitant of S in saying that this *part of S* is not an *element* of S. For this inhabitant, this means that it does not exist. For the ontologist, this means solely that $\mathfemale \subset S$ but that $\sim(\mathfemale \in S)$.

For the ontologist, given a quasi-complete situation S, *there exists a subset of the situation which is indiscernible within that situation.* It is a law of being that in every denumerable situation the state counts as one a part indiscernible within that situation, yet whose concept is in our possession: that of a generic correct part.

But our labours are not finished yet. Certainly, an indiscernible for S exists outside S—but where is the paradox? What we want is an indiscernible *internal to a situation.* Or, to be precise, a set which: *a.* is indiscernible in a situation; *b.* belongs to that situation. We want the set to *exist* in the very place in which it is indiscernible.

The entire question resides in knowing *to which situation ♀ belongs.* Its floating exteriority to S cannot satisfy us, because it is quite possible that it belongs to an as yet unknown extension of the situation, in which, for example, it would be constructible with statements of the situation, and thus completely discernible.

The most simple idea for studying this question is that of adding ♀ to the fundamental situation S. In this manner we would have a new situation to which ♀ would belong. The situation obtained by the adjunction of the indiscernible will be called a *generic extension* of S, and it will be written $S(♀)$. The extreme difficulty of the question lies in this 'addition' having to be made *with the resources of S,* otherwise it would be unintelligible for an inhabitant of S. Yet, ~(♀ ∈ S). How can any sense be made of this extension of S via a production that brings forth the belonging of the indiscernible which S includes? And what guarantee is there—supposing that we resolve the latter problem—that ♀ will be indiscernible in the generic extension $S(♀)$?

The solution consists in modifying and enriching not the situation itself, but its language, so as to be able to name *in S* the hypothetical elements of its extension by the indiscernible, thus anticipating—without presupposition of existence—the properties of the extension. In this language, an inhabitant of S will be able to say: 'If there exists a generic extension, then this name, which exists in S, designates such a thing within it.' This hypothetical statement will not pose any problems for her, because she disposes of the concept of genericity (which is void for her). From the outside, the ontologist will realize the hypothesis, because he knows that a generic set exists. For him, the referents of the names, which are solely articles of faith for an inhabitant of S, will be real terms. The *logic* of the development will be the same for whoever inhabits S and for us, but the *ontological status* of these inferences will be entirely different: faith in transcendence for one (because ♀ is 'outside the world'), position of being for the other.

3. THE NOMINATION OF THE INDISCERNIBLE

The striking paradox of our undertaking is that we are going to try to *name* the very thing which is impossible to *discern*. We are searching for a language for the unnameable. It will have to name the latter without naming it, it will instruct its vague existence without specifying anything whatsoever within it. The intra-ontological realization of this program, its sole resource the multiple, is a spectacular performance.

The names must be able to *hypothetically* designate, with S's resources alone, elements of $S(♀)$ (it being understood that $S(♀)$ exists for the external ontologist, and inexists for an inhabitant of S, or is solely a transcendental object of faith). The only *existent* things which touch upon $S(♀)$ in S are the conditions. A name will therefore combine a multiple of S with a condition. The 'strictest' idea would be to proceed such that a name itself is made up of couples of other names and conditions.

The definition of such a name is the following: a name is a multiple whose elements are pairs of names and conditions. That is; if u_1 is a name, $(a \in u_1) \rightarrow (a = <u_2,\pi>)$, where u_2 is a name, and π a condition.

Of course, the reader could indignantly point out that this definition is circular: I define a name by supposing that I know what a name is. This is a well-known aporia amongst linguists: how does one define, for example, the name 'name' without starting off by saying that it is a name? Lacan isolated the point of the real in this affair in the form of a thesis: there is no metalanguage. We are submerged in the mother tongue (*lalangue*) without being able to contort ourselves to the point of arriving at a separated thought of this immersion.

Within the framework of ontology, however, the circularity can be undone, and deployed as a hierarchy or stratification. This, moreover, is one of the most profound characteristics of this region of thought; it always stratifies successive constructions starting from the point of the void.

The essential instrument of this stratified unfolding of an apparent circle is again found in the series of ordinals. Nature is the universal tool for ordering—here, for the ordering of the names.

We start by defining the elementary names, or names of the nominal rank 0. These names are exclusively composed of pairs of the type $<\varnothing,\pi>$ where $\varnothing$ is the minimal condition (we have seen how $\varnothing$ is a condition, the one which conditions nothing), and π is an indeterminate condition. That is, if μ is a name (simplifying matters a little):

'μ is of the nominal rank 0' $\leftrightarrow [(\gamma \in \mu) \rightarrow \gamma = <\varnothing,\pi>]$

We then suppose that we have succeeded in defining all the names of the nominal rank β, where β is an ordinal smaller than an ordinal α (thus: $\beta \in \alpha$). Our goal is then to define a name of the nominal rank α. We will posit that such a name is composed of pairs of the type $<\mu_1,\pi>$ where μ_1 is a name of a nominal rank *inferior to* α, and π a condition:

'μ is of the nominal rank α' $\leftrightarrow [(\gamma \in \mu) \rightarrow (\gamma = <\mu_1,\pi>$, & '$\mu_1$ is of a nominal rank β smaller than α')]

The definition then ceases to be circular for the following reason: a name is always attached to a nominal rank named by an ordinal; let's say α. It is thus composed of pairs $<\mu,\pi>$, but where μ is of a nominal rank inferior to α and thus previously defined. We 'redescend' in this manner until we reach the names of the nominal rank 0, which are themselves explicitly defined (a set of pairs of the type $<\varnothing,\pi>$). The names are deployed starting from the rank 0 via successive constructions which engage nothing apart from the material defined in the previous steps. As such, a name of the rank 1 will be composed from pairs consisting of names of the rank 0 and conditions. But the pairs of the rank 0 are defined. Therefore, an element of a name of the rank 1 is also defined; it solely contains pairs of the type $< <\varnothing,\pi_1>, \pi_2>$, and so on.

Our first task is to examine whether this concept of name is intelligible for an inhabitant of S, and work out which names are in the fundamental situation. It is certain that they are not all there (besides, if $\copyright$ is not empty, the hierarchy of names *is not a set*, it inconsists, just like the hierarchy $\llcorner$ of the constructible—Meditation 29).

To start with, let's note that we cannot hope that nominal ranks 'exist' in S for ordinals which do not belong to S. Since S is transitive and denumerable, it solely contains denumerable ordinals. That is, $\alpha \in S \rightarrow \alpha \subset S$, and the cardinality of α cannot exceed that of S, which is equal to ω_0. Since 'being an ordinal' is absolute, we can speak of the *first* ordinal δ

which does not belong to S. For an inhabitant of S, only ordinals inferior to δ exist; therefore, recurrence on nominal ranks only makes sense up to and not including δ.

Immanence to the fundamental situation S therefore definitely imposes a substantial restriction upon the number of names which 'exist' in comparison to the names whose existence is affirmed by general ontology.

But what matters to us is whether an inhabitant of S possesses the concept of a name, such that she recognizes as names all the names (in the sense of general ontology) which belong to her situation, and, reciprocally, does not baptize multiples of her situation 'names' when they are not names for general ontology—that is, for the hierarchy of nominal ranks. In short, we want to verify that the *concept* of name is absolute, that 'being a name' *in* S coincides with 'being a name which belongs to S' in the sense of general ontology.

The results of this investigation are positive: they show that all the terms and all the operations engaged in the concept of name (ordinals, pairs, sets of pairs, etc.) are absolute for the quasi-complete situation S. These operations thus specify 'the same multiple'—if it belongs to S—for the ontologist as for the inhabitant of S.

We can thus consider, without further detours, the names of S, or names which exist in S, which belong to S. Of course, S does not necessarily contain all the names of a given rank α. But all the names that it contains, and those alone, are recognized as names by the inhabitant of S. From now on, when we speak of a name, it must be understood that we are referring to a name in S. It is with these names that we are going to construct a situation $S(\female)$ to which the indiscernible $\female$ will belong. A case in which it is literally the name that creates the thing.

4. $\female$-REFERENT OF A NAME AND EXTENSION BY THE INDISCERNIBLE

Let's suppose that a generic part $\female$ exists. Remember, this 'supposition' is a certitude for the ontologist (it can be shown that if S is denumerable, there exists a generic part), and a matter of theological faith for the inhabitant of S (because $\female$ does not belong to the universe S).

We are going to give the names a *referential value* tied to the indiscernible ♀. The goal is to have a name 'designate' a multiple which belongs to a situation in which we have forced the indiscernible ♀ to add itself to the fundamental situation. We will only use names known in S. We will write $R_♀(\mu)$ for the referential value of a name such as induced by the supposition of a generic part ♀. It is at this point that we start to fully employ the formal and supernumerary symbol ♀.

For elements, a name has pairs like $<\mu_1,\pi>$, where μ_1 is a name and π a condition. The referential value of a name can only be defined on the basis of these two types of multiples (names and conditions), since a pure multiple can only give what it possesses, which is to say what belongs to it. We will use the following simple definition: the referential value of a name for a supposed existent ♀ is the set of referential values of the names which enter into its composition and which are paired to a condition *which belongs to* ♀. Say, for example, that you observe that the pair $<\mu_1,\pi>$ is an element of the name μ. If π belongs to ♀, *then* the referential value of μ_1, that is, $R_♀(\mu_1)$, is an element of the referential value of μ. To summarize:

$$R_♀(\mu) = \{R_♀(\mu_1) \ / \ <\mu_1,\pi> \in \mu \ \& \ \pi \in ♀\}$$

This definition is just as circular as the definition of the name: you define the referential value of μ by supposing that you can determine that of μ_1. The circle is unfolded into a hierarchy by the use of the names' nominal rank. Since the names are stratified, the definition of their referential value can also be stratified.

– For names of the nominal rank *0*, which are composed of pairs $<\varnothing,\pi>$, we will posit:

- $R_♀(\mu) = \{\varnothing\}$, if there exists as element of μ, a pair $<\varnothing,\pi>$ with $\pi \in ♀$; in other words, if the name μ is 'connected' to the generic part in that one of its constituent pairs $<\varnothing,\pi>$ contains a condition which is in this part. Formally: $(\exists\mu)[<\varnothing,\pi> \in \mu \ \& \ \pi \in ♀] \leftrightarrow R_♀(\mu) = \{\varnothing\}$.
- $R_♀(\mu) = \varnothing$, if this is not the case (if no condition appearing in the pairs which constitute μ belongs to the generic part).

Observe that the assignation of value is explicit and depends uniquely on the belonging or non-belonging of conditions to the supposed generic part. For example, the name $\{<\varnothing,\pi>\}$ has the referential value $\{\varnothing\}$ if π belongs to ♀, and the value $\varnothing$ if π does not belong to ♀. All of this is clear to an inhabitant of S, who possesses a concept (void) of generic part, and can thus inscribe intelligible implications of the genre:

$$\pi \in \female \rightarrow R_\female(\mu) = \{\varnothing\}$$

which are of the type 'if . . . then', and do not require that a generic part *exists* (for her).

– Let's suppose that the referential value of the names has been defined for all names of a nominal rank inferior to the ordinal α. Take μ_1, a name of the rank α. Its referential value will be defined thus:

$$R_\female(\mu_1) = \{R_\female(\mu_2) \ / \ (\exists\pi)(<\mu_2,\pi> \in \mu_1 \ \& \ \pi \in \female)\}$$

The $\female$-referent of a name of the rank α is the set of $\female$-referents of the names which participate in its nominal composition, if they are paired with a condition which belongs to the generic part. This is a correct definition, because every element of a name μ_1 is of the type $<\mu_2,\pi>$, and it makes sense to ask whether $\pi \in \female$ or not. If it does belong, we take the value of μ_2, which is defined (for $\female$), since μ_2 is of inferior nominal rank.

We will then constitute, in a single step, another situation than the fundamental situation by taking all the values of all the names which belong to S. This new situation is constituted on the basis of the names; it is the generic extension of S. As announced earlier, it will be written $S(\female)$.

It is defined thus: $S(\female) = \{R_\female(\mu) \ / \ \mu \in S\}$

In other words: the generic extension by the indiscernible $\female$ is obtained by taking the $\female$-referents of all the names which exist in S. Inversely, 'to be an element of the extension' means: to be the value of a name of S.

This definition is comprehensible for an inhabitant of S, insofar as: $\female$ is solely a formal symbol designating an unknown transcendence; the concept of a generic description is clear for her; the names in consideration belong to S; and thus the definition via recurrence of the referential function $R_\female(\mu)$ is itself intelligible.

There are three crucial problems which have not yet been considered. First of all, is it really a matter of an *extension* of S here? In other words, do the elements of S also belong to the extension $S(\female)$? If not, it is a disjoint planet which is at stake, and not an extension—the indiscernible has not been added to the fundamental situation. Next, does the indiscernible $\female$ actually belong to the extension? Finally, does it remain indiscernible, thus becoming, within $S(\female)$, an intrinsic indiscernible?

5. THE FUNDAMENTAL SITUATION IS A PART OF ANY GENERIC EXTENSION, AND THE INDISCERNIBLE ♀ IS AN ELEMENT OF ANY GENERIC EXTENSION

a. Canonical names of elements of S

The 'nominalist' singularity of the generic extension lies in its elements being *solely* accessible via their names. This is one of the reasons why Cohen's invention is such a fascinating philosophical 'topos'. Being maintains therein a relation to the names which is all the more astonishing given that each and every one of them is thought there in its pure being, that is, as pure multiple. For a name is no more than an element of the fundamental situation. The extension $S(♀)$, despite existing for ontology —since ♀ exists if the fundamental situation is denumerable—thus appears to be an aleatory phantom with respect to which the sole certitude lies in the names.

If, for example, we want to show that the fundamental situation is included in the generic extension, that $S \subset S(♀)$—which alone guarantees the meaning of the word extension—we have to show that every element of S is also an element of $S(♀)$. But the generic extension is produced as a set of values—♀-referents—of names. What we have to show, therefore, is that for every element of S a name exists such that the value of this name in the extension is this element itself. The torsion is evident: say that $a \in S$, we want a name μ such that $R_♀(\mu) = a$. If such a μ exists, a, the value of this name, is an element of the generic extension.

What we would like is to have this torsion exist generally; that is, such that we could say: 'For *any* generic extension, the fundamental situation is included in the extension.' The problem is that the value of names, the function R, depends on the generic part supposed, because it is directly linked to the question of knowing which conditions are implied in it.

We can bypass this obstacle by showing that for every element a of S, there exists a name such that its referential value is a *whatever the generic part*.

This supposes the identification of something invariable in the genericity of a part, indeed in correct subsets in general. It so happens that this invariable exists; once again, it is the minimal condition, the condition $\varnothing$. It belongs to every non-void correct part, according to the rule Rd_1 which requires that if $\pi \in ♀$, any condition dominated by π also belongs to ♀. But the condition $\varnothing$ is dominated by any condition whatsoever. It follows that the referential value of a nominal pair of the type $<\mu,\varnothing>$ is *always*, whatever the $\venus$, the referential value of μ, because $\varnothing \in \venus$ in all cases.

We will thus use the following definition for the *canonical name* of an element a of the fundamental situation S: this name is composed of all the pairs $<\mu(\beta),\varnothing>$, where $\mu(\beta)$ is the canonical name of an element of a.

Here again we find our now classic circularity: the canonical name of a is defined on the basis of the canonical name of its elements. We break this circle by a direct recurrence *on belonging,* remembering that every multiple is woven from the void. To be more precise (systematically writing the canonical name of a as $\mu(a)$):

- if a is the empty set, we will posit: $\mu(\varnothing) = \varnothing$;
- in general, we will posit: $\mu(a) = \{<\mu(\beta),\varnothing> / \beta \in a\}$.

The canonical name of a is therefore the set of ordered pairs constituted by the canonical names of the elements of a and by the minimal condition $\varnothing$. This definition is correct: on the one hand because $\mu(a)$ is clearly a name, being composed of pairs which knot together names and a condition; on the other hand because—if $\beta \in a$—the name $\mu(\beta)$ has been previously defined, after the hypothesis of recurrence. Moreover, $\mu(a)$ is definitely a name known in S due to the absoluteness of the operations employed.

Now, and this is the crux of the affair, the referential value of the canonical name $\mu(a)$ is a itself *whatever the supposed generic part.* We always have $R_\venus(\mu(a)) = a$. These canonical names invariably name the multiple of S to which we have constructibly associated them.

What in fact is the referential value $R_\venus(\mu(a))$ of the canonical name of a? By the definition of referential value, and since the elements of $\mu(a)$ are the pairs $<\mu(\beta),\varnothing>$, it is the set of referential values of the $\mu(\beta)$'s when the condition $\varnothing$ belongs to $\venus$. But $\varnothing \in \venus$ whatever the generic part. Therefore, $R_\venus(\mu(a))$ is equal to the set of referential values of the $\mu(\beta)$, for $\beta \in a$. The hypothesis of recurrence supposes that for all $\beta \in a$ we definitely have $R_\venus(\mu(\beta)) = \beta$. Finally, the referential value of $\mu(a)$ is equal to all the β's which belong to a; that is, to a itself, which is none other than the count-as-one of all its elements.

The recurrence is complete: for $a \in S$, there exists a canonical name $\mu(a)$ such that the value of $\mu(a)$ (its referent) in *any* generic extension is the multiple a itself. Being the $\venus$-referent of a name for any $\venus$-extension of S, every element of S belongs to this extension. Therefore, $S \subset S(\venus)$, whatever the indiscernible $\venus$. We are thus quite justified in speaking of an *extension* of the fundamental situation; the latter is included in any extension by an indiscernible, whatever it might be.

b. Canonical name of an indiscernible part

What has not yet been shown is that the indiscernible belongs to the extension (we know that it does *not* belong to S). The reader may be astonished by our posing the question of the existence of ♀ within the extension $S(♀)$, given that it was actually built—by nominal projection—on the basis of ♀. But that ♀ proves to be an essential operator, *for the ontologist*, of the passage from S to $S(♀)$ does not mean that ♀ necessarily belongs to $S(♀)$; that is, that it exists for an inhabitant of $S(♀)$. It is quite possible that the indiscernible only exists in eclipse 'between' S and $S(♀)$, without there being ♀ ∈ $S(♀)$, which alone would testify to the *local* existence of the indiscernible.

To know whether ♀ belongs to $S(♀)$ or not, one has to demonstrate that ♀ *has a name* in S. Again, there are no other resources to be had apart from those found in tinkering with the names (Kunen puts it quite nicely as 'cooking the names').

The conditions π are elements of the fundamental situation. They thus have a canonical name $\mu(\pi)$. Let's consider the set: $\mu_♀ = \{<\mu(\pi),\pi> \, / \, \pi \in ©\}$; that is, the set of all the ordered pairs constituted by a canonical name of a condition, followed by that condition. This set is a name, by the definition of names, and it is a name in S, which can be shown by arguments of absoluteness. What could its referent be? It is certainly going to depend on the generic part ♀ which determines the value of the names. Take then a fixed ♀. By the definition of referential value $R_♀$, $\mu_♀$ is the set of values of the names $\mu(\pi)$ when $\pi \in$ ♀. But $\mu(\pi)$ being a canonical name, its value is always π. Therefore, the value of $\mu_♀$ is the set of π which belong to ♀, that is, ♀ itself. We have: $R_♀(\mu_♀) = ♀$. We can therefore say that $\mu_♀$ is the canonical name of the generic part, despite its value depending quite particularly on ♀, insofar as it is equal to it. The *fixed* name $\mu_♀$ will invariably designate, in a generic extension, the part ♀ from which the extension originates. We thus find ourselves in possession of a name for the indiscernible, a name, however, which does not discern it! For this nomination is performed by an identical name whatever the indiscernible. It is the name of *indiscernibility*, not the discernment of an indiscernible.

The fundamental point is that, having a fixed name, the generic part *always* belongs to the extension. This is the crucial result that we were looking for: the indiscernible belongs to the extension obtained on the basis of itself. The new situation $S(♀)$ is such that, on the one hand, S is one of its parts, and on the other hand, $♀$ is one of its elements. We have, through the mediation of the names, effectively *added an indiscernible to the situation in which it is indiscernible*.

6. EXPLORATION OF THE GENERIC EXTENSION

Here we are, capable of 'speaking' in S—*via* the names—of an enlarged situation in which a generic multiple *exists*. Remember the two fundamental results of the previous section:

- $S ⊂ S(♀)$, it is definitely an extension;
- $♀ ∈ S(♀)$, it is a *strict* extension, because $∼(♀ ∈ S)$.

There is some newness in the situation, notably an indiscernible of the first situation. But this newness does not prevent $S(♀)$ from sharing a number of characteristics with the fundamental situation S. Despite being quite distinct from the latter, in that an inexistent indiscernible of that situation exists within it, it is also very close. One striking example of this proximity is that the extension $S(♀)$ does not contain any supplementary ordinal with respect to S.

This point indicates the 'proximity' of $S(♀)$ to S. It signifies that the *natural* part of a generic extension remains that of the fundamental situation: extension via the indiscernible leaves the natural multiples invariant. The indiscernible is specifically the ontological schema of an *artificial* operator. And the artifice is here the intra-ontological trace of the foreclosed event. If the ordinals make up the most natural part of what there is in being, as determined by ontology, then the generic multiples form what is least natural, what is the most distanced from the *stability* of being.

How can it be shown that in adding the indiscernible $♀$ to the situation S, and in allowing this $♀$ to operate in the new situation (that is, we will also have in $S(♀)$ 'supplementary' multiples such as $ω_0 ∩ ♀$, or what the formula $λ$ separates in $♀$, etc.), no ordinal is added; that is, that the natural part of S is not affected by $♀$'s belonging to $S(♀)$? Of course, one has to use the names.

If there was an ordinal which belonged to $S(♀)$ without belonging to S, there would be (principle of minimality, Meditation 12 and Appendix 2) a smallest ordinal which possessed that property. Say that α is this minimum: it belongs to $S(\female)$, it does not belong to S, but every ordinal smaller than it—say $\beta \in \alpha$—belongs, itself, to S.

Because α belongs to $S(\female)$, it has a name in S. But in fact, we know of such a name. For the elements of α are the ordinals β *which belong to S*. They therefore all have a canonical name $\mu(\beta)$ whose referential value is β itself. Let's consider the name: $\mu = \{<\mu(\beta),\varnothing> \, / \, \beta \in \alpha\}$. It has the ordinal α as its referential value; because, given that the minimal condition $\varnothing$ always belongs to $\female$, the value of μ is the set of values of the $\mu(\beta)$'s, which is to say the set of β's, which is to say α itself.

What could the nominal rank of this name μ be? (Remember that the nominal rank is an ordinal.) It depends on the nominal rank of the canonical names $\mu(\beta)$. It so happens that *the nominal rank of $\mu(\beta)$ is superior or equal to β*. Let's show this by recurrence.

– The nominal rank of $\mu(\varnothing)$ is $\varnothing$ by definition.

– Let's suppose that, for every ordinal $\gamma \in \delta$, we have the property in question (the nominal rank of $\mu(\gamma)$ being superior or equal to γ). Let's show that δ also has this property. The canonical name $\mu(\delta)$ is equal to $\{<\mu(\gamma),\varnothing> \, / \, \gamma \in \delta\}$. It implies in its construction all the names $\mu(\gamma)$, and consequently its nominal rank is superior to that of all these names (the stratified character of the definition of names). It is therefore superior to all the ordinals γ because we supposed that the nominal rank of $\mu(\gamma)$ was superior to γ. An ordinal superior to all the ordinals γ such that $\gamma \in \delta$ is at least equal to δ. Therefore, the nominal rank of $\mu(\delta)$ is at least equal to δ. The recurrence is complete.

If we return to the name $\mu = \{<\mu(\beta),\varnothing>, / \, \beta \in \alpha\}$, we see that its nominal rank is superior to that of all the canonical names $\mu(\beta)$. But we have just established that the nominal rank of a $\mu(\beta)$ is itself superior or equal to β. Therefore, μ's rank is superior or equal to all the β's. It is consequently at least equal to α, which is the ordinal that comes after all the β's.

But we supposed that the ordinal α did *not* belong to the situation S. Therefore, there is no name, in S, of the nominal rank α. The name μ does not belong to S, and thus the ordinal α *is not named in S*. Not being named in S, it cannot belong to $S(\female)$ because 'belonging to $S(\female)$' means precisely 'being the referential value of a name which is in S'.

The generic extension does not contain any ordinal which is not already in the fundamental situation.

On the other hand, *all* the ordinals of S are in the generic extension, insofar as $S \subset S(\female)$. Therefore, the ordinals of the generic extension are exactly *the same* as those of the fundamental situation. In the end, the extension is neither more complex nor more natural than the situation. The addition of an indiscernible modifies it 'slightly', precisely because an indiscernible does not add explicit information to the situation in which it is indiscernible.

7. INTRINSIC OR IN-SITUATION INDISCERNIBILITY

I indicated (demonstrated) that ♀—which, in the eyes of the ontologist, is an indiscernible part of S for an inhabitant of S—does not exist in S (in the sense in which ~(♀ ∈ S)), but does exist in S(♀) (in the sense in which ♀ ∈ S(♀)). Does this existent multiple—for an inhabitant of S(♀)—remain indiscernible for this same inhabitant? This question is crucial, because we are looking for a concept of *intrinsic* indiscernibility; that is, a multiple which is effectively presented in a situation, but radically subtracted from the language of that situation.

The response is positive. The multiple ♀ is indiscernible for an inhabitant of S(♀): no explicit formula of the language separates it.

The demonstration we shall give of this point is of purely indicative value.

To say that ♀, which exists in the generic extension S(♀), remains indiscernible therein, is to say that no formula specifies the multiple ♀ in the universe constituted by that extension.

Let's suppose the contrary: the discernibility of ♀. A formula thus exists, $\lambda(\pi, a_1, \ldots a_n)$, with the parameters $a_1, \ldots a_n$ belonging to S(♀), such that for an inhabitant of S(♀) it *defines* the multiple ♀. That is:

$$\pi \in ♀ \leftrightarrow \lambda(\pi, a_1, \ldots a_n)$$

But it is then impossible for the parameters $a_1, \ldots a_n$ to belong to the fundamental situation S. Remember, ♀ is a part of ©, the set of conditions, which belongs to S. If the formula $\lambda(\pi, a_1, \ldots a_n)$ was parameterized in S, because S is a quasi-complete situation and the axiom of separation is veridical in it, this formula would separate out, for an inhabitant of S, the part ♀ of the existing set ©. The result would be that ♀ exists in S (belongs to S) and is also discernible therein. But we know that ♀, as a generic part, cannot belong to S.

By consequence, the n-tuplet $<a_1, \ldots a_n>$ belongs to S(♀) without belonging to S. It is part of the *supplementary* multiples introduced by the nomination, which is itself founded on the part ♀. It is evident that there is a circle in the supposed discernibility of ♀: the formula $\lambda(\pi, a_1, \ldots a_n)$ *already* implies, for the comprehension of the multiples $a_1, \ldots a_n$, that it is known which conditions belong to ♀.

To be more explicit: to say that in the parameters $a_1, \ldots a_n$ there are some which belong to $S(♀)$ without belonging to S, is to say that the names $\mu_1, \ldots \mu_n$, to which these elements correspond, are not all canonical names of elements of S. Yet whilst a canonical name does not depend (for its referential value) on the description under consideration (since $R_♀(\mu(a)) = a$ for whatever ♀), an indeterminate name entirely depends upon it. The formula which supposedly defines ♀ in $S(♀)$ can be written:

$$\pi \in ♀ \leftrightarrow \lambda(\pi, R_♀(\mu_1), \ldots R_♀(\mu_n))$$

insofar as all the elements of $S(♀)$ are the values of names. But exactly: for a non-canonical name μ_n, the value $R_♀(\mu_n)$ depends directly on knowing which conditions, amongst those that appear in the name μ_n, also appear in the generic part; such that we 'define' $\pi \in ♀$ on the basis of the knowledge of $\pi \in ♀$. There is no chance of a 'definition' of this sort founding the discernment of ♀, for it presupposes such.

Thus, for an inhabitant of $S(♀)$, there does not exist any intelligible formula in her universe which can be used to discern ♀. Although this multiple exists in $S(♀)$, it is indiscernible therein. We have obtained an *in-situation* or existent indiscernible. In $S(♀)$, there is at least one multiple which has a being but no name. The result is decisive: ontology recognizes the existence of *in-situation* indiscernibles. That it calls them 'generic'—an old adjective used by the young Marx when trying to characterize an entirely subtractive humanity whose bearer was the proletariat—is one of those unconscious conceits with which mathematicians decorate their technical discourse.

The indiscernible subtracts itself from any explicit nomination in the very situation whose operator it nevertheless is—having induced it in excess of the fundamental situation, in which its lack is thought. What must be recognized therein, when it inexists in the first situation under the supernumerary sign ♀, is nothing less than the purely formal mark of the event whose being is without being; and when its existence is indiscerned in the second situation, nothing less than the blind recognition, by ontology, of a possible being of truth.

PART VIII

Forcing: Truth and the Subject.
Beyond Lacan

MEDITATION THIRTY-FIVE
Theory of the Subject

I term *subject* any local configuration of a generic procedure from which a truth is supported.

With regard to the modern metaphysics still attached to the concept of the subject I shall make six preliminary remarks.

a. A subject is not a substance. If the word substance has any meaning it is that of designating a multiple counted as one in a situation. I have established that the part of a situation constituted by the true-assemblage of a generic procedure does not fall under the law of the count of the situation. In a general manner, it is subtracted from every encyclopaedic determinant of the language. The intrinsic indiscernibility in which a generic procedure is resolved rules out any substantiality of the subject.

b. A subject is not a void point either. The proper name of being, the void, is inhuman, and a-subjective. It is an ontological concept. Moreover, it is evident that a generic procedure is realized as multiplicity and not as punctuality.

c. A subject is not, in any manner, the organisation of a sense of experience. It is not a transcendental function. If the word 'experience' has any meaning, it is that of designating presentation as such. However, a generic procedure, which stems from an evental ultra-one qualified by a supernumerary name, does not coincide in any way with presentation. It is also advisable to differentiate truth and meaning. A generic procedure effectuates the post-evental truth of a situation, but the indiscernible multiple that is a truth does not deliver any meaning.

d. A subject is not an invariable of presentation. The subject is *rare*, in that the generic procedure is a diagonal of the situation. One could also say: the generic procedure of a situation being singular, every subject is rigorously singular. The statement 'there are some subjects' is aleatoric; it is not transitive to being.

e. Every subject is qualified. If one admits the typology of Meditation 31, then one can say that there are some individual subjects inasmuch as there is some love, some mixed subjects inasmuch as there is some art or some science, and some collective subjects inasmuch as there is some politics. In all this, there is nothing which is a structural necessity of situations. *The law does not prescribe there being some subjects*.

f. A subject is not a result—any more than it is an origin. It is the *local* status of a procedure, a configuration in excess of the situation.

Let's now turn to the details of the subject.

1. SUBJECTIVIZATION: INTERVENTION AND OPERATOR OF FAITHFUL CONNECTION

In Meditation 23 I indicated the existence of a problem of 'double origins' concerning the procedures of fidelity. There is the name of the event—the result of the intervention—and there is the operator of faithful connection, which rules the procedure and institutes the truth. In what measure does the operator depend on the name? Isn't the emergence of the operator a second event? Let's take an example. In Christianity, the Church is that through which connections and disconnections to the Christ-event are evaluated; the latter being originally named 'death of God' (cf. Meditation 21). As Pascal puts it, the Church is therefore literally 'the history of truth' since it is the operator of faithful connection and it supports the 'religious' generic procedure. But what is the link between the Church and Christ—or the death of God? This point is in perpetual debate and (just like the debate on the link between the Party and the Revolution) it has given rise to all the splits and heresies. There is always a suspicion that the operator of faithful connection is itself unfaithful to the event out of which it has made so much.

I term *subjectivization* the emergence of an operator, consecutive to an interventional nomination. Subjectivization takes place in the form of a Two. It is directed towards the intervention on the borders of the evental site. But it is also directed towards the situation through its coincidence with the rule of evaluation and proximity which founds the generic procedure. Subjectivization is interventional nomination *from the standpoint of the situation*, that is, the rule of the intra-situational effects of the supernumerary name's entrance into circulation. It could be said that subjectivization is a *special count*, distinct from the count-as-one which orders presentation, just as it is from the state's reduplication. What subjectivization counts is whatever is faithfully connected to the name of the event.

Subjectivization, the singular configuration of a rule, subsumes the Two that it is under a proper name's absence of signification. Saint Paul for the Church, Lenin for the Party, Cantor for ontology, Schoenberg for music, but also Simon, Bernard or Claire, if they declare themselves to be in love: each and every one of them a designation, via the one of a proper name, of the subjectivizing split between the name of an event (death of God, revolution, infinite multiples, destruction of the tonal system, meeting) and the initiation of a generic procedure (Christian Church, Bolshevism, set theory, serialism, singular love). What the proper name designates here is that the subject, as local situated configuration, is neither the intervention nor the operator of fidelity, but the advent of their Two, that is, the incorporation of the event into the situation in the mode of a generic procedure. The absolute singularity, subtracted from sense, of this Two is *shown* by the in-significance of the proper name. But it is obvious that this in-significance is also a reminder that what was summoned by the interventional nomination was the void, which is itself the proper name of being. Subjectivization is the proper name *in the situation* of this general proper name. It is an occurrence of the void.

The opening of a generic procedure founds, on its horizon, the assemblage of a truth. As such, subjectivization is that through which a truth is possible. It turns the event towards the truth of the situation for which the event is an event. It allows the evental ultra-one to be placed according to the indiscernible multiplicity (subtracted from the erudite encyclopaedia) that a truth is. The proper name thus bears the trace of both the ultra-one and the multiple, being that by which one happens within the other as the generic trajectory of a truth. Lenin is both the October revolution (the evental aspect) and Leninism, true-multiplicity of revolutionary politics for a half-century. Just as Cantor is both a madness which requires the thought of the pure multiple, articulating the infinite prodigality of being qua being to its void, and the process of the complete reconstruction of mathematical discursivity up to Bourbaki and beyond. This is because the proper name contains both the interventional nomination and the rule of faithful connection.

Subjectivization, aporetic knot of a name in excess and an un-known operation, is what *traces*, in the situation, the becoming multiple of the true, starting from the non-existent point in which the event convokes the void and interposes itself between the void and itself.

2. CHANCE, FROM WHICH ANY TRUTH IS WOVEN, IS THE MATTER OF THE SUBJECT

If we consider the local status of a generic procedure, we notice that it depends on a simple encounter. Once the name of the event is fixed, e_x, both the minimal gestures of the faithful procedure, positive ($e_x \square y$) or negative ($\sim(e_x \square y)$), and the enquiries, finite sets of such gestures, depend on the terms of the situation encountered by the procedure; starting with the evental site, the latter being the place of the first evaluations of proximity (this site could be Palestine for the first Christians, or Mahler's symphonic universe for Schoenberg). The operator of faithful connection definitely prescribes whether this or that term is linked or not to the supernumerary name of the event. However, it does not prescribe in any way whether such a term should be examined before, or rather than, any other. The procedure is thus ruled in its effects, but entirely aleatory in its trajectory. The only empirical evidence in the matter is that the trajectory begins at the borders of the evental site. The rest is lawless. There is, therefore, a certain chance which is essential to the course of the procedure. This chance *is not legible in the result of the procedure*, which is a truth, because a truth is the ideal assemblage of 'all' the evaluations, it is a *complete* part of the situation. But the subject does not coincide with this result. Locally, there are only illegal encounters, since there is nothing that determines, neither in the name of the event nor in the operator of faithful connection, that such a term be investigated at this moment and in this place. If we call the terms submitted to enquiry at a given moment of the generic procedure *the matter of the subject*, this matter, as multiple, does not have any assignable relation to the rule which distributes the positive indexes (connection established) and the negative indexes (non-connection). Thought in its operation, the subject is qualifiable, despite being singular: it can be resolved into a name (e_x) and an operator ($\square$). Thought in its multiple-being, that is, as the terms which appear with their indexes in effective enquiries, the subject is unqualifiable, insofar as these terms are arbitrary with regard to the double qualification which is its own.

The following objection could be made: I said (Meditation 31) that every finite presentation falls under an encyclopaedic determinant. In this sense, every *local* state of a procedure—thus every subject—being realized as a finite series of finite enquiries, is an object of knowledge. Isn't this a type of qualification? Do we not employ it in the form of the proper name when we speak of Cantor's theorem, or of Schoenberg's *Pierrot Lunaire*? Works and statements are, in fact, enquiries of certain generic procedures. If the subject is purely local, it is finite, and even if its matter is aleatoric, it is dominated by a knowledge. This is a classic aporia: that of the finitude of human enterprises. A truth alone is infinite, yet the subject is not coextensive with it. The truth of Christianity—or of contemporary music, or 'modern mathematics'—surpasses the finite support of those subjectivizations named Saint Paul, Schoenberg or Cantor; and it does so everywhere, despite the fact that a truth proceeds solely via the assemblage of those enquiries, sermons, works and statements in which these names are realized.

This objection allows us to grasp all the more closely what is at stake under the name of subject. Of course, an enquiry is a possible object of knowledge. But the *realization* of the enquiry, the enquiring of the enquiry, is not such, since it is completely down to chance that the particular terms evaluated therein by the operator of faithful connection find themselves presented in the finite multiple that it is. Knowledge can quite easily enumerate the constituents of the enquiries afterwards, because they come in finite number. Yet just as it cannot anticipate, in the moment itself, any meaning to their singular regrouping, knowledge cannot coincide with the subject, whose entire being is to encounter terms in a militant and aleatoric trajectory. Knowledge, in its encyclopaedic disposition, never encounters anything. It presupposes presentation, and represents it in language via discernment and judgement. In contrast, the subject is constituted by encountering its matter (the terms of the enquiry) without anything of its form (the name of the event and the operator of fidelity) prescribing such matter. If the subject does not have any other being-in-situation than the term-multiples it encounters and evaluates, its essence, since it has to include the chance of these encounters, is rather the trajectory which links them. However, this trajectory, being incalculable, does not fall under any determinant of the encyclopaedia.

Between the knowledge of finite groupings, their discernibility in principle, and the subject of the faithful procedure, there is an indifferent-difference which distinguishes between the result (some finite multiples of the situation) and the partial trajectory, of which this result is a local configuration. The subject is 'between' the terms that the procedure groups together. Knowledge, on the other hand, is the procedure's retrospective totalization.

The subject is literally separated from knowledge by chance. The subject is chance, vanquished term by term, but this victory, subtracted from language, is accomplished solely as truth.

3. SUBJECT AND TRUTH: INDISCERNIBILITY AND NOMINATION

The one-truth, which assembles to infinity the terms positively investigated by the faithful procedure, is indiscernible in the language of the situation (Meditation 31). It is a generic part of the situation insofar as it is an immutable excrescence whose entire being resides in regrouping presented terms. It is truth precisely inasmuch as it forms a one under the sole predicate of belonging, thus its only relation is to the being of the situation.

Because the subject is a *local* configuration of the procedure, it is clear that the truth is equally indiscernible 'for him'—the truth is global. 'For him' means the following precisely: a subject, which realizes a truth, is nevertheless incommensurable with the latter, because the subject is finite, and the truth is infinite. Moreover, the subject, being internal to the situation, can only know, or rather encounter, terms or multiples presented (counted as one) in that situation. Yet a truth is an un-presented part of the situation. Finally, the subject cannot *make a language* out of anything except combinations of the supernumerary name of the event and the language of the situation. It is in no way guaranteed that this language will suffice for the discernment of a truth, which, in any case, is indiscernible for the resources of the language of the situation alone. It is absolutely necessary to abandon any definition of the subject which supposes that it knows the truth, or that it is adjusted to the truth. Being the local moment of the truth, the subject falls short of supporting the latter's global sum. Every truth is transcendent to the subject, precisely because the latter's entire being resides in supporting the realization of truth. The subject is neither consciousness nor unconsciousness of the true.

The singular relation of a subject to the truth whose procedure it supports is the following: the subject believes that there is a truth, and this belief occurs in the form of a knowledge. I term this knowing belief *confidence*.

What does confidence signify? By means of finite enquiries, the operator of fidelity locally discerns the connections and disconnections between multiples of the situation and the name of the event. This discernment is an *approximative truth*, because the positively investigated terms are to come in a truth. This 'to come' is the distinctive feature of the subject who judges. Here, belief is what-is-to-come, or the future, under the *name* of truth. Its legitimacy proceeds from the following: the name of the event, supplementing the situation with a paradoxical multiple, circulates in the enquiries as the basis for the convocation of the void, the latent errant being of the situation. A finite enquiry therefore detains, in a manner both effective and fragmentary, the being-in-situation of the situation itself. This fragment materially declares the to-come—because even though it is discernible by knowledge, it is a fragment of an indiscernible trajectory. Belief is solely the following: that the operator of faithful connection does not gather together the chance of the encounters in vain. As a promise wagered by the evental ultra-one, belief represents the genericity of the true as detained in the local finitude of the stages of its journey. In this sense, the subject is confidence in itself, in that it does not coincide with the retrospective discernibility of its fragmentary results. A truth is posited as infinite determination of an indiscernible of the situation: such is the global and intra-situational result of the event.

That this belief occurs in the form of a knowledge results from the fact that *every subject generates nominations*. Empirically, this point is manifest. What is most explicitly attached to the proper names which designate a subjectivization is an arsenal of words which make up the deployed matrix of faithful marking-out. Think of 'faith', 'charity', 'sacrifice', 'salvation' (Saint Paul); or of 'party', 'revolution', 'politics' (Lenin); or of 'sets', 'ordinals', 'cardinals' (Cantor), and of everything which then articulates, stratifies and ramifies these terms. What is the exact function of these terms? Do they solely designate elements presented in the situation? They would then be redundant with regard to the established language of the situation. Besides, one can distinguish an ideological enclosure from the generic procedure of a truth insofar as the terms of the former, via displacements devoid of any signification, do no more than substitute for those already declared appropriate by the situation. In contrast, the names used by a subject—who supports the local configuration of a generic truth—*do not, in general, have a referent in the situation*. Therefore, they do not double the established language. But then what use are they? These are words which do designate terms, but terms which 'will have been' presented in a *new* situation: the one which results from the addition to the situation of a truth (an indiscernible) of that situation.

With the resources of the situation, with its multiples, its language, the subject generates names whose referent is in the future anterior: this is what supports belief. Such names 'will have been' assigned a referent, or a signification, when the situation will have appeared in which the indiscernible—which is only represented (or included)—is finally presented as a truth of the first situation.

On the surface of the situation, a generic procedure is signalled in particular by this nominal *aura* which surrounds its finite configurations, which is to say its subjects. Whoever is not taken up in the extension of the finite trajectory of the procedure—whoever has not been positively investigated in respect to his or her connection to the event—generally considers that these names are empty. Of course, he or she *recognizes* them, since these names are fabricated from terms of the situation. The names with which a subject surrounds itself are not indiscernible. But the external witness, noting that for the most part these names lack a referent inside the situation such as it is, considers that they make up an arbitrary and content-free language. Hence, any revolutionary politics is considered to maintain a utopian (or non-realistic) discourse; a scientific revolution is received with scepticism, or held to be an abstraction without a base in experiments; and lovers' babble is dismissed as infantile foolishness by the wise. These witnesses, in a certain sense, are right. The names generated—or rather, composed—by a subject are suspended, with respect to their signification, from the 'to-come' of a truth. Their local usage is that of supporting the belief that the positively investigated terms designate or describe an approximation of a new situation, in which the truth of the current situation will have been presented. Every subject can thus be recognized by the emergence of a language which is internal to the situation, but whose referent-multiples are *subject to the condition* of an as yet incomplete generic part.

A subject is separated from this generic part (from this truth) by an infinite series of aleatory encounters. It is quite impossible to anticipate or represent a truth, because it manifests itself solely through the course of the enquiries, and the enquiries are incalculable; they are ruled, in their succession, only by encounters with terms of the situation. Consequently, the reference of the names, from the standpoint of the subject, remains for ever suspended from the unfinishable condition of a truth. It is only possible to say: *if* this or that term, when it will have been encountered, turns out to be positively connected to the event, *then* this or that name will probably have such a referent, because the generic part, which remains indiscernible in the situation, will have this or that configuration, or partial property. A subject uses names to make hypotheses about the truth. But, given that it is *itself* a finite configuration of the generic procedure from which a truth results, one can also maintain that a subject uses names in order to make hypotheses about itself, 'itself' meaning the infinity whose finitude it is. Here, language (*la langue*) is the fixed order within which a finitude, subject to the condition of the infinity that it is realizing, practises the supposition of reference to-come. Language is the very being of truth via the combination of current finite enquiries and the future anterior of a generic infinity.

It can easily be verified that this is the status of names of the type 'faith', 'salvation', 'communism', 'transfinite', 'serialism', or those names used in a declaration of love. These names are evidently capable of supporting the future anterior of a truth (religious, political, mathematical, musical, existential) in that they combine local enquiries (predications, statements, works, addresses) with redirected or reworked names available in the situation. They *displace* established significations and leave the referent void: this void will have been filled if truth comes to pass as a new situation (the kingdom of God, an emancipated society, absolute mathematics, a new order of music comparable to the tonal order, an entirely amorous life, etc.)

A subject is what deals with the generic indiscernibility of a truth, which it accomplishes amidst discernible finitude, by a nomination whose referent is suspended from the future anterior of a condition. A subject is thus, by the grace of names, both the *real* of the procedure (the enquiring of the enquiries) and the *hypothesis* that its unfinishable result will introduce some newness into presentation. A subject emptily names the universe to-come which is obtained by the supplementation of the situation with an indiscernible truth. At the same time, the subject is the finite real, the local stage, of this supplementation. Nomination is solely empty inasmuch as it is full of what is sketched out by its own possibility. A subject is the self-mentioning of an empty language.

4. VERACITY AND TRUTH FROM THE STANDPOINT OF THE FAITHFUL PROCEDURE: FORCING

Since the language with which a subject surrounds itself is separated from its real universe by unlimited chance, what possible sense could there be in declaring a statement pronounced in this language to be veridical? The external witness, the man of knowledge, necessarily declares that these statements are devoid of sense ('the obscurity of a poetic language', 'propaganda' for a political procedure, etc.). Signifiers without any signified. Sliding without quilting point. In fact, the meaning of a subject-language is *under condition*. Constrained to refer solely to what the situation presents, and yet bound to the future anterior of the existence of an indiscernible, a statement made up of the names of a subject-language has merely a hypothetical signification. From inside the faithful procedure, it sounds like this: '*If* I suppose that the indiscernible truth contains or presents such or such a term submitted to the enquiry by chance, *then* such a statement in the subject-language will have had such a meaning and will (or won't) have been veridical.' I say 'will have been' because the veracity in question is relative to that *other* situation, the situation to-come in which a truth of the first situation (an indiscernible part) will have been presented.

A subject always declares meaning in the future anterior. What is *present* are terms of the situation on the one hand, and names of the subject-language on the other. Yet this distinction is artificial, because the names, being themselves presented (despite being empty), *are* terms of the situation. What exceeds the situation is the referential meaning of the names; such meaning exists solely within the retroaction of the *existence* (thus of the presentation) of an indiscernible part of the situation. One can therefore say: such a statement of the subject-language will have been veridical if the truth is such or such.

But of this 'such or such' of a truth, the subject solely controls—because it is such—the finite fragment made up of the present state of the enquiries. All the rest is a matter of confidence, or of knowing belief. Is this sufficient for the legitimate formulation of a hypothesis of connection between what a *truth* presents and the *veracity* of a statement that bears upon the names of a subject-language? Doesn't the infinite incompletion of a truth prevent any possible evaluation, *inside* the situation, of the veracity to-come of a statement whose referential universe is suspended from the chance, itself to-come, of encounters, and thus of enquiries?

When Galileo announced the principle of inertia, he was still separated from the truth of the new physics by all the chance encounters that are named in subjects such as Descartes or Newton. How could he, with the names he fabricated and displaced (because they were at hand—'movement', 'equal proportion', etc.), have supposed the veracity of his principle *for* the situation to-come that was the establishment of modern science; that is, the supplementation of his situation with the indiscernible and unfinishable part that one has to name 'rational physics'? In the same manner, when he radically suspended tonal functions, what musical veracity could Schoenberg have assigned to the notes and timbres prescribed in his scores in regard to that—even today—quasi-indiscernible part of the situation named 'contemporary music'? If the names are empty, and their system of reference suspended, what are the criteria, from the standpoint of the finite configurations of the generic procedure, of veracity?

What comes into play here is termed, of necessity, a *fundamental law of the subject* (it is also a law of the future anterior). This law is the following: if a statement of the subject-language is such that it will have been veridical for a situation in which a truth has occurred, this is because *a* term of the situation exists which both belongs to that truth (belongs to the generic part which *is* that truth) and maintains a particular relation with the names at stake in the statement. This relation is determined by the encyclopaedic determinants of the situation (of knowledge). This law thus amounts to saying that one can *know*, in a situation in which a post-eventel truth is being deployed, whether a statement of the subject-language has a chance of being veridical in the situation which adds to the initial situation a truth of the latter. It suffices to verify the existence of *one* term linked to the statement in question by a relation that is itself discernible in the situation. If such a term exists, then its belonging to the truth (to the indiscernible part which is the multiple-being of a truth) will impose the veracity of the initial statement within the *new* situation.

Of this law, there exists an ontological version, discovered by Cohen. Its lineaments will be revealed in Meditation 36. Its importance, however, is such that its concept must be explained in detail and illustrated with as many examples as possible.

Let's start with a caricature. In the framework of the scientific procedure that is Newtonian astronomy, I can, on the basis of observable perturbations in the trajectory of certain planets, state the following: 'An as yet unobserved planet distorts the trajectories by gravitational attraction.' The operator of connection here is pure *calculation*, combined with existing observations. It is certain that *if* this planet exists (in the sense in which observation, since it is in the process of being perfected, will end up encountering an object that it does classify amongst the planets), *then* the statement 'a supplementary planet exists' will have been veridical in the universe constituted by the solar system supplemented by scientific astronomy. There are two other possible cases:

– that it is impossible to justify the aberrations in the trajectory by the surmise of a supplementary planet belonging to the solar system (this *before* the calculations), and that it is not known what other hypothesis to make concerning their cause;
– or that the supposed planet does not exist.

What happens in these two cases? In the first case, I do not possess the *knowledge* of a fixed (calculable) relation between the statement 'something is inflecting the trajectory' (a statement composed of names of science—and 'something' indicates that one of these names is empty), and *a* term of the situation, a specifiable term (a planet with a calculable mass) whose scientifically observable existence in the solar system (that is, this system, plus its truth) would give meaning and veracity to my statement. In the second case, the relation exists (expert calculations allow the conclusion that this 'something' must be a planet); but I do not *encounter* a term within the situation which validates this relation. It follows that my statement is 'not yet' veridical in respect of astronomy.

This image illustrates two features of the fundamental law of the subject:

– Since the knowable relation between *a* term and a statement of the subject-language must exist within the encyclopaedia of the situation, it is quite possible that *no* term validate this relation for a given statement. In this case, I have no means of anticipating the latter's veracity, from the standpoint of the generic procedure.

   – It is also possible that there does exist a term of the situation which maintains with a statement of the subject-language the knowable relation in question, but that it has not yet been investigated, such that I do not know whether it belongs or not to the indiscernible part that is the truth (the result, in infinity, of the generic procedure). In this case, the veracity of the statement is *suspended*. I remain separated from it by the chance of the enquiries' trajectory. However, what I can anticipate is this: *if* I encounter this term, and it turns out to be connected to the name of the event, that is, to belong to the indiscernible multiple-being of a truth, *then*, in the situation to-come in which this truth exists, the statement will have been veridical.

Let's decide on the terminology. I will term *forcing* the relation implied in the fundamental law of the subject. That a term of the situation *forces* a statement of the subject-language means that the veracity of this statement in the situation to come is equivalent to the belonging of this term to the indiscernible part which results from the generic procedure. It thus means that this term, bound to the statement by the relation of forcing, belongs to the truth. Or rather, this term, encountered by the subject's aleatory trajectory, has been *positively* investigated with respect to its connection to the name of the event. A term forces a statement if its positive connection to the event forces the statement to be veridical in the new situation (the situation supplemented by an indiscernible truth). Forcing is a relation *verifiable by knowledge*, since it bears on a term of the situation (which is thus presented and named in the language of the situation) and a statement of the subject-language (whose names are 'cobbled-together' from multiples of the situation). What is *not* verifiable by knowledge is whether the term that forces a statement belongs or not to the indiscernible. Its belonging is uniquely down to the chance of the enquiries.

In regard to the statements which can be formulated in the subject-language, and whose referent (thus, the universe of sense) is suspended from infinity (and it is *for* this suspended sense that there is forcing of veracity), three possibilities can be identified, each discernible by knowledge inside the situation, and thus free of any surmise concerning the indiscernible part (the truth):

   a. The statement cannot be forced: it does not support the relation of forcing with *any* term of the situation. The possibility of it being veridical is thus ruled out, whatever the truth may be;

b. The statement can be universally forced: it maintains the relation of forcing with *all* the terms of the situation. Since some of these terms (an infinity) will be contained in the truth, whatever it may be, the statement will always be veridical in any situation to-come;

c. The statement can be forced by certain terms, but not by others. Everything depends, in respect to the future anterior of veracity, on the chance of the enquiries. If and when *a* term which forces the statement will have been positively investigated, the statement will be veridical in the situation to-come in which the indiscernible (to which this term belongs) supplements the situation for which it is indiscernible. However, this case is neither *factually* guaranteed (since I could still be separated from such an enquiry by innumerable chance encounters), nor guaranteed *in principle* (since the forcing terms could be negatively investigated, and thus not feature in a truth). The statement is thus not forced to be veridical.

A subject is a local evaluator of self-mentioning statements: he or she *knows*—with regard to the situation to-come, thus from the standpoint of the indiscernible—that these statements are either certainly wrong, or possibly veridical but suspended from the will-have-taken-place of *one* positive enquiry.

Let's try to make forcing and the distribution of evaluations tangible.

Take Mallarmé's statement: 'The poetic act consists in suddenly seeing an idea fragment into a number of motifs equal in value, and in grouping them.' It is a statement of the subject-language, a self-mentioner of the state of a finite configuration of the poetic generic procedure. The referential universe of this statement—in particular, the signifying value of the words 'idea' and 'motifs'—is suspended from an indiscernible of the literary situation: a state of poetry that will have been beyond the 'crisis in verse'. Mallarmé's poems and prose pieces—and those of others—are enquiries whose grouping-together defines this indiscernible as the truth of French poetry after Hugo. A local configuration of this procedure is a subject (for example, whatever is designated in pure presentation by the signifier 'Mallarmé'). Forcing is what a knowledge can discern of the relation between the above statement and this or that poem (or collection): the conclusion to be drawn is that if this poem is 'representative' of post-Hugo poetic truth, then the statement concerning the poetical act will be verifiable in knowledge—and so veridical—in the situation to-come in which this truth exists (that is, in a universe in which the 'new poetry', posterior to the crisis in verse, is actually presented and no longer merely announced). It is evident that such a poem must be the vector of relationships—discernible in the situation—between itself and, for example, those initially empty words 'idea' and 'motifs'. The existence of this *unique* poem—and what it detains in terms of encounters, evaluated positively, would guarantee the veracity of the statement 'The poetic act . . . ' in any poetic situation to-come which contained it—was termed by Mallarmé 'the Book'. But after all, the savant's study of *Un coup de dés . . .* in Meditation 19 is equivalent to a demonstration that the enquiry—the text—has definitely encountered a term which, at the very least, forces Mallarmé's statement to be veridical; that is, the statement that what is at stake in a modern poem is the motif of an idea (ultimately, the very idea of the event). The relation of forcing is here detained within the analysis of the text.

Now let's consider the statement: 'The factory is a political site.' This statement is phrased in the subject-language of the post-Marxist-Leninist political procedure. The referential universe of this statement requires the occurrence of that indiscernible of the situation which is politics in a non-parliamentary and non-Stalinian mode. The enquiries are the militant interventions and enquiries of the factory. It can be determined *a priori* (we can know) that workers, factory-sites, and sub-situations force the above statement to be veridical in every universe in which the existence of a currently indiscernible mode of politics will have been established. It is possible that the procedure has arrived at a point at which workers have been positively investigated, and at which the veracity to-come of the statement is guaranteed. It is equally possible that this not be the case, but then the conclusion to be drawn would be solely that the chance of the encounters must be pursued, and the procedure maintained. The veracity is merely suspended.

A contrario, if one examines the neo-classical musical reaction between the two wars, it is noticeable that no term of the musical situation defined in its own language by this tendency can force the veracity of the statement 'music is essentially tonal.' The enquiries (the neo-classical works) can continue to appear, one after the other, hereafter and evermore. However, Schoenberg having existed, not one of them ever encounters anything which is in a knowable relation of forcing with this statement. Knowledge alone decides the question here; in other words, the neo-classical procedure *is not generic* (as a matter of fact, it is constructivist—see Meditation 29).

Finally, a subject is at the intersection, via its language, of knowledge and truth. Local configuration of a generic procedure, it is suspended from the indiscernible. Capable of conditionally forcing the veracity of a statement of its language for a situation to-come (the one in which the truth exists) it is the savant of itself. A subject is a knowledge suspended by a truth whose finite moment it is.

5. SUBJECTIVE PRODUCTION: DECISION OF AN UNDECIDABLE, DISQUALIFICATION, PRINCIPLE OF INEXISTENTS

Grasped in its being, the subject is solely the finitude of the generic procedure, the local effects of an evental fidelity. What it 'produces' is the truth itself, an indiscernible part of the situation, but the infinity of this truth transcends it. It is abusive to say that truth is a subjective production. A subject is much rather *taken up* in fidelity to the event, and *suspended* from truth; from which it is forever separated by chance.

However, forcing does authorize partial descriptions of the universe to-come in which a truth supplements the situation. This is so because it is possible to know, under condition, which statements have at least a chance of being veridical in the situation. A subject measures the *newness* of the situation to-come, even though it cannot measure its own being. Let's give three examples of this capacity and its limit.

a. Suppose that a statement of the subject-language is such that certain terms force it and others force its negation. What can be known is that this statement is undecidable in the situation. If it was actually veridical (or erroneous) for the encyclopaedia in its current state, this would mean that, whatever the case may be, no term *of the situation* could intelligibly render it erroneous (or veridical, respectively). Yet this would have to be the case, if the statement is just as forceable positively as it is negatively. In other words, it is not possible to modify the established veracity of a statement by adding to a situation a truth of that situation; for that would mean that *in truth* the statement was *not* veridical in the situation. Truth is subtracted from knowledge, but it does not contradict it. It follows that this statement is undecidable in the encyclopaedia of the situation: it is impossible by means of the existing resources of knowledge alone to decide whether it is veridical or erroneous. It is thus possible that the chance of the enquiries, the nature of the event and of the operator of fidelity lead to one of the following results: either the statement will have been veridical in the situation to-come (if a term which forces its affirmation is positively investigated); or it will have been erroneous (if a term which forces its negation is positively investigated); or it will have remained undecidable (if the terms which force it, negatively and positively, are both investigated as unconnected to the name of the event, and thus *nothing* forces it in the truth which results from such a procedure). The productive cases are obviously the first two, in which an undecidable statement of the situation will have been decided for the situation to-come in which the indiscernible truth is presented.

The subject is able to take the measure of this decision. It is sufficient that within the finite configuration of the procedure, which is its being, an enquiry figures in which a term which forces the statement, in one sense or another, is reported to be connected to the name of the event. This term thus belongs to the indiscernible truth, and since it forces the statement we *know* that this statement will have been veridical (or erroneous) in the situation which results from the addition of this indiscernible. In that situation, that is, *in truth*, the undecidable statement will have been decided. It is quite remarkable, inasmuch as it crystallizes the aleatoric historicity of truth, that this decision can be—and not inconsequentially —either positive (veridical) or negative (erroneous). It depends in fact on the trajectory of the enquiries, and on the principle of evaluation contained in the operator of faithful connection. It *happens* that such an undecidable statement is decided in such or such a sense.

This capacity is so important that it is possible to give the following definition of a subject: that which decides an undecidable from the standpoint of an indiscernible. Or, that which forces a veracity, according to the suspense of a truth.

b. Since the situation to-come is obtained via supplementation (a truth, which was a represented but non-presented indiscernible excrescence, comes to pass in presentation), all the multiples of the fundamental situation are also presented in the new situation. They cannot disappear *on the basis of the new situation being new.* If they disappear, it is *according to* the ancient situation. I was, I must admit, a little misguided in *Théorie du sujet* concerning the theme of destruction. I still maintained, back then, the idea of an essential link between destruction and novelty. Empirically, novelty (for example, political novelty) is accompanied by destruction. But it must be clear that this accompaniment is not linked to intrinsic novelty; on the contrary, the latter is always a supplementation by a truth. *Destruction is the ancient effect of the new supplementation amidst the ancient.* Destruction can definitely be known; the encyclopaedia of the initial situation is sufficient. A destruction is not true: it is knowledgeable. Killing somebody is always a matter of the (ancient) state of things; it cannot be a prerequisite for novelty. A generic procedure circumscribes a part which is indiscernible, or subtracted from knowledge, and it is solely in a fusion with the encyclopaedia that it would believe itself authorized to reflect this operation as one of non-being. If indiscernibility and power of death are confused, then there has been a failure to maintain the process of truth. The autonomy of the generic procedure excludes any thinking in terms of a 'balance of power' or 'power struggles'. A 'balance of power' is a judgement of the encyclopaedia. What authorizes the subject is the indiscernible, the generic, whose supplementary arrival signs the global effect of an event. There is no link between deciding the undecidable and suppressing a presentation.

Thought in its novelty, the situation to-come presents everything that the current situation presents, but in addition, it presents a truth. By consequence, it presents innumerable new multiples.

What can happen, however, is the *disqualification* of a term. It is not impossible—given that the *being* of each term is safe—that certain statements are veridical in the new situation such as 'the first are last', or 'this theorem, previously considered important, is now no more than a simple case', or 'the theme will no longer be the organising element of musical discourse'. The reason is that the *encyclopaedia* itself is not invariable. In particular (as ontology establishes, cf. Meditation 36), quantitative evaluations and hierarchies may be upset in the new situation. What comes into play here is the interference between the generic procedure and the encyclopaedic determinants from which it is subtracted. Statements which determine this or that term, which arrange it within a hierarchy and name its place, are vulnerable to modification. We will distinguish, moreover, between 'absolute' statements which cannot be displaced by a generic procedure, and statements which, due to their attachment to artificial and hierarchical distinctions and their ties to the instability of the quantitative, can be forced in the sense of a disqualification. At base, the manifest *contradictions* of the encyclopaedia are not inalterable. What becomes apparent is that *in truth* these placements and differentiations did not have a legitimate grounding in the being of the situation.

A subject is thus also that which measures the possible disqualification of a presented multiple. And this is very reasonable, because the generic or one-truth, being an indiscernible part, is subtracted from the determinants of knowledge, and it is especially rebellious with regard to the most artificial qualifications. The generic is *egalitarian,* and every subject, ultimately, is ordained to equality.

c. A final remark: if a presentation's qualification *in the new situation* is linked to an inexistence, then this presentation was *already* qualified thus in the ancient situation. This is what I term *the principle of inexistents.* I said that a truth, as new or supplementary, does not suppress anything. If a qualification is negative, it is because it is reported that such a multiple does not exist in the new situation. For example, if, in the new situation, the statements 'to be unsurpassable in its genre' or 'to be absolutely singular' are veridical—their essence being that no term is presented which 'surpasses' the first, or is identical to the second—then the inexistence of such terms must *already* have been revealed in the initial situation, since supplementation by a truth cannot proceed from a destruction. In other words, inexistence is retroactive. If I remark it in the situation to-come, this is because *it already inexisted* in the first situation.

The positive version of the principle of inexistents runs as follows: a subject can bring to bear a disqualification, but never a de-singularization. What is singular in truth was such in the situation.

A subject is that which, finite instance of a truth, discerned realization of an indiscernible, forces decision, disqualifies the unequal, and saves the singular. By these three operations, whose rarity alone obsesses us, the event comes into being, whose insistence it had supplemented.

MEDITATION THIRTY-SIX

Forcing: from the indiscernible to the undecidable

Just as it cannot support the concept of truth (for lack of the event), nor can ontology formalize the concept of the subject. What it can do, however, is help think the type of being to which the fundamental law of the subject corresponds, which is to say forcing. This is the second aspect (after the indiscernible) of the unknown intellectual revolution brought about by Cohen. This time it is a matter of connecting the being of truth (the generic multiples) to the status of statements (demonstrable or undemonstrable). In the absence of any temporality, thus of any future anterior, Cohen establishes the ontological schema of the relation between the indiscernible and the undecidable. He thereby shows us that the existence of a subject is compatible with ontology. He ruins any pretension on the part of the subject to declare itself 'contradictory' to the general regime of being. Despite being subtracted from the saying of being (mathematics), the subject is in possibility of being.

Cohen's principal result on this point is the following: it is possible, in a quasi-complete fundamental situation, to determine under what conditions such or such a statement is veridical in the generic extension obtained by the addition of an indiscernible part of the situation. The tool for this determination is the study of certain properties of the names: this is inevitable; the names are all that the inhabitants of the situation know of the generic extension, since the latter does not exist in their universe. Let's be quite clear about the complexity of this problem: if we have the statement $\lambda(a)$, the supposition that a belongs to the generic extension is unrepresentable in the fundamental situation. What does make sense, however, is the statement $\lambda(\mu_1)$, in which μ_1 is a name for a hypothetical element a of the extension, an element which is thus written $R_♀(\mu_1)$, being the referential value of the name μ_1. There is obviously no reason why the veracity of $\lambda(a)$—$\lambda(R_♀(\mu_1))$—in the extension would imply that of $\lambda(\mu_1)$ in the situation. What we can hope for at the most is an implication of the genre: 'If the extension obeys such a prerequisite, then to $\lambda(\mu_1)$, a formula which makes sense in the situation, there must correspond a $\lambda(a)$ which is veridical in the extension, a being the referential value of the name μ_1 in that extension.' But it is necessary that the prerequisite be expressible *in* the situation. What can an inhabitant of the situation suppose concerning a generic extension? At the very most that such or such a condition appears in the corresponding generic part $♀$, insofar as within the situation we know the conditions, and we also possess the (empty) concept of that particular set of conditions which is a generic set. What we are looking for is thus a statement of the genre: 'If, in the situation, there is such a relation between some conditions and the statement $\lambda(\mu_1)$, then the belonging of these conditions to the part $♀$ implies, in the corresponding generic extension, the veracity of $\lambda(R_♀(\mu_1))$.'

This amounts to saying that from the exterior of the situation the ontologist will establish the equivalence between, on the one hand, a relation which is controllable in the situation (a relation between a condition π and a statement $\lambda(\mu_1)$ in the language of the situation), and, on the other hand, the veracity of the statement $\lambda(R_♀(\mu_1))$ in the generic extension. Thus, any veracity in the extension will allow itself to be *conditioned* in the situation. The result, and it is absolutely capital, will be the following: although an inhabitant of the situation does not know anything of the indiscernible, and so of the extension, she is capable of thinking that the belonging of such a condition to a generic description is equivalent to the veracity of such a statement within that extension. It is evident that this inhabitant is in the position of a subject of truth: she forces veracity at the point of the indiscernible. She does so with the nominal resources of the situation alone, without having to represent that truth (without having to know of the existence of the generic extension).

Note that 'inhabitant of S' is a metaphor, which does not correspond to any mathematical concept: ontology thinks the law of the subject, not the subject itself. It is this law which finds its guarantee of being in Cohen's great discovery: forcing. Cohen's forcing is none other than the determination of the relation we are looking for between a formula $\lambda(\mu_1)$, applied to the names, a condition π, and the veracity of the formula $\lambda(R_{♀}(\mu_1))$ in the generic extension when we have $\pi \in ♀$.

1. THE TECHNIQUE OF FORCING

Cohen's presentation of forcing is too 'calculatory' to be employed here. I will merely indicate its strategy.

Suppose that our problem is solved. We have a relation, written ≡, to be read 'forces', and which is such that:

- if a condition π forces a statement on the names, then, for any generic part ♀ such that $\pi \in ♀$, the same statement, this time bearing on the referential value of the names, is veridical in the generic extension $S(♀)$;
- reciprocally, if a statement is veridical in a generic extension $S(♀)$, there exists a condition π such that $\pi \in ♀$ and π forces the statement applied to the names whose values appear in the veridical statement in question.

In other words, the relation of forcing between π and the statement λ applied to the names is *equivalent* to the veracity of the statement λ in any generic extension $S(♀)$ such that $\pi \in ♀$. Since the relation 'π forces λ' is verifiable *in the situation S*, we become masters of the possible veracity of a formula in the extension $S(♀)$ without 'exiting' from the fundamental situation in which the relation ≡ (forces) is defined. The inhabitant of S can force this veracity without having to discern anything in the generic extension where the indiscernible resides.

It is thus a question of establishing that there exists a relation ≡ which verifies the equivalence above, that is:

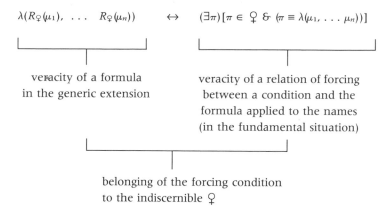

$$\lambda(R_\female(\mu_1), \ \ldots \ R_\female(\mu_n)) \qquad \leftrightarrow \qquad (\exists\pi)[\pi \in \female \ \& \ (\pi \equiv \lambda(\mu_1, \ldots \mu_n))]$$

veracity of a formula
in the generic extension

veracity of a relation of forcing
between a condition and the
formula applied to the names
(in the fundamental situation)

belonging of the forcing condition
to the indiscernible $\female$

The relation $\equiv$ operates between the conditions and the formulas. Its definition thus depends on the formalism of the language of set theory. A careful examination of this formalism—such as given in the technical note following Meditation 3—shows the following: the signs of a formula can ultimately be reduced to four logical signs ($\sim$, $\rightarrow$, $\exists$, $=$) and a specific sign ($\in$). The other logical signs ($\&$, or, $\leftrightarrow$, $\forall$) can be defined on the basis of the above signs (cf. Appendix 6). A simple reflection on the writing of the formulas which are applied to the names shows that they are then one of the five following types:

a. $\mu_1 = \mu_2$ (egalitarian atomic formula)

b. $\mu_1 \in \mu_2$ (atomic formula of belonging)

c. $\sim\lambda$ (where λ is an 'already' constructed formula)

d. $\lambda_1 \rightarrow \lambda_2$ (where λ_1 and λ_2 are 'already' constructed)

e. $(\exists\mu) \ \lambda(\mu)$ (where λ is a formula which contains μ as a free variable).

If we clearly define the value of the relation $\pi \equiv \lambda$ (the condition π forces the formula λ) for these five types, we will have a general definition by the procedure of recurrence on the length of the writings: this is laid out in Appendix 6.

It is equality which poses the most problems. It is not particularly clear how a condition can force, by its belonging to a generic part, two names μ_1 and μ_2 to have the same referential value in a generic extension. What we actually want is:

$$[\pi \equiv (\mu_1 = \mu_2)] \leftrightarrow [\pi \in \female \rightarrow [R_\female(\mu_1) = R_\female(\mu_2)]]$$

with the *sine qua non* obligation that the writing on the left of the equivalence be defined, with respect to its veracity, strictly within the fundamental situation.

This difficulty is contained by working on the nominal ranks (cf. Meditation 34). We start with the formulas $\mu_1 = \mu_2$ where μ_1 and μ_2 are of nominal rank 0, and we define $\pi \equiv (\mu_1 = \mu_2)$ for such names.

Once we have explained the forcing on names of the nominal rank 0, we then proceed to the general case, remembering that a name is composed of conditions and names of *inferior nominal rank* (stratification of the names). It is by supposing that forcing has been defined for these inferior ranks that we will define it for the following rank.

I lay out the forcing of equality for the names of nominal rank 0 in Appendix 7. For those who are curious, the completion of the recurrence is an exercise which generalizes the methods employed in the appendix.

Let's note solely that at the end of these laborious calculations we manage to define three possibilities:

- $\mu_1 = \mu_2$ is forced by the minimal condition $\varnothing$. Since this condition belongs to *any* generic part, $R_{\female}(\mu_1) = R_{\female}(\mu_2)$ is always veridical, whatever $\female$ may be.
- $\mu_1 = \mu_2$ is forced by π_1, a particular condition. Then $R_{\female}(\mu_1) = R_{\female}(\mu_2)$ is veridical in certain generic extensions (those such that $\pi_1 \in \female$), and erroneous in others (when $\sim(\pi_1 \in \female)$).
- $\mu_1 = \mu_2$ is not forceable. Then $R_{\female}(\mu_1) = R_{\female}(\mu_2)$ is not veridical in any generic extension.

Between their borders (statements always or never veridical) these three cases outline an aleatory field in which certain veracities can be forced *without them being absolute*—in the sense that solely the belonging of this or that condition to the description implies these veracities in the corresponding generic extensions. It is at this point that some λ statements of set theory (of general ontology) will turn out to be *undecidable*, being veridical in certain situations, and erroneous in others, according to whether a condition belongs or not to a generic part. Hence the essential bond, in which the law of the subject resides, between the indiscernible and the undecidable.

Once the problem of the forcing of formulas of the type $\mu_1 = \mu_2$ is resolved, we move on to the other elementary formulas, those of the type $\mu_1 \in \mu_2$. Here the procedure is much quicker, for the following reason: we will force an equality $\mu_3 = \mu_1$ (because we know how to do it), arranging beforehand that $R_♀(\mu_3) \in R_♀(\mu_2)$. This technique is based on the interdependence between equality and belonging, which is founded by the grand Idea of the same and the other which is the axiom of extension (Meditation 5).

How do we proceed for complex formulas of the type $\sim\lambda$, $\lambda_1 \rightarrow \lambda_2$, or $(\exists a) \, \lambda(a)$? Can they also be forced?

The response—positive—is constructed via recurrence on the length of writings (on this point cf. Appendix 6). I will examine one case alone—one which is fascinating for philosophy—that of negation.

We suppose that forcing is defined for the formula λ, and that $\pi_1 \equiv \lambda$ verifies the fundamental equivalence between forcing (in S) and veracity (in $S(♀)$). How can we 'pass' to the forcing of the formula $\sim(\lambda)$?

Note that if π_1 forces λ and π_2 dominates π_1, it is ruled out that π_2 force $\sim(\lambda)$. If π_2 actually forces $\sim(\lambda)$, this means that when $\pi_2 \in ♀$, $\sim(\lambda)$ is veridical in $S(♀)$ (fundamental equivalence between forcing and veracity once the forcing condition belongs to $♀$). But if $\pi_2 \in ♀$ and π_2 dominates π_1, we also have $\pi_1 \in ♀$ (rule Rd_1 of correct parts, cf. Meditation 33). If π_1 forces λ and $\pi_1 \in ♀$, then the formula λ is veridical in $S(♀)$. The result would then be the following: λ (forced by π_1) and $\sim(\lambda)$ (forced by π_2) would be simultaneously veridical in $S(♀)$—but this is impossible if the theory is coherent.

Hence the following idea: we will say that π forces $\sim(\lambda)$ if *no* condition dominating π forces λ:

$$[\pi \equiv \sim(\lambda)] \leftrightarrow [(\pi \subset \pi_1) \rightarrow \sim(\pi_1 \equiv \lambda)]$$

Negation, here, is based on there being no stronger (or more precise) condition of the indiscernible which forces the affirmation to be veridical. It is therefore, in substance, the unforceability of affirmation. Negation is thus a little evasive: it is suspended, not from the necessity of negation, but rather from the *non-necessity* of affirmation. In forcing, the concept of negation has something modal about it: it is possible to deny once one is not constrained to affirm. This modality of the negative is characteristic of subjective or post-evental negation.

After negation, considerations of pure logic allow us to define the forcing of $\lambda_1 \rightarrow \lambda_2$, on the supposition of the forcing of λ_1 and λ_2; and the same goes for $(\exists a) \, \lambda(a)$, on the supposition that the forcing of λ has been defined. We will thus proceed, via combinatory analysis, from the most simple formulas to the most complex, or from the shortest to the longest.

Once this construction is complete, we will verify that, for *any* formula λ, we dispose of a means to demonstrate *in* S whether there exists or not a condition π which forces it. If one such condition exists then its belonging to the generic part $\female$ implies that the formula λ is veridical in the extension $S(\female)$. Inversely, if a formula λ is veridical in a generic extension $S(\female)$, then a condition π exists which belongs to $\female$ and which forces the formula. The number of possible hypotheses in these conditions is three, just as we saw for the equality $\mu_1 = \mu_2$:

- the formula λ, forced by $\varnothing$, is veridical in *any* extension $S(\female)$;
- the formula λ, which is not forceable (there does not exist any π such that $\pi \equiv \lambda$), is not veridical in *any* extension $S(\female)$;
- the formula λ, forced by a condition π, is veridical in certain extensions $S(\female)$, those in which $\pi \in \female$, and not in others. This will lead to the ontological *undecidability* of this formula.

The result of these considerations is that given a formula λ in the language of set theory, we can ask ourselves whether it is necessary, impossible or possible that it be veridical in a generic extension. This problem makes sense for an inhabitant of S: it amounts to examining whether the formula λ, applied to names, is forced by $\varnothing$, is non-forceable, or forceable by a particular non-void condition π.

The first case to examine is that of the axioms of set theory, or the grand Ideas of the multiple. Since S, a quasi-complete situation, 'reflects' ontology, the axioms are all veridical within it. Do they remain so in $S(\female)$? The response is categorical: these axioms are all forced by $\varnothing$; they are therefore veridical in *any* generic extension. Hence:

2. A GENERIC EXTENSION OF A QUASI-COMPLETE SITUATION IS ALSO ITSELF QUASI-COMPLETE

This is the most important result of the technique of forcing, and it formalizes, within ontology, a crucial property of the effects of the subject: a truth, whatever veridical novelty it may support, remains homogeneous with the major characteristics of the situation whose truth it is. Mathematicians express this in the following manner: if S is a denumerable transitive model of set theory, then so is a generic extension $S(\female)$. Cohen himself declared; 'the intuition why it is so is difficult to explain. Roughly speaking . . . [it is because] no information can be extracted from the [indiscernible] set α which was not already present in M [the fundamental situation].' We can think through this difficulty: insofar as the generic extension is obtained through the addition of an indiscernible, generic, anonymous part, it is not such that we can, on its basis, discern invisible characteristics of the fundamental situation. A truth, forced according to the indiscernible produced by a generic procedure of fidelity, can definitely support *supplementary* veridical statements; this reflects the event in which the procedure originates being named in excess of the language of the situation. However, this supplement, inasmuch as the fidelity is inside the situation, cannot cancel out its main principles of consistency. This is, moreover, why it is the truth *of* the situation, and not the absolute commencement of another. The subject, which is the forcing production of an indiscernible included in the situation, cannot ruin the situation. What it can do is generate veridical statements that were previously undecidable. Here we find our definition of the subject again: support of a faithful forcing, it articulates the indiscernible with the decision of an undecidable. But first of all, we must establish that the supplementation it operates is adequate to the laws of the situation; in other words, that the generic extension is itself a quasi-complete situation.

To do so, it is a question of verifying, case by case, the existence of a forcing for all the axioms of set theory supposed veridical in the situation S. I give several simple and typical examples of such verification in Appendix 8.

The general sense of these verifications is clear: the conformity of the situation S to the laws of the multiple implies, by the mediation of forcing, the conformity of the generic extension $S(\female)$. Genericity conserves the laws of consistency. One can also say: a truth consists given the consistency of the situation whose truth it is.

3. STATUS OF VERIDICAL STATEMENTS WITHIN A GENERIC EXTENSION $S(\female)$: THE UNDECIDABLE

The examination of a particular connection may be inferred on the basis of everything which precedes this point: a connection which initiates the possibility of the being of the Subject; that between an indiscernible part of a situation and the forcing of a statement whose veracity is undecidable in that situation. We find ourselves here on the brink of a possible thought of the ontological substructure of a subject.

First, let's note the following: if one supposes that ontology is consistent—that no formal contradiction of the axioms of the theory of the pure multiple can be deduced—no veridical statement in a generic extension $S(\female)$ of a quasi-complete situation can ruin that consistency. In other words, if a statement λ is veridical in $S(\female)$, set theory (written ST) supplemented by the formula λ is consistent, once ST is. One can always supplement ontology by a statement whose veracity is forced from the point of an indiscernible $\female$.

Let's suppose that $ST + \lambda$ is not actually consistent, although ST alone is. This would mean that $\sim\lambda$ is a theorem of ST. That is, if a contradiction, let's say $(\sim\lambda_1 \, \& \, \lambda_1)$, is deducible from $ST + \lambda$, this means, by the theorem of deduction (cf. Meditation 22), that the implication $\lambda \rightarrow (\sim\lambda_1 \, \& \, \lambda_1)$ is deducible in ST alone. But, on the basis of $\lambda \rightarrow (\sim\lambda_1 \, \& \, \lambda_1)$, the statement $\sim\lambda$ can be deduced by simple logical manipulations. Therefore $\sim\lambda$ is a theorem of ST, a faithful statement of ontology.

The demonstration of $\sim\lambda$ only makes use of a finite number of axioms, like any demonstration. There exists, consequently, a denumerable quasi-complete situation S in which all of these axioms are veridical. They remain veridical in a generic extension $S(\female)$ of this situation. It follows that $\sim\lambda$, as a consequence of these veridical axioms, is also veridical in $S(\female)$. But then λ cannot be veridical in $S(\female)$.

We can trace back to the consistency of the situation S in a more precise manner: if both $\sim\lambda$ and λ are veridical in $S(\female)$ then a condition π_1 exists which forces λ, and a condition π_2 exists which forces $\sim\lambda$ (λ being applied this time to names). We thus have, *in S*, two veridical statements: $\pi_1 \equiv \lambda$ and $\pi_2 \equiv \sim\lambda$. Since $\pi_1 \in \female$ and $\pi_2 \in \female$, and given that λ and $\sim\lambda$ are veridical in $S(\female)$, there exists a condition π_3 which dominates both π_1 and π_2 (rule Rd_2 of correct sets). This condition π_3 forces both λ and $\sim\lambda$. Yet, according to the definition of the forcing of negation (see above) we have:

$$\pi_3 \equiv \sim\lambda \rightarrow \sim(\pi_3 \equiv \lambda), \text{ given that } \pi_3 \subset \pi_3.$$

If we also have $\pi_3 \equiv \lambda$, then in reality we have the formal contradiction: $(\pi_3 \equiv \lambda) \, \& \, \sim(\pi_3 \equiv \lambda)$, which is a contradiction expressed in the language of the situation S. That is to say, if $S(\female)$ validated contradictory statements, then so would S. Inversely, if S is consistent, $S(\female)$ must be such. It is thus impossible for a veridical statement in $S(\female)$ to ruin the supposed consistency of S, and finally of ST. We shall suppose, from now on, that ontology is consistent, and that if λ is veridical in $S(\female)$, then that statement is *compatible* with the axioms of *ST*. In the end, there are only two possible statutes available for a statement λ which forcing reveals to be veridical in a generic extension $S(♀)$:

- either λ is a theorem of ontology, a faithful deductive consequence of the Ideas of the multiple (of the axioms of *ST*);
- or λ is not a theorem of *ST*. But then, being nevertheless compatible with *ST*, it is an *undecidable statement* of ontology: that is, we can supplement the latter just as easily with λ as with ~λ, its consistency remains. In this sense, the Ideas of the multiple are powerless to *decide* the ontological veracity of this statement.

Indeed, if λ is compatible with *ST*, it is because the theory $ST + λ$ is consistent. But if λ is not a theorem of *ST*, the theory $ST + ~λ$ is equally consistent. If it was not such, one could deduce a contradiction in it, say ($~λ_1$ & $λ_1$). But, according to the theorem of deduction, we would then have in *ST* alone the deducible theorem: $~λ → (λ_1 & ~λ_1)$. A simple logical manipulation would then allow the deduction of λ, which contradicts the hypothesis according to which λ is not a theorem of *ST*.

The situation is finally the following: a veridical statement λ in a generic extension $S(♀)$ is either a theorem of ontology or a statement undecidable by ontology. In particular, if we know that λ is not a theorem of ontology, and that λ is veridical in $S(♀)$, we know that λ is undecidable.

The decisive point for us concerns those statements relative to the cardinality of the set of parts of a set, that is, to the state's excess. This problem commands the general orientations of thought (cf. Meditations 26 and 27). We already know that the statement 'statist excess is without measure' is not a theorem of ontology. In fact, within the constructivist universe (Meditation 29), this excess is measured and minimal: we have $| p(ω_a) | = ω_{S(a)}$. In this universe, the quantitative measure of statist excess is precise: as its cardinality, the set of parts possesses the successor cardinal to the one which measures the quantity of the situation. It is therefore compatible with the axioms of *ST* that such be the truth of this excess. If we find generic extensions $S(♀)$ where, on the contrary, it is veridical that $p(ω_a)$ has other values as its cardinality, even values that are more or less indeterminate, then we will know that the problem of statist excess is undecidable within ontology.

In this matter of the measure of excess, forcing via the indiscernible will establish the undecidability of what that measure is worth. There is errancy in quantity, and the Subject, who forces the undecidable in the place of the indiscernible, is the faithful process of that errancy. The following demonstration establishes that such a process is compatible with the thought of being-qua-being. It is best to keep in mind the main concepts of Meditations 34 and 35.

4. ERRANCY OF EXCESS (1)

We shall show that $| p(\omega_0) |$ can, in a generic extension $S(\female)$, surpass an absolutely indeterminate cardinal δ given in advance (remember that in the constructible universe L, we have $| p(\omega_0) | = \omega_1$).

Take a denumerable quasi-complete situation S. In that situation, there is necessarily ω_0, because ω_0, the first limit ordinal, is an absolute term. Now take a cardinal δ of the situation S. 'To be a cardinal' is generally *not* an absolute property. All this property means is that δ is an ordinal, and that between δ and all the smaller ordinals there is no one-to-one correspondence *which is itself found in the situation S*. We take such an indeterminate cardinal of S, such that it is superior to ω_0 (in S).

The goal is to show that in a generic extension $S(\female)$—which we will fabricate—there are at least as many parts of ω_0 as there are elements in the cardinal δ. Consequently, for an inhabitant of $S(\female)$, we have: $| p(\omega_0) | \geq \delta$. Since δ is an indeterminate cardinal superior to ω_0, we will have thereby demonstrated the errancy of statist excess, it being quantitatively as large as one wishes.

Everything depends on constructing the indiscernible $\female$ in the right manner. Remember: to underpin our intuition of the generic we employed finite series of 0's and 1's. This time, we are going to use finite series of *triplets* of the type $<a,n,0>$ or $<a,n,1>$; where a is an element of the cardinal δ, where n is a whole number, thus an element of ω_0, and where we then have either the mark 1 or 0. The information carried by such a triplet is implicitly of the type: if $<a,n,0> \in \female$, this means that a is *paired* with n. If it is rather $<a,n,1>$ which belongs to $\female$, this means that a is not paired with n. Therefore, we cannot have, in the same finite series, the triplet $<a,n,0>$ *and* the triplet $<a,n,1>$: they give contradictory information. We will posit that our set of conditions $\copyright$ is constructed in the following manner:

- An element of $\copyright$ is a finite set of triplets $<a,n,0>$ or $<a,n,1>$, with $a \in \delta$ and $n \in \omega_0$, it being understood that none of these sets can simultaneously contain, for a fixed a and a fixed n, the triplets $<a,n,0>$ and $<a,n,1>$.

For example, $\{<\alpha,5,1>, <\beta,4,0>\}$ is a condition, but $\{<\alpha,5,1>, <\alpha,5,0>\}$ is not.

– A condition dominates another condition if it contains all the triplets of the first one, thus, if the first is included in the second. For example: $\{<\alpha,5,1>, <\beta,4,0>\} \subset \{<\alpha,5,1>, <\beta,4,0>, <\beta,3,1>\}$
  This is the principle of order.

– Two conditions are compatible if they are dominated by a same third condition. This rules out their containing contradictory triplets like $<\alpha,5,1>$ and $<\alpha,5,0>$, because the third would have to contain both of them, and thus would not be a condition. This is the principle of coherency.

– It is clear that a condition is dominated by two conditions which are themselves incompatible. For example, $\{<\alpha,5,1>, <\beta,4,0>\}$ is dominated by $\{<\alpha,5,1>, <\beta,4,0>, <\beta,3,1>\}$ but also by $\{<\alpha,5,1>, <\beta,4,0>, <\beta,3,0>\}$. The two dominating conditions are incompatible. This is the principle of choice.

The conditions (the sets of appropriate triplets) will be written π_1, π_2, etc.

A correct subset of © is defined, exactly as in Meditation 33, by the rules Rd_1 and Rd_2: if a condition belongs to the correct set, any condition that it dominates also belongs to the latter (and so the void-set $\varnothing$ always belongs). If two conditions belong to the correct set, a condition also belongs to it which dominates both of them (and therefore these two conditions are compatible).

A generic correct part ♀ is defined by the fact that, for any domination D which belongs to S, we have ♀ $\cap$ $D \neq \varnothing$.

It is quite suggestive to 'visualize' what a domination is in the proposed example. Thus, 'contain a condition of the type $<\alpha,5,0>$ or $<\alpha,5,1>$' (in which we have fixed the number 5) defines a subset of conditions which is a domination, for if a condition π does not contain either of these, they can be added to it without contradiction. In the same manner, 'contain a condition of the type $<\alpha_1,n,1>$, $<\alpha_1,n,0>$' in which α_1 is a fixed element of the cardinal δ, also defines a domination, and so on. It is thus evident that ♀ is obliged to contain, in the conditions from which it is composed, 'all the n' and 'all the α', in that, due to its intersection with the dominations which correspond to a fixed α or a fixed n, for example, 5 and ω_0 (because δ is an infinite cardinal superior to ω_0, or $\omega_0 \in \delta$), there is always amongst its elements at least one triplet of the type $<\beta,5,0>$ or $<\beta,5,1>$, and also always one triplet of the type $<\omega_0,n,0>$ or $<\omega_0,n,1>$. This indicates to us both the genericity of ♀, its indeterminate nature, and signals that in $S(♀)$ there will be a type of correspondence between 'all the elements n of ω_0' and 'all the elements a of δ'. This is where the quantitative arbitrariness of excess will anchor itself.

One forces the adjunction of the indiscernible ♀ to S by nomination (Meditation 34), and one thus obtains the situation $S(♀)$, of which ♀ is then an element. We know, by forcing (see the beginning of this Meditation) that $S(♀)$ is also a quasi-complete situation: all the axioms of set theory 'currently in use' are true for an inhabitant of $S(♀)$.

Let's now consider, within the generic extension $S(♀)$, the sets $\gamma(n)$ defined as follows, for each γ which is an element of the cardinal δ.

$\gamma(n) = \{n \ / \ \{<\gamma,n,1>\} \in ♀\}$, that is, the set of whole numbers n which figure in a triplet $<\gamma,n,1>$ such that $\{<\gamma,n,1>\}$ is an element of the generic part ♀. Note that if a condition π of ♀ has such a triplet as an element, the singleton of this triplet—$\{<\gamma,n,1>\}$ itself—is included in π, and is thus dominated by π: as such it belongs to ♀ if π belongs to it (rule Rd_1 of correct parts).

These sets, which are parts of ω_0 (sets of whole numbers), belong to $S(♀)$ because their definition is clear for an inhabitant of $S(♀)$, quasi-complete situation (they are obtained by successive separations starting from ♀, and ♀ $\in S(♀)$). Moreover, since $\delta \in S$, $\delta \in S(♀)$, which is an extension of S. It so happens that we can show that within $S(♀)$, *there are at least as many parts of ω_0 of the type $\gamma(n)$ as there are elements in the cardinal δ*. And consequently, within $S(♀)$, $|\ p(\omega_0)\ |$ is certainly at least equal to δ, which is an arbitrary cardinal in S superior to ω_0. Hence the value of $|\ p(\omega_0)\ |$—the quantity of the state of the denumerable ω_0—can be said to exceed that of ω_0 itself by as much as one likes.

The detailed demonstration can be found in Appendix 9. Its strategy is as follows:

- It is shown that for every γ which is element of δ the part of ω_0 of the type $\gamma(n)$ is never empty;
- It is then shown that if γ_1 and γ_2 are *different* elements of δ, then the sets $\gamma_1(n)$ and $\gamma_2(n)$ are also different.

As such, one definitely obtains as many non-empty parts $\gamma(n)$ of ω_0 as there are elements γ in the cardinal δ.

The essence of the demonstration consists in revealing dominations in S, which *must* consequently be 'cut' by the generic part $♀$. This is how non-emptiness and differences are obtained in the sets $\gamma(n)$. Genericity reveals itself here to be prodigal in existences and distinctions: this is due to the fact that nothing in particular, no restrictive predicate, discerns the part $♀$.

Finally, given that for *each* $\gamma \in \delta$ we have defined a part $\gamma(n)$ of ω_0, that none of these parts are empty, and that all of them are different taken in pairs, there are as I said in $S(♀)$ *at least* δ different parts of ω_0. Thus, for the inhabitant of the generic extension $S(♀)$, it is certainly veridical that $| p(\omega_0) | \geq | \delta |$.

It would be quite tempting to say: that's it! We have found a quasi-complete situation in which it is veridical that statist excess has any value whatsoever, because δ is an indeterminate cardinal. We have *demonstrated errancy*.

Yes. But δ is a cardinal *in the situation S*, and our statement $| p(\omega_0) | \geq | \delta |$ is a veridical statement *in the situation $S(♀)$*. Is it certain that δ is still a cardinal in the generic extension? A one-to-one correspondence could appear, in $S(♀)$, between δ and a smaller ordinal, a correspondence absent in S. In such a case our statement could be trivial. If, for example, it turned out that in $S(♀)$ we had, in reality, $| \delta | = \omega_0$, then we would have obtained, after all our efforts, $| p(\omega_0) | \geq \omega_0$, which is even weaker than Cantor's theorem, and the latter is definitely demonstrable in any quasi-complete situation!

The possibility of a cardinal being *absented* in this manner—the Americans say 'collapsed'—by the passage to the generic extension is quite real.

5. ABSENTING AND MAINTENANCE OF INSTRINSIC QUANTITY

That quantity, the fetish of objectivity, is in fact evasive, and particularly dependent on procedures in which the being of the subject's effect resides, can be demonstrated in a spectacular manner—by reducing an indeterminate cardinal δ of the situation S to ω_0 in $S(♀)$. This generic operation absents the cardinal δ. Since ω_0 is an absolute cardinal, the operation only works for superior infinities, which manifest their instability here and their submission to forcings; forcings which, according to the system of conditions adopted, can ensure either the cardinal's maintenance or its absenting. We shall see how a 'minor' change in the conditions leads to catastrophic results for the cardinals, and thus for quantity insofar as it is thinkable inside the situations S and $S(\female)$.

Take, for example, as material for the conditions, triplets of the type $<n,a,0>$ or $<n,a,1>$, where $n \in \omega_0$ and $a \in \delta$ as always, and where δ is a cardinal of S. The whole number n is in first position this time. A condition is a finite series of such triplets, but this time with two restrictive rules (rather than one):

- if a condition, for a fixed n and a, contains the triplet $<n,a,1>$, it cannot contain the triplet $<n,a,0>$. This is the same rule as before;
- if a condition, for a fixed n and a, contains the triplet $<n,a,1>$, it cannot contain the triplet $<n,\beta,1>$ with β different from a. This is the supplementary rule.

The subjacent information is that $<n,a,1>$ is an atom of a *function* that establishes a correspondence between n and the element a. Therefore, it cannot at the same time establish a correspondence between it and a different element β.

Well! This 'minor' change—relative to the procedure in Section 4 of this Meditation—in the regulation of the triplets which make up the conditions has the following result: within an extension $S(\female)$ corresponding to these new rules, $|\delta| = \omega_0$ for an inhabitant of this extension. Although δ was a cardinal superior to ω_0 in S, it is a simple denumerable ordinal in $S(\female)$. What's more, the demonstration of this brutal absenting of a cardinal is not at all complicated: it is reproduced in its entirety in Appendix 10. Here again the demonstration is based on the revelation of dominations which constrain $\female$ to contain conditions such that, finally, for each element of δ there is a corresponding element of ω_0. Of course, this *multiple* δ, which is a cardinal superior to ω_0 in S, still exists as a pure multiple in $S(\female)$, but it can no longer be a cardinal in this new situation: the generic extension, by the conditions chosen in S, has *absented* it as cardinal. As multiple, it exists in $S(\female)$. However, its quantity has been deposed, and reduced to the denumerable.

The existence of such absentings imposes the following task upon us: we must show that in the generic extension of section 4 (via the triplets $<a,n,0>$ or $<a,n,1>$) the cardinal δ is *not* absented. And that therefore the conclusion $|p(\omega_0)| > |\delta|$ possesses the full sense of the veridical errancy of statist excess. We need to establish the prerequisites for a *maintenance* of cardinals. These prerequisites refer back to the space of conditions, and to what is quantitatively legible therein.

We establish a *necessary* condition for a cardinal δ of S to be absented in the generic extension $S(\female)$. This condition concerns the 'quantity' of pair by pair incompatible conditions that can be found in the set of conditions with which we work.

Let's term *antichain* any set of pair by pair incompatible conditions. Note that such a set is descriptively incoherent, insofar as it is inadequate for any correct part because it solely contains contradictory information. An antichain is in a way the opposite of a correct part. The following result can be shown: if, in a generic extension $S(\female)$, a cardinal δ of S superior to ω_0 is absented, this is because an antichain of conditions exists which is non-denumerable *in S* (thus for the inhabitant of S). The demonstration, which is very instructive with regard to the generic, is reproduced in Appendix 11.

Inversely, if S does not contain any non-denumerable antichain, the cardinals of S superior to ω_0 are not absented in the extension $S(\female)$. We shall say that they have been *maintained*. It is thus clear that the absenting or maintenance of cardinals depends uniquely on a quantitative property of the set of conditions, a property observable in S. This last point is crucial, since, for the ontologist, given that S is quasi-complete and thus denumerable, it is sure that every set of conditions is denumerable. But for an inhabitant of S, the same does not necessarily apply, since 'denumerable' is not an absolute property. There can thus exist, for this inhabitant, a non-denumerable antichain of conditions, and it is possible for a cardinal of S to be absented in $S(\female)$, in the sense in which, for an inhabitant of $S(\female)$, it will no longer be a cardinal.

We can recognize here the ontological schema of *disqualification*, such as may be operated by a subject-effect when the contradictions of the situation interfere with the generic procedure of fidelity.

6. ERRANCY OF EXCESS (2)

It has been shown above (section 4) that there exists an extension $S(\female)$ such that in it we have: $|p(\omega_0)| \geq |\delta|$, where δ is an indeterminate cardinal of S. What remains to be done is to verify that δ is definitely a cardinal of $S(\female)$, that it is maintained.

To do this, the criteria of the antichain must be applied. The conditions used were of the type $\pi =$ 'finite set of triplets of the type $<a,n,0>$ or

$<a,n,1>'$. How many such two by two incompatible conditions can there be?

In fact, it can be demonstrated (see Appendix 12) that when the conditions are made up of such triplets, an antichain of incompatible conditions cannot possess, in S, a cardinality superior to ω_0: any antichain is at the most denumerable. With such a set of conditions, the cardinals are all maintained.

The result is that the procedure used in Section 4 definitely leads to the veracity, in $S(\female)$, of the statement: $|p(\omega_0)| \geq |\delta|$, δ being an indeterminate cardinal of S, and consequently a cardinal of $S(\female)$, since it is maintained. Statist excess is effectively revealed to be without any fixed measure; the cardinality of the set of parts of ω_0 can surpass that of ω_0 in an arbitrary fashion. There is an essential undecidability, within the framework of the Ideas of the multiple, of the quantity of multiples whose count-as-one is guaranteed by the state (the metastructure).

Let's note in passing that if the generic extension can maintain or absent cardinals of the quasi-complete situation S, on the contrary, every cardinal of $S(\female)$ was already a cardinal of S. That is, if δ is a cardinal in $S(\female)$, it is because no one-to-one correspondence exists in $S(\female)$ between δ and a smaller ordinal. But then neither does such a correspondence exist in S, since $S(\female)$ is an extension in the sense in which $S \subset S(\female)$. If there were such a one-to-one correspondence in S, it would also exist in $S(\female)$, and δ would not be a cardinal therein. Here one can recognise the *subjective principle of inexistents*: in a truth (a generic extension), there are in general supplementary existents, but what inexists (as pure multiple) already inexisted in the situation. The subject-effect can *disqualify* a term (it was a cardinal, it is no longer such), but it cannot suppress a cardinal *in its being*, or as pure multiple.

A generic procedure can reveal the errancy of quantity, but it cannot cancel out the being in respect of which there is quantitative evaluation.

7. FROM THE INDISCERNIBLE TO THE UNDECIDABLE

It is time to recapitulate the ontological strategy run through in the weighty Meditations 33, 34 and 35: those in which there has emerged —though always latent—the articulation of a possible being of the Subject.

a. Given a quasi-complete denumerable situation, in which the Ideas of the multiple are for the most part veridical—thus, a multiple which realizes the schema of a situation in which the entirety of historical ontology is reflected—one can find therein a set of *conditions* whose principles, in the last analysis, are that of a partial order (certain conditions are 'more precise' than others), a coherency (criterion of compatibility), and a 'liberty' (incompatible dominants).

b. Rules intelligible to an 'inhabitant' of the situation allow particular sets of conditions to be designated as correct parts.

c. Certain of these correct parts, because they avoid any coincidence with parts which are definable or constructible or discernible within the situation, will be said to be *generic parts*.

d. Generally, a generic part does not exist in the situation, because it cannot belong to this situation despite being included therein. An inhabitant of the situation possesses the concept of generic part, but in no way possesses an existent multiple which corresponds to this concept. She can only 'believe' in such an existence. However, for the ontologist (thus, from the outside), if the situation is denumerable, there exists a generic part.

e. What do exist in the situation are *names*, multiples which bind together conditions and other names, such that the concept of a referential value of these names can be calculated on the basis of hypotheses concerning the unknown generic part (these hypotheses are of the type: 'Such a condition is supposed as belonging to the generic part.').

f. One terms *generic extension* of the situation the multiple obtained by the fixation of a referential value for all the names which belong to the situation. Despite being unknown, the elements of the generic extension are thus named.

g. What is at stake is definitely an extension, because one can show that every element of the situation has its own name. These are the *canonical names*, and they are independent of the particularity of the supposed generic part. Being nameable, all the elements of the situation are also elements of the generic extension, which contains all the referential values of the names.

h. The generic part, which is unknown in the situation, is on the contrary an element of the generic extension. Inexistent and indiscernible in the situation, it thus exists in the generic extension. However, it remains indiscernible therein. It is possible to say that the generic extension results from the adjunction to the situation of an indiscernible of that situation.

i. One can define, in the situation, a relation between conditions, on the one hand, and the formulas applied to names, on the other. This relation is called *forcing*. It is such that:

- if a formula $\lambda(\mu_1, \mu_2, \ldots \mu_n)$ bearing on the names is *forced* by a condition π, each time that this condition π belongs to a generic part, the statement $\lambda(R_\varphi(\mu_1), R_\varphi(\mu_2), \ldots R_\varphi(\mu_n))$ bearing on the referential values of these names is veridical in the corresponding generic extension;

- if a statement is veridical in a generic extension, there exists a condition π which forces the corresponding statement applied to the names of the elements at stake in the formula, and which belongs to the generic part from which that extension results.

Consequently, veracity in a generic extension is controllable *within the situation* by the relation of forcing.

j. In using forcing, one notices that the generic extension has all sorts of properties which were already those of the situation. It is in this manner that the axioms, or Ideas of the multiple, veridical in the situation, are also veridical in the generic extension. If the situation is quasi-complete, so is the generic extension: it reflects, in itself, the entirety of historical ontology within the denumerable. In the same manner the part of nature contained in the situation is the same as that contained by the generic extension, insofar as the ordinals of the second are exactly those of the first.

k. But certain statements which cannot be demonstrated in ontology, and whose veracity in the situation cannot be established, are veridical in the generic extension. It is in such a manner that sets of conditions exist which force, in a generic extension, the set of parts of ω_0 to surpass any given cardinal of that extension.

l. One can thus force an *indiscernible* to the point that the extension in which it appears is such that an *undecidable* statement of ontology is veridical therein, thus decided.

This ultimate connection between the indiscernible and the undecidable is literally the trace of the being of the Subject in ontology.

That its point of application be precisely the errancy of statist excess indicates that the breach in the ontological edifice, its incapacity to *close* the measureless chasm between belonging and inclusion, results from there being a textual interference between what is sayable of being-qua-being and the non-being in which the Subject originates. This interference results from the following: despite it depending on the event, which belongs to 'that-which-is-not-being-qua-being', the Subject must *be capable* of being.

Foreclosed from ontology, the event returns in the mode according to which the undecidable can only be decided therein by forcing veracity from the standpoint of the indiscernible.

For all the being of which a truth is capable amounts to these indiscernible inclusions: it allows, without annexing them to the encyclopaedia, their effects—previously suspended—to be retroactively pronounced, such that a discourse gathers them together.

Everything of the Subject which is its being—but *a* Subject is not its being—can be identified in its trace at the jointure of the indiscernible and the undecidable: a jointure that, without a doubt, the mathematicians were thoroughly inspired to blindly circumscribe under the name of forcing.

The impasse of being, which causes the quantitative excess of the state to err without measure, is in truth the pass of the Subject. That it be in this precise place that the axial orientations of all possible thought—constructivist, generic or transcendent—are fixed by being constrained to wager upon measure or un-measure, is clarified if one considers that the *proof* of the undecidability of this measure, which is the rationality of errancy, reproduces within mathematical ontology itself the chance of the generic procedure, and the correlative paradoxes of quantity: the absenting of cardinals, or, if they are maintained, the complete arbitrariness of the quantitative evaluation of the set of parts of a set.

A Subject alone possesses the capacity of indiscernment. This is also why it forces the undecidable to exhibit itself as such, on the substructure of being of an indiscernible part. It is thus assured that the impasse of being is the point at which a Subject convokes itself to a decision, because at least one multiple, subtracted from the language, proposes to fidelity and to the names induced by a supernumerary nomination the possibility of a decision without concept.

That it was necessary to intervene such that the event be in the guise of a name generates the following: it is not impossible to decide—without having to account for it—everything that a journey of enquiry and thought circumscribes of the undecidable.

Veracity thus has two sources: being, which multiplies the infinite knowledge of the pure multiple; and the event, in which a truth originates, itself multiplying incalculable veracities. Situated in being, subjective emergence forces the event to decide the true of the situation.

There are not only significations, or interpretations. There are truths, also. But the trajectory of the true is practical, and the thought in which it is delivered is in part subtracted from language (indiscernibility), and in part subtracted from the jurisdiction of the Ideas (undecidability).

Truth requires, apart from the presentative support of the multiple, the ultra-one of the event. The result is that it *forces decision*.

Every Subject passes in force, at a point where language fails, and where the Idea is interrupted. What it opens upon is an un-measure in which to measure itself; because the void, originally, was summoned.

The being of the Subject is to be symptom-(*of-*)being.

MEDITATION THIRTY-SEVEN
Descartes/Lacan

'[The *cogito*], as moment, is the detritus of a rejection of all knowledge,
but for all that it is supposed to found
a certain anchoring in being for the subject.'
'Science and Truth', *Écrits*

One can never insist enough upon the fact that the Lacanian directive of a return to Freud was originally doubled: he says—in an expression which goes back to 1946—'the directive of a return to Descartes would not be superfluous.' How can these two imperatives function together? The key to the matter resides in the statement that the subject of psychoanalysis is none other than the subject of science. This identity, however, can only be grasped by attempting to think the subject *in its place*. What localizes the subject is the point at which Freud can only be understood within the heritage of the Cartesian gesture, and at which he subverts, via dislocation, the latter's pure coincidence with self, its reflexive transparency.

What renders the *cogito* irrefutable is the form, that one may give it, in which the 'where' insists: '*Cogito ergo sum' ubi cogito, ibi sum*. The point of the subject is that *there* where it is thought that thinking it must be, it is. The connection between being and place founds the radical existence of enunciation as subject.

Lacan introduces us into the intricacies of this place by means of disturbing statements, in which he supposes 'I am not, there where I am the plaything of my thought; I think of what I am, there where I do not think I am thinking.' The unconscious designates that 'it thinks' there where I am not, but where I must come to be. The subject thus finds itself ex-centred from the place of transparency in which it pronounces itself to be: yet one is not obliged to read into this a complete rupture with Descartes. Lacan signals that he 'does not misrecognize' that the conscious certitude of existence, at the centre of the *cogito*, is not immanent, but rather transcendent. 'Transcendent' because the subject cannot coincide with the line of identification proposed to it by this certitude. The subject is rather the latter's *empty* waste.

In truth, this is where the entire question lies. Taking a short cut through what can be inferred as common to Descartes, to Lacan, and to what I am proposing here—which ultimately concerns the status of truth as generic hole in knowledge—I would say that the debate bears upon the localization of the void.

What *still* attaches Lacan (but this *still* is the modern perpetuation of sense) to the Cartesian epoch of science is the thought that the subject must be maintained in the pure void of its subtraction if one wishes to save truth. Only such a subject allows itself to be sutured within the logical, wholly transmissible, form of science.

Yes or no, is it of being qua being that the void-set is the proper name? Or is it necessary to think that it is the subject for which such a name is appropriate: as if its purification of any knowable depth delivered the truth, which speaks, only by ex-centering the null point eclipsed within the interval of multiples—multiples of that which guarantees, under the term 'signifier', material presence?

The choice here is between a structural recurrence, which thinks the subject-effect as void-set, thus as identifiable within the uniform networks of experience, and a hypothesis of the rarity of the subject, which suspends its occurrence from the event, from the intervention, and from the generic paths of fidelity, both returning the void to, and reinsuring it within, a function of suture to being, the knowledge of which is deployed by mathematics alone.

In neither case is the subject substance or consciousness. But the first option preserves the Cartesian gesture in its excentred dependency with regard to language. I have proof of this: when Lacan writes that 'thought founds being solely by knotting itself within the speech in which every operation touches upon the essence of language', he maintains the discourse of ontological foundation that Descartes encountered in the empty and apodictic transparency of the *cogito*. Of course, he organizes its processions in an entirely different manner, since for him the void is delocalized, and no purified reflection gives access to it. Nevertheless, the intrusion of this third term—language—is not sufficient to overturn this order which supposes that it is necessary *from the standpoint of the subject* to enter into the examination of truth as cause.

I maintain that it is not the truth which is cause for that suffering of false plenitude that is subjective anxiety ('yes, or no, what you [the psychoanalysts] do, does its sense consist in affirming that the truth of neurotic suffering is that of having the truth as cause?'). A truth is that indiscernible multiple whose finite approximation is supported by a subject, such that its ideality to-come, nameless correlate of the naming of an event, is that on the basis of which one can legitimately designate as subject the aleatory figure which, without the indiscernible, would be no more than an incoherent sequence of encyclopaedic determinants.

If it were necessary to identify a cause of the subject, one would have to return, not so much to truth, which is rather its stuff, nor to the infinity whose finitude it is, but rather to the event. Consequently, the void is no longer the eclipse of the subject; it is on the side of being, which is such that its errancy in the situation is convoked by the event, via an interventional nomination.

By a kind of inversion of categories, I will thus place the subject on the side of the ultra-one—despite it being itself the *trajectory* of multiples (the enquiries)—the void on the side of being, and the truth on the side of the indiscernible.

Besides, what is at stake here is not so much the subject—apart from undoing what, due to the supposition of its structural permanence, still makes Lacan a foundational figure who echoes the previous epoch. What is at stake is rather an opening on to a history of truth which is at last *completely* disconnected from what Lacan, with genius, termed exactitude or adequation, but which his gesture, overly soldered to language alone, allowed to subsist as the inverse of the true.

A truth, if it is thought as being solely a generic part of the situation, is a source of veracity once a subject forces an undecidable in the future anterior. But if veracity touches on language (in the most general sense of the term), truth only exists insofar as it is indifferent to the latter, since its procedure is generic inasmuch as it *avoids* the entire encyclopaedic grasp of judgements.

The essential character of the names, the names of the subject-language, is itself tied to the subjective capacity to anticipate, by forcing, what will have been veridical from the standpoint of a supposed truth. But names apparently create the thing only in ontology, where it is true that a generic extension results from the placement into being of the entire reference system of these names. However, even in ontology this creation is merely apparent, since the reference of a name depends upon the generic part, which is thus implicated in the particularity of the extension. The name only 'creates' its referent on the hypothesis that the indiscernible will have already been completely described by the set of conditions that, moreover, it is. A subject, up to and including its nominative capacity, is under the condition of an indiscernible, thus of a generic procedure, a fidelity, an intervention, and, ultimately, of an event.

What Lacan lacked—despite this lack being legible for us solely after having read what, in his texts, far from lacking, founded the very possibility of a modern regime of the true—is the radical suspension of truth from the supplementation of a being-in-situation by an event which is a separator of the void.

The 'there is' of the subject is the coming-to-being of the event, via the ideal occurrence of a truth, in its finite modalities. By consequence, what must always be grasped is that there is no subject, that there are no longer some subjects. What Lacan still owed to Descartes, a debt whose account must be closed, was the idea that there were always some subjects.

When the Chicago Americans shamelessly used Freud to substitute the re-educational methods of 'ego-reinforcement' for the truth from which a subject proceeds, it was quite rightly, and for everyone's salvation, that Lacan started that merciless war against them which his true students and heirs attempt to pursue. However, they would be wrong to believe they can win it, things remaining as they are; for it is not a question of an error or of an ideological perversion. Evidently, one could believe so if one supposed that there were 'always' some truths and some subjects. More seriously, the Chicago people, in their manner, took into account the withdrawal of truth, and with it, that of the subject it authorized. They were situated in a historical and geographical space where no fidelity to the events in which Freud, or Lenin, or Malevich, or Cantor, or Schoenberg had intervened was practicable any longer, other than in the inoperative forms of dogmatism or orthodoxy. Nothing generic could be supposed in that space.

Lacan thought that he was *rectifying* the Freudian doctrine of the subject, but rather, newly intervening on the borders of the Viennese site, he reproduced an operator of fidelity, postulated the horizon of an indiscernible, and persuaded us again that there are, in this uncertain world, some subjects.

If we now examine, linking up with the introduction to this book, what philosophical circulation is available to us within the modern referential, and what, consequently, our tasks are, the following picture may be drawn:

 a. It is possible to reinterrogate the entire history of philosophy, from its Greek origins on, according to the hypothesis of a mathematical regulation of the ontological question. One would then see a continuity and a periodicity unfold quite different to that deployed by Heidegger. In particular, the genealogy of the doctrine of truth will lead to a signposting, through singular interpretations, of how the categories of the event and the indiscernible, unnamed, were at work throughout the metaphysical text. I believe I have given a few examples.

 b. A close analysis of logico-mathematical procedures since Cantor and Frege will enable a thinking of what this intellectual revolution—a blind returning of ontology on its own essence—conditions in contemporary rationality. This work will permit the undoing, in this matter, of the monopoly of Anglo-Saxon positivism.

 c. With respect to the doctrine of the subject, the individual examination of each of the generic procedures will open up to an aesthetics, to a theory of science, to a philosophy of politics, and, finally, to the arcana of love; to an intersection without fusion with psychoanalysis. All modern art, all the incertitudes of science, everything ruined Marxism prescribes as a militant task, everything, finally, which the name of Lacan designates will be met with, reworked, and traversed by a philosophy restored to its time by clarified categories.

And in this journey we will be able to say—if, at least, we do not lose the memory of it being the event alone which authorizes being, what is called being, to found the finite place of a subject which decides—'Nothingness gone, the castle of purity remains.'

ANNEXES

APPENDIXES

The status of these twelve appendixes varies. I would distinguish four types.

1. Appendixes whose concern is to present a demonstration which has been passed over in the text, but which I judge to be interesting. This is the case for Appendixes 1, 4, 9, 10, 11 and 12. The first two concern the ordinals. The last four complete the demonstration of Cohen's theorem, since its strategy alone is given in Meditation 36.

2. Appendixes which sketch or exemplify methods used to demonstrate important results. This is the case for Appendix 5 (on the absoluteness of an entire series of notions), 6 (on logic and reasoning by recurrence), and 8 (on the veracity of axioms in a generic extension).

3. The 'calculatory' Appendix 7, which, on one example (equality), shows how one proceeds in defining Cohen's forcing.

4. Appendixes which in themselves are complete and significant expositions. Appendix 2 (on the concept of relation and the Heideggerean figure of forgetting in mathematics) and Appendix 3 (on singular, regular and inaccessible cardinals) which enriches the investigation of the ontology of quantity.

APPENDIX 1 (Meditations 12 and 18)
Principle of minimality for ordinals

Here it is a question of establishing that if an ordinal α possesses a property, an ordinal β exists which is the smallest to possess it, therefore which is such that no ordinal smaller than β has the property.

Let's suppose that an ordinal α possesses the property ψ. If it is not itself $\in$-minimal for this property, this is because one or several elements belong to it which also possess the property. These elements are themselves ordinals because an essential property of ordinals—emblematic of the homogeneity of nature—is that every element of an ordinal is an ordinal (this is shown in Meditation 12). Let's then separate, in α, all those ordinals which are supposed to possess the property Ψ. They form a set, according to the axiom of extensionality. It will be noted α_Ψ:

$$\alpha_\Psi = \{\beta \mid (\beta \in \alpha) \And \Psi(\beta)\}$$

(All the β which belong to α and have the property Ψ.)

According to the axiom of foundation, the set α_Ψ contains at least one element, let's say γ, which is such that it does not have any element in common with α itself. Indeed, the axiom of foundation posits that there is some Other in every multiple; that is, a multiple presented by the latter which no longer presents *anything* already presented by the initial multiple (a multiple on the edge of the void).

This multiple γ is thus such that:

- it belongs to α_Ψ. Therefore it belongs to α and possesses the property Ψ (definition of α_Ψ);

– no term δ belonging to it belongs to α_Ψ. Note that, nevertheless, δ also belongs, for its part, to α. That is, δ, which belongs to the ordinal γ, is an ordinal. Belonging, between ordinals, is a relation of order. Therefore, $(\delta \in \gamma)$ and $(\gamma \in \alpha)$ implies that $\delta \in \alpha$. The only possible reason for δ, which belongs to α, to not belong to α_Ψ, is consequently that δ does not possess the property Ψ.

The result is that γ is $\in$-minimal for Ψ, since no element of γ can possess this property, the property that γ itself possesses.

The usage of the axiom of foundation is essential in this demonstration. This is *technically* understandable because this axiom touches on the notion of $\in$-minimality. A foundational multiple (or multiple on the edge of the void) is, in a given multiple, $\in$-minimal for belonging to this multiple: it belongs to the latter, but what belongs to it in turn no longer belongs to the initial multiple.

It is also *conceptually* necessary because ordinals—the ontological schema of nature—are tied in a very particular manner to the exclusion of a being of the event. If nature always proposes an ultimate (or minimal) term for a given property, this is because in and by itself it excludes the event. Natural stability is incarnated by the 'atomic' stopping point that it ties to any explicit characterization. But this stability, whose heart is the maximal equilibrium between belonging and inclusion, structure and state, is only accessible at the price of an annulation of self-belonging, of the un-founded, thus of the pure 'there is', of the event as excess-of-one. If there is some minimality in natural multiples, it is because there is no ontological cut on the basis of which the ultra-one as convocation of the void, and as undecidable in respect to the multiple, would be interpreted.

APPENDIX 2 (Meditation 26)
A relation, or a function, is solely a pure multiple

For several millennia it was believed that mathematics could be defined by the singularity of its objects, namely numbers and figures. It would not be an exaggeration to say that this assumption of objectivity—which, as we shall see, is the mode of the forgetting of being proper to mathematics—formed the main obstacle to the recognition of the particular vocation of mathematics, namely, that of maintaining itself solely on the basis of being-qua-being through the discursive presentation of presentation in general. The entire work of the founder-mathematicians of the nineteenth century consisted in nothing other than *destroying* the supposed objects and establishing that they could all be designated as particular configurations of the pure multiple. This labour, however, left the structuralist illusion intact, with the result that mathematical technique requires that its own conceptual essence be maintained in obscurity.

Who hasn't spoken, at one time or another, of the relation 'between' elements of a multiple and therefore supposed that a difference in status opposed the elementary inertia of the multiple to its structuration? Who hasn't said 'take a set with a relation of order . . . ', thus giving the impression that this relation was itself something completely different from a set. Each time, however, what is concealed behind this assumption of order is that being knows no other figure of presentation than that of the multiple, and that thus the relation, inasmuch as it is, must be as multiple as the multiple in which it operates.

What we have to do is both to show—in conformity to the necessary ontological critique of the relation—how the setting-into-multiplicity of the structural relation is realized, and how the forgetting of what is said there of being is inevitable, once one is *in a hurry to conclude*—and one always is.

When I declare 'α has the relation R with β', or write $R(\alpha,\beta)$, I am taking two things into consideration: the *couple* made up of α and β, and the *order* according to which they occur. It is possible that $R(\alpha,\beta)$ is true but not $R(\beta,\alpha)$—if, for example, R is a relation of order. The constitutive ingredients of this relational atom $R(\alpha,\beta)$ are thus the idea of the pair, that is, of a multiple composed of two multiples, and the idea of dissymmetry between these two multiples, a dissymmetry marked in writing by the antecedence of α with respect to β.

I will have thus resolved in essence the critical problem of the reduction of any relation to the pure multiple if I succeed in inferring from the Ideas of the multiple—the axioms of set theory—that an ordered or dis-symmetrical pair really *is* a multiple. Why? Because what I will term 'relation' will be a set of ordered pairs. In other words, I will recognize that a multiple belongs to the genre 'relation' if all of its elements, or everything which belongs to it, registers as an ordered pair. If R is such a multiple, and if $<\alpha,\beta>$ is an ordered pair, my reduction to the multiple will consist in substituting, for the statement 'α has the relation R with β', the pure affirmation of the belonging of the ordered pair $<\alpha,\beta>$ to the multiple R; that is, $<\alpha,\beta> \in R$. Objects and relations have disappeared as conceptually distinct types. What remains is only the recognition of certain types of multiples: ordered pairs, and sets of such pairs.

The idea of 'pair' is nothing other than the general concept of the Two, whose existence we have already clarified (Meditation 12). We know that if α and β are two existent multiples, then there also exists the multiple $\{\alpha,\beta\}$, or the pair of α and β, whose sole elements are α and β.

To complete the ordering of the relation, I must now fold back onto the pure multiple the order of inscription of α and β. What I need is a multiple, say $<\alpha,\beta>$, such that $<\beta,\alpha>$ is clearly distinct from it, once α and β are themselves distinct.

The artifice of definition of this multiple, often described as a 'trick' by the mathematicians themselves, is in truth no more artificial than the linear order of writing in the inscription of the relation. It is solely a question of thinking dissymmetry as pure multiple. Of course, there are many ways of doing so, but there are just as many ways if not more to mark in writing that, with respect to another sign, a sign occupies an un-substitutable place. The argument of artifice only concerns this point:

the thought of a bond implies the place of the terms bound, and any inscription of this point is acceptable which maintains the order of places; that is, that α and β cannot be substituted for one another, that they are different. It is not the form-multiple of the relation which is artificial, it is rather the relation itself inasmuch as one pretends to radically distinguish it from what it binds together.

The canonical form of the ordered pair $<\alpha,\beta>$, in which α and β are multiples supposed existent, is written as the pair—the set with two elements—composed of the singleton of α and the pair $\{\alpha,\beta\}$. That is, $<\alpha,\beta>$ = $\{\{\alpha\},\{\alpha,\beta\}\}$. This set exists because the existence of α guarantees the existence of its forming-into-one, and that of α and β guarantees that of the pair $\{\alpha,\beta\}$, and finally the existence of $\{\alpha\}$ and $\{\alpha,\beta\}$ guarantees that of their pair.

It can be easily shown that if α and β are different multiples, $<\alpha,\beta>$ is different to $<\beta,\alpha>$; and, more generally, if $<\alpha,\beta>$ = $<\gamma,\delta>$ then $\alpha = \gamma$ and $\beta = \delta$. The ordered pair prescribes both its terms and their places.

Of course, no clear representation is associated with a set of the type $[\{\alpha\},\{\alpha,\beta\}]$. We will hold, however, that in this unrepresentable there resides the *form of being* subjacent to the idea of a relation.

Once the transliteration of relational formulas of the type $R(\alpha,\beta)$ into the multiple has been accomplished, a relation will be defined without difficulty, being a set such that all of its elements have the form of ordered pairs; that is, they realize within the multiple the figure of the dis-symmetrical couple in which the entire effect of inscribed relations resides. From then on, declaring that α maintains the relation R with β will solely mean that $<\alpha,\beta> \in R$; thus belonging will finally retrieve its unique role of articulating discourse upon the multiple, and folding within it that which, according to the structuralist illusion, would form an exception to it. A relation, R, is none other than a *species* of multiple, qualified by the particular nature of what belongs to it, which, in turn, is a species of multiple: the ordered pair.

The classical concept of function is a branch of the genre 'relation'. When I write $f(\alpha) = \beta$, I mean that *to* the multiple α I make the multiple β, and β alone, 'correspond.' Say that R_f is the multiple which is *the being of f*. I have, of course, $<\alpha,\beta> \in R_f$. But if R_f is a function, it is because for α fixed in the first place of the ordered pair β is unique. Therefore, a function is a multiple R_f exclusively made up of ordered pairs, which are also such that:

$$[(<a,\beta> \in R_f) \; \& \; (<a,\gamma> \in R_f)] \rightarrow (\beta = \gamma)$$

I have thus completed the reduction of the concepts of relation and function to that of a special type of multiple.

However the mathematician—and myself—will not burden himself for long with having to write, according to the being of presentation, not $R(\beta,\gamma)$ but $<\beta,\gamma> \in R$, with moreover, for β and γ elements of a, the consideration that R 'in a' is in fact an element of $p(p(p(a)))$. He will sooner say 'take the relation R defined on a', and write it $R(\beta,\gamma)$ or $\beta \; R \; \gamma$. The fact that the relation R is only a multiple is immediately concealed by this form of writing: it invincibly restores the conceptual difference between the relation and the 'bound' terms. In this point, the technique of abbreviation, despite being inevitable, nonetheless encapsulates a conceptual *forgetting*; and this is the form in which the forgetting of being takes place in mathematics, that is, the forgetting of the following: there is nothing presented within it save presentation. The structuralist illusion, which reconstitutes the operational autonomy of the relation, and distinguishes it from the inertia of the multiple, is the forgetful technical domination through which mathematics realizes the discourse on being-qua-being. It is necessary to mathematics to forget being in order to pursue its pronunciation. For the law of being, constantly maintained, would eventually prohibit writing by overloading it and altering it without mercy.

Being *does not want to be written*: the testimony to this resides in the following; when one attempts to render transparent the presentation of presentation the difficulties of writing become almost immediately irresolvable. The structuralist illusion is thus an imperative of reason, which overcomes the prohibition on writing generated by the weight of being by the forgetting of the pure multiple and by the conceptual assumption of the bond and the object. In this forgetting, mathematics is technically victorious, and pronounces being without knowing what it is pronouncing. We can agree, without forcing the matter, that the 'turn' forever realized, through which the science of being institutes itself solely by losing all lucidity with respect to what founds it, is literally the staging of beings (of objects and relations) instead of and in the place of being (the presentation of presentation, the pure multiple). Actual mathematics is thus the metaphysics of the ontology that it is. It is, in its essence, *forgetting of itself*.

The essential difference from the Heideggerean interpretation of metaphysics—and of its technical culmination—is that even if mathematical technique requires forgetting, by right, via a uniform procedure, it also authorizes at any moment the formal restitution of its forgotten theme. Even if I have accumulated relational or functional abbreviations, even if I have continually spoken of 'objects', even if I have ceaselessly propagated the structuralist illusion, I am guaranteed that I can immediately return, by means of a regulated interpretation of my technical haste, to original definitions, to the Ideas of the multiple: I can dissolve anew the pretension to separateness on the part of functions and relations, and re-establish the reign of the pure multiple. Even if practical mathematics is necessarily carried out within the forgetting of itself—for this is the price of its victorious advance—the option of de-stratification is always available: it is through such de-stratification that the structuralist illusion is submitted to critique; it restitutes the multiple alone as what is presented, there being no object, everything being woven from the proper name of the void. This availability means quite clearly that if the forgetting of being is the law of mathematical effectivity, what is just as forbidden for mathematics, at least since Cantor, is the forgetting of the forgetting.

I thus spoke incorrectly of 'technique' if this word is taken in Heidegger's sense. For him the empire of technique is that of nihilism, the loss of the forgetting itself, and thus the end of metaphysics inasmuch as metaphysics is still animated by that first form of forgetting which is the reign of the supreme being. In this sense, mathematical ontology is not technical, because the unveiling of the origin is not an unfathomable virtuality, it is rather an intrinsically available option, a permanent possibility. Mathematics regulates in and by itself the possibility of deconstructing the apparent order of the object and the liaison, and of retrieving the original 'disorder' in which it pronounces the Ideas of the pure multiple and their suture to being-qua-being by the proper name of the void. It is both the forgetting of itself and the critique of that forgetting. It is the *turn* towards the object, but also the *return* towards the presentation of presentation.

This is why, in itself, mathematics cannot—however artificial its procedures may be—stop belonging to Thought.

APPENDIX 3 (Meditation 26)
Heterogeneity of the cardinals: regularity and singularity

We saw (Meditation 14) that the homogeneity of the ontological schema of natural multiples—ordinals—admits a breach, that distinguishing successors from limit ordinals. The natural multiples which form the measuring scale for intrinsic size—the cardinals—admit a still more profound breach, which opposes 'undecomposable' or regular cardinals to 'decomposable' or singular cardinals. Just as the existence of a limit ordinal must be decided upon—this is the substance of the axiom of infinity—the existence of a regular limit cardinal superior to ω_0 (to the denumerable) cannot be inferred from the Ideas of the multiple, and so it presupposes a new decision, a kind of axiom of infinity for cardinals. It is the latter which detains the concept of an inaccessible cardinal. The progression towards infinity is thus incomplete if one confines oneself to the first decision. In the order of infinite quantities, one can still wager upon the existence of infinities which surpass the infinities previously admitted by as much as the first infinity ω_0 surpasses the finite. On this route, which imposes itself on mathematicians at the very place, the impasse, to which they were led by the errancy of the state, the following types of cardinals have been successively defined: weakly inaccessible, strongly inaccessible, Mahlo, Ramsey, measurable, ineffable, compact, supercompact, extendable, huge. These grandiose fictions reveal that the resources of being in terms of intrinsic size cause thought to falter and lead it close to the breaking point of language, since, as Thomas Jech says, 'with the definition of huge cardinals we approach the point of rupture presented by inconsistency.'

The initial conditions are simple enough. Let's suppose that a given cardinal is cut into pieces, that is, into parts such that their union would reassemble the entirety of the cardinal-multiple under consideration. Each of these pieces has itself a certain power, represented by a cardinal. It is sure that this power is *at the most* equal to that of the entirety, because it is a part which is at stake. Moreover, the number of pieces also has itself a certain power. A finite image of this manipulation is very simple: if you cut a set of 17 elements into one piece of 2, one of 5, and another of 10, you end up with a set of parts whose power is 3 (3 pieces), each part possessing a power inferior to that of the initial set (2, 5 and 10 are inferior to 17). The finite cardinal 17 can thus be decomposed into a *number* of *pieces* such that *both* this number *and* each of the pieces has a power inferior to its own. This can be written as:

$$17 = \underbrace{2 + 5 + 10}_{\text{3 parts}}$$

If, on the other hand, you consider the first infinite cardinal, ω_0—the set of whole numbers—the same thing does not occur. If a piece of ω_0 has an inferior power to that of ω_0, this is because it is finite, since ω_0 is the *first* infinite cardinal. And if the number of pieces is also inferior to ω_0, this is also because it is finite. However, it is clear that a finite number of finite pieces can solely generate, if the said pieces are 'glued back together' again, a finite set. We cannot hope to *compose* ω_0 out of pieces smaller than it (in the sense of intrinsic size, of cardinality) whose number is also smaller than it. At least one of these pieces has to be infinite *or* the number of pieces must be so. In any case, you will need the name-number ω_0 in order to compose ω_0. On the other hand, 2, 5 and 10, all inferior to 17, allow it to be attained, despite their number, 3, also being inferior to 17.

Here we have quantitative determinations which are very different, especially in the case of infinite cardinals. If you can decompose a multiple into a series of sub-multiples such that each is smaller than it, and also their number, then one can say that this multiple is composable 'from the base'; it is *accessible* in terms of quantitative combinations issued from what is inferior to it. If this is not possible (as in the case of ω_0), the intrinsic size is in position of rupture, it *begins with itself*, and there is no access to it proposed by decompositions which do not yet involve it.

A cardinal which is not decomposable, or accessible from the base, will be said to be *regular*. A cardinal which is accessible from the base will be said to be *singular*.

To be precise, a cardinal ω_a will be termed singular if there exists a smaller cardinal than ω_a, ω_β, and a family of ω_β parts of ω_a, each of these parts itself having a power inferior to ω_a, such that the union of this family reassembles ω_a.

If we agree to write the power of an indeterminate multiple as $|a|$ (that is, the cardinal which has the same power as it, thus the smallest ordinal which has the same power as it), the singularity of ω_a will be written in this manner, naming the pieces A_γ:

$$\underbrace{\omega_a = \bigcup_{\gamma \in \omega\beta} A_\gamma}_{\substack{\omega_a \text{ is reassembled} \\ \text{by } \dots}} \text{ with } \underbrace{A_\gamma \subset \omega_a}_{\text{pieces}} \And \underbrace{\omega_\beta < \omega_a}_{\substack{\text{in number} \\ \text{inferior to } \omega_a}} \And \underbrace{|A_\gamma| < \omega_a}_{\substack{\text{each piece having} \\ \text{itself a power inferior to } \omega_a}}$$

A cardinal ω_a is regular if it is not singular. Therefore, what is required for its composition is either that a piece already has the power ω_a, or that the number of pieces has the power ω_a.

1st question: Do regular infinite cardinals exist?

Yes. We saw that ω_0 is regular. It cannot be composed of a finite number of finite pieces.

2nd question: Do singular infinite cardinals exist?

Yes. I mentioned in Meditation 26 the limit cardinal $\omega_{(\omega_0)}$, which comes just 'after' the series $\omega_0, \omega_1, \dots, \omega_n, \omega_{S(n)}, \dots$ This cardinal is immensely larger than ω_0. However, it is singular. To understand how this is so, all one has to do is consider that it is the union of the cardinals ω_n, all of which are smaller than it. The number of these cardinals is precisely ω_0, since they are indexed by the whole numbers $0, 1, \dots n, \dots$ The cardinal $\omega_{(\omega_0)}$ can thus be composed on the basis of ω_0 elements smaller than it.

3rd question: Are there other regular infinite cardinals apart from ω_0?

Yes. It can be shown that every successor cardinal is regular. We saw that a cardinal ω_β is a successor if a ω_a exists such that $\omega_a < \omega_\beta$, and there is no other cardinal 'between them'; that is, that no ω_γ exists such that $\omega_a < \omega_\gamma < \omega_\beta$. It is said that ω_a is the successor of ω_β. It is clear that ω_0 and $\omega_{(\omega_0)}$ are not successors (they are limit cardinals), because if $\omega_n < \omega_{(\omega_0)}$, for example, there always remains an infinity of cardinals between ω_n and $\omega_{(\omega_0)}$, such as $\omega_{S(n)}$ and $\omega_{S(S(n))}, \dots$ All of this conforms to the concept of infinity used in Meditation 13.

That every successor cardinal be regular is not at all evident. This non-evidence assumes the technical form, in fact quite unexpected, of it being necessary to use the axiom of choice in order to demonstrate it. The form of intervention is thus required in order to decide that *each* intrinsic size obtained by 'one more step' (by a succession) is a pure beginning; that is, it cannot be composed from what is inferior to it.

This point reveals a general connection between intervention and the 'one more step'.

The common conception is that what happens 'at the limit' is more complex than what happens in one sole supplementary step. One of the weaknesses of the ontologies of Presence is their validation of this conception. The mysterious and captivating effect of these ontologies, which mobilize the resources of the poem, is that of installing us in the premonition of being as beyond and horizon, as maintenance and opening-forth of being-in-totality. As such, an ontology of Presence will always maintain that operations 'at the limit' present the real peril of thought, the moment at which opening to the bursting forth of what is serial in experience marks out the incomplete and the open through which being is delivered. Mathematical ontology warns us of the contrary. In truth, the cardinal limit does not contain anything more than that which precedes it, and whose union it operates. It is thus determined by the inferior quantities. The successor, on the other hand, is in a position of genuine excess, since it must locally surpass what precedes it. As such—and this is a teaching of great political value, or aesthetic value—it is not the global gathering together 'at the limit' which is innovative and complex, it is rather the realization, on the basis of the point at which one finds oneself, of the one-more of a step. Intervention is an instance of the point, not of the place. The limit is a composition, not an intervention. In the terms of the ontology of quantity, the limit cardinals, in general, are singular (they can be composed from the base), and the successor cardinals are regular, but to know this, we need the axiom of choice.

4th question: A singular cardinal is 'decomposable' into a number, which is smaller than it, of pieces which are smaller than it. But surely this decomposition cannot descend indefinitely?

Evidently. By virtue of the law of minimality supported by natural multiples (cf. Meditation 12 and Appendix 2), and thus by the cardinals, there necessarily exists a smallest cardinal ω_β which is such that the cardinal ω_α can be decomposed into ω_β pieces, all smaller than it. This is, one could say, the maximal decomposition of ω_α. It is termed the *cofinality* of ω_a, and we will write it as $c(\omega_a)$. A cardinal is singular if its cofinality really is smaller than it (it *is* decomposable); that is, if $c(\omega_a) < \omega_a$. With a regular cardinal, if one covers it with pieces smaller than it, then the number of these pieces has to be equal to it. In this case, $c(\omega_a) = \omega_a$.

5th question. Right; one has, for example, $c(\omega_0) = \omega_0$ (regular) and $c(\omega_{(\omega_0)}) = \omega_0$ (singular). If what you say about successor cardinals is true—that they are all regular—one has, for example, $c(\omega_3) = \omega_3$. But I ask you, aren't there limit cardinals, other than ω_0, which are regular? Because all the limit cardinals which I represent to myself—$\omega_{(\omega_0)}$, $\omega_{(\omega_0)(\omega_0)}$, and the others—are singular. They all have ω_0 as their cofinality.

The question immediately transports us into the depths of ontology, and especially those of the being of infinity. The first infinity, the denumerable, possesses the characteristic of combining the limit *and* this form of pure beginning which is regularity. It denies what I maintained above because it accumulates within itself the complexities of the one-more-step (regularity) and the apparent profundity of the limit. This is because the cardinal ω_0 is in truth the one-more-limit-step that is the tipping over of the finite into the infinite. It is a frontier cardinal between two regimes of presentation. It incarnates the ontological decision on infinity, a decision which actually remained on the horizon of thought for a very long time. It punctuates that instance of the horizon, and this is why it is the Chimera of a limit-point, that is, of a regular or undecomposable limit.

If there was another regular limit cardinal, it would relegate the infinite cardinals, in relation to its eminence, to the same rank as that occupied by the finite numbers in relation to ω_0. It would operate a type of 'finitization' of the preceding infinities, inasmuch as, despite being their limit, it would exceed them radically, since it would in no way be composable from them.

The Ideas of the multiple which we have laid out up to the present moment do not allow one to establish the existence of a regular limit cardinal apart from ω_0. It can be *demonstrated* that they would not allow such. The existence of such a cardinal (and necessarily it would be already absolutely immensely large) consequently requires an axiomatic decision, which confirms that what is at stake is a reiteration of the gesture by which thought opens up to the infinity of being.

A cardinal superior to ω_0 which is both regular and limit is termed *weakly accessible*. The axiom that I spoke of is stated as follows: 'A weakly accessible cardinal exists'. It is the first in the long possible series of *new* axioms of infinity.

APPENDIX 4 (Meditation 29)
Every ordinal is constructible

Just as the orientation of the entirety of ontology might lead one to believe, the schema of natural multiples is submitted to language. Nature is universally *nameable*.

First of all, let's examine the case of the first ordinal, the void.

We know that $L_0 = \varnothing$. The sole part of the void being the void (Meditation 8), it is enough to establish that the void is definable, In the constructible sense, within L_0—that is, within the void—to conclude that the void is the element of L_1. This adjustment of language's jurisdiction to the unpresentable is not without interest. Let's consider, for example, the formula $(\exists \beta)[\beta \in \gamma]$. If we restrict it to L_0, thus to the void, its sense will be 'there exists an element of the void which is an element of γ'. It is clear that no γ can satisfy this formula in L_0 because L_0 does not contain anything. Consequently, the part of L_0 separated by this formula is void. The void set is thus a definable part of the void. It is the unique element of the superior level, $L_{s(\varnothing)}$, or L_1, which is equal to $D(L_0)$. Therefore we have $L_{s(\varnothing)} = \{\varnothing\}$, the singleton of the void. The result is that $\varnothing \in L_{s(\varnothing)}$, which is what we wanted to demonstrate: the void *belongs* to a constructible level. It is therefore constructible.

Now, if not all the ordinals are constructible, there exists, by the principle of minimality (Meditation 12 and Appendix 1), a smallest non-constructible ordinal. Say that α is that ordinal. It is not the void (we have just seen that the void is constructible). For $\beta \in \alpha$, we know that β, smaller than α, is constructible. Let's suppose that it is possible to find a level L_γ, in which *all* the (constructible) elements β of α appear, and no other ordinal. The formula 'δ is an ordinal', with one free variable, will separate within

L_γ the definable part constituted from all these ordinals. It will do so because 'to be an ordinal' means (Meditation 12); 'to be a transitive multiple whose elements are all transitive', and this is a formula without parameters (it does not depend on any particular multiple—which would possibly be absent from L_γ). But the set of ordinals inferior to α is α itself, which is thus a definable part of L_γ, and is thus an element of $L_{S(\gamma)}$. In contradiction with our hypothesis, α is constructible.

What we have not yet established is whether there actually is *a* level L_γ, which contains all the constructible ordinals β, for $\beta \in \alpha$. To do so, it is sufficient to establish that every constructible level is transitive, that is, that $\beta \in L_\gamma \rightarrow \beta \subset L_\gamma$. For every ordinal smaller than an ordinal situated in a level will also belong to that level. It suffices to consider the level L_γ as the *maximum* for all the levels to which the $\beta \in \alpha$ belong: all of these ordinals will appear in it.

Hence the following lemma, which moreover clarifies the structure of the constructible hierarchy: every level L_α of the constructible hierarchy is transitive.

This is demonstrated by recurrence on the ordinals.

- $L_0 = \varnothing$ is transitive (Meditation 12);
- let's suppose that every level inferior to L_α is transitive, and show that L_α is also transitive.

1st case:

The set α is a limit ordinal. In this case, L_α is the union of all the inferior levels, which are all supposed transitive. The result is that if $\gamma \in L_\alpha$, a level L_β exists, with $\beta \in \alpha$, such that $\gamma \in L_\beta$. But since L_β is supposed to be transitive, we have $\gamma \subset L_\beta$. Yet L_α, union of the inferior levels, admits all of them as parts: $L_\beta \subset L_\alpha$. From $\gamma \subset L_\beta$ and $L_\beta \subset L_\alpha$, we get $\gamma \subset L_\alpha$. Thus the level L_α is transitive.

2nd case:

The set α is a successor ordinal, $L_\alpha = L_{S(\beta)}$.

Let's show first that $L_\beta \subset L_{S(\beta)}$ if L_β is supposed transitive (this is induced by the hypothesis of recurrence).

Say that γ_1 is an element of L_β. Let's consider the formula $\delta \in \gamma_1$. Since L_β is transitive, $\gamma_1 \in L_\beta \rightarrow \gamma_1 \subset L_\beta$. Therefore, $\delta \in \gamma_1 \rightarrow \delta \in L_\beta$. All the elements of γ_1 are also elements of L_β. The part of L_β defined by the formula $\delta \in \gamma_1$ coincides with γ_1 because all the elements δ of γ_1 are in L_β and as such this formula is clearly restricted to L_β. Consequently, γ_1 is *also* a definable part of L_β, whence it follows that it is an element of $\mathsf{L}_{s(\beta)}$. Finally we have: $\gamma_1 \in \mathsf{L}_\beta \rightarrow \gamma_1 \in \mathsf{L}_{s(\beta)}$, that is, $\mathsf{L}_\beta \subset \mathsf{L}_{s(\beta)}$.

This allows us to conclude. An element of $\mathsf{L}_{s(\beta)}$ is a (definable) part of L_β, that is: $\gamma \in \mathsf{L}_{s(\beta)} \rightarrow \gamma \subset \mathsf{L}_\beta$. But $\mathsf{L}_\beta \subset \mathsf{L}_{s(\beta)}$. Therefore, $\gamma \subset \mathsf{L}_{s(\beta)}$, and $\mathsf{L}_{s(\beta)}$ is transitive.

The recurrence is complete. The first level L_0 is transitive; and if all the levels up until L_a excluded are also transitive, so is L_a. Therefore every level is transitive.

APPENDIX 5 (Meditation 33)

On absoluteness

The task here is to establish the absoluteness of a certain number of terms and formulas for a quasi-complete situation. Remember, this means that the definition of the term is 'the same' relativized to the situation S as it is in general ontology, and that the formula relativized to S is equivalent to the general formula, once the parameters are restricted to belonging to S.

 a. $\varnothing$. This is obvious, because the definition of $\varnothing$ is negative (nothing belongs to it). It cannot be 'modified' in S. Moreover, $\varnothing \in S$, insofar as S is transitive and it satisfies the axiom of foundation. That is, the void alone (Meditation 18) can found a transitive multiple.
 b. $\alpha \subset \beta$ is absolute, in the sense in which *if α and β belong to S then* the formula $\alpha \subset \beta$ is true for an inhabitant of S if and only if it is true for the ontologist. This can be directly inferred from the transitivity of S: the elements of α and of β are also elements of S. Therefore, if all the elements of α (in the sense of S) belong to β—which is the definition of inclusion—then the same occurs in the sense of general ontology, and vice versa.
 c. ● $\alpha \cup \beta$: if α and β are elements of S, the set $\{\alpha,\beta\}$ also exists in S, by the validity within S of the axiom of replacement: applied, for example, to the Two that is $p(\varnothing)$, which exists in S, because $\varnothing \in S$ and because the axiom of the powerset is veridical in S (see this construction in Meditation 12). In passing, we can also verify that $p(\varnothing)$ is absolute (in general, $p(\alpha)$ is *not* absolute). In the same

manner, $\cup$ $\{\alpha,\beta\}$ exists within S, because the axiom of union is veridical in S. And $\cup$ $\{\alpha,\beta\} = \alpha \cup \beta$ by definition.

● $\alpha \cap \beta$ is obtained via separation within $\alpha \cup \beta$ via the formula '$\gamma \in \alpha$ & $\gamma \in \beta$'.

It is enough that *this* axiom of separation be veridical in S.

● $(\alpha - \beta)$, the set of elements of α which are not elements of β, is obtained in the same manner, via the formula '$\gamma \in \alpha$ & $\sim(\gamma \in \beta)$'.

d. We have just seen the pair $\{\alpha,\beta\}$ (in the absoluteness of $\alpha \cup \beta$). The ordered pair—to recall—is defined as follows, $<\alpha,\beta> = \{\{\alpha\},\{\alpha,\beta\}\}$ (see Appendix 2). Its absoluteness is then trivial.

e. 'To be an ordered pair' comes down to the formula; 'To be a simple pair whose first term is a singleton, and the second a simple pair of which one element appears in the singleton'. Exercise: write this formula in formal language, and meditate upon its absoluteness.

f. If α and β belong to S, the Cartesian product $\alpha \times \beta$ is defined as the set of ordered pairs $<\gamma,\delta>$ with $\gamma \in \alpha$ and $\delta \in \beta$. The elements of the Cartesian product are obtained by the formula 'to be an ordered pair whose first term belongs to α and the second to β'. This formula thus separates the Cartesian product within any set in which all the elements of α and all those of β appear. For example, in the set $\alpha \cup \beta$. $\alpha \times \beta$ is an absolute operation, and 'to be an ordered pair' an absolute predicate. It follows that the Cartesian product is absolute.

g. The formula 'to be an ordinal' has no parameters, and envelops transitivity alone (cf. Meditation 12). It is a simple exercise to work out its absoluteness (Appendix 4 shows the absoluteness of 'to be an ordinal' for the constructible universe).

h. ω_0 is absolute, inasmuch as it is defined as 'the smallest limit ordinal', that is, the 'smallest non-successor ordinal'. It is thus necessary to study the absoluteness of the predicate 'to be a successor ordinal'. Of course, the fact that $\omega_0 \in S$ may be inferred from S verifying the axiom of infinity.

i. On the basis that 'to be a limit ordinal' is absolute, one can infer that 'to be a function' is absolute. It is the formula: 'to have ordered pairs $<\alpha,\beta>$ as elements such that if $<\alpha,\beta>$ is an element and also $<\alpha,\beta'>$, then one has $\beta = \beta'$' (cf. the ontological definition of a function in Appendix 2). In the same manner, 'to be a one-to-one function' is absolute. A finite part is a set which is in one-to-one correspondence with a finite ordinal. Because ω_0 is absolute, the same thing goes for finite ordinals. Thus, if $\alpha \in S$, the predicate 'to be a finite part of S' is absolute. If, via this predicate, one separates within $[p(a)]^S$—which, itself, is not absolute—one clearly obtains all the finite parts of a (in the sense of general ontology), in spite of $[p(a)]^S$ *not* being identical, in general, to $p(a)$. This results from it being solely the *infinite* multiples amongst the elements of $p(a)$ which cannot be presented in S, such that $p(a) \neq [p(a)]^S$. But for the finite parts, given that 'to be a one-to-one function of a finite ordinal on a part of a' is absolute, the result is that they are all presented in S. Therefore, the set of finite parts of a is absolute.

All of these results authorize us to consider that conditions of the type 'all the finite series of triplets $<a,n,0>$ or $<a,n,1>$, where $a \in \delta$ and $n \in \omega_0$' can be *known* by an inhabitant of S (if δ is known), because the formula which defines such a multiple of conditions is absolute for S ('finite series', 'triplet', 0, 1, ω_0 ... are all absolute).

APPENDIX 6 (Meditation 36)
Primitive signs of logic and recurrence on the length of formulas

This Appendix completes Meditation 3's Technical Note, and shows how to reason via recurrence on the length of formulas. I use this occasion to speak briefly about reasoning via recurrence in general.

1. DEFINITION OF CERTAIN LOGICAL SIGNS

The complete array of logical signs (cf. the Technical Note at Meditation 3) should not be considered as made up of the same number of primitive signs. Just as inclusion, $\subset$, can be *defined* on the basis of belonging, $\in$ (cf. Meditation 5), one can define certain logical signs on the basis of others.

The choice of primitive signs is a matter of convention. Here I choose the signs $\sim$ (negation), $\rightarrow$ (implication), and $\exists$ (existential quantification). The derived signs are then introduced, by definitions, as *abbreviations* of certain writings made up of the primitive signs.

a. Disjunction (*or*): A *or* B is an abbreviation for $\sim$A $\rightarrow$ B;
b. Conjunction (&): A & B is an abbreviation for $\sim$(A $\rightarrow$ $\sim$B);
c. Equivalence ($\leftrightarrow$): A $\leftrightarrow$ B is an abbreviation for $\sim$((A $\rightarrow$ B) $\rightarrow$ $\sim$(B $\rightarrow$ A));
d. The universal quantifier ($\forall$): ($\forall a$)λ is an abbreviation for $\sim$($\exists a$)$\sim\lambda$.

Therefore, it is possible to consider that any logical formula is written using the signs $\sim$, $\rightarrow$ and $\exists$ alone. To secure the formulas of set theory, it suffices to add the signs = and $\in$, plus, of course, the variables a, β, γ etc., which designate the multiples, and also the punctuation.

We can then distinguish between:

- atomic formulas, without a logical sign, which are necessarily of the type $\alpha = \beta$ or $\alpha \in \beta$;
- and composed formulas, which are of the type $\sim\lambda$, $\lambda_1 \rightarrow \lambda_2$, or $(\exists\alpha)\lambda$, where λ is either an atomic formula, or a 'shorter' composed formula.

2. RECURRENCE ON THE LENGTH OF FORMULAS

Note that a formula is a finite set of signs, counting the variables, the logical signs, the signs = and $\exists$, and the parentheses, brackets, or square brackets. It is thus always possible to speak of the *length* of a formula, which is the (whole) number of signs which appear in it.

This association of a whole number with every formula allows the application to formulas of reasoning via recurrence, a form of reasoning that we have used often in this book for whole numbers and finite ordinals just as for ordinals in general.

Any reasoning by recurrence supposes that one can univocally speak of the 'next one' after a given set of terms under consideration. In fact, it is an operator for the rational mastery of infinity based on the procedure of 'still one more' (cf. Meditation 14). The subjacent structure is that of a well-ordering: because the terms which have *not yet* been examined contain a smallest element, this smallest element immediately *follows* those that I have already examined. As such, given an ordinal α, I know its unique successor $S(\alpha)$. Furthermore, given a set of ordinals, even infinite, I know *the one* that comes directly afterwards (which is perhaps a limit ordinal, but it does not matter).

The schema for this reasoning is thus the following (in three steps):

1. I show that the property to be established holds for *the smallest* term (or ordinal) in question. Most often, this means $\varnothing$.
2. I then show that *if* the property to be established holds for all the terms which are smaller than an indeterminate term α, *then* it holds for α itself, which is *the* one following the preceding terms.
3. I conclude that it holds for *all* of the terms.

This conclusion is valid for the following reason: if the property did not hold for all terms, *there would be a smallest term which would not possess it.*

Given all those terms smaller than the latter term; that is, all those which actually possess the property, this supposed smallest term without the property would have to possess it, by virtue of the second step of reasoning by recurrence. Contradiction. Therefore, all terms possess the property.

Let's return to the formulas. The 'smallest' formulas are the atomic ones $\alpha = \beta$ or $\alpha \in \beta$, which have three signs. Let's suppose that I have demonstrated a certain property, for example, forcing, for these, the shortest formulas (I consecrate Section 1 of Meditation 36, and Appendix 7 to this demonstration). This is the first step of reasoning by recurrence.

Now let's suppose that I have shown the theorem of forcing for all the formulas *of a length inferior to* $n + 1$ (which have less than $n + 1$ signs). The second step consists in showing that there is also forcing for formulas of $n + 1$ signs. But how can I obtain, on the basis of formulas with n signs at most, a formula of $n + 1$ signs? There are only three ways of doing so:

- if (λ) has n signs, $\sim(\lambda)$ has $n + 1$ signs;
- if (λ_1) and (λ_2) have n signs *together*, $(\lambda_1) \rightarrow (\lambda_2)$ has $n + 1$ signs;
- if (λ) has $n - 3$ signs, $(\exists a)(\lambda)$ has $n + 1$ signs.

Thus, I must finally show that *if* the formulas (λ), or the total of the formulas (λ_1) and (λ_2), have less than $n + 1$ signs, and verify the property (here, forcing), *then* the formulas with $n + 1$ signs, which are $\sim(\lambda)$, $(\lambda_1) \rightarrow (\lambda_2)$, and $(\exists a)(\lambda)$, also verify it.

I can then conclude (third step) that *all* the formulas verify the property, that forcing is *defined* for any formula of set theory.

APPENDIX 7 (Meditation 36)

Forcing of equality for names of the nominal rank 0

The task is to establish the existence of a relation of forcing, noted $\equiv$, defined in S, for formulas of the type '$\mu_1 = \mu_2$', where μ_1 and μ_2 are names of the rank 0 (that is, names made up of pairs $<\varnothing,\pi>$ in which π is a condition). This relation must hold such that:

$$[\pi \equiv (\mu_1 = \mu_2)] \leftrightarrow [(\pi \in \female) \rightarrow [R_\female(\mu_1) = R_\female(\mu_2)]]$$

First we will investigate the *direct* proposition (the forcing by π of the equality of names implies the equality of the referential values, given that $\pi \in \female$), and then we will look at the *reciprocal* proposition (if the referential values are equal, then a $\pi \in \female$ exists and it, π, forces the equality of the names). For the reciprocal proposition, however, we will only treat the case in which $R_\female(\mu_1) = \varnothing$.

1. DIRECT PROPOSITION

Let's suppose that μ_1 is a name of the nominal rank 0. It is made up of pairs $<\varnothing,\pi,>$, and its referential value is either $\{\varnothing\}$ or $\varnothing$ depending on whether or not at least one of the conditions π which appears in its composition belongs to $\female$ (cf. Meditation 34, Section 4).

Let's begin with the formula $\mu_1 = \varnothing$ (remember that $\varnothing$ is a name). To be certain that one has $R_\female(\mu_1) = R_\female(\varnothing) = \varnothing$, none of the conditions which appear in the name must belong to the generic part $\female$. What could force such a prohibition of belonging? The following: the part $\female$ contains a condition *incompatible* with all the other conditions which appear in the name μ_1. That is, the rule Rd_2 of correct parts (Meditation 33, Section 3) entails that all of the conditions of a correct part are compatible.

Let's write $Inc(\mu_1)$ for the set of conditions that are incompatible with all the conditions which appear in the name μ_1:

$Inc(\mu_1) = \{\pi \; / \; (<\varnothing, \pi_1> \in \mu_1) \to \pi$ and π_1 are incompatible$\}$

It is certain that if $\pi \in Inc(\mu_1)$, the belonging of π to a generic part $\female$ prohibits all the conditions which appear in μ_1 from belonging to this $\female$. The result is that the referential value of μ_1 in the extension which corresponds to this generic part is void.

We will thus pose that π forces the formula $\mu_1 = \varnothing$ (in which μ_1 is of the nominal rank 0) if $\pi \in Inc(\mu_1)$. It is clear that if π forces $\mu_1 = \varnothing$, we have $R_\female(\mu_1) = R_\female(\varnothing) = \varnothing$ in any generic extension such that $\pi \in \female$.

Thus, for μ_1 of the nominal rank 0 we can posit:

$[\pi \equiv (\mu_1 = \varnothing)] \leftrightarrow \pi \in Inc(\mu_1)$

The statement $\pi \in Inc(\mu_1)$ is entirely intelligible and verifiable *within* the fundamental situation. Nonetheless, it manages to force the statement $R_\female(\mu_1) = \varnothing$ to be veridical in any generic extension such that $\pi \in \female$.

Armed with this, the first of our results, we are going to attack the formula $\mu_1 \subset \mu_2$, again for names of the nominal rank 0. The strategy is the following: we know that '$\mu_1 \subset \mu_2$ and $\mu_2 \subset \mu_1$' implies $\mu_1 = \mu_2$. If we know, in a general manner, how to force $\mu_1 \subset \mu_2$, then we will know how to force $\mu_1 = \mu_2$.

If μ_1 and μ_2 are of the nominal rank 0, the referential values of these two names arc $\varnothing$ and $\{\varnothing\}$. We want to force the veracity of $R_\female(\mu_1) \subset R_\female(\mu_2)$. Table 3 shows the four possible cases.

$R_\female(\mu_1)$	$R_\female(\mu_2)$	$R_\female(\mu_1) \subset R_\female(\mu_2)$	**reason**
$\varnothing$	$\varnothing$	veridical	$\left.\begin{array}{c} \\ \\ \end{array}\right\} \; \varnothing$ is universal
$\varnothing$	$\{\varnothing\}$	veridical	part
$\{\varnothing\}$	$\{\varnothing\}$	veridical	$\{\varnothing\} \subset \{\varnothing\}$
$\{\varnothing\}$	$\varnothing$	erroneous	$\sim(\{\varnothing\} \subset \varnothing)$

If $R_\female(\mu_1) = \varnothing$, the veracity of the inclusion is guaranteed. It is also guaranteed if $R_\female(\mu_1) = R_\female(\mu_2) = \{\varnothing\}$. All we have to do is eliminate the fourth case.

Let's suppose, first of all, that $Inc(\mu_1)$ is not void: there exists $\pi \in Inc(\mu_1)$. We have seen that such a condition π forces the formula $\mu_1 = \varnothing$, that is, the veracity of $R_\female(\mu_1) = \varnothing$ in a generic extension such that $\pi \in \female$. It thus also forces $\mu_1 \subset \mu_2$, because then $R_\female(\mu_1) \subset R_\female(\mu_2)$ whatever the value of $R_\female(\mu_2)$ is.

If $Inc(\mu_1)$ is now void (in the fundamental situation, which is possible), let's note $App(\mu_1)$ the set of conditions which appear in the name μ_1.

$App(\mu_1) = \{\pi \; / \; \exists <\varnothing,\pi> \; [<\varnothing,\pi> \in \mu_1]\}$

Same thing for $App(\mu_2)$. Note that these are two sets of conditions. Let us suppose that a condition π_3 exists which dominates at least one condition of $App(\mu_1)$ and at least one condition of $App(\mu_2)$. If $\pi_3 \in \female$, the rule Rd_1 of correct parts entails that the dominated conditions also belong to it. Consequently, there is at least one condition of $App(\mu_1)$ and one of $App(\mu_2)$ which are in $\female$. It follows that, for this description, the referential value of μ_1 and of μ_2 is $\{\varnothing\}$. We then have $R_\female(\mu_1) \subset R_\female(\mu_2)$. It is thus possible to say that the condition π_3 forces the formula $\mu_1 \subset \mu_2$, because $\pi_3 \in \female$ implies $R_\female(\mu_1) \subset R_\female(\mu_2)$.

Let's generalize this procedure slightly. We will term *reserve of domination* for a condition π_1 any set of conditions such that a condition dominated by π_1 can always be found amongst them. That is, if R is a reserve of domination for π_1:

$(\exists \pi_2) \; [(\pi_2 \subset \pi_1) \; \& \; \pi_2 \in R]$

This means that if $\pi_1 \in \female$, one always finds in R a condition which also belongs to $\female$, because it is dominated by π_1. The condition π_1 being given, one can always verify *within the fundamental situation* (without considering any generic extension in particular) whether R is, or is not, a reserve of domination for π_1, since the relation $\pi_2 \subset \pi_1$ is absolute.

Let's return to $\mu_1 \subset \mu_2$, where μ_1 and μ_2 are of the nominal rank 0. Let's suppose that $App(\mu_1)$ and $App(\mu_2)$ are reserves of domination for a condition π_3. That is, there exists a $\pi_1 \in App(\mu_1)$, with $\pi_1 \subset \pi_3$, and there also exists a $\pi_2 \in App(\mu_2)$ with $\pi_2 \subset \pi_3$. Now, if π_3 belongs to $\female$, π_1 and π_2 also belong to it (rule Rd_1). Since π_1 and π_2 are conditions which appear in the names μ_1 and μ_2, the result is that the referential value of these names for this description is $\{\varnothing\}$. We therefore have $R_\female(\mu_1) \subset R_\female(\mu_2)$. Thus we can say that π_3 forces $\mu_1 \subset \mu_2$.

To recapitulate:

$$\pi_3 \equiv (\mu_1 \subset \mu_2) \leftrightarrow \begin{cases} \pi_3 \in Inc(\mu_1) \text{ if } Inc(\mu_1) \neq \varnothing \\ \\ \pi_3 \in \{\pi \text{ / } App(\mu_1) \text{ and } App(\mu_2) \text{ are reserves of domination for } \pi\} \text{ if } Inc(\mu_1) = \varnothing \end{cases}$$

Given two names μ_1 and μ_2 of the nominal rank 0, we know which conditions π_3 can force—if they belong to $\female$—the referential value of μ_1 to be included in the referential value of μ_2. Moreover, the relation of forcing is verifiable in the fundamental situation; in the latter, $Inc(\mu_1)$, $App(\mu_1)$, $App(\mu_2)$ and the concept of reserve of domination are all clear.

We can now say that π_3 forces $\mu_1 = \mu_2$ if π_3 forces $\mu_1 \subset \mu_2$ and also forces $\mu_2 \subset \mu_1$.

Note that $\mu_1 \subset \mu_2$ is not *necessarily* forceable. It is quite possible for $Inc(\mu_1)$ to be void, and that no condition π_3 exist such that $App(\mu_1)$ and $App(\mu_2)$ form reserves of domination for it. Everything depends on the names, on the conditions which appear in them. But *if* $\mu_1 \subset \mu_2$ is forceable by at least one condition π_3, *then* in any generic extension such that $\female$ contains π_3 the statement $R_\female(\mu_1) \subset R_\female(\mu_2)$ is veridical.

The general case (μ_1 and μ_2 have an indeterminate nominal rank) will be treated by recurrence: suppose that we have defined within S the statement 'π forces $\mu_1 = \mu_2$' for all the names of a nominal rank inferior to a. We then show that it can be defined for names of the nominal rank a. This is hardly surprising because a name μ is made up of pairs in the form $<\mu_1,\pi>$ *in which μ_1 is of an inferior nominal rank*. The instrumental concept throughout the entire procedure is that of the reserve of domination.

2. THE CONVERSE OF THE FORCING OF EQUALITY, IN THE CASE OF THE FORMULA $R_\female(\mu_1) = \varnothing$ IN WHICH μ_1 HAS THE NOMINAL RANK 0

This time we shall suppose that in a generic extension $R_\female(\mu_1) = \varnothing$ where μ_1 has the rank 0. What has to be shown is that there exists a condition π in $\female$ which forces $\mu_1 = \varnothing$. It is important to keep in mind the techniques and results from the preceding section (the direct proposition).

Lets consider the set D of conditions defined thus:

$$\pi \in D \leftrightarrow [\pi \equiv (\mu_1 = \varnothing) \text{ or } \pi \equiv [\mu_1 = [\{\varnothing\},\varnothing]]]$$

Note that since $\varnothing \in \female$, what is written on the right-hand side of the *or* in fact amounts to saying $\pi \in \female \rightarrow R_\female(\mu_1) = \{\varnothing\}$. The set of envisaged conditions D gathers together all those conditions which force μ_1 to have either one or the other of its possible referential values, $\varnothing$ or $\{\varnothing\}$. The key point is that this set of conditions is a domination (cf. Meditation 33, Section 4).

In other words, take an indeterminate condition π_2. Either $\pi_2 \equiv (\mu_1 = \varnothing)$, and π_2 belongs to the set D (first requisite), or π_2 does not force $\mu_1 = \varnothing$. If the latter is the case, according to the definition of forcing for the formula $\mu_1 = \varnothing$ (previous section), this is equivalent to saying $\sim(\pi_2 \in Inc(\mu_1))$. Consequently, there exists at least one condition π_3 with $<\varnothing, \pi_3> \in \mu_1$ and π_2 compatible with π_3. If π_2 is compatible with π_3, a π_4 exists which dominates π_2 and π_3. Yet for this π_4, $App(\mu_1)$ is a reserve of domination, because $\pi_3 \in App(\mu_1)$, and $\pi_3 \in \pi_4$. But apart from this, π_4 also dominates $\varnothing$. Therefore π_4 forces $\mu_1 = [\{\varnothing\}, \varnothing]$, because $App(\mu_1)$ and $App[\{\varnothing\}, \varnothing]$ are reserves of domination for π_4. The result is that $\pi_4 \in D$. And since $\pi_2 \subset \pi_4$, π_2 is clearly dominated by a condition of D. That is, whatever π_2 is at stake, D is a domination. If $\female$ is a generic part, $\female \cap D \neq \varnothing$.

We have supposed that $R_\female(\mu_1) = \varnothing$. It is therefore ruled out that a condition exist in $\female$ which forces $\mu_1 = [\{\varnothing\}, \varnothing]$, because we would then have $R_\female(\mu_1) = \{\varnothing\}$. It is therefore the alternative which is correct: $\{\female \cap [\pi / \pi \equiv (\mu_1 = \varnothing)]\} \neq \varnothing$. There is definitely a condition in $\female$ which forces $\mu_1 = \varnothing$.

Note that this time the genericity of the part $\female$ is explicitly convoked. The indiscernible determines the possibility of the equivalence: that between the veracity of the statement $R_\female(\mu_1) = \varnothing$ in the extension, and the existence of a condition in the multiple $\female$ which forces the statement $\mu_1 = \varnothing$, the latter bearing upon the names.

The general case is obtained via recurrence upon the nominal ranks. To obtain a domination D the following set will be used: 'All the conditions which force either $\mu_1 \subset \mu_2$, or $\sim(\mu_1 \subset \mu_2)$'.

APPENDIX 8 (Meditation 36)

Every generic extension of a quasi-complete situation is itself quasi-complete

It is not my intention to reproduce all the demonstrations here. In fact it is rather a question of verifying the following four points:

- if S is denumerable, so is $S(♀)$;
- if S is transitive, so is $S(♀)$;
- if an axiom of set theory which can be expressed in a unique formula (extensionality, powerset, union, foundation, infinity, choice, void-set) is veridical in S, it is also veridical in $S(♀)$;
- if, for a formula $\lambda(\alpha)$, and for $\lambda(\alpha,\beta)$, the corresponding axiom, respectively, of separation and of replacement, is veridical in S, then it is also veridical in $S(♀)$.

In short, in the mathematicians' terms: if S is a denumerable transitive model of set theory, then so is $S(♀)$.

Here are some indications and examples.

a. If S is denumerable so is $S(♀)$.

This goes without saying, because every element of $S(♀)$ is the referential value of a name μ_1 which belongs to the situation S. Therefore there cannot be more elements in $S(♀)$ than there are names in S, that is, more elements than S comprises. For ontology—from the outside—if S is denumerable, so is $S(♀)$.

b. The transitivity of $S(♀)$

We shall see in operation all the to-ing and fro-ing between what can be said of the generic extension, and the mastery, within S, of the names.

Take $\alpha \in S(\female)$, an indeterminate element of the generic extension. It is the value of a name. In other words, there exists a μ_1 such that $\alpha = R_\female(\mu_1)$. What does $\beta \in \alpha$ signify? It signifies that by virtue of the equality above, $\beta \in R_\female(\mu_1)$. But $R_\female(\mu_1) = \{R_\female(\mu_2) \ / \ <\mu_2,\pi> \in \mu_1 \ \& \ \pi \in \female\}$. Consequently, $\beta \in R_\female(\mu_1)$ means: there exists a μ_2 such that $\beta = R_\female(\mu_2)$. Therefore β is the $\female$-referent of the name μ_2, and belongs to the generic extension founded by the generic part $\female$.

It has been shown that $[\alpha \in S(\female) \ \& \ (\beta \in \alpha)] \rightarrow \beta \in S(\female)$, which means that α is also a part of $S(\female)$: $\alpha \in S(\female) \rightarrow \alpha \subset S(\female)$. The generic extension is thus definitely, as is S itself, a transitive set.

c. The axioms of the void, of infinity, of extensionality, of foundation and of choice are veridical in $S(\female)$.

This point is trivial for the void, because $\varnothing \in S \rightarrow \varnothing \in S(\female)$ (via the canonical names). The same occurs for infinity, $\omega_0 \in S \rightarrow \omega_0 \in S(\female)$, and, moreover, ω_0 is an absolute term because it is definable without parameters as 'the smallest limit ordinal'.

For extensionality, its veracity can be immediately inferred from the transitivity of $S(\female)$. That is, the elements of $\alpha \in S(\female)$ in the sense of general ontology are exactly the same as its elements in the sense of $S(\female)$, because if $S(\female)$ is transitive, $\beta \in \alpha \rightarrow \beta \in S(\female)$. Therefore, the comparison of two multiples via their elements gives the same identities (or differences) in $S(\female)$ as in general ontology.

I will leave the verification in $S(\female)$ of the axiom of foundation to you as an exercise—easy—and as another exercise—difficult—that of the axiom of choice.

d. The axiom of union is veridical in $S(\female)$.

Say μ_1 is the name for which α is the $\female$-referent. Since $S(\female)$ is transitive, an element β of α has a name μ_2. And an element of β has a name μ_3. The problem is to find a name whose value is exactly that of all these μ_3's, that is, the set of elements of elements of α.

We will thus take all the pairs $<\mu_3,\pi_3>$ such that:

- there exists a μ_2, and a π_2 with $<\mu_3,\pi_2> \in \mu_2$, itself such that;
- there exists a condition π_1 with $<\mu_2,\pi_1> \in \mu_1$.

For $<\mu_3,\pi_3>$ to definitely have a value, π_3 has to belong to $\female$. For this value to be one of the values which make up μ_2's values, because $<\mu_3,\pi_2> \in \mu_2$, we must have $\pi_2 \in \female$. Finally, for μ_2 to be one of the values which makes up μ_1's values, because $<\mu_2,\pi_1> \in \mu_1$, we must have $\pi_1 \in \female$. In other words, μ_3 will have as value an element of the union of a—whose name is μ_1—if, once $\pi_3 \in \female$, π_2 and π_1 also belong to $\female$. This situation is guaranteed (Rd_1 of correct parts) if π_3 dominates both π_2 and π_1, thus if we have $\pi_2 \subset \pi_3$ and $\pi_1 \subset \pi_3$. The union of a is thus named by the name which is composed of all the pairs $<\mu_3,\pi_3>$ such that there exists at least one pair $<\mu_2,\pi_1>$ belonging to μ_1, and such that there exists a condition π_2 with $<\mu_3,\pi_2> \in \pi_2$, and where we have, moreover, $\pi_2 \subset \pi_3$ and $\pi_1 \subset \pi_3$. We will pose:

$$\mu_4 = \{<\mu_3,\pi_3> \ / \ \exists <\mu_2,\pi_1> \in \mu_1 \ [(\exists \pi_2)<\mu_3,\pi_2> \in \mu_2 \ \& \ \pi_2 \subset \pi_3 \ \& \ \pi_1 \subset \pi_3]\}$$

The above considerations show that if $R_\female(\mu_1) = a$, then $R_\female(\mu_4) = \cup \ a$. Being the $\female$-referent of the name μ_4, $\cup \ a$ belongs to the generic extension.

The joy of names is evident.

e. If an axiom of separation is veridical in S, it is also veridical in $S(\female)$.

Notice that in the demonstrations given above (transitivity, union . . .) no use is made of forcing. In what follows, however, it is another affair; this time around, forcing is essential.

Take a formula $\lambda(a)$ and a fixed set $R_\female(\mu_1)$ of $S(\female)$. It is a matter of showing that, in $S(\female)$, the subset of $R_\female(\mu_1)$ composed of elements which verify $\lambda(a)$ is itself a set of $S(\female)$.

Let's agree to term the set of names which figure in the composition of the name μ_1, $Sna(\mu_1)$.

Consider the name μ_2 defined in the following manner:

$$\mu_2 - \{<\mu_3,\pi> \ / \ \mu_3 \in Sna(\mu_1) \ \& \ \pi \equiv [(\mu_3 \in \mu_1) \ \& \ \lambda(\mu_3)]\}$$

This is the name composed of all the pairs of names μ_3 which figure in μ_1, and of the conditions which force both $\mu_3 \in \mu_1$ and $\lambda(\mu_3)$. It is intelligible within the fundamental situation S for the following reason: given that the axiom of separation for λ is supposed veridical in S, the formula '$\mu_3 \in \mu_1$ & $\lambda(\mu_3)$' designates without ambiguity a multiple of S once μ_1 is a name in S.

It is clear that $R_\female(\mu_2)$ is what is separated by the formula λ in $R_\female(\mu_1)$. Indeed, an element of $R_\female(\mu_2)$ is of the form $R_\female(\mu_3)$, with $<\mu_3,\pi> \in \mu_2$, $\pi \in \female$, and $\pi \equiv [(\mu_3 \in \mu_1) \ \& \ \lambda(\mu_3)]$. By the theorems of forcing, we have $R_\female(\mu_3) \in R_\female(\mu_1)$ and $\lambda(R_\female(\mu_3))$. Therefore $R_\female(\mu_2)$ solely contains elements of $R_\female(\mu_1)$ which verify the formula λ.

Inversely, take $R_\female(\mu_3)$, an element of $R_\female(\mu_1)$ which verifies the formula λ. Since the formula $R_\female(\mu_3) \in R_\female(\mu_1)$ & $\lambda(R_\female(\mu_3))$ is veridical in $S(\female)$, there exists, by the theorems of forcing, a condition $\pi \in \female$ which forces the formula $\mu_3 \in \mu_1$ & $\lambda(\mu_3)$. It follows that $<\mu_3,\pi> \in \mu_2$, because apart from $R_\female(\mu_3) \in R_\female(\mu_1)$, one can infer that $\mu_3 \in Sna(\mu_1)$. And since $\pi \in \female$, we have $R_\female(\mu_3) \in R_\female(\mu_2)$. Therefore, every element of $R_\female(\mu_1)$ which verifies λ is an element of $R_\female(\mu_2)$.

f. The axiom of the powerset is veridical in $S(\female)$.

This axiom, as one would expect, is a much harder nut to crack, because it concerns a notion ('the set of subsets') which is not absolute. The calculations are abstruse and so I merely indicate the overall strategy.

Take $R_\female(\mu_1)$, an element of a generic extension. We shall cause parts to appear *within the name* μ_1, and use forcing, to obtain a name μ_4 such that $R_\female(\mu_4)$ has as *elements*, amongst others, all the parts of $R_\female(\mu_1)$. In this manner we will be sure of having enough names, in S, to guarantee, in $S(\female)$, the existence of all the parts of $R_\female(\mu_1)$ ('parts' meaning: parts in the situation $S(\female)$).

The main resource for this type of calculation lies in fabricating the names such that they combine parts of the name μ_1 with conditions that force the belonging of these parts to the name of a part of $R_\female(\mu_1)$. The detail reveals how the mastery of statements in $S(\female)$ passes via calculative intrications of referential value, of the consideration of the being of the names, and of the forcing conditions. This is precisely the practical art of the Subject: to move according to the triangle of the signifier, the referent and forcing. Moreover, this triangle, in turn, only makes sense due to the procedural supplementation of the situation by an indiscernible part. Finally, it is this art which allows us to establish that all the axioms of ontology which can be expressed in a unique formula are veridical in $S(\female)$.

To complete this task, all that remains to be done is the verification of the axioms of replacement which are veridical in S. In order to establish their veracity in $S(\female)$ one must combine the technique of forcing with the theorems of reflection. We will leave it aside.

APPENDIX 9 (Meditation 36)

Completion of the demonstration of $\mid p(\omega_0) \mid \geq \delta$ within a generic extension

We have defined sets of whole numbers (parts of ω_0), written $\gamma(n)$, where $[n \in \gamma(n)] \leftrightarrow \{<\gamma,n,1>\} \in \female$.

1. NONE OF THE SETS $\gamma(n)$ IS VOID

For a fixed $\gamma \in \delta$, let's consider in S the set D_γ of conditions defined in the following manner:

$D_\gamma = \{\pi \ / \ (\exists n)[<\gamma,n,1> \in \pi]\}$; that is, the set of conditions such that there exists at least one whole number n with $<\gamma,n,1>$ being an element of the condition. Such a condition $\pi \in D_\gamma$, if it belongs to $\female$, entails that $n \in \gamma(n)$, because then $\{<\gamma,n,1>\} \in \female$. It so happens that D_γ is a domination. If a condition π_1 does not contain any triplet of the type $<\gamma,n,1>$, one adds one to it, and it is always possible to do so without contradiction (it suffices, for example, to take an n which does not figure in any of the triplets which make up π_1). Therefore, π_1 is dominated by at least one condition of D_γ.

Moreover, $D_\gamma \in S$, because S is quasi-complete, and D_γ is obtained by separation within the set of conditions, and by absolute operations (in particular, the quantification $(\exists n)$ which is restricted to ω_0, absolute element of S). The genericity of $\female$ imposes the following: $\female \cap D_\gamma \neq \varnothing$, and consequently, $\female$ contains at least one condition which contains a triplet $<\gamma,n,1>$. The whole number n which figures in this triplet is such that $n \in \gamma(n)$, and therefore $\gamma(n) \neq \varnothing$.

2. THERE ARE AT LEAST δ SETS OF THE TYPE $\gamma(n)$

This results from the following: if $\gamma_1 \neq \gamma_2$, then $\gamma_1(n) \neq \gamma_2(n)$. Let's consider the set of conditions defined thus:

$D_{\gamma_1\gamma_2} = \{\pi \ / \ (\exists n) \ \{<\gamma_1,n,1> \in \pi \ \& \ <\gamma_2,n,0> \in \pi\}$
$or \ \{<\gamma_2,n,1> \in \pi \ \& \ <\gamma_1,n,0> \in \pi\}\}$

This $D_{\gamma_1\gamma_2}$ assembles all the conditions such that there is at least one whole number n which appears in triplets $<\gamma_1,n,x>$ and $<\gamma_2,n,x>$ which are elements of these conditions, but with the requirement that if $x = 1$ in the triplet in which γ_1 appears, then $x = 0$ in the triplet in which γ_2 appears, and vice versa. The subjacent information transmitted by these conditions is that there exists an n such that if it is 'paired' to γ_1, then it cannot be paired to γ_2, and vice versa. If such a condition belongs to $♀$, it imposes, for at least one whole number n_1:

- either that $\{<\gamma_2,n_1,1>\} \in ♀$, but then $\sim[\{<\gamma_2,n_1,1>\} \in ♀]$ (because $<\gamma_2,n_1,0>$ belongs to it, and because $<\gamma_2,n_1,1>$ and $<\gamma_2,n_1,0>$ are incompatible);
- or that $\{<\gamma_2,n_1,1>\} \in ♀$, but then $\sim[\{<\gamma_1,n_1,1>\} \in ♀]$ (for the same reasons).

One can therefore say that in this case the whole number n_1 separates γ_1 and γ_2 with respect to $♀$, because the triplet ending in 1 that it forms with one of the two γ's necessarily appears in $♀$; once it does so, the triplet ending in 1 that it forms with the other γ is necessarily absent from $♀$.

Another result is that $\gamma_1(n) \neq \gamma_2(n)$, because the whole number n_1 cannot be simultaneously an element of both of these two sets. Remember that $\gamma(n)$ is made up precisely of all the n such that $\{<\gamma,n,1>\} \in ♀$. Yet, $\{<\gamma_1,n_1,1>\} \in ♀ \rightarrow \sim[\{<\gamma_2,n_1,1>\} \in ♀]$, and vice versa.

But the set of conditions $D_{\gamma_1\gamma_2}$ is a domination (one adds the $<\gamma_1,n_1,1>$ and the $<\gamma_2,n_1,1>$, or vice versa, whichever are required, whilst respecting coherency) and belongs to S (by the axioms of set theory—which are veridical in S, quasi-complete situation—combined with some very simple arguments of absoluteness). The genericity of $♀$ thus imposes that $♀ \cap D_{\gamma_1\gamma_2} \neq \varnothing$. Consequently, in $S(♀)$, we have $\gamma_1(n) \neq \gamma_2(n)$, since there is at least one n_1 which separates them.

Since there are δ elements γ, because $\gamma \in \delta$, there are at least δ sets of the type $\gamma(n)$. We have just seen that they are all different. It so happens that these sets are parts of ω_0. Therefore, in $S(♀)$, there are at least δ parts of ω_0: $|p(\omega_0)| \geq \delta$.

APPENDIX 10 (Meditation 36)

Absenting of a cardinal δ of S in a generic extension

Take as a set of conditions the finite series of triplets of the type $<n,a,1>$ or $<n,a,0>$, with $n \in \omega_0$ and $a \in \delta$. See the rules concerning compatible triplets in Meditation 36, Section 5.

Say that $\female$ is a generic set of conditions of this type. It intersects every domination. It so happens that:

- The family of conditions which contains at least one triplet of the type $<n_1,a,1>$ for a fixed n_1, is a domination (the set of conditions π verifying the property $(\exists a)[<n_1,a,1> \in \pi]$). Simple exercise. Therefore, for every whole number $n_1 \in \omega_0$ there exists at least one $a \in \delta$ such that $\{<n_1,a,1>\} \in \female$.

- The family of conditions which contains at least one triplet of the type $<n,a_1,1>$ for a fixed a_1, is a domination (the set of conditions π verifying the property $(\exists n)[<n,a_1,1> \in \pi]$). Simple exercise. Therefore, for every ordinal $a_1 \in \delta$ there exists at least one $n \in \omega_0$ such that $\{<n,a_1,1>\} \in \female$.

What is beginning to take shape here is a one-to-one correspondence between ω_0 and δ: it will be absented in $S(\female)$.

To be precise: take f, the function of ω_0 towards δ defined as follows in $S(\female)$: $[f(n) = a] \leftrightarrow \{<n,a,1>\} \in \female$.

Given the whole number n, we will match it up with an a such that the condition $\{<n,a,1>\}$ is an element of the generic part $\female$. This function is defined for every n, since we have seen above that in $\female$, for a fixed n, there *always* exists a condition of the type $\{<n,a,1>\}$. Moreover, this function 'covers' all of δ, because, for a fixed $a \in \delta$, there always exists a whole number n such that the condition $\{<n,a,1>\}$ is in ♀. Furthermore, it is definitely a function, because to *each* whole number *one* element a and *one alone* corresponds. Indeed, the conditions $\{<n,a,1>\}$ and $\{<n,\beta,1>\}$ are incompatible if $a \neq \beta$, and there cannot be two incompatible conditions in ♀. Finally, the function f is clearly defined as a multiple of $S(♀)$—it is known by an inhabitant of $S(♀)$—for the following reasons: it is obtained by separation within ♀ ('all the conditions of the type $\{<n,a,1>\}$'); ♀ is an element of $S(♀)$; and, $S(♀)$ being a quasi-complete situation, the axiom of separation is veridical therein.

To finish, f, in $S(♀)$, is a function of ω_0 *on* δ, in the sense in which it finds for every whole number n a corresponding element of δ, and every element of δ is selected. It is thus ruled out that δ has in $S(♀)$, where the function exists, more elements than ω_0.

Consequently, in $S(♀)$, δ is not in any way a cardinal: it is a simple denumerable ordinal. The cardinal δ of S has been *absented* within the extension $S(♀)$.

APPENDIX 11 (Meditation 36)

Necessary condition for a cardinal to be absented in a generic extension: a non-denumerable antichain of conditions exists in S (whose cardinality in S is superior to ω_0).

Take a multiple δ which is a cardinal superior to ω_0 in a quasi-complete situation S. Suppose that it is absented in a generic extension $S(\female)$. This means that within $S(\female)$ there exists a function of an ordinal α smaller than δ over the entirety of δ. This rules out δ having more elements than α—for an inhabitant of $S(\female)$—and consequently δ is no longer a cardinal.

This function f, being an element of the generic extension, has a name μ_1, of which it is the referential value: $f = R\female(\mu_1)$. Moreover, we know that the ordinals of $S(\female)$ are the same as those of S (Meditation 34, Section 6). Therefore the ordinal α is an ordinal in S. In the same manner, the cardinal δ of S, if it is absented as a cardinal, remains an ordinal in $S(\female)$.

Since the statement 'f is a function of α over δ' is veridical in $S(\female)$, its application to the names is forced by a condition $\pi_1 \in \female$ according to the fundamental theorems of forcing. We have something like: $\pi_1 \Vdash [\mu_1$ is a function of $\mu(\alpha)$ over $\mu(\delta)]$, where $\mu(\alpha)$ and $\mu(\delta)$ are the canonical names of α and δ (see Meditation 34, Section 5 on canonical names).

For an element γ of the cardinal of S which is δ, and an element β of the ordinal α, let's consider the set of conditions written $\circledR(\beta\gamma)$ and defined as follows:

$$\circledR(\beta\gamma) = \{\pi \; / \; \pi_1 \subset \pi \; \& \; \pi \Vdash [\mu_1(\mu(\beta)) = \mu(\gamma)]\}$$

It is a question of conditions which dominate π_1, and which force the veracity in $S(\female)$ of $f(\beta) = \gamma$. If such a condition belongs to $\female$, on the one hand $\pi_1 \in \female$, therefore $R_\female(\mu_1)$ is definitely a function of α over δ, and on the other hand $f(\beta) = \gamma$.

Note that for a particular element $\gamma \in \delta$, there exists $\beta \in \alpha$ such that $\circledR(\beta\gamma)$ is not empty. Indeed, by the function f, every element γ of δ is the value of an element of α. There always exists at least one $\beta \in \alpha$ such that $f(\beta) = \gamma$ is veridical in $S(\female)$. And it exists in a condition π which forces $\mu_1(\mu(\beta)) = \mu(\gamma)$. Thus there exists (rule Rd_2) a condition of $\female$ which dominates both π and π_1.

That condition belongs to $\circledR(\beta\gamma)$.

Moreover, if $\gamma_1 \neq \gamma_2$, and $\pi_2 \in \circledR(\beta\gamma_1)$ and $\pi_3 \in \circledR(\beta\gamma_2)$, π_2 and π_3 are incompatible conditions.

Let's suppose that π_2 and π_3 are actually not incompatible. There then exists a condition π_4 which dominates both of them. There necessarily exists a generic extension $S'(\female)$ such that $\pi_4 \in \female$, for we have seen (Meditation 34, Section 2) that, given a set of conditions in a denumerable situation *for the ontologist* (that is, from the outside), one can construct a generic part which contains an indeterminate condition. But since π_2 and π_3 dominate π_1, in $S'(\female)$, $R_\female(\mu_1)$, that is, f, remains a function of α over δ, this quality being forced by π_1. Finally, the condition π_4

– forces that μ_1 is a function of β over δ
– forces $\mu_1(\mu(\beta)) = \mu(\gamma_1)$, thus prescribes that $f(\beta) = \gamma_1$
– forces $\mu_1(\mu(\beta)) = \mu(\gamma_2)$, thus prescribes that $f(\beta) = \gamma_2$

But this is impossible when $\gamma_1 \neq \gamma_2$, because a function f has one value alone for a given element β.

It thus follows that if $\pi_2 \in \circledR(\beta\gamma_1)$ and $\pi_3 \in \circledR(\beta\gamma_2)$, there does not exist any condition π_4 which dominates both of them, which means that π_2 and π_3 are incompatible.

Finally, we have constructed *in S* (and this can be verified by the absoluteness of the operations at stake) sets of conditions $\circledR(\beta\gamma)$ such that none of them are empty, and each of them solely contains conditions which are incompatible with the conditions contained by each of the others. Since these $\circledR(\beta\gamma)$ are indexed on $\gamma \in \delta$, this means that *there exist at least δ conditions which are incompatible pair by pair*. But, in S, δ is a cardinal superior to ω_0. There thus exists a set of mutually incompatible conditions which is not denumerable for an inhabitant of S.

If we term 'antichain' any set of pair by pair incompatible conditions, we therefore have the following: a necessary condition for a cardinal δ of S to be absented in an extension $S(\female)$ is that there exist in $\copyright$ an antichain of superior cardinality to ω_0 (for an inhabitant of S).

APPENDIX 12 (Meditation 36)
Cardinality of the antichains of conditions

We shall take as set © of conditions finite sets of triplets of the type $<a,n,0>$ or $<a,n,1>$ with $a \in \delta$ and $n \in \omega_0$, δ being a cardinal in S, with the restriction that in the same condition π, a and n being fixed, one cannot simultaneously have the triplet $<a,n,0>$ and the triplet $<a,n,1>$. An antichain of conditions is a set A of conditions pair by pair incompatible (two conditions are incompatible if one contains a triplet $<a,n,0>$ and the other a triplet $<a,n,1>$ for the same a and n).

Let's suppose that there exists an antichain of a cardinality superior to ω_0. There then exists one of the cardinality ω_1 (because, with the axiom of choice, the antichain contains subsets of all the cardinalities inferior or equal to its own). Thus, take an antichain $A \in ©$, with $|A| = \omega_1$.

A can be separated into disjointed pieces in the following manner:

- $A_0 = \varnothing$
- A_n = all the conditions of A which have the 'length' n, that is, which have exactly n triplets as their elements (since all conditions are *finite* sets of triplets).

As such, one obtains at the most ω_0 pieces, or a *partition* of A into ω_0 disjoint parts: each part corresponds to a whole number n.

Since ω_1 is a successor cardinal, it is regular (cf. Appendix 3). This implies that at least one of the parts has the cardinality ω_1, because ω_1 cannot be obtained with ω_0 pieces of the cardinality ω_0.

We thus have an antichain, all of whose conditions have the same length. Suppose that this length is $n = p + 1$, and that this antichain is written A_{p+1}. We shall show that there then exists an antichain B of the cardinality ω_1 *whose conditions have the length* p.

Say that π is a condition of A_{p+1}. This condition, which has $p+1$ elements, has the form:

$$\pi = \{<a_1,n_1,x_1>,<a_2,n_2,x_2>, \ldots <a_{p+1},n_{p+1},x_{p+1}>\}$$

where the $x_1, \ldots x_{p+1}$ are either 1's or 0's.

We will then obtain a partition of A_{p+1} into $p+2$ pieces in the following manner:

$$A_{p+1}^0 = \{\pi\}$$

$A_{p+1}^1 =$ the set of conditions of A_{p+1} which contain a triplet of the type $<a_1,n_1,x_1'>$, where $x_1' \neq x_1$ (one is 0 if the other is 1 or vice versa), and which, as such, are incompatible with π.

. . .

$A_{p+1}^q =$ the set of conditions of A_{p+1} which do not contain triplets incompatible with π of the type $<a_1,n_1,x_1'>, \ldots <a_{q-1},n_{q-1},x_{q-1}'>$, but which do contain an incompatible triplet $<a_q,n_q,x_q'>$.

. . .

$A_{p+1}^{p+1} =$ the set of conditions of A_{p+1} which do not contain any incompatible triplets of the type $<a_1,n_1,x_1'>, \ldots <a_p,n_p,x_p'>$, but which do contain one of the type $<a_{p+1},n_{p+1},x_{p+1}'>$.

A partition of A_{p+1} is thus definitely obtained, because every condition of A_{p+1} must be incompatible with π—A_{p+1} being an antichain—and must therefore contain as an element at least one triplet $<a,n,x'>$ such that there exists in π a triplet $<a,n,x>$ with $x \neq x'$.

Since there are $p+2$ pieces, at least one has the cardinality ω_1, because $|A_{p+1}| = \omega_1$, and a finite number ($p+2$) of pieces of the cardinality ω_0 would result solely in a total of the cardinality ω_0 (regularity of ω_1).

Let's posit that A_{p+1}^q is of the cardinality ω_1. All the conditions of A_{p+1}^q contain the triplet $<a_q,n_q,x_q'>$, with $x_q' \neq x_q$. But $x_q' \neq x_q$ completely determines x_q' (it is 1 if $x_q = 0$, and it is 0 if $x_q = 1$). All the conditions of A_{p+1}^q therefore contain *the same* triplet $<a_q,n_q,x_q'>$. However, these conditions are pair by pair incompatible. But they cannot be so due to their common element. If we remove this element from all of them we obtain pair by pair incompatible conditions of the length p (since all the conditions of A_{p+1}^q have the length $p+1$). Thus there exists a set B of pair by pair incompatible conditions, all of the length p, and this set always has the cardinality ω_1.

We have shown the following: if there exists an antichain of the cardinality ω_1, there also exists an antichain of the cardinality ω_1 all of whose conditions are of the same length. If that length is $p + 1$, thus superior to 1, there also exists an antichain of the cardinality ω_1 all of whose conditions have the length p. By the same reasoning, if $p \neq 1$, there then exists an antichain of the cardinality ω_1, all of whose conditions are of the length $p - 1$, etc. Finally, there must exist an antichain of the cardinality ω_1 all of whose conditions are of the length 1, thus being identical to singletons of the type $\{<a,n,x>\}$. However, this is impossible, because a condition of this type, say $<a,n,1>$, admits *one condition alone* of the same length which is incompatible with it, the condition $\{<a,n,0>\}$.

The initial hypothesis must be rejected: there is no antichain of the cardinality ω_1.

One could ask: does only one antichain of the cardinality ω_0 exist? The response is positive. It will be constructed, for example, in the following way:

To simplify matters let's write $\gamma_1, \gamma_2, \ldots \gamma_n$ for the triplets which make up a condition π: we have $\pi = \{\gamma_1, \gamma_2, \ldots \gamma_n\}$. Lets write $\bar{\gamma}$ for the triplet Incompatible with γ. We will posit that:

$\pi_0 = \{\gamma_0\}$, where γ_0 is an indeterminate triplet.

$\pi_1 = \{\bar{\gamma}_0, \gamma_1\}$ where γ_1 is an indeterminate triplet compatible with $\bar{\gamma}_0$.

$\ldots$

$\pi_n = \{\bar{\gamma}_0, \bar{\gamma}_1, \ldots \bar{\gamma}_{n-1}, \gamma_n\}$ where γ_n is an indeterminate triplet compatible with $\bar{\gamma}_0, \bar{\gamma}_1, \ldots \bar{\gamma}_{n-1}$.

$\ldots$

$\pi_{n+1} = \{\bar{\gamma}_0, \bar{\gamma}_1, \ldots \bar{\gamma}_n, \gamma_{n+1}\}$.

Each condition π_n is incompatible with all the others, because for a given π_q either $q < n$, and thus π_n contains $\bar{\gamma}_q$ whilst π_q contains γ_q, or $n < q$, and then π_q contains $\bar{\gamma}_n$ whilst π_n contains γ_n.

The set clearly constitutes an antichain of the cardinality ω_0. What blocked the reasoning which prohibited antichains of the cardinality ω_1 is the following point; the antichain above only contains *one* condition of a given length n, which is π_{n-1}. One cannot therefore 'descend' according to the length of conditions, in conserving the cardinality ω_0, as we did for ω_1.

Finally, every antichain of © is of a cardinality at the most equal to ω_0. The result is that in a generic extension $S(♀)$ obtained with that set of conditions, the cardinals are all maintained: they are the same as those of S.

Notes

In the Introduction I said that I would not use footnotes. The notes found here refer back to certain pages such that if the reader feels that some information is lacking there, they can see if I have furnished it here.

These notes also function as a bibliography. I have restricted it quite severely to only those books which were actually used or whose usage, in my opinion, may assist the understanding of my text. Conforming to a rule which I owe to M. I. Finley, who did not hesitate to indicate whether a recent text rendered obsolete those texts which had preceded it with respect to a certain point, I have referred, in general—except, naturally, for the 'classics'—to the most recent available books: especially in the scientific order these books 'surpass and conserve' (in the Hegelian sense) their predecessors. Hence the majority of the references concern publications posterior to 1960, indeed often to 1970.

The note on page 15 attempts to situate my work within contemporary French philosophy.

Page 1

The statement 'Heidegger is the last universally recognized philosopher' is to be read without obliterating the facts: Heidegger's Nazi commitment from 1933 to 1945, and even more his obstinate and thus decided silence on the extermination of the Jews of Europe. On the basis of this point alone it may be inferred that even if one allows that Heidegger was the thinker of his time, it is of the highest importance to leave both that time and that thought behind, in a clarification of just exactly what they were.

Page 4

On the question of Lacan's ontology see my *Théorie du sujet* (Paris: Seuil, 1982), 150–157.

Page 7

No doubt it was a tragedy for the philosophical part of the French intellectual domain: the premature disappearance of three men, who between the two wars incarnated the connection between that domain and postcantorian mathematics: Herbrand, considered by everyone as a veritable genius in pure logic, killed himself in the mountains; Cavaillès and Lautman, members of the resistance, were killed by the Nazis. It is quite imaginable that if they had survived and their work continued, the philosophical landscape after the war would have been quite different.

Page 12 and 13

For J. Dieudonné's positions on A. Lautman and the conditions of the philosophy of mathematics, see the preface to A. Lautman, *Essai sur l'unité des mathématiques* (Paris: UGE, 1977). I must declare here that Lautman's writings are nothing less than admirable and what I owe to them, even in the very foundational intuitions for this book, is immeasurable.

Page 15

Given that the method of exposition which I have adopted does not involve the discussion of the theses of my contemporaries, it is no doubt possible to identify, since nobody is solitary, nor in a position of radical exception from his or her times, numerous proximities between what I declare and what they have written. I would like to lay out here, in one sole gesture, the doubtlessly partial consciousness that I have of these proximities, restricting myself to living French authors. It is not a question of proximities alone, or of influence. On the contrary, it could be a matter of the most extreme distancing, but within a dialectic that maintains thought. The authors mentioned here are in any case those who make, for me, some *sense*.

– Concerning the ontological prerequisite, J. Derrida must certainly be mentioned. I feel closer, no doubt, to those who, after his work, have undertaken to *delimit* Heidegger by questioning him also on the point of his intolerable silence on the Nazi extermination of the Jews of Europe, and who search, at base, to bind the care of the political to the opening of poetic experience. I thus name J.-L. Nancy and P. Lacoue-Labarthe.

– Concerning presentation as pure multiple, it is a major theme of the epoch, and its principal names in France are certainly G. Deleuze and J.-F. Lyotard. It seems to me that, in order to think our *differends* as Lyotard would say, it is no doubt necessary to admit that the latent paradigm of Deleuze's work is 'natural' (even though it be in Spinoza's sense) and that of Lyotard juridical (in the sense of the Critique). Mine is mathematical.

– Concerning the Anglo-Saxon hegemony over the consequences of the revolution named by Cantor and Frege, we know that its inheritor in France is J. Bouveresse, constituting himself alone, in conceptual sarcasm, as tribunal of Reason. A liaison of another type, perhaps too restrictive in its conclusions, is proposed between mathematics and philosophy, by J. T. Desanti. And of the great Bachelardian tradition, fortunately my master G. Canguilheim survives.

– With respect to everything which gravitates around the modern question of the subject, in its Lacanian guise, one must evidently designate J.-A. Miller, who also legitimately maintains its organized connection with clinical practice.

– I like, in J. Rancière's work, the passion for equality.

– F. Regnault and J.-C. Milner, each in a manner both singular and universal, testify to the identification of procedures of the subject in other domains. The centre of gravity for the first is theatre, the 'superior art'. The second, who is also a scholar, unfolds the labyrinthine complexities of knowledge and the letter.

– C. Jambet and G. Lardreau attempt a Lacanian retroaction towards what they decipher as foundational in the gesture of the great monotheisms.

– L. Althusser must be named.

– For the political procedure, this time according to an intimacy of ideas and actions, I would single out Paul Sandevince, S. Lazarus, my fellow-traveller, whose enterprise is to formulate, in the measure of Lenin's institution of modern politics, the conditions of a new mode of politics.

Page 23

Concerning the one in Leibniz's philosophy, and its connection to the principle of indiscernibles, and thus to the constructivist orientation in thought, see Meditation 30.

Page 24

– I borrow the word 'presentation', in this sort of context, from J.-F. Lyotard.

– The word 'situation' has a Sartrean connotation for us. It must be neutralized here. A situation is purely and simply a space of structured multiple-presentation.

It is quite remarkable that the Anglo-Saxon school of logic has recently used the word 'situation' to attempt the 'real world' application of certain results which have been confined, up till the present moment, within the 'formal sciences'. A confrontation with set theory then became necessary. A positivist version of my enterprise can be found in the work of J. Barwise and J. Perry. There is a good summary of their work in J. Barwise, 'Situations, sets and the Axiom of Foundation', *Logic Colloquium '84* (North-Holland: 1986). The following definition bears citing: 'By situation, we mean a part of reality which can be understood as a whole, which interacts with other things.'

Page 27

I think (and such would be the stakes for a *disputatio*) that the current enterprise of C. Jambet (*La Logique des Orientaux* (Paris: Seuil, 1983)), and more strictly that of G. Lardreau (*Discours philosophique et Discours spirituel* (Paris: Seuil, 1985)), amount to suturing the two approaches to the question of being: the subtractive and the presentative. Their work necessarily intersects negative theologies.

Page 31

With respect to the typology of the hypotheses of the Parmenides, see F. Regnault's article 'Dialectique d'épistémologie' in *Cahiers pour l'analyse*, no. 9, Summer 1968 (Paris: Le Graphe/Seuil).

Page 32

The canonical translation for the dialogue *The Parmenides* is that of A. Diès (Paris: Les Belles Lettres, 1950). I have often modified it, not in order to correct it, which would be presumptuous, but in order to tighten, in my own manner, its conceptual requisition.

[Translator's note: I have made use of F. M. Cornford's translation, altering it in line with Badiou's own modifications ('Parmenides' in

E. Hamilton & H. Cairns (eds), *Plato: The Collected Dialogues* (Princeton: Princeton University Press, 1961)]

Page 33

The use of the other and the Other is evidently drawn from Lacan. For a systematic employment of these terms see Meditation 13.

Page 38

For the citations of Cantor, one can refer to the great German edition: G. Cantor, *Gesammelte Abhandlungen mathematischen und philosophischen Inhalts* (New York: Springer-Verlag, 1980). There are many English translations of various texts, and most are them are available. I would like to draw attention to the French translation, by J.-C. Milner, of very substantial fragments of *Fondements d'une théorie générale des ensembles* (1883), in *Cahiers pour l'analyse*, no. 10, Spring 1969. Having said that, the French translation used here is my own. [Translator's note: I have used Philip Jourdain's translation: Georg Cantor, *Contributions to the Founding of the Theory of Transfinite Numbers* (New York: Dover Publications, 1955)]

Parmenides' sentence is given in J. Beaufret's translation; *Parménide, le poème* (Paris: PUF, 1955). [Translator's note. I have directly translated Beaufret's phrasing. According to David Gallop the most common English translation is 'thinking and being are the same thing': see *Parmenides of Elea: Fragments* (trans. D. Gallop; Toronto: University of Toronto Press, 1984)]

Page 43

For Zermelo's texts, the best option is no doubt to refer to Gregory H. Moore's book *Zermelo's Axiom of Choice* (New York: Springer-Verlag, 1982).

The thesis according to which the essence of Zermelo's axiom is the limitation of the size of sets is defended and explained in Michael Hallett's excellent book, *Cantorian Set Theory and Limitation of Size* (Oxford: Clarendon Press, 1984). Even though I would contest this thesis, I recommend this book for its historical and conceptual introduction to set theory.

Page 47

On 'there is', and 'there are distinctions', see the first chapter of J.-C. Milner's book *Les Noms Indistincts* (Paris: Seuil, 1983).

NOTES

Page 60

Since the examination of set theory begins in earnest here let's fix some bibliographic markers.

– For the axiomatic presentation of the theory, there are two books which I would recommend without hesitation: in French, unique in its kind, there is that of J.-L. Krivine, *Théorie Axiomatique des ensembles* (Paris: PUF, 1969). In English there is K. J. Devlin's book, *Fundamentals of Contemporary Set Theory* (New York: Springer-Verlag, 1979).

– A very good book of intermediate difficulty: Azriel Levy, *Basic Set Theory* (New York: Springer-Verlag, 1979).

– Far more complete but also more technical books: K. Kunen, *Set Theory* (Amsterdam: North-Holland Publishing Company, 1980); and the monumental T. Jech, *Set Theory* (New York: Academic Press, 1978).

These books are all strictly mathematical in their intentions. A more historical and conceptual explanation—mind, its subjacent philosophy is positivist— is given in the classic *Foundations of Set Theory*, 2nd edn, by A. A. Fraenkel, Y. Bar-Hillel and A. Levy (Amsterdam: North-Holland Publishing Company, 1973).

Page 62

The hypothetical, or 'constructive', character of the axioms of the theory, with the exception of that of the empty set, is well developed in J. Cavaillès' book, *Méthode axiomatique et Formalisme*, written in 1937 and republished by Hermann in 1981.

Page 70

The text of Aristotle used here is *Physique*, text edited and translated by H. Carteron, 2nd edn, (Paris: Les Belles Lettres, 1952). With regard to the translation of several passages, I entered into correspondence with J.-C. Milner, and what he suggested went far beyond the simple advice of the exemplary Hellenist that he is anyway. However, the solutions adopted here are my own, and I declare J.-C. Milner innocent of anything excessive they might contain. [Translator's note: I have used the translation of R. P. Hardie and R. K. Gaye, altering it in line with Badiou's own modifications (in *The Complete Works of Aristotle* (J. Barnes (ed.); Princeton: Princeton University Press, 1984)]

Page 104

The clearest systematic exposition of the Marxist doctrine of the state remains, still today, that of Lenin; *The State and the Revolution* (trans. R. Service; London: Penguin, 1992). However, there are some entirely new contributions on this point (in particular with regard to the subjective dimension) in the work of S. Lazarus. [Translator's note: See S. Lazarus, *Anthropologie du nom* (Paris: Seuil, 1996)]

Page 112

The text of Spinoza used here, for the Latin, is the bilingual edition of C. Appuhn, *Ethique* (2 vols; Paris: Garnier, 1953), and for the French I have used the translation by R. Caillois in *Spinoza: Œuvres Complètes* (Paris: Gallimard, Bibliothèque de la Pléiade, 1954). I have adjusted the latter here and there. The references to Spinoza's correspondence have also been drawn from the Pléiade edition. [Translator's note: I have used Edwin Curley's translation, modified in line with Badiou's adjustments (Spinoza, *Ethics* (London: Penguin, 1996)]

Page 123

Heidegger's statements are all drawn from *Introduction à la Métaphysique* (trans. G. Kahn; Paris: PUF, 1958). I would not chance my arm in the labyrinth of translations of Heidegger, and so I have taken the French translation as I found it. [Translator's note: I have used the Ralph Manheim translation: M. Heidegger, *An Introduction to Metaphysics* (New Haven: Yale University Press, 1959)]

Page 124

For Heidegger's thought of the Platonic 'turn', and of what can be read there in terms of speculative aggressivity, see, for example, 'Plato's Doctrine on Truth' in M. Heidegger, *Pathmarks* (trans. T. Sheehan; Cambridge: Cambridge University Press, 1998).

Page 133

The definition of ordinals used here is not the 'classic' definition. The latter is the following: 'An ordinal is a transitive set which is well-ordered by the relation of belonging.' Its advantage, purely technical, is that it does not use the axiom of foundation in the study of the principal properties of ordinals. Its conceptual disadvantage is that of introducing well-ordering in a place where, in my opinion, it not only has no business but it also masks that an ordinal draws its structural or natural 'stability' from the concept of transitivity alone, thus from a specific relation between belonging and inclusion. Besides, I hold the axiom of foundation to be a crucial ontological Idea, even if its strictly mathematical usage is null. I closely follow J. R. Shoenfield's exposition in his *Mathematical Logic* (Reading MA: Addison-Wesley, 1967).

Page 157

The axiom of infinity is often not presented in the form 'a limit ordinal exists', but via a direct exhibition of the procedure of the already, the again, and of the second existential seal. The latter approach is adopted in order to avoid having to develop, prior to the statement of the axiom, part of the theory of ordinals. The axiom poses, for example, that there exists (second existential seal) a set such that the empty set is one of its elements (already), and such that if it contained a set, it would also contain the union of that set and its singleton (procedure of the again). I preferred a presentation which allowed one to think the natural character of this Idea. It can be demonstrated, in any case, that the two formulations are equivalent.

Page 161

The Hegel translation used here is that by P.-J. Labarrière and G. Jarczyk, *Science de la Logique* (3 vols; Paris: Aubier, 1972 for the 1st vol., used here). However, I was not able to reconcile myself to translating *aufheben* by *sursumer* (to supersede, to subsume), as these translations propose, because the substition of a technical neologism in one language for an everyday word from another language appears to me to be a renunciation rather than a victory. I have thus taken up J. Derrida's suggestion: '*relever*', '*relève*' [Translator's note: this word means to restore, set right, take up, take down, take over, pick out, relieve. See Hegel, *Science of Logic* (trans. A. V. Miller; London: Allen & Unwin, 1969)]

Page 189

What is examined in the article by J. Barwise mentioned above (in the note for page 24) is precisely the relation between a 'set theory' version of concrete situations (in the sense of Anglo-Saxon empiricism) and the axiom of foundation. It establishes via examples that there are non-founded situations (in my terms these are 'neutral' situations). However, its frame of investigation is evidently not the same as that which settles the ontico-ontological difference.

Page 191

The best edition of *Un coup de dés...* is that of Mitsou Ronat (Change Errant/d'atelier, 1980). [Translator's note: I have used Brian Coffey's translation and modified it when necessary: Stéphane Mallarmé, *Selected Poetry and Prose* (ed. M. A. Caws; New York: New Directions, 1982)]

One cannot overestimate the importance of Gardner Davies' work, especially *Vers une explication rationnelle du coupe de dès* (Paris: José Corti, 1953).

Page 197

The thesis of the axial importance of the number twelve, which turns the analysis via the theme of alexandrines towards the doctrine of literary forms, is supported by Mitsou Ronat's edition and introduction. She encounters an obstacle though, in the seven stars of the Great Bear. J.-C. Milner (in 'Libertés, Lettre, Matière,' *Conférences du Perroquet*, no. 3, 1985 [Paris: Perroquet]) interprets the seven as the invariable total of the figures which occupy two opposite sides of a die. This would perhaps neglect the fact that the seven is obtained as the total of *two* dice. My thesis is that the seven is a symbol of a figure without motif, absolutely random. Yet one can always find, at least up until twelve, esoteric significations for numbers. Human history has saturated them with signification: the seven branched candelabra . . .

Page 201

I proposed an initial approximation of the theory of the event and the intervention in *Peut-on penser la politique?* (Paris: Seuil, 1985). The limits of this first exposition—which was, besides, completely determined by the political procedure—reside in its separation from its ontological conditions. In particular, the function of the void in the interventional nomination is left untreated. However, reading the entire second section of this essay would be a useful accompaniment—at times more concrete—for Meditations 16, 17 and 20.

NOTES

Page 212

The edition of Pascal's *Pensées* used is that of J. Chevalier in Pascal, *Œuvres Complètes* (Paris: Gallimard, Bibliothèque de la Pléiade, 1954). My conclusion suggests that the order—the obligatory question of Pascalian editions —should be modified yet again, and there should be three distinct sections: the world, writing and the wager. [Translator's note: I have used and modified the following translations: Pascal, *Pascal's Pensées* (trans. M. Turnell; London: Harvill Press, 1962) and Pascal, *Pensées and Other Writings* (trans. H. Levi; Oxford: Oxford University Press, 1995)]

Page 223

On the axiom of choice the indispensable book is that of G. H. Moore, (cf. the note on page 43). A sinuous analysis of the genesis of the axiom of choice can be found in J. T. Desanti, *Les Idéalités mathématiques* (Paris: Seuil, 1968). The use, a little opaque nowadays, of a Husserlian vocabulary, should not obscure what can be found there: a tracing of the historical and subjective trajectory of what I call a great Idea of the multiple.

Page 225

For Bettazzi, and the reactions of the Italian school, see Moore (*op.cit.* note concerning page 43).

Page 226

For Fraenkel/Bar-Hillel/Levy see the note on page 60.

Page 242

For the concept of deduction, and for everything related to mathematical logic, the literature—especially in English—is abundant. I would recommend:

– For a conceptual approach, the introduction to A. Church's book, *Introduction to Mathematical Logic* (Princeton: Princeton University Press, 1956).

– For the classic statements and demonstrations:

– in French, J. F. Pabion, *Loqique Mathématique* (Paris: Hermann, 1976);

– in English, E. Mendelson, *Introduction to Mathematical Logic* (London: Chapman & Hall, 4th edn, 1997).

Page 247

There are extremely long procedures of reasoning via the absurd, in which deductive wandering within a theory which turns out to be inconsistent tactically links innumerable statements together before encountering, finally, an explicit contradiction. A good example drawn from set theory —and which is certainly not the longest—is the 'covering lemma', linked to the theory of constructible sets (cf. Meditation 29). Its statement is extremely simple: it says that if a certain set, defined beforehand, does not exist then every non-denumerable infinite set can be covered by a constructible set of ordinals of the same cardinality as the initial set. It signifies, in gross, that in this case (if the set in question does not exist), the constructible universe is 'very close' to that of general ontology, because one can 'cover' every multiple of the second by a multiple of the first which is no larger. In K. J. Devlin's canonical book, *Constructibility* (New York: Springer-Verlag, 1984), the demonstration via the absurd of this lemma of covering takes up 23 pages, leaves many details to the reader and supposes numerous complex anterior results.

Page 248

On intuitionism, the best option no doubt would be to read Chapter 4 of the book mentioned above by Fraenkel, Bar-Hillel and Levy (cf. note concerning page 60), which gives an excellent recapitulation of the subject, despite the eclecticism—in the spirit of our times—of its conclusion.

Page 250

On the foundational function within the Greek connection between mathematics and philosophy of reasoning via the absurd, and its consequences with respect to our reading of Parmenides and the Eléatics, I would back A. Szabo's book, *Les Débuts des mathématiques grecques* (trans. M. Federspiel; Paris: J. Vrin, 1977). [A. Szabo, *Beginnings of Greek Mathematics* (Dordrecht: Reidel Publishing, 1978)]

Page 254

Hölderlin.

Page 255

The French edition used for Hölderlin's texts is Hölderlin, *Œuvres* (Paris: Gallimard, Bibliothèque de la Pléiade, 1967). I have often modified the translation, or rather in this matter, searching for exactitude and density, I have followed the suggestions and advice of Isabelle Vodoz. [Translator's note: I have used Michael Hamburger's translation, modified again with the help of I. Vodoz: Friedrich Hölderlin, *Poems and Fragments* (London: Anvil, 3rd edn, 1994) as well as F. Hölderlin, *Bordeaux Memories: A Poem followed by five letters* (trans. K. White; Périgueux: William Blake & Co., 1984)]

On the orientation that Heidegger fixed with regard to the translation of Holderlin, I would refer to his *Approche de Hölderlin* (trans. H. Corbin, M. Deguy, F. Fédier and J. Launay; Paris: Gallimard, 1973). [Heidegger, *Elucidations of Hölderlin's Poetry* (trans. K. Hoeller; Amherst NY: Humanity Books, 2000); Heidegger, *Hölderlin's Hymn 'The Ister'* (trans. W. McNeill & J. Davis; Bloomington: Indiana University Press, 1996)]

Page 257

Everything which concerns Hölderlin's relationship to Greece, and more particularly his doctrine of the tragic, appears to me to be lucidly explored in several of Philippe Lacoue-Labarthe's texts. For example, there is the entire section on Hölderlin in *L'imitation des modernes* (Paris: Galilée, 1986). [P. Lacoue-Labarthe, *Typography: Mimesis, Philosophy, Politics* (C. Fynsk (ed.); Cambridge MA: Harvard University Press, 1989)]

Page 265

The references to Kant are to be found in the *Critique de la raison pure* in the section concerning the axioms of intuition (trans. J.-L. Delamarre and F. Marty; Paris: Bibliothèque de la Pléiade, 1980). [Translator's note: I have used the Kemp Smith translation: Kant, *Critique of Pure Reason* (London: Macmillan, 1929)]

Page 279

For a demonstration of Easton's theorem, it would be no doubt practical to:
– continue with this book until Meditations 33, 34 and 36;
– and complete this reading with Kunen (*op.cit.* cf. the note concerning page 60), 'Easton forcing', Kunen p.262, referring back as often as necessary (Kunen has excellent cross references), and mastering the small technical differences in presentation.

Page 281

That spatial content be solely 'numerable' by the cardinal $\mid p(\omega_0) \mid$ results from the following: a point of a straight line, once an origin is fixed, can be assigned to a real number. A real number, in turn, can be assigned to an infinite part of ω_0—to an infinite set of whole numbers—as its inscription by an unlimited decimal number shows. Finally, there is a one-to-one correspondence between real numbers and parts of ω_0, thus between the continuum and the set of parts of whole numbers. The continuum, quantitatively, is the set of parts of the discrete; or, the continuum is the state of that situation which is the denumerable.

Page 296

For a clear and succinct exposition of the theory of constructible sets one can refer to Chapter VIII of J.-L. Krivine's book (*op.cit.* note concerning page 60). The most complete book that I am aware of is that of K. J. Devlin, also mentioned in the note concerning page 60.

Page 305

The 'few precautions' which are missing, and which would allow this demonstration of the veridicity of the axiom of choice in the constructible universe to be conclusive, are actually quite essential: it is necessary to establish that well ordering exhibited in this manner does exist *within* the constructible universe; in other words, that all the operations used to indicate it are absolute for that universe.

Page 311

There is a canonical book on large cardinals: F. R. Drake, *Set Theory: an Introduction to Large Cardinals* (Amsterdam: North-Holland Publishing Company, 1974). The most simple case, that of inaccessible cardinals, is dealt with in Krivine's book (*op.cit.* note concerning page 60). A. Levy's book (cf. *ibid.*), which does not introduce forcing, contains in its ninth chapter all sorts of interesting considerations concerning inaccessible, compact, ineffable and measurable cardinals.

Page 314

A. Levy, *op.cit.*, in the note concerning page 60.

Page 315

The Leibniz texts used here are found in Leibniz, *Œuvres*, L. Prenant's edition (Paris: Aubier, 1972). It is a question of texts posterior to 1690, and in particular of 'The New System of Nature' (1695); 'On the Ultimate Origination of Things' (1697), 'Nature Itself' (1698), 'Letter to Varignon' (1707), 'Principles of Nature and of Grace' (1714), 'Monadology' (1714), Correspondence with Clarke (1715–16). I have respected the translations of this edition. [Translator's note: I have used and occasionally modified R. Ariew and D. Garber's translation in Leibniz, *Philosophical Essays* (Indianapolis: Hackett, 1989) and H. G. Alexander's in *The Leibniz–Clarke Correspondence* (New York: St Martin's Press: 1998)]

Page 322

For set theories with atoms, or 'Fraenkel-Mostowski models', see Chapter VII of J.-L. Krivine's book (cf. note concerning page 60).

Page 327

I proposed an initial conceptualization of the generic and of truth under the title 'Six propriétés de la vérité' in *Ornicar?*, nos 32 and 33, 1985 (Paris: Le Graphe/Seuil). That version was halfway between the strictly onto-logical exposition (concentrated here in Meditations 33, 34 and 36) and its metaontological precondition (Meditations 31 and 35). It assumed as axiomatic nothing less than the entire doctrine of situations and of the event. However, it is worth referring to because on certain points, notably with respect to examples, it is more explanatory.

Page 344

All of the texts cited from Rousseau are drawn from *Du contrat social, ou principes du droit politique*, and the editions abound. I used that of the Classiques (Paris: Garnier, 1954). [Translator's note: I have used Victor Gourevitch's translation, modifying it occasionally: Rousseau, *The Social Contract and other later political writings* (Cambridge: Cambridge University Press, 1997)]

Page 360

The theorem of reflection says the following precisely: given a formula in the language of set theory, and an indeterminate infinite set *E*, there exists a set R with E included in R and the cardinality of R not exceeding that of E, such that this formula, restricted to R (interpreted in R) is veridical in the latter if and only if it is veridical in general ontology. In other words, you can 'plunge' an indeterminate set (here E) into another (here R) which reflects the proposed formula. This naturally establishes that any formula (and thus also any *finite* set of formulas, which form one formula alone if they are joined together by the logical sign '&') can be reflected in a denumerable infinite set. Note that in order to demonstrate the theorem of reflection in a general manner, the axiom of choice is necessary. This theorem is a version *internal to set theory* of the famous Löwenheim–Skolem theorem: any theory whose language is denumerable admits a denumerable model.

A short bibliographic pause:

– On the Löwenheim–Skolem theorem, a very clear exposition can be found in J. Ladrière, 'Le théorème de Löwenheim–Skolem', *Cahiers pour l'analyse*, no. 10, Spring 1969 (Paris: Le Graphe/Seuil).

– On the theorem of reflection: one chapter of J.-L. Krivine's book bears the former as its title (*op.cit.*, cf. note concerning page 60). See also the book in which P. J. Cohen delivers his major discovery to the 'greater' public (genericity and forcing): *Set Theory and the Continuum Hypothesis* (New York: W. A. Benjamin, 1966)—paragraph eight of Chapter three is entitled 'The Löwenheim–Skolem theorem revisited'. Evidently one can find the theorem of reflection in all of the more complete books. Note that it was only published in 1961.

Let's continue: the fact of obtaining a denumerable model is not enough for us to have a quasi-complete situation. It is also necessary that this set be *transitive*. The argument of the Löwenheim–Skolem type has to be completed by another argument, quite different, which goes back to Mostowski (in 1949) and which allows one to prove that any extensional set (that is, any set which verifies the axiom of extensionality) is isomorphic to a transitive set.

The most suggestive clarification and demonstration of the Mostowski theorem can be found, in my opinion, in Yu. I. Manin's book: *A Course in Mathematical Logic* (trans. N. Koblitz; New York: Springer-Verlag, 1977). Chapter 7 of the second section should be read ('Countable models and Skolem's paradox').

With the reflection theorem *and* Mostowski's theorem, one definitely obtains the existence of a quasi-complete situation.

Page 362

The short books by J.-L. Krivine and K. J. Devlin (cf. note concerning page 60) either do not deal with the generic and forcing (Krivine) or they deal with these topics very rapidly (Devlin). Moreover they do so within a 'realist' rather than a conceptual perspective, which in my opinion represents the 'Boolean' version of Cohen's discovery.

My main reference, sometimes followed extremely closely (for the technical part of things) is Kunen's book (*op.cit.* note concerning page 60). But I think that in respect of the sense of the thought of the generic, the beginning of Chapter 4 of P. J. Cohen's book (*op.cit.* note concerning page 360), as well as its conclusion, is of great interest.

Page 397

For a slightly different approach to the concept of confidence see my *Théorie du sujet* (*op.cit.* note concerning page 4), 337–342.

Page 405

On the factory as a political place, cf. *Le Perroquet*, nos. 56–57, Nov.–Dec., 1985, in particular Paul Sandevince's article.

Page 411

I follow Kunen extremely closely (*op.cit.* note concerning page 60). The essential difference at the level of writing is that I write the domination of one condition by another as $\pi_1 \subset \pi_2$, whereas Kunen writes it, according to a usage which goes back to Cohen, as $\pi_2 \leq \pi_1$—thus 'backwards'. One of the consequences is that $\varnothing$ is termed a maximal condition and not a minimal condition, etc.

Page 418

By *ST* the formal apparatus of set theory must be understood, such as we have developed it from Meditation 3 onwards.

Page 431

The reference here is 'Science et verité' in J. Lacan, *Ecrits* (Paris: Seuil, 1966). ['Science and Truth' in *The Newsletter of the Freudian Field*, E. R. Sullivan (ed.); trans. B. Fink; vol. 3, 1989.]

Page 435

Mallarmé.

Page 445

On the demonstration that if $\langle a,\beta \rangle = \langle \gamma,\delta \rangle$, then $a = \gamma$ and $\beta = \delta$, see for example A. Levy's book (*op.cit.* note concerning page 60), 24–25.

Page 450

For complementary developments on regular and singular cardinals, see A. Levy's book (*op.cit.* note concerning page 60), Chapter IV, paragraphs 3 and 4.

Page 456

On absoluteness, there is an excellent presentation in Kunen (*op.cit.* note concerning page 60), 117–133.

Page 460

On the length of formulas and reasoning by recurrence, there are some very good exercises in J. F. Pabion's book (*op.cit.* note concerning page 242), 17–23.

Page 462

Definitions and complete demonstrations of forcing can be found in Kunen (*op.cit.* note concerning page 60) in particular on pages 192–201. Kunen himself holds these calculations to be 'tedious details'. It is a question, he says, of verifying whether the procedure 'really works'.

Page 467

On the veridicity of the axioms of set theory in a generic extension see Kunen, 201–203. However, there are a lot of presuppositions (in particular, the theorems of reflection).

Page 471

Appendixes 9, 10 and 11 follow Kunen extremely closely.

Dictionary

Some of the concepts used or mentioned in the text are defined here, and some crucial philosophical and ontological statements are given a sense. The idea is to provide a kind of rapid alphabetical run through the substance of the book. In each definition, I indicate by the sign (+) the words which have their own entry in the dictionary, and which I feel to be prerequisites for understanding the definition in question. The numbers between parentheses indicate the meditation in which one can find—unfolded, illustrated and articulated to a far greater extent—the definition of the concept under consideration.

It may be of some note that the Dictionary begins with ABSOLUTE and finishes with VOID.

ABSOLUTE, ABSOLUTENESS (29, 33, Appendix 5)

– A formula (+) λ is absolute for a set α if the veracity of that formula restricted (+) to α is equivalent, for values of the parameters taken from α, to its veracity in set theory without restrictions. That is, a formula is absolute if it can be demonstrated: $(\lambda)^\alpha \leftrightarrow \lambda$, once λ is 'tested' within α.

– For example: 'α is an ordinal inferior to ω_0' is an absolute formula for the level $L_{S(\omega_0)}$ of the constructible hierarchy (+).

– In general, quantitative considerations (cardinality (+), etc.) are not absolute.

ALEPH (26)

– An infinite (+) cardinal (+) is termed an aleph. It is written ω_a, the ordinal which indexes it indicating its place in the series of infinite cardinals (ω_a is the ath infinite cardinal. It is larger than any ω_β such that $\beta \in a$).

– The countable or denumerable infinity (+), ω_0, is the first aleph. The series continues: $\omega_0, \omega_1, \omega_2, \ldots \omega_n, \omega_{n+1}, \ldots \omega_0, \omega_{S(\omega_0)}, \ldots$

This is the series of alephs.

– Every infinite set has an aleph as its cardinality.

AVOIDANCE OF AN ENCYCLOPAEDIC DETERMINANT (31)

– An enquiry (+) avoids a determinant (+) of the encyclopaedia (+) if it contains a positive connection—of the type $\gamma(+)$—to the name of the event for a term γ which does not fall under the encyclopaedic determinant in question.

AXIOMS OF SET THEORY (3 and 5)

– The postcantorian clarification of the statements which found ontology (+), and thus all mathematics, as theory of the pure multiple.

– Isolated and extracted between 1880 and 1930, these statements are, in the presentation charged with the most sense, nine in number: extensionality (+), subsets (+), union (+), separation (+), replacement (+), void (+), foundation (+), infinity (+), choice (+). They concentrate the greatest effort of thought ever accomplished to this day by humanity.

AXIOM OF CHOICE (22)

– Given a set, there exists a set composed exactly of a representative of each of the (non-void) elements of the initial set. More precisely: there exists a function (+) f, such that, if a is the given set, and if $\beta \in a$, we have $f(\beta) \in \beta$.

– The function of choice exists, but in general it cannot be shown (or constructed). Choice is thus illegal (no explicit rule for the choice) and anonymous (no discernibility of what is chosen).

– This axiom is the ontological schema of intervention (+) but without the event (+): it is the being of intervention which is at stake, not its act.

– The axiom of choice, by a significant overturning of its illegality, is equivalent to the principle of maximal order: every set can be well-ordered.

AXIOM OF EXTENSIONALITY (5)

– Two sets are equal if they have the same elements.

– This is the ontological scheme of the same and the other.

AXIOM OF FOUNDATION (18)

– Any non-void set possesses at least one element whose intersection with the initial set is void (+); that is, an element whose elements are not elements of the initial set. One has $\beta \in \alpha$ but $\beta \cap \alpha = \varnothing$. Therefore, if $\gamma \in \beta$, we are sure that $\sim(\gamma \in \alpha)$. It is said that β founds α, or is on the edge of the void in α.

– This axiom implies the prohibition of self-belonging, and thus posits that ontology (+) does not have to know anything of the event (+).

AXIOM OF INFINITY (14)

– There exists a limit ordinal (+).

– This axiom poses that natural-being (+) admits infinity (+). It is post-Galilean.

AXIOM OF REPLACEMENT (5)

– If a set α exists, the set also exists which is obtained by replacing all of the elements of α by other existing multiples.

– This axiom thinks multiple-being (consistency) as transcendent to the particularity of elements. These elements can be substituted for, the multiple-form maintaining its consistency after the substitution.

AXIOM OF SEPARATION (3)

– If α is given, the set of elements of α which possess an explicit property (of the type $\lambda(\beta)$) also exists. It is a part (+) of α, from which it is said to be separated by the formula λ.

– This axiom indicates that being is anterior to language. One can only 'separate' a multiple by language within some already given being-multiple.

AXIOM OF SUBSETS OR OF PARTS (5)

– There exists a set whose elements are subsets (+) or parts (+) of a given set. This set, if α is given, is written $p(\alpha)$. What belongs (+) to $p(\alpha)$ is included (+) in α.

– The set of parts is the ontological scheme of the state of a situation (+).

AXIOM OF UNION (5)

– There exists a set whose elements are the elements of the elements of a given set. If α is given, the union of α is written $\cup\, \alpha$.

AXIOM OF THE VOID (5)

– There exists a set which does not have any element. This set is unique, and it has as its proper name the mark $\varnothing$.

BELONGING (3)

– The unique foundational sign of set theory. It indicates that a multiple β enters into the multiple-composition of a multiple α. This is written $\beta \in \alpha$, and it is said that 'β belongs to α' or 'β is an element of α'.

– Philosophically it would be said that a term (an element) belongs to a situation (+) if it is presented (+) and counted as one (+) by that situation. Belonging refers to presentation, whilst inclusion (+) refers to representation.

CANTOR'S THEOREM (26)

– The cardinality (+) of the set of parts (+) of a set is superior to that of the set. This is written:

$| a | < | p(a) |$

It is the law of the quantitative excess of the state of the situation over the situation.

– This excess fixes orientations in thought (+). It is the impasse, or point of the real, of ontology.

CARDINAL, CARDINALITY (26)

– A cardinal is an ordinal (+) such that there does not exist a one-to-one correspondence (+) between it and an ordinal smaller than it.

– The cardinality of an indeterminate set is the cardinal with which that set is in one-to-one correspondence. The cardinality of a is written $| a |$. Remember that $| a |$ is a cardinal, even if a is an indeterminate set.

– The cardinality of a set always exists, if one admits the axiom of choice (+).

COHEN-EASTON THEOREM (26, 36)

– For a very large number of cardinals (+), in fact for ω_0 and for all the successor cardinals, it can be demonstrated that the cardinality of the set of their parts (+) can take on more or less any value in the sequence of alephs (+).

To be exact, the fixation of a (more or less) indeterminate value remains coherent with the axioms of set theory (+), or Ideas of the multiple (+).

– As such, it is coherent with the axioms to posit that $| p(\omega_0) | = \omega_1$ (this is the continuum hypothesis (+)), but also to posit $| p(\omega_0) | = \omega_{18}$, or that $| p(\omega_0) | = \omega_{S(\omega_0)}$, etc.

– This theorem establishes the complete errancy of excess (+).

CONDITIONS, SET OF CONDITIONS (33)

– We place ourselves in a quasi-complete situation (+). A set which belongs to this situation is a set of conditions, written ©, if:

a. ∅ belongs to ©, that is, the void is a condition, the 'void condition'.

b. There exists, on ©, a relation, written ⊂. $\pi_1 \subset \pi_2$ reads 'π_2 dominates π_1'.

c. This relation is an order, inasmuch as if π_3 dominates π_2, and π_2 dominates π_1, then π_3 dominates π_1.

d. Two conditions are said to be compatible if they are dominated by the same third condition. If this is not the case they are incompatible.

e. Every condition is dominated by two conditions which are incompatible between themselves.

– Conditions provide both the material for a generic set (+), and information on that set. Order, compatibility, etc., are structures of information (they are more precise, coherent amongst themselves, etc.).

– Conditions are the ontological schema of enquiries (+).

CONSISTENT MULTIPLICITY (1)

– Multiplicity composed of 'many-ones', themselves counted by the action of structure.

CONSTRUCTIBLE HIERARCHY (29)

– The constructible hierarchy consists, starting from the void, of the definition of successive levels indexed on the ordinals (+), taking each time the definable parts (+) of the previous level.

– We therefore have: $L_0 = \varnothing$
$$L_{S(a)} = D(a)$$
$L_\beta = \cup \ \{L_0, L_1, \ldots L_\beta \ldots\}$ for all the $\beta \in a$, if β is a limit ordinal (+).

CONSTRUCTIBLE SET (29)

– A set is constructible if it belongs to one of the levels L_a of the constructible hierarchy (+).

– A constructible set is thus always related to an explicit formula of the language, and to an ordinal level (+). Such is the accomplishment of the constructivist vision of the multiple.

CONSTRUCTIVIST THOUGHT (27, 28)

– The constructivist orientation of thought (+) places itself under the jurisdiction of language. It only admits as existent those parts of a situation which are explicitly nameable. It thereby masters the excess (+) of inclusion (+) over belonging (+), or of parts (+) over elements (+), or of the state of the situation (+) over the situation (+), by reducing that excess to the minimum.

– Constructivism is the ontological decision subjacent to any nominalist thought.

– The ontological schema for such thought is Gödel's constructible universe (+).

CONTINUUM HYPOTHESIS (27)

– It is a hypothesis of the constructivist type (+). It posits that the set of parts (+) of the denumerable infinity (+), ω_0, has as its cardinality (+) the successor cardinal (+) to ω_0, that is, ω_1. It is therefore written $| p(\omega_0) | = \omega_1$.

– The continuum hypothesis is demonstrable within the constructible universe (+) and refutable in certain generic extensions (+). It is therefore undecidable (+) for set theory without restrictions.

– The word 'continuum' is used because the cardinality of the geometric continuum (of the real numbers) is exactly that of $p(\omega_0)$.

CORRECT SUBSET (OR PART) OF THE SET OF CONDITIONS (33)

– A subset of conditions (+)—a part of ©—is correct if it obeys the following two rules:

Rd_1: if a condition belongs to the correct part, all the conditions which it dominates also belong to the part.

Rd_2: if two conditions belong to the correct part, at least one condition which simultaneously dominates the other two also belongs to the part.

– A correct part actually 'conditions' *a* subset of conditions. It gives coherent information.

COUNT-AS-ONE (1)

– Given the non-being of the One, any one-effect is the result of an operation, the count-as-one. Every situation (+) is structured by such a count.

DEDUCTION (24)

– The operator of faithful connection (+) for mathematics (ontology). Deduction consists in verifying whether a statement is connected or not to the name of what has been an event in the recent history of mathematics. It then draws the consequences.

– Its tactical operators are *modus ponens*: from A and $A \rightarrow B$ draw B; and generalization: from $\lambda(a)$ where a is a free variable (+), draw $(\forall a)\lambda(a)$.

– Its current strategies are hypothetical reasoning and reasoning via the absurd, or apagogic reasoning. The last type is particularly characteristic because it is directly linked to the ontological vocation of deduction.

DEFINABLE PART (29)

– A part (+) of a given set a is definable—relative to a—if it can be separated within a, in the sense of the axiom of separation (+), by an explicit formula restricted (+) to a.

– The set of definable parts of a is written $D(a)$. $D(a)$ is a subset of $p(a)$.

– The concept of definable part is the instrument thanks to which the excess (+) of parts is limited by language. It is the tool of construction for the constructible hierarchy (+).

DENUMERABLE INFINITY ω_0 (14)

– If one admits that there exists a limit ordinal (+), as posited by the axiom of infinity (+), there exists a smallest limit ordinal according to the principle of minimality (+). This smallest limit ordinal—which is also a cardinal (+)—is written ω_0. It characterizes the denumerable infinity, the smallest infinity, that of the set of natural whole numbers, the discrete infinity.

– Every element of ω_0 will be said to be a finite ordinal.

– ω_0 is the 'frontier' between the finite and the infinite. An infinite ordinal is an ordinal which is equal or superior to ω_0 (the order here is that of belonging).

DOMINATION (33)

– A domination is a part D of the set © of conditions (+) such that, if a condition π is exterior to D, and thus belongs to © $- D$, there always exists in D a condition which dominates π.

– The set of conditions which do not possess a given property is a domination, if the set of conditions which do possess that property is a correct set (+): hence the intervention of this concept in the question of the indiscernible.

ELEMENT See Belonging.

ENCYCLOPAEDIC DETERMINANT (31)

– An encyclopaedic determinant (+) is a part (+) of the situation (+) composed of terms that have a property in common which can be formulated in the language of the situation. Such a term is said to 'fall under the determinant'.

ENCYCLOPAEDIA OF A SITUATION (31)

– An encyclopaedia is a classification of the parts of the situation which are discerned by a property which can be formulated in the language of the situation.

ENQUIRY (31)

– An enquiry is a finite series of connections, or of non-connections, observed—within the context of a procedure of fidelity (+)—between the terms of the situation and the name e_x of the event (+) such as it is circulated by the intervention.

– A minimal or atomic enquiry is a positive, $\gamma_1 \ \square \ e_x$, or negative, $\sim(\gamma_2 \ \square \ e_x)$, connection. It will also be said that γ_1 has been positively investigated (written $\gamma_1(+)$), and γ_2 negatively $(\gamma_2(-))$.

– It is said of an investigated term that it has been encountered by the procedure of fidelity.

EVENT (17)

– An event—of a given evental site (+)—is the multiple composed of: on the one hand, elements of the site; and on the other hand, itself (the event).

– Self-belonging is thus constitutive of the event. It is an element of the multiple which it is.

– The event interposes itself between the void and itself. It will be said to be an ultra-one (relative to the situation).

EVENTAL SITE (16)

– A multiple in a situation is an evental site if it is totally singular (+): it is presented, but none of its elements are presented. It belongs but it is radically not included. It is an element but in no way a part. It is totally ab-normal (+).

– It is also said of such a multiple that it is on the edge of the void (+), or foundational.

EXCESS (7, 8, 26)

– Designates the measureless difference, and especially the quantitative difference, or difference of power, between the state of a situation (+) and the situation (+). However, in a certain sense, it also designates the difference between being (in situation) and the event (+) (ultra-one). Excess turns out to be errant and unassignable.

EXCRESCENCE (8)

– A term is an excrescence if it is represented by the state of the situation (+) without being presented by the situation (+).

– An excrescence is included (+) in the situation without belonging (+) to it. It is a part (+) but not an element.

– Excrescence touches on excess (+).

FIDELITY, PROCEDURE OF FIDELITY (23)

– The procedure by means of which one discerns, in a situation, the multiples whose existence is linked to the name of the event (+) that has been put into circulation by an intervention (+).

– Fidelity distinguishes and gathers together the becoming of what is connected to the name of the event. It is a post-evental quasi-state.

– There is always an operator of connection characteristic of the fidelity. It is written □.

– For example, ontological fidelity (+) has deductive technique (+) as its operator of fidelity.

FORCING, AS FUNDAMENTAL LAW OF THE SUBJECT (35)

– If a statement of the subject-language (+) is such that it will have been veridical (+) for a situation in which a truth has occurred, this is because there exists a term of the situation which belongs to this truth and which maintains, with the names at stake in the statement, a fixed relation that can be verified by knowledge (+), thus inscribed in the encyclopaedia (+). It is this relation which is termed forcing. It is said that the term forces the decision of veracity for the statement of the subject-language.

– One can thus know, within the situation, whether a statement of the subject-language has a chance or not of being veridical when the truth will have occurred in its infinity.

– However, the verification of the relation of forcing supposes that the forcing term has been encountered and investigated by the generic procedure of fidelity (+). Thus it depends on chance.

FORCING, FROM COHEN (36, Appendixes 7 and 8)

– Take a quasi-complete situation (+) S, a generic extension (+) of S, $S(♀)$, Take a formula $\lambda(\alpha)$, for example, with one free variable. What is the truth value of this formula in the generic extension $S(♀)$, for example, for an element of $S(♀)$ substituted for the variable α?

– An element of $S(♀)$ is, by definition, the referential value (+) $R_♀(\mu_1)$ of a name (+) μ_1 which belongs to S. Let's consider the formula $\lambda(\mu_1)$, which substitutes the name μ_1 for the variable α. This formula can be understood by an inhabitant (+) of S, since $\mu_1 \in S$.

– One then shows that $\lambda[R_♀(\mu_1)]$ is veridical in $S(♀)$, thus for an inhabitant of $S(♀)$, if and only if there exists a condition (+) which belongs to ♀ and which maintains a relation—said to be that of forcing—with the statement $\lambda(\mu_1)$, a relation whose existence can be controlled in S, or by an inhabitant of S.

– The relation of forcing is written: ≡. We thus have:

$$\lambda[R♀(\mu_1)]^{S(♀)} \leftrightarrow (\exists\pi) \ [(\pi \in ♀) \ \& \ (\pi \equiv \lambda(\mu_1))]$$

It being understood that $\pi \equiv \lambda(\mu_1)$—which reads: π forces $\lambda(\mu_1)$—can be demonstrated or refuted in S.

– One can thus establish within S whether a statement $\lambda[R♀(\mu_1)]$ has a chance of being veridical in $S(♀)$: what is required, at least, is that there exist a condition π which forces $\lambda(\mu_1)$.

FORMING-INTO-ONE (5, 9)

– Operation through which the count-as-one (+) is applied to what is already a result-one. Forming-into-one produces the one of the one-multiple. Thus, {∅} is the forming-into-one of ∅; it is the latter's singleton (+).

– Forming-into-one is also a production on the part of the state of the situation (+). That is, if I form a term of the situation into one, I obtain a part of that situation, the part whose sole element is this term.

FORMULA (Technical Note at Meditation 3, Appendix 6)

– A set theory formula can be obtained in the following manner by using the primitive sign of belonging (+) ∈, equality =, the connectors (+), quantifiers (+), a denumerable infinity of variables (+) and parentheses:

    a. $\alpha \in \beta$ and $\alpha = \beta$ are atomic formulas;
    b. if λ is a formula, the following are also formulas: $\sim(\lambda)$; $(\forall\alpha)(\lambda)$; $(\exists\alpha)(\lambda)$;
    c. if λ_1 and λ_2 are formulas, so are the following: (λ_1) *or* (λ_2); (λ_1) & (λ_2); $(\lambda_1) \rightarrow (\lambda_2)$; $(\lambda_1) \leftrightarrow (\lambda_2)$.

FUNCTION (22, 26, Appendix 2)

– A function is nothing more than a species of multiple; it is not a distinct concept. In other words, the being of a function is a pure multiple. It is a multiple such that:

    a. all of its elements are ordered pairs (+) of the type $<\alpha,\beta>$;

b. if a pair <*α,β*> and a pair <*α,γ*> appear in a function, it is a fact that *β* = *γ*, and that these 'two' pairs are identical.

– We are in the habit of writing, instead of <*α,β*> ∈ *f* , *f*(*α*) = *β*. This is appropriate: the latter form is devoid of ambiguity since, (condition *b*) for a given *α*, one *β* alone corresponds.

GENERIC EXTENSION OF A QUASI-COMPLETE SITUATION (34)

– Take a quasi-complete situation (+), written *S*, and a generic part (+) of that situation, written ♀. We will term generic extension, and write as *S*(♀), the set constituted from the referential values (+), or ♀-referents, of all the names (+) which belong to *S*.

– Observe that it is the names which create the thing.

– It can be shown that ♀ ∈ *S*(♀), whilst ~(♀ ∈ *S*); that *S*(♀) is also a quasi-complete situation; and that ♀ is an indiscernible (+) intrinsic to *S*(♀).

GENERIC, GENERIC PROCEDURE (31)

– A procedure of fidelity (+) is generic if, for any determinant (+) of the encyclopaedia, it contains at least one enquiry (+) which avoids (+) this determinant.

– There are four types of generic procedure: artistic, scientific, political, and amorous. These are the four sources of truth (+).

GENERIC SET, GENERIC PART OF THE SET OF CONDITIONS (34)

– A correct subset (+) of conditions © is generic if its intersection with every domination (+) that belongs to the quasi-complete situation (+) in which © occurs is not void. A generic set is written ♀.

– The generic set, by 'cutting across' all the dominations, avoids being discernible within the situation.

– It is the ontological schema of a truth.

GENERIC THOUGHT (27, 31)

– The generic orientation of thought (+) assumes the errancy of excess (+), and admits unnameable or indiscernible (+) parts into being. It even sees in such parts the place of truth. For a truth (+) is a part indiscernible by language (against constructivism (+)), and yet it is not transcendent (+) (against onto-theology).

– Generic thought is the ontological decision subjacent to any doctrine which attempts to think of truth as a hole in knowledge (+). There are traces of such from Plato to Lacan.

– The ontological schema of such thought is Paul Cohen's theory of generic extensions (+).

HISTORICAL SITUATION (16)

– A situation to which at least one evental site (+) belongs. Note that the criteria (at least *one*) is local.

IDEAS OF THE MULTIPLE (5)

– Primordial statements of ontology. 'Ideas of the multiple' is the philosophical designation for what is designated ontologically (mathematically) as 'the axioms of set theory' (+).

INCLUSION (5, 7)

– A set β is included in a set α if all of the elements of β are also elements of α. This relation is written $\beta \subset \alpha$, and reads 'β is included in α'. We also say that β is a subset (English terminology), or a part (French terminology), of α.

– A term will be said to be included in a situation if it is a sub-multiple or a part of the latter. It is thus counted as one (+) by the state of the situation (+). Inclusion refers to (state) representation.

INCONSISTENT MULTIPLICITY (1)

– Pure presentation retrospectively understood as non-one, since being-one is solely the result of an operation.

INDISCERNIBLE (31, 33)

– A part of a situation is indiscernible if no statement of the language of the situation separates it or discerns it. Or: a part is indiscernible if it does not fall under any encyclopaedic determinant (+).

– A truth (+) is always indiscernible.

– The ontological schema of indiscernibility is non-constructibility (+). There is a distinction between extrinsic indiscernibility—the indiscernible part (in the sense of ⊂) of a quasi-complete situation does not belong (in the sense of ∈) to the situation—and intrinsic indiscernibility—the indiscernible part belongs to the situation in which it is indiscernible.

INFINITY (13)

– Infinity has to be untied from the One (theology) and returned to multiple-being, including natural-being (+). This is the Galilean gesture, and it is thought ontologically by Cantor.

– A multiplicity is infinite under the following conditions:

a. an initial point of being, an 'already' existing;
b. a rule of passage which indicates how I 'pass' from one term to another (concept of the other);
c. the recognition that, according to the rule, there is always 'still one more', there is no stopping point;
d. a second existent, a 'second existential seal', which is the multiple within which the 'one more' insists (concept of the Other).

– The ontological schema of natural infinity (+) is constructed on the basis of the concept of a limit ordinal (+).

INHABITANT OF A SET (29, 33)

– What is metaphorically termed 'inhabitant of α' or 'inhabitant of the universe α' is a supposed subject for whom the universe is uniquely made up of elements of α. In other words, for this inhabitant, 'to exist' means to belong to α, to be an element of α.

– For such an inhabitant, a formula λ is understood as $(\lambda)^\alpha$, as the formula restricted (+) to α. It is quantified within α, etc.

– Since self-belonging is prohibited, α does not belong to α. Consequently, an inhabitant of α does not know α. The universe of an inhabitant does not exist for that inhabitant.

INTERVENTION (20)

– The procedure by which a multiple is recognised as event (+), and which decides the belonging of the event to the situation in which it has its site (+).

– The intervention is shown to consist in making a name out of an unpresented element of the site in order to qualify the event whose site is this site. This nomination is both illegal (it does not conform to any rule of representation) and anonymous (the name drawn from the void is indistinguishable precisely because it is drawn from the void). It is equivalent to 'being an unpresented element of the site'.

– The name of the event, which is indexed to the void, is thus supernumerary to the situation in which it will circulate the event.

– Interventional capacity requires an event anterior to the one that it names. It is determined by a fidelity (+) to this initial event.

KNOWLEDGE (28, 31)

– Knowledge is the articulation of the language of the situation over multiple-being. Forever nominalist, it is the production of the constructivist orientation of thought (+). Its operations consist of discernment (this multiple has such a property) and classification (these multiples have the same property). These operations result in an encyclopaedia (+).

– A judgement classified within the encyclopaedia is said to be veridical.

LARGE CARDINALS (26, Appendix 3)

– A large cardinal is a cardinal (+) whose existence cannot be proven on the basis of the classic axioms of set theory (+), and thus has to form the object of a new axiom. What is then at stake is an axiom of infinity stronger than the one which guarantees the existence of a limit ordinal (+)

and authorizes the construction of the sequence of alephs (+). A large cardinal is a super-aleph.

– The simplest of the large cardinals are the inaccessible cardinals (cf. Appendix 3). One then goes much 'higher up' with Mahlo cardinals, Ramsey cardinals, ineffable cardinals, compact, super-compact or huge cardinals.

– None of these large cardinals forces a decision concerning the exact value of $p(a)$ for an infinite a. They do not block the errancy of excess (+).

LIMIT CARDINAL (26)

– A cardinal (+) which is neither $\varnothing$ nor a successor cardinal (+) is a limit cardinal. It is the union of the infinity of cardinals which precede it.

– The countable infinity (+), ω_0, is the first limit cardinal. The following one is ω_{ω_0}, which is the limit of the first segment of alephs (+): $\omega_0, \omega_1, \ldots \omega_n, \ldots$

LIMIT ORDINAL (14)

– A limit ordinal is an ordinal (+) different to $\varnothing$ and which is not a successor ordinal (+). In short, a limit ordinal is inaccessible via the operation of succession.

LOGICAL CONNECTORS (Technical Note at Meditation 3, Appendix 4)

– These are signs which allow us to obtain formulas (+) on the basis of other given formulas. There are five of them: $\sim$ (negation), *or* (disjunction), & (conjunction), $\rightarrow$ (implication), $\leftrightarrow$ (equivalence).

MULTIPLICITY, MULTIPLE (1)

– General form of presentation, once one assumes that the One is not.

NAMES FOR A SET OF CONDITIONS, OR ©-NAMES (34)

– Say that © is a set of conditions (+). A name is a multiple all of whose elements are ordered pairs (+) of names and conditions. These names are written μ, μ_1, μ_2, etc. Every element of a name μ thus has the form $<\mu_1,\pi>$, where μ_1 is a name and π a condition.

– The circularity of this definition is undone by stratifying the names. In the example above, the name μ_1 will always have to come from an inferior stratum (one defined previously) to that of the name μ, in whose composition it intervenes. The zero stratum is given by the names whose elements are of the type $<\varnothing,\pi>$.

NATURE, NATURAL (11)

– A situation is natural if all the terms it presents are normal (+), and if, in turn, all the terms presented by these terms are normal, and so on. Nature is recurrent normality. As such, natural-being generates a stability, a maximal equilibrium between presentation and representation (+), between belonging (+) and inclusion (+), between the situation (+) and the state of the situation (+).

– The ontological schema of natural multiples is constructed with the concept of ordinal (+).

NATURAL SITUATION (11)

– Any situation all of whose terms are normal (+); in addition, the terms of those terms are also normal, and so on. Note that the criteria (*all* the terms) is global.

NEUTRAL SITUATION (16)

– A situation which is neither natural nor historical.

NORMAL, NORMALITY (8)

– A term is normal if it is both presented (+) in the situation and represented (+) by the state of the situation (+). It is thus counted twice in its place: once by the structure (count-as-one) and once by the met-astructure (count-of-the-count).

– It can also be said that a normal term belongs (+) to the situation and is also included (+) in it. It is both an element and a part.

– Normality is an essential attribute of natural-being (+).

ONE-TO-ONE (function, correspondence) (26)

– A function (+) is one-to-one if, for two different multiples, there correspond, via the function, two different multiples. This is written: $\sim(\alpha = \beta) \rightarrow \sim[f(\alpha) = f(\beta)]$

– Two sets are in one-to-one correspondence if there exists a one-to-one function which, for every element of the first set, establishes a correspondence with an element of the second set, and this without remainder (all the elements of the second are used).

– The concept of one-to-one correspondence founds the ontological doctrine of quantity.

ON THE EDGE OF THE VOID (16)

– Characteristic of the position of an evental site within a situation. Since none of the elements of the site are presented 'underneath' the site there is nothing—within the situation—apart from the void. In other words, the dissemination of such a multiple does not occur in the situation, despite the multiple being there. This is why the one of such a multiple is, in the situation, right on the edge of the void.

– Technically, if $\beta \in \alpha$, it is said that β is on the edge of the void if, in turn, for every $\gamma \in \beta$ (every element of β) one has: $\sim(\gamma \in \alpha)$, γ itself not being an element of α. It is also said that β founds α (see the axiom of foundation (+)).

ONTICO-ONTOLOGICAL DIFFERENCE (18)

– It is attached to the following: the void (+) is solely marked (by $\varnothing$) within the ontological situation (+); in situation-beings, the void is foreclosed. The result is that the ontological schema of a multiple can be founded by the void (this is the case with ordinals (+)), whilst a historical situation-being (+) is founded by a forever non-void evental site. The mark of the void is what disconnects the thought of being (theory of the pure multiple) from the capture of beings.

ONTOLOGY (Introduction, 1)

– Science of being-qua-being. Presentation (+) of presentation. Realized as thought of the pure multiple, thus as Cantorian mathematics or set theory. It is and was already effective, despite being unthematized, throughout the entire history of mathematics.

– Obliged to think the pure multiple without recourse to the One, ontology is necessarily axiomatic.

ONTOLOGIST (29, 33)

– An ontologist is what we call an inhabitant (+) of the entire universe of set theory. The ontologist quantifies (+) and parameterizes (+) without restriction (+). For the ontologist, the inhabitant of a set a has quite a limited perspective on things. The ontologist views such an inhabitant from the outside.

– A formula is absolute (+) for the set a if it has the same sense (when it is parameterized in a) and the same veracity for the ontologist and for the inhabitant of a.

ORDERED PAIR (Appendix 2)

– The ordered pair of two sets a and β is the pair (+) of the singleton (+) of a and the pair $\{a,\beta\}$. It is written $<a,\beta>$. We thus have: $<a,\beta> = \{\{a\}, \{a,\beta\}\}$.

– The ordered pair fixes both its composition and its order. The 'places' of a and β—first place or second place—are determined. This is what allows the notions of relation and function (+) to be thought as pure multiples.

ORDINAL (12)

– An ordinal is a transitive (+) set all of whose elements are also transitive. It is the ontological schema of natural multiples (+).

– It can be shown that every element of an ordinal is an ordinal. This property founds the homogeneity of nature.

– It can be shown that any two ordinals, α and β, are ordered by presentation inasmuch as either one belongs to the other—$\alpha \in \beta$—or the other way round—$\beta \in \alpha$. Such is the general connection of all natural multiples.

– If $\alpha \in \beta$, it is said that α is smaller than β. Note that we also have $\alpha \subset \beta$ because β is transitive.

ORIENTATIONS IN THOUGHT (27)

– Every thought is orientated by a pre-decision, most often latent, concerning the errancy of quantitative excess (+). Such is the requisition of thought imposed by the impasse of ontology.

– There are three grand orientations: constructivist (+), transcendent (+), and generic (+).

PAIR (12)

– The pair of two sets α and β is the set which has as its sole elements α and β. It is written $\{\alpha,\beta\}$.

PARAMETERS (29)

– In a formula of the type $\lambda(\alpha, \beta_1, \ldots \beta_n)$, one can envisage treating the variables (+) $\beta_1, \ldots \beta_n$ as marks to be replaced by the proper names of fixed multiples. One then terms $\beta_1, \ldots \beta_n$ the parametric variables of the formula. A system of values of the parameters is an n-tuple $<\gamma_1, \ldots \gamma_n>$ of fixed, specified multiples (thus constants, or proper names). The formula $\lambda(\alpha, \beta_1, \ldots \beta_n)$ depends on the n-tuple $<\gamma_1, \ldots \gamma_n>$ chosen as value for the parametric variables. In particular, what this formula says of the free variable α depends on this n-tuple.

– For example, the formula $\alpha \in \beta_1$ is certainly false, whatever α is, if we take the empty set as the value of β_1, since there is no multiple α in existence such that $\alpha \in \varnothing$. On the other hand, the formula is certainly true if we take $p(\alpha)$ as the value of β_1, because for every set $\alpha \in p(\alpha)$.

– Comparison: the trinomial $ax^2 + bx + c$ has, or does not have, real roots, according to the numbers that are substituted for the parametric variables a, b and c.

PART OF A SET, OF A SITUATION (8) See *Inclusion*.

PRESENTATION (1)

– Primitive word of metaontology (or of philosophy). Presentation is multiple-being such as it is effectively deployed. 'Presentation' is reciprocal with 'inconsistent multiplicity' (+). The One is not presented, it results, thus making the multiple consist.

PRINCIPLE OF MINIMALITY OF ORDINALS, OR ∈-MINIMALITY (12, Appendix 1)

– If there exists an ordinal which possesses a given property, there exists a smallest ordinal which has that property: it possesses the property, but the smaller ordinals, those which belong to it, do not.

QUANTIFIERS (Technical Note at Meditation 3, Appendix 6)

– These are logical operators allowing the quantification of variables (+), that is, the clarification of significations such as 'for every multiple one has this or that', or 'there exists a multiple such that this or that'.

– The universal quantifier is written ∀. The formula (+) $(\forall a)\lambda$ reads; 'for every a, we have λ.'

– The existential quantifier is written ∃. The formula $(\exists a)\lambda$ reads; 'there exists a such that λ.'

QUANTITY (26)

– The modern (post-Galilean) difficulty with the concept of quantity is concentrated within infinite (+) multiples. It is said that two multiples are of the same quantity if there exists a one-to-one correspondence (+) between the two of them.

– See *Cardinal*, *Cardinality*, *Aleph*.

QUASI-COMPLETE SITUATION (33 and Appendix 5)

– A set is a quasi-complete situation and is written S if:

a. it is denumerably infinite (+);

b. it is transitive (+);

c. the axioms of the powerset (+), union (+), void (+), infinity (+), foundation (+), and choice (+), restricted to this set, are veridical in this set (the ontologist (+) can demonstrate their validity within S, and an inhabitant (+) of S can assume them without contradiction, as long as they are not contradictory for the ontologist);

d. all the axioms of separation (+) (for formulas λ restricted to S) or of replacement (+) (for substitutions restricted to S) which have been used by mathematicians up to this day—or will be, let's say, in the next hundred years to come (thus a finite number of such axioms) —are veridical under the same conditions.

– In other words, the inhabitant of S can understand and manipulate all of the theorems of set theory, both current and future (because there will never be an infinity of them to be effectively demonstrated), in their restricted-to-S versions; that is, inside its restricted universe. One can also say: S is a denumerable transitive model of set theory, considered as a finite set of statements.

– The necessity of confining oneself to actually practised (or historical) mathematics—that is, to a finite set of statements—which is obviously unobjectionable, is due to it being impossible to demonstrate within ontology the existence of what would be a complete situation, that is a model of all possible theorems, thus of all axioms of separation and replacement corresponding to the (infinite) series of separating or substituting formulas. The reason for this is that if we had done so, we would have demonstrated, within ontology, the coherence of ontology, and this is precisely what a famous logical theorem of Gödel proves to be impossible.

– However, one can demonstrate that there exists a quasi-complete situation.

REFERENTIAL VALUE OF A NAME, ♀-REFERENT OF A NAME (34)

– Given a generic part (+) of a quasi-complete situation (+), the referential value of a name (+) μ, written $R_{♀}(\mu)$, is the set of all the referential values of the names μ_1 such that:

a. there exists a condition π, with $<\mu_1,\pi> \in \mu$;

b. π belongs to ♀.

– The circularity of the definition is undone by stratification (see *Names*).

REPRESENTATION (8)

– Mode of counting, or of structuration, proper to the state of a situation (+). A term is said to be represented (in a situation) if it is counted as one by the state of the situation.

– A represented term is thus included (+) in the situation; that is, it is a part of the situation.

RESTRICTED FORMULA (29)

– A formula (+) is said to be restricted to a multiple α if:

a. All of its quantifiers (+) operate solely on elements of α. This means that $(\forall\beta)$ is followed by $\beta \in \alpha$ and $(\exists\beta)$ likewise. 'For all' then means 'for all elements of α' and 'there exists β' means 'there exists an element of α'.

b. All the parameters (+) take their fixed values in α: the substitution of values for parametric variables is limited to elements of α.

– The formula λ restricted to α is written $(\lambda)^\alpha$.

– The formula $(\lambda)^\alpha$ is the formula λ such as it is understood by an inhabitant of α.

SINGLETON (5)

– The singleton of a multiple α is the multiple whose unique element is α. It is the forming-into-one of α. It is written $\{\alpha\}$.

– If β belongs (+) to α, the singleton of β is itself included (+) in α. We have: $(\beta \in \alpha) \rightarrow (\{\beta\} \subset \alpha)$. As such we have $\{\beta\} \in p(\alpha)$: the singleton is an element of the set of parts (+) of α. This means: the singleton is a term of the state of the situation.

SINGULAR, SINGULARITY (8)

– A term is singular if it is presented (+) (in the situation) but not represented (+) (by the state of the situation). A singular term belongs to the situation but it is not included in it. It is an element but not a part.

– Singularity is opposed to excrescence (+), and to normality (+).

– It is an essential attribute of historical being, and especially of the evental site (+).

SITUATION (1)

– Any consistent presented multiplicity, thus: a multiple (+), and a regime of the count-as-one (+), or structure (+).

SET See *Belonging*.

SET THEORY See *Axioms of Set Theory*.

STATE OF THE SITUATION (8)

– The state of the situation is that by means of which the structure (+) of a situation is, in turn, counted as one (+). We will thus also speak of the count-of-the-count, or of metastructure.

– It can be shown that the necessity of the state results from the need to exclude any presentation of the void. The state secures and completes the plenitude of the situation.

STRUCTURE (1)

– What prescribes, for a presentation, the regime of the count-as-one (+). A structured presentation is a situation (+).

SUBJECT (35)

– A subject is a finite local configuration of a generic procedure (+). A subject is thus:

a. a finite series of enquiries (+);

b. a finite part of a truth (+).

It can thus be said that a subject occurs or is revealed locally.

– It can be shown that a subject, finite instance of a truth, realizes an indiscernible (+), forces a decision, disqualifies the unequal and saves the singular.

SUCCESSOR CARDINAL (26)

– A cardinal is the successor of a given cardinal a if it is the smallest cardinal which is larger than a. The successor cardinal of a is written a^+.

– The cardinal succession $a \rightarrow a^+$ should not be confused with the ordinal succession (+) $a \rightarrow S(a)$. There is a mass of ordinals between a and a^+, all of which have the cardinality (+) a.

– The first successor alephs (+) are ω_1, ω_2, etc.

SUCCESSOR ORDINAL (14)

– Say that a is an ordinal (+). The multiple $a \cup \{a\}$, which 'adds' the multiple a itself to the elements of a, is an ordinal (this can be shown). It has exactly one element more than a. It is termed a's successor ordinal, and it is written $S(a)$.

– Between a and $S(a)$ there is no ordinal. $S(a)$ is the successor of a.

– An ordinal β is a successor ordinal if it is the successor of an ordinal a; in other words, if $\beta = S(a)$.

– Succession is a rule of passage, in the sense implied by the concept of infinity (+).

SUBJECT-LANGUAGE (35)

– A subject (+) generates names, whose referent is suspended from the infinite becoming—always incomplete—of a truth (+). As such, the subject-language unfolds in the future anterior: its referent, and thus the veracity of its statements, depends on the completion of a generic procedure (+).

SUBSET (7) See *Inclusion*.

THEOREM OF THE POINT OF EXCESS (5)

– For every set a, it is established that there is necessarily at least one set which is an element of $p(a)$—the set of parts of a—but not an element of a. Thus, by virtue of the axiom of extensionality (+), a and $p(a)$ are different.

– This excess of $p(a)$ over a is a local difference. The Cohen–Easton theorem gives a global status to this excess.

– The theorem of the point of excess indicates that there always exists at least one excrescence (+). The state of the situation (+) thus cannot coincide with the situation.

TRANSCENDENT THOUGHT (27, Appendix 3)

– The orientation of transcendent thought places itself under the idea of a supreme being, of transcendent power. It attempts to master the errancy of excess from above, by hierarchically 'sealing off' its escape.

– It is the theological decision subjacent to metaphysics, in the Heideggerean sense of onto-theology.

– The ontological schema of such thought is the doctrine of the large cardinals (+).

TRANSITIVITY, TRANSITIVE SETS (12)

– A set a is transitive if every element β of a is also a part (+) of a; that is, if we have: $(\beta \in a) \to (\beta \subset a)$. This represents the maximum possible equilibrium between belonging (+) and inclusion (+).

Note that this can be written: $(\beta \in a) \to (\beta \in p(a))$; every element of a is also an element of the set of parts (+) of a.

– Transitivity is the ontological schema for normality (+): in a transitive set every element is normal; it is presented (by a) and it is represented (by $p(a)$).

TRUTH (Introduction, 31, 35)

– A truth is the gathering together of all the terms which will have been positively investigated (+) by a generic procedure of fidelity (+) supposed complete (thus infinite). It is thus, in the future, an infinite part of the situation.

– A truth is indiscernible (+): it does not fall under any determinant (+) of the encyclopaedia. It bores a hole in knowledge.

– It is truth of the entire situation, truth of the being of the situation.

– It must be remarked that if veracity is a criteria for statements, truth is a type of being (a multiple). There is therefore no contrary to the true, whilst the contrary of the veridical is the erroneous. Strictly speaking, the 'false' can solely designate what proves to be an obstacle to the pursuit of the generic procedure.

UNDECIDABLE (17, 36)

– Undecidability is a fundamental attribute of the event (+): its belonging to the situation in which its eventual site (+) is found is undecidable. The intervention (+) consists in deciding at and from the standpoint of this undecidability.

– A statement of set theory is undecidable if neither itself nor its negation can be demonstrated on the basis of the axioms. The continuum hypothesis (+) is undecidable; hence the errancy of excess (+).

UNICITY (5)

– For a multiple to be unique (or possess the property of unicity), the property which defines or separates (+) this multiple must itself imply that two different multiples cannot both possess it.

– Such is the multiple 'God', in onto-theology.

– The void-set (+), defined by the property 'to not have any element', is unique. So is the multiple defined, without ambiguity, as the 'smallest limit ordinal'. It is the denumerable (+) cardinal (+).

– Any unique multiple can receive a proper name, such as Allah, Yahweh, $\varnothing$ or ω_0.

VARIABLES, FREE VARIABLES, BOUND VARIABLES (Technical Note at Meditation 3)

– The variables of set theory are letters designed to designate a multiple 'in general'. When we write α, β, γ, ... etc., it means: an indeterminate multiple.

– The special characteristic of Zermelo's axiomatic is that it bears only one species of variable, thus inscribing the homogeneity of the pure multiple.

– In a formula (+), a variable is bound if it is contained in the field of a quantifier; otherwise it is free.

In the formula $(\exists\alpha)(\alpha \in \beta)$, α is bound and β is free.

– A formula which has a free variable expresses a supposed property of that variable. In the example above, the formula says: 'there exists an element of β'. It is false if β is void, otherwise it is true.

In general, a formula in which the variables $\alpha_1, \ldots \alpha_n$ are free is written $\lambda(\alpha_1, \ldots \alpha_n)$.

VERACITY, VERIDICAL (Introduction, 31, 35)

– A statement is veridical if it has the following form, verifiable by a knowledge (+): 'Such a term of the situation falls under such an encyclopaedic determinant (+)', or 'such a part of the situation is classified in such a manner within the encyclopaedia.'

– Veracity is the criteria of knowledge.

– The contrary of veridical is erroneous.

VOID (4)

– The void of a situation is the suture to its being. Non-one of any count-as-one (except within the ontological situation (+)), the void is that unplaceable point which shows that the that-which-presents wanders throughout the presentation in the form of a subtraction from the count.

– See *Axiom of the Void*.